BASEBALL
A LITERARY ANTHOLOGY

BASEBALL
A LITERARY ANTHOLOGY
Edited by Nicholas Dawidoff

WITHDRAWN

A Special Publication of
The Library of America

Design by Doyle Partners. This book is set in Stone Serif. Composition is by The Clarinda Company, printing and binding by R.R. Donnelley. Introduction, headnotes, and volume compilation © 2002 by Literary Classics of the United States, New York, N.Y All rights reserved. Printed in the United States of America. Some of the material in this volume is reprinted with the permission of holders of copyright and publication rights. See page 716 for acknowledgments. Published by The Library of America. Distributed to the trade in the United States by Penguin Putnam Inc. and in Canada by Penguin Books Canada, Ltd. Library of Congress Cataloging-in-Publication Data: Baseball: a literary anthology/ Nicholas Dawidoff, editor. p. cm.
ISBN 1-931082-09-X. 1. Baseball — Literary collections. 2. American literature collections. I. Dawidoff Nicholas.
PS 509.B37 B37 2002
810.8'0355—dc21
2 0 0 1 0 3
8   6   5
4

10 9 8 7 6 5 4 3 2 1

Contents

x   CONTENTS

. . . there is nothing now heard of, in our leisure hours, but ball—ball—ball.

—HENRY WADSWORTH LONGFELLOW
from a letter to his father written at
Bowdoin College, April 11, 1824

◆

. . . it's our game: that's the chief fact in connection with it: America's game: has the snap, go, fling of the American atmosphere—belongs as much to our institutions, fits into them as significantly as our constitutions, laws: is just as important in the sum total of our historic life.

—WALT WHITMAN
as quoted in Horace Traubel,
With Walt Whitman in Camden

◆

Baseball's time is seamless and invisible, a bubble within which players move at exactly the same pace and rhythms as all their predecessors. This is the way the game was played in our youth and in our fathers' youth, and even back then—back in the country days—there must have been the same feeling that time could be stopped.

—ROGER ANGELL
"The Interior Stadium"

Introduction

My grandfather, Alexander Gerschenkron, was born in Russia in 1904, fled to Austria during the Revolution, and lived there until Nazi soldiers began killing his neighbors in 1938, whereupon he left for England, and then finally came to America, settling in Cambridge in 1948. He was an instant and ardent American citizen, and it was in that patriotic spirit that he embraced the customs of the country. With a purpose he read droves of books by American writers, he debated American politics, he owned only American cars, and he bought himself a radio on which he listened to baseball, the National Game.

The Boston Red Sox became his team, and like most fans of that nine, he became immediately long-suffering. Every year the Red Sox filled their supporters with hope, and every year they found romantic ways of letting them down. The Red Sox even had a mortal enemy, the New York Yankees, whom my grandfather regarded with disdain because they always won, leaving nothing to the imagination, nothing, as A. J. Liebling said, to if about. In a sense, my grandfather was like the characters in the fiction of William Carlos Williams, James T. Farrell, and Eric Rolfe Greenberg, like real ballplayers such as Luis Tiant, Joe DiMaggio, and Moe Berg, like, in fact, so many Americans from immigrant families: he was using baseball as a means of cultural assimilation. He expressed great admiration for what he called "that truly democratic moment," the seventh-inning stretch, when, he said, all classes rose together in harmony as their passions cooled. By way of contrast, he pointed out that in Europe, class frustration was often expressed toward the end of soccer matches when riots broke out.

My grandfather liked that baseball had an underlying principle governing every possible occurrence, he liked that it rewarded quick wits as well as brute force, and he liked the way that the season unfurled across such a long time that it produced men of character. You had to have mettle and determination to succeed over that extended a calendar. He didn't confuse baseball with life but he did think baseball was a good prism through which to look over and think about life, to examine both those who played and those who watched. Life

3

is difficult to understand, and people tend to talk about things that are difficult to understand in terms of things that are easier to understand, so they use baseball to conjure with life. He thought that anyone who was going to be a person of true principle would get that way by proving his loyalty to small things, like the Red Sox. He urged his grandchildren to be fans of the Red Sox, but cautioned them never to blame the umpire for the team's many disappointments. He believed that a person—especially an American person—creates luck, and although my grandfather felt that fate, like God, was immutable, he also seemed to find it oddly beside the point. He was sure that a man stood a better chance if he ran out every routine ground ball to second base.

He was an economist, but his sensibility was undeniably literary, as was the way he thought about baseball. Tucked on his shelf beside stout volumes of Tolstoy and Dickens and Goethe and Flaubert were copies of *The Natural* by Bernard Malamud, *The Boys of Summer* by Roger Kahn, and neat stacks of *The New Yorker* which, in blessed weeks, contained the baseball writings of Roger Angell. My grandfather was an exceptionally well-read man, and when it came to baseball, his taste was impeccable. There was Malamud, who charged the game with mythical portent. And then Kahn, so adeptly using it to write moving elegies to a time (the 1940s and 1950s), a place (Brooklyn), a family (his own), and a team (the Dodgers). And finally Angell, who made games fresh by describing them with such original language and such penetrating insight, satisfying my grandfather's own belief that baseball was no ordinary sport, but something of depth and complexity enough to absorb any kind of mind across a lifetime.

This anthology consists of the very best baseball literature. By that I mean excellent writing about baseball in any form. I have gathered fiction long and short, poetry and doggerel, song lyrics, essays and scholarship, oral history, sections of biography and memoir, newspaper columns and reportage, the opening scene from a play (*Damn Yankees*), expert analysis of the inside game by shrewd journalists (like Paul Gallico) and also by players erudite (Moe Berg) and merely cerebral (Keith Hernandez), as well as Satchel Paige's timeless rules for staying young. There was a lot to choose from, because people have been writing about baseball for a long time.

The first literary references to "baseball" come from England, where those baseball forebears cricket and rounders were played. In 1744, the farmer and publisher John Newbery produced "A Little Pretty Pocket Book" of 26 children's games, with a game, a woodcut, and a scrap of verse for each letter of the alphabet. "B" was for "Baseball," with the lines "The ball once struck/Away flies the boy/ From each abandoned post/To the next with joy." Around 1800, Jane Austen referred to something called "baseball" in her novel *Northanger Abbey*. Here in the United States, Henry Wadsworth Longfellow and Oliver Wendell Holmes mention baseball as being part of their student days in the 1820s at Bowdoin and Harvard, respectively. That game was actually town ball, a baseball predecessor, and those writings, and many others like them, are not so much literature as archaeology—the broken jugs and fragments of bone that anticipate the advanced civilization to come. The same can be said for such engaging chestnuts as Ernest Thayer's mock-heroic tragedy "Casey at the Bat" and Jack Norworth's cheerful anthem "Take Me Out to the Ball Game." Baseball became a popular phenomenon long before it really had a literature worth speaking or singing about.

The most energetic early baseball writer was Albert Goodwill Spalding. Spalding was the president of the Chicago National League club, and from October 1888 to April 1889, he led a baseball exhibition tour around the world. (There are wonderful photographs of the ballplayers at the Pyramids in Egypt.) When Spalding and the players returned to America, he arranged a banquet for them in the plush quarters of Delmonico's in New York. Theodore Roosevelt was on hand, and so was Mark Twain. After dinner, Twain addressed the roomful of feasting sportsmen and declared baseball "the very symbol, the outward and visible expression of the drive, and push, and rush and struggle of the raging, tearing, booming nineteenth century!" Walt Whitman, too, admired baseball's energy. He said it had the "snap, go, fling of the American atmosphere—belongs as much to our institutions, fits into them as significantly as our constitutions, laws: is just as important in the sum total of our historic life." Like so many writers after them, Twain and Whitman thought baseball expressed something fundamental about America: it was wild, vigorous, improvisational, rushing toward the future. Much subsequent writing, however, has emphasized baseball's stately, pastoral quality, what

Roger Angell calls its "seamless and invisible" time, "a bubble within which players move at exactly the same pace and rhythms as all their predecessors."

To Spalding, baseball was an American religion, and he wanted that faith pure; he demanded plausible evidence that baseball was the "American game" and not a pagan descendant of English games like rounders (as had been asserted by Henry Chadwick, the preeminent nineteenth-century authority on the sport who wrote rule books, invented the box score, and was called the "Father of the Game" in his lifetime). In 1905, Spalding assembled a commission charged with proving the American origin of baseball. The commission's report gave baseball a creation myth with the story of Abner Doubleday, the Civil War general who was supposed to have invented the sport in the bucolic hamlet of Cooperstown, New York, in 1839. That was pure and vivid propaganda, but it appealed to the popular imagination. As the prose in his lively tract *America's National Game* suggests, Spalding was a fervid booster writing for a receptive audience. Americans wanted baseball to be from the rural heartland, and to be all theirs, and they willed it to be so.

The truth is that baseball evolved in a gradual way from rounders and cricket through various versions of town ball into a New York City game whose modern rules were codified in 1845, by a Manhattan bank employee named Alexander Joy Cartwright, and first used in a competition across the Hudson River on the liltingly named Elysian Fields of Hoboken, New Jersey. While it is commonly assumed that the exotic entertainment of antebellum eastern gentlemen became a national pastime after Appomattox, when Civil War soldiers brought baseball home with them, baseball was already broadly popular by the 1860s. The game was played all over the country, including in the deep rural South by both planters and slaves. During the war, combatants pitched and swung both outside the barracks and in prison camps. One boy who came of age in the late 1860s was Clarence Darrow, who would remember his youth in Kinsman, Ohio, by saying, "I have snatched my share of joys from the grudging hand of Fate as I have jogged along, but never has life held for me anything quite so entrancing as baseball." The professional game was thriving too.

Any reader of that superb baseball book, Lawrence Ritter's *The Glory of Their Times*, can readily see that by the early twentieth century baseball was a genuine national game, one played on lawns, lots, and pastures all across the United States by city boys, as well as by all manner of small-towners, many of them skilled bumpkins of the sort Ring Lardner met as a Chicago sportswriter covering the White Sox. Newspapers were filled with coverage of the local teams, and national publications like *The Sporting News* and *Baseball Magazine* were read by avid fans. The local pastime described by Carl Sandburg in his autobiography ("Our early games among the Berrien Street kids were played in the street, barefooted, keeping an eye out for broken glass or rusty cans with sharp edges sticking up") had become a mass entertainment whose players were household names. This was because of the popularity of organized play, but it was also due to the journalism of sportswriters like Damon Runyon, Charles E. Van Loan, and Heywood Broun. The literature of baseball begins here, when its mythology was just beginning to take shape, in the era of the first enduring baseball icons: Mathewson, Cobb, Wagner, McGraw.

Baseball really did reflect the contours of the country, and not all of them were attractive. In 1868, a want ad in the *Brooklyn Eagle* read: "The National Club of Washington are looking for a first baseman about here." The notice contained a caveat: "No Irish need apply." Barriers set up against other groups, most notably Jews and blacks, tarnished professional play well into the twentieth century. Baseball has received its share of criticism from those who have seen the uglier aspects of American life expressed on the field and in the bleachers. This included, but wasn't limited to, its policies of bias and exclusion. In "The American: His Morals," published in *The Smart Set* in 1913, H. L. Mencken (whose father had been part owner of a professional team in Baltimore) wrote that baseball stimulates "a childish and orgiastic local pride, a typical American weakness. . . . If the home club can't achieve the walloping unaided, the crowd helps—usually by means no worse than mocking or reviling, but sometimes with fists and beer bottles. And if, even then, the home club is drubbed, it becomes the butt itself and is lambasted even more brutally than the victims. The thirst of the crowd is for victims, and if it can't get them in one way it will get them in another." A similarly sardonic view was suggested by Sinclair Lewis in *Babbitt*, as he describes the conformist businessman's phony enthusiasm for the game: "Baseball, Babbitt determined, would be an excellent hobby. . . . He did go and support the team, and enhance the glory of Zenith, by yelling 'Attaboy!' and 'Rotten!' He performed the rite scrupulously. He wore a cotton handkerchief about his collar; he became sweaty; he opened his mouth in a wide loose grin; and drank lemon soda out of a bottle. . . . The game was a custom of his clan, and it gave outlet for the homicidal and side-taking instincts which Babbitt called 'patriotism' and 'love of sport.'"

By 1915, the comic baseball stories of Charles E. Van Loan and Zane Grey were meeting with popular success; a boys' literature built around sporting heroes such as Lester Chadwick's Baseball Joe had begun to flourish. Out of this mostly unexceptional mass of writing emerged the first important creator of baseball fiction, Ring Lardner. From the antics of Chisox rubes and bushers that he covered as a sportswriter Lardner made an epistolary novel, *You Know Me Al,* and a series of short stories published in magazines like *The Saturday Evening Post* that represent the real beginning of baseball writing as imaginative literature. Lardner set the standard for baseball fiction and has influenced the many novelists who have followed him onto the diamond, including Mark Harris, who in the four novels "told" by Henry "Author" Wiggen would create an unforgettable narrator in the tradition of *You Know Me Al,* complete with Lardnerian misspellings.

Lardner also inspired journalists to approach the game with flair. Because baseball is exciting, and because it is news, but not crucially important news, describing a baseball game has long been an opportunity for dramatic, even risky writing from men like Runyon, Broun, Gallico, and, later, Red Smith. Baseball gave writers the chance to tell their stories in ways that wouldn't have been appropriate in the coverage of weightier topics. One figure they all took on was Babe Ruth, the most popular player—and most popular literary subject—in baseball history. Nearly as compelling to baseball writers was Ruth's slugging contemporary, the illiterate Chicago White Sox outfielder "Shoeless" Joe Jackson, one of the tragic fixers accused of throwing the 1919 World Series. James T. Farrell, Nelson Algren, and James Maxwell, midwesterners all with boyhood ties to the corrupted Series, were just three of the writers who were taken with this story of American innocence betrayed. In 1925, F. Scott Fitzgerald used the crooked Series as a metaphor for the decadence of the Jazz Age in *The Great Gatsby.*

Throughout the history of baseball, a few men and a handful of games have received what may seem like disproportionate attention from the best baseball writers. I've mentioned Ruth and Jackson; there are also Joe DiMaggio and Ted Williams and the teams whose uniforms they wore, the triumphant Yankees and the tortured Red Sox. DiMaggio has inspired countless writers, among them Gay Talese, Stephen Jay Gould, and, more fleetingly, Ernest Hemingway (*The Old Man and the Sea*) and Paul Simon ("Mrs. Robinson"). The definitive essay on Williams remains John Updike's "Hub Fans Bid Kid Adieu." In the hands of these writers, the brilliant skills of the ballplayer are emblematic of something more broadly human. For Talese, the merciless modern reporter, the grace of DiMaggio becomes elusive in a way that is both holy and cold. With Updike watching, the intelligent, rancorous Williams has all the charisma the Bostons have always provided. Practically the only thing that team never offers its followers is a World Series victory, a succession of fascinating failures that Roger Angell imbues with the profundity of deep feeling. The lesson, it seems, is that baseball is interesting to writers because the game and its practitioners are as prone to fever and flaw as the real world they inhabit. Sometimes they take you away with beautiful play and illustrious feats. On other days, Ralph Branca slumps as he watches Bobby Thomson ruin the Dodgers' season. There is so much failure in baseball, and the good writers, like Don DeLillo, can never get enough of it.

Richard Ford once wrote that "sports really does cause very little of lasting value to happen in the world, except by accident. And this is the fundamental element of sports' character that sports writing has to wrestle with and overcome in order to make itself interesting." Baseball certainly is a diversion, but an uncommonly familiar one to a large number of people who summon from the daily nine-inning narrative a cast of heroes and villains, scraps of gossip, ethical conundrums, moments of despair, laughter, tears, plenty of hope, and the occasional lasting satisfaction. It acquires significance by virtue of the emotions that people invest in it. Perhaps the most important baseball games take place in the mind, memory, and imagination of the individual fan. The daily ballgame isn't as publicly important as the decisions of generals and politicians, but something that absorbs so many private imaginations has an emotional heft that cannot be dismissed. Baseball *matters* to people, and despite the reservations of skeptics like Mencken and Liebling, it can be seen as having a civilizing effect. Social workers talk about what baseball does for the spirits of people with low incomes and few options. By aligning themselves with a team, people feel part of something grand. In the same way, anyone who lived in Washington just after the Senators left town in 1971 will tell you that the loss of baseball immediately made the capital a less habitable city.

One of the oldest saws in literature holds that people write best about the things they know, and by the middle of the twentieth century Americans knew baseball. Just about everybody had played it or watched it, and no matter what their skill or level of interest, it was something they understood. So deep in the American grain was this game that it could accommodate any kind of literary sensibility, even Woody Allen's. In a stand-up bit describing his tenure as the captain of the Latent Paranoid Softball Team, Allen said, "We used to play all the neurotics on Sunday morning—Nailbiters against the Bedwetters, and if you've never seen neurotics play softball, it's really funny. I used to steal second base and feel guilty and go back to first."

All real baseball writers are also fans, and when writers owned up to that in the 1960s and 1970s, and wrote about the game more personally, baseball writing reached its full maturity. A writer wasn't simply describing the world of the ballgame, he was describing the meeting of that world and his own. For Amiri Baraka, this was segregated Newark. For Joel Oppenheimer, it was bohemian Greenwich Village. For Willie Morris, it was a small town in sorghum country. For Annie Dillard, it was in Pittsburgh, in her mother's kitchen. For Robert Creamer, it was inside the locker room, that masculine sanctum where he caught sight of Casey Stengel's lank posterior. Those old man's haunches mark another truth about baseball writing: for all of the valor and excitement of youth, experience and autumn are more interesting. From David Remnick's Reggie Jackson, to W. C. Heinz's Pete Reiser, to Jim Bouton's Jim Bouton, sunset is the hour when the hero becomes fully himself.

If it seems that New York teams receive an undue portion of attention, it's because the people whose business it is to make ballplayers interesting have tended to cluster in the nation's biggest city. In the same way that the Yankees usually win because their money and prestige lure the most skilled players into pinstripes, writers like Van Loan, Runyon, James Thurber, Red Smith, Roy Blount, and many more, have refined their skills elsewhere across the country, and then headed for New York to seek their literary fortunes. New York has provided them with publishers, stimulation, inspiration, worthy competition, the best salaries in the field, and a demanding and cultured audience. The writers, in turn, have made the New York ballclubs into literary folklore. Take the Mets. If the same team had played in St. Louis, they would simply have been the Browns. But the Browns never had someone like Jimmy Breslin, Murray Kempton, Roger Angell, or Joel Oppenheimer to watch over them. This makes a person wonder what we'd think of that legendary team, the Brooklyn Dodgers, had they not toiled in the city of mythmakers.

Anyone who edits an anthology of baseball writing owes a debt to such excellent earlier collections as the *Fireside* and *Armchair* baseball books. Some of what caught the attention of those books' editors did so for good reason. It's not easy to hit the curveball, and those who really can, like Heywood Broun (on Babe Ruth), W. C. Heinz (on Pete Reiser), Gay Talese (on Joe DiMaggio), and John Updike (on Ted Williams), belong in a big-league table of contents. So, of course, do other writers we couldn't include here. That's because the wonderful, irresistible game of baseball, so enduring in its rules and rhythms, so varied in its lore and lexicon, has everything a writer could ask for, most especially the opportunity for vivid characters to involve themselves in a highly dramatic activity. Baseball is governed by no clock, and there is no margin that spells ruin until the last inning is over. Because baseball is so fundamentally timeless, it is fundamentally prone to surprises. A ballgame is never just a ballgame—something that is true both for those who play and, perhaps especially, for those who watch. There are ten thousand ways to look at a ballgame; a select few can see the game in a way that is interesting to everyone. These are the ideal baseball companions, people who bring unusual powers of mind and imagination to this most familiar spectacle. That is the crowd assembled here, the company you will now be keeping, just as soon as you turn the page.

—NICHOLAS DAWIDOFF

Not long after Ernest L. Thayer (1863–1940) graduated from Harvard in 1885, this former editor of the *Harvard Lampoon* received a request from an old friend from the humor magazine. William Randolph Hearst was now editing a family newspaper, the *San Francisco Examiner,* and he wondered if Thayer would supply him with some pieces. Thayer agreed. His final contribution was a ballad published on June 3, 1888. Some months later in New York, a young comic named DeWolf Hopper learned that members of both the New York Giants and the Chicago White Stockings would be attending a performance of his, and as a salute to the ballplayers he recited the poem. With a delighted twitch of Giants catcher Buck Ewing's mustache, "Casey" became an instant national phenomenon, reprinted and remembered everywhere. Its inspired mock-heroic verse has been the fillip for countless take-offs, songs, stage shows, films, even an opera; its legion of parodists and imitators include the sportswriter Grantland Rice, Ray Bradbury (spoofing Melville in "Ahab at the Helm"), and Robert Coover (in his short story "McDuff on the Mound"). At Harvard, Thayer's friends William James and George Santayana had considered him a man of great promise, but Thayer was a one-hit wonder—and a bit of a Mighty Casey himself. Disdaining his fable as nonsense, he published nothing after his famous poem because he felt he had "nothing to say."

Ernest Lawrence Thayer

❥

Casey at the Bat

A Ballad of the Republic, Sung in the Year 1888

The outlook wasn't brilliant for the Mudville nine that day;
The score stood four to two with but one inning more to play.
And then when Cooney died at first, and Barrows did the same,
A sickly silence fell upon the patrons of the game.

A straggling few got up to go in deep despair. The rest
Clung to that hope which springs eternal in the human breast;
They thought if only Casey could but get a whack at that—
We'd put up even money now with Casey at the bat.

But Flynn preceded Casey, as did also Jimmy Blake,
And the former was a lulu and the latter was a cake;
So upon that stricken multitude grim melancholy sat,
For there seemed but little chance of Casey's getting to the bat.

But Flynn let drive a single, to the wonderment of all,
And Blake, the much despisèd, tore the cover off the ball;
And when the dust had lifted, and the men saw what had occurred,
There was Jimmy safe at second and Flynn a-hugging third.

Then from 5,000 throats and more there rose a lusty yell;
It rumbled through the valley, it rattled in the dell;
It knocked upon the mountain and recoiled upon the flat,
For Casey, mighty Casey, was advancing to the bat.

There was ease in Casey's manner as he stepped into his place;
There was pride in Casey's bearing and a smile on Casey's face.
And when, responding to the cheers, he lightly doffed his hat,
No stranger in the crowd could doubt 'twas Casey at the bat.

Ten thousand eyes were on him as he rubbed his hands with dirt;
Five thousand tongues applauded when he wiped them on his shirt.
Then while the writhing pitcher ground the ball into his hip,
Defiance gleamed in Casey's eye, a sneer curled Casey's lip.

And now the leather-covered sphere came hurtling through the air,
And Casey stood a-watching it in haughty grandeur there.
Close by the sturdy batsman the ball unheeded sped—
"That ain't my style," said Casey. "Strike one," the umpire said.

From the benches, black with people, there went up a muffled roar,
Like the beating of the storm-waves on a stern and distant shore.
"Kill him! Kill the umpire!" shouted some one on the stand;
And it's likely they'd have killed him had not Casey raised his hand.

With a smile of Christian charity great Casey's visage shone;
He stilled the rising tumult; he bade the game go on;
He signaled to the pitcher, and once more the spheroid flew;
But Casey still ignored it, and the umpire said, "Strike two."

"Fraud!" cried the maddened thousands, and echo answered fraud;
But one scornful look from Casey and the audience was awed.
They saw his face grow stern and cold, they saw his muscles strain,
And they knew that Casey wouldn't let that ball go by again.

The sneer is gone from Casey's lip, his teeth are clinched in hate;
He pounds with cruel violence his bat upon the plate.
And now the pitcher holds the ball, and now he lets it go,
And now the air is shattered by the force of Casey's blow.

———

Oh, somewhere in this favored land the sun is shining bright;
The band is playing somewhere, and somewhere hearts are light,
And somewhere men are laughing, and somewhere children shout;
But there is no joy in Mudville—mighty Casey has struck out.

●●●

"The Umpire Is a Most Unhappy Man" comes from the musical *The Umpire*, a big success in Chicago in 1905 that capitalized on the baseball craze then sweeping the nation. The show was created by the composer Joseph Howard and the librettist and lyricist team of Frank Adams and Will Hough. The trio was best known for "I Wonder Who's Kissing Her Now," later the title for a 1947 film about Howard which revived "The Umpire Is a Most Unhappy Man" for one of its musical numbers.

Will Hough & Frank Adams

♢

The Umpire Is a Most Unhappy Man

An umpire is a cross between a bullfrog and a goat,
He has a mouth that's flannel lined and brass tubes in his throat;
He needs a cool and level head, that isn't hard to hit,
So when the fans beat up his frame,
They'll have a nice place to sit;
The only job that's worse, is driver on a hearse.

Chorus:
How'd you like to be an umpire,
Work like his is merely play,
He don't even have to ask for,
All the things that come his way,
When the crowd yells, "knock his block off,"
"Soak him good," says ev'ry fan,
Then who wants to be an umpire,
The brick-bats whiz, when he gets his,
For the umpire is a most unhappy man.

Napoleon and Washington were generals of old,
Their lightest word moved regiments and armies we are told;
Where'er they led men followed them, but only came for hire,
Just think of all that gratis come,
To follow the bold umpire;
He leads them with such vim, because they're chasing him.

The vaudeville performer and songwriter Jack Norworth (1879–1959) was riding on the New York City subway one summer day in 1908 when he noticed an advertisement for a baseball game at the Polo Grounds. Although Norworth had no interest in baseball, he was a shrewd fellow, and by the time the ride was over he had written a 16-line lyric about a girl named Katie Casey who wanted nothing more than to be escorted to a ball game. Once the song was set to Albert Von Tilzer's melody and presented with nickelodeon slides illustrating Katie's progress from a lonely rocking chair to a place in the throng at the old ball game, the "sensational baseball song," as Norworth had called it, became a national sensation. Later it would become the title song of Busby Berkeley's classic 1949 musical about turn-of-the-century baseball, starring Gene Kelly and Frank Sinatra. For Norworth, 1908 turned out to be a very successful year, since he also found time to write the equally popular "Shine On, Harvest Moon."

Jack Norworth

♢

Take Me Out to the Ball Game

Katie Casey was baseball mad,
Had the fever and had it bad;
Just to root for the hometown crew,
Ev'ry sou, Katie blew.
On a Saturday, her young beau
Called to see if she'd like to go,
To see a show but Miss Kate said, "No,
I'll tell you what you can do":

Chorus:
Take me out to the ball game,
Take me out with the crowd.
Buy me some peanuts and cracker jack,
I don't care if I never get back.
Let me root, root, root for the home team,
If they don't win it's a shame.
For it's one, two, three strikes, you're out,
At the old ball game.

Franklin P. Adams (1881–1960)—F.P.A. to his readers—came from his hometown of Chicago to New York where he wrote humorously for a number of newspapers including the *Tribune*, the *World*, the *Herald Tribune*, the *Post*, and the *Evening Mail*. A vigorous man-about-town, Adams commanded a popular column, "The Conning Tower," and was a panelist on the radio quiz program *Information, Please!* With these eight lines, Adams made the Chicago Cubs' mediocre double-play combination so much a part of the language that in 1946 they all became members of the Baseball Hall of Fame. In 1947, Ogden Nash added his own variation to Adams' poem with his "Lineup for Yesterday: An ABC of Baseball Immortals": "E is for Evers/His jaw in advance/Never afraid/To Tinker with Chance."

George Edward Phair (1883–1965) was born in Milwaukee, where he worked for the *Sentinel* before moving on to the *Chicago American* and then the *New York American* from 1926 to 1938. In a time when many newspaper columnists led their daily dispatches with a few lines of verse, writers like Grantland Rice acknowledged Phair as the master of sporting doggerel. After a Cubs pitcher named Guy Bush defeated the Dodgers one day, Phair wrote: "A long and lanky lad named Bush/Wore little sideburns on his mush/Between his whiskers and his curves/He wrecked a lot of Brooklyn nerves." When Lawrence Ritter was compiling *The Glory of Their Times,* he was so taken with Phair's lines about the "old-fashioned hurler" that he made up a complementary panegyric to a hitter. Anyone who looks at the epigram preceding Lefty O'Doul's entry in *The Glory of Their Times* will discover "The Old-Fashioned Batter," a poem attributed to Phair which was actually written by the mischievous Ritter.

Newspaper Verse

♎

Baseball's Sad Lexicon

These are the saddest of possible words:
"Tinker to Evers to Chance."
Trio of bear cubs, and fleeter than birds,
Tinker and Evers and Chance.
Ruthlessly pricking our gonfalon bubble,
Making a Giant hit into a double—
Words that are heavy with nothing but trouble:
"Tinker to Evers to Chance."

F.P.A.

The Old-Fashioned Pitcher

How dear to my heart was the old-fashioned hurler
   Who labored all day on the old village green.
He did not resemble the up-to-date twirler
   Who pitches four innings and ducks from the scene.
The up-to-date twirler I'm not very strong for;
   He has a queer habit of pulling up lame.
And that is the reason I hanker and long for
   The pitcher who started and finished the game.

The old-fashioned pitcher,
   The iron-armed pitcher,
The stout-hearted pitcher,
   Who finished the game.

GEORGE E. PHAIR

••

As a young man, Charles Emmett Van Loan (1876–1919) worked at a meat-packing company and went to minor-league baseball games around Los Angeles with his boss. He began taking notes on what he saw, and when he converted them into dispatches and submitted them to the *Los Angeles Examiner,* he was on his way to becoming California's best baseball writer. He worked for the *Los Angeles Morning Herald* in 1904, and then for the *Denver Post,* where he met Damon Runyon. By 1910, the two men were house-mates in New York, colleagues at the sports department of the *American.* Over the next nine years Van Loan's journalism and short stories about boxing, horse-racing, golf, Hollywood, and of course baseball appeared in a number of publications, including *The Saturday Evening Post,* for which he served two stints as an editor. During the first, he became the editorial conduit for Ring Lardner's humorous sketches that would later be collected as the novel *You Know Me Al.* This piece, published in *The Outing* magazine in 1909, shows Van Loan's ample humor and his sophisticated understanding of the skills involved in baseball. The portraits of Ty Cobb and Hal Chase are especially interesting since they provide glimpses of the two players before a reputation for recalcitrance (Cobb) or dishonesty (Chase) overtook them.

Charles E. Van Loan

♡

Baseball as the Bleachers Like It

The man in the box office, whose swift, money-changing fingers play on the pulse of the amusement-loving public, will tell you that a baseball franchise in a large city is a "mint." The man in the box office cares little for sport; he views it with the sordid eye of one who thinks in figures and dreams in dollars. Those who make a study of the great business of providing amusement for a nation, will tell you that where other outdoor sports and "attractions" count their devotees by tens, baseball drags its hundreds and even thousands through the turnstiles. There must be some good reason for this state of affairs.

The same men sit on the bleachers day after day, their straw hats tilted down over keen eyes, their fingers fumbling score cards and pencils. Everything that the gallery is to the stage, the bleachers are to the diamond. The most merciless critic may be found somewhere behind first or third base where he can see everything which happens. The grand stand may be all very well for the thin-skinned ones who must mingle personal comfort with their amusement; the true baseball fan sits on the bleachers, trimmed down to his shirt sleeves. No wire nettings in front of him, if you please.

Why is he there day after day? He can hope to see nothing absolutely new, for in the present high stage of its development, professional baseball has reached a point where one new play a season is the average. What is the lure of this mighty magnet—this thing, half sport, half business, which draws its millions of dollars every year?

Is it the science of the game—the inside baseball?

Nine tenths of the men who go to the theater hope for one of two things: they want to be amused or thrilled. The problem play does not appeal to the man who has found life its own problem.

The man who goes to the race track for an afternoon's sport and does not sell his interest for a bookmaker's ticket hopes to see a great race with a nose-and-nose finish and three horses driving at the wire.

Patrons of the gentle art of the lamented Queensberry, hoot two clever men, who spar for points without damage or gore. These are the same men who make baseball profitable; what then do they see in the national game?

PROBLEM PLAYS ON THE DIAMOND

For example: it is the ninth inning; the score is 1 to 0, and it has been a battle of the pitchers from the clang of the gong. There have been a few scattering hits, a few brilliant bits of individual fielding, and many weak flies hoisted into the air. It has been a very scientific contest from first to last—so full of science that there has been little else. Ask your bleacher friend what he thinks of that sort of a game.

"We-ell," he will say, "Matty was good to-day and so was the other fellow. We won, of course, but. . . ."

Behind that "but" lurks the secret of the whole thing, the power of the game over its millions of devotees. The melodrama had been lacking; the sensational plays which stir the blood, the long sharp hits and the brilliant catches. It had been a problem play with two stars in the cast and sixteen walking gentlemen.

Now then, watch your friend in the last half of the eighth inning with the score 3 to 2 against the home team, two men out and the bases filled. It has been a slashing contest, full of free hitting, sharp fielding, and the brilliant double plays which hold the score in small figures.

The hard-hitting outfielder of the home team is at bat. Your friend is out on the edge of his seat. Any sort of a safe hit means a tied score; a long single might win the game, and a double . . . your friend hopes for a double! Watch his eyes when the umpire's right arm jerks upward as the first ball splits the plate.

"Aw, what was he waiting for? Might have known the first ball would be a groover!" Your friend seems peevish.

One ball. Wild cheering. Two balls. A demonstration and yells of "Going Up!" Ah! He missed that one! Well, he still has the big one left. Three balls.

From the box back of first base comes the sharp bark of the coacher.

"Three and two now, ole boy! Three and two! Make him be good!"

Watch your friend now. He has stopped breathing. His cigar is dying an unpleasant death. He does not care. Three and two! He has eyes and ears and a taste for one thing only—the drama spread out before him.

Once more the gray-clad pitcher cuddles the ball to his chest, nodding slightly in answer to the catcher's signal. Up goes his foot, back goes his body from the hips, a forward lunge, and the arm snaps out in a half circle like a powerful spring uncoiled. The ball flies straight for the catcher's mitt and at the same instant the three base runners flash into motion. Three and two and two men down—nothing to do but run.

The batter pivots with a mighty swing, there is a splitting crack as wood meets leather, and a white dot shoots out over the second baseman's head, mocking his futile leap. The center fielder is sheering off toward right, racing with a forlorn hope and the right fielder, wiser still, is already on his way toward the fence.

DELIRIUM ON THE BLEACHERS

How about your friend now? There he is, standing up in his place and tearing the air with a series of Comanche war whoops. All around you men, and women too, are screaming unintelligible words. The man beside you who gave you such a nasty look when you stepped on his feet, hammers you between the shoulder blades and bellows into your ear:

"A triple with bases full! A triple! What do you know about that, eh?"

What is the attraction in baseball? Your answer is out there on the bleachers, several thousand strong. Those leaping, howling, white-shirted dervishes have given it to you. It is the melodrama which makes baseball.

A baseball fan will go to a dozen poor games rather than miss that sort of a play, and when at last he recovers his breath he will tell you that he is amply repaid for his time and money.

The scientific contest interests him because he understands every move in the game, but if you want to bring him to his feet, you must give him melodrama.

Inside baseball? Yes, he knows something of that, too. He has made a study of inside baseball, sitting above the great masters. He recognizes and appreciates good pitching, but the thing which brings him to his feet with the howl of a timber wolf is the long clean drive to the fence, or the seemingly impossible catch. The melodrama "gets" him every time.

One of the grizzled old baseball generals once said:

"Give me a team of sluggers and I'll chance the errors." He knew what the fans wanted to see.

Ask the first youngster you meet to name the two greatest baseball players in the two big leagues. Nine times out of ten the answer will come like a flash:

"Hans Wagner and Ty Cobb!"

These are the names of the two great batters, Wagner in the National and Cobb in the American League.

The tenth youngster may take time to think and give you another answer. If you lift his hat you will find that youth has a high, intellectual brow. He will enjoy problem plays when he grows up.

The leading men of this national melodrama form interesting contrasts. Some of them have found it a long road from the sandlots to the pay roll of a big league team; others jumped into fame in a single week. Personal appearance counts for nothing; nationality counts for nothing; it is the man who "delivers the goods" who is always sure of his welcome from the lynx-eyed critics on the sunny seats.

Baseball fans are quick to recognize and identify the thing which we call "class." After your bleacher friend has watched a visiting team through an entire series he can place his finger on the weak spot in the organization; he can tell you how the games were lost and which players lost them.

Of the ball players who have jumped into prominence at a single bound, two might be mentioned: Hal Chase and Tyrus Cobb.

CHASE BREAKS INTO FAST COMPANY

A few years ago the Los Angeles team of the Pacific Coast League had need of a substitute first baseman. Frank Dillon, first baseman and team captain, had signed a contract to play with the Brooklyn club of the National League. Dillon was anxious to remain in California and did not report with the Eastern team for spring practice.

The manager of the Southern team, looking about him for a substitute player, engaged a boy from a small college team in central California, devoutly hoping that he might not have any use for him.

On the opening day of the league season, Dillon went out on the field to put the team through the preliminary practice, playing his old position at first base. The substitute sat on the bench. His face was unknown to the Southern baseball fans who immediately dubbed him a "bush leaguer" and forgot about him. The youngster sat there on the bench, nursing an odd-shaped pancake glove; a battered relic contrasting strangely with his new flannel uniform and spiked shoes.

It was his first appearance in "organized baseball." Success meant a chance to earn money; failure meant a ticket back to the prune orchards of Santa Clara County.

The gong clanged, announcing the opening of the game. The umpire drew a paper from his pocket, showed it to Dillon, and the captain and first baseman slowly left the field. He had been informed that every game in which he played would be declared forfeited. Baseball magnates have many ways of protecting themselves in business deals; Dillon had signed with Brooklyn and Brooklyn meant to have him.

The long-legged country boy arose and ambled out to Dillon's old position. The stands were in an uproar. Dillon had been the idol of the baseball public; the best first baseman in the league and the brainiest team captain the town had ever had. The contagion spread to the Los Angeles players, not one of whom had confidence in the raw college boy, thus thrust into an important position.

It would be hard to imagine a more unfortunate first appearance. The game opened with a rush. The first batter smashed a ground ball at the Los Angeles shortstop and tore down the line to first base. Mechanically the shortstop raced over, dropped his glove in front of the ball, and faced about to make the throw to first base. Instead of Dillon, there was the "bush league kid" on the bag.

The base runner was a fast man; in the twinkling of an eye the thing had been done—the panic was working. Instead of the perfect line "peg" to first base, the shortstop threw fully eight feet outside the bag and correspondingly high, shooting the ball with the speed of a rifle bullet. It would have been a vicious throw for a right-hander to care for, even though on his glove-hand side; the bush league boy was a left-handed player and wore the glove on his right hand. The ball was coming to his bare hand and coming with such speed that there was little chance to hold it, even if a man cared to risk injury by reaching for a wide ball with the bare hand.

"ACCIDENT" THAT BECAME A HABIT

With the fraction of a second in which to decide what to do, the country boy whirled with his back to the diamond, hooked the spikes of his left shoe in the bag, and thrust out a long right arm for a back-hand catch. The runner was beaten a stride on a circus catch which few big-leaguers would care to attempt.

After the cheering, the bleacherites decided that it had been a blind, back-hand stab or a lucky accident. Twenty minutes later every man inside the grounds knew that he was seeing first base played as no youngster had ever played it before. The infield, still in a state of panic, threw the ball high, wide, and on both sides of him, but the flat pancake glove was always there when it arrived.

The boy covered the ground with great loose-jointed strides, dug up impossible ground balls beyond the reach of an ordinary fielding first baseman, picked line drives out of the air, nipped bunts ten feet from the plate, caught advancing runners, and capped the climax by starting and finishing a double play thought to be possible with only one first baseman in America, Fred Tenney of the Nationals. There was but one verdict at the end of the game; the boy was the greatest first baseman ever seen on the Pacific Coast. He found his place in a single afternoon.

On the next opening day, the youngster wore a New York uniform. New York had heard of him as a marvel and a boy wonder, but New York accepts no verdict except her own. In less than a week Hal Chase was the baseball sensation of the season, and baseball critics burned up columns in an attempt to analyze his method of playing his position. In the end everybody agreed that it was not possible to understand a raw boy who broke into the fastest company in the business, ready-made, as it were. The veterans of the American League could not teach him anything about inside ball; he was a revelation to his team mates and a terror to opposing clubs.

Chase is still the premier first baseman of the country and the great star of baseball melodrama. He makes his plays by some unerring instinct which must have been born in him, and when it comes to handling bad throws at first base, there never was a player like him. Time after time he has been seen to turn his head away from a low-thrown ball and jam his glove down, making a blind catch of a ball which he could not have followed with his eyes.

Fielders have little trouble with ground balls, but this is because they can move about and suit the catch to the bound of the ball. The first baseman is anchored to the bag; he must play the ball as it comes to him or miss the base runner.

Other men have had more years of experience; many players are better at post-mortem analysis of a baseball problem, but when a ball is hit down to Hal Chase, you will see the bleachers come up as one man. The fans never know what he is going to do with the ball when he gets it, but they do know that there will be no fumbling or "booting," but a chain-lightning play directed at the one spot where the most damage can be done. Chase is the personification of baseball by instinct and the most popular first baseman the country has ever seen.

"TY" COBB'S FIRST BASEBALL MONEY

"Ty" Cobb was not so fortunate in his beginning. Tyrus was born in Georgia and early decided to be a semi-professional ball player. The difference between a professional and a semi-professional is that the former has a stated salary and always gets it, while the latter takes what he can get when he can get it.

Young Cobb walked six miles in the hot sun to play his first "money" game. When the receipts had been counted, Cobb's share was one dollar and twenty-five cents. He walked six miles to his home and on the way decided that there was a future in professional baseball.

The Charleston team secured him. He was a wild, erratic youngster who could bat like a demon, but never knew when to stop running bases. It is just as important to know when to stop running as it is to know when to begin. He gained the reputation of a crazy base runner and Charleston sold him to Augusta for one hundred and fifty dollars and was glad to get the money.

Augusta tried him and found the same fault. He could hit, but he was wild and discipline irked him. He was a firebrand on the team and he would fight on the field or off. Ty won and lost several battles with the Augusta players and then the management sold him to Detroit for seven hundred dollars—the greatest bargain in the history of the game.

In Detroit young Mr. Cobb, the firebrand, found men who made baseball a study. It was a slugging team, but mixed with the hitting was the judgment which wins games. The players took a hand in taming that hot Southern blood. They argued with him, but as Ty would rather fight than argue, most of the debates ended on the floor of the dressing room. Those cool, seasoned veterans of the Tiger team knew that in Cobb they had a phenomenon, so they went at him methodically, literally "licking him into shape." Some of them fought him more than once. Even to this day McIntyre plays left field and Cobb right field, because it is necessary to keep these two stars as far apart as possible.

Cobb has lost most of his rough edges. He has gone out of the rough-and-tumble business; he sheds no more blood in defense of his principles. He knows when to quit running bases, hits the ball hard and often, and makes doubles on hits which any other man would call legitimate singles.

He is as fast as a thunderbolt on the lines and the most daring man on a slide that baseball has seen in many a day. His slim, wiry legs are covered with bruises from April until October and he is always slightly lame until he hits the ball; then he forgets his soreness. Absolutely fearless, of great hitting ability, and a fighter every inch, Cobb is one of the great drawing cards in the baseball of to-day.

THE MAN WHO HITS EVERYTHING

Then there is the veteran Hans Wagner whose big stick has kept Pittsburgh in the first division for more years than he cares to remember. Hans is the last man in the world who would be taken for a great ball player. On appearance, he might be a piano mover. Immensely broad from shoulders to hips, awkward of gait, long armed, and bow-legged, this great German has won his place in baseball by his uncanny ability to hit the ball harder and more often than any living man.

Hans is no moving picture either in the field or at bat, but once he connects with the ball he becomes a human whirlwind. National League pitchers dream about him and call it a nightmare. The lucky man who strikes him out receives an ovation, for he has done something.

The only ball which worries Hans is the spit ball. He does not care for the wet ones, but they are all alike after he hits them. One of the spit-ball artists of the National League has this to say about Wagner:

"He'll hit anything anywhere. No pitcher ever scares him. He may hate to see you wetting that ball and when you say to him:

"'This is IT, you big Dutchman!' his eyes will get about as big as butter plates, but if he hits it! GOOD NIGHT!"

THE MOST SENSATIONAL OF ALL

The most sensational play ever made? Every fan will give a different answer to this question. Some will say that Chase made it when he saved a game by racing into the middle of the diamond on a pop fly, reaching the ball when it was only a few inches from the grass. Ed Walsh, the Chicago White Sox pitcher, thinks it was made at Detroit two years ago.

It happened in the game in which Walsh broke the Detroit hoodoo. The Tigers had beaten Walsh every time he faced them. They regarded him as their lawful prey. The game was played in Detroit, and Mullin, who started this season with eleven straight victories for the Tigers, was slated to pitch against Walsh.

Early in the contest George Davis, the veteran shortstop of the Chicago club, secured the only hit made off Mullin and it was enough to win the game. The ball, driven down the first base line into right field, struck a fire hose lying in the grass and bounded into the bleachers for a home run. After that Mullin was invincible.

Toward the end of the game, Detroit opened with the usual rally. Rossman, Detroit's first baseman, leading off in the inning, smashed the ball against the fence for a clean triple. "Dutch" Schaefer drew a base on balls. Schmidt, next at bat, gave the hit-and-run sign and, with both runners in motion, hit a hard bounder down toward third base where Tannehill of Chicago was playing. Tannehill made a perfect scoop and threw the ball to the plate twenty feet ahead of Rossman, who seeing that he was caught, doubled back on the line, hoping to dodge the tag long enough to allow Schaefer to reach third.

Sullivan raced down the line with the ball, driving Rossman before him. Rossman slipped and fell close to third base and just as Sullivan tagged him for the first out, Schaefer slid to third. In the meantime, Schmidt, a slow runner because of an injury to his ankle, had rounded first base and was well on his way to second. Sullivan straightened up and whipped the ball to Rohe who was covering second base and calling for the throw.

As Schmidt slid, Rohe's arm came down with a thump and Schmidt made the second out. The instant Sullivan threw the ball, Schaefer was on his feet and dashing home from third base. The plate had been left unprotected; Sullivan was down near third base. Walsh, the pitcher, yelled for the ball and raced Schaefer to the rubber, closely followed by George Davis. The two runners collided in front of the plate.

Walsh was stunned and Schaefer was thrown ten feet from the plate, alighting on his shoulders. Davis, who arrived about the same time, took the throw and dropped the ball on the struggling Tiger, completing the third out and the most sensational triple play ever made in the big leagues.

George Davis, who is a scientist, says that it was not a clean triple, but every man at the ball park went home talking about it in whispers. It is the melodrama of the game which counts in the penciled statement of the autocrat of the box office.

Generations of American children grew up reading about the exploits of heroic young ballplayers like Lester Chadwick's Baseball Joe, Gilbert Patten's (a pseudonym for Burt L. Standish) Frank Merriwell, John R. Tunis's Kid from Tomkinsville, and Clair Bee's Chip Hilton. Partly because he is frequently so unexemplary, the most interesting of these exemplars is John Humperdink "Dink" Stover, Owen Johnson's Lawrenceville School "Varmint" who later went to Yale. In a series of sketches first published in *The Saturday Evening Post,* Johnson (1878–1952), himself a Lawrenceville and Yale man, wrote about the picaresque prep school adventures of Stover and other eccentrically monikered characters such as Lovely Mead, the Gutter Pup, the Tennessee Shad, and Dennis de Brian de Boru Finnegan. The humor and intelligence of these tales give the youthful pranks and pains of *The Lawrenceville Stories,* like those of *Tom Sawyer,* their appeal to people of all ages. This is Chapter 6 of *The Varmint* (1910).

Owen Johnson

♢

from

The Varmint

D ink, under the influence of the new emotion, made a fairly full confession, merely overlooking the shoes that Flash did not carry over the Princeton goal line, and suppressing that detail of the Foundation House's supposed contribution, which had lent such a peculiar value to the souvenir crockery set. By four o'clock Butsey White had sufficiently recovered to remember the afternoon baseball match.

Ten minutes later Dink, lost in a lapping baseball suit lent by Cheyenne Baxter, re-enforced with safety pins, stationed himself in the outfield behind a catcher's mitt, for preliminary practice with little Susie Satterly and Beekstein Hall, who was shortsighted and wore glasses.

The result of five minutes' frantic chasing was that Dink, who surprised every one by catching a fly that somehow stuck in his glove, was promoted to centerfield; Susie Satterly, who had stopped two grounders, took left; while Beekstein was ignominiously escorted to a far position in rightfield and firmly requested to stop whatever he could with his chest.

The Cleve cohorts arrived, thirty strong, like banditti marching to sack a city, openly voicing their derision for the nine occupants of the Green House. The contest, which at first sight seemed unequal, was not in reality so, Tough McCarty and Cheyenne Baxter being an unusually strong battery, while the infield, with Butsey White at first, the White Mountain Canary at second, Stuffy Brown short-stop and the Coffee-colored Angel at third, quite outclassed the invaders. The trouble was in the outfield—where the trouble in such contests are sure to congregate.

Stover had never been so thoroughly frightened in his life. His imagination, boylike, was aghast at the unknown. A great question was to be decided in a few minutes, when his turn would come to step up to the box and expose himself to the terrific cannonade of Nick Carter, the lengthy pitcher of the Cleve. The curious thing was that on this point Stover himself was quite undecided. Was he a coward, or was he not? Would his legs go back on him, or would he stand his ground, knowing that the stinging ball might strike anywhere— on the tender wrist bones, shattering the point of the elbow, or landing with a deadly thud right over his temple, which he remembered was an absolutely fatal spot?

His first two innings in the field were a complete success—not a ball came his way. With his fielding average quite intact he came in to face the crisis.

"Brown to the bat, Stover on deck, Satterly in the hole," came the shrill voice of Fate in the person of Shrimp Davis, the official scorer.

Stover nervously tried one bat after another; each seemed to weigh a ton. Then Cheyenne Baxter joined him, crouching beside him for a word of advice.

"Now, Dink," he said in a whisper, keeping his eye on Stuffy Brown, who, being unable to hit the straightest ball, was pawing the plate and making terrific preparatory swings with his bat. "Now, Dink, listen here. (Pick out an easy one, Stuffy, and bang it on the nose. Hi-yi, good waiting, Stuffy.) Nick Carter's wild as a wet hen. All he's got is a fast outcurve. Now, what you want to do is to edge up close to the plate and let him hit you. (Oh, robber! That wasn't a strike! Say, Mr. Umpire, give us a square deal, will you?) Walk right into it, Dink, and if it happens to hit you on the wrist rub above the elbow like the mischief."

"Above the elbow?" said Dink in a hollow voice.

"That's it. You've got a chance to square yourself with the House. Step right into it. What? Three strikes? Say, Mr. Umpire, you're not taking Nick Carter's word for it, are you?"

Amid a storm of execrations Stuffy Brown retired, appealing frantically to the four quarters of the globe for justice and a judge.

Impelled by a resounding whack, Dink approached the plate as a balky horse tries his hoofs in a pool of water. He spread his feet and shouldered his bat, imitating the slightly-crouching position of Cheyenne Baxter. Then he looked out for a favorable opening. The field was thronged with representatives of the Cleve House. He turned to first base—it was miles away. He looked at Nick Carter, savagely preparing to mow him down, and he seemed to loom over him, infringing on the batter's box.

"Why the devil don't they stick the pitcher back and give a fellow a chance?" he thought, eying uneasily the quick, jerky preparations. "Why, at this distance a ball could go right through you."

"Come on, Nick, old boy," said a voice issuing from the iron mask at his elbow. "We've got an umpire that can't be bluffed. This is nothing but a Statue of Liberty. Chop him right down."

Dink shivered from the ground up, Carter's long arms gyrated spasmodically, and the ball, like the sweep of a swallow from the ground, sprang directly at him. Stover, with a yell, flung himself back, landing all in a heap.

"Ball one," said the umpire.

A chorus of taunts rose from the Green House nine.

"Trying to put him out, are you?"

"Mucker trick!"

"Put him out!"

"Good eye, Dinky!"

"That's the boy."

Stover rose, found his bat and ruthfully forced himself back to his position.

"I should have let it hit me," he said angrily, perceiving Baxter's frantic signals. "It might have broken a rib, but I'd have showed my nerve."

Clenching his bat fiercely he waited, resolved on a martyr's death. But the next ball coming straight for his head, he ducked horribly.

"Ball two—too high," said the umpire.

Stover tightened his belt, rapped the plate twice with his bat, as Butsey had done, and resumed his position. But the memory of the sound the ball had made when it had whistled by his ears had unnerved him. Before he could summon back his heroic resolves Carter, with a sudden jerk, delivered the ball. Involuntarily Stover stepped back, the ball easily and slowly passed him and cut the corner of the plate.

"Ball three," said the umpire hesitatingly.

The Cleve catcher hurled his mask to the ground, Carter cast down his glove and trod on it, while the second baseman fell on his bag and wept.

When order was restored Stover dodged the fourth wild ball and went in a daze to first, where to his amazement he was greeted with jubilant cheers.

"You're the boy, Dinky."

"You've got an eye like Charlie De Soto."

"They can't fool Rinky Dink."

"Why, he's a wonder."

"Watch him steal second."

Stover slapped his foot on first base with the joy of unhoped-for victory. He glowered about his own possessions. The perspective had suddenly changed; the field was open, all his, the Cleve House representatives were a lot of dubs, butterfingers and fumblers, anyhow! Under Cheyenne Baxter's directions he went plunging down to second, slid, all arms and legs, safely on to the bag, thanks to a wild pitch, and rose triumphantly, blowing the dust from his mouth.

There he remained, as Susie Satterly and Beekstein methodically struck out.

But the joy of that double voyage was still on him as he went back to centerfield, ready to master the hottest liner or retrieve the sky-scraping fly. It was a great game. He felt a special aptitude for it and wondered why he had never discovered the talent before. He began to dream of sizzling two-baggers and long home-runs over the fence.

"I wish I'd get a chance," he said, prancing about digging vicious holes in the glove, that looked like a chest protector. "I'd show 'em what I can do out here."

But no chance came. The battle was between pitchers, and to the surprise of every one the Green House came up to the last inning with the score of 2 to 1 in their favor, the solitary run of the Cleve being due to a fly that Beekstein had failed to notice.

The Green House nine went jubilantly out into the field for the last half of the ninth inning, determined to shut out the Cleve and end the season with at least one victory.

Dink ran out on his tiptoes, encased himself in his mitt and turned, tense and alert. He had gone through his first ordeal triumphantly. No chances had come to him in the field, but at bat he had accidently succeeded in being hit, and though he had struck out the next time he had hit a foul and knew the jubilant feeling that came with the crack of the bat.

"Give me a week and I'll soak 'em out," he said, moving restlessly, and he added to himself: "Strike 'em out, Cheyenne, old man! They're easy."

But the Cleves suddenly woke up and began to fight. One man beat out a grounder, and one struck out; another error of the temperamental White Mountain Canary put a man on third and one on second. Then Cheyenne, pulling himself together, made his second strike-out.

"Two out, play for the batter," came Cheyenne Baxter's warning hallo.

"Two out," said Dink to his fellow-fielders. "One more and we spink 'em. Come on, now!"

Both sides settled for the final play, the man on second leading well up toward third.

"Steady!" said Cheyenne.

Stover drew in his breath and rose to his toes, as he had done thirty times already.

Suddenly there was a sharp crack, and the ball meeting the bat, floated fair and free, out toward centerfield.

Dink did not have to move a step; in fact, the ball rose and fell straight for the massive mitt as though it had chosen his glove from all the other gloves in the field. It came slowly, endlessly, the easiest, gentlest, most perfect fly imaginable, directly for the large brown mitt that looked like a chest protector.

Stover, turned to stone, saw it strike fair in the middle, and then, irresistibly, slowly, while, horribly fascinated, he stood powerless, slowly trickle over the side of the mitt and drop to the ground.

Dink did not stop for a look, for a second thought, to hesitate or to deliberate. He knew! He gave a howl and broke for the House, and behind him, pell-mell, shrieking and murderous, like a pack of hounds in full cry, came the vanquished, thirsting body of the Green.

He cleared the fence with one hand, took the road with two bounds, fled up the walk, burst through the door, jumped the stairs, broke into his room, slammed the door, locked it, backed the bed against it and seized a chair.

Then the Green House struck the door like a salvo of grapeshot.

"Open up, you robber!"

"Open the door, you traitor!"

"You Benedict Arnold!"

"Open up, you white-livered pup!"

"You quitter!"

"You chickenheart!"

"You coward!"

Stover, his hair rising, seized the wooden chair convulsively, waiting for the door to burst in.

All at once the transom swung violently and the wolfish faces of Tough McCarty, the White Mountain Canary, Cheyenne and the Coffee-colored Angel crowded the opening.

"Get back or I'll kill you," said Dink in frantic fear, and, advancing, he swung the chair murderously. In a twinkling the transom was emptied.

The storm of voices rose again.

"The freshest yet!"

"The nerve of him!"

"Let's break in the door!"

"Come out!"

"Come out, Freshman!"

"He did it on purpose!"

"He chucked the game!"

"Wait till I get my hands on him!"

"I'll skin him!"

All at once the face of Butsey White appeared at the transom.

"Dink, you let me right in, you hear?"

No answer.

"You let me in right off!"

Still no answer.

"It's my room; you let me in to my room, do you hear?"

Stover continued silent.

"Dink," said Butsey in his loudest tones, "I'm coming right over the transom. Don't you dare to touch me!"

Stover again seized the chair.

Butsey White, supported from behind, carefully drew up one foot, and then convulsively disappeared as Stover charged with the chair.

There was a whispered consultation and then the battling face of Tough McCarty appeared with a new threat:

"You lay a hand on me and I'll rip the hide off you!"

"Keep back!" said Stover hoarsely.

"Put down that chair, you little varmint; do you hear me?"

"Don't you come over!"

"Yes, I'm coming over, and you don't dare to touch me. You don't——"

Stover was neither a coward nor a hero; he was simply in a panic and he was cornered. He rushed wildly to the breach and delivered the chair with a crash, Tough McCarty barely saving himself.

This open defiance of the champion angered the attacking party.

"He ought to be lynched!"

"The booby!"

"Wait till to-morrow!"

Tough McCarty reappeared for a brief second.

"I'll get you yet," he said, pointing a finger at the embattled Stover. "You're a muff, a low-down muff, in every sense of the word!"

Then succeeded the Coffee-colored Angel:

"Wait till I catch you, you Rinky Dink!"

Followed the White Mountain Canary:

"You'll reckon with *me* for this!"

Down to Beekstein Hall, with his black-rimmed spectacles, each member of the outraged nine climbed to the transom and expressed his unflattering opinion.

Stover sat down, his chin in his hands, his eyes on the great, lumbering mitt that lay dishonored on the floor.

"I'm disgraced," he said slowly, "disgraced. It's all over—all over. I'm queered—queered forever!"

The acerbic theater critic George Jean Nathan (1882–1958) came from Indiana to New York where he edited *The Smart Set* from 1914 to 1923 with his partner in venom, H. L. Mencken. The next year the two founded one of the most consistently brilliant and wide-ranging periodicals in United States history, *The American Mercury.* Nathan published extensively on the theater, and it seems only appropriate that one of the country's most self-assured arbiters of taste would have taken time to hold forth (in *Harper's Weekly* in 1910) on baseball's arbiters, the umpires.

George Jean Nathan

♥

Baiting the Umpire

B aseball is the national side-show. The baiting of umpires is the real big-tent entertainment. In Spain, by way of passing the time, they bait innocent bulls on holidays. In America, by way of the same thing, they bait inoffensive men in blue suits every day in the week during the warm season, and twice on Saturdays. What the Latins call "fêtes" the Americans call "double-headers." Also, what the Latins call "matadores" the Americans call "bleachers." Some years ago, the Spanish sport-loving public was satisfied with one bull in the ring, just as the American public was satisfied with one umpire. But, as taste became more hysterical and bloodthirsty, the Spaniards demanded at least two bulls for killing purposes, and the Americans, following suit, demanded two umpires. That is the real reason the Solons of baseball added the extra referee to the game. They told the second umpire he was supposed to "watch the bases." It was a snare. He was put there simply to gratify the public's augmented longing for "sport."

In comparing the national sports of Spain and the United States, it may be readily seen that the bull has a marked advantage over the umpire. The bull has two horns that he is allowed to use in self-defence. He is given a fair chance for his life. The umpire is not. The bull, furthermore, is not compelled to abide by any printed rules in the process of having his mortal coil unwound for him. The umpire is. He is not allowed to protect himself. Clause No. 65 of the rules governing baseball says that "under no circumstance shall a player dispute the accuracy of the umpire's judgment and decision on a play." When he applies for a job, the umpire is beguiled by that clause. But no sooner has he donned his blue serge suit and placed a lozenge in his mouth, than he perceives the trick that has been played on him. There is an unwritten law among the players that Clause No. 65 is in violation of their rights, and they feel justified in doing away with it, accordingly, whenever they see fit. There are twenty-five clauses telling the umpire what *he* must do, but only the solitary No. 65 telling what the *players* must not. And, as has been indicated, No. 65 does not count.

But the players do not concern us. They may feel like killing the umpire, but they must stand by and let the bleachers do the job for them. The bleachers are governed by no regulations and may "kill" umpires in any manner and at any time they, in their infinite wisdom, may choose.

The favorite way of doing away with this much-tried official is by word of mouth. Sometimes this is supplemented by leather cushions, pop-bottles, and apple cores, but usually the assault is committed verbally. It is rare sport. Hundreds of thousands of games of baseball were played in the United States during the season of 1909, and yet it is a matter of record that in only *one* of these contests was no umpire's scalp sought. The exception occurred in Jersey City, New Jersey, on Sunday, April 18th. The game in point was played between the Jersey City Eastern League team and the New York National League team, the latter winning by a score of six to three. Before the game, the management of the Jersey City club, as a safeguard against further Chancery Court proceedings to restrain the team from playing ball on Sundays, distributed cards to each spectator requesting the elimination of all loud speech. This was obeyed by the eighteen thousand persons present, and, as a consequence, a record was established. The entire nine innings were finished without any "umpire-killing" whatever. It was miraculous. You cannot kill an umpire in whispers. It is as unsatisfactory as it is impossible.

"Kill the umpire!" is the battle-cry of baseball. Compared to the umpire, the proverbial fat man is a universally loved individual. If there are twenty thousand men at a ball game, each one of the twenty thousand, as well as all the small boys on the near-by telegraph poles, hate the umpire. Every one itches to take his life. According to the shouted consensus of opinion, hanging is the favorite means for the disposition of the gentleman. "Hang the umpire!" sound the bleachers, in tones of thunder. The electric chair, the guillotine, asphyxiation, poison—none of these will do. The umpire must be hanged. Such is the lynch-law of the stands.

In the famous world's championship series last year between the Detroit and Pittsburg teams, Umpires Klem and Johnstone, of the National League, and Umpires O'Loughlin and Evans, of the American League, were "killed" in almost every inning of every game played. In fact, things got to such a point that the National Baseball Commission was forced to step in. The players had tried to do a little assassinating on their own account. For verbal assault with intent to kill, players Leach, Clarke, Camnitz, Maddox, and Donovan were fined twenty-five dollars each, while Miller, for insisting that one of the umpires must be killed at once because he had called a ball a strike in the fourth game when Miller knew very well it was no such thing, was fined twice that amount.

Once in a while, to vary the monotony of simply clamoring for the umpire's immediate demise, the spectators take it upon themselves to accomplish his death with their own hands. And once in a while they would succeed in their laudable purpose if it were not for the unwelcome intrusion of the police. Twice during last September at the Polo Grounds in New York, a squad of guardians of the law saw fit to spoil a good half-hour's amusement by escorting an umpire to the clubhouse, when a vast throng of lovers of clean sport longed to indulge in a little killing-bee. The umpire, in the second instance at least, *should* have been killed, according to the bleachers. There was justification a-plenty. Had he not robbed the home team of a game by calling a player out for not having touched a base? To be sure, the player should have touched the base according to the rules, and, to be sure, he failed to do so; but was that any reason for the umpire's decision? It most certainly was not. Any umpire who does not know enough to give favorable decisions to the home team in a case like this ought to be killed. The police are the greatest foes of good sport in this country. Thirty-seven times last season, in the two big leagues alone, did they interrupt the killing of umpires.

According to bleacher law, there are three particularly justifiable motives for doing away with umpires. An umpire may be killed, first, if he sees fit to adhere to the rules and make a decision against the home team at a close point in the game. Secondly, an umpire may be killed if he sends a member of the home team to the bench when the player in question has done absolutely nothing but call the umpire names and attempt to bite his ear off—an umpire has no business to be touchy. Thirdly (and this is a perfect defence against the charge of murder), an umpire may be killed if he calls any batter on the home team out on strikes when the player has not even struck at the balls pitched. That the balls go straight over the plate has nothing to do with the case.

It was estimated by a well-known baseball writer at the conclusion of last season that, judging solely from the newspaper records, three hundred and fifty-five umpires in the United States had been molested physically during the period stipulated. That is, three hundred and fifty-five of only the more spectacular instances had found their way into the prints. That the number of actual attempts to do physical injury to umpires was many times in excess of that chronicled cannot be doubted for a moment when it is remembered that there are, in this country, tens of thousands of professional and amateur teams which play a total of hundreds of thousands of games each season. And each game lasts at least nine innings. What a magnificent field of opportunity!

There is ample proof at hand to show that killing-the-umpire is a distinctively American sport. Other countries have tried baseball, but they have not tried killing-the-umpire. That is probably the reason why they have not waxed enthusiastic over baseball. For baseball without umpire-killing is like football without girls in the grand-stand. It simply can't be done. That foreign countries know nothing about our king of outdoor sports was indicated forcibly when, in the fall of 1909, the Detroit team made a trip to Cuba under the management of Outfielder McIntyre. In the entire series of twelve games with the Havana and Almendares nines, not one single objection was made by either the Cuban players or the silent Cuban spectators to a decision of the umpires. The Americans did not know what to think of it—until they counted up the gate receipts at the end of the series. Then they realized that, in their own country, it is the delight in killing-the-umpire rather than the pleasure in watching-the-game that draws the tremendous crowds through the turnstiles.

When the University of Wisconsin ball team went to Japan last fall at the invitation of the Keio team of Tokio, nine games were played on the Keio grounds at Mita Undoba and all nine games were umpired by one man—a Japanese named Nakano, a former player on the team representing Waseda University. Not once in any of the games did the Japanese spectators make any demonstration against Nakano, and, as a result, the games took on the appearance of "roll-the-ball"— the Japanese sport most familiar to Americans, bazar-goers, and Coney-Islanders. As one of the Wisconsin players said afterward, "For sheer excitement and outbursts of enthusiasm it rivalled a field-day at a deaf-mute asylum." In Victoria, Australia, where a determined effort is being made to popularize baseball, the prime movers in the campaign, appreciating full well the important and necessary relation that killing-the-umpire bears to the game, have tried the novel experiment of working up the hostile spirit toward the referee by playing the baseball contests—all or in part—before the huge football crowds. These crowds are demonstrative in the extreme, and it is hoped by the baseball promoters that part of the excess football emotional tumult may, in time, be directed against the umpires, thus insuring the success of the game. At Melbourne particularly, where baseball games have been tried on Saturday afternoons preceding the regular football matches, considerable progress has been noted in working up the feelings of the thirty thousand or more spectators against the umpires. Things are going so well, in fact, that there are now twenty-three baseball teams in Victoria as compared with five in 1904. The figures are vouched for by P. B. Seyffarth, one of the leading baseball campaigners in Australia.

In addition to the countries named, baseball has been tried recently in Great Britain, in Mexico, in Central America, in New Zealand, Canada, Italy, and in the Sandwich Islands. In none of these lands, save Australia and the Sandwich Islands, however, does it seem destined to become the national game. The reason is not far to seek. They have begun at the wrong end, these foreigners. You can't "institute" baseball. You must begin by building up a bleachers. The bleachers will "institute" killing-the-umpire, and then the game of baseball itself will begin to flourish. In Australia, the matter has been approached in the correct way. In the Sandwich Islands, baseball cannot possibly fail. The natives will take to umpires as naturally as they have taken to missionaries. Only with them, probably, the shout will be, "*Eat* the umpire!"

Albert Goodwill Spalding (1850–1915) was a farm boy from Byron, Illinois, who became one of baseball's first successful players, a businessman, a rule-maker, and a patron of the game. He was working as a clerk in a Rockford grocery store when returning Civil War soldiers introduced him to baseball. Between 1871 and 1875, as a member of the Boston Red Stockings, he was professional baseball's finest pitcher, leading the team to four pennants. He "jumped" to the Chicago White Stockings in 1876 and won 46 games that year. Later he became team president. The unrefined nature—and erratic supply—of early baseball equipment led Spalding to open a small sporting goods business, A. G. Spalding & Bros., which eventually became a conglomerate, supplying many Americans with their bats, gloves, and shin guards and Major League Baseball with its official balls until 1977. Spalding was instrumental in the formation of both the National and American leagues, and he was a tireless opponent of gambling in the sport. In 1905, he organized a commission to determine the American origins of baseball which popularized the apocryphal story that a Civil War general named Abner Doubleday had invented the game in Cooperstown, New York. A similar burst of patriotic gusto led him to write *America's National Game* (1911), the exuberant tract from which this excerpt is taken.

Albert G. Spalding

ᗢ

from

America's National Game

Have we, of America, a National Game? Is there in our country a form of athletic pastime which is distinctively American? Do our people recognize, among their diversified field sports, one standing apart from every other, outclassing all in its hold upon the interest and affection of the masses? If a negative reply may truthfully be given to all or any of these queries, then this book should never have been published—or written.

But, if we have a National Game; if we know a form of athletics which is peculiarly American, and have adopted it as our own; if it is American in its spirit, its character and its achievements; if it conforms in every way to the American temperament; if we have a field sport outranking all others in popularity, then it is indeed time that the writing, in personal reminiscence, of its story in book form should begin, "lest we forget" the salient points in the inception, evolution and development of so important a factor in the widespread entertainment of the American people and the physical upbuilding of our youth.

To enter upon a deliberate argument to prove that Base Ball is our National Game; that it has all the attributes of American origin, American character and unbounded public favor in America, seems a work of supererogation. It is to undertake the elucidation of a patent fact; the sober demonstration of an axiom; it is like a solemn declaration that two plus two equal four.

Every citizen of this country who is blessed with organs of vision knows that whenever the elements are favorable and wherever grounds are available, the great American game is in progress, whether in city, village or hamlet, east, west, north or south, and that countless thousands of interested spectators gather daily throughout the season to witness contests which are to determine the comparative excellence of competing local organizations or professional league teams.

The statement will not be successfully challenged that the American game of Base Ball attracts more numerous and larger gatherings of spectators than any other form of field sport in any land. It must also be admitted that it is the only game known for which the general public is willing day after day to pay the price of admission. In exciting political campaigns, Presidential candidates and brilliant orators will attract thousands; but let there be a charge of half a dollar imposed, and only Base Ball can stand the test.

I claim that Base Ball owes its prestige as our National Game to the fact that as no other form of sport it is the exponent of American Courage, Confidence, Combativeness; American Dash, Discipline, Determination; American Energy, Eagerness, Enthusiasm; American Pluck, Persistency, Performance; American Spirit, Sagacity, Success; American Vim, Vigor, Virility.

Base Ball is the American Game *par excellence,* because its playing demands Brain and Brawn, and American manhood supplies these ingredients in quantity sufficient to spread over the entire continent.

No man or boy can win distinction on the ball field who is not, as man or boy, an athlete, possessing all the qualifications which an intelligent, effective playing of the game demands. Having these, he has within him the elements of pronounced success in other walks of life. In demonstration of this broad statement of fact, one needs only to note the brilliant array of statesmen, judges, lawyers, preachers, teachers, engineers, physicians, surgeons, merchants, manufacturers, men of eminence in all the professions and in every avenue of commercial and industrial activity, who have graduated from the ball field to enter upon honorable careers as American citizens of the highest type, each with a sane mind in a sound body.

It seems impossible to write on this branch of the subject—to treat of Base Ball as our National Game—without referring to Cricket, the national field sport of Great Britain and most of her colonies. Every writer on this theme does so. But, in instituting a comparison between these games of the two foremost nations of earth, I must not be misunderstood. Cricket is a splendid game, for Britons. It is a genteel game, a conventional game—and our cousins across the Atlantic are nothing if not conventional. They play Cricket because it accords with the traditions of their country so to do; because it is easy and does not overtax their energy or their thought. They play it because they like it and it is the proper thing to do. Their sires, and grandsires, and great-grandsires played Cricket—why not they? They play Cricket because it is their National Game, and every Briton is a Patriot. They play it persistently—and they play it well. I have played Cricket and like it. There are some features about that game which I admire more than I do some things about Base Ball.

But Cricket would never do for Americans; it is too slow. It takes two and sometimes three days to complete a first-class Cricket match; but two hours of Base Ball is quite sufficient to exhaust both players and spectators. An Englishman is so constituted by nature that he can wait three days for the result of a Cricket match; while two hours is about as long as an American can wait for the close of a Base Ball game—or anything else, for that matter. The best Cricket team ever organized in America had its home in Philadelphia—and remained there. Cricket does not satisfy the red-hot blood of Young or Old America.

The genius of our institutions is democratic; Base Ball is a democratic game. The spirit of our national life is combative; Base Ball is a combative game. We are a cosmopolitan people, knowing no arbitrary class distinctions, acknowledging none. The son of a President of the United States would as soon play ball with Patsy Flannigan as with Lawrence Lionel Livingstone, provided only that Patsy could put up the right article. Whether Patsy's dad was a banker or boiler-maker would never enter the mind of the White House lad. It would be quite enough for him to know that Patsy was up in the game.

I have declared that Cricket is a genteel game. It is. Our British Cricketer, having finished his day's labor at noon, may don his negligee shirt, his white trousers, his gorgeous hosiery and his canvas shoes, and sally forth to the field of sport, with his sweetheart on one arm and his Cricket bat under the other, knowing that he may engage in his national pastime without soiling his linen or neglecting his lady. He may play Cricket, drink afternoon tea, flirt, gossip, smoke, take a whiskey-and-soda at the customary hour, and have a jolly, conventional good time, don't you know?

Not so the American Ball Player. He may be a veritable Beau Brummel in social life. He may be the Swellest Swell of the Smart Set in Swelldom; but when he dons his Base Ball suit, he says goodbye to society, doffs his gentility, and becomes—just a Ball Player! He knows that his business now is to play ball, and that first of all he is expected to attend to business. It may happen to be his business to slide; hence, forgetting his beautiful new flannel uniform, he cares not if the mud is four inches deep at the base he intends to reach. His sweetheart may be in the grandstand—she probably is—but she is not for him while the game lasts.

Cricket is a gentle pastime. Base Ball is War! Cricket is an Athletic Sociable, played and applauded in a conventional, decorous and English manner. Base Ball is an Athletic Turmoil, played and applauded in an unconventional, enthusiastic and American manner.

The founder of our National Game became a Major General in the United States Army! The sport had its baptism when our country was in the preliminary agonies of a fratricidal conflict. Its early evolution was among the men, both North and South, who, during the war of the sixties, played the game to relieve the monotony of camp life in those years of melancholy struggle. It was the medium by which, in the days following the "late unpleasantness," a million warriors and their sons, from both belligerent sections, passed naturally, easily, gracefully, from a state of bitter battling to one of perfect peace.

Base Ball, I repeat, is War! and the playing of the game is a battle in which every contestant is a commanding General, who, having a field of occupation, must defend it; who, having gained an advantage, must hold it by the employment of every faculty of his brain and body, by every resource of his mind and muscle.

But it is a bloodless battle; and when the struggle ends, the foes of the minute past are friends of the minute present, victims congratulating victors, conquerors pointing out the brilliant individual plays of the conquered.

It would be as impossible for a Briton, who had not breathed the air of this free land as a naturalized American citizen; for one who had no part or heritage in the hopes and achievements of our country, to play Base Ball, as it would for an American, free from the trammels of English traditions, customs, conventionalities, to play the national game of Great Britain.

Let such an Englishman stand at the batter's slab on an American ball field, facing the son of an American President in the pitcher's box, and while he was ruminating upon the propriety of hitting, in his "best form," a ball delivered by the hands of so august a personage, the President's boy would probably shoot three hot ones over the plate, and the Umpire's "Three strikes; you're out," would arouse our British cousin to a realization that we have a game too lively for any but Americans to play.

On the other hand, if one of our cosmopolitan ball artists should visit England, and attempt a game of Cricket, whether it were Cobb, Lajoie, Wagner, or any American batsman of Scandinavian, Irish, French or German antecedents; simply because he was an American, and even though the Cricket ball were to be bowled at his feet by King George himself, he would probably hit the sphere in regular Base Ball style, and smash all conventionalities at the same time, in his eager effort to clear the bases with a three-bagger.

The game of Base Ball is American as to another peculiar feature. It is the only form of field sport known where spectators have an important part and actually participate in the game. Time was, and not long ago, when comparatively few understood the playing rules; but the day has come when nearly every man and boy in the land is versed in all the intricacies of the pastime; thousands of young women have learned it well enough to keep score, and the number of matrons who know the difference between the short-stop and the back-stop is daily increasing.

But neither our wives, our sisters, our daughters, nor our sweethearts, may play Base Ball on the field. They may play Cricket, but seldom do; they may play Lawn Tennis, and win championships; they may play Basket Ball, and achieve laurels; they may play Golf, and receive trophies; but Base Ball is too strenuous for womankind, except as she may take part in grandstand, with applause for the brilliant play, with waving kerchief to the hero of the three-bagger, and, since she is ever a loyal partisan of the home team, with smiles of derision for the Umpire when he gives us the worst of it, and, for the same reason, with occasional perfectly decorous demonstrations when it becomes necessary to rattle the opposing pitcher.

But spectators of the sterner sex may play the game on field, in grandstand or on bleachers, and the influence they exert upon the contest is hardly less than that of the competitors themselves.

In every town, village and city is the local wag. He is a Base Ball fan from infancy. He knows every player in the League by sight and by name. He is a veritable encyclopædia of information on the origin, evolution and history of the game. He can tell you when the Knickerbockers were organized, and knows who led the batting list in every team of the National and American Leagues last year. He never misses a game. His witticisms, ever seasoned with spice, hurled at the visitors and now and then at the Umpire, are as thoroughly enjoyed by all who hear them as is any other feature of the sport. His words of encouragement to the home team, his shouts of derision to the opposing players, find sympathetic responses in the hearts of all present.

But it is neither the applause of the women nor the jokes of the wag which make for victory or defeat in comparison with the work of the "Rooter." He is ever present in large numbers. He is there to see the "boys" win. Nothing else will satisfy him. He is bound by no rules of the game, and too often, perhaps, by no laws of decorum. His sole object in life for two mortal hours is to gain victory for the home team, and that he is not overscrupulous as to the amount of racket emanating from his immediate vicinity need not be emphasized here.

And so it comes to pass that at every important game there is an exhibition in progress, in grandstand and on bleachers, that is quite as interesting in its features of excitement and entertainment as is the contest on the field of sport, and which, in its bearing upon the final result, is sometimes a factor nearly as potent as are the efforts of the contesting players.

It must be admitted that as the game of Base Ball has become more generally known; that is, as patrons of the sport are coming to be more familiar with its rules and its requirements, their enjoyment has immeasurably increased; because, just in so far as those in attendance understand the features presented in every play, so far are they able to become participators in the game itself. And beyond doubt it is to this growing knowledge on the part of the general public with the pastime that its remarkable popularity is due. For, despite the old adage, familiarity does *not* breed contempt, but fondness, and all America has come to regard Base Ball as its very own, to be known throughout the civilized world as the great American National Game.

Finally, in one other particular Base Ball has won its right to be denominated the American National Game. Ever since its establishment in the hearts of the people as the foremost of field sports, Base Ball has "followed the flag." It followed the flag to the front in the sixties, and received then an impetus which has carried it to half a century of wondrous growth and prosperity. It has followed the flag to Alaska, where, under the midnight sun, it is played on Arctic ice. It has followed the flag to the Hawaiian Islands, and at once supplanted every other form of athletics in popularity. It has followed the flag to the Philippines, to Porto Rico and to Cuba, and wherever a ship floating the Stars and Stripes finds anchorage to-day, somewhere on nearby shore the American National Game is in progress.

Alfred Damon Runyon (1884–1946) of Manhattan, Kansas, became a cultural icon of Manhattan, New York, by inventing a literary style that can be found in his Broadway play *A Slight Case of Murder* (1935), in his Broadway stories collected in *Guys and Dolls* (1932), which inspired the musical of the same name, or in the magnificent journalism and occasional light verse he contributed to the *New York American* and other Hearst newspapers. To be Runyonesque is to be clipped and familiar and yet simultaneously colorful and cunning—to put a swagger on everything, and especially on people with very little to swagger about. It was as a sportswriter that Runyon first made his mark, and these pieces, published in the *American* on consecutive days in July 1911, show how individual a talent he brought to that pursuit. Runyon was a master at capturing the carnival atmosphere of the ball park in boisterous, irresistible prose. His digressive, irreverent, energetically facetious reporting sought above all to entertain his readers; those interested in the facts could consult the box scores. "I always made covering a standard story like a big race or a ballgame more or less of a stunt," he recalled in a letter to his son. Among the characters described here are Fred Merkle, the first baseman who, by failing to touch base during a game with the Cubs, committed the tragic "boner" that cost the Giants the 1908 National League pennant; Roger Bresnahan, the Giants catcher who invented shin guards (appearing as player-manager for the St. Louis Cardinals); and George Wiltse, the pitcher who threw a 10-inning no-hitter in 1908 and once struck out seven consecutive batters in two innings (the third strike of one of the strikeouts was dropped by his catcher, none other than Roger Bresnahan).

Damon Runyon

ᘐ

Hail! Roger Merkle, Favorite of Toledo

Regular Christian Name is Fred, but We Call Him Roger in Order Not to Dim Bresnahan's Lustre.

Toledo is in Ohio, a statement which may be immediately verified by reference to any well-ordered map, railway guide or automobile prospectus.

The score yesterday afternoon was 4 to 2 in favor of the Giants.

It is a large and thriving mid-Western city, with paved streets, tramways and electric lights. It is noted chiefly for its imports of magazine writers considering the efficacy of the Golden Rule, as applied to municipal government, and for its exports of baseball players.

(Red Ames pitched agin 'em.)

The leading citizens of Toledo, in their order, are:

Roger Merkle,

Fred Bresnahan,

Brand Whitlock*

(*A member of the Ohio litterati.)

Some may argue that the Christian names of the first two have been misplaced. This is intentional. This is because these two gentlemen run a dead heat in point of public esteem in Toledo, and it would be an injustice to place either one first—a difficulty obviated as above.

(Humphries, ex-Philly, worked for Cincinnati. Soft.)

READ ABOUT THEIR FAVORITES

In Toledo, when the gentle Ohio night has drifted over the premises, the good people draw their chairs closely together in their parlors and read in their evening paper how fare their favorite sons on alien fields.

(Red allowed eight hits.)

In the Winter, when Roger Merkle and Fred Bresnahan pass down the principal aisle of Toledo activity, mayhap arm in arm, the population stand asunder and let them move as they may list, while the charioteers of the Seeing Toledo 'buses cry their names to the startled passengers.

This is mere preamble.

(The Reds got three men on in the sixth, with Larry McLean up— may be you think we were not scared!)

This is all merely preliminary to a statement that will cause the simple Toledo heart to rejoice. This is just an introduction to further words concerning their Citizen Merkle, for it is with Merkle that we have more directly to do, at the moment, Citizen Bresnahan coming later.

(Larry was an easy out.)

HIT HIMSELF THREE HITS

In a game of baseball at the Polo Grounds yesterday afternoon, your Mr. Merkle, Oh, City of Toledo, hit himself three large, and, as Harry Stevens would say, lovely, hits, two of which strung up a brace of runs for our boys, and were sadly needed ere the show closed.

(Griffith, Downey and Egan got canned. Goody, goody!)

One was a ringing ka-nock which wound up all out of shape in the left field bleachers, "one of the longest home runs of the season;" one was a resounding two-bagger, which crowded in a run, and the other was a common, or garden, single, which Merkle tried to stretch into a two-bagger. He did not do it.

(The Giants got a single and a double in the second, but nary run— Help!)

Well may Toledo, Ohio, lift a proud head, and say: "This is our son." Without those two runs for which Merkle was directly responsible, the terrible contest might be in progress right now, to the utter exclusion of other matters of more moment.

(Larry McLean was up again in the eighth with two men on, but flew out—Oh, you Larritickus!)

ANOTHER CARNIVAL OF NATIONS

Clarke Griffith gave the spectators another carnival of all nations, taking the blankets off both his Cubans, as well as Balenti, a Cheyenne Indian, who gained vast fame as a Carlisle footballer, and who went into the game yesterday as shortstop pro tem. Both of Griff's Cubans also passed in brief review as pinch hitters. They did not hit. Marsans went out on an infield tap in the seventh, and Almeda struck out when he showed up in the ninth. The editor of the Havana El Mundo groaned, and a fellow countryman of the tanned balltosser's fell in a fit in the stands, crying: "Mucho malo hombres!"

(Clarke Griffith said the same thing, but he said his in English, and you cannot get it through the mails in that condition.)

In addition to other things, this was ejection day for the Reds, Umpire Johnstone—he of the fiery dome—sticking his official thumb into the backs of a whole crowd of Ohioans and pushing them right off the field, Hon. Clarke Griffith bringing up the rear of the parade. Downey was the first to be chased away, this occurring in the second inning because he wailed in Johnstone's ear concerning a called strike. Balenti took his place.

In the sixth inning, when a squall blew up for Ames, due to Mitchell's triple, Balenti tapped to Bridwell, and Al whipped the ball in to Wilson in time to choke off Mitchell—or, at least, Johnstone viewed it in that light. The Reds—and a good many people in the stands—disagreed vociferously with the umpire's view, and Griffith and Egan kept speaking about the matter so often that they were both thrown out of the lot at the opening of the Giants' end of the inning.

Observe, now, the teeming third inning, done in the lingual fashion of the times. Devore singled to the infield, Balenti's brief bobble helping some. Doyle tripled and Devore scored. Doyle scored on a wild pitch, which bounced off McLean's toe, and after Snodgrass and Murray had gone out in order, Merkle crashed his homer into the bleachers.

In the fifth Doyle singled and Snodgrass sacrificed him to second, Snod going out at the plate without running, thinking his effort had gone foul. Murray flew out and Merkle's double scored Doyle.

LARRY DROPPED THE TOSS

In the Reds' end of the third Balenti walked, and after McLean had gone out on a fly, Humphries tapped to Bridwell and Doyle dropped Al's easy toss, putting Balenti on second and Humphries on first. Bescher fanned for the second time and Bates singled, scoring Balenti.

In the fourth Mitchell doubled over third and took third on Balenti's out, scoring on Grant's single.

The score:

CINCINNATI.	ab	r	h	po	a	e	NEW YORK.	ab	r	h	po	a	e
Bescher, lf	5	0	2	3	1	0	Devore, lf	4	1	1	0	0	0
Bates, cf	5	0	1	3	0	0	Doyle, 2b	4	2	2	3	2	1
H'tzel, 1b	4	0	0	9	1	0	S'dgrass, cf	3	0	1	2	0	0
Mitchell, rf	4	1	2	3	0	0	Murray, rf	4	0	1	2	0	0
Downey, ss	1	0	0	1	0	0	Merkle, 1b	4	1	3	10	0	0
Balenti, ss	3	0	1	1	2	0	Br'dwell, ss	4	0	1	1	7	0
Grant, 3b	2	0	1	0	2	0	Fletcher, 3b	4	0	1	0	3	0
Egan, 2b	2	1	1	0	1	0	Wilson, c	3	0	1	9	0	0
Esmo'd, 2b	1	0	0	0	0	0	Ames, p	3	0	0	0	3	0
McLean, c	4	0	0	3	1	0							
H'phries, p	2	0	0	1	3	0							
*Marsans	1	0	0	0	0	0							
Gaspar, p	0	0	0	0	1	0							
†Almeida	1	0	0	0	0	0							
Totals	35	2	8	24	12	0	Totals	33	4	11	27	15	1

*Batted for Humphries in the seventh inning.
†Batted for Gaspar in the ninth inning.
Cincinnati........................0   0   1   1   0   0   0   0   0—2
New York..........................0   0   3   0   1   0   0   0   x—4
Two-base hits—Wilson, Mitchell, Bescher, Merkle. Three-base hits—Doyle, Mitchell. Home run—Merkle. Sacrifice hit—Snodgrass. Stolen bases—Fletcher, Balenti. Left on base—New York, 6. Cincinnati, 9. Double play—Fletcher, Doyle and Merkle. Bases on balls—Off Ames, 1. Struck out—By Ames, 8; by Humphries, 1. Hits—Off Humphries, 9 in 6 innings; off Gaspar, 2 in 2 innings. Umpires—Johnstone and Eason. Time of game—One hour and fifty minutes.

Rajah's Pride Falls Before 'G. Hooks-em'

Two Weazened-Up Little Hits Sum Total Effort of Crushed St. Louis Band. Count 4 to 0.

As for you, Rajah Bresnahan, with your oily voice and city ways— take that! Zam! Bumpety-bump-bump! (Noise of villain falling off the front stoop, bleeding from the nose.)

Little did you think, Rajah Bresnahan, when you entered the doors of our humble cot in the shelter of Coogan's classic cliff, that we had a protector. Little did you think, when you came in that Olive street disguise, and wearing that hat, that the heavy hand of Retribution (nee George Hooks-em Wiltse) was hanging over your corrugated bean. It was 4 to 0.

It fell yesterday afternoon with the weight of a ton of tripe and a squashy sound, and the crime of Thursday, July 20, was avenged.

Last night the Man Who Owns St. Louis stood alone in front of his cheerless hotel, vainly searching his pockets for even so much as two little runs to rub, one against the other, while proud and haughty citizens who had been pleased to be seen in his glittering train passed hurriedly along without a word of recognition. They were on their way to attend the reception to George Hooks-em Wiltse, hero of the saucer scene yesterday.

Two weazened up little hits were all that the official scorer can reasonably inject into the record of the Gaekwar of Senloo, without perjuring himself—two very puny little hits.

Dusting off the upper shelves of the pantry where he stores his pitchers, in search of a crumb of twirling comfort, John J. McGraw ran across George Hooks-em Wiltse, lying there just trembling with anticipation.

"Feel my muscle," urged George. "Just feel it once, and set me on 'em."

"It might as well be you, George," said John J. McGraw, and so he pronounced his benediction upon the thin port wheeler, and sent him to the damp tee.

IT WAS HISTORY FOR WILTSE

The result now becomes history.

With his little black licorice-drop cap pulled down so tightly over his head that he probably had to use a can-opener to remove it; with his left arm bared to the shoulder, and looking as dark and sombre as the day itself, George Hooks-em Wiltse began slanting the ball sidewise and peculiar against the startled vision of the Cardinal Cleaners, who, thereupon, became the Cleaned.

The afternoon was cool, the sky was covered with a mask of clouds that shed a little rain before the game was concluded, and under these circumstances George Hooks-em Wiltse is at his very best— better than which there is none.

When the lank form of the left-hander loomed up amidships in the diamond, the twelve thousand spectators felt somewhat perturbed, recalling his last few previous starts, when he was out there with nothing much but his glove and uniform, but after he had gone three innings, the crowd sat back to enjoy a first-class exhibition of pitching.

For the first six innings just eighteen men faced the veteran southpaw. In the first inning Huggins, the first man up, waited with great patience until he had acquired a base on balls, but immediately thereafter Chief Meyers made a show of Miller on an attempted steal of second. In the second inning Evans drew a walk, but again the chief's strong right arm stopped an attempted steal. After that the celebrated Cleaners walked backward and forward from bench to bat with painful monotony.

ARTHUR RIGHT AFTER THE BALL

Sensational fielding by Arthur Fletcher was one of the brilliant features of the afternoon, and that young man who is said to have the most perfect hands in baseball displayed his lunch-hooks to considerable advantage in digging hard chances out of the turf and air.

In the seventh inning, with one out, Hauser got the first hit off Wiltse, a single as clean as a bugle, but George closed up again and made Rube Ellis, the leading citizen of Riviera, Cal., fan with mighty sweeps of a vast batting oar, while the lean Pole, Konetchy, flew out to Doyle.

In the ninth Huggins singled with two out, but Hauser was unable to help him.

In the Giants' end of the first inning Josh-way Devore led off with as clear a strike-out as ever was stricken, but J. Lawrence Doyle dealt Robert Harmon a resounding two-base thump. On the heels of this pleasant event came a two-satchel slam by Fred Snodgrass, and J. Lawrence Doyle rang up the first run. Snodgrass loitered far enough off second base to draw a random throw from Rajah, and the ball went out into centre field, while Snodgrass tallied. Murray struck out and Hauser made an acrobatic one-handed stop of a fast bounder from Merkle's bat and got the citizen of Toledo at first with the breadth of a span.

G. HOOKS ALSO SMITES IT

In the fifth inning Arthur Devlin, who was back in his old room on third, while Fletcher played the short field, awaiting the advent of Herzog, drew a base on balls and took third on J. Tortes Meyers's single to right. Meyers went to second on the throw-in, and G. Hooks Wiltse solemnly but very deliberately singled, scoring Devlin and Meyers, the Chief giving a grand ground and lofty exhibition of a cumbersome gentleman scoring from second on a comparatively short hit.

Doyle tapped gently to Harmon, and Wiltse was tagged out as he somberly galloped to third. Snodgrass hit into a double play.

Devore tripled with one out in the third, but subsequently went out at the plate on Doyle's fly to Evans. Snodgrass singled in the fourth, stole second on the Rajah, and reached third on Merkle's out, but proceeded no further.

The score:

ST. LOUIS.	ab	r	h	po	a	e	NEW YORK.	ab	r	h	po	a	e
Huggins, 2b	3	0	1	2	4	0	Devore, lf	4	0	1	1	0	0
Hanser ss	4	0	1	3	2	1	Doyle, 2b	4	1	2	3	1	0
Ellis, lf	3	0	0	2	0	0	S'dgrass, cf	4	1	2	0	0	0
Kon'y, 1b	3	0	0	8	1	1	Murray, rf	3	0	0	4	0	0
Evans, rf	2	0	0	1	1	0	Merkle, 1b	3	0	0	10	1	0
Smith, 3b	3	0	0	1	2	0	Fletcher, ss	3	0	1	2	3	0
McIver, cf	3	0	0	0	0	0	Devlin, 3b	1	1	0	0	2	0
Bres'n'n, e	3	0	0	6	3	1	Myers, c	3	1	1	6	2	0
Harmon, p	2	0	0	1	1	0	Wiltse, p	3	0	1	1	0	0
*Wowrey	1	0	0	0	0	0	Totals	28	4	8	27	9	0
Totals	27	0	2	24	14	3							

*Batted for Harmon in the ninth inning.

```
St. Louis..........................0    0    0    0    0    0    0    0    0——0
New York..........................2    0    0    0    2    0    0    0    x——4
```

First base on errors—New York, 1. Two-base hits—Doyle, Snodgrass. Three-base hits—Devore. Stolen bases—Snodgrass, 2. Left on bases—New York 2, St. Louis, 2. Double plays—Evans and Bresnahan; Hauser, Huggins and Konetchy, 2. Bases on balls—Off Wiltse, 2; off Harmon, 2. Struck out—By Wiltse, 6; by Harmon, 5. Umpires—O'Day and Emslie. Time of game—One hour and twenty-five minutes.

•••

Not long after Ty Cobb died in 1961, Lawrence Ritter, an economist at New York University, began a journey that would take him 75,000 miles before it ended in 1966. He was in search of old ballplayers who could tell his tape-recorder about their lives in baseball when it was still a somewhat disheveled pursuit and not quite yet the National Pastime. Ritter's conversations with the likes of Rube Marquard, Jimmy Austin, Edd Roush, and Sam Crawford were transformed into *The Glory of Their Times: The Story of Baseball Told by the Men Who Played It* (1966), a lucid, often moving, always gripping oral epic describing what it was like to play in the days when the crowds sang "Tessie" and second-stringers slept in the upper berth on road trips.

Lawrence S. Ritter

♥

from

The Glory of Their Times

Samuel Earl Crawford, who prefers to be called Wahoo Sam, played major-league baseball for 19 years, from 1899 through 1917. He was fast: he typically stole 25 to 30 bases a season. He could hit: the record books credit him with 2,964 major-league hits, a figure exceeded by only nine men in the history of baseball.* And he could hit with power: he led the National League in home runs in 1901, and the American League in 1908 and 1914.

---

* There is still considerable dispute over the total number of hits accumulated by Wahoo Sam. Some insist that the correct total should be 3,051. The case for the latter figure was best stated by H. G. Salsinger (in the Detroit *News* of May 20, 1957) upon the occasion of Sam Crawford's induction into the Baseball Hall of Fame:

"According to the official records, Crawford is credited with a lifetime total of 2,964 hits, but he should rightfully be credited with 3,051. When Crawford began his career, records were kept in a careless and haphazard manner. Crawford made his professional debut with Chatham in the Canadian League in 1899, but after 43 games he advanced to Grand Rapids in the Western League, where he made 87 hits and batted .334.

"Ban Johnson was president of the Western League in 1899. At the same time he was organizing the American League, which he launched in the spring of 1900. The National Commission ruled that any player from the Western League entering either the old National League or the new American League would be credited with all hits he made in the Western League.

"Crawford joined Cincinnati and was therefore entitled to the 87 hits he made for Grand Rapids. In compiling his lifetime record the statistician overlooked these 87 hits and gave him credit for 2,964 instead of his rightful 3,051."

In combination, these elements resulted in 312 major-league triples, still the most three-baggers ever hit by one man. It is almost inconceivable that this record will ever be broken. Willie Mays, the closest approximation to a modern-day Sam Crawford, has accumulated but 115 triples after 13 seasons in the majors.

Most baseball writers of that period agree that Sam Crawford was the out-standing power hitter of the dead-ball era. H. G. Salsinger, eminent Detroit sports writer who covered the Detroit Tigers throughout the era of Cobb and Crawford, recalls that "I have seen right fielders, playing against the fence, catch five fly balls off Crawford's bat in one game, five fly balls that would have cleared the fence any time after the season of 1920, when the jackrabbit ball was introduced."

I don't know how you found me, but since you're here you might as well come in and sit down. I don't have much time, though. Got a lot of things to do. But it's a hot day, so come in and rest awhile.

Yeah, I'm sort of hard to find. Still bounce around a lot, you know. Always on the move. Probably a hangover from all those years in baseball—Boston today, Detroit tomorrow, never long in one place. I do have a house down in Hollywood, but I can't take that town. Too much smog. Too many cars, all fouling up the air. Can hardly breathe down there. Too many people, too. Have to stand in line everywhere you go. Can't even get a loaf of bread without standing in line. Pretty soon they'll be standing in line to get into the john! That's not for me.

No, I don't have a telephone. If I had a lot of money I wouldn't have one. I *never* was for telephones. Just don't like them, that's all. Anybody wants to talk to you, they can come to see you. I do have a television over there—it was a gift—but I never turn it on. I'd rather read a book. Don't even watch the ball games. Oh, maybe the World Series, but that's about it. I like to do what I like to do, that's all. I don't see why I should watch television just because everybody else does. I'd rather read a book, or fix up the garden, or just take a walk with my wife, Mary, and see what's going on, you know.

Heck, I don't even buy a newspaper. Nothing but trouble in it. Just spoils your day. You get up in the morning, feel pretty good, get hold of a paper, and what do you see? Nothing but trouble. Big headlines about bombs and war and misery. It ruins the day. That's the way I look at it, anyway. Maybe I'm wrong, I don't know.

So you're doing a book about baseball in the old days. Why does a young fellow like you want to spend his time on something like that? Do you remember what Robert Ingersoll used to say? "Let the dead past bury its dead." That's what he used to say. Robert Ingersoll, remember him? A great man. I always admired him. He was a very famous lecturer in the late 1800's. Very famous and very controversial. He was supposed to be an atheist, but he wasn't really. More a skeptic, more an agnostic, than an atheist. You should read his *Lectures* some time. Very interesting. Now he's forgotten. Hardly anybody even remembers his name any more. That probably proves something, but I'm not sure what.

Anyway, those days are all back in the past. We're going to spend the rest of our lives in the future, not in the past: "Let the dead past bury its dead." On the other hand, Santayana said: "Those who forget the past are condemned to repeat it." So maybe there are two sides to this matter. But I don't think we'll ever repeat the old days in baseball. They'll never come back. Everything has changed too much.

You know, there were a lot of characters in baseball back then. Real individualists. Not conformists, like most ballplayers—and most people—are today. Rube Waddell, for instance. Boy, there was one of a kind. They never made another like him. I played on the same team with Rube back in 1899, the Grand Rapids club in the old Western League. We were both just starting out, but it wasn't hard to see even then that Rube was going to really be something. He won about 30 games for us that season and hardly lost any.

He used to pour ice water on his pitching arm. Yeah, ice water. We'd kid him, you know, tell him he didn't seem to have much on the ball that day, and ask him why he couldn't get it over the plate.

"Listen," he'd say, "I'll show you guys whether I've got anything or not. Fact is, I've got so much speed today I'll burn up the catcher's glove if I don't let up a bit."

And he'd go over to the water barrel—we had a barrel filled with ice water in the dugout—and dip the dipper in and pour ice water all over his left arm and shoulder.

"That's to slow me down a little," he'd say. And then he'd go out there and more likely than not he'd strike out the side.

Rube was just a big kid, you know. He'd pitch one day and we wouldn't see him for three or four days after. He'd just disappear, go fishing or something, or be off playing ball with a bunch of twelve-year-olds in an empty lot somewhere. You couldn't control him 'cause he was just a big kid himself. Baseball was just a game to Rube.

We'd have a big game scheduled for a Sunday, with posters all over Grand Rapids that the great Rube Waddell was going to pitch that day. Even then he was a big drawing card. Sunday would come and the little park would be packed way before game time, everybody wanting to see Rube pitch. But half the time there'd be no Rube. Nowhere to be found. The manager would be having a fit. And then just a few minutes before game time there'd be a commotion in the grandstand and you'd hear people laughing and yelling: "Here comes Rube, here comes Rube."

And there he'd come, right through the stands. He'd jump down on to the field, cut across the infield to the clubhouse, taking off his shirt as he went. In about three minutes—he never wore any under-wear—he'd run back out in uniform and yell, "All right, let's get 'em!"

By the end of that season—1899—we were both in the Big Leagues, Rube with Louisville and me with Cincinnati. I should say Big *League*, because there was only one major league then, the National League. The American League didn't start until a couple of years later, and it was a few years after that before the National League recognized it. It was sort of like the way it is now in professional football.

By 1903, though, we were both in the American League. I jumped to the Detroit Tigers and Rube went with Connie Mack's Philadelphia Athletics. We had some great battles after that, the Tigers and the A's, some great fights for the pennant. From 1905 through 1914, you know, either the Tigers or the A's won the pennant every year but two. The White Sox won it in 1906 and the Red Sox in 1912. But except for those two years, we won it in 1907, '08, and '09, and Connie won it the others.

Rube was at his peak those years he was with Connie. He was amazing. Way over 20 wins every season, and always leading the league in strikeouts. How good he'd have been if he'd taken baseball seriously is hard to imagine. Like I say, it was always just a game with Rube. He played 'cause he had fun playing, but as far as he was con-cerned it was all the same whether he was playing in the Big Leagues or with a bunch of kids on a sandlot.

The main thing you had to watch out for was not to get him mad. If things were going smoothly and everyone was happy, Rube would be happy too, and he'd just go along, sort of half pitching. Just fooling around, lackadaisical, you know. But if you got him mad he'd really bear down, and then you wouldn't have a chance. Not a chance.

Hughie Jennings, our manager at Detroit, used to go to the dime store and buy little toys, like rubber snakes or a jack-in-the-box. He'd get in the first-base coach's box and set them down on the grass and yell, "Hey, Rube, look." Rube would look over at the jack-in-the-box popping up and down and kind of grin, real slow-like, you know. Yeah, we'd do everything to get him in a good mood, and to distract him from his pitching.

When you think about people like Rube Waddell, and there were lots of other off-beat characters around then, also, you start to get some idea of how different it all used to be. Baseball players weren't too much accepted in those days, either, you know. We were considered pretty crude. Couldn't get into the best hotels and all that. And when we did get into a good hotel, they wouldn't boast about having us. Like, if we went into the hotel dining room—in a good hotel, that is—they'd quick shove us way back in the corner at the very end of the dining room so we wouldn't be too conspicuous. "Here come the ballplayers!" you know, and back in the corner we'd go.

I remember once—I think it was in 1903—I was with the Detroit club, and we all went into the dining room in this hotel, I believe in St. Louis. Well, this dining room had a tile floor, made out of little square tiles. We sat there—way down at the end, as usual—for about 20 minutes and couldn't get any waiters. They wouldn't pay any attention to us at all. Remember Kid Elberfeld? He was playing shortstop for us then, a tough little guy. Later he played for many years with the Yankees, up on the hilltop. Anyway, Kid Elberfeld says, "I'll get you some waiters, fellows."

Darned if he didn't take one of the plates and sail it way up in the air, and when it came down on that tile floor it smashed into a million pieces. In that quiet, refined dining room it sounded like The Charge of the Light Brigade. Sure enough, we had four or five waiters around there in no time.

Yeah, Kid Elberfeld, what a character he was. Kid Gleason was on the Detroit club about then, too. Another rugged little guy. Do you know that those guys actually *tried* to get hit with the ball when they were up at bat? They didn't care. They had it down to a fine art, you know. They'd look like they were trying to get out of the way, but they'd manage to let the ball just nick them. Anything to get on base. That was all part of the game then.

Kid Gleason used to be on that old Baltimore Oriole team in the 1890's. You know, with Willie Keeler and McGraw and Dan Brouthers and Hughie Jennings, who later became our manager at Detroit. That whole crew moved over to Brooklyn later. I played against those guys when I came up with Cincinnati, in 1899, and let me tell you, after you'd made a trip around the bases against them you knew you'd been somewhere. They'd trip you, give you the hip, and who knows what else. Boy, it was rough. There was only one umpire in those days, see, and he couldn't be everywhere at once.

Ned Hanlon used to manage that Baltimore club, but those old veterans didn't pay any attention to him. Heck, they all knew baseball inside out. You know, ballplayers were tough in those days, but they were real smart, too. Plenty smart. There's no doubt at all in my mind that the old-time ballplayer was smarter than the modern player. No doubt at all. That's what baseball was all about then, a game of strategy and tactics, and if you played in the Big Leagues you had to know how to think, and think quick, or you'd be back in the minors before you knew what in the world hit you.

Now the game is all different. All power and lively balls and short fences and home runs. But not in the old days. I led the National League in home runs in 1901, and do you know how many I hit? Sixteen. That was a helluva lot for those days. Tommy Leach led the league the next year—with six! In 1908 I led the American League with only seven. Do you know the most home runs Home Run Baker ever hit in one year? It was twelve. That was his best year. In 1914 Baker and I tied for the lead with the grand total of eight each. Now, little Albie Pearson will hit that many accidentally. So you see, the game is altogether different from what it was. Then it was strategy and quick thinking, and if you didn't play with your old noodle you didn't play at all.

Like I said, those old Baltimore Orioles didn't pay any more attention to Ned Hanlon, their manager, than they did to the batboy. When I came into the league, that whole bunch had moved over to Brooklyn, and Hanlon was managing them there, too. He was a bench manager in civilian clothes. When things would get a little tough in a game, Hanlon would sit there on the bench and wring his hands and start telling some of those old-timers what to do. They'd look at him and say, "For Christ's sake, just keep quiet and leave us alone. We'll win this ball game if you only shut up."

They would win it, too. If there was any way to win, they'd find it. Like Wee Willie Keeler. He was really something. That little guy couldn't have been over five feet four, and he only weighed about 140 pounds. But he played in the Big Leagues for 20 years and had a lifetime batting average of close to .350. Think of that! Just a little tiny guy.

"Hit 'em where they ain't," he used to say. And could he ever! He choked up on the bat so far he only used about half of it, and then he'd just peck at the ball. Just a little snap swing, and he'd punch the ball over the infield. You couldn't strike him out. He'd always hit the ball somewhere. And could he fly down to first! Willie was really fast. A real nice little guy too, very friendly, always laughing and kidding.

You know, there were a lot of little guys in baseball then. McGraw was a fine ballplayer and he couldn't have been over five feet six or seven. And Tommy Leach, with Pittsburgh—he was only five feet six and he couldn't have weighed over 140. He was a beautiful ballplayer to watch. And Bobby Lowe, who was the first player to ever hit four home runs in one game. He did that in 1894. That was something, with that old dead ball. Bobby and I played together for three or four years in Detroit, around 1905 or so.

Dummy Hoy was even smaller, about five-five. You remember him, don't you? He died in Cincinnati only a few years ago, at the age of ninety-nine. Quite a ballplayer. In my opinion Dummy Hoy and Tommy Leach should both be in the Hall of Fame.

Do you know how many bases Dummy Hoy stole in his major-league career? Over 600! That *alone* should be enough to put him in the Hall of Fame. We played alongside each other in the outfield with the Cincinnati club in 1902. He had started in the Big Leagues way back in the 1880's, you know, so he was on his way out then, and I had been up just a few years, but even that late in his career he was a fine out fielder. A *great* one.

I'd be in right field and he'd be in center, and I'd have to listen real careful to know whether or not he'd take a fly ball. He couldn't hear, you know, so there wasn't any sense in me yelling for it. He couldn't talk either, of course, but he'd make a kind of throaty noise, kind of a little squawk, and when a fly ball came out and I heard this little noise I knew he was going to take it. We never had any trouble about who was to take the ball.

Did you know that he was the one responsible for the umpire giving hand signals for a ball or a strike? Raising his right hand for a strike, you know, and stuff like that. He'd be up at bat and he couldn't hear and he couldn't talk, so he'd look around at the umpire to see what the pitch was, a ball or a strike. That's where the hand signs for the umpires calling balls and strikes began. That's a fact. Very few people know that.

Another interesting thing about Dummy Hoy was the unique doorbell arrangement he had in his house. He had a wife who was a deaf mute too, and they lived in Cincinnati. Instead of a bell on the door, they had a little knob. When you pulled this knob it released a lead ball which rolled down a wooden chute and then fell off onto the floor with a thud. When it hit the floor they felt the vibrations, through their feet, and they knew somebody was at the door. I thought that was quite odd and interesting, don't you?

It's funny how little things like that come back to you, after all these years. That was over 60 years ago when we played together. He was a little fellow, like I said, only five feet five. But he had real large, strong hands. He used to wear a diamond ring—we all did in those days—but his knuckles were so big that he had a ring with a hinge on it. A real hinge. He couldn't get a ring that would go over his big knuckles and still fit right, so he had one made with a hinge so that he could put it on and then close it and it would lock in place. Did you know that he once threw three men out at home plate in one game? From the outfield, I mean. That was in 1889. And still they don't give him a tumble for the Hall of Fame. It's not right.

In those days, believe it or not, it was tougher to throw a guy out at home than it is today. That might sound sort of silly, but it's true. One reason is that the ball was often lopsided. No kidding. We'd play a whole game with one ball, if it stayed in the park. Another reason is that when I broke in the Big Leagues we only had one umpire in a game, not four like they have today. And you *know* that one umpire just can't see everything at once. He'd stand behind the catcher until a man got on base, and then he'd move out and call balls and strikes from behind the pitcher. He'd be out there behind the pitcher with, say, a man on second base, and the batter would get a hit out to right field. Well, the umpire would be watching the ball and the batter rounding first and trying for second. Meanwhile, the guy who was on second would cut third base wide by fifteen feet on his way home. Never came anywhere close to third base, you know. We'd run with one eye on the ball and the other on the umpire!

Did you ever hear of Tim Hurst? He was a very famous umpire back then. A real tough character. He was wise to this deal, of course, where the runner doesn't come anywhere close to touching third base. Well, Jake Beckley was playing first base for us—with the Cincinnati club in 1899 or 1900 or so—and he came sliding into home one day. A real big slide, plenty of dust and all, even though no one was even trying to tag him out. Tim had been watching a play at second all the while.

"You're out!" yells Tim.

Jake screamed to high heaven. "What do you mean, I'm out?" he roared. "They didn't even make a play on me."

"You big S.O.B.," Tim said, "you got here *too* quick!"

Yeah, old Tim knew what was going on. I was an umpire too, for awhile, you know—in the Pacific Coast League from 1935 to 1938—long after I finished playing. Umpiring is a lonesome life. Thankless job. Thankless. You haven't got a friend in the place. Only your partner, that's all. He's the only man in the whole place who is for you. Everybody else is just waiting for you to make a mistake. There's a bench over here, and a bench over there, and thousands of people in the stands, and every eye in the whole damn place is watching like a hawk trying to get something on you.

I had a good partner, too. I booked in with a fellow named Jack Powell, a wonderful umpire and a wonderful person as well. He'd tell me not to fraternize with the players. I felt that I could kid around with them a little, you know. What the heck, I'd been a ballplayer myself. But he said, "Don't do it, don't fool with the players, don't have anything to do with them. If you do, sooner or later they'll put you on the spot."

And that's the way it turned out. He was right. It's a thankless and a lonely way to live, so I quit it.

But even then, in the thirties, the game was a lot different from the way it had been when I played. The lively ball and the home run were well entrenched by the thirties. Heck, like I said, we'd play a whole game with one ball, if it stayed in the park. Lopsided, and black, and full of tobacco juice and licorice stains. The pitchers used to have it all their way back then. Spitballs and emory balls and whatnot. But there were some great pitchers in those days: Jack Chesbro and Cy Young and Ed Walsh.

Ed Walsh, seemed like I was batting against that guy every other day. Great big, strong, good-looking fellow. He threw a spitball—I think that ball disintegrated on the way to the plate and the catcher put it back together again. I swear, when it went past the plate it was just the spit went by.

Of course, the greatest of them all was Walter Johnson. Boy, what a pitcher Walter was! He was the best I ever faced, without a doubt. Did you know that I was playing with Detroit the day Walter Johnson pitched his first major-league game? His very first. In fact, I beat him. I'm not being egotistical, you know, but it's a fact. I hit a home run off him and we beat him—I believe the score was 3–2.

I think that was late in 1907. We were after the pennant that year, our first pennant, and we needed that game badly. Big Joe Cantillon was managing Washington at the time. You know Joe? You know *of* him. He was a nice guy, Joe was, always kidding. Anyway, before the game Joe came over to the Detroit bench and said, "Well boys, I've got a great big apple-knocker I'm going to pitch against you guys today. Better watch out, he's plenty fast. He's got a swift."

He told us that, you know. And here comes Walter, just a string of a kid, only about eighteen or nineteen years old. Tall, lanky, from Idaho or somewhere. Didn't even have a curve. Just that fast ball. That's all he pitched, just fast balls. He didn't *need* any curve. We had a terrible time beating him. Late in the game I hit one—I can remember it as though it were yesterday—it went zooming out over the shortstop's head, and before they could get the ball back in I'd legged it all the way around. In those days the grounds were very big, you know, and if you hit one between the outfielders you could often make it all the way around the bases. Nowadays you very seldom see an inside-the-park home run, they've pulled those fences in so. But in those days most home runs were like that.

Yes, Joe Cantillon was a kidder, but he wasn't kidding that day. That Walter was fast! I batted against him hundreds of times after that, of course, and he never lost that speed. He was the fastest I ever saw, by far.

Did you ever see those pitching machines they have? That's what Walter Johnson always reminded me of, one of those compressed-air pitching machines. It's a peculiar thing, a lot of batters are afraid of those machines, because they can gear them up so that ball comes in there just like a bullet. It comes in so fast that when it goes by it *swooshes*. You hardly see the ball at all. But you *hear* it. *Swoosh*, and it smacks into the catcher's mitt. Well, that was the kind of ball Walter Johnson pitched. He had such an easy motion it looked like he was just playing catch. That's what threw you off. He threw so nice and easy—and then *swoosh*, and it was by you!

Walter was a wonderful person, too, you know. He was always afraid he might hit somebody with that fast ball. A wonderful man, in every way. Warm, and friendly, and wouldn't hurt a soul. Easily the greatest pitcher I ever saw. Of course, I never saw Grover Cleveland Alexander very much, or Christy Mathewson. They were in the National League, and from 1903 on I was with Detroit in the American League.

I must say, though, that the greatest all-around ballplayer I ever saw was in the National League. I played against him for four years, from 1899 through 1902, when I was with Cincinnati and he was first with Louisville and then with Pittsburgh. People always ask me about Ty Cobb, you know: "You played in the outfield next to Cobb for all those years. Don't you agree that he was the greatest player who ever lived?"

Cobb was great, there's no doubt about that; *one* of the greatest. But not *the* greatest. In my opinion, *the* greatest all-around player who ever lived was Honus Wagner.

Cobb could only play the outfield, and even there his arm wasn't anything extra special. But Honus Wagner could play any position. He could do everything. In fact, when I first played against him he was an outfielder, and then he became a third baseman, and later the greatest shortstop of them all. Honus could play any position except pitcher and be easily the best in the league at it. He was a wonderful fielder, terrific arm, very quick, all over the place grabbing sure hits and turning them into outs. And, of course, you know he led the league in batting eight times.

You'd never think it to look at him, of course. He looked so awkward, bowlegged, barrel-chested, about 200 pounds, a big man. And yet he could run like a scared rabbit. He had enormous hands, and when he scooped up the ball at shortstop he'd grab half the infield with it. But boy, Honus made those plays! He looked awkward doing it, not graceful like Larry Lajoie, but he could make every play Lajoie could make and more. Talk about speed. That bowlegged guy stole over 700 bases in the 21 years he played in the Big Leagues. A good team man, too, and the sweetest disposition in the world. The greatest ballplayer who ever lived, in my book.

Cobb and Wagner met head on in the 1909 World Series, you know, Detroit against Pittsburgh. We lost in seven games, the first time the Series went the full seven games. Wagner stole six bases in that Series, as many as our whole team, and Cobb stole only two. Honus was one of those natural ballplayers, you know what I mean? Like Babe Ruth and Willie Mays. Those fellows do everything by pure instinct. Mays is one of the few modern players who are just as good as the best of the old-timers. Although I guess the best center fielder of them all was Tris Speaker. He played in real close and could go back and get those balls better than anyone I ever saw.

Don't get me wrong. I'm not running Cobb down. He was terrific, no doubt about it. After all, he stole almost 900 bases and had a batting average of .367 over 24 years in the Big Leagues. You can't knock that. I remember one year I hit .378—in 1911, I think it was—and I didn't come anywhere close to leading the league: Joe Jackson hit .408 and Cobb hit .420. I mean, that's mighty rugged competition!

I played in the same outfield with Cobb for 13 years, from 1905 through 1917. I was usually in right, Cobb in center, and Davy Jones and then Bobby Veach in left. Davy Jones, he was the best lead-off man in the league. I've seen a lot of lead-off men, but I never saw one who came close to being Davy's equal. The lineup usually was Davy Jones, Donie Bush, Cobb, and Crawford, although sometimes I batted third and Cobb fourth. That Donie Bush was a superb shortstop, absolutely superb. I think he still holds a lot of records for assists and putouts.

They always talk about Cobb playing dirty, trying to spike guys and all. Cobb never tried to spike anybody. The base line belongs to the runner. If the infielders get in the way, that's their lookout. Infielders are supposed to watch out and take care of themselves. In those days, if they got in the way and got nicked they'd never say anything. They'd just take a chew of tobacco out of their mouth, slap it on the spike wound, wrap a handkerchief around it, and go right on playing. Never thought any more about it.

We had a trainer, but all he ever did was give you a rubdown with something we called "Go Fast." He'd take a jar of Vaseline and a bottle of Tabasco sauce—you know how hot that is—mix them together, and rub you down with that. Boy, it made you feel like you were on fire! That would *really* start you sweating. Now they have medical doctors and whirlpool baths and who knows what else.

But Ty was dynamite on the base paths. He really was. Talk about strategy and playing with your head, that was Cobb all the way. It wasn't that he was so fast on his feet, although he was fast enough. There were others who were faster, though, like Clyde Milan, for instance. It was that Cobb was so fast in his *thinking*. He didn't outhit the opposition and he didn't outrun them. He outthought them!

A lot of times Cobb would be on third base and I'd draw a base on balls, and as I started to go down to first I'd sort of half glance at Cobb, at third. He'd make a slight move that told me he wanted me to keep going—not to stop at first, but to keep on going to second. Well, I'd trot two-thirds of the way to first and then suddenly, without warning, I'd speed up and go across first as fast as I could and tear out for second. He's on third, see. They're watching him, and suddenly there I go, and they don't know what the devil to do.

If they try to stop me, Cobb'll take off for home. Sometimes they'd catch him, and sometimes they'd catch me, and sometimes they wouldn't get either of us. But most of the time they were too paralyzed to do anything, and I'd wind up at second on a base on balls. Boy, did that ever create excitement. For the crowd, you know; the fans were always wondering what might happen next.

Cobb was a great ballplayer, no doubt about it. But he sure wasn't easy to get along with. He wasn't a friendly, good-natured guy, like Wagner was, or Walter Johnson, or Babe Ruth. Did you ever read

Cobb's book? He wrote an autobiography, you know, and he spends a lot of time in there telling how terrible he was treated when he first came up to Detroit, as a rookie, in 1905. About how we weren't fair to him, and how we tried to "get" him.

But you have to look at the other side, too. We weren't cannibals or heathens. We were all ballplayers together, trying to get along. Every rookie gets a little hazing, but most of them just take it and laugh. Cobb took it the wrong way. He came up with an antagonistic attitude, which in his mind turned any little razzing into a life-or-death struggle. He always figured everybody was ganging up against him. He came up from the South, you know, and he was still fighting the Civil War. As far as he was concerned, we were all damn Yankees before he even met us. Well, who knows, maybe if he hadn't had that persecution complex he never would have been the great ballplayer he was. He was always trying to prove he was the best, on the field and off. And maybe he was, at that.

One thing that really used to get Ty's goat was when I'd have a good day and he didn't. Oh, would he ever moan then. Walter Johnson and I were very good friends, and once in a while Walter would sort of "give" me a hit or two, just for old-time's sake. But when Ty came up there, Walter always bore down all the harder. There was nothing he enjoyed more than fanning Ty Cobb.

You see, Walter always liked my model bat. Somehow he got the idea that my bats were lucky for him. So very often when the Senators came to Detroit Walter would come into our clubhouse and quietly ask me if I could spare a bat for him.

"Sure, Walter," I'd say, "go take any one you want."

He'd go over to my locker, look them over, pick one out, and quietly leave. Well, whenever the occasion arose when it wouldn't affect a game, Walter would let up a bit on me and I'd have a picnic at the plate—like, if Washington had a good lead and it was late in the game. I'd come up to bat and Gabby Street, Walter's catcher, would whisper, "Walter likes you today, Sam."

That was the cue that the next pitch would be a nice half-speed fast ball. So I'd dig in and belt it. Of course, if it was a close game all that was out the window. The friendship deal was off then. Cobb never did figure out why I did so well against Walter, while he couldn't hit him with a ten-foot pole.

Well, this is more than I've talked in years, and it's good. I don't see many people, and even when I do I don't talk about baseball too much. I read a lot. My favorite writer is Balzac. A wonderful writer. But I rarely talk about baseball. There are very few people around, you know, who remember those old days. Once in a while I meet some elderly man who says, "I can remember seeing you play. My father took me to see you when I was a kid." But very seldom.

It's like when I got elected to the Hall of Fame, back in 1957. I was living in a little cabin at the edge of the Mojave Desert, near a little town called Pearblossom. Nobody around there even knew I'd been a ballplayer. I never talked about it. So there I was, sitting there in that cabin, with snow all around—it was February—and all of a sudden the place is surrounded with photographers and newspapermen and radio-TV reporters and all. I didn't know what in the world was going on.

"You've just been elected to the Hall of Fame," one of them said to me.

The people living around there—what few of them there were— were all excited. They couldn't figure out what was happening. And when they found out what it was all about, they couldn't believe it. "Gee, you mean old Sam? He used to be a ballplayer? We didn't even know it. Gee!"

From then on, of course, I've gotten thousands of letters. I still get a lot. Mostly from kids, wanting autographs. Sometimes they send a stamped envelope, and sometimes they don't. But I've answered every one by hand. In 1957, when I was elected to the Hall, I also went back to Detroit. It was the fiftieth anniversary of all the players who were still alive who had been on that 1907 pennant-winning team. I enjoyed that, but I wouldn't put on a uniform. I went out in civilian clothes and waved to the fans, but I refused to put on a uniform. I want to be remembered the way I used to be. When they think of Sam Crawford in a Detroit uniform I want them to think of me the way I was way back then, and no other way.

Yes, those were days I'll never forget. There were always a lot of laughs playing ball back then. I guess it must still be that way today. A lot of sadness and disappointment, too, like losing three straight World Series and never winning a pennant after 1909. But always a lot of laughs. Like ballplayers and their superstitions. I'm only a little superstitious. I won't walk under a ladder, that's all. But a lot of them were obsessed with that stuff. For instance, butterflies flying across the field. A white butterfly meant something, and a red one meant something else. Particularly those big red ones—monarchs, they called them—they really meant something special. The manager would look out and say, "Boy, oh boy, oh boy, there goes a red one." They really believed that stuff, you know.

Before Hughie Jennings became the manager at Detroit—that was in 1907—Bill Armour was our manager. He had managed Cleveland before that, and in 1905 he became the Detroit manager. He'd go nuts if he saw a cross-eyed bat boy. Bill would take one look at him and get an expression on his face like he was about to die.

"Get rid of him, get rid of him," he'd yell. "Or leave him stay, but get him out of my sight. I don't want to see him."

Naturally, we spent half our time searching for cross-eyed kids, so we could sneak them in as bat boys!

Everything wasn't gay and carefree, of course. In lots of ways it wasn't the easiest life in the world. We had to travel a lot, you know, and travel conditions were pretty rugged then. We had sleeper trains in the Big Leagues in 1899 and 1900, when I broke in, but the sleepers had gaslights in them, not electric lights. They used to go around and light them up at night. We spent a lot of our lives living out of our grips, on trains and in hotels. The hotels weren't the best in the world, and the trains had coal-burning engines. So you'd wake up in the morning covered with cinders. They had fine little screens on the train windows, but the cinders would still come through.

And there were tragedies, you know, like the death of Big Ed Delahanty in the middle of the 1903 season. Ed was only in his mid-thirties and was still going strong as an outfielder with Washington when he died. I think Ed was the best right-handed hitter I ever saw, really a great hitter. It's hard to choose between him and Honus. He was the second man in history to hit four home runs in a game. Bobby Lowe did it in 1894, and Ed a couple of years later, and then nobody did it again for 40 or 50 years. Twice he got six hits in one game. Quite a hitter. I think his lifetime batting average was close to .350.

Ed was born and raised in Cleveland, the oldest of six brothers. And five of them became Big League ballplayers. We had one of them with the Tigers—Jimmy, a second baseman. Ed's death was tragic. The

Washington club was coming back from somewhere—I don't remember where—and their train had come to the suspension bridge there at Niagara Falls. It stopped before it went across, and Ed got off for a minute. But the train started up without him, and Ed began to walk across the bridge. The watchman, the guard at the bridge, tried to stop him, and they had a fight or something. Nobody knows just what happened. Anyway, Ed fell off the bridge and was killed. They found his body a couple of miles below the Falls. It was too bad. He was a nice guy.

How did I get started in baseball? Well, I played ball all the time as a kid, you know. I always loved it. I grew up in Wahoo, Nebraska. "Wahoo Sam." I insisted they put that on my plaque at the Hall of Fame. That's my home town, and I'm proud of it. Darryl Zanuck came from Wahoo, did you know that? Also Howard Hanson, of the Eastman Conservatory of Music. I remember when Darryl Zanuck was a little towheaded kid running around the streets. His mother and father owned the hotel there in Wahoo. That was a long time ago. My dad ran a general store, just a little country store where they sold everything.

In those days baseball was a big thing in those little towns. The kids would be playing ball all the time. Nowadays basketball and football seem to be as popular among kids as baseball, maybe more so, but not then. And we didn't have radio, you know, or television, or automobiles. I guess, when you come to think of it, we spent most of our childhood playing ball.

Heck, we used to make our own baseballs. All the kids would gather string and yarn and we'd get hold of a little rubber ball for the center. Then we'd get our mothers to sew a cover on the ball to hold it all together. We didn't use tape to tape up the outside, like kids did 10 or 20 years later. We didn't see much tape in those days, about 1890 or so. Of course, they had tape then, electrical tape, but not much.

I can remember very well the first electric lights in Wahoo, on the street corner. Just one loop of wire, kind of reddish. We used to go down to the corner and watch this light go on. That was a big deal. Then we'd go over to the powerhouse, where the dynamos were, and see where they made the electricity. After that came the arc lights, with two carbons coming together. That was the next step. But the first ones were just one loop of wire in the bulb, and they gave kind of a reddish glow.

Of course, there were regular baseballs made back then. We'd call them league balls. But we couldn't afford to buy them, not us kids. That was for the men to play with. For bats we'd find some broken bat and nail it up, or sometimes even make our own.

Every town had its own town team in those days. I remember when I made my first baseball trip. A bunch of us from around Wahoo, all between sixteen and eighteen years old, made a trip overland in a wagon drawn by a team of horses. One of the boys got his father to let us take the wagon. It was a lumber wagon, with four wheels, the kind they used to haul the grain to the elevator, and was pulled by a team of two horses. It had room to seat all of us—I think there were 11 or 12 of us—and we just started out and went from town to town, playing their teams.

One of the boys was a cornet player, and when we'd come to a town he'd whip out that cornet and sound off. People would all come out to see what was going on, and we'd announce that we were the Wahoo team and were ready for a ball game. Every little town out there on the prairie had its own ball team and ball grounds, and we challenged them all. We didn't have any uniforms or anything, just baseball shoes maybe, but we had a manager. I pitched and played the outfield both.

It wasn't easy to win those games, as you can imagine. Each of those towns had its own umpire, so you really had to go some to win. We played Freemont, and Dodge, and West Point, and lots of others in and around Nebraska. Challenged them all. Did pretty well, too.

We were gone three or four weeks. Lived on bread and beefsteak the whole time. We'd take up a collection at the games—pass the hat, you know—and that paid our expenses. Or some of them, anyway. One of the boys was the cook, but all he could cook was round steak. We'd get 12 pounds for a dollar and have a feast. We'd drive along the country roads, and if we came to a stream, we'd go swimming; if we came to an apple orchard, we'd fill up on apples. We'd sleep anywhere. Sometimes in a tent, lots of times on the ground, out in the open. If we were near some fairgrounds, we'd slip in there. If we were near a barn, well . . .

That tour led to my getting started in professional baseball. We beat the West Point team, and after the tour was over I got a letter from the manager at West Point, Nebraska, asking if I wanted to play with them. He said they'd pay me, or at least get me a job. I was apprenticing to be a barber at the time. So I went up there, and there I met a fellow from Omaha who had been with Chatham in the Canadian League. His name was Johnny McElvaine. He was going back the next season and wanted me to go along with him. So Johnny wrote the manager of the Chatham team and told him about me, and they sent back transportation money for both of us. That was in 1899. I was only nineteen at the time.

Yeah, I was going to be a barber. But then baseball came along, and I never went back to barbering. I was learning the trade the hard way, there in Wahoo. And I do mean the hard way. Cleaning cuspidors, and washing windows, and mopping the floor. Then sometimes they'd let me lather somebody and get them ready for the real barber. And sometimes a tramp would come through and want a haircut, and I could practice on him. That's the way we learned in those days.

That was a tough way to make a living. Stand on your feet from seven in the morning to ten or eleven o'clock on a Saturday night. Saturday was the big haircutting day. All the farmers would come in then, hay in their hair and all. We used to give a haircut and a shave and a shampoo for thirty-five cents. Ten cents for a shave, twenty-five for a haircut, and they'd throw in the shampoo. Now a haircut alone costs two dollars. Looks like the same old quarter haircut to me.

So when I got this chance to play professional ball, I didn't think twice about it. At Chatham I got $65 a month, plus board. That was pretty good. A dollar was a dollar in those days, you know. That Canadian League was just a little six-club league. Folded up about July. From there I was sold to Grand Rapids in the Western League, where I played with Rube Waddell, and in September they sold me to Cincinnati in the National League. All three leagues in one year, and I hit over .300 in all of them. So there I was, in 1898 touring Nebraska with the Wahoo team in a wagon, and in 1899 playing in the Big Leagues with the Cincinnati Reds.

All that was pretty exciting for a nineteen-year-old kid. I'd never been anywhere before that. At Cincinnati I made about $150 a month, which was a lot of money in those days, especially for me.

There were a lot of old-timers on that Cincinnati club in 1899: Buck Ewing, who was managing, Biddy McPhee, Tommy Corcoran, Harry Steinfeldt, Al Selbach, Jake Beckley, Noodles Hahn—lots of them. Biddy McPhee played second base for 18 years in Cincinnati, one position. From 1882 to 1899. And Noodles Hahn, you never hear his name anymore. He was a first-rate left-hander. Talk about starting and finishing games, that guy pitched 41 complete games in 1901. Between 1899 and 1904 he started something like 225 games and completed about 210 of them.

Well, then the American League started up, about 1900 or so, and the players started jumping back and forth, from one league to the other. Larry Lajoie and Elmer Flick jumped from the Phillies to Cleveland, Ed Delahanty from the Phillies to Washington, Jack Chesbro from the Pirates to the Yankees—they were the Highlanders then—and Willie Keeler from Brooklyn to the Yankees. I left Cincinnati and went over to Detroit in 1903, and stayed there for 15 years.

Boy, here I am still talking. Hard to believe. I hope I haven't said anything I shouldn't. There are a lot of the old-timers still left, you know, and they're liable to say, "That fathead, who the hell does he think he is, anyway, popping off like that!"

I wouldn't want them to say that. Because I'd rather they remember me as a pretty straight sort of a guy, you know. So that when I kick off they'll say, "Well, good old Sam, he wasn't such a bad guy, after all. Everything considered, he was pretty fair and square. We'll miss him."

That's the way I'd like it to be.

Ringgold Wilmer Lardner, Jr., (1885–1933) was born in Niles, Michigan, and worked as a sportswriter for the *South Bend Times,* the *Chicago Examiner, The Sporting News,* and the *Chicago Tribune.* Lardner reveled in baseball and in the company of Chicago ballplayers until disclosure that the White Sox had fixed the 1919 World Series somewhat disenchanted him with the sport. His mordant sense of humor, his matchless ear for dialogue, and an undeniable misanthropic streak helped Lardner create the short fiction that won him praise from Virginia Woolf, H. L. Mencken, and a cast of literary acquaintances ranging from F. Scott Fitzgerald to Dashiell Hammett. Many of the best of these pieces feature ballplayers—tall tales about clever double-talkers, lucky stiffs, and hard-case hicks like "Alibi Ike," "Horseshoes," "My Roomy," and "Where Do You Get That Noise?"

Lardner is at his unsentimental best in *You Know Me Al,* an epistolary novel in which a brash, self-deluded rookie pitcher, Jack Keefe, sends news of the big leagues to his "Friend Al" Blanchard back home in the Indiana bushes. Like many of Lardner's characters, Jack Keefe was modeled after the major leaguers he covered as a journalist, including Butcher Boy Joe Benz, a notable unsophisticate who once pitched an exhibition game for the White Sox while dressed in hip boots. *You Know Me Al* first appeared in a series of *Saturday Evening Post* installments in 1914 and 1915, and immediately made Lardner both a famous man and the seminal writer of baseball literature. Here, the hardheaded hayseed describes the climax of his rivalry with Joe Hill, the husband of Violet, one of Keefe's former fiancées.

Ring Lardner

♥

from

You Know Me Al

Detroit, Michigan, April 28.

FRIEND AL: What do you think of a rotten manager that bawls me out and fines me $50.00 for loosing a 1 to 0 game in 10 innings when it was my 1st start this season? And no wonder I was a little wild in the 10th when I had not had no chance to work and get control. I got a good notion to quit this rotten club and jump to the Federals where a man gets some kind of treatment. Callahan says I

81

throwed the game away on purpose but I did not do no such a thing Al because when I throwed that ball at Joe Hill's head I forgot that the bases was full and besides if Gleason had not of starved me to death the ball that hit him in the head would of killed him.

And how could a man go to 1st base and the winning run be forced in if he was dead which he should ought to of been the lucky left handed stiff if I had of had my full strenth to put on my fast one instead of being ½ starved to death and weak. But I guess I better tell you how it come off. The papers will get it all wrong like they generally allways does.

Callahan asked me this A.M. if I thought I was hard enough to work and I was tickled to death, because I seen he was going to give me a chance. I told him Sure I was in good shape and if them Tigers scored a run off me he could keep me setting on the bench the rest of the summer. So he says All right I am going to start you and if you go good maybe Gleason will let you eat some supper.

Well Al when I begin warming up I happened to look up in the grand stand and who do you think I seen? Nobody but Violet. She smiled when she seen me but I bet she felt more like crying. Well I smiled back at her because she probily would of broke down and made a seen or something if I had not of. They was not nobody warming up for Detroit when I begin warming up but pretty soon I looked over to their bench and Joe Hill Violet's husband was warming up. I says to myself Well here is where I show that bird up if they got nerve enough to start him against me but probily Jennings don't want to waste no real pitcher on this game which he knows we got cinched and we would of had it cinched Al if they had of got a couple of runs or even 1 run for me.

Well, Jennings come passed our bench just like he allways does and tried to pull some of his funny stuff. He says Hello are you still in the league? I says Yes but I come pretty near not being. I came pretty near being with Detroit. I wish you could of heard Gleason and Callahan laugh when I pulled that one on him. He says something back but it was not no hot comeback like mine.

Well Al if I had of had any work and my regular control I guess I would of pitched a 0 hit game because the only time they could touch me was when I had to ease up to get them over. Cobb was out of the game and they told me he was sick but I guess the truth is that he knowed I was going to pitch. Crawford got a couple of lucky scratch hits off of me because I got in the hole to him and had to let up. But the way that lucky left handed Hill got by was something awful and if I was as lucky as him I would quit pitching and shoot craps or something.

Our club can't hit nothing anyway. But batting against this bird was just like hitting fungos. His curve ball broke about ½ a inch and you could of wrote your name and address on his fast one while it was comeing up there. He had good control but who would not when they put nothing on the ball?

Well Al we could not get started against the lucky stiff and they could not do nothing with me even if my suport was rotten and I give a couple or 3 or 4 bases on balls but when they was men waiting to score I zipped them threw there so as they could not see them let alone hit them. Every time I come to the bench between innings I looked up to where Violet was setting and give her a smile and she smiled back and once I seen her clapping her hands at me after I had made Moriarty pop up in the pinch.

Well we come along to the 10th inning, 0 and 0, and all of a sudden we got after him. Bodie hits one and Schalk gets 2 strikes and 2 balls and then singles. Callahan tells Alcock to bunt and he does it but Hill sprawls all over himself like the big boob he is and the bases is full with nobody down. Well Gleason and Callahan argude about should they send somebody up for me or let me go up there and I says Let me go up there because I can murder this bird and Callahan says Well they is nobody out so go up and take a wallop.

Honest Al if this guy had of had anything at all I would of hit 1 out of the park, but he did not have even a glove. And how can a man hit pitching which is not no pitching at all but just slopping them up? When I went up there I hollered to him and says Stick 1 over here now you yellow stiff. And he says Yes I can stick them over allright and that is where I got something on you.

Well Al I hit a foul off of him that would of been a fare ball and broke up the game if the wind had not of been against it. Then I swung and missed a curve that I don't see how I missed it. The next 1 was a yard outside and this Evans calls it a strike. He has had it in for me ever since last year when he tried to get funny with me and I says something back to him that stung him. So he calls this 3d strike on me and I felt like murdering him. But what is the use?

I throwed down my bat and come back to the bench and I was glad Callahan and Gleason was out on the coaching line or they probily would of said something to me and I would of cut loose and beat them up. Well Al Weaver and Blackburne looked like a couple of rums up there and we don't score where we ought to of had 3 or 4 runs with any kind of hitting.

I would of been all O.K. in spite of that peace of rotten luck if this big Hill had of walked to the bench and not said nothing like a real pitcher. But what does he do but wait out there till I start for the box and I says Get on to the bench you lucky stiff or do you want me to hand you something? He says I don't want nothing more of yourn. I allready got your girl and your goat.

Well Al what do you think of a man that would say a thing like that? And nobody but a left hander could of. If I had of had a gun I would of killed him deader than a doornail or something. He starts for the bench and I hollered at him Wait till you get up to that plate and then I am going to bean you.

Honest Al I was so mad I could not see the plate or nothing. I don't even know who it was come up to bat 1st but whoever it was I hit him in the arm and he walks to first base. The next guy bunts and Chase tries to pull off 1 of them plays of hisn instead of playing safe and he don't get nobody. Well I kept getting madder and madder and I walks Stanage who if I had of been myself would not foul me.

Callahan has Scotty warming up and Gleason runs out from the bench and tells me I am threw but Callahan says Wait a minute he is going to let Hill hit and this big stiff ought to be able to get him out of the way and that will give Scotty a chance to get warm. Gleason says You better not take a chance because the big busher is hogwild, and they kept argueing till I got sick of listening to them and I went back to the box and got ready to pitch. But when I seen this Hill up there I forgot all about the ball game and I cut loose at his bean.

Well Al my control was all O.K. this time and I catched him square on the fourhead and he dropped like as if he had been shot. But pretty soon he gets up and gives me the laugh and runs to first base. I did not know the game was over till Weaver come up and pulled me off the field. But if I had not of been ½ starved to death and weak so as I could not put all my stuff on the ball you can bet that Hill never would of ran to first base and Violet would of been a widow and probily a lot better off than she is now. At that I never should ought to of tried to kill a left-hander by hitting him in the head.

Well Al they jumped all over me in the clubhouse and I had to hold myself back or I would of gave somebody the beating of their life. Callahan tells me I am fined $50.00 and suspended without no pay. I asked him What for and he says They would not be no use in telling you because you have not got no brains. I says Yes I have to got some brains and he says Yes but they is in your stumach. And then he says I wish we had of sent you to Milwaukee and I come back at him. I says I wish you had of.

Well Al I guess they is no chance of getting square treatment on this club and you won't be supprised if you hear of me jumping to the Federals where a man is treated like a man and not like no white slave.

Yours truly,   JACK.

Where Do You Get That Noise?

The trade was pulled wile the Phillies was here first trip. Without knockin' nobody, the two fellas we give was worth about as much as a front foot on Main Street, Belgium. And the fella we got had went better this spring than any time since he broke in. So when the news o' the deal come out I says to Dode, I says:

"What's the matter with Pat—tradin' Hawley? What's he goin' to do with them two he's gettin'—make ticket takers out of 'em? What's the idear?"

"It does look like a bad swap for us," says Dode. "Hawley's worth six like them you're givin' us, and he ain't only twenty-seven years old."

"That's what I'm tellin' you," I says. "The deal looks like you was tryin' to help us out."

"We are," says Dode. "Didn't we just get through helpin' you out o' the first division?"

"Save that for the minstrels," I says. "Give me the inside on this business: Is they somethin' the matter with him? The trade's made now already and it won't hurt you none to come clean. Didn't him and Pat get along?"

"Sure! Why not?" says Dode. "Did you ever see a guy that Pat couldn't get along with him?"

"Well then," says I, "what's the answer? Don't keep me in suspenders."

"I ain't sure myself," says Dode, "but I and Bobby was talkin' it over and we figured that Pat just plain got sick o' hearin' him talk."

"Feed that to the goldfish," I says. "If Pat couldn't stand conversation he wouldn't of never lasted this long."

"Conversation, yes," Dode says; "but it's a different thing when a bird makes an argument out of everything that's said. They wasn't a day passed but what Hawley just as good as called everybody on the club a liar. And, it didn't make no difference whether you was talkin' to him or not. If I happened to be tellin' you that my sister was the champion chess player o' Peanut County, he'd horn right in and say she wasn't no such a thing; that So-and-So was the champion. And they wouldn't be no use to argue with him because you couldn't even get a draw. He'd say he was born in the county seat o' Peanut County and empired all the chess tournaments there. They wasn't no subject that he didn't know all about it better'n anybody else. They wasn't no town he wasn't born and brought up in. His mother or his old man is first cousins to everybody in the United States. He's been operated on for every disease in the hospital. And if he's did all he says he's did he'll be eight hundred and twenty-two years old next Halloween."

"They's lots o' fellas like that," I says.

"You think so?" says Dode. "You wait a wile. Next time I see you, if you don't say he's all alone in the Argue League I'll give you my bat."

"If he's that good," I says, "he'll be soup for Carey."

"He will at first, maybe," says Dode; "but Carey'll get sick of him, just like Pat and all the rest of us did."

II

I didn't lose no time tellin' Carey about Dode's dope, and Carey didn't lose no time tryin' it out. It was the second day after Hawley joined us. It looked like rain, as usual, and we was stallin' in the club-house, thinkin' they'd maybe call it off before we had to dress.

"I see in some paper," says Carey, "where the heavy artillery fire over in Europe is what makes all this duck weather."

He didn't get no rise; so he wound up again.

"It seems like it must be somethin' that does it because they wasn't never no summer like this before," he says.

"What do you mean—no summer like this?" says Hawley.

"No summer with so much rain as they's been this summer," Carey says.

"Where do you get that stuff?" says Hawley. "This here summer's been dry, you might say."

"Yes," says Carey; "and you might say the Federals done well in Newark."

"I mean," says Hawley, "that this here summer's been dry compared to other summers."

"I s'pose," says Carey, "they wasn't never such a dry summer?"

"They's been lots of 'em," Hawley says. "They's been lots o' summers that was drier and they's been lots o' summers when they was more rain."

"Not in the last twenty years," says Carey.

"Yes, in the last twenty years too," says Hawley. "Nineteen years ago this summer made this here one look like a drought. It come up a storm the first day o' May and they wasn't a day from then till the first o' September when it didn't rain one time or another."

"You got some memory," says Carey—"goin' back nineteen years."

"I guess I ought to remember it," says Hawley. "That was the first year my old man left me go to the ball games alone, and they wasn't no games in our town from April till Labor Day. They wasn't no games nowheres because the railroads was all washed out. We lived in Cleveland and my old man was caught in New York when the first o' the floods come and couldn't get back home for three months."

"Couldn't he hire a canoe nowheres?" says Carey.

"Him and some others was thinkin' about tryin' the trip on a raft," says Hawley, "but my old lady was scared to have him try it; so she wrote and told him to stay where he was."

"She was lucky to have a carrier pigeon to take him the letter," says Carey. "Or did you swim East with it?"

"Swim!" Hawley says. "Say, you wouldn't talk about swim if you'd saw the current in them floods!"

"I'm sorry I missed it," says Carey. "I was still over in Portugal yet that year."

"It dried up in time for the world serious," says Hawley.

"The world serious between who?" ast Carey.

"The clubs that won out in the two leagues," says Hawley.

"I didn't know they was two leagues in '96," says Carey. "Who did they give the pennants to—the clubs that was ahead when it begin to sprinkle?"

"Sprinkle!" says Hawley. "Say, you'd of called it a sprinkle if you'd saw it. Sprinkle! Say, I guess that was some sprinkle!"

"I guess it must of been some sprinkle!" says Carey. "It must of made this summer look like a sucker."

"No," says Hawley; "this summer's been pretty bad."

"But nowheres near like nineteen year ago," says Carey.

"Oh, I guess they's about the same rainfall every year," Hawley says. "But, still and all, we've had some mighty wet weather since the first o' May this year, and I wouldn't be su'prised if the heavy artillery fire in Europe had somethin' to do with it."

"That's ridic'lous," says Carey.

"Ridic'lous!" says Hawley. "Where do you get that stuff? Don't you know that rain can be started with dynamite? Well, then, why wouldn't all that shootin' affect the weather? They must be some explanation."

"Did you make him?" says Carey to me afterward. "He trimmed me both ways. Some day he'll single to right field and throw himself out at first base. I seen I was in for a lickin', so I hedged to get a draw, and the minute I joined his league he jumped to the outlaws. But after this I'm goin' to stick on one side of it. He goes better when he's usin' his own stuff."

III

In battin' practice the next day Carey hit one up against them boards in right center on a line.

"Good night!" says Smitty. "I bet that's the hardest wallop that was ever made on these grounds."

"I know I didn't never hit one harder here," says Carey. "I don't never hit good in this park. I'd rather be on the road all the wile. I hit better on the Polo Grounds than anywheres else. I s'pose it's on account o' the background."

"Where do you get that stuff?" says Hawley. "Everybody hits better in New York that they do here. Do you want to know why? Because it's a clean town, without no dirt and cinders blowin' in your eyes. This town's all smoke and dirt, and it ain't no wonder a man's handicapped. The fellas that's with clubs in clean towns has got it all over us. Look at Detroit—one o' the cleanest towns in the country! And look how Cobb and Crawford hit! A man in one o' these smoke holes can't never pile up them big averages, or he can't last as long, neither."

"No," says Carey; "and that accounts for Wagner's rotten record in Pittsburgh."

Do you think that stopped him? Not him!

"Yes," he says; "and how much would Wagner of hit if he'd been playin' in New York or Detroit all the wile? He wouldn't never been below .500. And he'd of lasted just twicet as long."

"But on account of him landin' in Pittsburgh," says Carey, "the poor kid'll be all through already before he's fairly started yet. It's a crime and the grand jury should ought to take steps."

"Have you ever been to Washington?" says I.

"Have I ever been to Washington?" says Hawley. "Say, I know Washington like a book. My old man's brother's a senator there in Congress. You must of heard o' Senator Hawley."

"Oh, yes," says Carey; "the fella that made the speech that time."

"That's the fella," says Hawley. "And a smart fella too. Him and Woodruff Wilson's just like brothers. They're always to each other's houses. That's where I met Wilson—was at Uncle Zeke's. We fanned together for a couple hours. You wouldn't never know he was the President. He don't let on like he was any better than I or you."

"He ain't as good as you; that's a pipe!" says Carey.

"Where does your cousin live?" says Smitty.

"Cousin Zeke's got the swellest apartment in Washington," says Hawley. "Right next to the Capitol, on Pennsylvania Street."

"I wisht I could live there," I says. "It's the best town in the country for my money. And it's the cleanest one too."

"No factories or smoke there," says Carey.

"I wonder how it comes," I says, "that most o' the fellas on the

Washington Club, playin' in the cleanest town in the country most o' the wile, can't hardly foul a ball—let alone hit it."

"Maybe the silver dust from the mint gets in their eyes," says Carey.

"Where do you get that noise?" says Hawley. "The mint ain't nowheres near the ball orchard."

"Well then," I says, "how do you account for the club not hittin'?"

"Say," says Hawley, "it ain't no wonder they don't hit in that town. We played a exhibition game there last spring and we didn't hit, neither."

"Who pitched against you—Johnson?" I ast him.

"Yes; Johnson," says Hawley.

"But that don't explain why the Washington bunch can't hit," says Carey. "He ain't mean enough to turn round and pitch against his own club."

"They won't nobody hit in that town," says Hawley, "and I don't care if it's Johnson pitchin' or the mayor."

"What's the trouble?" I says.

"The heat gets 'em!" says Carey.

"No such a thing!" says Hawley. "That shows you don't know nothin' about it. It's the trees."

"The trees!" I says. "Do they play out in the woods or somewheres?"

"No," says Hawley. "If they did they'd be all right. Their ball park's just like any ball park; they ain't no trees in it. But they's trees all over the rest o' the town. It don't make no difference where you go, you're in the shade. And then, when you get to the ball park you're exposed to the sun all of a sudden and it blinds you."

"I should think it would affect their fieldin' too," says Carey.

"They wear goggles in the field," says Hawley.

"Do the infielders wear goggles?" ast Carey.

"No; but most o' the balls they got to handle comes on the ground. They don't have to look up for 'em," says Hawley.

"S'pose somebody hits a high fly ball that's comin' down right in the middle o' the diamond," says Carey. "Who gets it?"

"It ain't got," says Hawley. "They leave it go and it gen'ally almost always rolls foul."

"If I was Griffith," says Carey, "I'd get the Forestry Department to cut away the trees in some part o' town and then make all my ball players live there so's they'd get used to the sun."

"Or he might have a few big maples planted round the home plate some Arbor Day," I says.

"Yes," says Carey; "or he might trade Johnson to the Pittsburgh Federals for Oakes."

"He'd be a sucker to trade Johnson," says Hawley.

IV

Well, we played down in Cincy one Saturday to a crowd that might of all came out in one street car without nobody ridin' in the motor-man's vest pocket. We was discussin' it that night at supper.

"It's no more'n natural," I says. "The home club's been goin' bad and you can't expect the whole population to fight for a look at 'em."

"Yes," says Carey; "but it ain't only here. It's everywheres. We didn't hardly draw our breath at St. Louis and the receipts o' that last double-header at home with Pittsburgh wouldn't buy enough shavin' soap to lather a gnat. All over the circuit it's the same way, and in the other leagues too. It's a off year, maybe; or maybe they's reasons for it that we ain't doped out."

"Well," I says, "the war's hurt business, for one thing, and people ain't got no money to spend on box seats. And then golf's gettin' better all the wile. A man'd naturally rather do some exercisin' him-self than watch somebody else do it. Besides that, automobiles has got so cheap that pretty near everybody can buy 'em, and the people that owns 'em takes their friends out in the country instead o' comin' to the ball yard. And besides that," I says, "they's too much baseball and the people's sick of it."

Hawley come in and set down with us wile I was still talkin' yet.

"What's the argument?" he says.

"We was tryin' to figure out why we can't get a quorum out to the games no more," says Carey.

"Well," says Hawley, "you know the real reason, don't you?"

"No," says Carey; "but I bet we're goin' to hear it. I bet you'll say it's on account o' the Gulf Stream."

"Where do you get that noise?" says Hawley.

"If you want to know the real reason, the war's the real reason."

"That's what I was sayin'," says I. "The war's hurt business and people ain't got no money to blow on baseball."

"That shows you don't know nothin' about it," says Hawley.

"Then I got you tied," I says, "because you just sprung the same thing yourself."

"No such a thing!" says Hawley. "You're talkin' about the war hurtin' business and I'm talkin' about the war hurtin' baseball."

"What's the difference?" I says.

"All the difference in the world," says Hawley. "If everybody was makin' twicet as much money durin' the war as they made before the war started yet, the baseball crowds wouldn't be no bigger than they have been."

"Come acrost with the answer," says Carey. "The strain's somethin' awful."

"Well, boys," says Hawley, "they ain't nobody in this country that ain't pullin' for one side or the other in this here war. Is that right or wrong?"

"Which do you say it is?" says Carey.

"I say it's right because I know it's right," says Hawley.

"Well then," says Carey, "don't ask us boobs."

"No matter what a man says about he bein' neutral," says Hawley, "you can bet that down in his heart he's either for the Dutchmen or the Alleys; I don't care if he's Woodruff Wilson or Bill Klem. We all got our favorites."

"Who's yours?" I says.

"Don't you tell!" says Carey. "It wouldn't be fair to the other side."

"I don't mind tellin'," says Hawley. "I'd be a fine stiff to pull for the Dutchmen after all King George done for my old man."

"What did he do for him?" says Carey.

"Well, it's a long story," says Hawley.

"That's all right," says Carey. "They's only one game to-morrow."

"I'll give it to you some other time," Hawley says.

"I hope you don't forget it," says Carey.

"Forget it!" says Hawley. "When your old man's honored by the royalties you ain't liable to forget it."

"No," says Carey; "but you could try."

"Here!" I says. "I'm waitin' to find out how the war cuts down the attendance."

"I'm comin' to that," says Hawley. "When you figure it out they couldn't nothin' be simpler."

"It does sound simple, now it's been explained," says Carey.

"It ain't been explained to me," I says.

"You're in too big a hurry," Hawley says. "If you wouldn't interrupt a man all the wile you might learn somethin'. You admit they ain't nobody that's neutral. Well then, you can't expect people that's for the Alleys to come out to the ball park and pull for a club that's mostly Dutchmen, and you can't expect Dutchmen to patronize a club that's got a lot o' fellas with English and French names."

"Wait a minute!" says Carey. "I s'pose they ain't no Germans here in Cincinnati, is they?"

"Sure!" says Hawley. "The place is ran over with 'em."

"Then," says Carey, "why don't they break all records for attendance at this park, with Heine Groh and Fritz Mollwitz and Count Von Kolnitz and Wagner and Schneider and Herzog on the ball club?"

"Because they's others on the team that offsets 'em," says Hawley. "We'll say they's a Dutchman comes out to the game to holler for some o' them boys you mentioned. We'll say that Groh kicks a ground ball and leaves three runs score and puts the club behind. And then we'll say that Clarke comes up in the ninth innin' and wins the game for Cincinnati with a home run. That makes the Dutchman look like a rummy, don't it? Or we'll say Schneider starts to pitch a game and gets knocked out, and then Dale comes in and they can't foul him. Your German friend wishes he had of stayed home and washed part o' the dashhound."

"Yes," says Carey; "but wouldn't he want to come to the game again the next day in hopes he'd get his chancet to holler?"

"No," says Hawley; "because, whatever happened, they'd be somethin' about it he wouldn't like. If the Reds win the Alleys on the club'd feel just as good as the Dutchmen, and that'd make him sore. And if they lost he'd be glad on account o' the Alleys; but he'd feel sorry for the Germans."

"Then they's only one thing for Garry Herrmann to do," I says: "he should ought to trade off all his Alleys for Dutch."

"That'd help the attendance at home," says Hawley; "but when his club played in Boston who'd go out to see 'em?"

"Everybody that could borrow a brick," says Carey.

"Accordin' to your dope," I says, "they's only one kind of a club that'd draw everywheres, and that's a club that didn't have no Dutchmen or Alleys—neither one."

"That's the idear," says Hawley: "a club made up o' fellas from countries that ain't got nothin' to do with the war—Norwegians, Denmarks, Chinks, Mongrels and them fellas. A guy that had brains enough to sign up that kind of a club would make a barrel o' money."

"A guy'd have a whole lot o' trouble findin' that kind of a club," I says.

"He'd have a whole lot more trouble," says Carey, "findin' a club they could beat."

V

Smitty used to get the paper from his home town where his folks lived at, somewheres near Lansing, Michigan. One day he seen in it where his kid brother was goin' to enter for the state golf championship.

"He'll just about cop it too," says Smitty. "And he ain't only seventeen years old. He's been playin' round that Wolverine Country Club, in Lansing, and makin' all them birds like it."

"The Wolverine Club, in Lansing?" says Hawley.

"That's the one," Smitty says.

"That's my old stampin' grounds," says Hawley. "That's where I learned the game at."

"The kid holds the record for the course," says Smitty.

"He don't no such a thing!" says Hawley.

"How do you know?" says Smitty.

"I guess I'd ought to know," Hawley says. "The guy that holds that record is talkin' to you."

"What's your record?" says Smitty.

"What'd your brother make?" says Hawley.

"Plain seventy-one," says Smitty; "and if you ever beat that you can have my share o' the serious money."

"You better make a check right now," says Hawley. "The last time I played at that club I rolled up seventy-three."

"That beats me," Smitty says.

"If you're that good," says Carey, "I'd like to take you on sometime. I can score as high as the next one."

"You might get as much as me now because I'm all out o' practice," says Hawley; "but you wouldn't of stood no show when I was right."

"What club was you best with?" ast Carey.

"A heavy one," says Hawley. "I used to play with a club that they couldn't hardly nobody else lift."

"An iron club?" says Smitty.

"Well," says Hawley, "it felt like they was iron in it."

"Did you play all the wile with one club?" ast Carey.

"You bet I did," Hawley says. "I paid a good price and got a good club. You couldn't break it."

"Was it a brassie?" says Smitty.

"No," says Hawley. "It was made by some people right there in Lansing."

"I'd like to get a hold of a club like that," says Carey.

"You couldn't lift it," Hawley says; "and even if you could handle it I wouldn't sell it for no price—not for twicet what it cost."

"What did it cost?" Smitty ast him.

"Fifty bucks," says Hawley; "and it'd of been more'n that only for the people knowin' me so well. My old man used to do 'em a lot o' good turns."

"He must of stood in with 'em," says Carey, "or they wouldn't of never left go of a club like that for fifty."

"They must of sold it to you by the pound," I says—"about a dollar a pound."

"Could you slice a ball with it?" says Carey.

"That was the trouble—the balls wouldn't stand the gaff," Hawley says. "I used to cut 'em in two with it."

"How many holes did they have there when you was playin'?" Smitty ast.

"Oh, three or four," he says; "but they didn't feaze me."

"They got eighteen now," says Smitty.

"They must of left the course run down," Hawley says. "You can bet they kept it up good when my old man was captain."

"Has your brother ever been in a big tourney before?" I says to Smitty.

"He was in the city championship last summer," says Smitty.

"How'd he come out?" Hawley ast.

"He was second highest," says Smitty. "He'd of win, only he got stymied by a bumblebee."

"Did they cauterize it?" says Carey.

"Where do you get that noise?" says Hawley.

"They ain't no danger in a bee sting if you know what to do. Just slip a piece o' raw meat on it."

"Was you ever stymied by a bee?" says Carey.

"Was I!" says Hawley. "Say, I wisht I had a base hit for every time them things got me. My old lady's dad had a regular bee farm down in Kentucky, and we'd go down there summertimes and visit and help gather the honey. I used to run round barefooted and you couldn't find a square inch on my legs that wasn't all et up."

"Must of kept your granddad broke buyin' raw meat," says Carey.

"Meat wasn't so high in them days," says Hawley. "Besides he didn't have to buy none. He had his own cattle."

"I should think the bees would of stymied the cattle," says Carey.

"Cattle's hide's too tough; a bee won't go near 'em," says Hawley.

"Why didn't you hire a cow to go round with you wile you collected honey?" says Carey.

"What'd you quit golf for?" ast Smitty.

"A fella can't play golf and hit good," says Hawley.

"I should think it'd help a man's hittin'," Carey says. "A golf ball's a whole lot smaller than a baseball, and a baseball should ought to look as big as a balloon to a man that's been playin' golf."

"Where do you get that noise?" says Hawley. "Golf's bad for a man's battin'; but it ain't got nothin' to do with your swing or your eye or the size o' the ball."

"What makes it bad, then?" I ast him.

"Wait a minute and I'll tell you," he says. "They's two reasons: In the first place they's genally almost always some people playin' ahead o' you on a golf course and you have to wait till they get out o' reach. You get in the habit o' waitin' and when you go up to the plate in a ball game and see the pitcher right in front o' you and the infielders and baserunners clost by, you're liable to wait for 'em to get out o' the way for the fear you'll kill 'em. And wile you're waitin' the pitcher's liable to slip three over in the groove and you're struck out."

"I wasn't never scared o' killin' no infielder," says Carey.

"And what's the other reason?" I says.

"The other reason," says Hawley, "is still better yet than the one I give you."

"Don't say that!" says Smitty.

"When you're playin' golf you pay for the balls you use," says

Hawley; "so in a golf game you're sort of holdin' back and not hittin' a ball as far as you can, because it'll cost you money if you can't find it. So you get used to sort o' holdin' back; and when you get up there to the plate you don't take a good wallop for the fear you'll lose the ball. You forget that the balls is furnished by the club."

"And besides that," says Carey, "you're liable to get to thinkin' that your bat cost fifty bucks, the same as your golf racket, and you don't swing hard because you might break it."

"You don't know nothin' about it," says Hawley.

VI

Now I don't care how big a goof a man is, he'd ought to know better than get smart round a fella that's slumped off in his battin'. Most o' the time they ain't no better-natured fella in the world than Carey; but when him and first base has been strangers for a wile, lay offen him!

That's how Hawley got in bad with Carey—was talkin' too much when the old boy wasn't in no mood to listen.

He begin to slump off right after the fourth o' July double-header. In them two games a couple o' the boys popped out when they was sent up to sacrifice. So Cap got sore on the buntin' game and says we'd hit and run for a wile. Well, in the first innin', every day for the next three days, Bishop led off with a base on balls and then started down when he got Carey's sign. And all three times Carey cracked a line drive right at somebody and they was a double play. After the last time he come in to the bench tryin' to smile.

"Well," he says, "I guess that's about a record."

"A record! Where do you get that stuff?" says Hawley. "I come up four times in Philly in one game and hit into four double plays."

"You brag too much!" says Carey; but you could see he didn't want to go along with it.

Well, that last line drive seemed to of took the heart out of him or somethin', because for the next week he didn't hardly foul one—let alone gettin' it past the infield.

When he'd went through his ninth game without a blow Hawley braced him in the clubhouse. "Do you know why you ain't hittin'?" he says.

"Yes," says Carey. "It's because they don't pitch where I swing."

"It ain't no such a thing!" says Hawley. "It's because you don't choke up your bat enough."

"Look here!" says Carey. "I been in this league longer'n you and I've hit better'n you. When I want advice about how to hold my bat I'll get you on the wire."

You know how clost the clubs was bunched along in the middle o' July. Well, we was windin' up a series with Brooklyn and we had to cop the last one to break even.

We was tied up in the ninth and one out in their half when Wheat caught a-hold o' one and got three bases on it. Cutshaw raised one a little ways back o' second base and it looked like a cinch Wheat couldn't score if Carey got her. Well, he got her all right and Wheat come dashin' in from third like a wild man.

Now they ain't no better pegger in the league than this same Carey and I'd of bet my life Wheat was runnin' into a double play. I thought he was a sucker for makin' the try. But Carey throwed her twenty feet to one side o' the plate. The run was in and the game was over.

Hawley hadn't hardly got in the clubhouse before he started in.

"Do you know what made you peg bad?" he says.

"Shut up!" says Smitty. "Is that the first bad peg you ever seen? Does they have to be a reason for all of 'em? He throwed it bad because he throwed it bad."

"He throwed it bad," says Hawley, "because he was in center field instead o' left field or right field. A center fielder'll peg wide three times to the others' oncet. And you know why it is, don't you?"

Nobody answered him.

"I'll tell you why it is," he says. "They's a foul line runnin' out in right field and they's a foul line runnin' out in left field, and them two lines gives a fielder somethin' to guide his throw with. If they was a white line runnin' from home plate through second base and out in center field you wouldn't see so many bad pegs from out there.

"But that ain't the only reason," says Hawley. "They's still another reason. The old boy ain't feelin' like hisself. He's up in the air because he ain't hittin'."

That's oncet where Hawley guessed right. But Carey didn't say a word—not till we was in the Subway.

"I know why I ain't hittin' and why I can't peg," he told me. "I'm so sick o' this Wisenheimer that I can't see. I can't see what they're pitchin' and I can't see the bases. I'm lucky to catch a fly ball."

"Forget him!" I says. "Let him rave!"

"I can't stop him from ravin'," says Carey; "but he's got to do his ravin' on another club."

"What do you mean?" I says. "You ain't manager."

"You watch me!" says Carey. "I ain't goin' to cripple him up or nothin' like that, but if he's still with us yet when we come offen this trip I'll make you a present o' my oldest boy."

"Have you got somethin' on him?"

"No," says Carey; "but he's goin' to get himself in wrong. And I think he's goin' to do it to-night."

VII

He done it—and that night too. I guess you know that, next to winnin', Cap likes his missus better'n anything in the world. She is a nice gal, all right, and as pretty as they make 'em.

Cap's as proud of her as a colleger with a Charlie Chaplin mustache. When the different papers would print Miss So-and So's pitcher and say she was the handsomest girl in this, that or the other place, Cap'd point it out to us and say: "My gal makes her look like a bad day outdoors."

Cap's wife's a blonde; and—believe me, boy—she dresses! She wasn't with us on this trip I'm speakin' of. She hasn't been with us all season, not since the trainin' trip. I think her mother's sick out there in St. Joe. Anyway, Hawley never seen her—that is, to know who she was.

Well, Carey framed it up so's I and him and Cap went in to supper together. Hawley was settin' all alone. Carey, brushin' by the head waiter, marches us up to Hawley's table and plants us. Carey's smilin' like he didn't have a care in the world. Hawley noticed the smile.

"Yattaboy!" he says. "Forget the base hits and cheer up!"

"I guess you'd cheer up, too, if you'd seen what I seen," says Carey. "Just lookin' at her was enough to drive away them Ockaway Chinese blues."

"That ain't no way for a married man to talk," says Cap.

"Well," says Carey, "gettin' married don't mean gettin' blind."

"What was she like?" ast Cap.

"Like all the prettiest ones," says Carey. "She was a blonde."

"Where do you get that noise?" says Hawley, buttin' in. "I s'pose they ain't no pretty dark girls?"

"Oh, yes," says Carey—"octoroons and them."

"Well," says Hawley, "I never seen no real pretty blondes. They ain't a blonde livin' that can class up with a pretty brunette."

"Where do you get that noise?" says Carey.

"Where do I get it!" says Hawley. "Say, I guess I've saw my share o' women. When you seen as many as I seen you won't be talkin' blonde."

"I seen one blonde that's the prettiest woman in this country," says Carey.

"The one you seen just now?" says Hawley.

"No sir; another one," says Carey.

"Where at?" Hawley ast him.

"She's in Missouri, where she first come from," says Carey; "and she's the prettiest girl that was ever in the state."

"That shows you don't know what you're talkin' about," Hawley says. "I guess I ought to know the prettiest girl in Missouri. I was born and raised there, and the prettiest girl in Missouri went to school with me."

"And she was a blonde?" says Carey.

"Blonde nothin'!" says Hawley. "Her hair was as black as Chief Meyers'. And when you see a girl with black hair you know it's natural color. Take a blonde and you can't tell nothin' about it. They ain't one in a thousand of 'em that ain't dyed their hair."

Cap couldn't stand it no longer.

"You talk like a fool!" he says. "You don't know nothin' about women."

"I guess I know as much as the next one," says Hawley.

"You don't know nothin'!" says Cap. "What was this girl's name?"

"What girl's name?" says Hawley.

"This black girl you're talkin' about—this here prettiest girl in Missouri," says Cap.

"I forget her name," says Hawley.

"You never knowed her name," says Cap. "You never knowed nothin'! We traded nothin' to get you and we got stung at that. If you want your unconditional release, all you got to do is ask for it.

And if you don't want it I'll get waivers on you and send you down South where you can be amongst the brunettes. We ain't got no room on this club for a ball player that don't know nothin' on no subject. You're just as smart about baseball as you are about women. It's a wonder your head don't have a blow-out! If a torpedo hit a boat you was on and you was the only one drownded, the captain'd send a wireless: 'Everybody saved!' "

Cap broke a few dishes gettin' up from the table and beat it out o' the room.

Hawley was still settin', with his mouth wide open, lookin' at his prunes. After a wile I and Carey got up and left him.

"He ain't a bad fella," I says when we was outside. "He don't mean nothin'. It looks to me like a raw deal you're handin' him."

"I don't care how it looks to you or anybody else," says Carey. "I still got a chancet to lead this league in hittin' and I ain't goin' to be talked out of it."

"Do you think you'll hit when he's gone?"

"You bet I'll hit!" says Carey.

Cap ast for waivers on Hawley, and Pittsburgh claimed him.

"I wisht it had of been some other club," he says to me. "That's another o' them burgs where the smoke and cinders kills your battin'."

But I notice he's been goin' good there and he should ought to enjoy hisself tellin' Wagner how to stand up to the plate.

The day after he'd left us I kept pretty good track o' Carey. He popped out twicet, grounded out oncet and hit a line drive to the pitcher.

Few writers have been more popular in their time than the poet, biographer, guitar-slinging singer, and storyteller of the prairies, Carl Sandburg (1878–1967). The son of a Galesburg, Illinois, railroad blacksmith, Sandburg attended local Lombard College where he played baseball and flunked English grammar. He left before graduating, and spent years "deadbeating," living a peripatetic experience of America that would help form his unkempt, full-bodied vision of the democratic heartland. It is not surprising that Sandburg, romancer of smokestacks, slaughterhouses, and cornfields, should turn out to have been a frustrated ballplayer, as he recounted in this excerpt from his autobiography *Always the Young Strangers* (1953). The poetic tribute to the game included here is from his 1918 collection *Cornhuskers*.

Carl Sandburg

♢

Hits and Runs

I remember the Chillicothe ball players grappling the Rock Island
    ball players in a sixteen-inning game ended by darkness.
And the shoulders of the Chillicothe players were a red smoke
    against the sundown and the shoulders of the Rock Island
    players were a yellow smoke against the sundown.
And the umpire's voice was hoarse calling balls and strikes and outs
    and the umpire's throat fought in the dust for a song.

from

Always the Young Strangers

I have played baseball on a summer day starting at eight o'clock in
the morning, running home at noon for a quick meal, playing
again till six o'clock in the evening, and then a run home for a quick
meal and again with fielding and batting till it was too dark to see the

leather spheroid. On many a Saturday I had sold the *Sporting News* at five cents a copy, and I had read about the "leather spheroid."

Four lots to the east of our house was a vacant double lot where we laid out a small diamond. At the time a good-natured Jersey cow was pastured there for a few weeks. We never knocked a ball that hit the cow but when the ball landed near her and the fielder ran toward her it disturbed her. Also it disturbed the owner of the cow, who said he would have the police on us. So we played in the street till the day the cow was gone and we heard it had been sold. Then we went back to our pasture.

On the narrow lot next to the pasture lived Mrs. Moore, widow of a Civil War veteran, living alone on a Federal pension. She was a tall woman with dark hair streaked with gray and a face we liked well enough. She was a peaceable, quiet woman, smoking her tobacco in a clay pipe, keeping to herself and raising vegetables and flowers. She had the nicest all-round flower garden in our block, the front of her lot filled with hollyhocks, begonias, salvia, asters, and morning-glories climbing the fences. We had no ill will toward Mrs. Moore. But first base was only ten feet or so from her fence and every so often a fly or a foul ball would go over the fence into her potatoes, carrots, and hollyhocks. A boy would climb the fence and go stomping around hunting the lost ball. At such times as Mrs. Moore stood between the boy and the place where he believed the ball fell it was not pleasant for either party concerned. "Why must you boys do this to my place?" she would ask. When the boy answered, "We'll try never to do it again," her reply would come, "See that you don't do it again. I don't want to make trouble for you boys."

Again and again we sent the ball over into her well-kept yard. She tried scolding us but she just naturally wasn't a scold. She quietly hinted she might have to go to the police. She tried to look at us mean but couldn't manage it. It hurt her to see us scrounging among her garden plants. We were a nuisance and she could have gone to the police and had us abolished. And she didn't go to the police or to our parents living near by. She had property rights and we were trespassing on her property, and she forgave us our trespasses even though we went on trespassing. I would say now that she was a woman of rare inner grace who had gathered wisdom from potatoes and hollyhocks.

What is this fascination about making a hickory stick connect with a thrown ball and sending the ball as a high fly or a hot grounder for a safe hit? What is this fascination about picking up a hot grounder and throwing it to first for a putout—or running for a fly and leaping in the air for a one-handed catch and a putout? What is this peculiar shame of standing under a high fly and it falls smack in your hands and you muff it? What is this nameless embarrassment of being at bat with three men on bases and you fan the air three times with your bat and it's "side out" and you hear someone say, "You're all right only there was a hole in the bat"? These questions have gone round and round in the heads of millions of American boys for generations. I have many a night gone to bed and before falling asleep I imagined myself sliding to second, sliding to third, and stealing home. And I have had dreams of playing deep outfield and muffing a high fly with three men on bases and two of them scoring. Before falling asleep I would make plays that astonished players and people on the side lines. But in my dreams I always muffed the ball or when I tried to steal a base I was tagged out.

Our early games among the Berrien Street kids were played in the street, barefooted, keeping an eye out for broken glass or rusty cans with sharp edges sticking up. The bat was a broom handle, the ball was handmade—a five-cent rubber ball wrapped round with grocery string. The home plate was a brick, first base a brick, second base a tin can, third another tin can. We played barehanded till we learned how to get a large man-sized glove and stuff it with cotton, wool, or hair to take the sting out of a fast ball hitting the palm or fingers.

The days came when we played in the cow pasture with a Spalding big-league regulation ball. We gathered round the boy who first brought it to us and said we could play with it. "Well, what do you know!" we said. "A dollar and a half." And we told it around as a kind of wonder, "We been playin today with a dollar and a half." We would hear "Fatty" Beckman ask, "Is Skinny Seeley comin today with that dollar and a half?" Sure he was. He was bringing the same ball that Amos Rusie was throwing in the big league, the same ball Big Bill Lange was hitting so hard with the Chicago team. We had played many a game with a dollar-and-a-half ball that had the leather cover off and we could hit it and catch it but there wasn't the feel of that same leather spheroid that Big Bill Lange was hitting. When I carried

Chicago newspapers and read sports news I learned about the "elusive pill" thrown by Amos Rusie. I was among those who grieved later to hear of Amos Rusie taking to drink, being dropped from major and minor clubs, and being found one day digging gas mains at a dollar-fifty a day. He was doing ten cents a day better than my father at the Q. shop but still I was more sorry for him than for my father.

Across a few years I could from day to day name the leading teams and the tailenders in the National League and the American Association. I could name the players who led in batting and fielding and the pitchers who had won the most games. I filled my head with this knowledge and carried it around. There were times my head seemed empty of everything but baseball names and figures. I could hear them rattling around in my head. I had my opinions about who was better than anybody else in the national game. Therefore I now understand the Great American Ball Fan and all his follies. I was an addict and I know why pop bottles have been thrown at umpires, though I have never at a season end thrown a good straw hat on the grandstand floor and jumped on it to crush the life out of it.

When Galesburg played Chillicothe or Peoria or Rock Island on the Knox campus grounds, there were always two fans to perform. Jim O'Brien, chief of the fire department, was on hand and took his stand near first base with an umbrella to keep the sun off him. And when the home team had a streak of luck, his umbrella would go into the air and he would catch it coming down and go into a fancy umbrella dance. Also there was the dentist Doc Olson. He could yell, whistle, and juggle a straw hat and make faces at the visiting team and cut up didoes. No matter how poor the home team played, these two fans performed and entertained those who paid their two bits to get in.

The Berrien Street kids lacking the two bits' admission watched the games on the Knox campus through knotholes in the fence. Or we climbed a tree fifty yards from the home plate, found a crotch to sit in, and had as much fun as though we were in the two-bit bleachers.

The most exciting baseball year the town had in that time was when a City League was organized and played one or two games a week. The Main Street clerks had one team, the railroad shopmen another, and there were two other teams. I remember the pitching styles of Bob Switzer, "Kill" Bruner, and Nelson Willard, the work at shortstop and second base of Bay Sanderson and Grant Beadle. One notable player was "Hump" Ostrander in right field for the railway shopmen. In his younger days he had hopped a railroad train and slipped and lost his left arm. The stump of it hung from his left shoulder. All catches he made were one-handed. When he stepped to bat at the plate he swung with one arm and hand. Hump's record was fair and when he caught a fly or slammed out a base hit he got extra cheers as a phenomenon. I had come to like him when we sat across the aisle from each other in Swedish summer school and studied *"Biblisk historia"* (Bible history) together.

Out of the tall grass around Victoria came a team that had surprises. Galesburg had picked the best nine in the town to meet them and the word was that maybe Galesburg would "goose-egg" them. But the country boys played fast ball, among them the Spratt brothers, Bob and Jack, who later went into minor-league clubs. Their center fielder was a tall gawk wearing a derby hat. He may have had a cap at home and couldn't find it. It was the first time the town had seen in a regular ball game a player crowned with a derby. As the game got going Victoria took the lead by one or two runs and kept the lead till near the closing inning, when Galesburg with one out got two men on bases and one of its heaviest sluggers came to bat. He hit the ball high and handsome and sent it sailing away out to deep center field. The tall gawk in the derby made a fast run, made a leap for it, caught it with one hand and threw it straight to second to catch a man off base—so Victoria was victorious in one of the craziest, sweetest pieces of baseball drama I have ever seen.

One year Galesburg had a semi-pro team, its second baseman a professional named Bud Fowler, a left-handed Negro, fast and pretty in his work. A traveling salesman named Dushane, a stubby Frenchman with a brown mustache and every hair curled to the right moment, played third base one year. When the home team made a double play he would leap in the air, turn a somersault, and light on his feet. The crowd watched for it. It came in handy when the home team was losing, which it usually was when playing minor-league clubs.

An idea began growing in me that if I played and practiced a lot I might become good enough to get on a team where my talent was appreciated. Once on a minor-league team I would have my chance to show what I could do and I might end up in the majors—who knows about a thing like that? I didn't mention it. It was a secret ambition. I nursed it along and in what spare time I could find I played where the boys were playing, did fairly well in left field on a scrub team.

Then came an afternoon in early October. I was sixteen. Skinny Seeley and I went to a pasture in the second block north of the Lombard campus. Skinny and I knocked up flies. He was hitting some long and high ones to me. I had managed to buy secondhand a fielder's glove, a regular big-league affair I was proud of. I was running for a high one. I believed I would make a brilliant catch of it, the kind of catch I would make when maybe one of the minor-league clubs had taken me on. I was running at top speed. Suddenly my right foot stashed into a hole and I fell on my knees and face. When I looked at what had happened to my right foot I saw a gash in the shoe leather and blood oozing from the tangled yarn of the sock. I saw too that in the eight-inch hole there was a beer bottle, broken in half, standing on its bottom end, and into the top of this my foot had crashed.

I limped across the pasture, about a block, to the house of Dr. Taggart. He was at home. Out on his front porch he had me take off the shoe, then slowly the sock. He cleaned out the bleeding cut, picked out yarn and glass, applied antiseptic. Then he brought out a curved needle and sewed four stitches at about the middle of the foot just below the instep. I didn't let out a moan or a whimper through the whole operation. After my fall, when I saw the gashed shoe and the broken bottle, I did cry out, "Jesus wept! Jesus wept!" I moaned and groaned going toward the doctor's house, but when I found him in and when I watched the cool, sure, easy way he handled me, I gritted my teeth and smiled to him and told him I was lucky. He bandaged my foot and I limped home. My mother spoke sorrow and pity. My father asked when would I ever learn any sense and quit wasting my time with baseball.

From that day on I was completely through with any and all hopes and dreams of becoming a big-time ballplayer. I went on playing occasional games and have never lost a certain odd tingle of the hands at holding a bat or catching a baseball. Those four stitches in the right foot marked the end of my first real secret ambition. I began a hunt for new secret ambitions, but they were slow in coming.

Brooklyn-born Heywood Broun (1888–1939) wrote for a number of New York newspapers, including the *World,* where his long-running column "It Seems to Me" appeared, as did this piece. An iconoclast who at various times used his column, as well as the pages of *The Nation* and *The New Republic,* as a forum for radical social criticism, Broun achieved notoriety for his sympathetic coverage of Sacco and Vanzetti during their 1921 trial. He was also a skilled baseball writer and the frequent companion of both Christy Mathewson—they played a lot of checkers together—and Babe Ruth. It is Ruth, then a relatively young Yankee fly swatter, who is Broun's subject for this 1923 World Series story, with its classic lead.

Heywood Broun

◊

Ruth Comes Into His Own With 2 Homers, Clinching Second for Yanks, 4 to 2

The Ruth is mighty and shall prevail. He did yesterday. Babe made two home runs and the Yankees won from the Giants at the Polo Grounds by a score of 4 to 2. This evens up the World's Series, with one game for each contender.

It was the first game the Yankees won from the Giants since Oct. 10, 1921, and it ended a string of eight successive victories for the latter, with one tie thrown in.

Victory came to the American League champions through a change in tactics. Miller Huggins could hardly fail to have observed Wednesday that terrible things were almost certain to happen to his men if they paused any place along the line from first to home.

In order to prevent blunders in base running he wisely decided to eliminate it. The batter who hits a ball into the stands cannot possibly be caught napping off any base.

HAMMER BALL OUT OF PARK

The Yankees prevented Kelly, Frisch and the rest from performing tricks in black magic by consistently hammering the ball out of the park or into sections of the stand where only amateurs were seated.

Through simplicity itself, the system worked like a charm. Three of the Yankees' four runs were the product of homers, and this was enough for a winning total. Erin Ward was Ruth's assistant. Irish Meusel of the Giants also made a home run, but yesterday's show belonged to Ruth.

For the first time since coming to New York, Babe achieved his full brilliance in a World's Series game. Before this he has varied between pretty good and simply awful, but yesterday he was magnificent.

Just before the game John McGraw remarked:

"Why shouldn't we pitch to Ruth? I've said before, and I'll say it again, we pitch to better hitters than Ruth in the National League."

McGRAW CLINGS TO HIS HERESY

Ere the sun had set on McGraw's rash and presumptuous words, the Babe had flashed across the sky fiery portents which should have been sufficient to strike terror and conviction into the hearts of all infidels. But John McGraw clung to his heresy with a courage worthy of better cause.

In the fourth inning Ruth drove the ball completely out of the premises. McQuillan was pitching at the time, and the count was two balls and one strike. The strike was a fast ball shoulder high, at which Ruth had lunged with almost comic ferocity and ineptitude.

Snyder peeked at the bench to get a signal from McGraw. Catching for the Giants must be a terrific strain on the neck muscles, for apparently it is etiquette to take the signals from the bench manager furtively. The catcher is supposed to pretend he is merely glancing around to see if the girl in the red hat is anywhere in the grand stand, although all the time his eyes are intent on McGraw.

THE BAMBINO TIES THE RECORD

Of course the nature of the code is secret, but this time McGraw scratched his nose to indicate: "Try another of those shoulder high fast ones on the Big Bam and let's see if we can't make him break his back again."

But Babe didn't break his back, for he had something solid to check his terrific swing. The ball started climbing from the moment it left the plate. It was a pop fly with a brand new gland and, though it flew high, it also flew far.

When last seen the ball was crossing the roof of the stand in deep right field at an altitude of 315 feet. We wonder whether new baseballs conversing in the original package ever remark: "Join Ruth and see the world."

In the fifth Ruth was up again and by this time McQuillan had left the park utterly and Jack Bentley was pitching. The count crept up to two strikes and two balls. Snyder sneaked a look at the little logician deep in the dugout. McGraw blinked twice, pulled up his trousers and thrust the forefinger of his right hand into his left eye. Snyder knew that he meant: "Try the Big Bozo on a slow curve around his knees and don't forget to throw to first if you happen to drop the third strike."

Snyder called for the delivery as directed and Ruth half topped a line drive over the wall of the lower stand in right field. With that drive the Babe tied a record. Benny Kauff and Duffy Lewis are the only other players who ever made two home runs in a single World's Series game.

But was McGraw convinced and did he rush out of the dugout and kneel before Ruth with a cry of "Maestro" as the Babe crossed the plate? He did not. He nibbled at not a single word he has ever uttered in disparagement of the prowess of the Yankee slugger. In the ninth Ruth came to bat with two out and a runner on second base. By every consideration of prudent tactics an intentional pass seemed indicated.

Snyder jerked his head around and observed that McGraw was blowing his nose. The Giant catcher was puzzled, for that was a signal he had never learned. By a process of pure reasoning he attempted to figure out just what it was that his chief was trying to convey to him.

"Maybe he means if we pitch to Ruth we'll blow the game," thought Snyder, but he looked toward the bench again just to make sure.

Now McGraw intended no signal at all when he blew his nose. That was not tactics, but only a head cold. On the second glance, Snyder observed that the little Napoleon gritted his teeth. Then he proceeded to spell out with the first three fingers of his right hand: "The Old Guard dies, but never surrenders." That was a signal Snyder recognized, although it never had passed between him and his manager before.

McGraw was saying: "Pitch to the big bum if he hammers every ball in the park into the North River."

And so, at Snyder's request, Bentley did pitch to Ruth and the Babe drove the ball deep into right centre; so deep that Casey Stengel could feel the hot breath of the bleacherites on his back as the ball came down and he caught it. If that drive had been just a shade to the right it would have been a third home run for Ruth. As it was, the Babe had a great day with two home runs, a terrific long fly and two bases on balls.

YOUNG BOOED FOR BAD TACTICS

Neither pass was intentional. For that McGraw should receive due credit. His fame deserves to be recorded along with the man who said, "Lay on, MacDuff," "Sink me the ship, Master Gunner, split her in twain," and "I'll fight it out on this line if it takes all summer." For John McGraw also went down eyes front and his thumb on his nose.

Some of the sportsmanship of the afternoon was not so admirable. In the sixth inning Pep Young prevented a Yankee double play by diving at the legs of Ward, who was just about to throw to first after a force-out. Tack Hardwick never took out an opposing back more neatly. Half the spectators booed Young and the other half applauded him.

It did not seem to us that there was any very good reason for booing Young, since the tradition of professional baseball always has been agreeably free of chivalry. The rule is, "Do anything you can get away with."

But Young never should have been permitted to get away with that interference. The runner on first ought to have been declared out. In coming down to second Young had complete rights to the baseline and the bag, but those rights should not have permitted him the privilege of diving all the way across the bag to tackle Ward around the ankles.

It was a most palpably incompetent decision by Hart, the National League umpire on second base. Fortunately the blunder had no effect on the game, since the next Giant batter hit into a double play in which the Giant rushline was unable to reach Ward in time to do anything about it.

Ruth crushed to earth shall rise again. Herb Pennock, the assistant hero of the afternoon, did the same thing. In the fourth inning, Jack Bentley toppled the slim Yankee left-hander into a crumpled heap by hitting him in the back with a fast ball. Pennock went down with a groan which could be heard even in the $1 seats. All the players gathered around him as he writhed, and what with sympathy and some judicious massage, he was up again within three or four minutes, and his pitching efficiency seemed to be in nowise impaired. It was, of course, wholly an accident, as the kidney punch is barred in baseball.

Entirely aside from his injury, Pennock looked none too stalwart. He is a meagre athlete who winds up with great deliberation, as if fearful about what the opposing batter will do with the ball. And it was mostly slow curves that he fed to the Giants, but they did nothing much in crucial moments. Every now and then Pennock switched to a fast one and the change of pace had McGraw's men baffled throughout.

Just once Pennock was in grave danger. It looked as if his three-run lead might be swept away in the sixth inning. Groh, Frisch and Young, the three Giants to face him at that point, all singled solidly. It seemed the part of wisdom to remove Pennock immediately after Young's single had scored Groh. Here Huggins was shrewd. He guessed wisely and stuck to Pennock.

Irish Meusel forced Young, and it would have been a double play but for Young's interference with Ward's throw. Cunningham, who followed, did hit into a double play, Scott to Ward to Pipp. The Giants' rally thus was limited to one run.

Their other score came in the second inning, when Irish Meusel drove a home run into the upper tier of the left field stands. It was a long wallop and served to tie the score at that stage of the game, as Erin Ward had made a home run for the Yankees in the first half of the inning. Ward's homer was less lusty, but went in the same general direction.

In the fourth the Yankees broke the tie. Ruth began it with his over-the-fence smash, and another run came across on a single by Pipp Schang's hit to right—which Young fumbled long enough to let Pipp reach third—and Scott's clean line hit to centre. This is said to be Scott's last year as a regular and he seems intent on making a good exit, for, in addition to fielding spryly, he made two singles.

The defensive star of the afternoon was Joe Dugan, third baseman of the Yankees. He specialized on bunts. McQuillan caught him flat-footed with an unexpected tap in the third inning, and Dugan made a marvelous throw on the dead run in time to get his man at first.

Again he made a great play against Kelly, first batter up in the last half of the ninth. Kelly just nicked the ball with a vicious swing and the result was a treacherous spinning grounder that rolled only half way down to third. Dugan had to run and throw in conjunction this time, too, but he got his man.

For the Giants, Frisch, Young and Meusel batted hard, and Jack Bentley pitched well after relieving McQuillan in the fourth. He was hit fairly hard and he was a trifle wild, but the only run scored against him was Ruth's homer in the fifth.

As for the local color, the only bit we saw was around the neck of a spectator in a large white hat. The big handkerchief, which was spread completely over the gentleman's chest, was green and yellow, with purple spots. The rooter said his name was Tom Mix, but offered no other explanation.

In 1943, Jerome Holtzman graduated from high school and took a job as a copy boy in the *Chicago Daily Times* sports department. Over his long career he contributed frequent dispatches to *The Sporting News* and invented a baseball statistic, the "save," a means of quantifying the success of relief pitchers. Today, he is a *Chicago Tribune* baseball columnist, the acknowledged dean of Chicago sportswriters, and a sartorial anachronism who prowls the nation's raffish press rows in handsomely tailored three-piece suits that give him the look of one of the dapper interwar sports correspondents whose oral histories he collected in *No Cheering in the Press Box* (1974). This excerpt is from his conversation with Richards Vidmer, the stylish *New York Times* and *New York Herald Tribune* reporter who played golf, toed the bar rail, and did other things as well with his good friend Babe Ruth.

Jerome Holtzman

♥

from

No Cheering in the Press Box

Richards Vidmer

I wasn't a good reporter. I always figured you could read a box score and know what happened. I still do. When I'd write a ball game, I'd write about some particular thing, not "In the first inning Gehrig singled to right, in the second inning Meusel tripled to center, and in the third inning so-and-so grounded into a double play." The hell with that.

Oh, I'd bring it all in—who won and the important plays—but I used to start my stories with some angle—like, well, there was the day the Yankees had the bases filled with two outs in the ninth inning and they sent Mike Gazella to pinch hit. An awfully nice guy. Went to Lafayette. And he stood up there and got a base on balls to force in the winning run. So I started off, "He also serves who only stands and waits."

I played a lot of golf. I played every morning on the road. As a result, I was generally late to the ball games. I'd get to the press box in the third inning and ask someone to fill me in. One time, in St. Louis, I got there pretty late in the game, maybe the fifth or sixth inning, and I asked Will Wedge—he was the baseball man at the *Sun*—if anything special had happened.

"Oh," he says, "Babe hit another home run," which was routine in those days. But he said they had broadcast on the loudspeaker that they wanted the ball back.

I said, "What for? Was it especially long or something?"

Wedge didn't know, but he said a little Italian kid had retrieved the ball and had given it to the Babe. Wedge gave me the kid's name.

Then I remember that Babe and Claire—that was his wife—and I had been to a movie a couple of nights before, and Babe happened to say, "Well, the next one I hit will be my five hundredth."

Now you know what a big to-do there is today when a guy hits five hundred home runs. Writers and photographers follow him around for weeks. But Babe had just mentioned it casually. I was probably the only writer who knew it was his five hundredth.

So I sat down and wrote how Babe had hit this home run and this little kid in the alley, an Italian kid, had chased the ball, and how he'd been trying to get a ball all these years but he never got one because the bigger kids had always beaten him to it. Finally, he gets a ball, his big moment, and a cop comes up and says to the kid, "Come with me."

The kid's scared.

He says, "I ain't done nuthin', I ain't done nuthin'."

And the cop says, "Babe Ruth wants to see you."

Now the kid knows he's in trouble.

So they bring him into the Yankee dugout and Babe Ruth gives him five bucks and a brand new ball.

That was my story for the next day, not the fact that the Yankees won 18–4 or 9–1, or something like that. What the hell, you can see that in the box score. Hell, I'd have it moving. I'd have some drama in it, or romance, or some damn thing. Not like they do it today.

But don't get the wrong impression. I wasn't a big scoop artist. Christ, no! That's why I had so many friends. I never could see blowing the whistle on somebody just for a big headline, a one-day sensation. I'll give you an example.

The day Lou Gehrig took himself out of the lineup and went up to the Mayo Clinic, I wasn't traveling with the Yankees. I was writing a column then, and the Yankees were on the road when Lou took himself out. When the club came home I went into the clubhouse and said, "What the hell's the matter with you, Lou? When you going to get back in the lineup?" I was always kidding with him.

He said, "Wait a minute," and called this fellow over. It was his doctor. He said to the doctor, "Talk to him." And the doctor looked at Lou and Lou said, "Go ahead, tell him anything you want. He's my pal." And Lou walks away.

I asked the doctor, "What's the matter with Lou?"

The doctor told me he's got a creeping paralysis. Nobody knows what causes it. If they knew they could cure it, or at least stop it.

"What are his chances?"

"Well," the doctor says, "there has been much progress made in paralysis these last few years because of President Roosevelt. We hope we'll discover the cause and cure it in time."

"Suppose you don't?"

"Well, I'd say two years is the limit."

I'm the only writer who knows what's the matter with Lou. But I didn't write it. And why the hell should I? The public has to be informed, my ass! None of the public's damned business as long as he plays ball or doesn't play. That's the way I felt, and that's why Lou told the doctor he could level with me. Lou knew damn well I wasn't going to rush into print for the sake of a headline.

Then, maybe two weeks later, Jimmy Powers found out and he spreads it all over the *News*—saying how all of Lou's teammates are afraid to sit next to him in the dugout, and so on, which was a God damn lie. But it was sensational, all right.

I was always reticent about writing anything that was going to hurt somebody, and of course, I would never write anything told to me in confidence. I only read excerpts of the Bouton book. I thought it was damned interesting and amusing—and true. I had seen the same thing, or similar things, thirty years before. Sure, ball players are like that. All athletes are like that. For God's sake, all men are like that. But I just don't see where a public figure's private life is anybody's business.

Hell, I could have written a story every day on the Babe. But I never wrote about his personal life, not if it would hurt him. Babe couldn't say no to certain things. Hot dogs was the least of 'em. There were other things that were worse. Hell, sometimes I thought it was one long line, a procession.

I remember once we were coming north, at the end of spring training. We used to barnstorm and stop at all the little towns. We traveled on the train. Babe and some of the other ball players and myself, we'd play bridge between the exhibition games, in the morning before they had to go to the ball park, and then after the ball game until the train left, generally about eleven o'clock that night. In those days they used to start the games at one o'clock, or one-thirty. We'd be through by three and we'd go back to the hotel to Babe's room and start playing bridge, and surer than hell the phone would ring. I'd always answer it.

"Is Babe Ruth there?"

And I'd say, "No, he's not here right now. This is his secretary. Can I tell him who called?"

"This is Mildred. Tell him Mildred called."

And I'd say, "Mildred"—and the Babe would shake his head, meaning no. Get rid of her.

I'd say, "I'm sorry, he's not here right now, but I'll tell him that you called."

Well, before I could finish, Babe would be across the room, grab the phone, and say, "Hello, babe, c'mon up."

He couldn't say no.

Up she'd come and interrupt the bridge game for ten minutes or so. They'd go in the other room. Pretty soon they'd come out and the girl would leave. Babe would say, "So long, kid," or something like that. Then he'd sit down and we'd continue our bridge game. That's all. That was it. While he was absent we'd sit and talk, wait for him.

One evening in Philadelphia I was in the dining room and Babe had me paged. I went to the phone and Babe said, "What are you doing tonight?"

I said, "Nothing in particular."

And he said, "Come up about nine o'clock, will ya?"

I didn't know what he wanted, but I went up there at nine o'clock. Babe was in his dressing gown. There was some whiskey and ice, soda and whatnot on the table. Babe always had a suite. We had two or three drinks and chatted away about a lot of crap. He talked about Joe McCarthy. Babe had ambitions to be a manager and he never liked

McCarthy. He always said McCarthy was a dumb Irishman who didn't know anything. After about a half-hour of this I saw a shadow at the door in the other room, the bedroom, and I said, "Say, Claire isn't down with you, is she?"

He says, "No, she didn't come down this trip."

So I says, "Have you got a doll in there?"

And he said, "Yeah."

"Jesus, Babe, why didn't you tell me? I've been sitting here chewing the fat with you, and all the time you've got a doll in there."

"No, no," he says. "That's why I wanted you to come up. I thought I'd need a rest."

Oh, sure, that sort of thing is funny, but I didn't think it would add anything to the public image of the Babe. The public already had a good picture of him.

If you weren't around in those times, I don't think you could appreciate what a figure the Babe was. He was bigger than the President. One time, coming north, we stopped at a little town in Illinois, a whistle stop. It was about ten o'clock at night and raining like hell. The train stopped for ten minutes to get water, or something. It couldn't have been a town of more than five thousand people, and by God, there were four thousand of them down there standing in the rain, just waiting to see the Babe.

Babe and I and two other guys were playing bridge. Babe was sitting next to the window. A woman with a little baby in her arms came up and started peering in at the Babe. She was rather good looking. Babe looked at her and went on playing bridge. Then he looked at her again and finally he leaned out and said, "Better get away from here, lady. I'll put one in the other arm."

William Carlos Williams (1883–1963) was a man of numerous and passionate enthusiasms, among them athletics, of which he exulted in *The Autobiography* (1951): "The sweat, the breathlessness, the injuries—that's what sport is." His favorite sport was baseball. "The crowd at the ball game" is part of *Spring and All* (1923), a radically innovative sequence that mixes poetry and prose in unpredictable ways. *White Mule* (1937) is the first novel in a trilogy based on the early life of Williams' wife, Flossie. It recounts her first two years as a sickly infant born to immigrant parents, Joe and Gurlie Stecher, who are struggling to adjust to life in New York City. A doubleheader between the New York Giants and the St. Louis Cardinals is described late in the novel as Joe, an expert printer, considers quitting his job and opening a shop of his own. As well as providing a less flattering glimpse of Giants pitcher George Wiltse than the one given by Damon Runyon (see page 57), this chapter from *White Mule* offers a vivid account of how a man with troubles on his mind spectates at a ballgame.

William Carlos Williams

◊

The crowd at the ball game
is moved uniformly

by a spirit of uselessness
which delights them—

all the exciting detail
of the chase

and the escape, the error
the flash of genius—

all to no end save beauty
the eternal—

So in detail they, the crowd,
are beautiful

for this
to be warned against

saluted and defied—
It is alive, venomous

it smiles grimly
its words cut—

The flashy female with her
mother, gets it—

The Jew gets it straight—it
is deadly, terrifying—

It is the Inquisition, the
Revolution

It is beauty itself
that lives

day by day in them
idly—

This is
the power of their faces

It is summer, it is the solstice
the crowd is

cheering, the crowd is laughing
in detail

permanently, seriously
without thought

from

White Mule

Fourth of July Doubleheader

The Giants were in second place, one game behind the leading Cards. If they won both today the standings would be reversed and they would go into first position. It meant a lot to both teams. Every now and then a loud boom could be heard coming from the streets or the rat-a-tat-tat of a handful of firecrackers exploding somewhere to remind you of what was going on outside. But inside the park it was another world.

But it hadn't started too well for George Wiltze, McGraw's lanky right hander. Bauer, the Card's lead-off man, scratched an infield hit on a slow bounder toward second. Then Johnson, the second man up, drove a hot one past third, Bauer stopping at second. Not so good. And with two on and nobody out Archer, the Cards' big first sacker, drove the first ball on a line between center and left for two bases. It looked like curtains for Wiltze.

Six weeks from today bids will be opened . . . It'll be a dirty fight. But we'll lick 'em because they're guilty and they know it and we're . . .

Take him out! Take him out! yelled a fan sitting immediately in front of Joe. What is this, a procession?

But I got 'em when it comes to the paper—I got 'em there. That's what's going to hurt. Can't get around that. Must sleep more though, can't afford to get sick now. Take it easy because that's only going to be the beginning. Only the start . . .

Time was called while the Giants' infield gathered around Wiltze near the pitcher's box, looking down and kicking imaginary pebbles in the dirt for the most part. But after a couple of minutes they ran back to their positions and the tall right hander got a cheer as he pulled his cap down and took his stand once more.

Better tell 'em tomorrow I'll be quitting at the end of the week. Need a rest. No. Just quitting, that's all. Give 'em no reason. No, that'll make them suspicious. Can't afford that right now. Stick it out for the month. Looks nasty staying in and plotting to take away their business. Not though. What must I do? Cut my throat to do them a favor. Bid's 'r open to the public. Would they consider me? Should say not. A fair bid's a fair bid. They never made a fair bid in their existence. Got to play safe, that's all. Got to out-guess 'em. No other way. Got to stick it out and fool 'em. They'll make it plenty hot anyway when they find out—sooner or later.

Two in and nobody out with a man on second waiting to go. Strike one! Yeay! yelled Joe in his gruff laughing voice, that's the stuff. Give him another in the same place. Strike two!

Then it happened again. The same queer feeling. Wiltze leaned far forward, recovered, took a slow look toward second, then whipped over a third strike while the crowd howled. Joe recognized every move as it happened. That'd happened before, just the way Wiltze had gone through it now. Not another play like it but the *same play*. Twice. Every move. From the time Wiltze had first leaned forward until the pitch had been delivered Joe's mind had preceded every move an instant before, action for action. He'd seen that play before, at some other time, in some other place. That identical play. Twice during the last half hour he'd had that same strange feeling. Agh, he said aloud and took out a cigar. But he didn't light it and after a moment put it back into his pocket.

One down. The next two men were retired on easy ground balls and the inning was over. That's pitching, said Joe. But his eyes were bothering him a little and he rubbed them with both hands.

Wonder when Gurlie will be wanting to come home.

In their half of the first the Giants got one back. Fletcher started it with a clean single and promptly stole second. A very close play. The Cards swarmed around the ump but Fletcher stayed where he was and advanced to third a moment later on an infield out, scoring when Merkle, on a well executed squeeze play, tapped along the first base line. It was smart base-ball, just the stuff Joe delighted to see, the sort of ball McGraw taught his boys. A great afternoon.

Everything has to be thought of. Can't trust anybody. Too bad but can't help it. Every smallest detail down in black and white—perfect, to the last penny, minute detail. Counting devices for each press, every sheet numbered serially—every coupon, in fact. Even after they come off the presses, still danger—greatest danger of all in fact. Wears you out. Can't help it. Got to think of everything. Got to play safe. McGraw thinks of everything. Just the same a man might slip . . .

The fourth inning now coming up. Joe in his favorite position back of first base, his coat off, men all around him smoking and fanning themselves with their hats, entirely at home. Knock him out of the box! yelled the man in front. Send him to the showers. Get that big stiff.

Not today, said Joe. They had their chance. Too late now. Knock him out of the box, yelled the man addressing himself to the field in general. He's got nothing on the ball.

They'll ask plenty questions. Not so dumb. Tell 'em I'm going back to Buffalo. More money. Bet they double me. Too late now, boys. No, tell 'em nothing. They'll have me watched. Won't be able to go anywhere after that. Can't quit till everything's settled—then I'll take them fishing. Got to work through someone else after that. Gurlie can help.

Wham! the first man up in the Cardinal's half of the fourth poled a triple to deep right. There they go! What'd I tell you he was no good? Take him out! Take that big bum out of there. Joe couldn't tell which side the man was rooting for—if it wasn't a grudge against Wiltze himself, maybe. But the next batter, trying to put it into the stands, went down swinging, Wiltze making it two in a row on the next and knocking down a smash through the box with his bare hand and tossing easily to first for the final out. What a man! Joe was delighted.

Up to now the Giants had seemed small and at a disadvantage and the St. Louis team much abler and more rugged. But now it began to change. Last half of the fourth, St. Louis still leading 2 to 1. Wiltze himself at the plate. One to tie and two to win. Wiltze swung viciously but only succeeded in knocking three fouls into the stands, one after the other. Then he watched a third strike go by, waist high, and retired to the dugout with bowed head.

The next man followed with a hard smash to short and was thrown out on a fast play by Clancy of the Cards. Good work Clancy. The Giants were meeting the ball but couldn't seem to drop them safe. Two out. So that when Magee, reaching for a wide one, managed to tap a short fly safe behind first nobody thought anything of it, Joe along with the others. But the next man singled and the next after that and before you knew it two runs were in and . . .

Looked all right, ought to hold anything I want to put on it. That's something they'd like to know—28 Center St. Right across from the jail. Better get building inspector to look it over before presses begin to move. G. W. Hoe and Co. Three lithographic presses. That's what costs. Never thought I'd have the cash to buy those. They'll be watching.

Pandemonium broke loose as the second run crossed the plate. The stands which had been mainly quiet hitherto, morose as a child, were screaming now, yelling their heads off. Joe bit the end of his cigar and lit it, smiling to himself with satisfaction.

That's something like it he said to himself grimly, absorbed and amused. Yes, that looks a little better, answered a voice from the seat to his left. A little startled Joe turned slightly and saw a straight-shouldered man of about fifty, red faced and wearing a striped blue suit, white shirt, black cross tie and a cloth cap. He did not return Joe's look but remained with his face unemotionally fixed toward the diamond.

With two runs already in, two out and a man on first Jansen, for the Cards, lost his steadiness, passed two and was yanked unceremoniously from the scene of action. Well, well. It happens to the best of them, thought Joe. But that's baseball. The game was stopped while the new pitcher strolled in slowly from the St. Louis bullpen and the twenty or thirty thousand waited.

That'll be the big day—when the contracts are opened. They'll have two bids in as usual, one high and one—cut-throat, to kill off all competition if necessary. Do it at a loss to hold it. They'll be watching. Mustn't even be in Washington. Stay home. Go fishing, really. All through some inconspicuous . . .

Nobody can underbid my figures—if it's a fair bid. Unless it's crooked. Unless they've got it fixed, in ways I don't know, in the post office department itself. Page has always been honest though. Never can tell. But I'll fight it if it takes me to the very White House. I'll show 'em up in the papers. I'll bust the whole crooked business wide open. I will. I will. Family or no family. Building, presses, ink . . . payroll.

Nobody scored in the sixth. The seventh inning now coming up. The lucky seventh. Peanuts. Here y'are, get your fresh roasted peanuts. Fi' cents a bag. Sasprilla. Ginger ale. Pass it in, will ya Buddy? Joe took the bottle gingerly and handed it down the line. Then he passed back the nickel. Wonder what some people come to a ball game for anyway, said the man in the next seat. Joe looked again. A tall, deep-chested man looking straight ahead at the playing field as before.

Just enough breeze to lift the flags along the upper edge of the north stands and let them fall again lazily. The diamond and outfield, sharply cut, were a bright velvet carpet to Joe's eyes. As the players ran back and forth on it he could feel with envy its turfy spring and wished for—something, nearer definition now than ever before in his life.

Wonder how they're making out in the country up there. Some day, some day—pretty soon, maybe.

The Cards were unable to score in their half of the seventh. And now it was the Giants' turn. Everybody up! It felt good to stand and stretch once more. But the Cards' new pitcher, a bespectacled rookie named Williams, let our Giants down one, two, three without a man reaching first. And so it ran into the eighth frame, New York still leading by the slim margin of one run. Archer up for the Cards, the man who had poled out the long double in the first scoring his team's only runs so far.

With two balls and one strike on him the hefty first baseman caught the next one on the end of his bat and sent it high toward the left field stands. Going! Going! It seemed to take minutes as Joe watched it ride, clear over the top of the stands and bounce way up onto the elevated tracks beyond them—outside the park. Gone! Wow! What a hit—tying the score.

That's the stuff, said Joe in spite of himself. Knock it out of the park.

The man in front was on his feet at the crack of the bat. There it goes! There goes your old ball game. What'd I tell you? As the big runner ambled around the bases the crowd sat stunned.

That don't mean a thing, said Joe's neighbor. That can happen to anybody. They'll get that back. Wait and see.

Put in Mathewson! yelled the wild-eyed rooter in front. Put in a pitcher. Hey you, McGraw! why don't you put in a pitcher and give us a break for our money?

Guys like that ought to be put in cages, said Joe's neighbor out of the corner of his mouth. Mathewson! he added with contempt. All you hear now is Mathewson. I'll admit he's a good ball player but you'd think to hear some of them talk it was him invented the game. I been waiting for that.

As Wiltze still remained on the mound the man in the front row made a great show of slumping back in his seat. Good *night!* There was however no more scoring in that frame and it went into the ninth still tied up, 3 to 3.

High over the field a flock of pigeons wheeled into sight—swooping suddenly in a swift flow of wings. Joe watched them and tried to count them as they rose again, circling back over the field. Pretty though, pigeons, flying that way in the sunlight and fresh air— cleaner up there than down here, like on a mountain.

And in the ninth the Cards broke loose again, pushed over another run on a free pass, a wild pitch, an infield out and a long fly to center. So that when Bresnahan faced the St. Louis hurler in the last half of the ninth, the Giants were trailing again by one run.

Hit that ball! Hit it! Joe implored. And that's just what Bresnahan did, a smashing single straight over second. He was advanced, following McGraw's usual strategy, on a sacrifice bunt. Then Wiltze himself shot an unexpected safety along the first base line just out of Archer's straining grasp. One away with a run needed to tie and two to win, both of them now on the bags. Looks good, said Joe's neighbor. Thought he might put in a pinch hitter that time but I guess it worked out all right at that.

Better take out some more insurance, thought Joe, while I have the chance. You never can tell.

But Fletcher popped out, close to the stands, and the Giants were two down and it was up to Donlin, now or never, to bring home the bacon. The stands were absolutely still as the New York second baseman walked to the plate, knocked the dirt from his cleats with his bat handle and faced the mound.

The first pitch drove him back in a hurry. The next clipped the outside corner. The next was high. But on the next the big Irishman swung with everything he had and met the ball square, a beautiful drive between first and second. Bresnahan was already at the plate when Wiltze, legging it for second, saw the ball coming, tried to dodge but it hit him in the side of the foot—and the game was over. St. Louis 4, New York 3.

Well, there it is, said Joe's friend on the left straightening his back and stretching. Nice game, barring a few accidents. I used to play with this outfit myself, twenty years ago. Tip Meehan. Ever hear the name? No, Joe couldn't remember that he had. Yes, I've caught 'em all, from Amos Rusie right on down the line.

Joe wanted to ask him what he was doing now.

I still like to watch 'em. You wouldn't take me for a man of sixty, would you? I should say not, said Joe. Well, that's what I am. Sixty-one at my next birthday. Coming up? said he, rising.

No, said Joe. Not just now. Well, take care of yourself. Do my best, said Joe.

Rush, rush, rush! For what, my God? For what? Money, that's all. And when you've got it, what?

A small place in the suburbs, not too far from the city—with a green, well-kept lawn. Flowers, a few trees about it. *Ein Obstgarten.* Blue, red and white grapes on an arbor. A tree of good late apples. A plum tree. Greengages, they're the best. He remembered being told— no, he'd seen it himself—that if a tree won't bear fruit you drive eight or ten good iron nails into it. Good strong nails. Take an apple tree or a plum tree, for instance. Pick a good spot and drive in enough iron nails. Next year you'll see fruit. Doesn't seem to hurt the tree either. But a lawn, that's something else again. Requires a lot of care. Pretty hard to have a really good lawn, moles get into it, weeds—like this playing field for instance, without a man to care for it every day. Nothing finer though than a fine green lawn. Nothing finer. But is it worth it?

Batteries for the second game! For St. Louis, Slezak and Meyer. For New York, Mathewson and . . . Shut up! Shut up! shouted Joe. But it was no use. At the mere mention of Mathewson's name the crowd burst into an uproar. Joe looked instinctively to his companion on the left—but that notable had not returned for the second game. In fact there wasn't much to it. Matty proved to be in such fine form that all the Giants needed was the one run they picked up in the second—though they got a few more later—and that ended it. None of the excitement of the first encounter.

As the crowd filed out Joe followed those who were going down the aisle instead of up, toward the playing field. He had no place in particular to go, he might as well take his time.

A little self-consciously he wandered toward the pitcher's mound. He hadn't realized how much raised it was above the rest of the diamond. That's just it, he said, when you really get up close to a thing . . . And the way they whip that ball in! Walking in toward the plate he looked back to where Wiltze had stood. But when several fourteen to sixteen year old boys approached he turned and walked back across the infield, past second base out into the soft grass beyond. It was coarser than he had thought it to be from the stands, much more uneven and full of worm casts.

As he passed through the center gate with the other stragglers of the crowd he thought he saw, ahead of him, the old fellow who had sat beside him during the first game. Wonder where he's been. And so out into the dirty street under the elevated tracks. And home.

Donald Honig is a prolific author who has written books for children, Civil War books, mysteries (including one about a plot to murder Jackie Robinson), and a farrago of nonfiction baseball books about everything from managers to the World Series to centerfielders. After reading Lawrence Ritter's *The Glory of Their Times,* Honig began compiling baseball oral histories himself. This spoken profile of James "Cool Papa" Bell is taken from *Baseball When the Grass Was Real* (1975). Bell died in 1991, four years after the street in St. Louis where he lived was renamed in his honor.

Donald Honig

ᗢ

from

Baseball When the Grass Was Real

James "Cool Papa" Bell

JAMES BELL
Born: 1903, Starkville, Mississippi

James "Cool Papa" Bell was for more than two decades a star of the Negro Leagues. Considered by many one of the game's all-time ranking center fielders, a peer of Speaker, Mays, and DiMaggio, Bell's speed and baserunning feats were legendary. It was commonplace for him to score from second base on fly balls and groundouts. Kept from his true place as a major league star because of the color barrier, Bell played baseball all over the United States, as well as in Mexico, Cuba, Dominican Republic, Puerto Rico, for nearly thirty years.

In 1974 Bell's extraordinary talents were given belated recognition by organized baseball when he was inducted into the Hall of Fame at Cooperstown.

Of course, most of the time nobody kept any records, so I don't know what my lifetime batting average is. Nobody knows. If I had to guess, I'd say around .340 or .350. I batted .437 one year, in the

Mexican League. I batted .407 in 1944, .411 in 1946. I played twenty-nine years of baseball, and the lowest I ever batted was .308, in 1945. Other than that it was .340 on up to .400. That's twenty-nine seasons, 1922 through 1950. Plus twenty-one winter seasons. That makes a total of fifty seasons. That's the way you have to count it, by seasons.

I was born in Starkville, Mississippi, in 1903; at least that's what I always figured, because that's what I was told. See, in Jackson, Mississippi, they've got two different ages for me. They didn't keep good age records back then. I went by what my mother told me, and she said it was 1903.

I started playing ball as soon as I could, just like the average kid. Everybody played baseball; there were neighborhood teams, but no uniforms or anything like that.

My mother always said that when we got old enough to work, she would send us away from Starkville because she didn't want us to come up the way she came up. She wanted us to try to get the best education we could. We didn't have a high school in Starkville, which meant I wasn't going to get much education there. So she sent me to St. Louis, in 1920.

I had brothers already living in St. Louis, you see, which is why she sent me there. I told my mother I'd go to school, but once I got to the big city, there was so much going on I didn't have time for school. So I hired on at the packinghouse, at fifty-three cents an hour. It was my first job in St. Louis.

I had five brothers, all good athletes. When I got to St. Louis, four of them were playing with a semipro team, the Compton Hill Cubs. I joined up with them, as a left-hand pitcher. I didn't have any trouble making the team; I'd been playing ball with grown men since I was thirteen. I never had trouble making any team, as a matter of fact.

I was a pretty good pitcher, but I wanted to play every day. I was with the Cubs about a year and a half, playing Sundays and holidays and during the week working in the packinghouse.

Then one day I pitched a good game against the St. Louis Stars, a professional team with a lot of first-rate ballplayers. A few nights later my brother, who owned a restaurant, said to me, "The manager of the St. Louis Stars was over here. Wants you to play ball."

Well, that sounded pretty good to me. But my mother and my sister didn't want me to play professional baseball. My sister wrote home to my mother and said I was going to play ball and leave St. Louis and they wouldn't see me anymore. But my brother said, "Now look, you go ahead on and play. It doesn't matter if you make a whole lot of money or not. You can live here when you're in St. Louis and don't worry about the rent, and you can eat here, too. Just so you can say you played pro ball."

So I went with the Stars and pitched for them for two years, making $90 a month. Then they switched me to the outfield. See, every time I pitched I'd get two or three hits. Some of the older fellows on the team told me I should be playing every day, and then the manager got the same idea. That was in 1924.

We played five days a week. We were in what they called the Western League, and we played against Chicago, Indianapolis, Detroit, Kansas City, Cleveland, Dayton, and Toledo. Then there was an Eastern League, with teams in the East. It was on the same basis as the white major leagues, only it was a lower scale. But the fields were pretty good, and in 1928 or '29 we installed lights, years before the major leagues did. We drew crowds of 3,000 to 5,000, and more than that once we got the lights.

When I started, they thought I was going to be afraid playing in front of big crowds, because I was a country boy. When I joined the team, Gatewood, the manager, said to me, "We're going on the road for a month. Now you just watch everything. You got a lot to learn."

Our first stop was Indianapolis. They beat us three games. So Gatewood said, "What the heck, I'd just as soon put you in there. But don't be afraid. Don't pay any attention to the crowd."

We got a big lead in the fourth game, and he put me in to pitch the last two innings. I struck a couple of them out, and some of the fellows said, "Hey, that kid's mighty cool. He takes everything cool."

So they started calling me Cool. When I'd go in, they'd yell, "C'mon, Cool," like that. But that didn't sound right. That's not enough of a name, they said, got to put something else on it. They added Papa to it and started calling me Cool Papa. That's where it came from. In 1922.

I was with the Stars from 1922 through 1931. Then the league broke up and I went with the Homestead Grays in Pittsburgh. I played with them in part of 1932, but then they stopped paying us. That was the worst of the Depression then, 1932. So I moved from there to the Kansas City Monarchs and finished the season with them. No salary there either. We were on percentage, barnstorming around. We wound up playing in Mexico City that winter, but still hardly making any money.

———

'Cool Papa' Bell's Foot Ease

(Remedy By A Famous Ball Player)
QUICK RELIEF
DIRECTIONS: — Apply on corn for three nights (for hard corn bandage). Remove with knife.
Price 25c

I used to have a soft corn between my toes, and I'd mix up a salve to put on it. I made it up myself. It contained plain ol' wash soap, turpentine, and lots of other stuff. Just mixed it all up. A newspaper reporter heard about what I put on and asked me to give him some. He must've liked it, because he suggested I start making the salve for sale and get a patent on it. He said he'd write it up for me. So he wrote an ad. I saw the ad and didn't like it. It didn't sound so good: "Remove with knife. . . ." He said he'd straighten it out, but he never did. I had a lot of the stuff but didn't sell much. Ended up giving most of it away.

———

In the Negro Leagues the audience was mixed but mostly colored. Even down South there were some white people at the games. When we played the Birmingham Black Barons in their park, there were always lots of whites in the crowd, but they were separated by a rope. You could be sitting right next to a white man, but that rope was always there. That was the system they had in those days. That's what they called states' rights. States' rights doesn't mean much to the Negro. You don't get justice with states' rights. Which is a bad thing to happen.

In 1933 I joined the Pittsburgh Crawfords and stayed with them four years. Left there in 1937 to go to the Dominican Republic. Remember Trujillo, the dictator? He was killed a few years ago, you know. Well, they were fixin' to do that back in 1937. But they like baseball down there and they were having championship games, and they said if he would win, they would keep him in office.

So Trujillo got a lot of boys from the States, as well as from Cuba and Panama and Puerto Rico. Mostly he wanted Satchel Paige. We were down in New Orleans in spring training in 1937 and Trujillo's men came there to get Satchel. But he didn't want to go. He kept ducking them for three or four days, but finally one day they trailed him to the hotel and came in looking for him—leaving their chauffeur out in the car. Paige slipped out the side door and jumped in his car to try to get away, but they crossed their car over the street and blocked it.

They told him they wanted him to go down there, and he said he didn't want to go. See, he'd just jumped his team in North Dakota the year before, and everybody was still mad at him, and he didn't want to jump again. That's why he was ducking them. But they showed him a lot of money, offered him a big salary, and he jumped again and went to the Dominican Republic.

But even with Satchel they needed some more ballplayers, because they were losing. So they asked him to send back and get some players from the Negro Leagues. He called Pittsburgh, where I was with the Crawfords. Now, I never did jump nowhere unless something was going bad, and that year it was going bad. The owner of the Crawfords was losing money, and he was giving us ballplayers a tough time, not paying us. Matter of fact, the whole league was going bad at that time. So I was *looking* for somewhere to go when Satchel called.

"We're in trouble down here," he said. "We're supposed to win this championship. I want you and some of the boys to come down. They'll give you eight hundred dollars, your transportation, and all your expenses for six weeks. Will you do it?"

"No," I said. "But make it a thousand and I'll say yes."

Satchel put the head man on the phone, and he said okay, he'd give us each $1,000. Then I said how about us getting some of the money before we get there.

"No," he said, "we can't do that."

"I have to have *something* before I leave," I said.

He said he would talk to his people about it and call us back. When he called back, he said, "Okay, we'll give you half of it in Miami, before you get here. We'll have the consul in Miami meet your plane on your way down, and he'll give each of you five hundred dollars."

They sent us the tickets, and we went to Miami. This man met us at the airport, and he took us to a restaurant. He never mentioned money, and he sure didn't look like he had any on him. But after we ate, he finally gave each of us the $500.

When we got to the Dominican Republic, we went to San Pedro de Macorís—about 40 miles from Santo Domingo—which is the little town they kept the ball club in. And there was Satchel. Boy, was he happy to see us.

They kept us under guard at a private club. Had a head man there with us all the time, with a .45 pistol. We were allowed out on only two days of the week. They said they were going to kill Trujillo if we didn't win.

The best team there was Santiago, and we beat them, finally, and we won the championship. We won it the last day of the season. I guess we saved Trujillo's life, but the people finally got rid of him later.

Then from 1938 through 1941 I played in Mexico, first with Tampico, then with Torreón. In 1942 I came back to the United States and played with the Chicago American Giants.

In 1943 the Giants wouldn't give me the money they'd promised me the year before, and at the same time the Memphis team wanted me. The owner of the Memphis team told me to come there; he promised to pay my way down. But when I got there, he said, "No, I never pay transportation for no ballplayers." And then he said, "Also, I have to fix your teeth. All my ballplayers have a got to have their teeth fixed."

"There's nothing wrong with my teeth," I said.

"Yes, there is," he said.

See, besides owning the ball club, he was a dentist. All his players had to have their teeth fixed by him. Then he'd take his pay out of their salary.

"Look," I said, "it don't seem like we're gonna get along here. If this is the way you run your team, then I'm going home."

The Homestead Grays had been trying to get me, and I got in touch with them. So they started fighting over my contract. But that didn't mean anything. We always had contracts, but they didn't mean much. They wouldn't pay you your money, and that was that. You'd just go somewhere else.

In those days, the thirties, after the big-league season was over, the major leaguers would go barnstorming. We played against all of them. In 1931 Max Carey brought a team to St. Louis to play us. Bill Walker—he'd had a great year with the Giants—was scheduled to pitch the first game. We knocked him out in the very first inning. We beat 'em about 18–3. They had a good team, too: O'Neill catching, Bill Terry at first, Durocher at short, Wally Berger and the two Waner boys in the outfield, and some others I can't remember.

We played a team of big leaguers in 1929, with Charlie Gehringer on it. He was one of the best ballplayers I ever saw. That was a good team we played against. They had O'Neill and Wally Schang catching, Art Shires playing first base, Gehringer at second, Red Kress at short, Manush, Simmons, and Bing Miller in the outfield, Willis Hudlin, Bob Quinn, Earl Whitehill, and George Uhle pitching. We won six out of eight. Gehringer was the only one who looked good. He was some ballplayer.

Here's the thing. In a short series we could beat those guys. In a whole summer, with the team we had, we couldn't. We only had fourteen or fifteen men to a team. We'd play about 130 league games, and *another* 130 exhibition games. Anywhere from 250 to 300 games a season.

Later on there were those famous games where Satchel pitched against Dizzy Dean. I was in center field most all of those games. Dean was a good pitcher, no mistake about that. The feature for those games was always Paige and Dean. Nobody else got any publicity.

Dean beat us a game in New York broke our heart. We had beaten them four in a row, and we went to New York, and everybody said we couldn't do it again. Dean shut us out, 3–0, at Yankee Stadium.

There was a play that day I still remember. I was on second, and Josh Gibson was up. He hit one on a line way back in deep center field. Jimmy Ripple caught it, and I tagged up and rounded third and came all the way home. The ball came in to the catcher—Mike Ryba— the same time I did, but high, and I slid in under it before he came down with the tag. And the umpire said, "Out!" I said I was safe, but the umpire laughed, and said, "I'm not gonna let you do that on major leaguers. Maybe you can do that in *your* league, but not against major leaguers."

Heck, I often scored from second on a long outfield fly.

We went from there to York, Pennsylvania. Dizzy was supposed to pitch. They had guaranteed him $350, but the people were kind of slow coming in, so the man in charge decided to hold the game up a while till the crowd got bigger. Dizzy said he wouldn't pitch a ball until he got his $350. I was told he was afraid the receipts wouldn't cover his guarantee.

Finally the crowd got a little bigger, though not by much. The promoter came to us and said, "Look, you boys play here several times a year. All we've taken in is a little more than I've already promised Dean. Would you play anyway?"

So we said, "Okay, we're here, so we might as well."

Then Dizzy came into the clubhouse and said, "Listen, don't you all hit me. I just pitched Sunday, and my arm is still tired. So don't hit me, y'hear." He wanted to look good, you know.

Sure, Diz, we told him. Then we went out and got four runs the first inning. First three men got on, and Gibson hit a home run, and the score was 4–0 before Dean knew what happened. Then four more in the second inning. People were booing and everything. Dizzy wouldn't pitch anymore, and he went to play second base, which he couldn't do very well.

We wound up winning by a big score, and all we got was about $7 apiece, while Dean got his $350.

It was rough barnstorming. We traveled by bus, you see. You'd be surprised at the conditions we played under. We would frequently play two and three games a day. We'd play a twilight game, ride 40 miles, and play another game, under the lights. This was in the 1940's. On Sundays you'd play three games—a doubleheader in one town and a single night game in another. Or three single games in three different towns. One game would start about one o'clock, a second about four, and a third at about eight. Three different towns, mind you. Same uniform all day, too. We'd change socks and sweat shirts, but that's about all. When you got to the town, they'd be waiting for you, and all you'd have time to do would be to warm your pitcher up. Many a time I put on my uniform at eight o'clock in the morning and wouldn't take it off till three or four the next morning.

Every night they'd have to find us places to stay if we weren't in a big city up North. Some of the towns had hotels where they'd take us. Colored hotels. Never a mixed hotel. In New York we'd stay at the Theresa, in Harlem, or the Woodside. In the larger cities in the South we'd stay at colored hotels. In smaller towns we'd stay at rooming houses or with private families, some of us in each house.

You could stay better in small towns in the South than you could in the North, because in a small town in the North you most of the time don't find many colored people living there. And those that are there have no extra rooms. But in a small town in the South there are enough colored people living there so you can find room in their homes.

Once we were going from Monroe, Louisiana, to New Orleans. We had to cross the bridge over the river at Vicksburg, Mississippi. We were planning to eat lunch at a little town called Picayune. We stopped at a colored restaurant and asked if they had any food.

"Oh, not for all those men," they said. "It'll take us too long to fix food for all those men." It was spring training, and we had about twenty-five men.

When the restaurant people went outside and looked at our bus standing there, they said, "Say, whose bus is this? Any white boys in it?"

"No," we said.

"Who owns it?"

"We have an owner."

"Is he white or colored?"

"Colored."

"And all these boys on the bus are colored?"

"Yeah," we said.

"Well," they said, "you all better get out of the state of Mississippi quick as you can."

"Why?"

" 'Cause if you don't, they gonna take this bus and all you guys in it and put you all working on that farm out there. They need farm workers real bad. There's a lot of people now out there on the farm they caught passing through. They jail 'em for speeding and put 'em to serving their sentence out on that farm."

So we got back on the bus and drove straight through till we were out of the state of Mississippi.

When I was manager of the Kansas City Monarchs' farm team, we played a lot against the House of David. That was in 1948, '49, '50. They had a lot of ex-minor- and -major-league players on their teams. They had to wear a beard. We barnstormed with them through California, Colorado, Nebraska, Iowa, North and South Dakota, and Canada.

We met a lot of good people, but also a lot that weren't so good. Some of them wanted to be good. All the people that you see that say, "I don't want you to do this or that"—they aren't bad people, they're worried people a lot of time, worried about the public. When we traveled with the House of David, they had no trouble finding accommodations, so they had all their reservations made out before the season started. But we had to go to places where we never did know whether we could sleep. Most of the time we'd stay in these cabins on the edge of town. They call them motels today, but in those days they called them cabins.

We went into a lot of small towns where they'd never seen a colored person. In some of those places we couldn't find anyplace to sleep, so we slept on the bus. If we had to, we could convert the seats into beds. We'd just pull over to the side of the road, in a cornfield or someplace, and sleep until the break of day, and then we'd go on into the next town, hoping we'd find a restaurant that would be willing to serve colored people.

All those things we experienced, today people wouldn't believe it. The conditions and the salaries, and what we had to go through. Lots of time for months and months I played on percentage—all of us did—and we'd be lucky to make $5 a game.

But I had a lot of fun in baseball. Saw a lot of great ballplayers. Guys you probably never heard of. Pitcher named Theodore Trent. He'd beat Paige an awful lot of the time. And he never lost a game to a big-league team barnstorming. When we played Max Carey's all-stars, Trent struck those guys out again and again, with that great curveball he had. One game he struck Bill Terry out four times.

Trent was a great pitcher, but he got TB and died young.

Satchel was the fastest, though. I never saw a pitcher throw harder; you could hardly time him. I've seen Walter Johnson, I've seen Dizzy Dean, Bob Feller, Lefty Grove, all of them. Also Dick Redding and Smokey Joe Williams among our boys. *None* of them threw as hard as Paige at the time I saw them. All he threw for years was that fastball; it'd be by you so fast you could hardly turn. And he had control. He could throw that ball right by your knees all day.

Josh Gibson was a good catcher, but not outstanding. He didn't have good hands, and he wasn't the best receiver, though he had a strong arm. But he was a hitter, one of the greatest you ever saw. The most powerful. Never swung hard at the ball either. Just a short swing. Never swung all the way around. Pretty big man. About 190, 195 pounds. About 6'1". He died when he was only thirty-six.

Ruth used to hit them *high*. Not Gibson. He hit them *straight*. Line drives, but they kept going. His power was to center field, right over the pitcher's head. I played against Foxx, but Gibson hit harder and further more often than Foxx or any other player I ever saw.

But they rate Oscar Charleston the greatest Negro ballplayer of them all. He played outfield and first base. Then there was Buck Leonard, a very powerful hitter, and Judy Johnson, a wonderful third baseman, one of the best ever. So many of them, so many great players.

After I was through playing, I tried to get a coaching or scouting job in organized baseball, but nobody would hire me. The one man who might have given me a job was Bill Veeck, but I never could get to see him. Every time I went to see Mr. Veeck when he had the St. Louis Browns' franchise the people in the front office wouldn't let me in to see him. I'd been in baseball all my life and wanted to stay in it, but nobody wanted me.

But I'm not looking back at the past; I'm looking ahead to the future. I'm not angry at Mississippi or anyplace else. That's the way it was in those days. I pray that we can all live in peace together.

The remarkable career of James Weldon Johnson (1871–1938) is a litany of firsts: at the age of 23, after establishing the first African-American high school in Florida, Johnson founded the *Jacksonville Daily American,* the nation's first African-American daily newspaper. The following year he entered law school and became the first African-American to pass the Florida bar. With his brother J. Rosamond Johnson, he wrote the lyrics to "Lift Every Voice and Sing" (often called the "Negro National Anthem") and vaudeville hits such as "Under the Bamboo Tree" and "The Congo Love Song." Fluent in Spanish from a young age, Johnson worked for the State Department from 1906 to 1912, serving as consul in Venezuela and Nicaragua. In 1916, he was named field secretary for the N.A.A.C.P. and later became the organization's executive secretary. His writings include *The Autobiography of an Ex-Colored Man* (1912), a groundbreaking novel about racial passing; *Black Manhattan* (1930), a history of African-American life in New York City; and three volumes of poetry. It seems that nothing was beyond Johnson's grasp—he could even throw a mean curveball, as he recalled in *Along This Way* (1933), his autobiography.

James Weldon Johnson

♡

from

Along This Way

The games I learned to play at school were: marbles, tops, shinny, and baseball. Baseball was my game; the one in which I developed more than ordinary expertness. I was well adapted to the game physically, being slight of figure but muscular. And I not only practiced steadily but studied assiduously. I worked to master what is now known as "inside" baseball. I read regularly a weekly publication called *Sporting Life,* which was devoted chiefly to baseball, so I was familiar with the names and records of all the noted professional players. My favorite club was the old Detroit, and my particular heroes of the diamond were Fred Dunlap and Dan Brouthers, its famous second baseman and first baseman. Before I left Stanton to go to Atlanta University, one of the pitchers on the "Cuban Giants," the crack Negro professional team of New York, imparted to me the secrets of the art of curve pitching. (The Cuban Giants were originally organized from among the waiters at the Ponce de Leon Hotel in St. Augustine. They played professional ball in the North in the summer but for a number of seasons they worked in winter in the St. Augustine hotels and played ball, principally for the entertainment of the guests.) Under my instructor, who had taken a liking to me because he thought I showed the makings of a real player, I gained control of a wide out-curve, a sharp in-shoot, a slow and tantalizing "drop" and a deceptive "rise." I was at the time the only local colored boy who could do the trick. I practiced by the hour with my friend Sam Grant as catcher. We were the battery of our nine, "The Domestics" (why we chose this name I cannot tell), a club made up of boys ranging from fourteen to sixteen years of age. Our fame as a battery began to spread.

My first taste of athletic glory came when Sam and I were called on to serve as the battery for "The Roman Cities" (I am more puzzled by the significance of this name than by that of the club to which I belonged), the leading colored club of Jacksonville and, thereby, the best club in the whole city, in a big game with a formidable team from Savannah. The Roman Cities was a first-rate club. The chief strength of the team was Bill Broad, so nicknamed because of the abnormal breadth of his face. Bill Broad was a wonderful outfielder and, I think, the best natural batter I have ever seen. In either capacity his most strenuous exertions always appeared to be effortless. There were other good players on The Roman Cities, but the team was a little apprehensive over the impending game, and decided to take a chance on strengthening their offensive with my style of pitching, which they had watched. They tried to fit Sam and me out in the blue and red uniforms of the club, but those were all too large; so we played in the white flannel suits, white caps and black stockings of our own club.

The crowd was big and vociferous. It was made up of both whites and blacks. (A good Negro team was then as great a drawing card for whites in the South as one is now for whites in the North.) The white people of Jacksonville were ardent boosters for The Roman Cities, especially when the club played against a team from a Georgia town. For this game a good many shops were closed, and street cars and hacks went out to the grounds loaded beyond capacity. When the visiting nine took the field, I glued my eyes on the opposing pitcher. He was a tall, slender fellow and a fine exponent of the classic style of pitching. He stood holding the ball in front of him in both hands while he intently studied the batter. Then shifting his entire weight to the right foot, he slowly twirled his body round to the right until he almost faced second base, his left foot rising from the ground as his body turned; then back again he twirled with accelerating speed. At the same time his right arm swung back, under, upward, forward and under, describing an almost complete figure 8. He turned swiftly. His left foot came down and dug into the earth, holding the momentum of his body in check, while the right rose into the air, and the ball shot out, projected by every ounce of his weight and energy. The motion began in a gentle sweeping curve and culminated in a pose, held for an instant, of tense power. It was an exhibition of the perfection of masculine grace. Beautiful pitching like that is among the lost arts.

This pitcher's strategy lay in a ball of blinding speed, change of pace, and the ability to trim the corners of the plate. I guessed at once that Sam and I would make a poor showing at the bat; and I guessed right. But we counterbalanced all that. When I ran out to go into the box for the home team, there was every reason for me to feel nervous, but I didn't. No medicine man ever appeared before the tribe with more confidence in his magic than I had in mine when I faced the crowd. As I stooped and picked up a handful of dirt to rub into the cover of the ball to roughen it somewhat, and glanced at the hulking young giant who came to bat, if I had the presumption to draw an analogy between myself and little David choosing his five smooth stones from the brook, I ought, perhaps, to be pardoned. But the analogy was not so far-fetched, at that; David used long-range artillery against a short sword, and I had up my sleeve what was practically a magic power, the power to make the ball suddenly change its course and dart out of the path of the on-coming bat. The advantage, over those to whom it was new, was so great as to amount to unfairness. Yet it was not apparent enough to prevent my being greeted by a chorus of groans and yells as well as applause and cheers.

My delivery was, necessarily, quite different from that of my opponent. It was overhand, rapid, even jerky, and ended with the quick snap of the wrist required to produce the curve. I started with the use of a wide out-curve aimed at the plate, and the break timed so as to tempt the batter to fan the air; varying it by aiming straight at the batter so that the break was over the plate, my purpose being to cause the batter to duck and have a strike called. The coaches finally solved this, and cautioned the batters, "When you see it coming for the plate, don't hit at it. Wait till you see it coming at you." Of course, I immediately began working in a straight ball, an in-shoot, and the drop; and the mystery deepened. As the game went on it assumed a humorous aspect. As many spectators as could do so crowded behind the catcher to watch the vagaries of the ball, and yells of derision greeted bewildered batters, especially when they lunged at the elusive, wide-breaking out-curves. The Roman Cities won the game by a one-sided score. I struck out sixteen men and held the others down to ineffectiveness. My reward was a pretty full cup of the sensation of being a popular hero.

One of the most interested spectators at the game was a man named Haines Spearing. He was a colored sport and said to be the best-dressed man in Jacksonville. He loudly declared that the whole thing was a hoax, a physical impossibility, merely an optical illusion—or words to that effect—and offered to bet that it could not be demonstrated. I couldn't cover his bet, but offered to give him a demonstration free of any risk on his part. I did what I had often done in practice and what I was confident I could do ninety-five times out of a hundred. A group followed us to where two trees stood ten or twelve feet apart. I took my stand in line with the trees and about fifty feet away. I stepped a couple of feet to the left and threw the ball so that it passed to the right of the first tree, between the two, and out to the left of the second. Q.E.D.

Thomas Wolfe (1900–1938) was born in North Carolina, just like his fictional alter ego Eugene Gant, the protagonist of *Look Homeward, Angel* (1929). The following scene is taken from its sequel, *Of Time and the River* (1935). Ben Gant, Eugene's scornful, defiant brother whose death at a young age is described early in *Look Homeward, Angel*, re-creates the events of a faraway World Series for an enraptured crowd of baseball fans. Another Wolfe character, Nebraska Crane from *The Web and the Rock* and *You Can't Go Home Again,* is a big-league player, and as part of his research, Wolfe attended the annual dinner of the Baseball Writers Association of America in 1938. Afterwards, in a letter of thanks to his host Arthur Mann, Wolfe expounded on the game with inimitable gusto and protraction: "One reason I have always loved baseball so much is that it has been not merely 'the great national game' but really a part of the whole weather of our lives, of the thing that is our own, of the whole fabric, the million memories of America. For example, in the memory of almost every one of us, is there anything that can evoke spring—the first fine days of April—better than the sound of the ball smacking into the pocket of the big mitt, the sound of the bat as it hits the horsehide: for me, at any rate, and I am being literal and not rhetorical—almost everything I know about spring is in it—the first leaf, the jonquil, the maple tree, the smell of grass upon your hands and knees, the coming into flower of April. And is there anything that can tell more about an American summer than, say, the smell of the wooden bleachers in a small-town baseball park, that resinous, sultry, and exciting smell of old dry wood."

Thomas Wolfe

♡

from

Of Time and the River

Ben stands there in the window, for a moment idle, his strong, lean fingers resting lightly on his bony hips, his gray eyes scowling fiercely, bitterly and contemptuously over the laughing and exuberant faces of the crowd. For a moment more he scowls fixedly at them with an expression of almost savage contempt. Then scornfully he turns away from them. The bitter, lean and pointed face, the shapely, flashing, close-cropped head jerks upward, backward, he

laughs briefly and with pitying contempt as he speaks to that unknown and invisible auditor who all his life has been the eternal con-
fidant and witness of his scorn:

"Oh my God!" he says, jerking his scornful head out towards the
crowd again. "Listen to this, will you?"

They look at him with laughing and exuberant faces, unwounded
by his scorn. They look at him with a kind of secret and unspoken
tenderness which the strange and bitter savor of his life awakes in
people always. They look at him with faith, with pride, with the joy
and confidence and affection which his presence stirs in every one.
And as if he were the very author of their fondest hopes, as if he were
the fiat, not the helpless agent, of the thing they long to see accomplished, they yell to him in their unreasoning exuberance: "All right,
Ben! Give us a hit now! A single's all we need, boy! Bring him in!" Or
others, crying with the same exuberance of faith: "Strike him out,
Ben! Make him fan!"

But now the crowd, sensing the electric thrill and menace of a
decisive conflict, has grown still, is waiting with caught breath and
pounding hearts, their eyes fixed eagerly on Ben. Somewhere, a thousand miles to the North, somewhere through the reddened, slanting
and fast-fading light of that October day, somewhere across the il-
limitable fields and folds and woods and hills and hollows of America, across the huge brown earth, the mown fields, the vast wild
space, the lavish, rude and unfenced distances, the familiar, homely,
barren, harsh, strangely haunting scenery of the nation; somewhere
through the crisp, ripe air, the misty, golden pollenated light of all
her prodigal and careless harvest; somewhere far away at the heart
of the great sky-soaring, smoke-gold, and enchanted city of the
North, and of their vision—the lean right arm of the great pitcher
Mathewson is flashing like a whip. A greyhound of a man named
Speaker, quick as a deer to run, sharp as a hawk to see, swift as a cat
to strike, stands facing him. And the huge terrific stands, packed to
the eaves incredibly with mounting tiers of small white faces, now
all breathless, silent, and intent, all focused on two men as are the
thoughts, the hearts, the visions of these people everywhere in little
towns, soar back, are flung to the farthest edges of the field in a vision of power, of distance, space and lives unnumbered, fused into
a single unity that is so terrific that it bursts the measures of our

comprehension and has a dream-like strangeness of reality even when we see it.

The scene is instant, whole and wonderful. In its beauty and design that vision of the soaring stands, the pattern of forty thousand empetalled faces, the velvet and unalterable geometry of the playing field, and the small lean figures of the players, set there, lonely, tense and waiting in their places, bright, desperate solitary atoms encircled by that huge wall of nameless faces, is incredible. And more than anything, it is the light, the miracle of light and shade and color— the crisp, blue light that swiftly slants out from the soaring stands and, deepening to violet, begins to march across the velvet field and towards the pitcher's box, that gives the thing its single and incomparable beauty.

The batter stands swinging his bat and grimly waiting at the plate, crouched, tense, the catcher, crouched, the umpire, bent, hands clasped behind his back, and peering forward. All of them are set now in the cold blue of that slanting shadow, except the pitcher who stands out there all alone, calm, desperate, and forsaken in his isolation, with the gold-red swiftly fading light upon him, his figure legible with all the resolution, despair and lonely dignity which that slanting, somehow fatal light can give him. Deep lilac light is eating swiftly in from every corner of the field now, and far off there is a vision of the misty, golden and October towers of the terrific city. The scene is unforgettable in the beauty, intoxication and heroic feeling of its incredible design, and yet, as overwhelming as the spectacle may be for him who sees it, it is doubtful if the eye-witness has ever felt its mystery, beauty, and strange loveliness as did that unseen and unseeing audience in a little town.

But now the crowd, sensing the menaceful approach of a decisive moment, has grown quiet and tense and breathless, as it stands there in the street. In the window, Ben sets the earphones firmly with his hands, his head goes down, the scowl between his gray eyes deepens to a look of listening intensity. He begins to speak sharply to a young man standing at a table on the floor behind him. He snaps his fingers nervously, a card-board placard is handed to him, he looks quickly at it, and then thrusts it back, crying irritably:

"No, no, no! Strike one, I said! Damn it, Mac, you're about as much help to me as a wooden Indian!"

The young man on the floor thrusts another placard in his hand. Ben takes it quickly, swiftly takes out a placard from the complicated frame of wires and rows and columns in the window (for it is before the day of the electric scoreboard, and this clumsy and complicated system whereby every strike, ball, substitution, or base hit—every possible movement and event that can occur upon the field—must be indicated in this way by placards printed with the exact information, is the only one they know) and thrusts a new placard on the line in place of the one that he has just removed. A cheer, sharp, lusty, and immediate, goes up from the crowd. Ben speaks sharply and irritably to the dark and sullen-featured youth whose name is Foxey and Foxey runs outside quickly with another placard inscribed with the name of a new player who is coming in. Swiftly, Foxey takes out of its groove the name of the departing player, shoves the new one into place, and this time the rival partisans in the crowd cheer for the pinch hitter.

In the street now there is the excited buzz and hum of controversy. The people, who, with a strange and somehow moving loyalty, are divided into two groups supporting the merits of two teams which they have never seen, are eagerly debating, denying, making positive assertions of what is likely to happen, which are obviously extravagant and absurd in a contest where nothing can be predicted, and so much depends on fortune, chance, and the opportunity of the moment.

In the very forefront of the crowd, a little to the right as Ben stands facing them, a well-dressed man in the late fifties can be seen excitedly discussing the prospect of the game with several of his companions. His name is Fagg Sluder, a citizen well known to every one in town. He is a man who made a fortune as a contractor and retired from active business several years ago, investing part of his wealth in two or three large office buildings, and who now lives on the income he derives from them.

He is a nervous energetic figure of a man, of middle height, with graying hair, a short, cropped mustache, and the dry, spotted, slightly concave features which characterize many Americans of his age. A man who, until recent years, has known nothing but hard work since his childhood, he has now developed, in his years of leisure, an enthusiastic devotion to the game, that amounts to an obsession.

He has not only given to the town the baseball park which bears his name, he is also president of the local Club, and uncomplainingly makes good its annual deficit. During the playing season his whole time is spent in breathing, thinking, talking baseball all day long: if he is not at the game, bent forward in his seat behind the home plate in an attitude of ravenous absorption, occasionally shouting advice and encouragement to the players in his rapid, stammering, rather high-pitched voice that has a curiously incisive penetration and carrying power, then he is up on the Square before the fire department going over every detail of the game with his cronies and asking eager, rapid-fire questions of the young red-necked players he employs, and towards whom he displays the worshipful admiration of a school-boy.

Now this man who, despite his doctor's orders, smokes twenty or thirty strong black cigars a day, and in fact is never to be seen without a cigar in his fingers or in his mouth—may be heard all over the crowd speaking eagerly in his rapid, stammering voice to a man with a quiet and pleasant manner who stands behind him. This is the assistant chief of the fire department and his name is Bickett:

"Jim," Mr. Sluder is saying in his eager and excited way, "I—I—I—I tell you what I think! If—if—if Speaker comes up there again with men on bases—I—I—I just believe Matty will strike him out—I swear I do. What do you think?" he demands eagerly and abruptly.

Mr. Bickett, first pausing to draw slowly and languorously on a cigarette before casting it into the gutter, makes some easy, quiet and non-committal answer which satisfies Mr. Sluder completely, since he is paying no attention to him anyway. Immediately, he claps the chewed cigar which he is holding in his stubby fingers into his mouth, and nodding his head briskly and vigorously, with an air of great decision, he stammers out again:

"Well—I—I—I just believe that's what he's going to do: I—I—I don't think he's afraid of that fellow at all! I—I—I think he knows he can strike him out any time he feels like it."

The boy knows every one in the crowd as he looks around him. Here are the other boys of his own age, and older—his fellow route-boys in the morning's work, his school companions, delivery boys employed by druggists, merchants, clothiers, the sons of the more wealthy and prominent people of the town. Here are the boys from

the eastern part of town from which he comes and in which his father's house is built—the older, homelier, and for some reason more
joyful and confident part of town to him—though why he does not
know, he cannot say. Perhaps it is because the hills along the eastern
borders of the town are near and close and warm, and almost to be
touched. But in the western part of town, the great vistas of the soaring ranges, the distant summits of the Smokies fade far away into the
west, into the huge loneliness, the haunting desolation of the unknown distance, the red, lonely light of the powerful retreating sun.

But now the old red light is slanting swiftly, the crowd is waiting
tense and silent, already with a touch of sorrow, resignation, and the
winter in their hearts, for summer's over, the game is ending, and October has come again, has come again. In the window, where the red
slant of the sun already falls, Ben is moving quickly, slipping new
placards into place, taking old ones out, scowling, snapping his hard,
white fingers in command, speaking curtly, sharply, irritably to the
busy figures, moving at his bidding on the floor. The game—the last
game of the series—is sharp, close, bitterly contested. No one can say
as yet which way the issue goes, which side will win, when it will
end—but that fatality of red slanting light, the premonitory menace
of the frost, the fatal certitude of victory and defeat, with all the sorrow and regret that both can bring to men, are in their hearts.

From time to time, a wild and sudden cheer breaks sharply from
the waiting crowd, as something happens to increase their hope of
victory, but for the most part they are tense and silent now, all waiting for the instant crisis, the quick end.

Behind Ben, seated in a swivel chair, but turned out facing toward
the crowd, the boy can see the gouty bulk of Mr. Flood, the owner of
the paper. He is bent forward heavily in his seat, his thick apoplectic
fingers braced upon his knees, his mouth ajar, his coarse, jowled, ve-
nously empurpled face and bulging yellow eyes turned out upon the
crowd, in their constant expression of slow stupefaction. From time
to time, when the crowd cheers loudly, the expression of brutal
surprise upon Mr. Flood's coarse face will deepen perceptibly and
comically, and in a moment he will say stupidly, in his hoarse and
phlegmy tones:

"Who done that? . . . What are they yelling for? . . . Which side's
ahead now? . . . What happened that time, Ben?"

To which Ben usually makes no reply whatever, but the savage scowl between his gray eyes deepens with exasperation, and finally, cursing bitterly, he says:

"Damn it, Flood! What do you think I am—the whole damned newspaper? For heaven's sake, man, do you think all I've got to do is answer damn-fool questions! If you want to know what's happening, go outside where the rest of them are!"

"Well, Ben, I just wanted to know how—" Mr. Flood begins hoarsely, heavily, and stupidly.

"Oh, for God's sake! Listen to this, won't you?" says Ben, laughing scornfully and contemptuously as he addresses the invisible auditor of his scorn, and jerking his head sideways toward the bloated figure of his employer as he does so, "Here!" he says, in a disgusted manner. "For God's sake, some one go and tell him what the score is, and put him out of his misery!" And scowling savagely, he speaks sharply into the mouthpiece of the phone and puts another placard on the line.

And suddenly, even as the busy figures swarm and move there in the window before the waiting crowd, the bitter thrilling game is over! In waning light, in faint shadows, far, far away in a great city of the North, the 40,000 small empetalled faces bend forward, breathless, waiting—single and strange and beautiful as all life, all living, and man's destiny. There's a man on base, the last flash of the great right arm, the crack of the bat, the streaking white of a clean-hit ball, the wild, sudden, solid roar, a pair of flashing legs have crossed the rubber, and the game is over!

And instantly, there at the city's heart, in the great stadium, and all across America, in ten thousand streets, ten thousand little towns, the crowd is breaking, flowing, lost forever! That single, silent, most intolerable loveliness is gone forever. With all its tragic, proud and waiting unity, it belongs now to the huge, the done, the indestructible fabric of the past, has moved at last out of that inscrutable maw of chance we call the future into the strange finality of dark time.

Now it is done, the crowd is broken, lost, exploded, and 10,000,000 men are moving singly down 10,000 streets—toward what? Some by the light of Hesperus which, men say, can bring all things that live on earth to their own home again—flock to the fold, the father to his child, the lover to the love he has forsaken—and the proud of heart, the lost, the lonely of the earth, the exile and the wanderer—to what? To pace again the barren avenues of night, to pass before the bulbous light of lifeless streets with half-averted faces, to pass the thousand doors, to feel again the ancient hopelessness of hope, the knowledge of despair, the faith of desolation.

And for a moment, when the crowd has gone, Ben stands there silent, lost, a look of bitter weariness, disgust, and agony upon his gray gaunt face, his lonely brow, his fierce and scornful eyes. And as he stands there that red light of waning day has touched the flashing head, the gaunt, starved face, has touched the whole image of his fiercely wounded, lost and scornful spirit with the prophecy of its strange fatality. And in that instant as the boy looks at his brother, a knife is driven through his entrails suddenly, for with an instant final certitude, past reason, proof, or any visual evidence, he sees the end and answer of his brother's life. Already death rests there on his proud head like a coronal. The boy knows in that one instant Ben will die.

Paul Gallico (1897–1976), the son of musical parents who met at a conservatory in Vienna, wrote lyrically about sports for New York's *Daily News* from 1923 to 1936, before leaving journalism for a career as a novelist. His books include *The Snow Goose* (1941), *Mrs. 'Arris Goes to Paris* (1958), and *The Poseidon Adventure* (1969). As a sportswriter, Gallico invented the stunt—later refined by George Plimpton—of jumping into the ring with an athlete and then writing about the experience. Gallico sparred with the heavyweight Jack Dempsey (the Champ knocked him out cold), played tennis with Helen Wills, caught Dazzy Vance's fastball, and golfed with Bobby Jones. Gallico belonged, as he admitted to Jerome Holtzman, to "the 'gee-whiz' group of sportswriters," by which he meant that he was overly impressed by athletes. His enduring fascination with games and the people who play them is evident from *Farewell to Sport,* a classic 1937 collection from which this lithe essay is taken.

Paul Gallico

◻

Inside the Inside

B aseball can be the most fascinating game in the world to watch and also the dullest, depending very often upon circumstances— that is to say, the quality of the play, the caliber and situation of the competing teams, and also what you yourself bring into the park. All games are alike in form and intent. One man tries to beat another man, or one group of men try to worst another group through skill, courage, and physical condition. It is merely the materials with which they are provided for this purpose, the rules, and the playing grounds that differ. The more intricate the game and tangled the rules and complicated the materials, the more difficult it is to understand, but the more fascinating it becomes when you do understand it.

When two men face each other in a boxing ring with gloves on their hands and begin to fight when the bell rings, and stop fighting when it rings again after three minutes, it is reasonably obvious to anyone what is going on and what they are trying to do to each other and the means they are employing. The struggle is a simple hand-to-hand trial for complete mastery within certain time limits, and because the struggle sometimes gets atavistic, abysmal, and terrifying, with show of blood, it is arresting and arousing. The novice spectator becomes an expert after witnessing his first prizefight or boxing match because everything is plain and simple and easy to see. It takes rather longer to know what is going on on a baseball field, what the trials and the problems of the various players are, what can be done and what cannot be done; and even so, many people who have been going to games for years do not know exactly what it is all about because they have never taken the trouble to find out. They love it, though, because they do realize that there is a fine balance struck between offense and defense and that, by a lucky accident in the laying out of the playing field and the development of the game, you may sit by and witness the development of real drama and the working of keen wits in fast bodies.

Baseball talk is a great bore, baseball-players are not exactly intellectual giants, and baseball figures, box scores and averages even duller. But the things that take place on the field in a tight game played to the hilt by a couple of major-league clubs can be completely captivating.

If games as a whole bore you, you will never like baseball. But if you can take pleasure in the story of conflict unfolded before your eyes, it is only necessary to become a little more familiar with the materials used by baseball-players and the rules under which they operate to find something that can be quite as fascinating, for instance, as the theater. In one afternoon at the ball yard you may, if you know where and how to look for it, come upon half a dozen split-second races between a running man and a thrown ball, in which the hundredth part of a second is all the difference between success and failure, dozens of examples of skill triumphant, skill defeated, traps baited and snapped shut upon victims, human courage, human folly, and human cowardice, narrow escapes, heroes, villains, individual deeds that verge upon the miraculous, bits of co-operation between two men or among three or four that are really beautiful to see in their rhythm and perfection, heroes turned suddenly into clowns and goats, clowns becoming heroes, speed, grace, and sometimes even a curious beauty, the beauty of the perfection of a well-pitched, well-defended game.

The patterns of the game are of themselves interesting and pleasing to the eye. The rich chocolate-brown or pale tan of the infield is contrasted with the fine soothing green of the outfield. The base paths are neatly geometrical, and the white foul lines on either side of the home plate start their diverging roads towards infinity. There is a place for everyone and every place is neatly marked off with white lime. There is a base at each corner of the square, and a player stationed at, or close to, each base. The outfield is divided into three sections, right, center, and left field, and each field has a patrolman stationed in his appointed place. Pitcher and catcher stand on a line that is the hypotenuse of the right-angle triangle made by the three bases, home, first, and second. And pleasingly anti-geometrical is the shortstop, who is placed with no heed to design at all, midway between second and third base, upsetting the whole scheme of regularity like a tiny beauty mark on the cheek of a pretty girl.

One team dresses in white, the other in gray. And the action is static rather than fluid, with sharp, refreshing changes from tension and immobility to quick, brilliant bursts of motion. You may see this curiously exaggerated in newsreel photographs of ball games, because the camera cuts in usually just a second before the flashes of action on the diamond. You catch a glimpse of them stock still first, and then suddenly men are streaking around the bases, heads down, legs twinkling, while fielders glide in to make their quick, graceful defensive moves.

But the plot behind the patterns is even more exciting. Let us take a simple example; the score is tied, there is one out, a runner is on first base, and a heavy hitter is at bat, crouched a little over the plate, waving his mace back and forth gently but menacingly. And, incidentally, he doesn't do this in hopes of frightening the pitcher. He is merely keeping his bat moving because the action he is to be called upon to meet is so fast that he will be hopelessly beaten if he hasn't begun to move a little in advance of it.

There they are, then, the eleven men involved at the moment in what from the point of view of the eventual outcome of the game may be definitely the crisis. The first baseman is dividing his attention between keeping the runner at his base from gaining too much of a lead, and still covering his territory defensively. If the ball is hit, the runner on first will come charging at full clip into second base. Depending upon where the ball is hit to, either the second baseman or the shortstop will have to get there to take the throw and the shock. Or he may not even wait for a hit, but try to steal in the little bit of time between the start of the pitcher's delivery and the passage of the ball to catcher and thence to second baseman. The shortstop is intent upon the delicate problem of starting a successful double play and retiring the side. The third baseman has moved in a little to speed up the fielding of a possible bunt or roller in the infield, and yet he must not leave the space around his base unprotected through which a sharply driven ball may scoot for two or three bases and disaster.

The outfielders have shifted their positions to suit the known batting habits of the hitter. The burly, powerful figure squatting behind the bat, the catcher, is the man in control of the entire situation, and the pitcher is his tool, obeying his brain and his strategy, telegraphed to him by means of finger signals. Or perhaps the catcher is merely an intermediary who transmits the signals and will of an even better strategic mind in the person of the manager sitting on the bench. And the batter is one lone man playing the other nine men, their speed and skill, the intelligence of the catcher in playing his weaknesses, and the control of the pitcher and his ability to obey the orders of the catcher, combined against him. Every move that follows will have a direct bearing upon the outcome of the game. Nothing is unimportant. A double play will badly hurt the morale of the side thus retired with victory in its grasp. A hit or an error or a stolen base may equally upset the equilibrium of the defending team. But still more fascinating and exciting is the fact that all of the men involved are playing a match against time and distance and dealing with the smallest fragments of seconds that can be split on the dial of a delicate stop watch.

The baseball diamond is no diamond at all, but actually a square set up on one of its points, and the bases, home to first, first to second, second to third, and third to home, are each exactly 90 feet apart. The pitcher's box is 60½ feet from home plate. The distance from home plate to second base, which is the line on which the catcher throws in the attempt to catch a man out who is stealing, is a fraction over 127 feet. And the entire science and thrill of the American game of baseball, developed from an old English game called rounders, lie tucked away in those measurements. They are very rarely examined, and still more rarely thought of, even by the players.

Most of the men who play the game haven't the vaguest notion of the miracles of timing and precision that they perform.

The infielders, for instance, have a fraction under three seconds in which to field a batted ball and get it over to first base ahead of the runner, because the batter only has to run a distance of thirty yards to reach first. From a standing start a fast man can do it in three and two tenths seconds, and a left-handed batter perhaps one or two tenths of a second faster, because he is on the right-hand side of the plate and a yard closer to his goal. If the fielder can get that ball to first base in just under three seconds, the runner is out. A few tenths of a second over the three seconds and he is safe and a potential run is menacing the defense.

Now, look at the second hand of your watch and note the time it takes for three seconds to tick off—one . . . two . . . three and gone. In this time, the infielder judges the speed and direction of a ball hit with all the weight and force behind the body of a man, moves in to meet it, figuring the hop as he does so, and the number of steps he must take to reach it, catches it and throws it again all in one motion while still moving forward. There is nothing prettier for timing and rhythm in any sport than to watch a shortstop or third baseman (whose problems are greater because, of the infielders, they are farthest removed from first base and have a greater distance to throw) come in fast for a slow roller, and as he is moving, swoop on the ball like a gull dropping for a fish, and with a continuation of the same movement with which he picked it up, get it away on a line for first base with an underhand throw across his forward-bending body. So precious and vital are those tenths of seconds that if he tries to straighten up, or draw his arm back to gain more speed and accuracy, the play is over. The runner has crossed first base.

How much faster, then, and more beautiful in speed and execution is the double play when three men handle the ball in the same length of time and retire two runners on the one play, the man speeding to second (and he has a good head start) and the batter heading for first. Three seconds flat or better, and yet the shortstop fields the batted ball, or rather scoops it over to the second baseman, who sends it on to first. It would take a delicate timing instrument to measure the fraction of a second that the shortstop actually has possession of the ball. Crack! goes the bat. Step, and flip, goes the shortstop! The second baseman in that time has run from his position perhaps five or six yards from the bag as the ball is started towards him by the shortstop. Ball and man meet on the base, and likewise with the same motion, in which there is no check or hesitation, the second baseman whirls and lines the ball down to first. He can whip that ball the ninety feet from second to first in three fifths of a second. And he is lucky to have that much time left.

The catcher has a pretty problem to throw out a man who is trying to steal. A good base-runner will take a lead of from two to three or four yards from first base before he suddenly ducks his head and breaks for second with every ounce of speed he can muster. He can make it in something around three seconds flat, or even a tenth or two under. Unlike a force-out, where it is merely necessary to touch the bag once the ball is in the fielder's possession, the second baseman or shortstop, who receives the throw at second, must touch the runner with the ball before his spikes cut into the bag or he hooks it with his leg. Here is a fine, brisk bit of juggling with time. The runner starts his dash with the wind-up of the pitcher or, as he rarely winds up with a man on base, with his first move to pitch the ball to the batter, usually the first tension or drawing back of the arm. From that time on, the hurler is committed and must go through with the pitch.

The ball travels the sixty feet to the plate, and, just to be mother's little helping hand, the batter takes a cut at it to make it more difficult for the catcher and throw him off if he can. The catcher must receive the ball perfectly, straighten up, whip off his heavy mask, draw back his arm, and fire the ball on a line, not in the general direction of second base, but to the foot of the bag, about ankle-high, so that the receiver is spared that precious tenth of a second or more in getting it onto the sliding runner. If the maneuver is completed inside of three seconds and the throw is accurate, the runner is out. Anything over that and he is safe. It takes a ten-second man to steal a base successfully these days—that is, a man who can run a hundred yards in ten seconds. And every inch of ground that he can chisel by increasing his lead off first without getting caught at it and thrown out at first, is important and vital to the success of this maneuver and has a direct bearing upon the eventual outcome of the game. Those seemingly endless throws that the pitcher makes over to first base to hold the runner close to the bag are not made for exercise or to annoy the customers.

The purpose is to reduce those inches. The inches otherwise will be translated into hundredths of a second around second base and spell the difference between safe and out. A man can score from second on a single. Runs depend upon those tiny measurements.

As a matter of fact, no game in the world is as tidy and dramatically neat as baseball, with cause and effect, crime and punishment, motive and result, so cleanly defined. The consequences of a single error or failure pyramid inexorably as the game goes on and finally prove to be the events that have won or lost the day, exactly as the minor, unnoticed incidents unfolded at the beginning of a well-constructed play suddenly loom up as prime and all-important to the climax.

Pretty, too, is the personal duel between pitcher and batter, or rather between the pitcher and his alter or commanding ego, the catcher, and the man who is trying to hit. The problem of the batter seems tremendously magnified when one considers what might be termed the ballistics and forces under which he operates.

The distance between the pitcher's box and home plate, as has been noted, is 60½ feet. And a fast ball will make the trip from the hand of the thrower to the mitt of the catcher somewhere between three and four tenths of a second. That doesn't exactly give a batter much time to turn the matter over in his head and make up his mind whether he will take a cut at it or let it pass for a ball, though it is true the average pitch is somewhat slower and the ball takes four to five tenths of a second for its flight. The average baseball bat is only about three feet long, and the batter's arm permits it to extend for another foot or so. Actually, out of that entire distance of 60½ feet that is traversed by the ball in less than half a second, it is in position to be hit safely by the batter for only three feet of the journey. This brings the time element in which a ball remains in a position where it may be met with the bat close to an absurdity, an impossibility; something around two one-hundredths of a second, which is cutting it rather fine. And still the batsmen manage, on an average, to hit safely one third of the baseballs thrown at them.

To assist the batter and to strike a better balance between him and the pitcher, the latter is forced, if he wishes to register a called strike, to throw the ball to the hitter down a groove a little more than a foot wide, the width of the home plate. And if the pitcher throws more than four of them outside this groove, the batter, as everyone knows, is entitled to the equivalent of a hit, a free passage to first base. The batter is further permitted two misses without penalty. If he misses the third time he is out.

Thus, the activity centered on home plate is really very simple to understand; three strikes out, four balls a walk. But the drama that is packed into that simple arrangement of figures, the swift changes of fortune and situation whereby first one and then the other finds himself in difficulties which with stunning suddenness are liable to mushroom into the loss of the game, explain a good deal of the fascination of the sport.

For instance, the so-called three strikes allotted the batter are a great snare and delusion. In point of fact it is only two strikes, for he is allowed to miss the ball only twice, but nobody but the batter ever thinks of that. The third time he misses it he is out. And yet there is magic in that number "three" and he strides to the plate with great confidence in his allotment of three strikes, a confidence that is only slightly dented upon the calling or taking of the first one, because, after all, there are still two more chances left. Two strikes and he is in for it. Now he *must* hit. The margin of possible failure has been wiped out. The pressure has suddenly become almost unbearable. And three chances had seemed such a safe margin when he first stepped up to the plate!

But note how the balance of power seesaws between pitcher and hitter. Batter up! The first one comes over—a ball. The batter smirks and pounds the plate with satisfaction. The advantage lies with him now. If the pitcher throws another wide one it means that three out of his next four pitches must be in that groove or the batter walks. Very nice. And so the next throw will bear looking at very closely, because the chances are it will be a strike. There is a little pressure on the pitcher and none whatsoever on the batter. He can afford to relax a little and let the pitcher commit himself on the next ball. He does. Ball two! Ha! Two balls and no strikes. Lovely. The batsman begins to preen himself a little and the pitcher to perspire. That man serving 'em up from the little mound is in for it now. Strike one! Oh, oh! Now the batter is doing a little more thinking. The next one will be more of a problem. Shall he let it pass and hope it will be a third ball, putting the pitcher definitely on the spot, or should he reason that the latter will try to burn it over and get *him* in the hole? Ugh! Strike two! Swung at it and missed it by a foot. Guessed wrong. The pitcher fooled him (or rather the catcher). He should have let it go. Out-guessed. Now the batter begins to sweat. The advantage lies with the enemy now. Two balls and two strikes and the pitcher has another ball to waste and can tease him with a bad one, or take a chance of breaking a fast one over the corner of the plate and getting him out. Hardly a moment ago the batter had the situation well in hand. Now he is in a mess. That confounded pitcher is just playing with him. Look at him grinning up there on the mound. All the confidence has oozed out of the hitter and into the hurler. Here it comes—zip! Has the umpire's right arm flashed up? No! A ball! Three and two! Switch again. Now the pitcher is in deep trouble, although the batter is not feeling any too good about the situation. But the odds have passed to the batter because the pitcher must commit himself first. Once that ball leaves his fingers it is irrevocable. There is no calling it back or changing his mind. True, the hitter has only that tenth of a second in which to make his decision as to what he will do with the next pitch, but in a game of such delicate fractions of time it is a decided advantage. He knows that the pitcher cannot afford to walk him, especially if there is only one out, or none, or another man on base already. And if the bases are full the corresponding pressure upon the pitcher is all the greater. No, he must throw the ball down that nice, one-foot groove in which the bat may work to deadliest advantage. His only chance is to put so much spin, or "stuff," on the ball that when it meets the bat instead of rifling off into the outfield for a clean hit, it will deflect to the ground and give the fielders a chance to scoop it up, or glance off high into the air to be caught on the fly. But he might decide to risk it and make the eager hitter bite at one and strike out.

This goes on every minute of the game, and never seems to be twice the same, as the individual duels go on, inning after inning, changing in their nature and intensity according to the situation of the game. Pitching to batters with runners on base increases the pitcher's worries and problems a hundred-fold. Batting in pinches piles pressure upon the batsmen. The situation is always different, and they drive on relentlessly, piling up and piling up to a certain climax as the final innings of the game are reached, increasing in intensity as the pitcher begins to tire and it is a question how long he can respond with accuracy and control to the dictates of the brain behind the bat.

The game is as full of surprises as a mystery play. The plot and its ending may be perfectly apparent up to the ninth inning and the last man at bat, and then with stunning suddenness change entirely and go on to a new ending. A pitcher will often be the hero of a closely fought battle in which his side leads 1–0 for eight innings and the rival batsmen have been looking sillier and sillier as they fanned the air, clawing at curves and drops, or standing with their bats on their shoulders while the ball broke across the plate for perfect called strikes. A batter in the hands of a masterful pitcher is a pitiful sight, anyway. He releases enough energy with each swing to cave in the side of a building and it does nothing but create a mild breeze as bat fails to meet ball. He swings himself clear off his feet and sits awkwardly in the dust from the force of his useless blow. Or he stands looking like a big zany, with his ears turning a beautiful shade of cerise, while a perfect third strike burns past his bosom and the umpire calls him out and the catcher laughs sardonically and makes unpleasant remarks out of the side of his mouth.

These are moments of pure glory and unadulterated satisfaction for the pitcher and his battery mate and their adherents in the grandstands. Or the batter actually connects with the ball with a mighty swipe destined to rip the hide from it, but all that happens is that the ball takes one hop into the hands of the second baseman, who, to show his contempt for the puny effort, tosses the ball underhand to the first baseman.

Even in the ninth inning when an obviously astigmatic umpire, with two out and none on base, calls what was obviously a third strike a fourth ball, and a man reaches first base, there is no cause for alarm. The batters that day are lugging useless timber to the plate and have had no more than three safe hits the entire game. They might just as well have match-sticks in their fingers. And the next man up, the final hitter, is a weak sister, relegated to the lower half of the batting order because he has no reputation or record as a dangerous slugger. The crowd is already beginning to head for the exits, chuckling to themselves at the helplessness of the batters, admiring the skill and control of the pitcher. The catcher calls for a sizzler over the plate, loaded with spin. The weak hitter will ground it to a fielder and the game will be over. In anticipation the pitcher is already standing beneath a cooling shower, listening to the laudatory words of his comrades, and reading the "SHUT-OUT" headlines in the morning papers. Next year he must ask for a raise. He winds up—let the man on base go down to second if he wants to. Now he is in a knot. Now he unwinds. Now he pitches. And now, too, it happens. For, working silently and without warning, the poisons of fatigue in that arm that seemed to be made of steel and whipcord have worked their changes. The pitcher has given the same twist, the same flip of his wrist, the same leverage and follow-through with his body, only instead of slanting towards the batter with blinding speed, the ball comes floating down the groove, all stitches showing, and looking just a shade smaller than a full moon. The batter doesn't have to be a Babe Ruth to nudge that one. He says: "Oh, baby, come to Papa!" laces it into the grandstand for a home run, and that is that.

The game is over. The pitcher has lost 2–1. All he could do was stand there with his hands on his hips, feeling his ears growing long and furry, watching the ball sail over the whisky advertisement affixed to the top balcony. The fielders cannot even make a play for it. The right fielder dutifully has his rump pressed up against the right-field wall, but he would have to be a hundred feet tall to get his hands on that ball and he can do little more than wave it a regretful farewell as it disappears into the crowd.

There you have it. One tiny, uncontrollable slip and the hero has become the dunce, the goat, and the villain. All the failures of the batters that day are forgotten and forgiven, wiped out by that one blow. The sports-writers, some of them, angrily tear sheets of paper from their typewriters, on which they have already begun to write: "In one of the most masterful exhibitions of plain and fancy hurling ever seen at the Polo Grounds, Joie Dokes, diminutive southpaw of the New York Giants, shut out the St. Louis Cardinals 1–0 here yesterday afternoon, letting them down with three hits," etc., etc., insert a fresh piece of paper, and start all over again: "Elmer Crabtree, veteran shortstop of the Cards, hasn't been hitting the length of his cap all year, but yesterday afternoon in the ninth inning of a brilliant pitchers' duel, he stepped to the plate with two out, the score 1–0 against him, and a comrade on base due to walk, and with the count two and two on him," etc., etc., etc.

There are hundreds of these situations brought on during the course of the game, and one could write endlessly of them. I don't mean to do so. But that is why I have liked baseball and always will. It is endlessly intriguing, and when the human element is added to the weird mechanics of the sport, the wise, foxy veterans, the brash, cocky young kids, the eccentric and screwy characters who play the game, it becomes truly a part of the national scene.

But I like, too, the freedom of baseball and the physical and emotional simplicity of the relationship between player and spectator. It is the only game in the world where the onlooker is permitted to heckle, hoot, cheer, and advise the player to his heart's content. I am not particularly concerned whether it is sportsmanlike for an individual concealed beyond hope of detection in some section of the crowd, to howl, purple-faced, as a batter retires from the plate with his tail between his legs after having fanned in a clutch: "Oh, you bum! Go lay down, you bum, yah yeller. Oh, you bum!" but I know that it makes the abusive individual feel wonderful, because I have sat next to him and watched him wipe the sweat off his brow with a damp handkerchief after his tirade, tilt a bottle of pop to his lips, and then look around him to take in the admiring glances of some of the less daring and articulate fans. He has established himself as an expert and a critic. He has hoisted something off his chest. I know him, the poor little man; not man, but mouse. In the office he sits under the thumb of his niggling superior and at home under both thumbs of his wife. Taxi-drivers curse him as he scuttles out from beneath their wheels, waiters ignore him, policemen bawl him out, nobody loves him, nobody pays any attention to him. But in the ball park he can rise up on his hind legs and abuse a player. It's good for him, and it doesn't hurt the player any.

So, too, the crowd as a whole plays the role of Greek chorus to the actors on the field below. It reflects every action, every movement, every changing phase of the game. It keens. It rejoices. It moans. It jeers. It applauds and gives great swelling murmurs of surprise and appreciation, or finds relief in huge, Gargantuan laughs. I can stand outside of a ball park and listen to the crowd and come close to telling exactly what is happening on the diamond inside. That quick, sharp explosive roar that rises in crescendo and is suddenly shut off sharply as though someone had laid a collective thumb on the windpipe of the crowd, followed by a gentle pattering of applause, tells its own story, of a briskly hit ball, a fielder racing for it, a runner dashing for the base. The throw nips the runner and the noise too. That steady "Clap-clap-clap-clap-clap. . . ." Tight spot. Men on base, crowd trying to rattle the pitcher. A great roar turning into a groan that dies away to nothing—a potential home run, with too much slice on it, that just went foul. The crowd lives the actions of the players more than in any other game. It is a release and something of a purge. It is the next best thing to participation.

Moe Berg (1902–1972) grew up in Newark, New Jersey, and studied modern languages at Princeton, graduating near the top the class of 1923. He was also the star of the baseball team. The day after graduation he joined the Brooklyn Dodgers to earn tuition money—he wanted to do graduate work at the Sorbonne in Paris. By 1930, Berg had earned a degree from Columbia Law School, and had become the Chicago White Sox starting catcher. This most erudite major leaguer was also a talented writer. In 1941, Berg, then a Red Sox coach, received a letter from Edward Weeks, editor of *The Atlantic Monthly,* who said he wondered about pitchers and asked Berg to write him a "paper" on what it takes "to be better than average." The piece, so redolent of both Berg's learning and his exotic personality, amounts to a concise primer on the essential workings of the game, and remains the best "inside baseball" essay ever written by a major-league practitioner.

Moe Berg

♥

Pitchers and Catchers

I

Baseball men agree with the philosopher that perfection—which means a pennant to them—is attainable only through a proper combination of opposites. A team equally strong in attack and in defense, well-proportioned as a unit, with, of course, those intangibles, morale, enthusiasm, and direction—that is the story of success in baseball. Good fielding and pitching, without hitting, or vice versa, is like Ben Franklin's half a pair of scissors—ineffectual. Lopsided pennant failures are strewn throughout the record books. Twenty-game winners or .400 hitters do not ensure victory. *Ne quid nimis.* Ty Cobb, baseball genius, helped win pennants early in his career, but from 1909 through 1926, his last year at Detroit, he and his formidable array of hitters failed—they never found the right combination. Ed Walsh, the great White Sox spitball pitcher, in 1908 won forty or practically half of his club's games, to this day an individual pitching record, but alone he couldn't offset his own 'hitless wonders.' Walter Johnson the swift, with over 400 victories, waited almost twenty years before his clubmates at Washington helped him to a championship. Every pennant winner must be endowed both at the plate and in the field. Even Babe Ruth's bat, when it loomed largest, couldn't obscure the Yankees' high-calibre pitching and their tight defense in key spots.

With all the importance that hitting has assumed since the Babe and home runs became synonymous, I note that Connie Mack, major-league manager for almost half a century, household name for strategy wherever the game is played, still gives pitching top rating in baseball.

A Walter Johnson, a Lefty Grove, a Bob Feller, cannon-ball pitchers, come along once in a generation. By sheer, blinding speed they overpower the hitter. Johnson shut out the opposition in 113 games, more than the average pitcher wins in his major-league lifetime. Bob Feller continues this speed-ball tradition. We accept these men as pitching geniuses, with the mere explanation that, thanks to their strong arms, their pitches are comparatively untouchable. When Walter Johnson pitched, the hitter looked for a fast ball and got it; he looked—but it didn't do him much good. Clark Griffith, then manager of the Washington Club, jestingly threatened Walter with a fine any time he threw a curve. 'Griff' knew that no variation in the speed king's type of pitch was necessary. But what of the other pitchers who are not so talented?

Many times a pitcher without apparent stuff wins, whereas his opponent, with what seems to be a great assortment, is knocked out of the box in an early inning. The answer, I believe, lies in the bare statement, 'Bat meets ball'; any other inference may lead us into the danger of overcomplication. The player himself takes his ability for granted and passes off his success or lack of it with 'You do or you don't.' Call it the law of averages.

Luck, as well as skill, decides a game. The pitcher tries to minimize the element of luck. Between the knees and shoulders of the hitter, over a plate just 17 inches wide, lies the target of the pitcher, who throws from a rectangular rubber slab on a mound 60 feet, 6 inches distant. The pitcher has to throw into this area with enough on the ball to get the hitter out—that is his intention. Control, natural or acquired, is a prerequisite of any successful pitcher: he must have direction, not only to be effective, but to exist.

Because of this enforced concentration of pitches, perhaps the game's most interesting drama unfolds within the limited space of the ball-and-strike zone. The pitcher toes the mound; action comes with the motion, delivery, and split-second flight of the ball to the catcher. With every move the pitcher is trying to fool the hitter, using his stuff, his skill and wiles, his tricks and cunning, all his art to win.

Well known to ball players is the two-o'clock hitter who breaks down fences in batting practice. There is no pressure; the practice pitcher throws ball after ball with the same motion, the same delivery and speed. If the practice pitcher varies his windup or delivery, the hitters don't like it—not in batting practice—and they show their dislike by sarcastically conceding victory by a big score to the batting practice pitcher and demanding another. This is an interesting phenomenon. The hitter, in practice, is adjusting himself to clock-like regularity of speed, constant and consistent. He is concentrating on his timing. He has to coördinate his vision and his swing. This coördination the opposing pitcher wants to upset from the moment he steps on the rubber and the game begins. The very duration of the stance itself, the windup and motion, and the form of delivery are all calculated to break the hitter's equilibrium. Before winding up, the pitcher may hesitate, outstaring the notoriously anxious hitter in order to disturb him. Ted Lyons, of the Chicago White Sox, master student of a hitter's habits, brings his arms over his head now once, now twice, three or more times, his eyes intent on every move of the hitter, slowing up or quickening the pace of his windup and motion in varying degrees before he delivers the pitch. Cy Young, winner of most games in baseball history,—he won 511,—had four different pitching motions, turning his back on the hitter to hide the ball before he pitched. Fred Marberry, the great Washington relief pitcher, increased his effectiveness by throwing his free, non-pivot foot as well as the ball at the hitter to distract him.

In 1884, when Connie Mack broke in as a catcher for Meriden, Charlie Radbourne—who won 60 games for Providence—could have cuffed, scraped, scratched, finger-nailed, applied resin, emery, or any other foreign substance to, or spit on the two balls the teams started and finished the game with. 'Home-Run' Baker, who hit two balls out of the park in the 1911 World Series to win his nickname,—and never more than twelve in a full season,—characterizes a defensive era in the game. During the last war it was impossible to get some of the nine foreign ingredients that enter into the manufacture of our baseball. To make up for the lack of the superior foreign yarn, our machines were adjusted to wind the domestic product tighter. In 1919, when the war was over, the foreign yarn was again available, but the same machines were used. The improved technique, the foreign ingredients, Babe Ruth and bat, conspired to revolutionize baseball. It seems prophetic, with due respect to the Babe, that our great American national game, so native and representative, could have been so completely refashioned by happenings on the other side of the world.

II

The importance of the bat has been stressed to such an extent that, since 1920, foreign substances have been barred to the pitcher, and the spitball outlawed. The resin bag, the sole concession, is used on the hands only to counteract perspiration. The cover of the ball, in two sections, is sewed together with stitches, slightly raised, in one long seam; today's pitcher, after experimentation and experience, takes whatever advantage he can of its surface to make his various pitches more effective by gripping the ball across or along two rows of stitches, or along one row or on the smooth surface. The pitcher is always working with a shiny new ball. A game today will consume as many as eight dozen balls instead of the two roughed and battered ones which were the limit in 1884.

With the freak pitch outlawed and the accent put on hitting in the modern game, the pitcher has to be resourceful to win. He throws fast, slow, and breaking balls, all with variations. He is fortunate if his fast ball hops or sinks, slides or sails, because, if straight as a string or too true, it is ineffective. The ball has to do something at the last moment. The curve must break sharply and not hang. To add to his repertory of balls that break, the pitcher may develop a knuckle ball (fingers applied to the seam, knuckled against, instead of gripping the ball), a fork ball (the first two fingers forking the ball), or a screw ball (held approximately the same as an orthodox fast or curve ball but released with a twist of the wrist the reverse of a curve). The knuckle and fork balls flutter through the air, wavering, veering, or taking a sudden lurch, without revolving like the other pitches; they are the modern counterpart of the spitball, a dry spitter.

The pitcher studies the hitter's stance, position at the plate, and swing, to establish the level of his natural batting stroke and to detect any possible weakness. Each hitter has his own individual style. The pitcher scouts his form and notes whether he holds the bat on the end or chokes it, is a free swinger or a chop hitter. He bears in mind whether the hitter crowds, or stands away from, the plate, in front of or behind it, erect or crouched over it. Whether he straddles his legs or strides forward to hit, whether he lunges with his body or takes a quick cut with wrist and arm only, whether he pulls a ball, hits late or through the box—all these things are telltale and reveal a hitter's liking for a certain pitch, high or low, in or out, fast, curve, or slow.

To fool the hitter—there's the rub. With an assortment at his disposal, a pitcher tries to adapt the delivery, as well as the pitch, to the hitter's weakness. Pitchers may have distinct forms of delivery and work differently on a given hitter; a pitcher throws overhand, three-quarter overhand (which is about midway between overhand and side-arm), side-arm, or underhand. A cross-fire is an emphasized side-arm pitch thrown against the forward foot as the body leans to the same side as the pitching arm at the time of the motion and delivery. Not the least important part of the delivery is the body follow-through to get more stuff on the pitch and to take pressure off the arm. Having determined the hitter's weakness, the pitcher can throw to spots—for example, 'high neck in,' low outside, or letter high. But he never forgets that, with all his equipment, he is trying to throw the hitter off his timing—probably the best way to fool him, to get him out. Without varying his motion, he throws a change-of-pace fast or curve ball, pulls the string on his fast ball, slows up, takes a little off or adds a little to his fast ball.

Just as there are speed kings, so there are hitters without an apparent weakness. They have unusual vision, power, and great ability to coördinate these in the highest degree. They are the ranking, top hitters who hit everything in the strike zone well—perhaps one type of pitch less well than another. To these hitters the pitcher throws his best pitch and leaves the result to the law of averages. Joe DiMaggio straddles in a spread-eagle stance with his feet wide apart and bat already cocked. He advances his forward foot only a matter of inches, so that, with little stride, he doesn't move his head, keeping his eyes steadily on the ball. He concentrates on the pitch; his weight equally distributed on both feet, he has perfect wrist action and power to drive the ball for distance. Mel Ott, on the other hand, lifts the front foot high just as the pitcher delivers the ball; he is not caught off balance or out of position, because he sets the foot down only after he has seen what type of pitch is coming. With DiMaggio's stance one must have good wrist action and power. With Ott's, there is a danger of taking a long step forward before one knows what is coming. But Mel does not commit himself.

Rogers Hornsby, one of the game's greatest right-hand hitters, invariably took his position in the far rear corner of the batter's box, stepped into the pitch, and hit to all fields equally well. Ty Cobb was always a step ahead of the pitcher. He must have been because he led the American League in hitting every year but one in the thirteen-year period 1907–1919. He outstudied the pitcher and took as many positions in the batter's box as he thought necessary to counteract the type of motion and pitch he was likely to get. He adapted his stance to the pitcher who was then on the mound; for Red Faber, whose spitball broke sharply down, Cobb stood in front of the plate; for a curve-ball left-hander, Ty took a stance behind the plate in order to hit the curve after it broke, because, as Ty said, he could see it break and get hold of it the better. For Lefty O'Doul, one of the greatest teachers of hitting in the game, there are no outside pitches. Lefty stands close to the plate; his bat more than covers it, he is a natural right-field pull hitter. Babe Ruth, because of his tremendous, unequaled home-run power, and his ability to hit equally well all sorts of pitches with a liberal stride and a free swing, and consistently farther than any other player, has demonstrated that he had the greatest coördination and power of any hitter ever known. Ted Williams, of the Boston Red Sox, the only current .400 hitter in the game, completely loose and relaxed, has keen enough eyes never to offer at a bad pitch; he has good wrist and arm action, leverage, and power. Jimmy Foxx, next to Babe Ruth as a home-run hitter, steps into a ball, using his tremendous wrists and forearms for his powerful, long and line drives. These hitters do not lunge with the body; the front hip gives way for the swing, and the body follows through.

III

The game is carried back and forth between the pitcher and the hitter. The hitter notices what and where the pitchers are throwing. If the pitcher is getting him out consistently, for example, on a curve outside, the hitter changes his mode of attack. Adaptability is the hallmark of the big-league hitter. Joe Cronin, playing manager of the Red Sox, has changed in his brilliant career from a fast-ball, left-field pull hitter to a curve-ball and a right-field hitter, to and fro through the whole cycle and back again, according to where the pitchers are throwing. He has no apparent weakness, hits to all fields, and is one of the greatest 'clutch' hitters in the game. *Plus ça change, plus c'est la même chose.*

Like Walter Johnson, Lefty Grove was a fast-ball pitcher, and the hitters knew it. The hitters looked for this pitch; Lefty did not try to fool them by throwing anything else, but most of them were fooled, not by the type of pitch, but by his terrific speed. With two strikes on the hitter, Lefty did throw his curve at times, and that, too, led almost invariably to a strike-out. In 1935, Lefty had recovered from his first serious sore arm of the year before. Wear and tear, and the grind of many seasons, had taken their toll. Now he had changed his tactics, and was pitching curves and fast balls, one or the other. His control was practically perfect. On a day in that year in Washington, Heinie Manush, a great hitter, was at bat with two men on the bases. The game was at stake; the count was three balls and two strikes. Heinie stood there, confident, looking for Lefty's fast ball. 'Well,' thought Heinie, 'it might be a curve.' Lefty was throwing the curve more and more now, but the chances with the count of three and two were that Lefty would throw his fast ball with everything he had on it. Fast or curve—he couldn't throw anything else; he had nothing else to throw. Heinie broke his back striking out on the next pitch, the first fork ball Grove ever threw. For over a year, on the side lines, in the bullpen, between pitching starts, Lefty had practised and perfected this pitch before he threw it, and he waited for a crucial spot to use it. Lefty had realized his limitations. The hitters were getting to his fast and curve balls more than they used to. He wanted to add to his pitching equipment; he felt he had to. Heinie Manush anticipated, looked for, guessed a fast ball, possibly a curve, but Lefty fooled him with his new pitch, a fork ball.

Here was the perfect setup for out-guessing a hitter. Lefty Grove's development of a third pitch, the fork ball, is the greatest example in our time of complete, successful change in technique by one pitcher. When a speed-ball pitcher loses his fast one, he has to compensate for such loss by adding to his pitching equipment. Lefty both perfected his control and added a fork ball. Carl Hubbell's screw ball, practically unhittable at first, made his fast ball and curve effective. Lefty Gomez, reaching that point in his career where he had to add to his fast and curve ball, developed and threw his first knuckle ball this year. Grove, Gomez, and Hubbell, three outstanding left-handers,—Grove and Gomez adding a fork ball and a knuckle ball respectively to their fast and curve balls when their speed was waning, Hubbell developing a screw ball early in his career to make it his best pitch and to become one of the game's foremost southpaws,—so you have the build-up of great pitchers.

At first, the superspeed of Grove obviated the necessity of pitching brains. But, when his speed began to fade, Lefty turned to his head. With his almost perfect control and the addition of his fork ball, Lefty now fools the hitter with his cunning. With Montaigne, we conceive of Socrates in place of Alexander, of brain for brawn, wit for whip. And this brings us to a fascinating part of the pitcher-hitter drama: Does a hitter guess? Does a pitcher try to outguess him? When the pitching process is no longer mechanical, how much of it is psychological? When the speed of a Johnson or a Grove is fading or gone, can the pitcher outguess the hitter?

IV

We know that the pitcher studies the strength and weakness of every hitter and that the hitter notes every variety of pitch in the pitcher's repertory; that the big-league hitter is resourceful, and quick to meet every new circumstance. Does he anticipate what the pitcher is going to throw? He can regulate his next pitch arbitrarily by the very last-second flick of the wrist. There is no set pattern for the order of pitches. Possible combinations are so many that a formula of probability cannot be established. He may repeat the fast ball or curve ball indefinitely, or pitch them alternately; there is no mathematical certainty what the pitch will be. There is no harmony in the pattern of a pitcher's pitches. And no human being has the power of divination.

But does this prevent a hitter from guessing? Does he merely hit what he sees if he can? Is it possible for a hitter to stand at the plate and use merely his vision, without trying to figure out what the pitcher might throw? The hitter bases his anticipation on the repertory of the pitcher, taking into account the score of the game, what the pitcher threw him the last time at bat, whether he hit that pitch or not, how many men are on base, and the present count on him. The guess is more than psychic, for there is some basis for it, some precedent for the next move; what is past is prologue.

The few extraordinary hitters whose exceptional vision and power to coördinate must be the basis for their talent can afford to be oblivious of anything but the flight of the ball. Hughie Duffy, who has the highest batting average in baseball history (he hit .438 in 1894), or Rogers Hornsby, another great right-hand hitter, may even deny that he did anything but hit what he saw. But variety usually makes a hitter think. When Ty Cobb changed his stance at the plate to hit the pitcher then facing him, he anticipated not only a certain type of motion but also the pitch that followed it. He studied past performance. Joe DiMaggio hit a home run to break Willie Keeler's consecutive-games hitting record of 44, standing since 1897, and has since carried the record to 56 games. In hitting the home run off Dick Newsome, Red Sox pitcher, who has been very successful this year because of a good assortment of pitches, Joe explains: 'I hit a fast ball; I knew he would come to that and was waiting for it; he had pitched knucklers, curves, and sinkers.' Jimmie Foxx looks for a particular pitch when facing a pitcher—for example, a curve ball against a notorious curve-ball pitcher—and watches any other pitch go by. But when he has two strikes he cancels all thought of what the pitcher might throw; he then hits what he sees. Jimmie knows that if he looks for a certain pitch and guesses wrong, with two strikes on him, he will be handcuffed at the plate watching the pitch go by. Hank Greenberg, full of imagination, has guessed right most of the time—he hit 58 home runs one year.

Just as Lefty Grove perfected control of his not-so-speedy fast ball and curve, and added the fork ball to give him variety, so even the outstanding hitters have to change their mode of attack later when their vision and reactions are not quite so sharp as they used to be.

V

The catcher squatting behind the hitter undoubtedly has the coign of vantage in the ball park; all the action takes place before him. Nothing is outside his view except the balls-and-strikes umpire behind him—which is at times no hardship. The receiver has a good pair of hands, shifts his feet gracefully for inside or outside pitches, and bends his knees, not his back, in an easy, rhythmic motion, as he stretches his arms to catch the ball below his belt. The catcher has to be able to cock his arm from any position, throw fast and accurately to the bases, field bunts like an infielder, and catch foul flies like an outfielder. He must be adept at catching a ball from any angle, and almost simultaneously tagging a runner at home plate. The catcher is the Cerberus of baseball.

These physical qualifications are only a part of a catcher's equipment. He signals the pitcher what to throw, and this implies superior baseball brains on his part. But a pitcher can put a veto on a catcher's judgment by shaking him off and waiting for another sign. The game cannot go on until he pitches. Every fan has seen a pitcher do this—like the judge who kept shaking his head from time to time while counsel was arguing; the lawyer finally turned to the jury and said, 'Gentlemen, you might imagine that the shaking of his head by His Honor implied a difference of opinion, but you will notice if you remain here long enough that when His Honor shakes his head there is nothing in it.' (Judges, if you are reading, please consider this *obiter.*) One would believe that a no-hit, no-run game, the acme of perfection, the goal of a pitcher, would satisfy even the most exacting battery mate. Yet, at the beginning of the seventh inning of a game under those conditions, 'Sarge' Connally, White Sox pitcher, said to his catcher, 'Let's mix 'em up; why don't you call for my knuckler?' 'Sarge' was probably bored with his own infallibility. He lost the no-hitter and the game on an error.

Of course, no player monopolizes the brains on a ball club. The catcher gives the signals only because he is in a better position than the pitcher to hide them. In a squatting position, the catcher hides the simple finger, fist, or finger-wiggle signs between his legs, complicating them somewhat with different combinations only when a runner on second base in direct line of vision with the signals may look in, perhaps solve them, and flash back another signal to the hitter.

Signal stealing is possible in many ways. The most prevalent self-betrayals are made by the pitcher and catcher themselves. Such detection requires the closest observation. A catcher, after having given the signal, gets set for the pitch; in doing so he may unintentionally, unconsciously, make a slight move—for example, to the right, in order to be in a better position to catch a right-hander's curve ball. But more often it is the pitcher who reveals something either to the coaches on the base lines or—what is more telling—to the hitter standing in the batter's box.

The pitcher will betray himself if he makes two distinct motions for two different pitches—as, for example, a side-arm delivery for the curve and overhand for the fast ball. A pitcher may also betray himself in his windup by raising his arms higher for the fast ball than for the curve. In some cases his eyes are more intent on the plate for one pitch than for another. Usually the curve is more difficult to control. If a pitcher has to make facial distortions, they should be the same for one pitch as for another.

A pitcher covers up the ball with his glove as he fixes it, to escape detection. Otherwise he may reveal that he is holding the ball tighter for a curve than for a fast ball, or even gripping the stitches differently for one than for the other. Eddie Collins, all-time star second baseman, was probably the greatest spy on the field or at bat in the history of the game. He was a master at 'getting' the pitch for himself somewhere in the pitcher's manipulation of the ball or in his motion. This ability in no small part helped make him the great performer that he was.

Ball players would rather detect these idiosyncrasies for themselves, as they stand awaiting the pitch, than get a signal from the coach. The coach, on detecting something, gives a sign to the hitter either silently by some move—for instance, touching his chest—or by word of mouth—'Come on,' for a curve. But this is dangerous unless the coach detects the pitches with one hundred per cent accuracy. There must be no doubt. Many times, in baseball, a club knows every pitch thrown and still loses. The hitter may be too anxious if he actually knows what is coming, or a doubt might upset him. And there is always the danger of a pitcher's suspecting that he is 'tipping' himself off. He then deals in a bit of counter-espionage by making more emphatic to the opposition his revealing mannerism to encourage them, only to cross them up at a crucial time.

The whole club plays as a unit to win. The signs that the pitcher and catcher agree on reflect the collective ideas, the judgment of all the players on how to get the opposition out. Preventing runs from scoring is as important as making them. The players know how the pitcher intends to throw to each opponent. They review their strategy before game time, as a result of which they know how the battery is going to work, and they play accordingly. The shortstop and second baseman see the catcher's signs and get the jump on the ball; sometimes they flash it by prearranged signal to the other players who are not in a position to see it. The outfielders can then lean a little, but only after the ball is actually released.

He is a poor catcher who doesn't know at least as well as the pitcher what a hitter likes or doesn't like, to which field he hits, what he did the last time, what he is likely to do this time at bat. The catcher is an on-the-spot witness, in a position to watch the hitter at first hand. He has to make quick decisions, bearing in mind the score, the inning, the number of men on the bases, and other factors.

VI

Pitchers and catchers are mutually helpful. It is encouraging to a pitcher when a catcher calls for the ball he wants to throw and corroborates his judgment. The pitcher very seldom shakes a catcher off, because they are thinking alike in a given situation. By working together they know each other's system. Pitchers help catchers as much as catchers do pitchers. One appreciative catcher gives due credit to spit-baller Red Faber, knuckle-baller Ted Lyons, and fast-baller Tommy Thomas, all of the Chicago White Sox, for teaching him, as he caught them, much about catching and working with pitchers. Bill Dickey, great Yankee catcher, will readily admit that Herb Pennock taught him battery technique merely by catching a master and noting how he mixed up his pitches. Ray Schalk, Chicago White Sox, and Steve O'Neill, Cleveland Indians, were two of the greatest receivers and all-round workmen behind the plate in baseball history. Gabby Hartnett and Mickey Cochrane stood out as hitters as well as catchers, Mickey being probably the greatest inspirational catcher of our time.

The catcher works in harmony with the pitcher and dovetails his own judgment with the pitcher's stuff. He finds out quickly the pitcher's best ball and calls for it in the spots where it would be most effective. He knows whether a hitter is in a slump or dangerous enough to walk intentionally. He tries to keep the pitcher ahead of the hitter. If he succeeds, the pitcher is in a more advantageous position to work on the hitter with his assortment of pitches. But if the pitcher is in a hole—a two and nothing, three and one, or three and two count—he knows that the hitter is ready to hit. The next pitch may decide the ball game. The pitcher tries not to pitch a 'cripple'— that is, tries not to give the hitter the ball he hits best. But it is also dangerous to overrefine. Taking the physical as well as the psychological factors into consideration, the pitcher must at times give even the best hitter his best pitch under the circumstances. He pitches hard, lets the law of averages do its work, and never second-guesses himself. The pitcher throws a fast ball through the heart of the plate, and the hitter, surprised, may even take it. The obvious pitch may be the most strategic one.

The pitcher may throw overhand to take full advantage of the white shirts in the bleacher background. Breaking balls are more effective when thrown against the resistance of the wind. In the latter part of a day, when shadows are cast in a stadium ball park, the pitcher may change his tactics by throwing more fast balls than he did earlier in the game.

The players are not interested in the score, but merely in how many runs are necessary to tie and to win. They take nothing for granted in baseball. The idea is to win. The game's the thing.

The great American humorist James Thurber (1894–1961) was born in Columbus, Ohio, and in his early thirties went to work for *The New Yorker.* Although
he always suffered from poor eyesight and eventually went blind, Thurber
remained a fan of baseball in general—in *Is Sex Necessary?* he describes the
game as "a sex substitute"—and of the Brooklyn Dodgers' broadcaster Red
Barber in particular. Thurber took a signature phrase of Barber's, "the catbird
seat," for the title of one of his best short stories. It was another redhead,
Red Smith, who contended that Thurber's "You Could Look It Up" (1941)—
adopted by Casey Stengel as *his* signature phrase—inspired Bill Veeck to hire a
real midget to bat for the St. Louis Browns. (Veeck always denied it.) Doubtless
true is something else Smith said not long after Thurber's death: "You don't
hear people laugh the way they used to."

James Thurber

◔

You Could Look It Up

It all begun when we dropped down to C'lumbus, Ohio, from Pittsburgh to play a exhibition game on our way out to St. Louis. It was
gettin' on into September, and though we'd been leadin' the league
by six, seven games most of the season, we was now in first place by
a margin you could 'a' got it into the eye of a thimble, bein' only a
half a game ahead of St. Louis. Our slump had given the boys the
leapin' jumps, and they was like a bunch a old ladies at a lawn fete
with a thunderstorm comin' up, runnin' around snarlin' at each
other, eatin' bad and sleepin' worse, and battin' for a team average of
maybe .186. Half the time nobody'd speak to nobody else, without it
was to bawl 'em out.

Squawks Magrew was managin' the boys at the time, and he was
darn near crazy. They called him "Squawks" 'cause when things was
goin' bad he lost his voice, or perty near lost it, and squealed at you
like a little girl you stepped on her doll or somethin'. He yelled at
everybody and wouldn't listen to nobody, without maybe it was me.
I'd been trainin' the boys for ten year, and he'd take more lip from

178

me than from anybody else. He knowed I was smarter'n him, anyways, like you're goin' to hear.

This was thirty, thirty-one year ago; you could look it up, 'cause it was the same year C'lumbus decided to call itself the Arch City, on account of a lot of iron arches with electric-light bulbs into 'em which stretched acrost High Street. Thomas Albert Edison sent 'em a telegram, and they was speeches and maybe even President Taft opened the celebration by pushin' a button. It was a great week for the Buckeye capital, which was why they got us out there for this exhibition game.

Well, we just lose a double-header to Pittsburgh, 11 to 5 and 7 to 3, so we snarled all the way to C'lumbus, where we put up at the Chittaden Hotel, still snarlin'. Everybody was tetchy, and when Billy Klinger took a sock at Whitey Cott at breakfast, Whitey throwed marmalade all over his face.

"Blind each other, whatta I care?" says Magrew. "You can't see nothin' anyways."

C'lumbus win the exhibition game, 3 to 2, whilst Magrew set in the dugout, mutterin' and cursin' like a fourteen-year-old Scotty. He bad-mouthed everybody on the ball club and he bad-mouthed everybody offa the ball club, includin' the Wright brothers, who, he claimed, had yet to build a airship big enough for any of our boys to hit it with a ball bat.

"I wisht I was dead," he says to me. "I wisht I was in heaven with the angels."

I told him to pull hisself together, 'cause he was drivin' the boys crazy, the way he was goin' on, sulkin' and bad-mouthin' and whinin'. I was older'n he was and smarter'n he was, and he knowed it. I was ten times smarter'n he was about this Pearl du Monville, first time I ever laid eyes on the little guy, which was one of the saddest days of my life.

Now, most people name of Pearl is girls, but this Pearl du Monville was a man, if you could call a fella a man who was only thirty-four, thirty-five inches high. Pearl du Monville was a midget. He was part French and part Hungarian, and maybe even part Bulgarian or somethin'. I can see him now, a sneer on his little pushed-in pan, swingin' a bamboo cane and smokin' a big cigar. He had a gray suit with a big black check into it, and he had a gray felt hat with one of them rain-bow-colored hatbands onto it, like the young fellas wore in them days. He talked like he was talkin' into a tin can, but he didn't have no foreign accent. He might a been fifteen or he might a been a hundred, you couldn't tell. Pearl du Monville.

After the game with C'lumbus, Magrew headed straight for the Chittaden bar—the train for St. Louis wasn't goin' for three, four hours—and there he set, drinkin' rye and talkin' to this bartender.

"How I pity me, brother," Magrew was tellin' this bartender. "How I pity me." That was alwuz his favorite tune. So he was settin' there, tellin' this bartender how heart-breakin' it was to be manager of a bunch a blindfolded circus clowns, when up pops this Pearl du Monville outa nowheres.

It give Magrew the leapin' jumps. He thought at first maybe the D.T.'s had come back on him; he claimed he'd had 'em once, and little guys had popped up all around him, wearin' red, white and blue hats.

"Go on, now!" Magrew yells. "Get away from me!"

But the midget clumb up on a chair acrost the table from Magrew and says, "I seen that game today, Junior, and you ain't got no ball club. What you got there, Junior," he says, "is a side show."

"Whatta ya mean, 'Junior'?" says Magrew, touchin' the little guy to satisfy hisself he was real.

"Don't pay him no attention, mister," says the bartender. "Pearl calls everybody 'Junior,' 'cause it alwuz turns out he's a year older'n anybody else."

"Yeh?" says Magrew. "How old is he?"

"How old are you, Junior?" says the midget.

"Who, me? I'm fifty-three," says Magrew.

"Well, I'm fifty-four," says the midget.

Magrew grins and asts him what he'll have, and that was the beginnin' of their beautiful friendship, if you don't care what you say.

Pearl du Monville stood up on his chair and waved his cane around and pretended like he was ballyhooin' for a circus. "Right this way, folks!" he yells. "Come on in and see the greatest collection of freaks in the world! See the armless pitchers, see the eyeless batters, see the infielders with five thumbs!" and on and on like that, feedin' Magrew gall and handin' him a laugh at the same time, you might say.

You could hear him and Pearl du Monville hootin' and hollerin' and singin' way up to the fourth floor of the Chittaden, where the boys was packin' up. When it come time to go to the station, you can imagine how disgusted we was when we crowded into the doorway of that bar and seen them two singin' and goin' on.

"Well, well, well," says Magrew, lookin' up and spottin' us. "Look who's here. . . . Clowns, this is Pearl du Monville, a monseer of the old, old school. . . . Don't shake hands with 'em, Pearl, 'cause their fingers is made of chalk and would bust right off in your paws," he says, and he starts guffawin' and Pearl starts titterin' and we stand there givin' 'em the iron eye, it bein' the lowest ebb a ball-club manager'd got hisself down to since the national pastime was started.

Then the midget begun givin' us the ballyhoo. "Come on in!" he says, wavin' his cane. "See the legless base runners, see the outfielders with the butter fingers, see the southpaw with the arm of a little chee-ild!"

Then him and Magrew begun to hoop and holler and nudge each other till you'd of thought this little guy was the funniest guy than even Charlie Chaplin. The fellas filed outa the bar without a word and went on up to the Union Depot, leavin' me to handle Magrew and his new-found crony.

Well, I got 'em outa there finely. I had to take the little guy along, 'cause Magrew had a holt onto him like a vise and I couldn't pry him loose.

"He's comin' along as masket," says Magrew, holdin' the midget in the crouch of his arm like a football. And come along he did, hollerin' and protestin' and beatin' at Magrew with his little fists.

"Cut it out, will ya, Junior?" the little guy kept whinin'. "Come on, leave a man loose, will ya, Junior?"

But Junior kept a holt onto him and begun yellin', "See the guys with the glass arm, see the guys with the cast-iron brains, see the fielders with the feet on their wrists!"

So it goes, right through the whole Union Depot, with people starin' and catcallin', and he don't put the midget down till he gets him through the gates.

"How'm I goin' to go along without no toothbrush?" the midget asts. "What'm I goin' to do without no other suit?" he says.

"Doc here," says Magrew, meanin' me—"doc here will look after you like you was his own son, won't you, doc?"

I give him the iron eye, and he finely got on the train and prob'ly went to sleep with his clothes on.

This left me alone with the midget. "Lookit," I says to him. "Why don't you go on home now? Come mornin', Magrew'll forget all about you. He'll prob'ly think you was somethin' he seen in a nightmare maybe. And he ain't goin' to laugh so easy in the mornin', neither," I says. "So why don't you go on home?"

"Nix," he says to me. "Skiddoo," he says, "twenty-three for you," and he tosses his cane up into the vestibule of the coach and clam'ers on up after it like a cat. So that's the way Pearl du Monville come to go to St. Louis with the ball club.

I seen 'em first at breakfast the next day, settin' opposite each other; the midget playin' "Turkey in the Straw" on a harmonium and Magrew starin' at his eggs and bacon like they was a uncooked bird with its feathers still on.

"Remember where you found this?" I says, jerkin' my thumb at the midget. "Or maybe you think they come with breakfast on these trains," I says, bein' a good hand at turnin' a sharp remark in them days.

The midget puts down the harmonium and turns on me. "Sneeze," he says; "your brains is dusty." Then he snaps a couple drops of water at me from a tumbler. "Drown," he says, tryin' to make his voice deep.

Now, both them cracks is Civil War cracks, but you'd of thought they was brand new and the funniest than any crack Magrew'd ever heard in his whole life. He started hoopin' and hollerin', and the midget started hoopin' and hollerin', so I walked on away and set down with Bugs Courtney and Hank Metters, payin' no attention to this weak-minded Damon and Phidias acrost the aisle.

Well, sir, the first game with St. Louis was rained out, and there we was facin' a double-header next day. Like maybe I told you, we lose the last three double-headers we play, makin' maybe twenty-five errors in the six games, which is all right for the intimates of a school for the blind, but is disgraceful for the world's champions. It was too wet to go to the zoo, and Magrew wouldn't let us go to the movies, 'cause they flickered so bad in them days. So we just set around, stewin' and frettin'.

One of the newspaper boys come over to take a pitture of Billy Klinger and Whitey Cott shakin' hands—this reporter'd heard about the fight—and whilst they was standin' there, toe to toe, shakin' hands, Billy give a back lunge and a jerk, and throwed Whitey over his shoulder into a corner of the room, like a sack a salt. Whitey come back at him with a chair, and Bethlehem broke loose in that there room. The camera was tromped to pieces like a berry basket. When we finely got 'em pulled apart, I heard a laugh, and there was Magrew and the midget standin' in the door and givin' us the iron eye.

"Wrasslers," says Magrew, cold like, "that's what I got for a ball club, Mr. Du Monville, wrasslers—and not very good wrasslers at that, you ast me."

"A man can't be good at everythin'," says Pearl, "but he oughta be good at somethin'."

This sets Magrew guffawin' again, and away they go, the midget taggin' along by his side like a hound dog and handin' him a fast line of so-called comic cracks.

When we went out to face that battlin' St. Louis club in a double-header the next afternoon, the boys was jumpy as tin toys with keys in their back. We lose the first game, 7 to 2, and are trailin', 4 to 0, when the second game ain't but ten minutes old. Magrew set there like a stone statue, speakin' to nobody. Then, in their half a the fourth, some-body singled to center and knocked in two more runs for St. Louis.

That made Magrew squawk. "I wisht one thing," he says. "I wisht I was manager of a old ladies' sewin' circus 'stead of a ball club."

"You are, Junior, you are," says a familyer and disagreeable voice.

It was that Pearl du Monville again, poppin' up outa nowheres, swingin' his bamboo cane and smokin' a cigar that's three sizes too big for his face. By this time we'd finely got the other side out, and Hank Metters slithered a bat acrost the ground, and the midget had to jump to keep both his ankles from bein' broke.

I thought Magrew'd bust a blood vessel. "You hurt Pearl and I'll break your neck!" he yelled.

Hank muttered somethin' and went on up to the plate and struck out.

We managed to get a couple runs acrost in our half a the sixth, but they come back with three more in their half a the seventh, and this was too much for Magrew.

"Come on, Pearl," he says. "We're gettin' outa here."

"Where you think you're goin'?" I ast him.

"To the lawyer's again," he says cryptly.

"I didn't know you'd been to the lawyer's once, yet," I says.

"Which that goes to show how much you don't know," he says.

With that, they was gone, and I didn't see 'em the rest of the day, nor know what they was up to, which was a God's blessin'. We lose the nightcap, 9 to 3, and that puts us into second place plenty, and as low in our mind as a ball club can get.

The next day was a horrible day, like anybody that lived through it can tell you. Practice was just over and the St. Louis club was takin' the field, when I hears this strange sound from the stands. It sounds like the nervous whickerin' a horse gives when he smells somethin' funny on the wind. It was the fans ketchin' sight of Pearl du Monville, like you have prob'ly guessed. The midget had popped up onto the field all dressed up in a minacher club uniform, sox, cap, little letters sewed onto his chest, and all. He was swingin' a kid's bat and the only thing kept him from lookin' like a real ballplayer seen through the wrong end of a microscope was this cigar he was smokin'.

Bugs Courtney reached over and jerked it outa his mouth and throwed it away. "You're wearin' that suit on the playin' field," he says to him, severe as a judge. "You go insultin' it and I'll take you out to the zoo and feed you to the bears."

Pearl just blowed some smoke at him which he still has in his mouth.

Whilst Whitey was foulin' off four or five prior to strikin' out, I went on over to Magrew. "If I was as comic as you," I says, "I'd laugh myself to death," I says. "Is that any way to treat the uniform, makin' a mockery out of it?"

"It might surprise you to know I ain't makin' no mockery outa the uniform," says Magrew. "Pearl du Monville here has been made a bone-of-fida member of this so-called ball club. I fixed it up with the front office by long-distance phone."

"Yeh?" I says. "I can just hear Mr. Dillworth or Bart Jenkins agreein' to hire a midget for the ball club. I can just hear 'em." Mr. Dillworth was the owner of the club and Bart Jenkins was the secretary, and they never stood for no monkey business. "May I be so bold as to inquire," I says, "just what you told 'em?"

"I told 'em," he says, "I wanted to sign up a guy they ain't no pitcher in the league can strike him out."

"Uh-huh," I says, "and did you tell 'em what size of a man he is?"

"Never mind about that," he says. "I got papers on me, made out legal and proper, constitutin' one Pearl du Monville a bone-of-fida member of this former ball club. Maybe that'll shame them big babies into gettin' in there and swingin', knowin' I can replace any one of 'em with a midget, if I have a mind to. A St. Louis lawyer I seen twice tells me it's all legal and proper."

"A St. Louis lawyer would," I says, "seein' nothin' could make him happier than havin' you makin' a mockery outa this one-time baseball outfit," I says.

Well, sir, it'll all be there in the papers of thirty, thirty-one year ago, and you could look it up. The game went along without no scorin' for seven innings, and since they ain't nothin' much to watch but guys poppin' up or strikin' out, the fans pay most of their attention to the goin's-on of Pearl du Monville. He's out there in front a the dugout, turnin' handsprings, balancin' his bat on his chin, walkin' a imaginary line, and so on. The fans clapped and laughed at him, and he ate it up.

So it went up to the last a the eighth, nothin' to nothin', not more'n seven, eight hits all told, and no errors on neither side. Our pitcher gets the first two men out easy in the eighth. Then up come a fella name of Porter or Billings, or some such name, and he lammed one up against the tobacco sign for three bases. The next guy up slapped the first ball out into left for a base hit, and in come the fella from third for the only run of the ball game so far. The crowd yelled, the look a death come onto Magrew's face again, and even the midget quit his tom-foolin'. Their next man fouled out back a third, and we come up for our last bats like a bunch a schoolgirls steppin' into a pool of cold water. I was lower in my mind than I'd been since the day in Nineteen-four when Chesbro throwed the wild pitch in the ninth inning with a man on third and lost the pennant for the Highlanders. I knowed something just as bad was goin' to happen, which shows I'm a clairvoyun, or was then.

When Gordy Mills hit out to second, I just closed my eyes. I opened 'em up again to see Dutch Muller standin' on second, dustin' off his pants, him havin' got his first hit in maybe twenty times to the plate. Next up was Harry Loesing, battin' for our pitcher, and he got a base on balls, walkin' on a fourth one you could a combed your hair with.

Then up come Whitey Cott, our lead-off man. He crotches down in what was prob'ly the most fearsome stanch in organized ball, but all he can do is pop out to short. That brung up Billy Klinger, with two down and a man on first and second. Billy took a cut at one you could a knocked a plug hat offa this here Carnera with it, but then he gets sense enough to wait 'em out, and finely he walks, too, fillin' the bases.

Yes, sir, there you are; the tyin' run on third and the winnin' run on second, first a the ninth, two men down, and Hank Metters comin' to the bat. Hank was built like a Pope-Hartford and he couldn't run no faster'n President Taft, but he had five home runs to his credit for the season, and that wasn't bad in them days. Hank was still hittin' better'n anybody else on the ball club, and it was mighty heartenin', seein' him stridin' up towards the plate. But he never got there.

"Wait a minute!" yells Magrew, jumpin' to his feet. "I'm sendin' in a pinch hitter!" he yells.

You could a heard a bomb drop. When a ball-club manager says he's sendin' in a pinch hitter for the best batter on the club, you know and I know and everybody knows he's lost his holt.

"They're goin' to be sendin' the funny wagon for you, if you don't watch out," I says, grabbin' a holt of his arm.

But he pulled away and run out towards the plate, yellin', "Du Monville battin' for Metters!"

All the fellas begun squawlin' at once, except Hank, and he just stood there starin' at Magrew like he'd gone crazy and was claimin' to be Ty Cobb's grandma or somethin'. Their pitcher stood out there with his hands on his hips and a disagreeable look on his face, and the plate umpire told Magrew to go on and get a batter up. Magrew told him again Du Monville was battin' for Metters, and the St. Louis manager finely got the idea. It brung him outa his dugout, howlin' and bawlin' like he'd lost a female dog and her seven pups.

Magrew pushed the midget towards the plate and he says to him, he says, "Just stand up there and hold that bat on your shoulder. They ain't a man in the world can throw three strikes in there 'fore he throws four balls!" he says.

"I get it, Junior!" says the midget. "He'll walk me and force in the tyin' run!" And he starts on up to the plate as cocky as if he was Willie Keeler.

I don't need to tell you Bethlehem broke loose on that there ball field. The fans got onto their hind legs, yellin' and whistlin', and everybody on the field begun wavin' their arms and hollerin' and shovin'. The plate umpire stalked over to Magrew like a traffic cop, waggin' his jaw and pointin' his finger, and the St. Louis manager kept yellin' like his house was on fire. When Pearl got up to the plate and stood there, the pitcher slammed his glove down onto the ground and started stompin' on it, and they ain't nobody can blame him. He's just walked two normal-sized human bein's, and now here's a guy up to the plate they ain't more'n twenty inches between his knees and his shoulders.

The plate umpire called in the field umpire, and they talked a while, like a couple doctors seein' the bucolic plague or somethin' for the first time. Then the plate umpire come over to Magrew with his arms folded acrost his chest, and he told him to go on and get a bat-ter up, or he'd forfeit the game to St. Louis. He pulled out his watch, but somebody batted it outa his hand in the scufflin', and I thought there'd be a free-for-all, with everybody yellin' and shovin' except Pearl du Monville, who stood up at the plate with his little bat on his shoulder, not movin' a muscle.

Then Magrew played his ace. I seen him pull some papers outa his pocket and show 'em to the plate umpire. The umpire begun lookin' at 'em like they was bills for somethin' he not only never bought it, he never even heard of it. The other umpire studied 'em like they was a death warren, and all this time the St. Louis manager and the fans and the players is yellin' and hollerin'.

Well, sir, they fought about him bein' a midget, and they fought about him usin' a kid's bat, and they fought about where'd he been all season. They was eight or nine rule books brung out and everybody was thumbin' through 'em, tryin' to find out what it says about midgets, but it don't say nothin' about midgets, 'cause this was some-thin' never'd come up in the history of the game before, and nobody'd ever dreamed about it, even when they has nightmares. Maybe you can't send no midgets in to bat nowadays, 'cause the old game's changed a lot, mostly for the worst, but you could then, it turned out.

The plate umpire finely decided the contrack papers was all legal and proper, like Magrew said, so he waved the St. Louis players back to their places and he pointed his finger at their manager and told him to quit hollerin' and get on back in the dugout. The manager says the game is percedin' under protest, and the umpire bawls, "Play ball!" over 'n' above the yellin' and booin', him havin' a voice like a hog-caller.

The St. Louis pitcher picked up his glove and beat at it with his fist six or eight times, and then got set on the mound and studied the situation. The fans realized he was really goin' to pitch to the midget, and they went crazy, hoopin' and hollerin' louder'n ever, and throwin' pop bottles and hats and cushions down onto the field. It took five, ten minutes to get the fans quieted down again, whilst our fellas that was on base set down on the bags and waited. And Pearl du Monville kept standin' up there with the bat on his shoulder, like he'd been told to.

So the pitcher starts studyin' the setup again, and you got to admit it was the strangest setup in a ball game since the players cut off their beards and begun wearin' gloves. I wisht I could call the pitcher's name—it wasn't old Barney Pelty nor Nig Jack Powell nor Harry Howell. He was a big right-hander, but I can't call his name. You could look it up. Even in a crotchin' position, the ketcher towers over the midget like the Washington Monument.

The plate umpire tries standin' on his tiptoes, then he tries crotchin' down, and he finely gets hisself into a stanch nobody'd ever seen on a ball field before, kinda squattin' down on his hanches.

Well, the pitcher is sore as a old buggy horse in fly time. He slams in the first pitch, hard and wild, and maybe two foot higher'n the midget's head.

"Ball one!" hollers the umpire over 'n' above the racket, 'cause everybody is yellin' worsten ever.

The ketcher goes on out towards the mound and talks to the pitcher and hands him the ball. This time the big right-hander tried a undershoot, and it comes in a little closer, maybe no higher'n a foot,

foot and a half above Pearl's head. It would a been a strike with a human bein' in there, but the umpire's got to call it, and he does.

"Ball two!" he bellers.

The ketcher walks on out to the mound again, and the whole infield comes over and gives advice to the pitcher about what they'd do in a case like this, with two balls and no strikes on a batter that oughta be in a bottle of alcohol 'stead of up there at the plate in a big-league game between the teams that is fightin' for first place.

For the third pitch, the pitcher stands there flat-footed and tosses up the ball like he's playin' ketch with a little girl.

Pearl stands there motionless as a hitchin' post, and the ball comes in big and slow and high—high for Pearl, that is, it bein' about on a level with his eyes, or a little higher'n a grown man's knees.

They ain't nothin' else for the umpire to do, so he calls, "Ball three!"

Everybody is onto their feet, hoopin' and hollerin', as the pitcher sets to throw ball four. The St. Louis manager is makin' signs and faces like he was a contorturer, and the infield is givin' the pitcher some more advice about what to do this time. Our boys who was on base stick right onto the bag, runnin' no risk of bein' nipped for the last out.

Well, the pitcher decides to give him a toss again, seein' he come closer with that than with a fast ball. They ain't nobody ever seen a slower ball throwed. It come in big as a balloon and slower'n any ball ever throwed before in the major leagues. It come right in over the plate in front of Pearl's chest, lookin' prob'ly big as a full moon to Pearl. They ain't never been a minute like the minute that followed since the United States was founded by the Pilgrim grandfathers.

Pearl du Monville took a cut at that ball, and he hit it! Magrew give a groan like a poleaxed steer as the ball rolls out in front a the plate into fair territory.

"Fair ball!" yells the umpire, and the midget starts runnin' for first, still carryin' that little bat, and makin' maybe ninety foot an hour. Bethlehem breaks loose on that ball field and in them stands. They ain't never been nothin' like it since creation was begun.

The ball's rollin' slow, on down towards third, goin' maybe eight, ten foot. The infield comes in fast and our boys break from their bases like hares in a brush fire. Everybody is standin' up, yellin' and hollerin', and Magrew is tearin' his hair outa his head, and the midget is scamperin' for first with all the speed of one of them little dashhounds carryin' a satchel in his mouth.

The ketcher gets to the ball first, but he boots it on out past the pitcher's box, the pitcher fallin' on his face tryin' to stop it, the shortstop sprawlin' after it full length and zaggin' it on over towards the second baseman, whilst Muller is scorin' with the tyin' run and Loesing is roundin' third with the winnin' run. Ty Cobb could a made a three-bagger outa that bunt, with everybody fallin' over theirself tryin' to pick the ball up. But Pearl is still maybe fifteen, twenty feet from the bag, toddlin' like a baby and yeepin' like a trapped rabbit, when the second baseman finely gets a holt of that ball and slams it over to first. The first baseman ketches it and stomps on the bag, the base umpire waves Pearl out, and there goes your old ball game, the craziest ball game ever played in the history of the organized world.

Their players start runnin' in, and then I see Magrew. He starts after Pearl, runnin' faster'n any man ever run before. Pearl sees him comin' and runs behind the base umpire's legs and gets a holt onto 'em. Magrew comes up, pantin' and roarin', and him and the midget plays ring around-a-rosy with the umpire, who keeps shovin' at Magrew with one hand and tryin' to slap the midget loose from his legs with the other.

Finely Magrew ketches the midget, who is still yeepin' like a stuck sheep. He gets holt of that little guy by both his ankles and starts whirlin' him round and round his head like Magrew was a hammer thrower and Pearl was the hammer. Nobody can stop him without gettin' their head knocked off, so everybody just stands there and yells. Then Magrew lets the midget fly. He flies on out towards second, high and fast, like a human home run, headed for the soap sign in center field.

Their shortstop tries to get to him, but he can't make it, and I knowed the little fella was goin' to bust to pieces like a dollar watch on a asphalt street when he hit the ground. But it so happens their center fielder is just crossin' second, and he starts runnin' back, tryin' to get under the midget, who had took to spiralin' like a football 'stead of turnin' head over foot, which give him more speed and more distance.

I know you never seen a midget ketched, and you prob'ly never even seen one throwed. To ketch a midget that's been throwed by a heavy-muscled man and is flyn' through the air, you got to run under him and with him and pull your hands and arms back and down when you ketch him, to break the compact of his body, or you'll bust him in two like a match-stick. I seen Bill Lange and Willie Keeler and Tris Speaker make some wonderful ketches in my day, but I never seen nothin' like that center fielder. He goes back and back and still further back and he pulls that midget down outa the air like he was liftin' a sleepin' baby from a cradle. They wasn't a bruise onto him, only his face was the color of cat's meat and he ain't got no air in his chest. In his excitement, the base umpire, who was runnin' back with the center fielder when he ketched Pearl, yells, "Out!" and that give hysteries to the Bethlehem which was ragin' like Niagry on that ball field.

Everybody was hoopin' and hollerin' and yellin' and runnin', with the fans swarmin' onto the field, and the cops tryin' to keep order, and some guys laughin' and some of the women fans cryin', and six or eight of us holdin' onto Magrew to keep him from gettin' at that midget and finishin' him off. Some of the fans picks up the St. Louis pitcher and the center fielder, and starts carryin' 'em around on their shoulders, and they was the craziest goin's-on knowed to the history of organized ball on this side of the 'Lantic Ocean.

I seen Pearl du Monville strugglin' in the arms of a lady fan with a ample bosom, who was laughin' and cryin' at the same time, and him beatin' at her with his little fists and bawlin' and yellin'. He clawed his way loose finely and disappeared in the forest of legs which made that ball field look like it was Coney Island on a hot summer's day.

That was the last I ever seen of Pearl du Monville. I never seen hide nor hair of him from that day to this, and neither did nobody else. He just vanished into the thin of the air, as the fella says. He was ketched for the final out of the ball game and that was the end of him, just like it was the end of the ball game, you might say, and also the end of our losin' streak, like I'm goin' to tell you.

That night we piled onto a train for Chicago, but we wasn't snarlin' and snappin' any more. No, sir, the ice was finely broke and a new spirit come into that ball club. The old zip come back with the disappearance of Pearl du Monville out back a second base. We got to laughin' and talkin' and kiddin' together, and 'fore long Magrew was laughin' with us. He got a human look onto his pan again, and he quit whinin' and complainin' and wishtin' he was in heaven with the angels.

Well, sir, we wiped up that Chicago series, winnin' all four games, and makin' seventeen hits in one of 'em. Funny thing was, St. Louis was so shook up by that last game with us, they never did hit their stride again. Their center fielder took to misjudgin' everything that come his way, and the rest a the fellas followed suit, the way a club'll do when one guy blows up.

'Fore we left Chicago, I and some of the fellas went out and bought a pair of them little baby shoes, which he had 'em golded over and give 'em to Magrew for a souvenir, and he took it all in good spirit. Whitey Cott and Billy Klinger made up and was fast friends again, and we hit our home lot like a ton of dynamite and they was nothin' could stop us from then on.

I don't recollect things as clear as I did thirty, forty year ago. I can't read no fine print no more, and the only person I got to check with on the golden days of the national pastime, as the fella says, is my friend, old Milt Kline, over in Springfield, and his mind ain't as strong as it once was.

He gets Rube Waddell mixed up with Rube Marquard, for one thing, and anybody does that oughta be put away where he won't bother nobody. So I can't tell you the exact margin we win the pennant by. Maybe it was two and a half games, or maybe it was three and a half. But it'll all be there in the newspapers and record books of thirty, thirty-one year ago and, like I was sayin', you could look it up.

George Rolfe Humphries (1894–1969) lived in Pennsylvania, California, New York, Washington, and Massachusetts, taught Latin and coached athletics, served in World War I, made remarkable translations of Lorca and Virgil, and published eight volumes of poetry. He liked baseball and wrote about it with brio—not surprisingly, since his father, Jack Humphries, played professional ball in the 1880s. In "Night Game," he describes the particular pleasure of fans streaming together from the ballpark toward the subway: "This mood, this music, part of the human race/Alike and different, after the game is over." "Polo Grounds," his tribute to Giants baseball, is suffused with rueful eloquence.

Rolfe Humphries

♢

Polo Grounds

Time is of the essence. This is a highly skilled
And beautiful mystery. Three or four seconds only
From the time that Riggs connects till he reaches first,
And in those seconds Jurges goes to his right,
Comes up with the ball, tosses to Witek at second
For the force on Reese, Witek to Mize at first,
In time for the out—a double play.

(Red Barber crescendo. Crowd noises, obbligato;
Scattered staccatos from the peanut boys,
Loud in the lull, as the teams are changing sides) . . .

Hubbell takes the sign, nods, pumps, delivers—
A foul into the stands. Dunn takes a new ball out,
Hands it to Danning, who throws it down to Werber;
Werber takes off his glove, rubs the ball briefly,
Tosses it over to Hub, who goes to the rosin bag,
Takes the sign from Danning, pumps, delivers—
Low, outside, ball three. Danning goes to the mound,
Says something to Hub, Dunn brushes off the plate,

Adams starts throwing in the Giant bullpen,
Hub takes the sign from Danning, pumps, delivers,
Camilli gets hold of it, a *long* fly to the outfield,
Ott goes back, back, back, against the wall, gets under it,
Pounds his glove, and takes it for the out.
That's all for the Dodgers. . . .

Time is of the essence. The rhythms break,
More varied and subtle than any kind of dance;
Movement speeds up or lags. The ball goes out
In sharp and angular drives, or long, slow arcs,
Comes in again controlled and under aim;
The players wheel or spurt, race, stoop, slide, halt,
Shift imperceptibly to new positions,
Watching the signs, according to the batter,
The score, the inning. Time is of the essence.

Time is of the essence. Remember Terry?
Remember Stonewall Jackson, Lindstrom, Frisch,
When they were good? Remember Long George Kelly?
Remember John McGraw and Benny Kauff?
Remember Bridwell, Tenney, Merkle, Youngs,
Chief Myers, Big Jeff Tesreau, Shufflin' Phil?
Remember Matthewson, and Ames, and Donlin,
Buck Ewing, Rusie, Smiling Mickey Welch?
Remember a left-handed catcher named Jack Humphries,
Who sometimes played the outfield, in '83?

Time is of the essence. The shadow moves
From the plate to the box, from the box to second base,
From second to the outfield, to the bleachers.

Time is of the essence. The crowd and players
Are the same age always, but the man in the crowd
Is older every season. Come on, play ball!

Wendell Smith (1914–1972) grew up in Detroit, where his father worked as a cook for Henry Ford. After attending West Virginia State College, where he was both a student journalist and a student athlete—legend holds that he invented the one-handed jumpshot—Smith went to work for one of the country's leading African-American newspapers, the *Pittsburgh Courier*. There his persistent and highly polemical reporting advocated the integration of major-league baseball; it was Smith who recommended to Branch Rickey that he choose Jackie Robinson to break the color line. The passion of Smith's writing at its best can be gauged from a May 1938 piece in which he expressed years of frustration at watching black audiences pay money to attend ballgames from which black players were excluded: "We have been fighting for years in an effort to make owners of major league baseball teams admit Negro players. But they won't do it, probably never will. We keep on crawling, begging and pleading for recognition just the same. We know that they don't want us, but we still keep giving them our money." The piece included here is written in a contrasting tone of triumph. It appeared in the *Courier* on the day Robinson played his first game for the Montreal Royals, the Brooklyn Dodgers' best minor-league team. In 1947, Smith began writing for the *Chicago American*, becoming the first black sportswriter with a byline at that or any other major American daily. He also was the first black member of the Baseball Writers Association of America.

Wendell Smith

♥

It Was a Great Day in Jersey

JERSEY CITY, N. J.—The sun smiled down brilliantly in picturesque Roosevelt Stadium here Thursday afternoon and an air of excitement prevailed throughout the spacious park, which was jammed to capacity with 25,000 jabbering, chattering opening day fans . . . A seething mass of humanity, representing all segments of the crazy-quilt we call America, poured into the magnificent ball park they named after a man from Hyde Park—Franklin D. Roosevelt—to see Montreal play Jersey City and the first two Negroes in modern baseball history perform, Jackie Robinson and Johnny Wright . . . There was the usual fanfare and color, with mayor Frank Hague chucking out the first ball, the band music, kids from Jersey City schools putting on an exhibition of running, jumping and acrobatics . . . There was also the hot dogs, peanuts and soda pop . . . And some guys in the distant bleachers whistled merrily: "Take Me Out to the Ball Game" . . . Wendell Willkie's "One World" was right here on the banks of the Passaic River.

The outfield was dressed in a gaudy green, and the infield was as smooth and clean as a new-born babe . . . And everyone sensed the significance of the occasion as Robinson and Wright marched with the Montreal team to deep centerfield for the raising of the Stars and Stripes and the "Star-Spangled Banner" . . . Mayor Hague strutted proudly with his henchmen flanking him on the right and left . . . While the two teams, spread across the field, marched side by side with military precision and the band played on . . . We all stood up—25,000 of us—when the band struck up the National Anthem . . . And we sang lustily and freely, for this was a great day . . . Robinson and Wright stood out there with the rest of the players and dignitaries, clutching their blue-crowned baseball caps, standing erect and as still as West Point cadets on dress parade.

WHAT WERE THEY THINKING ABOUT?

No one will ever know what they were thinking right then, but I have traveled more than 2,000 miles with their courageous pioneers during the past nine weeks—from Sanford, Fla., to Daytona Beach to Jersey City—and I feel that I know them probably better than any newspaperman in the business . . . I know that their hearts throbbed heavily and thumped a steady tempo with the big drum that was pounding out the rhythm as the flag slowly crawled up the centerfield mast.

And then there was a tremendous roar as the flag reached its crest and unfurled gloriously in the brilliant April sunlight . . . The 25,000 fans settled back in their seats, ready for the ballgame as the Jersey City Giants jogged out to their positions . . . Robinson was the second batter and as he strolled to the plate the crowd gave him an enthusiastic reception . . . They were for him . . . They all knew how he had overcome many obstacles in the deep South, how he had been barred from playing in Sanford, Fla., Jacksonville, Savannah and Richmond . . . And yet, through it all, he was standing at the plate as the second baseman of the Montreal team . . . The applause they gave so willingly was a salute of appreciation and admiration . . . Robinson then socked a sizzler to the shortstop and was thrown out by an eyelash at first base.

The second time he appeared at the plate marked the beginning of what can develop into a great career. He got his first hit as a member of the Montreal Royals . . . It was a mighty home run over the left-field fence . . . With two mates on the base paths, he walloped the first pitch that came his way and there was an explosive "crack" as bat and ball met . . . The ball glistened brilliantly in the afternoon sun as it went hurtling high and far over the leftfield fence . . . And, the white flag on the foul-line pole in left fluttered lazily as the ball whistled by.

HE GOT A GREAT OVATION FROM TEAM, FANS

Robinson jogged around the bases—his heart singing, a broad smile on his beaming bronze face as his two teammates trotted home-ward ahead of him . . . When he rounded third, Manager Clay Hop-per, who was coaching there, gave him a heavy pat on the back and shouted: "That's the way to hit that ball!" . . . Between third and home-plate he received another ovation from the stands, and then the entire Montreal team stood up and welcomed him to the bench . . . White hands slapping him on his broad back . . . Deep Southern voices from the bench shouted, "Yo sho' hit 'at one, Robbie, nice goin' kid!" . . . Another said: "Them folks 'at wouldn't let you play down in Jacksonville should be hee'ah now. Whoopee!" . . . And still another: "They cain't stop ya now, Jackie, you're really goin' places, and we're going to be right there with ya!" . . . Jackie Robinson laughed softly and smiled . . . Johnny Wright, wearing a big, blue pitcher's jacket, laughed and smiled . . . And, high up in the press box, Joe Bostic of the Amsterdam News and I looked at each other knowingly, and, we, too, laughed and smiled . . . Our hearts beat just a bit faster, and the thrill ran through us like champagne bubbles . . . It was a great day in Jersey . . . It was a great day in baseball!

But he didn't stop there, this whirlwind from California's gold coast . . . He ran the bases like a wild colt from the Western plains. He laid down two perfect bunts and slashed a hit into rightfield . . . He befuddled the pitchers, made them balk when he was roaring up and down the base paths, and demoralized the entire Jersey City team . . . He was a hitting demon and a base-running maniac . . . The crowd gasped in amazement . . . The opposing pitchers shook their heads in helpless agony . . . His understanding teammates cheered him on with unrivaled enthusiasm . . . And Branch Rickey, the man who had the fortitude and courage to sign him, heard the phenomenal news via telephone in the offices of the Brooklyn Dodgers at Ebbets Field and said admiringly—"He's a wonderful boy, that Jackie Robinson—a wonderful boy!"

THEY MOBBED HIM AFTER THE GAME

When the game ended and Montreal had chalked up a 14 to 1 triumph, Robinson dashed for the club house and the showers . . . But before he could get there he was surrounded by a howling mob of kids, who came streaming out of the bleachers and stands . . . They swept down upon him like a great ocean wave and he was drowned in a sea of adolescent enthusiasm . . . There he was—this Pied Piper of the diamond—perspiration rolling off his bronze brow, idolizing kids swirling all around him, autograph hounds tugging at him . . . And big cops riding prancing steeds trying unsuccessfully to disperse the mob that had cornered the hero of the day . . . One of his own teammates fought his way through the howling mob and finally "saved" Robinson . . . It was Red Durrett, who was a hero in his own right because he had pounded out two prodigious home runs himself, who came to the "rescue." He grabbed Robinson by the arm and pulled him through the crowd. "Come on," Durrett demanded, "you'll be here all night if you don't fight them off. They'll mob you. You can't possibly sign autographs for all those kids."

So, Jackie Robinson, escorted by the red-head outfielder, finally made his way to the dressing room. Bedlam broke loose in there, too . . . Photographers, reporters, kibitzers and hangers-on fenced him in . . . It was a virtual madhouse . . . His teammates, George Shuba, Stan Breard, Herman Franks, Tom Tatum, Marvin Rackley and all the others, were showering congratulations on him . . . They followed him into the showers, back to his locker and all over the dressing room . . . Flash bulbs flashed and reporters fired questions with machine-gun like rapidity . . . And Jackie Robinson smiled through it all.

As he left the park and walked out onto the street, the once-brilliant sun was fading slowly in the distant western skies . . . His petite and dainty little wife greeted him warmly and kindly. "You've had quite a day, little man," she said sweetly.

"Yes," he said softly and pleasantly, "God has been good to us today!"

James Farl Powers (1917–1999) was born to a Catholic family in Jacksonville, Illinois, and lived in midwestern college towns and at a seaside home in Ireland, where his friend, the novelist Sean O'Faolain, joked that Powers spent his mornings setting down a comma and his afternoons wondering if he should replace it with a semicolon. He was not prolific, but he was a master, famous among writers if never a best seller. His 1963 novel about a priest, *Morte D'Urban*, won a National Book Award, yet his greatest talent, perhaps, was for what he called "little stories," like this one from his first collection, *Prince of Darkness* (1947).

J. F. Powers

♥

Jamesie

There it was, all about Lefty, in Ding Bell's Dope Box.

"We don't want to add coals to the fire, but it's common knowledge that the Local Pitcher Most Likely To Succeed is fed up with the home town. Well, well, the boy's good, which nobody can deny, and the scouts are on his trail, but it doesn't say a lot for his team spirit, not to mention his civic spirit, this high-hat attitude of his. And that fine record of his—has it been all a case of him and him alone? How about the team? The boys have backed him up, they've given him the runs, and that's what wins ball games. They don't pay off on strike-outs. There's one kind of player every scribe knows—and wishes he didn't—the lad who gets four for four with the willow, and yet, somehow, his team goes down to defeat—but does that worry this gent? Not a bit of it. He's too busy celebrating his own personal success, figuring his batting average, or, if he's a pitcher, his earned run average and strike-outs. The percentage player. We hope we aren't talking about Lefty. If we are, it's too bad, it is, and no matter where he goes from here, especially if it's up to the majors, it won't remain a secret very long, nor will he . . . See you at the game Sunday. Ding Bell."

"Here's a new one, Jamesie," his father said across the porch, holding up the rotogravure section.

With his father on Sunday it could be one of three things—a visit to the office, fixing up his mother's grave in Calvary, or just sitting on the porch with all the Chicago papers, as today.

Jamesie put down the *Courier* and went over to his father without curiosity. It was always Lindy or the *Spirit of St. Louis,* and now without understanding how this could so suddenly be, he was tired of them. His father, who seemed to feel that a growing boy could take an endless interest in these things, appeared to know the truth at last. He gave a page to the floor—that way he knew what he'd read and how far he had to go—and pulled the newspaper around his ears again. Before he went to dinner he would put the paper in order and wish out loud that other people would have the decency to do the same.

Jamesie, back in his chair, granted himself one more chapter of *Baseball Bill in the World Series.* The chapters were running out again, as they had so many times before, and he knew, with the despair of a narcotic, that his need had no end.

Baseball Bill, at fifty cents a volume and unavailable at the library, kept him nearly broke, and Francis Murgatroyd, his best friend . . . too stingy to go halves, confident he'd get to read them all as Jamesie bought them, and each time offering to exchange the old Tom Swifts and Don Sturdys he had got for Christmas—as though that were the same thing!

Jamesie owned all the Baseball Bills to be had for love or money in the world, and there was nothing in the back of this one about new titles being in preparation. Had the author died, as some of them did, and left his readers in the lurch? Or had the series been discontinued—for where, after *Fighting for the Pennant* and *In the World Series,* could Baseball Bill go? *Baseball Bill, Manager,* perhaps. But then what?

"A plot to *fix* the World Series! So that was it! Bill began to see it all. . . . The mysterious call in the night! The diamond necklace in the dressing room! The scribbled note under the door! With slow fury Bill realized that the peculiar odor on the note paper was the odor in his room now! It was the odor of strong drink and cigar smoke! And it came from his midnight visitor! The same! Did he represent the powerful gambling syndicate? Was *he* Blackie Humphrey himself? Bill held his towering rage in check and smiled at his visitor in his friendly, boyish fashion. His visitor must get no inkling of his true thoughts. Bill must play the game—play the very fool they took him for! Soon enough they would discover for themselves, but to their everlasting sorrow, the courage and daring of Baseball Bill . . ."

Jamesie put the book aside, consulted the batting averages in the *Courier,* and reread Ding Bell. Then, not waiting for dinner and certain to hear about it at supper, he ate a peanut butter sandwich with catsup on it, and left by the back door. He went down the alley calling for Francis Murgatroyd. He got up on the Murgatroyd gate and swung—the death-defying trapeze act at the circus—until Francis came down the walk.

"Hello, Blackie Humphrey," Jamesie said tantalizingly.

"Who's Blackie Humphrey?"

"You know who Blackie Humphrey is all right."

"Aw, Jamesie, cut it out."

"And you want me to throw the World Series!"

"Baseball Bill!"

"In the World Series. It came yesterday."

"Can I read it?"

Jamesie spoke in a hushed voice. "So you're Blackie Humphrey?"

"All right. But I get to read it next."

"So you want me to throw the World Series, Blackie. Is that it? Say you do."

"Yes, I do."

"Ask me again. Call me Bill."

"Bill, I want you to throw the World Series. Will you, Bill?"

"I might." But that was just to fool Blackie. Bill tried to keep his towering rage in check while feigning an interest in the nefarious plot. "Why do you want me to throw it, Blackie?"

"I don't know."

"Sure you know. You're a dirty crook and you've got a lot of dough bet on the other team."

"Uh, huh."

"Go ahead. Tell me that."

While Blackie unfolded the criminal plan Bill smiled at him in his friendly, boyish fashion.

"And who's behind this, Blackie?"

"I don't know."

"Say it's the powerful gambling syndicate."

"It's them."

"Ah, ha! Knock the ash off your cigar."

"Have I got one?"

"Yes, and you've got strong drink on your breath, too."

"Whew!"

Blackie should have fixed him with his small, piglike eyes.

"Fix me with your small, piglike eyes."

"Wait a minute, Jamesie!"

"Bill. Go ahead. Fix me."

"O.K. But you don't get to be Bill all the time."

"Now blow your foul breath in my face."

"There!"

"Now ask me to have a cigar. Go ahead."

Blackie was offering Bill a cigar, but Bill knew it was to get him to break training and refused it.

"I see through you, Blackie." No, that was wrong. He had to conceal his true thoughts and let Blackie play him for a fool. Soon enough his time would come and . . . "Thanks for the cigar, Blackie," he said. "I thought it was a cheap one. Thanks, I'll smoke it later."

"I paid a quarter for it."

"Hey, that's too much, Francis!"

"Well, if I'm the head of the powerful——"

Mr. Murgatroyd came to the back door and told Francis to get ready.

"I can't go to the game, Jamesie," Francis said. "I have to caddy for him."

Jamesie got a ride with the calliope when it had to stop at the corner for the light. The calliope was not playing now, but yesterday it had roamed the streets, all red and gold and glittering like a hussy among the pious, black Fords parked on the Square, blaring and showing off, with a sign, Jayville vs. Beardstown.

The ball park fence was painted a swampy green except for an occasional new board. Over the single ticket window cut in the fence hung a sign done in the severe black and white railroad manner, "Home of the Jayville Independents," but everybody called them the "Indees."

Jamesie bought a bottle of Green River out of his savings and made the most of it, swallowing it in sips, calling upon his will power under the sun. He returned the bottle and stood for a while by the ticket window making designs in the dust with the corrugated soles of his new tennis shoes. Ding Bell, with a pretty lady on his arm and carrying the black official scorebook, passed inside without paying, and joked about it.

The Beardstown players arrived from sixty miles away with threatening cheers. Their chartered bus stood steaming and dusty from the trip. The players wore gray suits with "Barons" written across their chests and had the names of sponsors on their backs—Palms Café, Rusty's Wrecking, Coca-Cola.

Jamesie recognized some of the Barons but put down a desire to speak to them.

The last man to leave the bus, Jamesie thought, must be Guez, the new pitcher imported from East St. Louis for the game. Ding Bell had it in the Dope Box that "Saliva Joe" was one of the few spitters left in the business, had been up in the Three Eye a few years, was a full-blooded Cuban, and ate a bottle of aspirins a game, just like candy.

The dark pitcher's fame was too much for Jamesie. He walked alongside Guez. He smelled the salt and pepper of the gray uniform, saw the scarred plate on the right toe, saw the tears in the striped stockings—the marks of bravery or moths—heard the distant chomp of tobacco being chewed, felt—almost—the iron drape of the flannel, and was reduced to friendliness with the pitcher, the enemy.

"Are you a real Cuban?"

Guez looked down, rebuking Jamesie with a brief stare, and growled, "Go away."

Jamesie gazed after the pitcher. He told himself that he hated Guez—that's what he did, hated him! But it didn't do much good. He looked around to see if anybody had been watching, but nobody had, and he wanted somebody his size to vanquish—somebody who might think Guez was as good as Lefty. He wanted to bet a million dollars on Lefty against Guez, but there was nobody to take him up on it.

The Indees began to arrive in ones and twos, already in uniform but carrying their spikes in their hands. Jamesie spoke to all of them except J. G. Nickerson, the manager. J. G. always glared at kids. He thought they were stealing his baseballs and laughing about it behind his back. He was a great one for signaling with a score card from the bench, like Connie Mack, and Ding Bell had ventured to say that managers didn't come any brainier than Jayville's own J. G. Nickerson, even in the big time. But if there should be a foul ball, no matter how tight the game or crucial the situation, J. G. would leap up, straining like a bird dog, and try to place it, waving the bat boy on without taking his eyes off the spot where it disappeared over the fence or in the weeds. That was why they called him the Foul Ball.

The Petersons—the old man at the wheel, a red handkerchief tied tight enough around his neck to keep his head on, and the sons, all players, Big Pete, Little Pete, Middle Pete, and Extra Pete—roared up with their legs hanging out of the doorless Model T and the brass radiator boiling over.

The old man ran the Model T around in circles, damning it for a runaway horse, and finally got it parked by the gate.

"Hold 'er, Knute!" he cackled.

The boys dug him in the ribs, tickling him, and were like puppies that had been born bigger than their father, jollying him through the gate, calling him Barney Oldfield.

Lefty came.

"Hi, Lefty," Jamesie said.

"Hi, kid," Lefty said. He put his arm around Jamesie and took him past the ticket taker.

"It's all right, Mac," he said.

"Today's the day, Lefty," Mac said. "You can do it, Lefty."

Jamesie and Lefty passed behind the grandstand. Jamesie saw Lefty's father, a skinny, brown-faced man in a yellow straw katy.

"There's your dad, Lefty."

Lefty said, "Where?" but looked the wrong way and walked a little faster.

At the end of the grandstand Lefty stopped Jamesie. "My old man is out of town, kid. Got that?"

Jamesie did not see how this could be. He knew Lefty's father. Lefty's father had a brown face and orange gums. But Lefty ought to know his own father. "I guess it just looked like him, Lefty," Jamesie said.

Lefty took his hand off Jamesie's arm and smiled. "Yeah, that's right, kid. It just looked like him on account of he's out of town—in Peoria."

Jamesie could still feel the pressure of Lefty's fingers on his arm. They came out on the diamond at the Indees bench near first base. The talk quieted down when Lefty appeared. Everybody thought he had a big head, but nobody could say a thing against his pitching record, it was that good. The scout for the New York Yankees had invited him only last Sunday to train with them next spring. The idea haunted the others. J. G. had shut up about the beauties of teamwork.

J. G. was counting the balls when Jamesie went to the suitcase to get one for Lefty. J. G. snapped the lid down.

"It's for Lefty!"

"Huh!"

"He wants it for warm up."

"Did you tell this kid to get you a ball, Left?"

"Should I bring my own?" Lefty said.

J. G. dug into the suitcase for a ball, grunting, "I only asked him." He looked to Jamesie for sympathy. He considered the collection of balls and finally picked out a fairly new one.

"Lefty, he likes 'em brand new," Jamesie said.

"Who's running this club?" J. G. bawled. But he threw the ball back and broke a brand new one out of its box and tissue paper. He ignored Jamesie's ready hand and yelled to Lefty going out to the bull pen, "Coming at you, Left," and threw it wild.

Lefty let the ball bounce through his legs, not trying for it. "Nice throw," he said.

Jamesie retrieved the ball for Lefty. They tossed it back and forth, limbering up, and Jamesie aped Lefty's professional indolence.

When Bugs Bidwell, Lefty's battery mate, appeared with his big mitt, Jamesie stood aside and buttoned his glove back on his belt. Lefty shed his red blanket coat with the leather sleeves and gave it to Jamesie for safe-keeping. Jamesie folded it gently over his arm, with the white chenille "J" showing out. He took his stand behind Bugs to get a good look at Lefty's stuff.

Lefty had all his usual stuff—the fast one with the two little hops in it, no bigger than a pea; his slow knuckler that looked like a basketball, all the stitches standing still and staring you in the face; his sinker that started out high like a wild pitch, then dipped a good eight inches and straightened out for a called strike. But something was wrong—Lefty with nothing to say, no jokes, no sudden whoops, was not himself. Only once did he smile at a girl in the bleachers and say she was plenty . . . and sent a fast one smacking into Bugs' mitt for what he meant.

That, for a moment, was the Lefty that Jamesie's older cousins knew about. They said a nice kid like Jamesie ought to be kept away from him, even at the ball park. Jamesie was always afraid it would get back to Lefty that the cousins thought he was poor white trash, or that he would know it in some other way, as when the cousins passed him on the street and looked the other way. He was worried, too, about what Lefty might think of his Sunday clothes, the snow-white blouse, the floppy sailor tie, the soft linen pants, the sissy clothes. His tennis shoes—sneakers, he ought to say—were all right, but not the golf stockings that left his knees bare, like a rich kid's. The tough guys, because they were tough or poor—he didn't know which—wore socks, not stockings, and they wore them rolled down slick to their ankles.

Bugs stuck his mitt with the ball in it under his arm and got out his Beechnut. He winked at Jamesie and said, "Chew?"

Jamesie giggled. He liked Bugs. Bugs, on loan from the crack State Hospital team, was all right—nothing crazy about him; he just liked it at the asylum, he said, the big grounds and lots of cool shade, and he was not required to work or take walks like the regular patients. He was the only Indee on speaking terms with Lefty.

Turning to Lefty, Bugs said, "Ever seen this Cuban work?"

"Naw."

"I guess he's got it when he's right."

"That so?" Lefty caught the ball with his bare hand and spun it back to Bugs. "Well, all I can promise you is a no-hit game. It's up to you clowns to get the runs."

"And me hitting a lousy .211."

"All you got to do is hold me. Anyhow what's the Foul Ball want for his five bucks—Mickey Cochrane?"

"Yeah, Left."

"I ought to quit him."

"Ain't you getting your regular fifteen?"

"Yeah, but I ought to quit. The Yankees want me. Is my curve breaking too soon?"

"It's right in there, Left."

———

It was a pitchers' battle until the seventh inning. Then the Indees pushed a run across.

The Barons got to Lefty for their first hit in the seventh, and when the next man bunted, Lefty tried to field it instead of letting Middle Pete at third have it, which put two on with none out. Little Pete threw the next man out at first, the only play possible, and the runners advanced to second and third. The next hitter hammered a line drive to Big Pete at first, and Big Pete tried to make it two by throwing to second, where the runner was off, but it was too late and the runner on third scored on the play. J. G. from the bench condemned Big Pete for a dumb Swede. The next man popped to short center.

Jamesie ran out with Lefty's jacket. "Don't let your arm get cold, Lefty."

"Some support I got," Lefty said.

"Whyn't you leave me have that bunt, Lefty?" Middle Pete said, and everybody knew he was right.

"Two of them pitches was hit solid," Big Pete said. "Good anywhere."

"Now, boys," J. G. said.

"Aw, dry up," Lefty said, grabbing a blade of grass to chew. "I ought to quit you bums."

Pid Kirby struck out for the Indees, but Little Pete walked, and Middle Pete advanced him to second on a long fly to left. Then Big Pete tripled to the weed patch in center, clear up against the Chevrolet sign, driving in Little Pete. Guez whiffed Kelly Larkin, retiring the side, and the Indees were leading the Barons 2 to 1.

The first Baron to bat in the eighth had J. G. frantic with fouls. The umpire was down to his last ball and calling for more. With trembling fingers J. G. unwrapped new balls. He had the bat boy and the bat boy's assistant hunting for them behind the grandstand. When one fell among the automobiles parked near first, he started to go and look for himself, but thought of Jamesie and sent him instead. "If anybody tries to hold out on you, come and tell me."

After Jamesie found the ball he crept up behind a familiar blue Hupmobile, dropping to his knees when he was right under Uncle Pat's elbow, and then popping up to scare him.

"Look who's here," his cousin said. It had not been Uncle Pat's elbow at all, but Gabriel's. Uncle Pat, who had never learned to drive, sat on the other side to be two feet closer to the game.

Jamesie stepped up on the running board, and Gabriel offered him some popcorn.

"So you're at the game, Jamesie," Uncle Pat said, grinning as though it were funny. "Gabriel said he thought that was you out there."

"Where'd you get the cap, Jamesie?" Gabriel said.

"Lefty. The whole team got new ones. And if they win today J. G. says they're getting whole new uniforms."

"Not from me," Uncle Pat said, looking out on the field. "Who the thunder's wearing my suit today?"

"Lee Coles, see?" Gabriel said, pointing to the player. Lee's back— Mallon's Grocery—was to them.

Uncle Pat, satisfied, slipped a bottle of near beer up from the floor to his lips and tipped it up straight, which explained to Jamesie the foam on his mustache.

"You went and missed me again this week," Uncle Pat said broodingly. "You know what I'm going to do, Jamesie?"

"What?"

"I'm going to stop taking your old *Liberty* magazine if you don't bring me one first thing tomorrow morning."

"I will." He would have to bring Uncle Pat his own free copy and erase the crossword puzzle. He never should have sold out on the street. That was how you lost your regular customers.

Uncle Pat said, "This makes the second time I started in to read a serial and had this happen to me."

"Is it all right if the one I bring you tomorrow has got 'Sample Copy' stamped on it?"

"That's all right with me, Jamesie, but I ought to get it for nothing." Uncle Pat swirled the last inch of beer in the bottle until it was all suds.

"I like the *Post*," Gabriel said. "Why don't you handle the *Post*?"

"They don't need anybody now."

"What he ought to handle," Uncle Pat said, "is the *Country Gentleman*."

"How's the Rosebud coming, Jamesie?" Gabriel asked. "But I don't want to buy any."

Uncle Pat and Gabriel laughed at him.

Why was that funny? He'd had to return eighteen boxes and tell them he guessed he was all through being the local representative. But why was that so funny?

"Did you sell enough to get the bicycle, Jamesie?"

"No." He had sold all the Rosebud salve he could, but not nearly enough to get the Ranger bicycle. He had to be satisfied with the Eveready flashlight.

"Well, I got enough of that Rosebud salve now to grease the Hup," Gabriel said. "Or to smear all over me the next time I swim the English Channel—with Gertrude Ederle. It ought to keep the fishes away."

"It smells nice," Uncle Pat said. "But I got plenty."

Jamesie felt that they were protecting themselves against him.

"I sent it all back anyway," he said, but that was not true; there were six boxes at home in his room that he had to keep in order to get the flashlight. Why was that the way it always worked out? Same way with the flower seeds. Why was it that whenever he got a new suit at Meyer Brothers they weren't giving out ball bats or compasses? Why was it he only won a half pound of bacon at the carnival, never a Kewpie doll or an electric fan? Why did he always get tin whistles and crickets in the Crackerjack, never a puzzle, a ring, or a badge? And one time he had got nothing! Why was it that the five-dollar bill he found on South Diamond Street belonged to Mrs. Hutchinson? But he *had* found a quarter in the dust at the circus that nobody claimed.

"Get your aunt Kate to take that cap up in the back," Uncle Pat said, smiling.

Vaguely embarrassed, Jamesie said, "Well, I got to get back."

"If that's Lefty's cap," Gabriel called after him, "you'd better send it to the cleaners."

When he got back to the bench and handed the ball over, J. G. seemed to forget all about the bases being crowded.

"Thank God," he said. "I thought you went home with it."

The Barons were all on Lefty now. Shorty Parker, their manager, coaching at third, chanted, "Take him out . . . Take him out . . . Take him out."

The Barons had started off the ninth with two clean blows. Then

Bugs took a foul ball off the chicken wire in front of the grandstand
for one out, and Big Pete speared a drive on the rise for another. Two
down and runners on first and third. Lefty wound up—bad baseball—
and the man on first started for second, the batter stepping into the
pitch, not to hit it but to spoil the peg to second. The runner was safe;
the man on third, threatening to come home after a false start, slid
yelling back into the sack. It was close and J. G. flew off the bench to
protest a little.

After getting two strikes on the next batter, Lefty threw four balls,
so wide it looked like a deliberate pitchout, and that loaded the bases.

J. G. called time. He went out to the mound to talk it over with
Lefty, but Lefty waved him away. So J. G. consulted Bugs behind the
plate. Jamesie, lying on the grass a few feet away, could hear them.

"That's the first windup I ever seen a pitcher take with a runner on
first."

"It was pretty bad," Bugs said.

"And then walking that last one. He don't look wild to me, neither."

"He ain't wild, J. G.; I'll tell you that."

"I want your honest opinion, Bugs."

"I don't know what to say, J. G."

"Think I better jerk him?"

Bugs was silent, chewing it over.

"Guess I better leave him in, huh?"

"You're the boss, J. G. I don't know nothing for sure."

"I only got Extra Pete to put in. They'd murder him. I guess I got to
leave Lefty in and take a chance."

"I guess so."

When J. G. had gone Bugs walked halfway out to the mound and
spoke to Lefty. "You all right?"

"I had a little twinge before."

"A little what?"

Lefty touched his left shoulder.

"You mean your arm's gone sore?"

"Naw. I guess it's nothing."

Bugs took his place behind the plate again. He crouched, and Jamesie, from where he was lying, saw two fingers appear below the mitt—
the signal. Lefty nodded, wound up, and tried to slip a medium-fast
one down the middle. Guez, the batter, poled a long ball into left—foul

by a few feet. Bugs shook his head in the mask, took a new ball from the umpire, and slammed it hard at Lefty.

Jamesie saw two fingers below the mitt again. What was Bugs doing? It wasn't smart baseball to give Guez another like the last one!

Guez swung and the ball fell against the left field fence—fair. Lee Coles, the left fielder, was having trouble locating it in the weeds. Kelly Larkin came over from center to help him hunt. When they found the ball, Guez had completed the circuit and the score was 5 to 2 in favor of the Barons.

Big Pete came running over to Lefty from first base, Little Pete from second, Pid Kirby from short, Middle Pete from third. J. G., calling time again, walked out to them.

"C'mere, Bugs," he said.

Bugs came slowly.

"What'd you call for on that last pitch?"

"Curve ball."

"And the one before that?"

"Same."

"And what'd Lefty give you?"

"It wasn't no curve. It wasn't much of anything."

"No," J. G. said. "It sure wasn't no curve ball. It was right in there, not too fast, not too slow, just right—for batting practice."

"It slipped," Lefty said.

"Slipped, huh!" Big Pete said. "How about the other one?"

"They both slipped. Ain't that never happened before?"

"Well, it ain't never going to happen again—not to me, it ain't," J. G. said. "I'm taking you out!"

He shouted to Extra Pete on the bench, "Warm up! You're going in!" He turned to Lefty.

"And I'm firing you. I just found out your old man was making bets under the grandstand—and they wasn't on us! I can put you in jail for this!"

"Try it," Lefty said, starting to walk away.

"If you knew it, J. G.," Big Pete said, "whyn't you let us know?"

"I just now found it out, is why."

"Then I'm going to make up for lost time," Big Pete said, following Lefty, "and punch this guy's nose."

Old man Peterson appeared among them—somebody must have told him what it was all about. "Give it to him, son!" he cackled.

Jamesie missed the fight. He was not tall enough to see over all the heads, and Gabriel, sent by Uncle Pat, was dragging him away from it all.

"I always knew that Lefty was a bad one," Gabriel said on the way home. "I knew it from the time he used to hunch in marbles."

"It reminds me of the Black Sox scandal of 1919," Uncle Pat said. "I wonder if they'll hold the old man, too."

Jamesie, in tears, said, "Lefty hurt his arm and you don't like him just because he don't work, and his father owes you at the store! Let me out! I'd rather walk by myself than ride in the Hupmobile—with you!"

He stayed up in his room, feigning a combination stomach-ache and headache, and would not come down for supper. Uncle Pat and Gabriel were down there eating. His room was over the dining room, and the windows were open upstairs and down, but he could not quite hear what they said. Uncle Pat was laughing a lot—that was all for sure—but then he always did that. Pretty soon he heard no more from the dining room and he knew they had gone to sit on the front porch.

Somebody was coming up the stairs. Aunt Kate. He knew the wavering step at the top of the stairs to be hers, and the long pause she used to catch her breath—something wrong with her lungs? Now, as she began to move, he heard ice tinkling in a glass. Lemonade. She was bringing him some supper. She knocked. He lay heavier on the bed and with his head at a painful angle to make her think he was suffering. She knocked again. If he pinched his forehead it would look red and feverish. He did. Now.

"Come in," he said weakly.

She came in, gliding across the room in the twilight, tall and white as a sail in her organdy, serene before her patient. Not quite opening his eyes, he saw her through the lashes. She thought he was sick all right, but even if she didn't, she would never take advantage of him to make a joke, like Uncle Pat, prescribing, "A good dose of salts! That's the ticket!" Or Gabriel, who was even meaner, "An enema!"

He had Aunt Kate fooled completely. He could fool her every time. On Halloween she was the kind of person who went to the door every time the bell rang. She was the only grownup he knew with whom it was not always the teeter-totter game. She did not raise herself by lowering him. She did not say back to him the things he said, slightly changed, accented with a grin, so that they were funny. Uncle Pat did. Gabriel did. Sometimes, if there was company, his father did.

"Don't you want the shades up, Jamesie?"

She raised the shades, catching the last of that day's sun, bringing the ballplayers on the wall out of the shadows and into action. She put the tray on the table by his bed.

Jamesie sat up and began to eat. Aunt Kate was the best one. Even if she noticed it, she would say nothing about his sudden turn for the better.

She sat across from him in the rocker, the little red one he had been given three years ago, when he was just a kid in the first grade, but she did not look too big for it. She ran her hand over the front of his books, frowning at Baseball Bill, Don Sturdy, Tom Swift, Horatio Alger, Jr., and the *Sporting News*. They had come between him and her.

"Where are the books we used to read, Jamesie?"

"On the bottom shelf."

She bent to see them. There they were, his old friends and hers— hers still. Perseus. Theseus. All those old Greeks. Sir Lancelot. Merlin. Sir Tristram. King Arthur. Oliver Twist. Pinocchio. Gulliver. He wondered how he ever could have liked them, and why Aunt Kate still did. Perhaps he still did, a little. But they turned out wrong, most of them, with all the good guys dying or turning into fairies and the bad guys becoming dwarfs. The books he read now turned out right, if not until the very last page, and the bad guys died or got what was coming to them.

"Were they talking about the game, Aunt Kate?"

"Your uncle was, and Gabriel."

Jamesie waited a moment. "Did they say anything about Lefty?"

"I don't know. Is he the one who lost the game on purpose?"

"That's a lie, Aunt Kate! That's just what Uncle Pat and Gabriel say!"

"Well, I'm sure I don't know——"

"You *are* on their side!"

Aunt Kate reached for his hand, but he drew it back.

"Jamesie, I'm sure I'm not on anyone's side. How can I be? I don't know about baseball—and I don't care about it!"

"Well, I *do*! And I'm not one bit sick—and you thought I was!"

Jamesie rolled out of bed, ran to the door, turned, and said, "Why don't you get out of my room and go and be with them! You're on their side! And Uncle Pat drinks *near beer*!"

He could not be sure, but he thought he had her crying, and if he did it served her right. He went softly down the stairs, past the living room, out the back door, and crept along the house until he reached the front porch. He huddled under the spiraea bushes and listened to them talk. But it was not about the game. It was about President Coolidge. His father was for him. Uncle Pat was against him.

Jamesie crept back along the house until it was safe to stand up and walk. He went down the alley. He called for Francis.

But Francis was not home—still with his father, Mrs. Murgatroyd said.

Jamesie went downtown, taking his own special way, through alleys, across lots, so that he arrived on the Square without using a single street or walking on a single sidewalk. He weighed himself on the scales in front of Kresge's. He weighed eighty-three pounds, and the little card said, "You are the strong, silent type, and silence is golden." He weighed himself in front of Grant's. He weighed eighty-four pounds, and the card said, "Cultivate your good tastes and make the most of your business connections."

He bought a ball of gum from the machine in front of the Owl Drugstore. It looked like it was time for a black one to come out, and black was his favorite flavor, but it was a green one. Anyway he was glad it had not been white.

He coveted the Louisville Sluggers in the window of the D. & M. Hardware. He knew how much they cost. They were autographed by Paul Waner, Ty Cobb, Rogers Hornsby, all the big league stars, and if Lefty ever cracked his, a Paul Waner, he was going to give it to Jamesie, he said.

When Lefty was up with the Yankees—though they had not talked about it yet—he would send for Jamesie. He would make Jamesie the bat boy for the Yankees. He would say to Jake Ruppert, the owner of the Yankees, "Either you hire my friend, Jamesie, as bat boy or I quit."

Jake Ruppert would want his own nephew or somebody to have the job, but what could he do? Jamesie would have a uniform like the regular players, and get to travel around the country with them, living in hotels, eating in restaurants, taking taxicabs, and would be known to everybody as Lefty's best friend, and they would both be Babe Ruth's best friends, the three of them going everywhere together. He would get all the Yankees to write their names on an Official American League ball and then send it home to Francis Murgatroyd, who would still be going to school back in Jayville—poor old Francis; and he would write to him on hotel stationery with his own fourteen-dollar fountain pen.

And then he was standing across the street from the jail. He wondered if they had Lefty locked up over there, if Uncle Pat and Gabriel had been right—not about Lefty throwing a game—that was a lie!—but about him being locked up. A policeman came out of the jail. Jamesie waited for him to cross the street. He was Officer Burkey. He was Phil Burkey's father, and Phil had shown Jamesie his father's gun and holster one time when he was sleeping. Around the house Mr. Burkey looked like anybody else, not a policeman.

"Mr. Burkey, is Lefty in there?"

Mr. Burkey, through for the day, did not stop to talk, only saying, "Ah, that he is, boy, and there's where he deserves to be."

Jamesie said "Oh yeah!" to himself and went around to the back side of the jail. It was a brick building, painted gray, and the windows were open, but not so you could see inside, and they had bars over them.

Jamesie decided he could do nothing if Mr. Burkey was off duty. The street lights came on; it was night. He began to wonder, too, if his father would miss him. Aunt Kate would not tell. But he would have to come in the back way and sneak up to his room. If it rained tomorrow he would stay in and make up with Aunt Kate. He hurried home, and did not remember that he had meant to stay out all night, maybe even run away forever.

The next morning Jamesie came to the jail early. Mr. Burkey, on duty, said he might see Lefty for three minutes, but it was a mystery to him why anyone, especially a nice boy like Jamesie, should want to see the bum. "And don't tell your father you was here."

Jamesie found Lefty lying on a narrow iron bed that was all springs and no covers or pillow.

"Lefty," he said, "I came to see you."

Lefty sat up. He blinked at Jamesie and had trouble getting his eyes to see.

Jamesie went closer. Lefty stood up. They faced each other. Jamesie could have put his hand through the bars and touched Lefty.

"Glad to see you, kid."

"Lefty," Jamesie said, "I brought you some reading." He handed Lefty Uncle Pat's copy of *Liberty* magazine.

"Thanks, kid."

He got the box of Rosebud salve out of his pocket for Lefty.

"Well, thanks, kid. But what do I do with it?"

"For your arm, Lefty. It says 'recommended for aches and pains.'"

"I'll try it."

"Do you like oranges, Lefty?"

"I can eat 'em."

He gave Lefty his breakfast orange.

A funny, sweet smell came off Lefty's breath, like perfume, only sour. Burnt matches and cigar butts lay on the cell floor. Did Lefty smoke? Did he? Didn't he realize what it would do to him?

"Lefty, how do you throw your sinker?"

Lefty held the orange and showed Jamesie how he gripped the ball along the seams, how he snapped his wrist before he let it fly.

"But be sure you don't telegraph it, kid. Throw 'em all the same—your fast one, your floater, your curve. Then they don't know where they're at."

Lefty tossed the orange through the bars to Jamesie.

"Try it."

Jamesie tried it, but he had it wrong at first, and Lefty had to reach through the bars and show him again. After that they were silent, and Jamesie thought Lefty did not seem very glad to see him after all, and remembered the last gift.

"And I brought you this, Lefty."

It was *Baseball Bill in the World Series*.

"Yeah?" Lefty said, momentarily angry, as though he thought Jamesie was trying to kid him. He accepted the book reluctantly.

"He's a pitcher, Lefty," Jamesie said. "Like you, only he's a right-hander."

The sour perfume on Lefty's breath came through the bars again, a little stronger on a sigh.

Wasn't that the odor of strong drink and cigar smoke—the odor of Blackie Humphrey? Jamesie talked fast to keep himself from thinking. "This book's all about Baseball Bill and the World Series," he gulped, "and Blackie Humphrey and some dirty crooks that try to get Bill to throw it, but . . ." He gave up; he knew now. And Lefty had turned his back.

After a moment, during which nothing happened inside him to explain what he knew now, Jamesie got his legs to take him away, out of the jail, around the corner, down the street—away. He did not go through alleys, across lots, between buildings, over fences. No. He used the streets and sidewalks, like anyone else, to get where he was going—away—and was not quite himself.

James A. Maxwell (1912–1984) wrote frequently for *The New Yorker,* the *Atlantic,* and other magazines in the 1940s and 1950s and also had a long career as an editor. Short stories based on his experiences in the Army counterintelligence corps in North Africa during World War II were collected in the book *I Never Saw an Arab Like Him* (1948). This nonfiction piece is about the scandalous "Black Sox," players from the Chicago White Sox who conspired with gamblers to throw the 1919 World Series to the Cincinnati Reds. To many Americans, the Black Sox story came to represent not only baseball's loss of innocence, but the country's. It had so many tragic elements, from the underpaid players who corrupted themselves for pennies they never saw, to the little boy who called to the illiterate outfielder Shoeless Joe Jackson, "Say it ain't so, Joe." That young naif was probably the creation of the journalist Hugh Fullerton, making him the first of many American writers to be inspired by the Black Sox, including F. Scott Fitzgerald, Nelson Algren, Bernard Malamud, Harry Stein, and the Canadian novelist W. P. Kinsella.

James A. Maxwell

♡

Shine Ball

In Cincinnati, baseball has always been less a sport than a kind of psychosis. It is to the natives what bullfighting is to the citizens of Madrid, and is approached with the same passionate enthusiasm and subjected to the same universally expert consideration. There is, I feel sure, a larger percentage of true baseball aficionados in Cincinnati than in any other city in the country. The obsession traditionally seizes the inhabitants at an early age, and most local children can name the infield of the Reds long before they have learned to distinguish between Andrew Jackson and Andrew Johnson. Just why the Reds, a team usually to be found mired in the lower depths of the National League, should engender such loyalty is not clear. They have won the pennant only three times in history, but the hopes of their followers have been perpetually bright.

It is a fair guess that 1919 is likely to be remembered by a Cincinnatian not as the first whole year of peace after World War I, or as the

219

year prohibition began, but, rather, as the year in which the Reds won their first pennant. Feverish excitement came early in the season that year. The team was obviously good, and the city trembled with expectation. I was seven at the time, and I recall that my schoolwork was badly disrupted by baseball hysteria throughout late May and early June. It was almost impossible to concentrate on spelling and arithmetic when all my thoughts were on Hod Eller's famous shine ball, Edd Roush's batting average, Jake Daubert's flawless playing at first base.

As soon as the school term ended, I began going to almost all the home games. I lived only about a mile from the ballpark, and at that time the management admitted children free to the weekday games if they were accompanied by adults, so my friends and I hung around the box office and asked ticket buyers to let us walk in with them. It was a beautiful and thrilling summer.

When the team was on the road, we clustered each afternoon before the front window of Ahler's Café, a neighborhood saloon that had a ticker. Mr. Ahler got the inning-by-inning score from the long yellow ribbon of paper we could occasionally see coming out of it, as well as brief notices of any such spectacular occurrences as home runs or double plays, and he chalked all this information on a big scoreboard that hung where we could easily see it through the window.

Following the games in this fashion was often maddeningly unsatisfactory, but our imagination supplied a good deal of the action we were missing. When the ticker was inactive and the Reds were at bat, for instance, we were sure that our heroes were staging a great rally and that the operator of the ticker was merely waiting for the end of the inning to send all the good news at once. If there was a considerable lull while the opposing team was at bat, we kept our spirits strong by saying that there must have been a fight on the field, or that it had begun to rain, or that the pitcher was taking a long time to warm up.

The most agonizing period for us was while the ticker was working. When it was quiet, the saloon's customers usually stood at the bar, drinking what was presumably near-beer, but as soon as the machine began to spew out its ribbon, they crowded around it. The saloon was in an old building with thick walls, and I suppose it was cooler with the door closed. In any case, the door always was closed, and we could see only that the men were laughing and slapping one another's backs or making dour faces and gestures of disgust. These pantomimes, unaccompanied by concrete information, would sometimes agitate us to a point of near-hysteria, and we would rap on the window to hurry Mr. Ahler to the board. It was a rash thing to do, for if his rheumatism was troubling him, he was likely to come out in a rage and order us away.

About the middle of September, after weeks of constant nervous strain for all Cincinnatians, the Reds clinched the National League pennant. The city erupted into celebration, but once the first outburst had passed, everyone began to worry about the Reds' opponents in the forthcoming World Series, the Chicago White Sox. Fearsome stories of Shoeless Joe Jackson's hitting power, of the impenetrability of the Chicago infield, of the pitching of Ed Cicotte circulated freely among the faithful. I heard my father and grandfather discuss the relative merits of the two teams again and again, and they always agreed that a Chicago victory was almost certain. This adult opinion made me somewhat uneasy but did not entirely obliterate my hope.

The Series began at last, and on the first two afternoons a half dozen of my friends and I, A.W.O.L. from school, stationed ourselves in the street just outside the ballpark long before game time. There was no way for us to get inside for those games, of course, but I don't recall that any of us felt especially envious of the fortunate people who went past us through the gates. I know that I, at least, was completely happy just to be near the action. The excitement and noise of the crowd, the bellowed commands of policemen, the honking horns of taxis, the impatient clanging of streetcar bells, the cries of the hawkers selling peanuts, soft drinks, and score cards, the pervading sense of drama were sufficient reward for being there, and even for just being alive.

Once the game started, we reveled in the flat, revolverlike cracks of the bats, the explosive bursts of hoarse voices, and the moments of tense quiet, when we could hear only the shouts of the venders. Inside the stadium, some men stood with their backs against a grating high above us, and from time to time we got the attention of one of them and learned the score.

The Reds won the first two games, making me forget that I had ever doubted their invincibility. Then the teams went to Chicago for the next three games. My friends and I attended school on those afternoons, though to little purpose, and as soon as classes were dismissed, we raced to Ahler's Café. The Reds lost the first game in Chicago and won the two others. They needed only one more victory. (In 1919, it took five games to win the championship.)

On the evening of the day the Reds won their fourth game, my father, who had been reading the paper, lowered it and stared at the wall for a moment. "This doesn't make sense," he said. "The Reds aren't that good and Chicago isn't that bad. I can't figure it out."

I looked up from the homework I was doing on the floor beside his chair. "It's the shine ball," I said firmly. "They can't hit the shine ball." I had no clear idea what a shine ball was, but it was the specialty of my favorite pitcher, Hod Eller, and to me the name suggested that he did something mysterious to the ball that caused it to reflect light, like a mirror, thus temporarily blinding the opposing batter.

"It just couldn't happen this way," Father said to himself, ignoring me.

The teams came back to Cincinnati. Those of us who had stayed out of school for the first two games of the Series had been punished with extra homework assignments, but our number had been so great that our principal dismissed school an hour early for the Reds' sixth Series game, and, after Chicago won that, for the seventh, too.

My companions and I returned to our posts by the ballpark, and when the Reds lost the sixth game, we consoled ourselves with the thought that their lead was too great to be overcome. When they were defeated again the following afternoon, however, Chicago was within one game of tying the Series. Doubt invaded all of us, and we walked away from the park with scarcely a word to say to one another.

"The percentages are beginning to pay off," my father said at dinner that evening. He spoke in the unhappy, yet satisfied, tone of a man who has correctly predicted a disaster. "That Chicago team has everything—pitching, hitting, fielding—and they were bound to get their stride. With the last two games on their home field, it doesn't look good for the Reds," he concluded, and for the first time in my life I was unable to eat dessert.

The next day was Thursday, and our group skipped school again and gathered outside Ahler's Café a few minutes before game time. My spirits were somewhat higher than they had been the night before. Hod Eller was to pitch for the Reds, and I had an almost mystic faith in his shine ball. The game began, and we waited what seemed an interminable while for the ticker to give the score. I knew the batting order by heart, of course, and I visualized the scene in Chicago, recalling the idiosyncrasies of the various players—how this one tugged at the peak of his cap before each pitch, how that one always swung four bats before going to the plate, how another never failed to knock the dirt from his spikes. Finally, we heard the faint, staccato clicking of the ticker and saw the men in the saloon gather around the machine. After a few moments, there was a great roar, and some of the men pounded one another on the back while three or four danced the jig. My friends and I almost broke Mr. Ahler's front window trying to hurry him to the scoreboard, and, for once, he didn't glower at us as he went toward it with a strip of yellow ticker paper in his hand. He waved to us gaily, then picked up the chalk and marked five runs for the Reds. We shouted until we were breathless.

There was never any doubt about the outcome after that first inning, and the game ended with the Reds the winners by a score of 10–5. As soon as it was over, we ran up and down the street screeching the news at the tops of our high, pre-adolescent voices. Heads popped out of windows, and before long many adults had joined us.

I talked and played little but baseball that year until snow and Christmas provided new interests. Christmas was especially thrilling in 1919 because my Uncle Dave, who lived in Chicago, came to Cincinnati for the holidays. He had been gassed during the war, had spent several months in a government hospital, and had recently become the operator of a racing handbook in Chicago. He was by far the most romantic figure in our family, and my affection for him was great.

He arrived the day before Christmas, still looking pale and considerably underweight, but he was full of vivacity. According to family custom, we gathered at my grandparents' home that evening and exchanged presents. I must have received many gifts that night, but all

I recall is opening a large white box from Uncle Dave and finding in it a blue-gray baseball uniform with the word "Reds" spelled out in crimson felt across the shirt front. I walked toward Uncle Dave with the shirt in one hand and a blue-and-white striped stocking dangling from the other, but when I tried to thank him, my voice quavered, and all the adults laughed.

On the Sunday evening between Christmas and New Year's, Uncle Dave and my father sat in the living room after dinner, smoking their pipes and talking, while I lay on the floor next to the sofa and read the comic sheet from the morning paper. I paid no attention to their conversation until I heard my father say, "What did you think of the World Series?"

"Not much," Uncle Dave said. I looked up with interest.

Father laughed. "We thought the Reds did pretty well," he said. "They weren't exactly the favorites, you know."

"They *should* have done pretty well," Uncle Dave said. "They had a lot more than nine men playing for them."

Father looked puzzled. "What are you talking about, Dave?" he asked.

"I mean the Series was fixed," Uncle Dave said. "The White Sox threw those games."

I looked at the two men to see if they were enjoying some joke I didn't understand, but neither of them was smiling. Father was staring blankly at my uncle. For a while neither of them spoke. "You're kidding," my father said, at last.

"Kidding, hell!" Uncle Dave said. "Shoeless Joe Jackson, Cicotte— damn near the whole Chicago team was *trying* to lose that Series."

A cold, wet band seemed to wrap itself around my chest, chilling my body and making breathing difficult.

"My God!" Father said softly.

"Every gambler in Chicago knew that the Series was in the bag for Cincinnati," Uncle Dave said. His voice sounded tired. "Why do you think the odds on the Reds went to hell before the first game? The Sox seemed a cinch to win, but there wasn't a dime's worth of smart money on them." I didn't understand much of what he said from then on, but I knew it was all bad.

"Of course," Father said. "Of course. It had to be something like that. It's the only explanation that makes sense."

"The Reds didn't win the Series," Uncle Dave said. "The Sox gave it to them."

I found myself suddenly on my feet. "That's a lie!" I shouted. "That's a dirty lie!"

The two men looked at me in astonishment. They had probably forgotten I was in the room. "Jim!" my father said to me sternly.

"You're just mad because Chicago lost!" I said. "You're a dirty loser! A dirty loser!"

"Jim, stop that!" my father said, getting up from his chair.

"Dirty loser!" I cried once more, and then I turned, ran upstairs to my room, and slammed the door. I stood there in the dark for what seemed a long time, with my face and body pressed against the wall, my hands and arms rigid at my sides, trying to control my trembling. My eyes were tightly closed, and I remember that the plaster was cool against my forehead. My stomach tightened and I fought against being sick. My breath came out with a harsh, rasping sound, but I didn't, or couldn't cry.

Finally, the door opened and Uncle Dave came quietly into the room. He didn't turn on the light, but the lamp in the hall lightened the darkness somewhat. Uncle Dave stood directly behind me. "I'm sorry, Jim," he said gently. "I know how you feel." He didn't touch me, but I pushed myself harder against the wall. "I know how you feel," he repeated sadly, and then he left, closing the door behind him.

It was in the fall of 1920, almost a year later, that the newspapers began to print the story of what came to be known as the Black Sox Scandal. Uncle Dave's correspondence with my family usually consisted of infrequent brief notes, but in November of that year—just a few weeks after the Chicago players had admitted before a grand jury that bribes had been accepted—I received a long, carefully documented letter that, I realize now, must have taken him hours of research to prepare. He had gone through the complete records of the 1919 World Series. By making his own deductions from figures I didn't wholly understand, he contrived to demonstrate to me that, as far as statistics went, nobody could say the White Sox hadn't tried their best to win, despite having been paid by the gamblers to lose. He pointed out, among other things, that Joe Jackson had tied the batting record for a World Series with twelve hits and had averaged .375, and that Chicago had made no more fielding errors than Cincinnati had. "The Reds would have won anyway," he concluded. "Remember that. The Reds would have won anyway."

My Uncle Dave was an able man with percentages, and I have never seen any reason to question his interpretation of those he sent me. As a result, I suppose I am one of the few baseball fans in the country who are still convinced that the Reds were the real champions in 1919.

The hardnosed writer Nelson Algren (1909–1981) was the son of a Chicago machinist who couldn't hold a job because of his habit of hitting foremen. Algren wrote about dilapidated outcasts, winos, horseplayers, junkies, glass-jawed fighters, and women with skirts too short and heels too high. In 1950, he won the first National Book Award for *The Man with the Golden Arm,* a novel about a heroin addict. A year later he published a classic portrait of his hustler-hometown, *Chicago: City on the Make,* from which this excerpt is taken. Writing in *The New York Times,* Budd Schulberg called Algren's Chicago "a kind of American annex to Dante's inferno." Among his other books are the novel *A Walk on the Wild Side* (1956) and the story collection *The Neon Wilderness* (1947).

Nelson Algren

ᘐ

from

Chicago: City on the Make

The Silver-Colored Yesterday

All that long-ago August day the sun lay like shellac on the streets, but toward evening a weary small breeze wandered out of some saloon or other, toured Cottage Grove idly awhile, then turned, aimlessly as ever, west down Seventy-first.

The year was 1919, Shoeless Joe Jackson was out-hitting Ty Cobb, God was in his Heaven, Carl Wanderer was still a war hero, John Dillinger was an Indiana farm boy and the cops were looking cautiously, in all the wrong corners, for Terrible Tommy O'Connor.

And every Saturday evening the kid called Nephew and I hauled a little red wagon load of something called the *Saturday Evening Blade,* a rag if there ever was one, down Cottage Grove to the wrought-iron Oakwoods Cemetery gate. There to hawk it past the long-moldering graves of Confederate prisoners who had died at Camp Douglas in some long-ago wrought-iron war.

When we sold out we'd just hang around the gate waiting for

Nephew's Uncle Johnson to break out of the saloon directly across the way. The bartender ran us off if we came near the doors without the iron-clad alibi of having a fight to watch, and Uncle J. was the white hope of that corner.

If no brawl developed of itself the barflies were certain to arrange something for poor Johnson, an oversized spastic with a puss like a forsaken moose, whose sole idea in battle was to keep his hands in front of his eyes. Some white hope.

Uncle's whole trouble, Nephew confided in me as half owner of the little red wagon, was that he had gone to work too young.

Some uncle. We used to hear him hymning at the bar—

> Oh he walks wit' me
> 'N he talks wit' me—

and the barflies encouraging him mockingly.

He was deeply religious, and the barflies encouraged him in every-thing—drinking, hymning or fighting, fornication or prayer. As though there were something wondrously comical about everything Uncle attempted.

I remember that poor hatless holy Johnson yet, lurching upon some unsaved little tough with a face shadowed by a cap and a lit cig-arette on his lip—the cigarette bobbles and Uncle reels back, blood from his nose coming into his mouth. The Cap yanks him forward, feints his hands down off his eyes and raps him a smashing banneger in the teeth. "It's a case of a good little man whipppin' a good big man, that's all," Nephew advised me confidentially, holding our little red wagon behind him. Then the soft shuffle-shuffle of The Cap's shoes imitating the White City professionals.

"Finish the clown off," Nephew encourages The Cap softly. That's the kind of family it was.

Uncle had never learned to fall down. He'd reel, lurch, bleed, bel-low and bawl until the bartender would break the thing up at last, wiping Uncle's ashen face with a bar towel in the arc-lamp's ashen light. Till the others came crowding with congratulations right out of the bottle, pouring both into Uncle right there on the street. Then a spot of color would touch his cheeks and he'd break out into that ter-rible lament—

'N he tells me I am his own.

to show us all he'd won again. Uncle had some such spiritual triumph every Saturday night.

I used to hang open-mouthed around that sort of thing, coming away at last feeling nothing save some sort of city-wide sorrow. Like something had finally gone terribly wrong between the cross atop St. Columbanus and that wrought-iron gate, out of an old wrought-iron war, forever guarding the doubly-dead behind us.

No one could tell me just what.

The wisest thing to do was simply to go beer-cork hunting behind the saloon. With the city spreading all about. Like some great diseased toadstool under a sheltering, widespread sky. Then to haul our little red wagon slowly home, with Nephew humming all to himself, "Be my little bay-bee bum-bul bee, buzz buzz buzz."

Maybe the whole town went to work too young.

For it's still a Godforsaken spastic, a cerebral-palsy natural among cities, clutching at the unbalanced air: topheavy, bleeding and blind. Under a toadstool-colored sky.

Maybe we all went to work too young.

Yet that was a time of several treasures: one sun-bright-yellow beer cork with a blood-red owl engraved upon it, a Louisville slugger bat autographed by Swede Risberg, and a Comiskey Park program from one hot and magic Sunday afternoon when Nephew and I hid under the cool bleachers for three hours before game time. To come out blinking at last into the roaring stands, with the striped sun on them. And Eddie Cicotte shutting out Carl Mays.

The morning we moved from the far Southside to North Troy Street I had all three treasures on me. And Troy Street led, like all Northside streets—and alleys too—directly to the alien bleachers of Wrigley Field.

"Who's yer fayvrut player?" the sprouts in baseball caps waiting in front of the house had to know before I could pass. I put the horn of the Edison victrola I was carrying down on the sidewalk at my feet before replying. It didn't sound like something asked lightly.

But the suddenly far-distant White Sox had had a competent sort of athlete at short and I considered myself something of a prospect in that position too. "Swede Risberg," I answered confidently, leaning on the Louisville slugger with the autograph turned too casually toward the local loyalty board.

I didn't look like such a hot prospect to North Troy Street, I could tell that much right there and then. "It got to be a National Leaguer," the chairman advised me quietly. So that's how the wind was blowing.

I spent three days leaning on that autograph, watching the other sprouts play ball. They didn't even use American League bats. "Charley Hollocher then," I finally capitulated, naming the finest fielding shortstop in the National League, "account I t'row righty too."

"Hollocher belongs to Knifey," I was informed—but I could fight Knifey for him, I had the right.

I wouldn't have fought Knifey's baby sister for Grover Cleveland Alexander and Bill Killefer thrown in. And could only think nostalgically of the good simple life of the far Southside, where kids had names like "Nephew" and "Cousin," and where a man's place among men could be established by the number of *Saturday Evening Blades* he sold. I went through the entire roster of National League shortstops before finding one unclaimed by anyone else on Troy Street—Ivan Olson, an ex-American Leaguer coming to the end of his career with the team then known as the Brooklyn Robins.

But Olson was taking a lot of booing from the Flatbush crowd that season because he had a habit of protesting a called third strike by throwing his bat in the air—and every time he did it an umpire would pick it up and toss it higher. No eleven-year-old wants to be on the side of any player who isn't a hero to the stands. "If I *got* to pick a Swede"—I stood up to The Committee at last—"I'll stick to Risberg—I seen him play once is why."

Well, you could say your old man was a millionaire if that was your mood and nobody would bother to make you take it back. You might even hint that you knew more about girls than you were telling and still get by. But there wasn't one of those Troy Street wonders who'd yet seen his "fayvrut player" actually play. You had to back that sort of statement up. I pulled out the Comiskey Park program hurriedly.

They handed it around in a circle, hand to grubby hand, examining the penciled score for fraud. When it came back to my own hand I was in.

In without selling out: I'd kept the faith with The Swede.

The reason I never got to play anything but right field the rest of that summer I attribute to National League politics pure and simple.

Right field was a coal-shed roof with an American League sun suspended directly overhead. A height from which I regarded with quiet scorn the worshipers of false gods hitting scratchy little National League bloopers far below. There wasn't one honest-to-God American League line drive all summer.

It wasn't till a single sunless morning of early Indian summer that all my own gods proved me false: Risberg, Cicotte, Jackson, Weaver, Felsch, Gandil, Lefty Williams and a utility infielder whose name escapes me—wasn't it McMillen? The Black Sox were the Reds of that October and mine was the guilt of association.

And the charge was conspiracy.

Benedict Arnolds! Betrayers of American Boyhood, not to mention American Girlhood and American Womanhood and American Hoodhood. Every bleacher has-been, newspaper mediocrity and pulpit inanity seized the chance to regain his lost pride at the expense of seven of the finest athletes who ever hit into a double play. And now stood stripped to the bleacher winds in the very sight of Comiskey and God.

I was the eighth. I climbed down from right field to find The Committee waiting.

"Let's see that score card again."

I brought it forth, yellow now with a summer of sun and honest sweat, but still legible. When it came back this time I was only allowed to touch one corner, where a grubby finger indicated the date in July of 1920. Risberg had sold out in the preceding September and I was coming around Troy Street almost a year later pretending I believed Risberg to be an honest man. I'd gone out to the ball park, seen him play in person and was now insisting I'd seen nothing wrong, nothing wrong at all. The moving finger stopped on Risberg's sorrowful name: four times at bat without a hit, caught sleeping off second, and a wild peg to first. And I still pretended I hadn't suspected a *thing*?

"I wasn't there when he *really* thrun the game," I tried to hedge. "It was a different day when he played bum on purpose."

The Tobey of *that* committee was a sprout who had a paying thing going, for weekdays, in the resale of colored paper-picture strips of major-league players. He bought them ten for a penny and resold them to us for two, making himself as high as a dollar a week, of which fifty cents went to his Sunday-school collection plate. I'd once seen his lips moving at the plate, praying for a hit. "What do *you* think he was doin' tossin' wild to first?" this one wanted to know now.

"I figure he was excited, it was a real close play."

"You mean for your all-time All-American fayvrut player you pick a guy who gets excited on the close ones?"

"I didn't know it was for all time," was all I could think to reply. "I thought it was just for this year."

"What kind of American *are* you anyhow?" he wanted to know. He had me. I didn't know what kind I was.

"No wonder you're always in right field where nothin' ever comes—nobody could trust you in center." He was really cutting me up, this crusader.

"Well, I asked for Hollocher in the first place," I recalled.

"You could still fight Knifey for him."

"I'll just take Ivan Olson."

"That's not the question."

"What *is* the question?"

"The question is who was the guy, he knock down two perfec' pegs to the plate in a world-series game, one wit' the hand 'n one wit' the glove?"

"Cicotte done *that*."

"'N who was Cicotte's roommate?"

Too late I saw where the trap lay: Risberg. I was dead.

"We all make mistakes, fellas," I broke at last. "We all goof off, we're all human—it's what *I* done, I goofed off too—it just goes to show you guys I'm human too. I ain't mad at you guys, you're all good guys, don't be made at *me*." Choked with guilt and penitence, crawling on all fours like a Hollywood matinee idol, I pleaded to be allowed, with all my grievous faults, to go along with the gang. "Can I still have Olson, fellas? Can I keep my job if I bum-rap some people for you?"

Out of the welter of accusations, half denials and sudden silences a single fact drifted down: that Shoeless Joe Jackson couldn't play bad baseball even if he were trying to. He hit .875 that series and played errorless ball, doing everything a major-leaguer could to win. Nearing sixty today, he could probably still outhit anything now wearing a National League uniform.

Only, I hadn't picked Shoeless Joe. I'd picked the man who, with Eddie Cicotte, bore the heaviest burden of all our dirty Southside guilt. The Black Sox had played scapegoat for Rothstein and I'd played the goat for The Swede.

So wound up that melancholy season grateful to own the fast-fading Olson. When he went back to Rochester or somewhere they started calling me "Olson" too. Meaning I ought to go back to Rochester too. I took that. But when they began calling me "Svenska" that was too much. I fought.

And got the prettiest trimming you'd ever care to see. Senator Tobey himself administered it, to ringing applause, his Sunday-school change jingling righteously with his footwork. Leaving me at last with two chipped teeth, an orchid-colored shiner and no heart left, even for right field, for days.

However do senators get so close to God? How is it that front-office men never conspire? That matinee idols feel such guilt? Or that winners never pitch in a bill toward the price of their victory?

I traded off the Risberg bat, so languid had I become, for a softball model autographed only by Klee Brothers, who were giving such bats away with every suit of boy's clothing bought on the second floor. And flipped the program from that hot and magic Sunday when Cicotte was shutting out everybody forever, and a triumphant right-hander's wind had blown all the score cards across home plate, into the Troy Street gutter.

I guess that was one way of learning what Hustlertown, sooner or later, teaches all its sandlot sprouts. "Everybody's out for The Buck. Even big-leaguers."

Even Swede Risberg.

•••

James Joseph Victor Cannon (1910–1973) grew up in a cold-water apartment
in the "unfreaky part of Greenwich Village," and went uptown as a teenager
to make his name as a big-city reporter. There he became the literary ward of
Damon Runyon, who told him, "The best way to be a bum and make a living
is to be a sportswriter." Cannon loved fighters and ballplayers—especially the
Joes, Louis and DiMaggio—and he liked the city's sporting-life set, but mostly
he kept company with his typewriter. His passionate, colorful, frequently re-
sentful, occasionally mawkish newspaper dispatches made him the most admired, most imitated man-on-the-street voice of his time. When he submitted
a typical line like "baseball is music played on an adding machine," it is easy
to see why. His observations about spring training are taken from *Who Struck
John?* (1956), a collection of some of his best columns from the *New York Post*.

Jimmy Cannon

♢

Nice Work

G oing South with the ball clubs is the most pleasant assignment
of a sportswriter's year. It is a good trip even when the wind
blows and the gulf turns turbulent and the afternoon skies writhe
with touselled clouds. It is that place on the pier at Clearwater where
they serve the boiled shrimps in wire baskets. It means sitting on the
green wooden bench against the wall of the Floridan Hotel in Tampa
listening to the baseball scouts argue with their guarded opinions as
they try to frisk one another's minds.

There were nights in St. Pete when the Cardinals had a jug band
and they played concerts on the porch of their hotel with the old
people standing on the sidewalk. It is being touched by the elderly
couples who sit with such serenity at the horse-pitching joint and
betting on the dogs at night with Yogi Berra handicapping for me.
There was one year when all the waitresses at the Fort Harrison Hotel
in Clearwater were beauties and had degrees from either Smith or
Vassar.

It is the fishermen on the causeways who seem contented in their
loneliness, standing there all day, their lines slack and bait unnibbled.

There was a saloon, across the way from the Fort Harrison, when the Dodgers trained there, where a juke box had the hiccups but couldn't hurt the record Ray Noble made of George and Ira Gershwin's "London Town." It was a new song then.

The broken guys, sallow and crabbed, used to stand in front of the Dempsey-Vanderbilt Hotel in Miami. Solvent people walked around the block to duck the bites. We went to a night club on an island across a canal from the beach. It was run by Bill Dwyer, the old bootlegger.

It was a big joint and recently decorated with famous acts in the floor show. It had opened only a few days before but we were the only party in the place. The night before they had backed up the wagon and taken out the gambling equipment and told them the okay was off.

"The same guy that took my money," Dwyer said, "come back and closed me up three nights later. I can't figure those Americans down here."

The joint didn't last a week.

After the war the Colonial Inn was dealing across the county line. It was dangerous to dance because the women wore diamond bracelets and going around the floor was like trying to walk through a series of barbed wire fences. You were lucky if you weren't cut by the jewelry. It was '46 and women wore their diamonds and mink coats over their bathing suits and sweltered in the sun.

The black market thieves gambled big but they didn't know the price of the points on the dice. They let their money ride even when they won. They didn't pick up unless the dealers told them to. Winning seemed to be a disgrace.

It was a year when it was proof of social prestige to be able to announce the hotel where you stopped was run by a burglar. No one talked about the comfort of his accommodations. The price was all he discussed. It seems too long ago. It was only '46.

It is seeing Charlie Keller in his first exhibition game with Newark and knowing he couldn't fail. It is Bob Feller showing you the slider he had learned in the Navy. It is Joe McCarthy grumpily wondering why ball players bothered with golf. It is the jockeys talking about the races in the tack room at Hialeah and sounding like a flock of mice.

It is the horse rooms in Palm Beach which were like bus terminals and all the credentials you needed to gamble was money. It is the Calumet II, a fishing boat, that Joe DiMaggio chartered. It was a stormy February and we only got out in it for a couple of days. It was so cold we slept in our overcoats most of the time. It is dinner in the Cuban restaurant of Tampa.

It is Lefty Gomez who knew his fast ball was gone and the way he concealed his apprehension and turned it into a gag. It is all the kids coming up and the older guys fading and knowing it and what the hell. You do or you don't and why dramatize it? It's the same in all the other businesses, too. It is seeing Ted Williams for the first time and realizing this was a hitter of genuine greatness.

It is riding around in the station wagon of Gabe Paul and making the circuit with Pat Patterson and Ted McGrew, the scouts, and watching Bill Stewart, the umpire, demonstrating the balk motion with a belligerent pride. It is Jocko Conlon singing Irish ballads and the kids at Vero Beach, where the Dodgers are, away from home for the first time and frightened by the possibility of failure. It is Stone Crab Joe's in Miami and the restaurant in St. Pete where the organ plays love songs very softly.

It is a fly ball rising into a flock of pelicans and a sail boat leaning with the wind and the creak of rockers on the verandas and the jazz of the big night clubs. It is a promise that, before long, on the grass of big cities, there will soon be baseball. And never on rainy days.

Tallulah Bankhead (1903–1968) grew up in a minor-league town, Huntsville, Alabama, but it was in London, New York, and Hollywood that this daughter of a prominent politician became such a famous actress that when anyone heard a raspy, seductive "Hello, dahling," they knew just which leopardskin-clad glamour-puss was in the room. Dazzling on stage in plays like *The Little Foxes* and *The Skin of Our Teeth,* she was almost as charismatic in the drawing room. Her quick-witted autobiography nicely captured her dynamic and sometimes overbearing personality.

Tallulah Bankhead

▽

from

Tallulah

Though I remain serene when confronted with royalty, I get downright hysterical when looking at a champion in action. About to fly to England to start my radio season in "The Big Show" in the fall of '51, my enthusiasm was chilled because I would miss the "Sugar Ray" Robinson–Randy Turpin fight, would be out of touch with the Giants, panting, when I left, on the heels of the Dodgers.

Attending a Giant game with me, say my cronies, is an experience comparable to shooting the Snake River rapids in a canoe. When they lose I taste wormwood. When they win I want to do a tarantella on top of the dugout. A Giant rally brings out the roman candle in me. The garments of adjoining box-holders start to smolder.

I once lured the young Viennese actor, Helmut Dantine, to a set-to between the Giants and the Pirates. Mr. Dantine had never seen a game before. My airy explanations confused the *émigré.* Rapt in his attention to my free translation of the sacrifice hit, Helmut was almost decapitated by a foul ball. Mr. Dantine looked upon the *faux pas* as a hostile act. He felt I had tricked him into a false sense of security that the hitter might have an unsuspecting target. He left before the ninth, a grayer if not a wiser man.

It's true I run a temperature when watching the Giants trying to come from behind in the late innings, either at the Polo Grounds or on my TV screen. I was hysterical for hours after Bobby Thomson belted Ralph Branca for that ninth inning homer in the final game of the Dodger-Giant playoff in '51. The Giants had to score four runs in the ninth to win. Remember? There was blood on the moon that night in Bedford Village. But I don't know nearly as much about base-ball as Ethel Barrymore. Ethel is a real fan, can give you batting aver-ages, the text of the infield fly rule and comment on an umpire's vision.

Someone has said that Ethel Barrymore has the reticence born of assurance whereas my monologues indicate my insecurity. The point is moot. It's unlikely I'll ever submit to a psychiatrist's couch. I don't want some stranger prowling around through my psyche, monkeying with my id. I don't need an analyst to tell me that I have never had any sense of security. Who has?

My devotion to the Giants, dating back to 1939, has drawn the fire of renegades, eager to deflate me. One of these wrote that on my first visit to Ebbets Field in Brooklyn I rooted all afternoon for Dolph Camilli, the Dodger first baseman. I had been tricked into this trea-son, swore my enemy, because I wasn't aware that the Giants wore gray uniforms when traveling, the residents white. Though I invaded Flatbush to cheer Mel Ott, Giant right fielder, I wound up in hysterics over Camilli, because both had the numeral "4" on the back of their uniform. Stuff, balderdash and rot, not to use a few other words too hot to handle in a memoir.

A daughter of the deep South, I have little time for the "Yankees." They're bleak perfectionists, insolent in their confidence, the snobs of the diamond. The Yankees are all technique, no color or juice. But they keep on winning pennants year after year. Not the Giants! They've won one flag in the last fourteen years.

I blew my first fuse over the Giants in the summer of '39, when in-troduced to Harry Danning and Mel Ott. Ott was so good-looking, so shy, so gentlemanly—and from Louisiana. For two weeks I got up in the middle of the night—around noon by the actor's clock—to charge up to the Polo Grounds.

I worked myself up into such a fever that I invited the team to see a performance of *The Little Foxes*. After the play I served them a buffet supper, and drinks compatible with their training rules, on the

promenade which fringed the rear of the balcony. The Giants, following this soiree, dropped eight games in a row. Had I hexed them? The
suspicion chilled me. I denied myself the Polo Grounds and they
started to win again.

I have proved a hoodoo to more than one champion. I first got in-
flamed over sports in London. The tennis championships were being
held at Wimbledon and Bill Tilden dropped into my house in Farm
Street. Most Americans dropped in there, after visiting Madame
Tussaud's Waxworks and the Tower, in line of duty. Tilden was temperamental, brilliant. He dramatized every lob, every serve. I was
seething in the grandstand when he played the singles' final with
Henri Cochet. To insure Bill's victory, I gave him a four-leaf clover to
carry in his shirt pocket. Cochet was dull and methodical, completely
lacking in color. Tilden won the first two sets, was at point, set, match
in the third set when Cochet broke his service and went on to take
the set and the next two as well.

I also carried an emotional banner for Joe Louis. When he fought
Max Schmeling, the scowling Nazi, the first time, I sent him Daddy's
bull's-eye, a charm of spectacular potency. I urged Joe to carry it in his
robe the night of the battle. He did carry it, and was knocked stiff in
the twelfth round.

When Joe and Schmeling met the second time I was there with
my husband, John Emery, carrying a rug, a pair of field glasses, and a
flask—just in case of snake bite. When Joe knocked the Uhlan cold
in the first round, I leaped to my feet before seventy thousand people and screamed: "I told you so, you sons-of-bitches." I was addressing four bundsmen sitting directly behind us. An hour and three
drinks later, Edie Smith, my secretary, phoned me at "21": "Oh, *Die
Donner,* all that money you spent and it only lasted two minutes."
"Edie," I said, "had it lasted a minute longer I would have died in the
Stadium."

Looking back on my fiascos with wishbones and four-leaf clovers
reminds me that I once put the whammy on Daddy. I went to a
ball game between a team of Congressmen and the Washington
firemen's nine, played in behalf of charity. Daddy had been a great
athlete at the University of Alabama. I was sure that he would distinguish himself. To my horror he fanned three times. I was crushed
for days.

My heroes are not necessarily headliners. I swooned over Burgess Whitehead, Giant second baseman, because he moved like a ballet dancer. He was a Phi Beta Kappa, a brilliant fielder, but he couldn't hit his way out of a paper bag. Then there was Lou Chiozza. One of his traducers said that he weighed 170 and hit the same figure. Pursuing an outfield fly Lou collided so violently with Jo-Jo Moore that he broke his ankle. When he was carted off to the hospital, I banked his bed with flowers. Two visiting teammates were paralyzed with fright, on walking into his dimly lit room. They found their white-clad comrade asleep in a profusion of lilies and came to the conclusion he was dead. Why was I fascinated with Chiozza? He was born in Tallulah, Louisiana.

Brooklyn-born Bernard Malamud (1914–1986) was teaching English composition classes at Oregon State University in 1952 when he published *The Natural,* a novel about the doomed slugger Roy Hobbs. Hobbs may have been inspired by Phillies first baseman Eddie Waitkus, who was shot by a female admirer in his Chicago hotel room in 1949 (another camp claims Chicago Cubs shortstop Billy Jurges, who was shot in the ribs by a dancer named Violet Valli in 1932, as the character's model). To some degree, Malamud's first novel can be read as an allegory for the end of the American dream. A lean book, it overflows with classical allusion; "I threw *everything* in," Malamud once said. By creating a character who is part Ulysses, part Babe Ruth, and part Shoeless Joe Jackson, *The Natural* broke new ground in baseball fiction. In this early scene, the young Roy Hobbs is on a train bound from the West Coast to Chicago, where he will try out for the Cubs. As Eddie, the railroad porter, notices, Roy's luggage consists of a bassoon case. Roy's traveling companion is an alcoholic former big-league catcher and former big-league scout named Sam Simpson. By delivering Roy to the Cubs, Sam hopes to find professional redemption—and to get his scouting job back. Also on the train is the holdout major-league slugger Walter "the Whammer" Wambold, Max Mercy, a nationally syndicated sportswriter, and Harriet Bird, a strange woman "with heartbreaking legs" who seems much taken with the Whammer. Roy has noticed her too and is "marvelously interested." The day's newspaper headlines tell the lurid story of an unknown woman who has killed two young West Coast athletes in the past twenty-four hours by shooting them with silver bullets.

Bernard Malamud

◊

from

The Natural

Toward late afternoon the Whammer, droning on about his deeds on the playing field, got very chummy with Harriet Bird and before long had slipped his fat fingers around the back of her chair so Roy left the club car and sat in the sleeper, looking out of the window, across the aisle from where Eddie slept sitting up. Gosh, the size of the forest. He thought they had left it for good yesterday and here it still was. As he watched, the trees flowed together and so did the hills and clouds. He felt a kind of sadness, because he had lost the feeling of a particular place. Yesterday he had come from somewhere, a place he knew was there, but today it had thinned away in space—how vast he could not have guessed—and he felt like he would never see it again.

The forest stayed with them, climbing hills like an army, shooting down like waterfalls. As the train skirted close in, the trees leveled out and he could see within the woodland the only place he had been truly intimate with in his wanderings, a green world shot through with weird light and strange bird cries, muffled in silence that made the privacy so complete his inmost self had no shame of anything he thought there, and it eased the body-shaking beat of his ambitions. Then he thought of here and now and for the thousandth time wondered why they had come so far and for what. Did Sam really know what he was doing? Sometimes Roy had his doubts. Sometimes he wanted to turn around and go back home, where he could at least predict what tomorrow would be like. Remembering the white rose in his pants pocket, he decided to get rid of it. But then the pine trees flowed away from the train and slowly swerved behind blue hills; all at once there was this beaten gold, snow-capped mountain in the distance, and on the plain several miles from its base lay a small city gleaming in the rays of the declining sun. Approaching it, the long train slowly pulled to a stop.

Eddie woke with a jump and stared out the window.

"Oh oh, trouble, we never stop here."

He looked again and called Roy.

"What do you make out of that?"

About a hundred yards ahead, where two dirt roads crossed, a moth-eaten model-T Ford was parked on the farther side of the road from town, and a fat old man wearing a broadbrimmed black hat and cowboy boots, who they could see was carrying a squat doctor's satchel, climbed down from it. To the conductor, who had impatiently swung off the train with a lit red lamp, he flourished a yellow telegram. They argued a minute, then the conductor, snapping open his watch, beckoned him along and they boarded the train. When they passed through Eddie's car the conductor's face was sizzling with irritation but the doctor was unruffled. Before disappearing through the door, the conductor called to Eddie, "Half hour."

"Half hour," Eddie yodeled and he got out the stool and set it outside the car so that anyone who wanted to stretch, could.

Only about a dozen passengers got off the train, including Harriet Bird, still hanging on to her precious hat box, the Whammer, and Max Mercy, all as thick as thieves. Roy hunted up the bassoon case just if the train should decide to take off without him, and when he had located Sam they both got off.

"Well, I'll be jiggered." Sam pointed down about a block beyond where the locomotive had halted. There, sprawled out at the outskirts of the city, a carnival was on. It was made up of try-your-skill booths, kiddie rides, a freak show and a gigantic Ferris wheel that looked like a stopped clock. Though there was still plenty of daylight, the carnival was lit up by twisted ropes of blinking bulbs, and many banners streamed in the breeze as the calliope played.

"Come on," said Roy, and they went along with the people from the train who were going toward the tents.

Once they had got there and fooled around a while, Sam stopped to have a crushed cocoanut drink which he privately spiked with a shot from a new bottle, while Roy wandered over to a place where you could throw three baseballs for a dime at three wooden pins, shaped like pint-size milk bottles and set in pyramids of one on top of two, on small raised platforms about twenty feet back from the counter. He changed the fifty-cent piece Sam had slipped him on leaving the train, and this pretty girl in yellow, a little hefty but with a sweet face and nice ways, who with her peanut of a father was waiting on trade, handed him three balls. Lobbing one of them, Roy easily knocked off the pyramid and won himself a naked kewpie doll. Enjoying the game, he laid down another dime, again clattering the pins to the floor in a single shot and now collecting an alarm clock. With the other three dimes he won a brand-new boxed baseball, a washboard, and baby potty, which he traded in for a six-inch harmonica. A few kids came over to watch and Sam, wandering by, indulgently changed another half into dimes for Roy. And Roy won a fine leather cigar case for Sam, a "God Bless America" banner, a flashlight, can of coffee, and a two-pound box of sweets. To the kids' delight, Sam, after a slight hesitation, flipped Roy another half dollar, but this time the little man behind the counter nudged his daughter and she asked Roy if he would now take a kiss for every three pins he tumbled.

Roy glanced at her breasts and she blushed. He got embarrassed too. "What do you say, Sam, it's your four bits?"

Sam bowed low to the girl. "Ma'am," he said, "now you see how dang foolish it is to be a young feller."

The girl laughed and Roy began to throw for kisses, flushing each pyramid in a shot or two while the girl counted aloud the kisses she owed him.

Some of the people from the train passed by and stayed to watch when they learned from the mocking kids what Roy was throwing for.

The girl, pretending to be unconcerned, tolled off the third and fourth kisses.

As Roy fingered the ball for the last throw the Whammer came by holding over his shoulder a Louisville Slugger that he had won for himself in the batting cage down a way. Harriet, her pretty face flushed, had a kewpie doll, and Max Mercy carried a box of cigars. The Whammer had discarded his sun glasses and all but strutted over his performance and the prizes he had won.

Roy raised his arm to throw for the fifth kiss and a clean sweep when the Whammer called out to him in a loud voice, "Pitch it here, busher, and I will knock it into the moon."

Roy shot for the last kiss and missed. He missed with the second and third balls. The crowd oohed its disappointment.

"Only four," said the girl in yellow as if she mourned the fifth.

Angered at what had happened, Sam hoarsely piped, "I got ten dollars that says he can strike you out with three pitched balls, Wambold."

The Whammer looked at Sam with contempt.

"What d'ye say, Max?" he said.

Mercy shrugged.

"Oh, I love contests of skill," Harriet said excitedly. Roy's face went pale.

"What's the matter, hayfoot, you scared?" the Whammer taunted.

"Not of you," Roy said.

"Let's go across the tracks where nobody'll get hurt," Mercy suggested.

"Nobody but the busher and his bazooka. What's in it, busher?"

"None of your business." Roy picked up the bassoon case.

The crowd moved in a body across the tracks, the kids circling around to get a good view, and the engineer and fireman watching from their cab window.

Sam cornered one of the kids who lived nearby and sent him home for a fielder's glove and his friend's catcher's mitt. While they were waiting, for protection he buttoned underneath his coat the washboard Roy had won. Max drew a batter's box alongside a piece of slate. He said he would call the throws and they would count as one of the three pitches only if they were over or if the Whammer swung and missed.

When the boy returned with the gloves, the sun was going down, and though the sky was aflame with light all the way to the snowy mountain peak, it was chilly on the ground.

Breaking the seal, Sam squeezed the baseball box and the pill shot up like a greased egg. He tossed it to Mercy, who inspected the hide and stitches, then rubbed the shine off and flipped it to Roy.

"Better throw a couple of warm-ups."

"My arm is loose," said Roy.

"It's your funeral."

Placing his bassoon case out of the way in the grass, Roy shed his coat. One of the boys came forth to hold it.

"Be careful you don't spill the pockets," Roy told him.

Sam came forward with the catcher's glove on. It was too small for his big hand but he said it would do all right.

"Sam, I wish you hadn't bet that money on me," Roy said.

"I won't take it if we win, kiddo, but just let it stand if we lose," Sam said, embarrassed.

"We came by it too hard."

"Just let it stand so."

He cautioned Roy to keep his pitches inside, for the Whammer was known to gobble them on the outside corner.

Sam returned to the plate and crouched behind the batter, his knees spread wide because of the washboard. Roy drew on his glove and palmed the ball behind it. Mercy, rubbing his hands to warm them, edged back about six feet behind Sam.

The onlookers retreated to the other side of the tracks, except Harriet, who stood without fear of fouls up close. Her eyes shone at the sight of the two men facing one another.

Mercy called, "Batter up."

The Whammer crowded the left side of the plate, gripping the heavy bat low on the neck, his hands jammed together and legs plunked evenly apart. He hadn't bothered to take off his coat. His eye on Roy said it spied a left-handed monkey.

"Throw it, Rube, it won't get no lighter."

Though he stood about sixty feet away, he loomed up gigantic to Roy, with the wood held like a caveman's ax on his shoulder. His rocklike frame was motionless, his face impassive, unsmiling, dark.

Roy's heart skipped a beat. He turned to gaze at the mountain.

Sam whacked the leather with his fist. "Come on, kiddo, wham it down his whammy."

The Whammer out of the corner of his mouth told the drunk to keep his mouth shut.

"Burn it across his button."

"Close your trap," Mercy said.

"Cut his throat with it."

"If he tries to dust me, so help me I will smash his skull," the Whammer threatened.

Roy stretched loosely, rocked back on his left leg, twirling the right a little like a dancer, then strode forward and threw with such force his knuckles all but scraped the ground on the follow-through.

At thirty-three the Whammer still enjoyed exceptional eyesight. He saw the ball spin off Roy's fingertips and it reminded him of a white pigeon he had kept as a boy, that he would send into flight by flipping it into the air. The ball flew at him and he was conscious of its bird-form and white flapping wings, until it suddenly disappeared from view. He heard a noise like the bang of a firecracker at his feet and Sam had the ball in his mitt. Unable to believe his ears he heard Mercy intone a reluctant strike.

Sam flung off the glove and was wringing his hand.

"Hurt you, Sam?" Roy called.

"No, it's this dang glove."

Though he did not show it, the pitch had bothered the Whammer no end. Not just the speed of it but the sensation of surprise and strangeness that went with it—him batting here on the railroad tracks, the crazy carnival, the drunk catching and a clown pitching, and that queer dame Harriet, who had five minutes ago been patting him on the back for his skill in the batting cage, now eyeing him coldly for letting one pitch go by.

He noticed Max had moved farther back.

"How the hell you expect to call them out there?"

"He looks wild to me." Max moved in.

"Your knees are knockin'," Sam tittered.

"Mind your business, rednose," Max said.

"You better watch your talk, mister," Roy called to Mercy.

"Pitch it, greenhorn," warned the Whammer.

Sam crouched with his glove on. "Do it again, Roy. Give him something simular."

"Do it again," mimicked the Whammer. To the crowd, maybe to Harriet, he held up a vaunting finger showing there were other pitches to come.

Roy pumped, reared and flung.

The ball appeared to the batter to be a slow spinning planet looming toward the earth. For a long light-year he waited for this globe to whirl into the orbit of his swing so he could bust it to smithereens that would settle with dust and dead leaves into some distant cosmos. At last the unseeing eye, maybe a fortuneteller's lit crystal ball—anyway, a curious combination of circles—drifted within range of his weapon, or so he thought, because he lunged at it ferociously, twisting round like a top. He landed on both knees as the world floated by over his head and hit with a *whup* into the cave of Sam's glove.

"Hey, Max," Sam said, as he chased the ball after it had bounced out of the glove, "how do they pernounce Whammer if you leave out the W?"

"Strike," Mercy called long after a cheer (was it a jeer?) had burst from the crowd.

"What's he throwing," the Whammer howled, "spitters?"

"In the pig's poop." Sam thrust the ball at him. "It's drier than your granddaddy's scalp."

"I'm warning him not to try any dirty business."

Yet the Whammer felt oddly relieved. He liked to have his back crowding the wall, when there was a single pitch to worry about and a single pitch to hit. Then the sweat began to leak out of his pores as he stared at the hard, lanky figure of the pitiless pitcher, moving, despite his years and a few waste motions, like a veteran undertaker of the diamond, and he experienced a moment of depression.

Sam must have sensed it, because he discovered an unexpected pity in his heart and even for a split second hoped the idol would not be tumbled. But only for a second, for the Whammer had regained confidence in his known talent and experience and was taunting the greenhorn to throw.

Someone in the crowd hooted and the Whammer raised aloft two fat fingers and pointed where he would murder the ball, where the gleaming rails converged on the horizon and beyond was invisible.

Roy raised his leg. He smelled the Whammer's blood and wanted it, and through him the worm's he had with him, for the way he had insulted Sam.

The third ball slithered at the batter like a meteor, the flame swallowing itself. He lifted his club to crush it into a universe of sparks but the heavy wood dragged, and though he willed to destroy the sound he heard a gong bong and realized with sadness that the ball he had expected to hit had long since been part of the past; and though Max could not cough the fatal word out of his throat, the Whammer understood he was, in the truest sense of it, out.

The crowd was silent as the violet evening fell on their shoulders.

For a night game, the Whammer harshly shouted, it was customary to turn on lights. Dropping the bat, he trotted off to the train, an old man.

The ball had caught Sam smack in the washboard and lifted him off his feet. He lay on the ground, extended on his back. Roy pushed everybody aside to get him air. Unbuttoning Sam's coat, he removed the dented washboard.

"Never meant to hurt you, Sam."

"Just knocked the wind outa me," Sam gasped. "Feel better now." He was pulled to his feet and stood steady.

The train whistle wailed, the echo banging far out against the black mountain.

Then the doctor in the broadbrimmed black hat appeared, flustered and morose, the conductor trying to pacify him, and Eddie hopping along behind.

The doctor waved the crumpled yellow paper around. "Got a telegram says somebody on this train took sick. Anybody out here?"

Roy tugged at Sam's sleeve.

"Ixnay."

"What's that?"

"Not me," said Roy.

The doctor stomped off. He climbed into his Ford, whipped it up and drove away.

The conductor popped open his watch. "Be a good hour late into the city."

"All aboard," he called.

"Aboard," Eddie echoed, carrying the bassoon case.

The buxom girl in yellow broke through the crowd and threw her arms around Roy's neck. He ducked but she hit him quick with her pucker four times upon the right eye, yet he could see with the other that Harriet Bird (certainly a snappy goddess) had her gaze fastened on him.

Walter Wellesley Smith (1905–1982) was born in Green Bay, Wisconsin, attended Notre Dame, and worked his way toward New York (the *Herald Tribune* and later the *Times*) by writing for newspapers in Milwaukee, St. Louis, and Philadelphia. Smith always called himself a "newspaper stiff" writing about "the games little boys play," but wry self-deprecation was just one of the many qualities colleagues admired in America's finest sports columnist. Of course he knew how good he was. One of those colleagues, a young *Sports Illustrated* reporter named Amy Lennard, covered a wall of her office with Red Smith columns. Eventually she summoned the nerve to send Smith a fan letter in which she praised his prose and mentioned her wallpaper pattern. Smith replied: "Dear Ms. Lennard: Thank you. And I think you should do something about the other three walls. Yours—Red Smith."

This account of Carl Erskine's masterful pitching against the Yankees in the 1953 World Series (which the Yankees went on to win, four games to two, setting an all-time record of five consecutive World Series titles) showcases Smith's abilities as a beat reporter. He was also a prolific writer of obituaries; "The Terrible-Tempered Mr. Grove," first published in 1975, was collected in *To Absent Friends* (1982), a gathering of more than one hundred eulogies.

Red Smith

▽

Dodgers Defeat Yanks, 3–2, as Erskine Fans 14

The late lamented stirred fitfully yesterday, twitched, moaned softly and got shakily to their knees, helped up by a plump old gentleman with a busted paw and a young accident case of two days earlier. Yesterday the Dodgers was dead. Today they is weak and gasping for breath, but the breath is still in them.

Two days after he tripped, fell and was mangled by the Yankee juggernaut in one cruel inning, Brooklyn's Carl Erskine pitched a six-hit ball game in which he broke the famous World Series strikeout record established twenty-four years ago. Two days after a pitched ball smashed a knuckle on his right hand and rendered him apparently useless as a batter, ample old Roy Campanella wrapped his aching fist around a bat and slugged a home run that won for Erskine and the Dodgers, 3 to 2.

After one of the most grandly exciting games since rounders became a national religion, the Dodgers still must win three of four games to achieve their first world championship. Trailing the Yankees, two victories to one, they aren't in what you'd call boisterous health, but at least they aren't three games behind.

That they would surely be if it weren't for Erskine, Campanella and Jackie Robinson, aided by a curious balk committed by the Yankees' fine pitcher, Vic Raschi.

It was a brute of a ball game. It was stiff with tension from the first pitch until the last one was batted gently back into Erskine's glove by Joe Collins, with the issue even then undecided. A peddler of pills for the pale and nervous could have found 35,270 buyers in Ebbets Field.

Erskine, of course, is the story. Brooklyn's only twenty-game winner started the first game on Wednesday and was ruined in a four-run first inning. Yesterday he had a no-hitter for four innings, yielded a one-run lead in the fifth which the Dodgers immediately erased, lost a one-run lead in the eighth, and never had another pitch batted out of the infield.

Of all World Series records, possibly the one which has been talked about most often was established on Oct. 8, 1929, when Connie Mack flabbergasted even his own Philadelphia players by starting beat-up old Howard Ehmke, in the first game against the Cubs, whereupon Ehmke struck out thirteen batters.

Yesterday Erskine fanned Joe Collins four times, Mickey Mantle four times, and had twelve strikeouts when Don Bollweg opened the ninth inning as a pinch-hitter. Down went the rookie swinging and the record was tied. Up came John Mize, whose pinch-hits mutilated the Dodgers last year.

Mize took two called strikes, fouled off the third pitch, swung at the fourth and missed. The old record was dead but the Yankees were still alive. Irv Noren, a third pinch-hitter, walked.

Now Collins could tie the record that a Yankee pitcher, George Pipgras, made in 1932 by striking out five times, or he could win the game with a two-run homer. He tapped gently to Erskine who brandished the ball in a triumphant fist and tossed it to Gil Hodges at first base for the last easy play.

It was pretty nearly the only easy play of the afternoon. Among those that will be remembered longest, the most curious occurred in the home fifth after Jackie Robinson doubled with one out. Raschi, conscious of Robinson on base behind him, hesitated in his pitching motion and Robinson called the balk himself, the umpires concurring.

Robinson trotted to third, whence he got home on Billy Cox's squeeze bunt, tying the score. Possibly Cox might have batted him home from second or maybe Erskine, who singled after the squeeze, would have knocked the run in. Maybe not, too.

Now melodrama thickened. With none out and runners on first and second, Campanella tried to bunt in the sixth because it seemed certain he couldn't hit. He popped out to Raschi.

This was the fourth time since he was hurt that Campanella had come up with big runs on the bases, and he hadn't gotten a ball out of the infield. He did not look like a man who would deliver the winning hit.

Before the sixth inning ended, Robinson singled home a run which put Brooklyn ahead, but in the eighth the Yankees made trouble again. Hank Bauer singled with one out and for the second time Erskine hit Yogi Berra with a pitch, bringing applause from fans who boo when a pitch crowds Brooklyn's batters.

Up came Mantle, three times a strikeout victim. He stood still for two strikes. Casey Stengel burst from the dugout, furious. He swung an imaginary bat in a gesture of rage: "Swing, dammit!" Then, leaning against a post at the dugout's mouth, he stood glowering. His posture has already been described:

> "With neck out-thrust, you fancy how,
>   Legs wide, arms locked behind
> As if to balance the prone brow
>   Oppressive with its mind."

Obediently, Mantle swung and missed. The manager turned his back as the young man returned to the dugout regarding his own toes as though he'd never seen them before.

Gene Woodling's single then tied the score again, but that was all except for Campanella—a considerable exception. Incidentally, Robinson and Campanella had led the Dodgers in a special batting practice session at 10 a.m. They have been practicing batting all their lives.

Maybe those few extra minutes were just what they needed.

The Terrible-Tempered Mr. Grove

Lefty Grove was a pitcher who, in the classic words of Bugs Baer, "could throw a lamb chop past a wolf." One day in Yankee Stadium he threw them past three wolves named Babe Ruth, Lou Gehrig and Bob Meusel. The Philadelphia Athletics were leading, 1–0, when Mark Koenig led off the Yankees' ninth inning with a triple. Grove threw three pitches to Ruth, three to Gehrig, and three to Meusel, all strikes. Meusel hit one of them foul. Another time Grove relieved Jack Quinn with the bases full of Yankees. That day it required ten pitches to strike out Ruth, Gehrig and Tony Lazzeri, who hit two fouls. In still another game he relieved Roy Mahaffey in Chicago with runners on second and third and nobody out. Again he struck out the side on ten pitches. When Don Honig's book *Baseball When the Grass Was Real* comes out, it will include George Pipgras's account of batting against Walter Johnson for the first time. He took two strikes, stepped out of the box and said to Muddy Ruel, Johnson's catcher, "Muddy, I never saw those pitches."

"Don't let it worry you," Muddy said. "He's thrown a few that Cobb and Speaker are still looking for."

Grove's fastball was like that, but he didn't have Johnson's comforting control. (One season when Johnson won thirty-four games he gave up only thirty-eight bases on balls; batters could oppose this gentleman confident that they wouldn't be hit in the head by accident or design.) Along with his blinding swift, Grove had the quality that Uncle Wilbert Robinson described as "pleasingly wild."

"But Groves wasn't a pitcher in those days," Connie Mack once said. "He was a thrower until after we sold him to Boston and he hurt his arm. Then he learned to pitch, and he got so he just knew, somehow, when the batter was going to swing."

It was typical of Connie Mack that he could pay an all-time record of $100,600 for a man—$600 more than the Yankees gave the Red Sox for Ruth—manage the guy for nine years, win three pennants and two world championships with him, and never learn to pronounce his name. To Connie, Lefty was always "Groves," Lou Boudreau was "Mr. Bordeer," and Zeke Bonura and Babe Barna were both "Bernair."

Robert Moses Grove was a tall, genial gentleman of seventy-five with a head of lustrous white hair who loved to sit around at baseball gatherings cutting up old touches. Lefty Grove, who threw bullets past Ruth and Gehrig and the rest, stood six-foot-three and wore an expression of sulky anger stuck on top of a long, thin neck.

He was a fierce competitor who made little effort to subdue a hair-trigger temper. His natural speed had dazzled and overpowered minor league hitters, and he wasn't accustomed to adversity when he got to the American League. When things went bad he raged blindly, blaming anybody who was handy.

One team that drove him wild was the Washington Senators. Before reaching the majors he had worked against them in an exhibition game. He was wild and they combed him over without mercy. When Clark Griffith heard about his old friend Connie paying all that money for Grove he said it would be a cold day in August before that busher ever beat his club, or words to that effect. Chances are some thoughtful soul relayed the remark to Grove. At any rate, the Senators whipped him the first seventeen times he worked against them.

Lefty threw his most memorable tantrum in St. Louis on August 23, 1931. He had won sixteen straight, tying the American League record shared by Smoky Joe Wood and Walter Johnson, and was going for his seventeenth against the tractable St. Louis Browns. While Dick Coffman was pitching a shutout, Goose Goslin got a bloop single off Grove and ran home when Jimmy Moore, a substitute for the injured Al Simmons in left field, misjudged an ordinary liner by Jack Burns. Beaten, 1–0, Grove took the visitors' clubhouse apart locker by locker, cursing Moore, Coffman, Goslin, Burns and especially Simmons, who was home in Milwaukee consulting his doctor.

The press found Grove surly and laconic and put him away as a grouch, although it wouldn't have been hard to discover what made him the way he was. A product of the bituminous fields of the western Maryland mountains, he had little experience with strangers and no exposure to social graces. People who had more schooling than he or had traveled more widely made him uneasy. Retreating into a shell, he became one of the great lobby-sitters of his time, a graven image shrouded in cigar smoke.

On the mound he was poetry. He would rock back until the knuckles of his left hand almost brushed the earth behind him, then come up and over with the perfect follow-through. He was the only 300-game winner between Grover Alexander and Warren Spahn, a span of thirty-seven years. He had the lowest earned-run average in the league nine different years, and nobody else ever did that more than five times. If the old records can be trusted, Alexander, Christy Mathewson, Johnson and Sandy Koufax each won five ERA titles. Some men would say these were the best pitchers that ever lived. Are the records trying to tell us Old Man Mose was twice as good as any of them?

Grove held at least one record that doesn't appear in the books. In 1920 Martinsburg, West Virginia, got a franchise in the Blue Ridge League and hired Grove at $125 a month. Martinsburg had no ball parks but the team opened on the road and a little jerrybuilt grandstand was flung up before the first home game. There was no money for a fence, however, so Grove was sold to Jack Dunn's Baltimore team for $3,000. That makes Old Mose the only player ever traded for an outfield fence.

•••

As a student, professor, and dean, the French-born historian and critic Jacques Barzun (b. 1907) was a fixture at Columbia University for decades. His works include *Darwin, Marx, Wagner: Critique of a Heritage* (1941), *Berlioz and the Romantic Century* (1950), *Race: A Study in Superstition* (1965), and *From Dawn to Decadence: 500 Years of Western Cultural Life* (2000). Barzun brings to the topic of baseball a sensibility steeped in European intellectual history but open to peculiarly American forms of expression, including those of sport. These remarks appear in Barzun's 1954 book about his adopted homeland, which was tellingly subtitled "A Declaration of Love Spiced with a Few Harsh Words."

Jacques Barzun

◊

from

God's Country and Mine

People who care less for gentility manage things better. They don't bother to leave the arid city but spend their surplus there on pastimes they can enjoy without feeling cramped. They follow boxing and wrestling, burlesque and vaudeville (when available), professional football and hockey. Above all, they thrill in unison with their fellow man the country over by watching baseball. The gods decree a heavyweight match only once in a while and a national election only every four years, but there is a World Series with every revolution of the earth around the sun. And in between, what varied pleasure long drawn out!

Whoever wants to know the heart and mind of America had better learn baseball, the rules and realities of the game—and do it by watching first some high school or small-town teams. The big league games are too fast for the beginner and the newspapers don't help. To read them with profit you have to know a language that comes easy only after philosophy has taught you to judge practice. Here is scholarship that takes effort on the part of the outsider, but it is so bred into the native that it never becomes a dreary round of technicalities.

The wonderful purging of the passions that we all experienced in the fall of '51, the despair groaned out over the fate of the Dodgers, from whom the league pennant was snatched at the last minute, give us some idea of what Greek tragedy was like. Baseball *is* Greek in being national, heroic, and broken up in the rivalries of city-states. How sad that Europe knows nothing like it! Its Olympics generate anger, not unity, and its interstate politics follow no rules that a people can grasp. At least Americans understand baseball, the true realm of clear ideas.

That baseball fitly expresses the powers of the nation's mind and body is a merit separate from the glory of being the most active, agile, varied, articulate, and brainy of all group games. It is of and for our century. Tennis belongs to the individualistic past—a hero, or at most a pair of friends or lovers, against the world. The idea of baseball is a team, an outfit, a section, a gang, a union, a cell, a commando squad—in short, a twentieth-century setup of opposite numbers.

Baseball takes its mystic nine and scatters them wide. A kind of individualism thereby returns, but it is limited—eternal vigilance is the price of victory. Just because they're far apart, the outfield can't dream or play she-loves-me-not with daisies. The infield is like a steel net held in the hands of the catcher. He is the psychologist and historian for the staff—or else his signals will give the opposition hits. The value of his headpiece is shown by the iron-mongery worn to protect it. The pitcher, on the other hand, is the wayward man of genius, whom others will direct. They will expect nothing from him but virtuosity. He is surrounded no doubt by mere talent, unless one excepts that transplanted acrobat, the shortstop. What a brilliant invention is his role despite its exposure to ludicrous lapses! One man to each base, and then the free lance, the trouble shooter, the movable feast for the eyes, whose motion animates the whole foreground.

The rules keep pace with this imaginative creation so rich in allusions to real life. How excellent, for instance, that a foul tip muffed by the catcher gives the batter another chance. It is the recognition of Chance that knows no argument. But on the other hand, how wise and just that the third strike must not be dropped. This points to the fact that near the end of any struggle life asks for more than is needful in order to clinch success. A victory has to be won, not snatched. We find also our American innocence in calling "World Series" the annual games between the winners in each big league. The world doesn't know or care and couldn't compete if it wanted to, but since it's us children having fun, why, the world is our stage. I said baseball was Greek. Is there not a poetic symbol in the new meaning—our meaning—of "Ruth hits Homer"?

Once the crack of the bat has sent the ball skimmiting left of second between the infielder's legs, six men converge or distend their defense to keep the runner from advancing along the prescribed path. The ball is not the center of interest as in those vulgar predatory games like football, basketball, and polo. Man running is the force to be contained. His getting to first or second base starts a capitalization dreadful to think of: every hit pushes him on. Bases full and a homer make four runs, while the defenders, helpless without the magic power of the ball lying over the fence, cry out their anguish and dig up the sod with their spikes.

But fate is controlled by the rules. Opportunity swings from one side to the other because innings alternate quickly, keep up spirit in the players, interest in the beholders. So does the profusion of different acts to be performed—pitching, throwing, catching, batting, running, stealing, sliding, signaling. Blows are similarly varied. Flies, Texas Leaguers, grounders, baseline fouls—praise God the human neck is a universal joint! And there is no set pace. Under the hot sun, the minutes creep as a deliberate pitcher tries his feints and curves for three strikes called, or conversely walks a threatening batter. But the batter is not invariably a tailor's dummy. In a hundredth of a second there may be a hissing rocket down right field, a cloud of dust over first base—the bleachers all a-yell—a double play, and the other side up to bat.

Accuracy and speed, the practiced eye and hefty arm, the mind to take in and readjust to the unexpected, the possession of more than one talent and the willingness to work in harness without special orders—these are the American virtues that shine in baseball. There has never been a good player who was dumb. Beef and bulk and mere endurance count for little, judgment and daring for much. Baseball is among group games played with a ball what fencing is to games of combat. But being spread out, baseball has something sociable and friendly about it that I especially love. It is graphic and choreographic. The ball is not shuttling in a confined space, as in tennis.

Nor does baseball go to the other extreme of solitary whanging and counting stopped on the brink of pointlessness, like golf. Baseball is a kind of collective chess with arms and legs in full play under sunlight.

How adaptable, too! Three kids in a back yard are enough to create the same quality of drama. All of us in our tennis days have pounded balls with a racket against a wall, for practice. But that is nothing compared with batting in an empty lot, or catching at twilight, with a fella who'll let you use his mitt when your palms get too raw. Every part of baseball equipment is inherently attractive and of a most enchanting functionalism. A man cannot have too much leather about him; and a catcher's mitt is just the right amount for one hand. It's too bad the chest protector and shinpads are so hot and at a distance so like corrugated cardboard. Otherwise, the team is elegance itself in its stripped knee breeches and loose shirts, colored stockings and peaked caps. Except for brief moments of sliding, you can see them all in one eyeful, unlike the muddy hecatombs of football. To watch a football game is to be in prolonged neurotic doubt as to what you're seeing. It's more like an emergency happening at a distance than a game. I don't wonder the spectators take to drink. Who has ever seen a baseball fan drinking within the meaning of the act? He wants all his senses sharp and clear, his eyesight above all. He gulps down soda pop, which is a harmless way of replenishing his energy by the ingestion of sugar diluted in water and colored pink.

Happy the man in the bleachers. He is enjoying the spectacle that the gods on Olympus contrived only with difficulty when they sent Helen to Troy and picked their teams. And the gods missed the fun of doing this by catching a bat near the narrow end and measuring hand over hand for first pick. In Troy, New York, the game scheduled for 2 P.M. will break no bones, yet it will be a real fight between Southpaw Dick and Red Larsen. For those whom civilized play doesn't fully satisfy, there will be provided a scapegoat in a blue suit—the umpire, yell-proof and even-handed as justice, which he demonstrates with outstretched arms when calling "Safe!"

And the next day in the paper: learned comment, statistical summaries, and the verbal imagery of meta-euphoric experts. In the face of so much joy, one can only ask, Were you there when Dogface Joe parked the pellet beyond the pale?

Robert Frost (1874–1963) was for many the greatest American poet of the 20th century. Born in San Francisco, he went to New England when his father died, and worked as a millhand, reporter, teacher, and farmer. Frost was also an instructor at the University of Michigan, Harvard, and Amherst College, where he enjoyed playing softball with his students. His lines in "Birches" describing "Some boy too far from town to learn baseball,/Whose only play was what he found himself," are among the most poignant poetic references to the sport. In 1956, *Sports Illustrated,* which had asked William Faulkner the year before to write about ice hockey and the Kentucky Derby, commissioned from Frost an essay on baseball. This is what he wrote.

Robert Frost

♥

Perfect Day—A Day of Prowess

Americans would rather watch a game than a play a game. Statement true or false? Why, as to these thousands here today to watch the game and not play it, probably not one man-jack but has himself played the game in his athletic years and got himself so full of bodily memories of the experience (what we farmers used to call kinesthetic images) that he can hardly sit still. We didn't burst into cheers immediately, but an exclamation swept the crowd as if we felt it all over in our muscles when Boyer at third made the two impossible catches, one a stab at a grounder and the other a leap at a line drive that may have saved the day for the National League. We all winced with fellow feeling when Berra got the foul tip on the ungloved fingers of his throwing hand.

As for the ladies present, they are here as next friends to the men, but even they have many of them pitching arms and batting eyes. Many of them would prefer a league ball to a pumpkin. You wouldn't want to catch them with bare hands. I mustn't count it against them that I envision one in the outfield at a picnic with her arms spread wide open for a fly ball as for a descending man-angel. Luckily it didn't hit her in the mouth which was open too, or it might have hurt her beauty. It missed her entirely.

How do I know all this and with what authority do I speak? Have I not been written up as a pitcher in *The New Yorker* by the poet, Raymond Holden?—though the last full game I pitched in was on the grounds of Rockingham Park in Salem, New Hampshire, before it was turned into a race track. If I have shone at all in the all-star games at Breadloaf in Vermont it has been as a relief pitcher with a soft ball I despise like a picture window. Moreover I once took an honorary degree at Williams College along with a very famous pitcher, Ed Lewis, who will be remembered and found in the record to have led the National League in pitching quite a long time ago. His degree was not for pitching. Neither was mine. His was for presiding with credit over the University of New Hampshire and the Massachusetts College of Agriculture. He let me into the secret of how he could make a ball behave when his arm was just right. It may sound superstitious to the uninitiated, but he could push a cushion of air up ahead of it for it to slide off from any way it pleased. My great friendship for him probably accounts for my having made a trivial 10¢ bet on the National League today. He was a Welshman from Utica who, from having attended eisteddfods at Utica with his father, a bard, had like another Welsh friend of mine, Edward Thomas, in England, come to look on a poem as a performance one had to win. Chicago was my first favorite team because Chicago seemed the nearest city in the league to my original home town, San Francisco. I have conquered that prejudice. But I mean to see if the captain of it, Anson my boyhood hero, is in the Hall of Fame at Cooperstown where he belongs.

May I add to my self-citation that one of my unfulfilled promises on earth was to my fellow in art, Alfred Kreymborg, of an epic poem some day about a ball batted so hard by Babe Ruth that it never came back, but got to going round and round the world like a satellite. I got up the idea long before any artificial moon was thought of by the scientists. I meant to begin something like this:

> It was nothing to nothing at the end of the tenth
> And the prospects good it would last to the nth.

It needs a lot of work on it before it can take rank with *Casey at the Bat.*

In other words, some baseball is the fate of us all. For my part I am never more at home in America than at a baseball game like this in

Clark Griffith's gem of a field, gem small, in beautiful weather in the capital of the country and my side winning. Here Walter Johnson flourished, who once threw a silver dollar across the Potomac (where not too wide) in emulation of George Washington, and here Gabby Street caught the bullet-like ball dropped from the top of George Washington's monument. It is the time and the place. And I have with me as consultant the well-known symbolist, Howard Schmitt of Buffalo, to mind my baseball slang and interpret the incidentals. The first player comes to the bat, Temple of the Redlegs, swinging two bats as he comes, the meaning of which or moral of which, I find on application to my consultant, is that we must always arrange to have just been doing something beforehand a good deal harder than what we are just going to do.

But when I asked him a moment later what it symbolized when a ball got batted into the stands and the people instead of dodging in terror fought each other fiercely to get and keep it and were allowed to keep it, Howard bade me hold on; there seemed to be a misunderstanding between us. When he accepted the job it was orally; he didn't mean to represent himself as a symbolist in the high-brow or middle-brow sense of the word, that is as a collegiate expounder of the double entendre for college classes; he was a common ordinary cymbalist in a local band somewhere out on the far end of the Eeryie Canal. We were both honest men. He didn't want to be taken for a real professor any more than I wanted to be taken for a real sport. His utmost wish was to contribute to the general noise when home runs were made. He knew they would be the most popular hits of the day. And they were—four of them from exactly the four they were expected from, Musial, Williams, Mays and Mantle. The crowd went wild four times. Howard's story would have been more plausible if he had brought his cymbals with him. I saw I would have to take care of the significances myself. This comes of not having got it in writing. The moral is always get it in writing.

Time was when I saw nobody on the field but the players. If I saw the umpire at all it was as an enemy for not taking my side. I may never have wanted to see bottles thrown at him so that he had to be taken out by the police. Still I often regarded him with the angry disfavor that the Democratic Party showed the Supreme Court in the '30s and other parties have shown it in other crises in our history. But now grown psychological, shading 100, I saw him as a figure of justice, who stood forth alone to be judged as a judge by people and players with whom he wouldn't last a week if suspected of the least lack of fairness or the least lack of faith in the possibility of fairness. I was touched by his loneliness and glad it was relieved a little by his being five in number, five in one so to speak, *e pluribus unum*. I have it from high up in the judiciary that some justices see in him an example to pattern after. Right there in front of me for reassurance is the umpire brought up perhaps in the neighborhood of Boston who can yet be depended upon not to take sides today for or against the American League the Boston Red Sox belong to. Let me celebrate the umpire for any influence for the better he may have on the Supreme Court. The justices suffer the same predicaments with him. I saw one batter linger perceptibly to say something to the umpire for calling him out on a third strike. I didn't hear what the batter said. One of the hardest things to accept as just is a called third strike.

It has been a day of prowess in spite of its being a little on the picnic side and possibly not as desperately fought as it might be in a World Series. Prowess, prowess, in about equal strength for both sides. Each team made 11 hits, two home runs and not a single error. The day was perfect, the scene perfect, the play perfect. Prowess of course comes first, the ability to perform with success in games, in the arts and, come right down to it, in battle. The nearest of kin to the artists in college where we all become bachelors of arts are their fellow performers in baseball, football and tennis. That's why I am so particular college athletics should be kept from corruption. They are close to the soul of culture. At any rate the Greeks thought so. Justice is a close second to prowess. When displayed toward each other by antagonists in war and peace, it is known as the nobility of noble natures. And I mustn't forget courage, for there is neither prowess nor justice without it. My fourth, if it is important enough in comparison to be worth bringing in, is knowledge, the mere information we can't get too much of and can't ever get enough of, we complain, before going into action.

As I say, I never feel more at home in America than at a ball game be it in park or in sandlot. Beyond this I know not. And dare not.

The author of the coming-of-age trilogy *Studs Lonigan* (1932–35) was born, grew up, and was educated, at parochial schools and at the University of Chicago, on Chicago's South Side. He was raised by his grandmother, a native of County Westmeath, Ireland, who came to the United States during the Civil War. As a boy, Farrell (1904–1979) watched her dress up and go off to Ladies Day ballgames at Comiskey Park. Her interest was an outgrowth of his—Farrell bought a bat with his first dollar—and his novels would teem with baseball scenes. In 1957 he published *My Baseball Diary,* from which "My Grandmother Goes to Comiskey Park" is taken.

James T. Farrell

♢

My Grandmother Goes to Comiskey Park

My grandmother is no more. She passed away in her sleep in 1931. I was raised by her and probably she wanted to see a baseball game because I was so full of baseball in my boyhood, and she most likely wondered what it was which interested her grandson, her son, Tom, and so many of the men.

She was born in County Westmeath, Ireland, and emigrated to America during the Civil War. Working as a domestic in Brooklyn, her lady one day sent her to a nearby bakery. She heard tell that Mr. Lincoln was dead, shot. She always retained much of her Irish peasant girlhood in her speech and way of seeing life. She never quite understood all the change that was going on in this country. Baseball was part of the excitement and strangeness of her new country. But once she saw a game, she wanted to see more, and as a little old woman, in her Sunday black dress, she went to ladies day games alone in the early 1920's. Not telling anyone where she was going, she would dress up of a Friday afternoon and go to Comiskey Park on the street car. She came home exited. She liked to see the way the men would "lep" and run.

Baseball to her was part of the new world of America, but she saw it with the wonder of an unlettered peasant woman who had run the fields of Ireland as a girl in bare feet.

My grandmother knew absolutely nothing about baseball. At home, we talked of it incessantly, and whenever my brother and I, or my uncle and I went to a game, she always questioned us about it. She seemed keenly interested in who won, even though she knew nothing of the rules of the game. Hearing that Friday was Ladies Day at Comiskey Park and that women were admitted free, she decided to see a game. She dressed up in her Sunday black silk dress, put on the new hat which she wore to Sunday Mass, and off we went to Comiskey Park.

This was in 1912, and the first Ladies Day game we saw was a contest between the New York Highlanders and the White Sox.

That year, as I've already indicated in one of these essays, Ping Bodie was one of my favorites. Late in this particular Ladies Day game, Ping was on third base. With a pitch, he lit out to steal home. There was the slide and the cloud of dust. I thought that he had been called out. In disappointment, I let out a shrill cry:

"Hard luck, Ping."

But my disappointment was needless. Ping Bodie safely stole home. It so happened that Earl was at the game that day, seated at another end of the park. He told me that night that he had heard my shout when Ping Bodie stole home.

My grandmother plied me with questions, root-beer, hot dogs and Cracker-Jack. She was intensely excited and bewildered. She watched everything and understood nothing.

"Son, why is the man leppin' for the ball?"

"Son, why do they make him out?"

"Why don't they let him run?"

I tried to answer her questions, and all about me there were genially amused men watching and listening to the talk between the little boy with glasses and curly hair and the little old Irish woman in her Sunday black clothes.

A man tried to explain a point of the game to her and she told him:

"Don't be making free with me. Sure and I know all about the baseball."

A few moments later she was leaning forward and asking the man:

"Mister, are you married?"

He told her no.

"Sure and a fine man like you, you should have a wife. Me oldest son isn't married. He supports me."

My grandmother went often to the Ladies Day games, and became a familiar figure in the grandstand back of the White Sox dugout near third base. She would, of course, take me and she would always wear her Sunday best clothes. And I never was able to explain to her what the game was about. She loved it even though until her dying day she didn't know what the plays meant.

Her favorite team was the Boston Red Sox. She was convinced that the best of all baseball teams was Boston because many of her relatives from the old country had settled in that city. They were fine people and if Boston was their home, then the Boston baseball team had to be the best of all, just as Westmeath was the best county in Ireland.

Several times, she took me to see the Boston Red Sox play the White Sox and whenever we saw these two teams play, the Red Sox won. This made her proud and happy. At supper on those nights, she would tell my uncle with great enthusiasm:

"Tom, the Bostons won. Tom, you should see the way the Bostons lep for the ball."

"Mother, did you understand the game?"

"Indeed I did, and you should see the men play. Ah, the Bostons are fine men. Me mother's cousin settled in Boston town . . ."

She would then be off on her relatives.

She never learned to read or write and was always asking someone to read the newspaper to her. She would ask one of us to do this and would invariably give the command:

"Read me the death notices."

Then she would say: "Read me about the Bostons."

When I came in at night with the box score edition of the evening paper, she would ask:

"Son, did the Bostons win?"

If the Red Sox had won, she would brag and crow. Sometimes at supper she would tell my uncle:

"Tom, the Bostons won again."

In 1914, I was ten years old. One Friday afternoon we went to the Ladies Day game as usual. I used to be let in without charge at the turnstile where women were admitted. But this time, the man at the turnstile refused to admit me and told my grandmother that she would have to pay for me. At first she was surprised and she said:

"The little boy is me grandson."

This didn't move the man. I stood there disappointed and a little ashamed. I wanted to ask my grandmother to pay for me and didn't want her to argue with the man.

But argue she did, until she had attracted a small crowd.

"If you don't let me grandson in with me, I'll never darken this place as long as I live," she said in anger.

And she said more.

"'Tis the last time I come here!"

"I'll tell me cousin, Alderman Willie O'Toole, and he'll fix you. He'll fix you for insultin' me and me little grandson."

I was quite embarrassed. I pulled at her skirt and weakly said:

"Mother . . ."

"Be still, Son," she said, and looking up at the man:

"I'll tell the man that owns the ball park."

The man at the turnstile tried to explain to her that only ladies were admitted without the price of admission. This meant nothing to my grandmother. She gave him one of her best tongue-lashings. Then in a gesture of pride and with her head raised in dignity, she took my hand and said:

"Come on, Son, we'll never be seen here again."

My hopes were gone. But just as she started to lead me away, the man at the turnstile relented:

"All right, Lady, come on in and the boy too."

She proudly passed through the turnstile, her head held high. Then she said to the man:

"'Tis well for you you let me grandson in."

"That's all right, Lady . . ."

"Aw, you're a fine man. Tell me, are you married?"

"Yes, Lady."

"Well, God will bless you and your wife."

After 1914, I didn't go often to the games with her. But then, she would go alone. When she came home she would always say:

"I hied meself down to the baseball. It would do your heart good to see the men and the way they ran and lep for the ball."

She kept going to Ladies Day games on into the middle 1920's, and invariably, she came home excited and happy. And she never deserted the Bostons. They always remained her favorites.

She loved baseball and understood absolutely nothing about the game.

In Douglass Wallop's 1954 novel *The Year the Yankees Lost the Pennant* a middle-aged Washington Senators fan sells his soul to the devil in order to become the youthful ballplayer who will lead them to the pennant. Only a year later *Damn Yankees,* Richard Adler and Jerry Ross's musical version of the novel (with a book by Wallop and legendary director George Abbott), became a Broadway triumph with no little help from Gwen Verdon and Ray Walston as the diabolical tempters. The show-stopping assertion that "you've gotta have heart" has been echoed countless times since, and the show was later reprised as an equally successful movie. This opening scene vividly plays out two dilemmas: the frustration of the fan whose team never wins, and the loneliness of the sports widow.

from

Damn Yankees

ACT ONE

SCENE I

The curtain is made of alternately colored strings of baseballs.

The curtain lifts, disclosing a typical suburban front porch and living room. JOE *is watching a ball game on television.* MEG *sits nearby sewing. It is a very warm evening. They are a comfortable couple in their forties.*

JOE

A strike—you're nuts. He's nuts.

MEG

Back home in Hannibal we had heat over 100 lots of times.

JOE
(Slides down in his chair)

Slide.

MEG

Casper Niles tried to fry an egg on the sidewalk in front of his drugstore one time.

JOE

Good old Smokey, he got a hit.

269

MEG

In Hannibal they were always saying cool air was on its way from Canada. I certainly don't see any sign of it here, do you? (*No reply*) Do you?

JOE

Do I what?

MEG

See any sign of cool air . . . ?

JOE

You're blind, Ump. You're blind. See any sign of what, dear?

MEG

Never mind. (*Music begins*) It wasn't important. (*She continues to sew as she sings*)

When we met in nineteen thirty-eight, it was November
When I said that I would be his mate, it was December
I reasoned he would be the greatest husband that a girl had ever
    found.
That's what I reasoned
That's what I reasoned
Then April rolled around.

JOE

(JOE *leans forward in his chair, begins to sing to the television set*)
Strike three, ball four, walk a run'll tie the score.
Yer blind, Ump,
Yer blind, Ump,
Ya mus' be out-a yer mind, Ump!

MEG

Six months out of every year
I might as well be made of stone
Six months out of every year when I'm with him
I'm alone.

JOE

He caught the corner.

MEG

Six months out of every year
He doesn't take me anywhere

Six months out of every year, when I play cards
Solitaire.
> (*She rises, walks to the screen door and leans against it*)

The other six months out of every year
We are hardly ever seen apart
But then the Washington Senators take over my place in his heart.
Six months out of every year
I might as well be wearing crepe
Life is just an awful bore from which I find no escape
Six months out of every year.
> (*A chorus of men from the neighborhood enters. All are wearing the same tie and slacks as* JOE. *They kneel downstage and sing.*)

BOYS

Strike three
Ball four
Walk a run'll tie the score
Fly ball
Double play
Yankees win again today.
Those damn Yankees
Why can't we beat 'em?
He's out, he's safe, he's out, he's safe, he's out, he's safe, he's out.
> (*A chorus of neighborhood women, all in identical gaily colored aprons, enters. Takes the other side of stage*)

Yer blind Ump,
Yer blind Ump, you must be out of yer mind Ump.

GIRLS

> (*Now the stage is divided equally between the men and women and they sing against each other*)

Six months out of every year
He lives by the television set.

BOYS

He's out, he's safe, he's out!

GIRLS

If you see that man of mine
How does he look?
I forget.

BOYS

Le-e-ets go!

GIRLS

Six months out of every year
We know there is no other dame
If he isn't home by six,

BOYS

He's out, he's safe, he's out!

GIRLS

It's six to one
There's a game

BOYS

Le-e-ets go!

GIRLS

Six months out of every year when we cook for them it never
    pays

BOYS

Aahh!

GIRLS

Instead of praising our goulash
They are appraising the plays of Willie Mays!

BOYS

He's out, he's safe, he's out!

GIRLS

Six months out of every year

BOYS

Strike three ball four walk a run'll tie the score

GIRLS

We might as well be wearing crepe

BOYS

Fly ball double play, Yankees win again today

GIRLS

Life is just an awful bore
From which there is no escape.

BOYS

Those damn Yankees. Why can't we beat em?
He's out, he's safe, he's out, he's safe, he's out, he's safe, he's out.
Yer blind Ump, yer blind Ump
Ya must be out-a yer mind Ump.

> (*Girls snake across the stage and line up in front of the men.*)

GIRLS

We're dying for the mercury to drop to three below

BOYS

Yay team

GIRLS

We're crying for the happy days of icicles and snow

BOYS

Yay team

GIRLS

We don't mind sleepin' solo, that is once a year or so,

BOYS

Those damn Yankees

GIRLS

But with them it's a career

BOYS

What are ya waitin' for?
April, May, June, July, August, September

GIRLS

April, May, June, July, August, September
Six months out of every year

BOYS

Yer blind Ump, yer blind Ump, ya must be out-a yer mind Ump.

> (*Neighbors exit in both directions and we see* MEG *standing by the screen door and* JOE *watching television as before.*)

ALL

April, May, June, July, August, September.
April, May, June, July, August, September.

MEG

Six months out of every year.
(*Goes back to her chair and knitting.*)

JOE

Yer blind ump, yer blind ump, ya must be . . .
(*Speaks*)
O.K. Sohovik, don't try to murder it. . . . Just slip one through the infield . . . Come on, Sohovik, get lucky . . . Oh boy . . . (*To her*) The ball's in the dirt and he swings. That does it!
(JOE *snaps off the television.*)

MEG

Did the Washington Senators win, dear? (*He grunts*) Oh, I'm sorry. Well, maybe they will next time.

JOE

Damn Yankees.

MEG

What, dear?

JOE

I'd like to lick those damn Yankees just once.

Wilfred Charles Heinz (b. 1915) served as a war correspondent for the *New York Sun* and is the author of *The Professional* (1958), which Ernest Hemingway called "the only good novel I've ever read about a fighter." A frail Damon Runyon scribbled Heinz's name on a bar napkin along with the comment "very good" (underlined three times) when an editor from Hearst magazines asked him for a recommendation. Writers _____ _____ _____ long admired Heinz _____ _____ the _____ _____ ipt "to rig up events as _____ _____ _____ _____ tences that describe ol _____ _____ _____ _____ d out-fielder Pete Reis _____ was _____

W. C. Heinz

⌂

The Rocky Road of Pistol Pete

"Out in Los Angeles," says Garry Schumacher, who was a New York baseball writer for 30 years and is now assistant to Horace Stoneham, president of the San Francisco Giants, "they think Duke Snider is the best center fielder they ever had. They forget Pete Reiser. The Yankees think Mickey Mantle is something new. They forget Reiser, too."

Maybe Pete Reiser was the purest ballplayer of all time. I don't know. There is no exact way of measuring such a thing, but when a man of incomparable skills, with full knowledge of what he is doing, destroys those skills and puts his life on the line in the pursuit of his endeavor as no other man in his game ever has, perhaps he is the truest of them all.

"Is Pete Reiser there?" I said on the phone.

This was last season, in Kokomo. Kokomo has a population of about 50,000 and a ball club, now affiliated with Los Angeles and called the Dodgers, in the Class D Midwest League. Class D is the bottom of the barrel of organized baseball, and this was the second season that Pete Reiser had managed Kokomo.

"He's not here right now," the woman's voice on the phone said. "The team played a double-header yesterday in Dubuque, and they didn't get in on the bus until 4:30 this morning. Pete just got up a few minutes ago and he had to go to the doctor's."

"Oh?" I said. "What has he done now?"

In two and a half years in the minors, three seasons of Army ball and ten years in the majors, Pete Reiser was carried off the field 11 times. Nine times he regained consciousness either in the clubhouse or in hospitals. He broke a bone in his right elbow, throwing. He broke both ankles, tore a cartilage in his left knee, ripped the muscles in his left leg, sliding. Seven times he crashed into outfield walls, dislocating his left shoulder, breaking his right collarbone and, five times, ending up in an unconscious heap on the ground. Twice he was beaned, and the few who remember still wonder today how great he might have been.

"I didn't see the old-timers," Bob Cooke, who is sports editor of the New York *Herald Tribune*, was saying recently, "but Pete Reiser was the best ballplayer I ever saw."

"We don't know what's wrong with him," the woman's voice on the phone said now. "He has a pain in his chest and he feels tired all the time, so we sent him to the doctor. There's a game tonight, so he'll be at the ball park about 5 o'clock."

Pete Reiser is 39 years old now. The Cardinals signed him out of the St. Louis Municipal League when he was 15. For two years, because he was so young, he chauffeured for Charley Barrett, who was scouting the Midwest. They had a Cardinal uniform in the car for Pete, and he used to work out with the Class C and D clubs, and one day Branch Rickey, who was general manager of the Cardinals then, called Pete into his office in Sportsman's Park.

"Young man," he said, "you're the greatest young ballplayer I've ever seen, but there is one thing you must remember. Now that you're a professional ballplayer you're in show business. You will perform on the biggest stage in the world, the baseball diamond. Like the actors on Broadway, you'll be expected to put on a great performance every day, no matter how you feel, no matter whether it's too hot or too cold. Never forget that."

Rickey didn't know it at the time, but this was like telling Horatius that, as a professional soldier, he'd be expected someday to stand his ground. Three times Pete sneaked out of hospitals to play. Once he went back into the lineup after doctors warned him that any blow on the head would kill him. For four years he swung the bat and made the throws when it was painful for him just to shave and to comb his hair. In the 1947 World Series he stood on a broken ankle to pinch hit, and it ended with Rickey, then president of the Dodgers, begging him not to play and guaranteeing Pete his 1948 salary if he would just sit that season out.

"That might be the one mistake I made," Pete says now. "Maybe I should have rested that year."

"Pete Reiser?" Leo Durocher, who managed Pete at Brooklyn, was saying recently. "What's he doing now?"

"He's managing Kokomo," Lindsey Nelson, the TV sportcaster, said.

"Kokomo?" Leo said.

"That's right," Lindsey said. "He's riding the buses to places like Lafayette and Michigan City and Mattoon."

"On the buses," Leo said, shaking his head and then smiling at the thought of Pete.

"And some people say," Lindsey said, "that he was the greatest young ballplayer they ever saw."

"No doubt about it," Leo said. "He was the best I ever had, with the possible exception of Mays. At that, he was even faster than Willie." He paused. "So now he's on the buses."

The first time that Leo ever saw Pete on a ball field was in Clearwater that spring of '39. Pete had played one year of Class D in the Cardinal chain and one season of Class D for Brooklyn. Judge Kenesaw Mountain Landis, who was then Baseball Commissioner, had sprung Pete and 72 others from what they called the "Cardinal Chain Gang," and Pete had signed with Brooklyn for $100.

"I didn't care about money then," Pete says. "I just wanted to play."

Pete had never been in a major-league camp before, and he didn't know that at batting practice you hit in rotation. At Clearwater he was grabbing any bat that was handy and cutting in ahead of Ernie Koy or Dolph Camilli or one of the others, and Leo liked that.

One day Leo had a chest cold, so he told Pete to start at shortstop. His first time up he hit a homer off the Cards' Ken Raffensberger, and that was the beginning. He was on base his first 12 times at bat that spring, with three homers, five singles and four walks. His first time against Detroit he homered off Tommy Bridges. His first time against the Yankees he put one over the fence off Lefty Gomez.

Durocher played Pete at shortstop in 33 games that spring. The Dodgers barnstormed North with the Yankees, and one night Joe McCarthy, who was managing the Yankees, sat down next to Pete on the train.

"Reiser," he said, "you're going to play for me."

"How can I play for you?" Pete said. "I'm with the Dodgers."

"We'll get you," McCarthy said. "I'll tell Ed Barrow, and you'll be a Yankee."

The Yankees offered $100,000 and five ballplayers for Pete. The Dodgers turned it down, and the day the season opened at Ebbets Field, Larry MacPhail, who was running things in Brooklyn, called Pete on the clubhouse phone and told him to report to Elmira.

"It was an hour before game time," Pete says, "and I started to take off my uniform and I was shaking all over. Leo came in and said: 'What's the matter? You scared?' I said: 'No. MacPhail is sending me to Elmira.' Leo got on the phone and they had a hell of a fight. Leo said he'd quit, and MacPhail said he'd fire him—and I went to Elmira.

"One day I'm making a throw and I heard something pop. Every day my arm got weaker and they sent me to Johns Hopkins and took X rays. Dr. George Bennett told me: 'Your arm's broken.' When I came to after the operation, my throat was sore and there was an ice pack on it. I said: 'What happened? Your knife slip?' They said: 'We took your tonsils out while we were operating on your arm.'"

Pete's arm was in a cast from the first of May until the end of July. His first two weeks out of the cast he still couldn't straighten the arm, but a month later he played ten games as a left-handed outfielder until Dr. Bennett stopped him.

"But I can't straighten my right arm," Pete said.

"Take up bowling," the doctor said.

When he bowled, though, Pete used first one arm and then the other. Every day that the weather allowed he went out into the back yard and practiced throwing a rubber ball left-handed against a wall.

Then he went to Fairgrounds Park and worked on the long throw, left-handed, with a baseball.

"At Clearwater that next spring," he says, "Leo saw me in the outfield throwing left-handed, and he said: 'What do you think you're doin'?' I said: 'Hell, I had to be ready. Now I can throw as good with my left arm as I could with my right.' He said: 'You can do more things as a right-handed ballplayer. I can bring you into the infield. Go out there and cut loose with that right arm.' I did and it was okay, but I had that insurance."

So at 5 o'clock I took a cab from the hotel in Kokomo to the ball park on the edge of town. It seats about 2,200, 1,500 of them in the white-painted fairgrounds grandstand along the first base line, and the rest in chairs behind the screen and in bleachers along the other line.

I watched them take batting practice; trim, strong young kids with their dreams, I knew, of someday getting up there where Pete once was, and I listened to their kidding. I watched the groundskeeper open the concession booth and clean out the electric popcorn machine. I read the signs on the outfield walls, advertising the Mid-West Towel and Linen Service, Basil's Nite Club, the Hoosier Iron Works, UAW Local 292 and the Around the Clock Pizza Café. I watched the Dubuque kids climbing out of their bus, carrying their uniforms on wire coat hangers.

"Here comes Pete now," I heard the old guy setting up the ticket box at the gate say.

When Pete came through the gate he was walking like an old man. In 1941 the Dodgers trained in Havana, and one day they clocked him, in his baseball uniform and regular spikes, at 9.8 for 100 yards. Five years later the Cleveland Indians were bragging about George Case and the Washington Senators had Gil Coan. The Dodgers offered to bet $1,000 that Reiser was the fastest man in baseball, and now it was taking him forever to walk to me, his shoulders stooped, his whole body heavier now, and Pete just slowly moving one foot ahead of the other.

"Hello," he said, shaking hands but his face solemn. "How are you?"

"Fine," I said, "but what's the matter with you?"

"I guess it's my heart," he said.

"When did you first notice this?"

"About eleven days ago. I guess I was working out too hard. All of a sudden I felt this pain in my chest and I got weak. I went into the clubhouse and lay down on the bench, but I've had the same pain and I'm weak ever since."

"What did the doctor say?"

"He says it's lucky I stopped that day when I did. He says I should be in a hospital right now, because if I exert myself or even make a quick motion I might go—just like that."

He snapped his fingers. "He scared me," he said. "I'll admit it. I'm scared."

"What are you planning to do?"

"I'm going home to St. Louis. My wife works for a doctor there, and he'll know a good heart specialist."

"When will you leave?"

"Well, I can't just leave the ball club. I called Brooklyn, and they're sending a replacement for me, but he won't be here until tomorrow."

"How will you get to St. Louis?"

"It's about 300 miles," Pete says. "The doctor says I shouldn't fly or go by train, because if anything happens to me they can't stop and help me. I guess I'll have to drive."

"I'll drive you," I said.

Trying to get to sleep in the hotel that night I was thinking that maybe, standing there in that little ball park, Pete Reiser had admitted out loud for the first time in his life that he was scared. I was thinking of 1941, his first full year with the Dodgers. He was beaned twice and crashed his first wall and still hit .343 to be the first rookie and the youngest ballplayer to win the National League batting title. He tied Johnny Mize with 39 doubles, led in triples, runs scored, total bases and slugging average, and they were writing on the sports pages that he might be the new Ty Cobb.

"Dodgers Win On Reiser HR," the headlines used to say. "Reiser Stars As Brooklyn Lengthens Lead."

"Any manager in the National League," Arthur Patterson wrote one day in the New York *Herald Tribune*, "would give up his best man to obtain Pete Reiser. On every bench they're talking about him. Rival players watch him take his cuts during batting practice, announce when he's going to make a throw to the plate or third base during outfield drill. They just whistle their amazement when he scoots down the first base line on an infield dribbler or a well-placed bunt."

He was beaned the first time at Ebbets Field five days after the season started. A sidearm fast ball got away from Ike Pearson of the Phillies, and Pete came to at 11:30 that night in Peck Memorial Hospital.

"I was lying in bed with my uniform on," he told me once, "and I couldn't figure it out. The room was dark, with just a little night light, and then I saw a mirror and I walked over to it and lit the light and I had a black eye and a black streak down the side of my nose. I said to myself: 'What happened to me?' Then I remembered.

"I took a shower and walked around the room, and the next morning the doctor came in. He looked me over, and he said: 'We'll keep you here for five or six more days under observation.' I said: 'Why?' He said: 'You've had a serious head injury. If you tried to get out of bed right now, you'd fall down.' I said: 'If I can get up and walk around this room, can I get out?' The doc said: 'All right, but you won't be able to do it.'"

Pete got out of bed, the doctor standing ready to catch him. He walked around the room. "I've been walkin' the floor all night," Pete said.

The doctor made Pete promise that he wouldn't play ball for a week, but Pete went right to the ball park. He got a seat behind the Brooklyn dugout and Durocher spotted him.

"How do you feel?" Leo said.

"Not bad," Pete said.

"Get your uniform on," Leo said.

"I'm not supposed to play," Pete said.

"I'm not gonna play you," Leo said. "Just sit on the bench. It'll make our guys feel better to see that you're not hurt."

Pete suited up and went out and sat on the bench. In the eighth inning it was tied, 7–7. The Dodgers had the bases loaded, and there was Ike Pearson again, coming in to relieve.

"Pistol," Leo said to Pete, "get the bat."

In the press box the baseball writers watched Pete. They wanted to see if he'd stand right in there. After a beaning they are all entitled to shy, and many of them do. Pete hit the first pitch into the center-field stands, and Brooklyn won, 11 to 7.

"I could just barely trot around the bases," Pete said when I asked him about it. "I was sure dizzy."

Two weeks later they were playing the Cardinals, and Enos Slaughter hit one and Pete turned in center field and started to run. He made the catch, but he hit his head and his tail bone on that corner near the exit gate.

His head was cut, and when he came back to the bench they also saw blood coming through the seat of his pants. They took him into the clubhouse and pulled his pants down and the doctor put a metal clamp on the cut.

"Just don't slide," he told Pete. "You get it sewed up after the game."

In August of that year big Paul Erickson was pitching for the Cubs and Pete took another one. Again he woke up in a hospital. The Dodgers were having some pretty good beanball contests with the Cubs that season, and Judge Landis came to see Pete the next day.

"Do you think that man tried to bean you?" he asked Pete.

"No sir," Pete said. "I lost the pitch."

"I was there," Landis said, "and I heard them holler: 'Stick it in his ear.'"

"That was just bench talk," Pete said. "I lost the pitch."

He left the hospital the next morning. The Dodgers were going to St. Louis after the game, and Pete didn't want to be left in Chicago.

Pete always says that the next year, 1942, was the year of his downfall, and the worst of it happened on one play. It was early July and Pete and the Dodgers were tearing the league apart. In a four-game series in Cincinnati he got 19 for 21. In a Sunday double-header in Chicago he went 5 for 5 in the first game, walked three times in the second game and got a hit the one time they pitched to him. He was hitting .381, and they were writing in the papers that he might end up hitting .400.

When they came into St. Louis the Dodgers were leading by ten and a half games. When they took off for Pittsburgh they left three games of that lead and Pete Reiser behind them.

"We were in the twelfth inning, no score, two outs and Slaughter hit it off Whit Wyatt," Pete says. "It was over my head and I took off.

I caught it and missed that flagpole by two inches and hit the wall and dropped the ball. I had the instinct to throw it to Peewee Reese, and we just missed gettin' Slaughter at the plate, and they won, 1–0.

"I made one step to start off the field and I woke up the next morning in St. John's Hospital. My head was bandaged, and I had an awful headache."

Dr. Robert Hyland, who was Pete's personal physician, announced to the newspapers that Pete would be out for the rest of the season. "Look, Pete," Hyland told him. "I'm your personal friend. I'm advising you not to play any more baseball this year."

"I don't like hospitals, though," Pete was telling me once, "so after two days I took the bandage off and got up. The room started to spin, but I got dressed and I took off. I snuck out, and I took a train to Pittsburgh and I went to the park.

"Leo saw me and he said: 'Go get your uniform on, Pistol.' I said: 'Not tonight, Skipper.' Leo said: 'Aw, I'm not gonna let you hit. I want these guys to see you. It'll give 'em that little spark they need. Besides, it'll change the pitching plans on that other bench when they see you sittin' here in uniform.' "

In the fourteenth inning the Dodgers had a runner on second and Ken Heintzelman, the left-hander, came in for the Pirates. He walked Johnny Rizzo, and Durocher had run out of pinch hitters.

"Damn," Leo was saying, walking up and down. "I want to win this one. Who can I use? Anybody here who can hit?"

Pete walked up to the bat rack. He pulled out his stick. "You got yourself a hitter," he said to Leo.

He walked up there and hit a line drive over the second baseman's head that was good for three bases. The two runs scored, and Pete rounded first base and collapsed.

"When I woke up I was in a hospital again," he says. "I could just make out that somebody was standin' there and then I saw it was Leo. He said: 'You awake?' I said: 'Yep.' He said: 'By God, we beat 'em! How do you feel?' I said: 'How do you think I feel?' He said: 'Aw, you're better with one leg and one eye than anybody else I've got.' I said: 'Yeah, and that's the way I'll end up—on one leg and with one eye.'

"I'd say I lost the pennant for us that year," Pete says now, although he still hit .310 for the season. "I was dizzy most of the time and I couldn't see fly balls. I mean balls I could have put in my pocket, I couldn't get near. Once in Brooklyn when Mort Cooper was pitching for the Cards I was seeing two baseballs coming up there. Babe Pinelli was umpiring behind the plate, and a couple of times he stopped the game and asked me if I was all right. So the Cards beat us out the last two days of the season."

The business office of the Kokomo ball club is the dining room of a man named Jim Deets, who sells insurance and is also the business manager of the club. His wife, in addition to keeping house, mothering six small kids, boarding Pete, an outfielder from Venezuela and a shortstop from the Dominican Republic, is also the club secretary.

"How do you feel this morning?" I asked Pete. He was sitting at the dining-room table, in a sweat shirt and a pair of light-brown slacks, typing the game report of the night before to send it to Brooklyn.

"A little better," he said.

Pete has a worn, green 1950 Chevy, and it took us eight and a half hours to get to St. Louis. I'd ask him how the pain in his chest was and he'd say that it wasn't bad or it wasn't so good, and I'd get him to talking again about Durocher or about his time in the Army. Pete played under five managers at Brooklyn, Boston, Pittsburgh and Cleveland, and Durocher is his favorite.

"He has a great mind, and not just for baseball," Pete said. "Once he sat down to play gin with Jack Benny, and after they'd played four cards Leo read Benny's whole hand to him. Benny said: 'How can you do that?' Leo said: 'If you're playin' your cards right, and I give you credit for that, you have to be holding those others.' Benny said: 'I don't want to play with this guy.'

"One spring at Clearwater there was a pool table in a room off the lobby. One night Hugh Casey and a couple of other guys and I were talking with Leo. We said: 'Gee, there's a guy in there and we've been playin' pool with him for a couple of nights, but last night he had a real hot streak.' Leo said: 'How much he take you for?' We figured it out and it was $2,000. Leo said: 'Point him out to me.'

"We went in and pointed the guy out and Leo walked up to him and said: 'Put all your money on the table. We're gonna shoot for it.' The guy said: 'I never play like that.' Leo said: 'You will tonight. Pick your own game.' Leo took him for $4,000, and then he threw him out. Then he paid us back what we'd gone for, and he said: 'Now, let that be a lesson. That guy is a hustler from New York. The next time it happens I won't bail you out.' Leo hadn't had a cue in his hands for years."

It was amazing that they took Pete into the Army. He had wanted to enlist in the Navy, but the doctors looked him over and told him none of the services could accept him. Then his draft board sent him to Jefferson Barracks in the winter of 1943, and the doctors there turned him down.

"I'm sittin' on a bench with the other guys who've been rejected," he was telling me, "and a captain comes in and says: 'Which one of you is Reiser?' I stood up and I said: 'I am.' In front of everybody he said: 'So you're trying to pull a fast one, are you? At a time like this, with a war going on, you came in here under a false name. What do you mean, giving your name as Harold Patrick Reiser? Your name's Pete Reiser, and you're the ballplayer, aren't you?' I said: 'I'm the ballplayer and they call me Pete, but my right name is Harold Patrick Reiser.' The captain says: 'I apologize. Sergeant, fingerprint him. This man is in.'"

They sent him to Fort Riley, Kansas. It was early April and raining and they were on bivouac, and Pete woke up in a hospital. "What happened?" he said.

"You've got pneumonia," the doctor said. "You've been a pretty sick boy for six days. You'll be all right, but we've been looking you over. How did you ever get into this Army?"

"When I get out of the hospital," Pete was telling me, "I'm on the board for a discharge and I'm waitin' around for about a week, and still nobody there knows who I am. All of a sudden one morning a voice comes over the bitch box in the barracks. It says: 'Private Reiser, report to headquarters immediately.' I think: 'Well, I'm out now.'

"I got over there and the colonel wants to see me. I walk in and give my good salute and he says: 'Sit down, Harold.' I sit down and he says: 'Your name really isn't Harold, is it?' I say: 'Yes, it is, sir.' He says: 'But that isn't what they call you where you're well known, is it? You're Pete Reiser the ballplayer, aren't you?' I say: 'Yes, sir.' He says: 'I thought so. Now, I've got your discharge papers right there, but we've got a pretty good ball club and we'd like you on it. We'll make a deal. You say nothing, and you won't have to do anything but play ball. How about it?' I said: 'Suppose I don't want to stay in?'

"He picked my papers up off his desk," Pete was saying, "and he tore 'em right up in my face. I can still hear that 'zip' when he tore 'em. He said: 'You see, you have no choice.'

"Then he picked up the phone and said something and in a minute a general came in. I jumped up and the colonel said: 'Don't bother to salute, Pete.' Then he said to the general: 'Major, this is Pete Reiser, the great Dodger ballplayer. He was up for a medical discharge, but he's decided to stay here and play ball for us.'

"So, the general says: 'My, what a patriotic thing for you to do, young man. That's wonderful. Wonderful.' I'm sittin' there, and when the general goes out the colonel says: 'That major, he's all right.' I said: 'But he's a general. How come you call him a major?' The colonel says: 'Well, in the regular Army he's a major and I'm a full colonel. The only reason I don't outrank him now is that I've got heart trouble. He knows it, but I never let him forget it. I always call him major.' I thought: 'What kind of an Army am I in?' "

Joe Gantenbein, the Athletics' outfielder, and George Scharein, the Phillies' infielder, were on that team with Pete, and they won the state and national semipro titles. By the time the season was over, however, the order came down to hold up all discharges.

The next season there were 17 major-league ballplayers on the Fort Riley club, and they played four nights a week for the war workers in Wichita. Pete hit a couple of walls, and the team made such a joke of the national semipro tournament that an order came down from Washington to break up the club.

"Considering what a lot of guys did in the war," Pete says, "I had no complaints, but five times I was up for discharge, and each time something happened. From Riley they sent me to Camp Livingston. From there they sent me to New York Special Services for twelve hours and I end up in Camp Lee, Virginia, in May of 1945.

"The first one I meet there is the general. He says: 'Reiser, I saw you on the list and I just couldn't pass you up.' I said: 'What about my discharge?' He says: 'That will have to wait. I have a lot of celebrities down here, but I want a good baseball team.' "

Johnny Lindell, of the Yankees, and Dave Philley, of the White Sox, were on the club and Pete played left field. Near the end of the season he went after a foul fly for the third out of the last inning, and he went right through a temporary wooden fence and rolled down a 25-foot embankment.

"I came to in the hospital, with a dislocated right shoulder," he says, "and the general came over to see me and he said: 'That was one of the greatest displays of courage I've ever seen, to ignore your future in baseball just to win a ball game for Camp Lee.' I said: 'Thanks.'

"Now it's November and the war is over, but they're still shippin' guys out, and I'm on the list to go. I report to the overseas major, and he looks at my papers and says: 'I can't send you overseas. With everything that's wrong with you, you shouldn't even be in this Army. I'll have you out in three hours.' In three hours, sure enough, I've got those papers in my hand, stamped, and I'm startin' out the door. Runnin' up to me comes a Red Cross guy. He says: 'I can get you some pretty good pension benefits for the physical and mental injuries you've sustained.' I said: 'You can?' He said: 'Yes, you're entitled to them.' I said: 'Good. You get 'em. You keep 'em. I'm goin' home.'"

When we got to St. Louis that night I drove Pete to his house and the next morning I picked him up and drove him to see the heart specialist. He was in there for two hours, and when he came out he was walking slower than ever.

"No good," he said. "I have to go to the hospital for five days for observation."

"What does he think?"

"He says I'm done puttin' on that uniform. I'll have to get a desk job."

Riding to the hospital I wondered if that heart specialist knew who he was tying to that desk job. In 1946, the year he came out of the Army, Pete led the league when he stole 34 bases, 13 more than the runner-up Johnny Hopp of the Braves. He also set a major-league record that still stands, when he stole home eight times.

"Nine times," he said once. "In Chicago I stole home and Magerkurth hollered: 'You're out!' Then he dropped his voice and he said: '——, I missed it.' He'd already had his thumb in the air. I had nine out of nine."

I suppose somebody will beat that some day, but he'll never top the way Pete did it. That was the year he knocked himself out again trying for a diving catch, dislocated his left shoulder, ripped the muscles in his left leg and broke his left ankle.

"Whitney Kurowski hit one in the seventh inning at Ebbets Field," he was telling me. "I dove for it and woke up in the clubhouse. I was in Peck Memorial for four days. It really didn't take much to knock me out in those days. I was comin' apart all over. When I dislocated my shoulder they popped it back in, and Leo said: 'Hell, you'll be all right. You don't throw with it anyway.'"

That was the year the Dodgers tied with the Cardinals for the pennant and dropped the play-off. Pete wasn't there for those two games. He was in Peck Memorial again.

"I'd pulled a charley horse in my left leg," Pete was saying. "It's the last two weeks of the season, and I'm out for four days. We've got the winning run on third, two outs in the ninth and Leo sends me up. He says: 'If you don't hit it good, don't run and hurt your leg.'

"The first pitch was a knockdown and, when I ducked, the ball hit the bat and went down the third base line, as beautiful a bunt as you've ever seen. Well, Ebbets Field is jammed. Leo has said: 'Don't run.' But this is a big game. I take off for first, and we win and I've ripped the muscles from my ankle to my hip. Leo says: 'You shouldn't have done it.'

"Now it's the last three days of the season and we're a game ahead of the Cards and we're playin' the Phillies in Brooklyn. Leo says to me: 'It's now or never. I don't think we can win it without you.' The first two up are outs and I single to right. There's Charley Dressen, coachin' on third, with the steal sign. I start to get my lead, and a pitcher named Charley Schanz is workin' and he throws an ordinary lob over to first. My leg is stiff and I slide and my heel spike catches the bag and I hear it snap.

"Leo comes runnin' out. He says: 'Come on. You're all right.' I said: 'I think it's broken.' He says: 'It ain't stickin' out.' They took me to Peck Memorial, and it was broken." ·

We went to St. Luke's Hospital in St. Louis. In the main office they told Pete to go over to a desk where a gray-haired, semistout woman was sitting at a typewriter. She started to book Pete in, typing his answer on the form. "What is your occupation, Mr. Reiser?" she said.

"Baseball," Pete said.

"Have you ever been hospitalized before?"

"Yes," Pete said.

In 1946 the Dodgers played an exhibition game in Springfield, Missouri. When the players got off the train there was a young radio announcer there, and he was grabbing them one at a time and asking them where they thought they'd finish that year.

"In first place," Reese and Casey and Dixie Walker and the rest were saying. "On top" . . . "We'll win it."

"And here comes Pistol Pete Reiser!" the announcer said. "Where do you think you'll finish this season, Pete?"

"In Peck Memorial Hospital," Pete said.

After the 1946 season Brooklyn changed the walls at Ebbets Field. They added boxes, cutting 40 feet off left field and dropping center field from 420 to 390 feet. Pete had made a real good start that season in center, and on June 5 the Dodgers were leading the Pirates by three runs in the sixth inning when Culley Rikard hit one.

"I made my turn and ran," Pete says, "and, where I thought I still had that thirty feet, I didn't."

"The crowd," Al Laney wrote the next day in the New York *Herald Tribune*, "which watched silently while Reiser was being carried away, did not know that he had held on to the ball . . . Rikard circled the bases, but Butch Henline the umpire, who ran to Reiser, found the ball still in Reiser's glove. . . . Two outs were posted on the scoreboard after play was resumed. Then the crowd let out a tremendous roar."

In the Brooklyn clubhouse the doctor called for a priest, and the Last Rites of the Church were administered to Pete. He came to, but lapsed into unconsciousness again and woke up at 3 A.M. in Peck Memorial.

For eight days he couldn't move. After three weeks they let him out, and he made that next western trip with the Dodgers. In Pittsburgh he was working out in the outfield before the game when Clyde King, chasing a fungo, ran into him and Pete woke up in the clubhouse.

"I went back to the Hotel Schenley and lay down," he says. "After the game I got up and had dinner with Peewee. We were sittin' on the porch, and I scratched my head and I felt a lump there about as big as half a golf ball. I told Peewee to feel it and he said: 'Gosh!' I said: 'I don't think that's supposed to be like that.' He said: 'Hell, no.'"

Pete went up to Rickey's room and Rickey called his pilot and had Pete flown to Johns Hopkins in Baltimore. They operated on him for a blood clot.

"You're lucky," the doctor told him. "If it had moved just a little more you'd have been gone."

Pete was unable to hold even a pencil. He had double vision and, when he tried to take a single step, he became dizzy. He stayed for three weeks and then went home for almost a month.

"It was August," he says, "and Brooklyn was fightin' for another pennant. I thought if I could play the last two months it might make the difference, so I went back to Johns Hopkins. The doctor said: 'You've made a remarkable recovery.' I said: 'I want to play.' He said: 'I can't okay that. The slightest blow on the head can kill you.'"

Pete played. He worked out for four days, pinch hit a couple of times and then, in the Polo Grounds, made a diving catch in left field. They carried him off, and in the clubhouse he was unable to recognize anyone.

Pete was still having dizzy spells when the Dodgers went into the 1947 Series against the Yankees. In the third game he walked in the first inning, got the steal sign and, when he went into second, felt his right ankle snap. At the hospital they found it was broken.

"Just tape it, will you?" Pete said.

"I want to put a cast on it," the doctor said.

"If you do," Pete said, "they'll give me a dollar-a-year contract next season."

The next day he was back on the bench. Bill Bevens was pitching for the Yankees and, with two out in the ninth, it looked like he was going to pitch the first no-hitter in World Series history.

"Aren't you going to volunteer to hit?" Burt Shotton, who was managing Brooklyn, said to Pete.

Al Gionfriddo was on first and Bucky Harris, who was managing the Yankees, ordered Pete walked. Eddie Miksis ran for him, and when Cookie Lavagetto hit that double, the two runs scored and Brooklyn won, 3–2.

"The next day," Pete says, "the sports writers were second-guessing Harris for putting me on when I represented the winning run. Can you imagine what they'd have said if they knew I had a broken ankle?"

At the end of that season Rickey had the outfield walls at Ebbets Field padded with one-inch foam rubber for Pete, but he never hit them again. He had headaches most of the time and played little. Then he was traded to Boston, and in two seasons there he hit the wall a couple of times. Twice his left shoulder came out while he was making diving catches. Pittsburgh picked Pete up in 1951, and the next year he played into July with Cleveland and that was the end of it.

Between January and September of 1953, Pete dropped $40,000 in the used-car business in St. Louis, and then he got a job in a lumber mill for $100 a week. In the winter of 1955 he wrote Brooklyn asking for a part-time job as a scout, and on March 1, Buzzy Bavasi, the Dodger vice-president, called him on the phone.

"How would you like a manager's job?" Buzzy said.

"I'll take it," Pete said.

"I haven't even told you where it is. It's Thomasville, Georgia, in Class D."

"I don't care," Pete said. "I'll take it."

At Vero Beach that spring, Mike Gaven wrote a piece about Pete in the New York *Journal American*.

"Even in the worn gray uniform of the Class D Thomasville, Georgia, club," Mike wrote, "Pete Reiser looks, acts and talks like a big leaguer. The Dodgers pitied Pete when they saw him starting his comeback effort after not having handled a ball for two and a half years. They lowered their heads when they saw him in a chow line with a lot of other bushers, but the old Pistol held his head high. . . ."

The next spring, Sid Friedlander, of the New York *Post*, saw Pete at Vero and wrote a column about him managing Kokomo. The last thing I saw about him in the New York papers was a small item out of Tipton, Indiana, saying that the bus carrying the Kokomo team had collided with a car and Pete was in a hospital in Kokomo with a back injury.

"Managing," Pete was saying in that St. Louis hospital, "you try to find out how your players are thinking. At Thomasville one night one of my kids made a bad throw. After the game I said to him: 'What were you thinking while that ball was coming to you?' He said: 'I was saying to myself that I hoped I could make a good throw.' I said: 'Sit down.' I tried to explain to him the way you have to think. You know how I used to think?"

"Yes," I said, "but you tell me."

"I was always sayin': 'Hit it to me. Just hit it to me. I'll make the catch. I'll make the throw.' When I was on base I was always lookin' over and sayin': 'Give me the steal sign. Give me the sign. Let me go.' That's the way you have to think."

"Pete," I said, "now that it's all over, do you ever think that if you hadn't played it as hard as you did, there's no telling how great you might have been or how much money you might have made?"

"Never," Pete said. "It was my way of playin'. If I hadn't played that way I wouldn't even have been whatever I was. God gave me those legs and the speed, and when they took me into the walls that's the way it had to be. I couldn't play any other way."

A technician came in with an electrocardiograph. She was a thin, dark-haired woman and she set it up by the bed and attached one of the round metal disks to Pete's left wrist and started to attach another to his left ankle.

"Aren't you kind of young to be having pains in your chest?" she said.

"I've led a fast life," Pete said.

On the way back to New York I kept thinking how right Pete was. To tell a man who is this true that there is another way for him to do it is to speak a lie. You cannot ask him to change his way of going, because it makes him what he is.

Three days after I got home I had a message to call St. Louis. I heard the phone ring at the other end and Pete answered. "I'm out!" he said.

"Did they let you out, or did you sneak out again?" I said.

"They let me out," he said. "It's just a strained heart muscle, I guess. My heart itself is all right."

"That's wonderful."

"I can manage again. In a couple of days I can go back to Kokomo."

If his voice had been higher he would have sounded like a kid at Christmas.

"What else did they say?" I said.

"Well, they say I have to take it easy."

"Do me a favor," I said.

"What?"

"Take their advice. This time, please take it easy."

"I will," he said. "I'll take it easy."

If he does it will be the first time.

Across the century, several major-league pitchers published analyses and reminiscences of the vocation. In 1908, for instance, Candy Cummings described "How I Pitched the First Curve," and four years later Christy Mathewson published the seductively titled, tediously constructed *Pitching in a Pinch*. The journeyman reliever Jim Brosnan (b. 1929) played with four teams in nine seasons; his diary of the summer of 1959, which he spent with the Cardinals and Reds, made him a real-life equivalent of Mark Harris's Henry Wiggen, expressing with candor and dry wit how it really feels to try to throw baseballs past Hank Aaron for a living and then go home to a wife who calls you "Meat."

Jim Brosnan

▽

from

The Long Season

MAY 6—PHILADELPHIA

Lord God, will sorrows never cease.

I had just finished my last chew of the night in the ninth as we scored three runs to knock Robin Roberts out of the box. We then led 7–3. The phone rang in the cage next to the bullpen in Philly and Pollet answered it. He waved to me as he hung up and said, "Jim, you might as well get loose in case he needs somebody."

Mizell had retired seven straight batters and I didn't think there would be much need for help. But by the time I'd taken off my jacket, found my glove under the bench, walked to the bullpen mound and stuck a piece of gum in my mouth, Wilmer was just about out of the game. Wally Post hit the second pitch for a single and Anderson slammed a high curve off the scoreboard for one run.

Hal Smith ambled out to talk to Mizell, taking as much time as he could. But what can a catcher say but good-by? Keane, who had been running the club since the third when Hemus was thumbed, also took his time before calling me in from the bullpen. I heard Venzon, the umpire, yell to me that I was to come on to the mound, but I kept throwing so that he'd have to come down the left field line to get me. I *like* Tony, and all that, but I needed time to get warm. I threw two more quick curves before he got to me to yell, "Let's go, Brosnan. Didn't you hear me call you?"

I was tempted to get smart and say, "You're the one with the rabbit ears, not me," but I like Tony; really I do. Sticking my nose in the air, I walked by Venzon and out to the mound thinking to myself, "I'm ready."

I could have been more ready, I guess.

I couldn't have looked worse, I know.

Willie Jones was the first hitter, and I knew I could get him out if I kept everything away, and wasted maybe one pitch inside. But he hit a pitch that was just not quite far enough away from him. His fly ball fell a foot inside the right field line for a double. Philadelphia was just two runs down and still had nobody out.

Freese bounced a slider back to me, and I felt better. But Dave Philley batted for Hegan and hit a low slider away from him to left field for a single. It wasn't too bad a pitch. Had it broken down slightly instead of staying flat Philley might have hit it into the ground instead of on a line. Then, too, White might have caught the ball in left field had he been an outfielder instead of a first baseman.

Bowman batted for the pitcher and I was trying to decide how to pitch him, when Keane ran out of the dugout, yelling for time. He ran all the way to the mound and said, "We're going to let Jackson pitch to him." I assumed that what Keane said came from Hemus, shrugged my shoulders, and walked to the clubhouse. At this critical moment I was willing to accept anyone's opinion. The Philadelphia fans were roaring. Do they sense disaster, those miserable fans?

Jackson pitched to four men. Two of them singled, and two of them walked as the Phillies' radio broadcaster snorted and brayed fanatically. As I uncapped the aspirin bottle in the dressing room, the winning run crossed the plate. I swallowed two pills at once, pocketed two for later, and sat down on the table to wait for the explosion.

The tension was thick. The locker room steamed nervously, the damp walls reflecting every player's breath. I heard the clatter of muddy spiked shoes being banged on the floor; and the scratching of matches as cigarettes were lit.

"That's the worst exhibition I ever saw!"

That's all that was said.

There wasn't much anyone could say. I, personally, didn't say anything for hours except "Let me have another one"—at the hamburger grill across the street from the Warwick Hotel.

Eighteen hours later as we dressed for the second game of the series the locker room atmosphere was still somewhat subdued. Usually the professional ballplayer manages to put aside the memories of catastrophic disappointments. He says, "I just won't think about it. You can't win 'em in the clubhouse. That's the way it goes. You win some, lose some, and some are rained out." Eventually he talks himself back into the state of self-confidence in which he performs best. The aplomb of the eighty-time loser is not always complacency. He knows that a certain percentage of games must be lost because the other team is better for certain games. Again, he knows that his team will occasionally give away a game that should have been won. He comes right back, smiling and fighting. (Lose ninety times in a season, though, and it shows in the face. A close-up reveals frown lines, crow's-feet, and an extra tint of red in the eyeballs from too much regretting.)

We had lost many games, but that was the first one we had given away. Hemus's daily preachment—"You lose because you're making mistakes"—had been emphatically demonstrated. The most grievous fault of a ballplayer is to give a ball game away.

Usually a ballplayer replays a losing game immediately afterward. A conversational autopsy quickly spots the blame. Two martinis and a rare steak later, the game is forgotten till the newspapers come out and rehash it. "The worst exhibition (he) ever saw" wasn't replayed by the bullpen till the next game started.

"Well, that's not the last one we'll give away, either," I said, finally.

"Let's try to forget last night," said Pollet in the seventh inning. "We got this game to worry about."

"Doesn't look like he's gonna use anybody down here tonight, Howie," said Green.

Kellner had started the game and had served up two tremendous home runs to Wally Post, and another one to Hammer. We were down 6–4 as the seventh started. Durham batted for Kellner and bounced out. The phone rang in the bullpen.

"Give me Nunn, I guess," said Hemus.

Nunn pitched the last of the seventh and retired three men in a row. He took a shower in our half of the eighth, when we came up with four big ones to go ahead by two. Again, Hemus called the bullpen.

Pollet turned away from the phone, looked over his crew as if he were the master of ceremonies on "Who Do You Trust?" and pointed to me. "He wants to know how you feel."

"Give me the ball, Coach," I said, and stood up to take off my jacket.

The eighth was easy. As I started out of the dugout in the Phillies' half of the ninth, Hemus reached up to pat me on the back, apparently thought better of it and said, instead, "Let's see you bear down now, big man. Get that first hitter."

I didn't.

That damn Willie Jones, again. He has an odd behavior at the plate. He'll take a hard swing at a pitch, miss it, and look out at the pitcher, his face purple with rage. It's hard to tell whether he's mad at you for making him miss the ball or mad at himself for not hitting it. Or, he'll take a half-ass swing at a pitch, and you swear you had him fooled. But just set him up for the same pitch later and he'll hit it like he knew it was coming.

So, he hit a pretty good slider into right center. The ball might have been caught had Flood been playing Jones straight away. But I saw at a glance that Curt wasn't going to catch up with the ball. I headed toward the Phillies' clubhouse to back up third base. Jones made it, easily; and he scored when Freese hit a long fly to right field.

Bowman batted for the catcher and singled. The Philly fans yelled for an encore of my previous evening's performance. Out of the dugout came Hemus. He pawed the ground, cleared his throat, looked at the bullpen, and said, "Can you get him out?"

I looked at Dave Philley, who had been announced as a pinch-hitter. He had knocked me out just twenty-four hours earlier. I shrugged my shoulders and said. "Hell, yes."

Hemus looked at me for a moment, then turned and walked back to the bench. Cunningham, who had run back to first, wheeled around and ran back to the mound, a slightly mischievous grin on his face. He asked me, "Is everything all right, Professor?" turned and ran back to first base.

I relaxed, took a deep breath, and shook off Green's signal for the slider.

"No slide balls," I said to myself. "Nothing but power this time. I'm going to throw this ball right by him."

And I did.

Robert Francis (1901–1987) was born in Upland, Pennsylvania, and for most of his years lived an austere and often solitary existence in Amherst, Massachusetts. The fruit of that life was a rich body of contemplative poems, collected in such volumes as *The Sound I Listened For* (1944), *The Orb Weaver* (1960), and *A Certain Distance* (1976), that move freely, unpredictably, and often wittily between the natural and human worlds. In everything—including baseball—he finds matter of the deepest import.

Robert Francis

◊

Pitcher

His art is eccentricity, his aim
How not to hit the mark he seems to aim at,

His passion how to avoid the obvious,
His technique how to vary the avoidance.

The others throw to be comprehended. He
Throws to be a moment misunderstood.

Yet not too much. Not errant, arrant, wild,
But every seeming aberration willed.

Not to, yet still, still to communicate
Making the batter understand too late.

The Base Stealer

Poised between going on and back, pulled
Both ways taut like a tightrope-walker,
Fingertips pointing the opposites,
Now bouncing tiptoe like a dropped ball
Or a kid skipping rope, come on, come on,
Running a scattering of steps sidewise,
How he teeters, skitters, tingles, teases,
Taunts them, hovers like an ecstatic bird,
He's only flirting, crowd him, crowd him,
Delicate, delicate, delicate, delicate—now!

"He was sometimes unbearable," wrote Ted Williams' biographer Ed Linn on the occasion of Williams' final game at Fenway Park, "but he was never dull." John Updike's account of The Kid's last at-bats for the Red Sox captures Boston's contentious love affair with the last of the .400 hitters. For many Red Sox fans, the effect of his swan-song home run hinged on a simple gesture. Updike simply records Williams' refusal to tip his cap as he floated around the bases "like a feather in a vortex." The Kid's own remarks were more defiant: "I thought about my hat, and I thought about it. I hit second base, and I said, no, I'll never tip my hat. And I came into home plate more than ever convinced that I wouldn't. It was that type of feeling." Apart from this piece, published in *The New Yorker* and collected, with added footnotes, in *Assorted Prose* (1965), Updike (b. 1932) has written sparingly about baseball, though he meditated on "Tao in the Yankee Stadium Bleachers" in his first book of poems, *The Carpenter Hen, and Other Tame Creatures* (1958).

John Updike

▽

Hub Fans Bid Kid Adieu

Fenway Park, in Boston, is a lyric little bandbox of a ballpark. Everything is painted green and seems in curiously sharp focus, like the inside of an old-fashioned peeping-type Easter egg. It was built in 1912 and rebuilt in 1934, and offers, as do most Boston artifacts, a compromise between Man's Euclidean determinations and Nature's beguiling irregularities. Its right field is one of the deepest in the American League, while its left field is the shortest; the high left-field wall, three hundred and fifteen feet from home plate along the foul line, virtually thrusts its surface at right-handed hitters. On the afternoon of Wednesday, September 28th, 1960, as I took a seat behind third base, a uniformed groundkeeper was treading the top of this wall, picking batting-practice home runs out of the screen, like a mushroom gatherer seen in Wordsworthian perspective on the verge of a cliff. The day was overcast, chill, and uninspirational. The Boston team was the worst in twenty-seven seasons. A jangling medley of incompetent youth and aging competence, the Red Sox were finishing in seventh place only because the Kansas City Athletics had locked them out of the cellar. They were scheduled to play the Baltimore Orioles, a much nimbler blend of May and December, who had been dumped from pennant contention a week before by the insatiable Yankees. I, and 10,453 others, had shown up primarily because this was the Red Sox's last home game of the season, and therefore the last time in all eternity that their regular left fielder, known to the headlines as TED, KID, SPLINTER, THUMPER, TW, and, most cloyingly, MISTER WONDERFUL, would play in Boston. "WHAT WILL WE DO WITHOUT TED? HUB FANS ASK" ran the headline on a newspaper being read by a bulb-nosed cigar smoker a few rows away. Williams' retirement had been announced, doubted (he had been threatening retirement for years), confirmed by Tom Yawkey, the Red Sox owner, and at last widely accepted as the sad but probable truth. He was forty-two and had redeemed his abysmal season of 1959 with a—considering his advanced age—fine one. He had been giving away his gloves and bats and had grudgingly consented to a sentimental ceremony today. This was not necessarily his last game; the Red Sox were scheduled to travel to New York and wind up the season with three games there.

I arrived early. The Orioles were hitting fungos on the field. The day before, they had spitefully smothered the Red Sox, 17–4, and neither their faces nor their drab gray visiting-team uniforms seemed very gracious. I wondered who had invited them to the party. Between our heads and the lowering clouds a frenzied organ was thundering through, with an appositeness perhaps accidental, "You *maaaade* me love you, I didn't wanna do it, I didn't wanna do it. . . ."

The affair between Boston and Ted Williams was no mere summer romance; it was a marriage composed of spats, mutual disappointments, and, toward the end, a mellowing hoard of shared memories. It fell into three stages, which may be termed Youth, Maturity, and Age; or Thesis, Antithesis, and Synthesis; or Jason, Achilles, and Nestor.

First, there was the by now legendary epoch* when the young

---

* This piece was written with no research materials save an outdated record book and the Boston newspapers of the day; and Williams' early career preceded the dawning of my *Schlagballewusstsein* (Baseball-consciousness). Also for reasons of perspective was my account of his

bridegroom came out of the West and announced "All I want out of life is that when I walk down the street folks will say 'There goes the greatest hitter who ever lived.'" The dowagers of local journalism attempted to give elementary deportment lessons to this child who spake as a god, and to their horror were themselves rebuked. Thus began the long exchange of backbiting, bat-flipping, booing, and spitting that has distinguished Williams' public relations.* The spitting

---

beginnings skimped. Williams first attracted the notice of a major-league scout—Bill Essick of the Yankees—when he was a fifteen-year-old pitcher with the San Diego American Legion Post team. As a pitcher-outfielder for San Diego's Herbert Hoover High School, Williams recorded averages of .586 and .403. Essick balked at signing Williams for the $1,000 his mother asked; he was signed instead, for $150 a month, by the local Pacific Coast League franchise, the newly created San Diego Padres. In his two seasons with this team, Williams hit merely .271 and .291, but his style and slugging (23 home runs the second year) caught the eye of, among others, Casey Stengel, then with the Boston Braves, and Eddie Collins, the Red Sox general manager. Collins bought him from the Padres for $25,000 in cash and $25,000 in players. Williams was then nineteen. Collins' fond confidence in the boy's potential matched Williams' own. Williams reported to the Red Sox training camp in Sarasota in 1938 and, after showing more volubility than skill, was shipped down to the Minneapolis Millers, the top Sox farm team. It should be said, perhaps, that the parent club was equipped with an excellent, if mature, outfield, mostly purchased from Connie Mack's dismantled A's. Upon leaving Sarasota, Williams is supposed to have told the regular outfield of Joe Vosmik, Doc Cramer, and Ben Chapman that he would be back and would make more money than the three of them put together. At Minneapolis he hit .366, batted in 142 runs, scored 130, and hit 43 home runs. He also loafed in the field, jabbered at the fans, and smashed a water cooler with his fist. In 1939 he came north with the Red Sox. On the way, in Atlanta, he dropped a foul fly, accidentally kicked it away in trying to pick it up, picked it up, and threw it out of the park. It would be nice if, his first time up in Fenway Park, he had hit a home run. Actually, in his first Massachusetts appearance, the first inning of an exhibition game against Holy Cross at Worcester, he *did* hit a home run, a grand slam. The Red Sox season opened in Yankee Stadium. Facing Red Ruffing, Williams struck out and, the next time up, doubled for his first major-league hit. In the Fenway Park opener, against Philadelphia, he had a single in five trips. His first home run came on April 23, in that same series with the A's. Williams was then twenty, and played *right* field. In his rookie season he hit .327; in 1940, .344.

* See *Ted Williams*, by Ed Linn (Sport Magazine Library), Chapter 6, "Williams vs. the Press." It is Linn's suggestion that Williams walked into a circulation war among the seven Boston newspapers, who in their competitive zeal headlined incidents that the New York papers, say, would have minimized, just as they minimized the less genial side of the moody and aloof DiMaggio and smoothed Babe Ruth into a folk hero. It is also Linn's thought, and an interesting one, that Williams thrived on even adverse publicity, and needed a hostile press to elicit, contrariwise, his defiant best. The statistics (especially of the 1958 season, when he snapped a slump by spitting in all directions, and inadvertently conked an elderly female fan with a tossed bat) seem to corroborate this. Certainly Williams could have had a truce for the asking, and his industrious perpetuation of the war, down to his last day in uniform, implies its usefulness to him. The actual and intimate anatomy of the matter resides in locker rooms and hotel corridors fading from memory. When my admiring account was printed, I received a letter from a sports reporter who hated Williams with a bitter and explicit immediacy. And even Linn's hagiology permits some glimpses of Williams' locker-room manners that are not pleasant.

incidents of 1957 and 1958 and the similar dockside courtesies that Williams has now and then extended to the grandstand should be judged against this background: the left-field stands at Fenway for twenty years have held a large number of customers who have bought their way in primarily for the privilege of showering abuse on Williams. Greatness necessarily attracts debunkers, but in Williams' case the hostility has been systematic and unappeasable. His basic offense against the fans has been to wish that they weren't there. Seeking a perfectionist's vacuum, he has quixotically desired to sever the game from the ground of paid spectatorship and publicity that supports it. Hence his refusal to tip his cap* to the crowd or turn the other cheek to newsmen. It has been a costly theory—it has probably cost him, among other evidences of good will, two Most Valuable Player awards, which are voted by reporters†—but he has held to it. While his critics, oral and literary, remained beyond the reach of his discipline, the opposing pitchers were accessible, and he spanked them to the tune of .406 in 1941.‡ He slumped to .356 in 1942 and went off to war.

In 1946, Williams returned from three years as a Marine pilot to the second of his baseball avatars, that of Achilles, the hero of incomparable prowess and beauty who nevertheless was to be found

---

* But he did tip his cap, high off his head, in at least his first season, as cartoons from that period verify. He also was extravagantly cordial to taxi-drivers and stray children. See Linn, Chapter 4, "The Kid Comes to Boston": "There has never been a ballplayer—anywhere, any-time—more popular than Ted Williams in his first season in Boston." To this epoch belong Williams' prankish use of the Fenway scoreboard lights for rifle practice, his celebrated ex-pressed preference for the life of a fireman, and his determined designation of himself as "The Kid."

† In 1947 Joe DiMaggio and in 1957 Mickey Mantle, with seasons inferior to Williams', won the MVP award because sportswriters, who vote on ballots with ten places, had venge-fully placed Williams ninth, tenth, or nowhere at all. The 1941 award to Joe DiMaggio, even though this was Williams' .406 year, is more understandable, since this was also the *annus miraculorum* when DiMaggio hit safely in 56 consecutive games.

‡ The sweet saga of this beautiful decimal must be sung once more. Williams, after hitting above .400 all season, had cooled to .39955 with one doubleheader left to play, in Philadel-phia. Joe Cronin, then managing the Red Sox, offered to bench him to safeguard his average, which was exactly .400 when rounded to the third decimal place. Williams said (I forget where I read this) that he did not want to become the .400 hitter with just his toenails over the line. He played the first game and singled, homered, singled, and singled. With less to gain than to lose, he elected to play the second game and got two more hits, including a double that dented a loudspeaker horn on the top of the right-field wall, giving him six-for-eight on the day and a season's average that, in the forty years between Rogers Hornsby's .403 (1925) and the present, stands as unique.

sulking in his tent while the Trojans (mostly Yankees) fought through to the ships. Yawkey, a timber and mining maharajah, had surrounded his central jewel with many gems of slightly lesser water, such as Bobby Doerr, Dom DiMaggio, Rudy York, Birdie Tebbetts, and Johnny Pesky. Throughout the late forties, the Red Sox were the best paper team in baseball, yet they had little three-dimensional to show for it, and if this was a tragedy, Williams was Hamlet. A succinct review of the indictment—and a fair sample of appreciative sports-page prose—appeared the very day of Williams' valedictory, in a column by Huck Finnegan in the Boston *American* (no sentimentalist, Huck):

> Williams' career, in contrast [to Babe Ruth's], has been a series of failures except for his averages. He flopped in the only World Series he ever played in (1946) when he batted only .200. He flopped in the playoff game with Cleveland in 1948. He flopped in the final game of the 1949 season with the pennant hinging on the outcome (Yanks 5, Sox 3). He flopped in 1950 when he returned to the lineup after a two-month absence and ruined the morale of a club that seemed pennant-bound under Steve O'Neill. It has always been Williams' records first, the team second, and the Sox non-winning record is proof enough of that.

There are answers to all this, of course. The fatal weakness of the great Sox slugging teams was not-quite-good-enough pitching rather than Williams' failure to hit a home run every time he came to bat. Again, Williams' depressing effect on his teammates has never been proved. Despite ample coaching to the contrary, most insisted that they *liked* him. He has been generous with advice to any player who asked for it. In an increasingly combative baseball atmosphere, he continued to duck beanballs docilely. With umpires he was gracious to a fault. This courtesy itself annoyed his critics, whom there was no pleasing. And against the ten crucial games (the seven World Series games with the St. Louis Cardinals, the 1948 playoff with the Cleveland Indians, and the two-game series with the Yankees at the end of the 1949 season, when one victory would have given the Red Sox the pennant) that make up the Achilles' heel of Williams' record, a mass of statistics can be set showing that day in and day out he was no slouch in the clutch.* The correspondence columns of the Boston papers now and then suffer a sharp flurry of arithmetic on this score; indeed, for Williams to have distributed all his hits so they did nobody else any good would constitute a feat of placement unparalleled in the annals of selfishness.

Whatever residue of truth remains of the Finnegan charge those of us who love Williams must transmute as best we can, in our own personal crucibles. My personal memories of Williams began when I was a boy in Pennsylvania, with two last-place teams in Philadelphia to keep me company. For me, "W'ms, lf" was a figment of the box scores who always seemed to be going 3-for-5. He radiated, from afar, the hard blue glow of high purpose. I remember listening over the radio to the All-Star Game of 1946, in which Williams hit two singles and two home runs, the second one off a Rip Sewell "blooper" pitch; it was like hitting a balloon out of the park. I remember watching one of his home runs from the bleachers of Shibe Park; it went over the first baseman's head and rose methodically along a straight line and was still rising when it cleared the fence. The trajectory seemed qualitatively different from anything anyone else might hit. For me, Williams is the classic ballplayer of the game on a hot August weekday, before a small crowd, when the only thing at stake is the tissue-thin difference between a thing done well and a thing done ill. Baseball is a game of the long season, of relentless and gradual averaging-out. Irrelevance—since the reference point of most individual contests is remote and statistical—always threatens its interest, which can be maintained not by the occasional heroics that sportswriters feed upon but by players who always *care*; who care, that is to say, about themselves and their art. Insofar as the clutch hitter is not a sportswriter's myth, he is a vulgarity, like a writer who writes only for money. It may be that, compared to such managers' dreams as the manifestly classy Joe DiMaggio and the always helpful Stan Musial, Williams was an icy star. But of all team sports, baseball, with its graceful intermittences of action, its immense and tranquil field

---

* For example: In 1948, the Sox came from behind to tie the Indians by winning three straight; in those games Williams went two for two, two for two; and two for four. In 1949, the Sox overtook the Yankees by winning nine in a row; in that streak, Williams won four games with home runs.

sparsely settled with poised men in white, its dispassionate mathematics, seems to me best suited to accommodate, and be ornamented by, a loner. It is an essentially lonely game. No other player visible to my generation concentrated within himself so much of the sport's poignance, so assiduously refined his natural skills, so constantly brought to the plate that intensity of competence that crowds the throat with joy.

By the time I went to college, near Boston, the lesser stars Yawkey had assembled around Williams had faded, and his rigorous pride of craftsmanship had become itself a kind of heroism. This brittle and temperamental player developed an unexpected quality of persistence. He was always coming back—back from Korea, back from a broken collarbone, a shattered elbow, a bruised heel, back from drastic bouts of flu and ptomaine poisoning. Hardly a season went by without some enfeebling mishap, yet he always came back, and always looked like himself. The delicate mechanism of timing and power seemed sealed, shockproof, in some case deep within his frame.* In addition to injuries, there was a heavily publicized divorce, and the usual storms with the press, and the Williams Shift—the maneuver, custom-built by Lou Boudreau of the Cleveland Indians, whereby three infielders were concentrated on the right side of the infield.† Williams could easily have learned to punch singles through the vacancy on his left and fattened his average hugely. This was what Ty Cobb, the Einstein of average, told him to do. But the game had changed since Cobb; Williams believed that his value to the club and to the league was as a slugger, so he went on pulling the ball, trying

* Two reasons for his durability may be adduced. A non-smoker, non-drinker, habitual walker, and year-round outdoorsman, Williams spared his body the vicissitudes of the seasonal athlete. And his hitting was in large part a mental process; the amount of cerebration he devoted to such details as pitchers' patterns, prevailing winds, and the muscular mechanics of swinging a bat would seem ridiculous, if it had not paid off. His intellectuality, as it were, perhaps explains the quickness with which he adjusted, after the war, to the changed conditions—the night games, the addition of the slider to the standard pitching repertoire, the new cry for the long ball. His reaction to the Williams Shift, then, cannot be dismissed as unconsidered.

† Invented, or perpetrated (as a joke?) by Boudreau on July 14, 1946, between games of a doubleheader. In the first game of the doubleheader, Williams had hit three homers and batted in eight runs. The shift was not used when men were on base and, had Williams bunted or hit late against it immediately, it might not have spread, in all its variations, throughout the league. The Cardinals used it in the lamented World Series of that year. Toward the end, in 1959 and 1960, rather sadly, it had faded from use, or degenerated to the mere clockwise twitching of the infield customary against pull hitters.

to blast it through three men, and paid the price of perhaps fifteen points of lifetime average. Like Ruth before him, he bought the occasional home run at the cost of many directed singles—a calculated sacrifice certainly not, in the case of a hitter as average-minded as Williams, entirely selfish.

After a prime so harassed and hobbled, Williams was granted by the relenting fates a golden twilight. He became at the end of his career perhaps the best *old* hitter of the century. The dividing line falls between the 1956 and the 1957 seasons. In September of the first year, he and Mickey Mantle were contending for the batting championship. Both were hitting around .350, and there was no one else near them. The season ended with a three-game series between the Yankees and the Sox, and, living in New York then, I went up to the Stadium. Williams was slightly shy of the four hundred at-bats needed to qualify; the fear was expressed that the Yankee pitchers would walk him to protect Mantle. Instead, they pitched to him. It was wise. He looked terrible at the plate, tired and discouraged and unconvincing. He never looked very good to me in the Stadium.* The final outcome in 1956 was Mantle .353, Williams .345.

The next year, I moved from New York to New England, and it made all the difference. For in September of 1957, in the same situation, the story was reversed. Mantle finally hit .365; it was the best season of his career. But Williams, though sick and old, had run away from him. A bout of flu had laid him low in September. He emerged from his cave in the Hotel Somerset haggard but irresistible; he hit four successive pinch-hit home runs. "I feel terrible," he confessed, "but every time I take a swing at the ball it goes out of the park." He ended the season with thirty-eight home runs and an average of .388, the highest in either league since his own .406, and, coming from a decrepit man of thirty-nine, an even more supernal figure. With eight or so of the "leg hits" that a younger man would have beaten out, it would have been .400. And the next year, Williams, who in 1949 and 1953 had lost batting championships by decimal whiskers to

---

* Shortly after his retirement, Williams, in *Life*, wrote gloomily of the Stadium, "There's the bigness of it. There are those high stands and all those people smoking—and, of course, the shadows. . . . It takes at least one series to get accustomed to the Stadium and even then you're not sure." Yet his lifetime batting average there is .340, only four points under his median average.

George Kell and Mickey Vernon, sneaked in behind his teammate Pete Runnels and filched his sixth title, a bargain at .328.

In 1959, it seemed all over. The dinosaur thrashed around in the .200 swamp for the first half of the season, and was even benched ("rested," Manager Mike Higgins tactfully said). Old foes like the late Bill Cunningham began to offer batting tips. Cunningham thought Williams was jiggling his elbows;* in truth, Williams' neck was so stiff he could hardly turn his head to look at the pitcher. When he swung, it looked like a Calder mobile with one thread cut; it reminded you that since 1954 Williams' shoulders had been wired together. A solicitous pall settled over the sports pages. In the two decades since Williams had come to Boston, his status had imperceptibly shifted from that of a naughty prodigy to that of a municipal monument. As his shadow in the record books lengthened, the Red Sox teams around him declined, and the entire American League seemed to be losing life and color to the National. The inconsistency of the new super-stars—Mantle, Colavito, and Kaline—served to make Williams appear all the more singular. And off the field, his private philanthropy—in particular, his zealous chairmanship of the Jimmy Fund, a charity for children with cancer—gave him a civic presence matched only by that of Richard Cardinal Cushing. In religion, Williams appears to be a humanist, and a selective one at that, but he and the abrasive-voiced Cardinal, when their good works intersect and they appear in the public eye together, make a handsome pair of seraphim.

Humiliated by his '59 season, Williams determined, once more, to come back. I, as a specimen Williams partisan, was both glad and fearful. All baseball fans believe in miracles; the question is, how *many* do you believe in? He looked like a ghost in spring training. Manager Jurges warned us ahead of time that if Williams didn't come through he would be benched, just like anybody else. As it turned out, it was Jurges who was benched. Williams entered the 1960 season needing eight home runs to have a lifetime total of 500; after

---

* It was Cunningham who, when Williams first appeared in a Red Sox uniform at the 1938 spring training camp, wrote with melodious prescience: "The Sox seem to think Williams is just cocky enough and gabby enough to make a great and colorful outfielder, possibly the Babe Herman type. Me? I don't like the way he stands at the plate. He bends his front knee inward and moves his foot just before he takes a swing. That's exactly what I do just before I drive a golf ball and knowing what happens to the golf balls I drive, I don't believe this kid will ever hit half a singer midget's weight in a bathing suit."

one time at bat in Washington, he needed seven. For a stretch, he was hitting a home run every second game that he played. He passed Lou Gehrig's lifetime total, and finished with 521, thirteen behind Jimmy Foxx, who alone stands between Williams and Babe Ruth's un-approachable 714. The summer was a statistician's picnic. His two-thousandth walk came and went, his eighteen-hundredth run batted in, his sixteenth All-Star Game. At one point, he hit a home run off a pitcher, Don Lee, off whose father, Thornton Lee, he had hit a home run a generation before. The only comparable season for a forty-two-year-old man was Ty Cobb's in 1928. Cobb batted .323 and hit one homer. Williams batted .316 but hit twenty-nine homers.

In sum, though generally conceded to be the greatest hitter of his era, he did not establish himself as "the greatest hitter who ever lived." Cobb, for average, and Ruth, for power, remain supreme. Cobb, Rogers Hornsby, Joe Jackson, and Lefty O'Doul, among players since 1900, have higher lifetime averages than Williams' .344. Unlike Foxx, Gehrig, Hack Wilson, Hank Greenberg, and Ralph Kiner, Williams never came close to matching Babe Ruth's season home-run total of sixty.* In the list of major-league batting records, not one is held by Williams. He is second in walks drawn, third in home runs, fifth in lifetime average, sixth in runs batted in, eighth in runs scored and in total bases, fourteenth in doubles, and thirtieth in hits.† But if we allow him merely average seasons for the four-plus seasons he lost to two wars, and add another season for the months he lost to in-juries, we get a man who in all the power totals would be second, and not a very distant second, to Ruth. And if we further allow that these years would have been not merely average but prime years, if we allow for all the months when Williams was playing in sub-par con-dition, if we permit his early and later years in baseball to be some sort of index of what the middle years could have been, if we give him a right-field fence that is not, like Fenway's, one of the most dis-tant in the league, and if—the least excusable "if"—we imagine him condescending to outsmart the Williams Shift, we can defensibly as-semble, like a colossus induced from the sizable fragments that do remain, a statistical figure not incommensurate with his grandiose

---

* Written before Roger Maris's fluky, phenomenal sixty-one.
† Again, as of 1960. Since then, Musial may have surpassed him in some statistical areas.

ambition. From the statistics that are on the books, a good case can be made that in the *combination* of power and average Williams is first; nobody else ranks so high in both categories. Finally, there is the witness of the eyes; men whose memories go back to Shoeless Joe Jackson—another unlucky natural—rank him and Williams together as the best-looking hitters they have seen. It was for our last look that ten thousand of us had come.

Two girls, one of them with pert buckteeth and eyes as black as vest buttons, the other with white skin and flesh-colored hair, like an underdeveloped photograph of a redhead, came and sat on my right. On my other side was one of those frowning chestless young-old men who can frequently be seen, often wearing sailor hats, attending ball games alone. He did not once open his program but instead tapped it, rolled up, on his knee as he gave the game his disconsolate attention. A young lady, with freckles and a depressed, dainty nose that by an optical illusion seemed to thrust her lips forward for a kiss, sauntered down into the box seat right behind the roof of the Oriole dugout. She wore a blue coat with a Northeastern University emblem sewed to it. The girls beside me took it into their heads that this was Williams' daughter. She looked too old to me, and why would she be sitting behind the visitors' dugout? On the other hand, from the way she sat there, staring at the sky and French-inhaling, she clearly was *somebody*. Other fans came and eclipsed her from view. The crowd looked less like a weekday ballpark crowd than like the folks you might find in Yellowstone National Park, or emerging from automobiles at the top of scenic Mount Mansfield. There were a lot of competitively well-dressed couples of tourist age, and not a few babes in arms. A row of five seats in front of me was abruptly filled with a woman and four children, the youngest of them two years old, if that. Someday, presumably, he could tell his grandchildren that he saw Williams play. Along with these tots and second-honeymooners, there were Harvard freshmen, giving off that peculiar nervous glow created when a sufficient quantity of insouciance is saturated with enough insecurity; thick-necked Army officers with brass on their shoulders and steel in their stares; pepperings of priests; perfumed bouquets of Roxbury Fabian fans; shiny salesmen from Albany and Fall River; and those gray, hoarse men—taxi drivers, slaughterers, and bartenders—

who will continue to click through the turnstiles long after everyone else has deserted to television and tramporamas. Behind me, two young male voices blossomed, cracking a joke about God's five proofs that Thomas Aquinas exists—typical Boston College levity.

The batting cage was trundled away. The Orioles fluttered to the sidelines. Diagonally across the field, by the Red Sox dugout, a cluster of men in overcoats were festering like maggots. I could see a splinter of white uniform, and Williams' head, held at a self-deprecating and evasive tilt. Williams' conversational stance is that of a six-foot-three-inch man under a six-foot ceiling. He moved away to the patter of flash bulbs, and began playing catch with a young Negro outfielder named Willie Tasby. His arm, never very powerful, had grown lax with the years, and his throwing motion was a kind of muscular drawl. To catch the ball, he flicked his glove hand onto his left shoulder (he batted left but threw right, as every schoolboy ought to know) and let the ball plop into it comically. This catch session with Tasby was the only time all afternoon I saw him grin.

A tight little flock of human sparrows who, from the lambent and pampered pink of their faces, could only have been Boston politicians moved toward the plate. The loudspeakers mammothly coughed as someone huffed on the microphone. The ceremonies began. Curt Gowdy, the Red Sox radio and television announcer, who sounds like everybody's brother-in-law, delivered a brief sermon, taking the two words "pride" and "champion" as his text. It began, "Twenty-one years ago, a skinny kid from San Diego, California . . ." and ended, "I don't think we'll ever see another like him." Robert Tibolt, chairman of the board of the Greater Boston Chamber of Commerce, presented Williams with a big Paul Revere silver bowl. Harry Carlson, a member of the sports committee of the Boston Chamber, gave him a plaque, whose inscription he did not read in its entirety, out of deference to Williams' distaste for this sort of fuss. Mayor Collins, seated in a wheelchair, presented the Jimmy Fund with a thousand-dollar check.

Then the occasion himself stooped to the microphone, and his voice sounded, after the others, very Californian; it seemed to be coming, excellently amplified, from a great distance, adolescently young and as smooth as a butternut. His thanks for the gifts had not died from our ears before he glided, as if helplessly, into "In spite of all the terrible things that have been said about me by the knights of the keyboard up there. . . ." He glanced up at the press rows suspended behind home plate. The crowd tittered, appalled. A frightful vision flashed upon me, of the press gallery pelting Williams with erasers, of Williams clambering up the foul screen to slug journalists, of a riot, of Mayor Collins being crushed. ". . . And they *were* terrible things," Williams insisted, with level melancholy, into the mike. "I'd like to forget them, but I can't." He paused, swallowed his memories, and went on, "I want to say that my years in Boston have been the greatest thing in my life." The crowd, like an immense sail going limp in a change of wind, sighed with relief. Taking all the parts himself, Williams then acted out a vivacious little morality drama in which an imaginary tempter came to him at the beginning of his career and said, "Ted, you can play anywhere you like." Leaping nimbly into the role of his younger self (who in biographical actuality had yearned to be a Yankee), Williams gallantly chose Boston over all the other cities, and told us that Tom Yawkey was the greatest owner in baseball and we were the greatest fans. We applauded ourselves lustily. The umpire came out and dusted the plate. The voice of doom announced over the loudspeakers that after Williams' retirement his uniform number, 9, would be permanently retired—the first time the Red Sox had so honored a player. We cheered. The national anthem was played. We cheered. The game began.

Williams was third in the batting order, so he came up in the bottom of the first inning, and Steve Barber, a young pitcher born two months before Williams began playing in the major leagues, offered him four pitches, at all of which he disdained to swing, since none of them were within the strike zone. This demonstrated simultaneously that Williams' eyes were razor-sharp and that Barber's control wasn't. Shortly, the bases were full, with Williams on second. "Oh, I hope he gets held up at third! That would be wonderful," the girl beside me moaned, and, sure enough, the man at bat walked and Williams was delivered into our foreground. He struck the pose of Donatello's David, the third-base bag being Goliath's head. Fiddling with his cap, swapping small talk with the Oriole third baseman (who seemed delighted to have him drop in), swinging his arms with a sort of prancing nervousness, he looked fine—flexible, hard, and not unbecomingly substantial through the middle. The long neck, the small head, the knickers whose cuffs were worn down near his ankles—all these clichés of sports cartoon iconography were rendered in the flesh.

With each pitch, Williams danced down the baseline, waving his arms and stirring dust, ponderous but menacing, like an attacking goose. It occurred to about a dozen humorists at once to shout "Steal home! Go, go!" Williams' speed afoot was never legendary. Lou Clinton, a young Sox outfielder, hit a fairly deep fly to center field. Williams tagged up and ran home. As he slid across the plate, the ball, thrown with unusual heft by Jackie Brandt, the Oriole center fielder, hit him on the back.

"Boy, he was really loafing, wasn't he?" one of the collegiate voices behind me said.

"It's cold," the other voice explained. "He doesn't play well when it's cold. He likes heat. He's a hedonist."

The run that Williams scored was the second and last of the inning. Gus Triandos, of the Orioles, quickly evened the score by plunking a home run over the handy left-field wall. Williams, who had had this wall at his back for twenty years,* played the ball flawlessly. He didn't budge. He just stood still, in the center of the little patch of grass that his patient footsteps had worn brown, and, limp with lack of interest, watched the ball pass overhead. It was not a very interesting game. Mike Higgins, the Red Sox manager, with nothing to lose, had restricted his major-league players to the left-field line— along with Williams, Frank Malzone, a first-rate third baseman, played the game—and had peopled the rest of the terrain with unpredictable youngsters fresh, or not so fresh, off the farms. Other than Williams' recurrent appearances at the plate, the *maladresse* of the Sox infield was the sole focus of suspense; the second baseman turned every grounder into a juggling act, while the shortstop did a breathtaking impersonation of an open window. With this sort of assistance, the Orioles wheedled their way into a 4–2 lead. They had early replaced Barber with another young pitcher, Jack Fisher. Fortunately (as it turned out), Fisher is no cutie; he is willing to burn the ball through the strike zone, and inning after inning this tactic punctured Higgins' string of test balloons.

* In his second season (1940) he was switched to left field, to protect his eyes from the right-field sun.

Whenever Williams appeared at the plate—pounding the dirt from his cleats, gouging a pit in the batter's box with his left foot, wringing resin out of the bat handle with his vehement grip, switching the stick at the pitcher with an electric ferocity—it was like having a familiar Leonardo appear in a shuffle of *Saturday Evening Post* covers. This man, you realized—and here, perhaps, was the difference, greater than the difference in gifts—really desired to hit the ball. In the third inning, he hoisted a high fly to deep center. In the fifth, we thought he had it; he smacked the ball hard and high into the heart of his power zone, but the deep right field in Fenway and the heavy air and a casual east wind defeated him. The ball died. Al Pilarcik leaned his back against the big "380" painted on the right-field wall and caught it. On another day, in another park, it would have been gone. (After the game, Williams said, "I didn't think I could hit one any harder than that. The conditions weren't good.")

The afternoon grew so glowering that in the sixth inning the arc lights were turned on—always a wan sight in the daytime, like the burning headlights of a funeral procession. Aided by the gloom, Fisher was slicing through the Sox rookies, and Williams did not come to bat in the seventh. He was second up in the eighth. This was almost certainly his last time to come to the plate in Fenway Park, and instead of merely cheering, as we had at his three previous appearances, we stood, all of us, and applauded. I had never before heard pure applause in a ballpark. No calling, no whistling, just an ocean of handclaps, minute after minute, burst after burst, crowding and running together in continuous succession like the pushes of surf at the edge of the sand. It was a sombre and considered tumult. There was not a boo in it. It seemed to renew itself out of a shifting set of memories as the Kid, the Marine, the veteran of feuds and failures and injuries, the friend of children, and the enduring old pro evolved down the bright tunnel of twenty-two summers toward this moment. At last, the umpire signalled for Fisher to pitch; with the other players, he had been frozen in position. Only Williams had moved during the ovation, switching his bat impatiently, ignoring everything except his cherished task. Fisher wound up, and the applause sank into a hush.

Understand that we were a crowd of rational people. We knew that a home run cannot be produced at will; the right pitch must be perfectly met and luck must ride with the ball. Three innings before, we had seen a brave effort fail. The air was soggy, the season was exhausted. Nevertheless, there will always lurk, around the corner in a pocket of our knowledge of the odds, an indefensible hope, and this was one of the times, which you now and then find in sports, when a density of expectation hangs in the air and plucks an event out of the future.

Fisher, after his unsettling wait, was low with the first pitch. He put the second one over, and Williams swung mightily and missed. The crowd grunted, seeing that classic swing, so long and smooth and quick, exposed. Fisher threw the third time, Williams swung again, and there it was. The ball climbed on a diagonal line into the vast volume of air over center field. From my angle, behind third base, the ball seemed less an object in flight than the tip of a towering, motionless construct, like the Eiffel Tower or the Tappan Zee Bridge. It was in the books while it was still in the sky. Brandt ran back to the deepest corner of the outfield grass, the ball descended beyond his reach and struck in the crotch where the bullpen met the wall, bounced chunkily, and vanished.

Like a feather caught in a vortex, Williams ran around the square of bases at the center of our beseeching screaming. He ran as he always ran out home runs—hurriedly, unsmiling, head down, as if our praise were a storm of rain to get out of. He didn't tip his cap. Though we thumped, wept, and chanted "We want Ted" for minutes after he hid in the dugout, he did not come back. Our noise for some seconds passed beyond excitement into a kind of immense open anguish, a wailing, a cry to be saved. But immortality is nontransferable. The papers said that the other players, and even the umpires on the field, begged him to come out and acknowledge us in some way, but he refused. Gods do not answer letters.

Every true story has an anticlimax. The men on the field refused to disappear, as would have seemed decent, in the smoke of Williams' miracle. Fisher continued to pitch, and escaped further harm. At the end of the inning, Higgins sent Williams out to his left-field position, then instantly replaced him with Carrol Hardy, so we had a long last look at Williams as he ran out there and then back, his uniform jogging, his eyes steadfast on the ground. It was nice, and we were grateful, but it left a funny taste.

One of the scholasticists behind me said, "Let's go. We've seen everything. I don't want to spoil it." This seemed a sound aesthetic decision. Williams' last word had been so exquisitely chosen, such a perfect fusion of expectation, intention, and execution, that already it felt a little unreal in my head, and I wanted to get out before the castle collapsed. But the game, though played by clumsy midgets under the feeble glow of the arc lights, began to tug at my attention, and I loitered in the runway until it was over. Williams' homer had, quite incidentally, made the score 4–3. In the bottom of the ninth inning, with one out, Marlin Coughtry, the second-base juggler, singled. Vic Wertz, pinch-hitting, doubled off the left-field wall, Coughtry advancing to third. Pumpsie Green walked, to load the bases. Willie Tasby hit a double-play ball to the third baseman, but in making the pivot throw Billy Klaus, an ex-Red Sox infielder, reverted to form and threw the ball past the first baseman and into the Red Sox dugout. The Sox won, 5–4. On the car radio as I drove home I heard that Williams, his own man to the end, had decided not to accompany the team to New York. He had met the little death that awaits athletes. He had quit.

Over the 20 years he pitched in the Negro Leagues, and the six more he threw in the majors, the ageless Leroy "Satchel" Paige (1906–1982) was among the most gifted and flamboyant characters in American baseball history. As the star of the Pittsburgh Crawfords, the Kansas City Monarchs, and barnstorming teams in the U.S., Mexico, and the Caribbean, Paige delighted in stunts like calling in his outfield and then striking out the side. He loved to give his pitches names like the Jump Ball, the Bee Ball, and the Long Tom. Like the memorable one-liners of Dizzy Dean ("If you can do it, it ain't braggin'"), Casey Stengel, and Yogi Berra, Paige's rules for staying young are gems of baseball vernacular. Often quoted while he was alive, these words appear on his gravestone. A fuller account of Paige's career can be found in his autobiography *Maybe I'll Pitch Forever* (1962).

Satchel Paige

▽

Rules for Staying Young

Avoid fried meats which angry up the blood.

If your stomach disputes you, lie down and pacify it with cool thoughts.

Keep the juices flowing by jangling around gently as you move.

Go very light on the vices, such as carrying on in society—the social ramble ain't restful.

Avoid running at all times.

And don't look back. Something might be gaining on you.

••

Bill Veeck (1914–1987) grew up in Chicago, where his father was president of the Cubs. After a childhood of mixing with gangsters and ballplayers, Veeck would have it that he spent his adult life doing more of the same. As an owner of major- and minor-league teams, he loathed most of his executive peers and delighted in provoking them with a stream of publicity stunts—nobody in baseball ever did more with fireworks and swaybacked horses, not to mention men of limited height. There were more serious accomplishments: in 1947, while operating the Cleveland Indians, he hired Larry Doby, the first black player in the American League. When it came time to write his memoirs, Veeck chose baseball's finest ghostwriter to assist him, the former *Sport* magazine staff member—and Ted Williams biographer—Ed Linn. The result, *Veeck As In Wreck* (1962), is the irresistible account of a rambunctious character.

Bill Veeck

ᗉ

A Can of Beer, a Slice of Cake— and Thou, Eddie Gaedel

In 1951, in a moment of madness, I became owner and operator of a collection of old rags and tags known to baseball historians as the St. Louis Browns.

The Browns, according to reputable anthropologists, rank in the annals of baseball a step or two ahead of Cro-Magnon man. One thing should be made clear. A typical *Brownie* was more than four feet tall. Except, of course, for Eddie Gaedel, who was 3'7" and weighed 65 lbs. Eddie gave the Browns their only distinction. He was, by golly, the best darn midget who ever played big-league ball. He was also the only one.

Eddie came to us in a moment of desperation. Not his desperation, ours. After a month or so in St. Louis, we were looking around desperately for a way to draw a few people into the ball park, it being perfectly clear by that time that the ball club wasn't going to do it unaided. The best bet seemed to be to call upon the resources of our radio sponsors, Falstaff Brewery. For although Falstaff only broadcast our games locally, they had distributors and dealers all over the state.

It happened that 1951 was the Fiftieth Anniversary of the American League, an event the league was exploiting with its usual burst of inspiration by sewing special emblems on the uniforms of all the players. It seemed to me that a birthday party was clearly called for. It seemed to me, further, that if I could throw a party to celebrate the birthdays of both the American League and Falstaff Brewery, the sponsors would be getting a nice little tie-in and we would have their distributors and dealers hustling tickets for us all over the state. Nobody at Falstaff's seemed to know exactly when their birthday was, but that was no great problem. If we couldn't prove it fell on the day we chose, neither could anyone prove that it didn't. The day we chose was a Sunday doubleheader against the last-place Detroit Tigers, a struggle which did not threaten to set the pulses of the city beating madly.

Rudie Schaffer, the Browns' business manager, and I met with the Falstaff people—Mr. Griesedieck Sr., the head of the company, Bud and Joe Griesedieck and their various department heads—to romance our project. "In addition to the regular party, the acts and so on," I told Bud, "I'll do something for you that I have never done before. Something so original and spectacular that it will get you national publicity."

Naturally, they pressed me for details. Naturally, I had to tell them that much as I hated to hold out on them, my idea was so explosive I could not afford to take the slightest chance of a leak.

The Falstaff people, romantics all, went for it. They were so anxious to find out what I was going to do that they could hardly bear to wait out the two weeks. I was rather anxious to find out what I was going to do, too. The real reason I had not been willing to let them in on my top-secret plan was that I didn't have any plan.

What can I do, I asked myself, that is so spectacular that *no one* will be able to say he had seen it before? The answer was perfectly obvious. I would send a midget up to bat.

Actually, the idea of using a midget had been kicking around in my head all my life. I have frequently been accused of stealing the idea from a James Thurber short story, "You Could Look It Up." Sheer libel. I didn't steal the idea from Thurber, I stole it from John J. McGraw.

McGraw had been a great friend of my father's in the days when McGraw was managing the New York Giants and my daddy was president of the Chicago Cubs. Once or twice every season he would come to the house, and one of my greatest thrills would be to sit quietly at the table after dinner and listen to them tell their lies. McGraw had a little hunchback he kept around the club as a sort of good-luck charm. His name, if I remember, was Eddie Morrow. Morrow wasn't a midget, you understand, he was a sort of gnome. By the time McGraw got to the stub of his last cigar, he would always swear to my father that one day before he retired he was going to send his gnome up to bat.

All kids are tickled by the incongruous. The picture of McGraw's gnome coming to bat had made such a vivid impression on me that it was there, ready for the plucking, when I needed it.

I put in a call to Marty Caine, the booking agent from whom I had hired all my acts when I was operating in Cleveland, and asked him to find me a midget who was somewhat athletic and game for anything. "And Marty," I said, "I want this to be a secret."

I never told Marty what I wanted him for. Only five other people knew. Mary Frances, my wife; Rudie Schaffer; Bob Fishel, our publicity man; Bill Durney, our traveling secretary; and, of course, Zack Taylor, our manager.

Marty Caine found Eddie Gaedel in Chicago and sent him down to be looked over. He was a nice little guy, in his mid-twenties. Like all midgets, he had sad little eyes, and like all midgets, he had a squeaky little voice that sounded as if it were on the wrong speed of a record player.

"Eddie," I said, "how would you like to be a big-league ballplayer?"

When he first heard what I wanted him to do, he was a little dubious. I had to give him a sales pitch. I said, "Eddie, you'll be the only midget in the history of the game. You'll be appearing before thousands of people. Your name will go into the record books for all time. You'll be famous, Eddie," I said. "Eddie," I said, "you'll be immortal."

Well, Eddie Gaedel had more than a little ham in him. The more I talked, the braver he became. By the time I was finished, little Eddie was ready to charge through a machine-gun nest to get to the plate.

I asked him how much he knew about baseball. "Well," he said, "I know you're supposed to hit the white ball with the bat. And then you run somewhere."

Obviously, he was well schooled in the fundamentals. "I'll show you what I want you to do," I told him.

I picked up a little toy bat and crouched over as far as I could, my front elbow resting on my front knee. The rules of the game say that the strike zone is between the batter's armpits and the top of his knees "when he assumes his natural stance." Since Gaedel would bat only once in his life, whatever stance he took was, by definition, his natural one.

When Eddie went into that crouch, his strike zone was just about visible to the naked eye. I picked up a ruler and measured it for posterity. It was 1½ inches. Marvelous.

Eddie practiced that crouch for awhile, up and down, up and down, while I cheered him on lustily from the sidelines. After a while, he began to test the heft of the bat and glare out toward an imaginary pitcher. He sprang out of his crouch and took an awkward, lunging swing.

"No, no," I said. "You just stay in that crouch. All you have to do is stand there and take four balls. Then you'll trot down to first base and we'll send someone in to run for you."

His face collapsed. You could see his visions of glory leaking out of him. All at once, I remembered that the twist in the James Thurber story was that the midget got ambitious, swung at the 3–0 pitch and got thrown out at first base because it took him an hour and a half to run down the baseline.

"Eddie," I said gently, "I'm going to be up on the roof with a high-powered rifle watching every move you make. If you so much as look as if you're going to swing, I'm going to shoot you dead."

Eddie went back to Chicago with instructions to return on Saturday, August 18, the day before the game. In the meantime, there were details to be attended to. First of all, there was the question of a uniform. No problem. Bill DeWitt Jr., the seven-year-old son of our vice-president, had a little Browns' uniform hanging in the locker room. Rudie stole it and sent it out to get the number 1/8 sewed on the back. Scorecards are traditionally printed up on the morning of the game, so listing him would be no problem at all.

Just for the heck of it, I took out a $1,000,000 insurance policy to protect us in case of sudden death, sudden growth or any other pernicious act of nature. Somehow no opportunity to tell anybody about that policy ever came up, no great loss since the whole thing cost me about a buck and a half.

We were hiring Eddie for one day at $100, the minimum AGVA scale for a midget act. Still, if he was going to play in an official game he had to be signed to a standard player's contract, with a salary set on an annual basis and a guaranteed 30-day payment upon termination. That was no real problem, either. We computed the salary on the basis of $100 a game and typed in an additional clause in which Eddie agreed to waive the 30-day notice.

I must admit that by the time Eddie came back to St. Louis we were playing the cloak-and-dagger stuff a bit strong. Eddie went directly to a hotel suite we had hired for him about ten blocks from the park. Instead of bringing the contract to his room, Bob Fishel set up a meeting on a street corner a block or two from the hotel. Bob drove up in his old Packard and Eddie slid into the front seat, scribbled his signature on two contracts and jumped back out. One of the contracts was mailed to league headquarters on Saturday night, which meant that it would not be delivered until Monday morning. The other contract was given to Zack Taylor, in case our promising rookie was challenged by the umpires. The morning of the game, I wired headquarters that we were putting player Edward Gaedel on our active list.

On Sunday morning, we smuggled Eddie up to the office for further instruction on the fine art of crouching. That was a little dangerous. I have always taken the doors off my office and encouraged people to walk right in to see me. We posted a lookout and from time to time either Mary Frances or Bob or Rudie would have to hustle Eddie out to the farm-system offices in the back. Always they'd come back with the same story. As soon as Eddie got out of my sight he'd turn tiger and start swinging his little bat. "He's going to foul it up," they all told me. "If you saw him back there you'd know he's going to swing."

"Don't worry," I'd tell them, worrying furiously. "I've got the situation well in hand."

Don't worry. . . . Just as I was leaving the office to circulate among the customers as they arrived at the park, Eddie asked me, "Bill . . . ? How tall was Wee Willie Keeler?"

Oh, boy. . . .

"Eddie," I said, "I've got your life insured for a million dollars. I've got a gun stashed up on the roof. But don't you let any of that bother you. You just crouch over like you've been doing and take four pitches, huh?"

As I was going out the door, I turned back one final time. "Wee Willie Keeler," I told him, "was six-feet-five."

Falstaff came through nobly. We had a paid attendance of better than 18,000, the biggest crowd to see the Browns at home in four years. Since our customers were also our guests for the Falstaff Birthday Party, we presented everybody with a can of beer, a slice of birthday cake and a box of ice cream as they entered the park. I also gave out one of Falstaff's own promotional gimmicks, salt-and-pepper shakers in the shape of a Falstaff bottle. The tie-in there was that we were giving the fans *midget* beer bottles as souvenirs of the day, a subtlety which managed to elude everybody completely.

The most surprising thing to me, as I moved through the crowd during the first game, was that nobody seemed to have paid the slightest attention to the rather unique scorecard listing:

1/8 Gaedel

Harry Mitauer of the *Globe-Democrat* did ask Bob Fishel about it up in the press box, but Roberto was able to shunt the question aside. (The next day, we had a hundred or so requests from collectors, so I suppose there are quite a few of the Gaedel scorecards still in existence around the country.)

Every baseball crowd, like every theatre audience, has its own distinctive attitude and atmosphere. You can usually tell as they are coming into the park whether it is going to be a happy, responsive crowd or a dead and sullen one. With the Birthday Party and the gifts and the busfuls of people from the outlying towns, the crowd arrived in a gay and festive mood. Not even the loss of the first game could dampen their spirit.

We went all out in our between-games Birthday Celebration. We had a parade of old-fashioned cars circling the field. We had two men and two women, dressed in Gay Ninety costumes, pedaling around the park on a bicycle-built-for-four. Troubadours roamed through the stands to entertain the customers. Our own band, featuring Satchel Paige on the drums, performed at home plate. Satch, who is good enough to be a professional, stopped the show cold.

In our own version of a 3-ring circus, we had something going on at every base—a hand-balancing act at first base, a trampoline act on second and a team of jugglers at third. Max Patkin, our rubber-boned clown, pulled a woman out of the grandstand and did a wild jitterbug dance with her on the pitcher's mound.

Eddie Gaedel had remained up in the office during the game, under the care of big Bill Durney. Between games, Durney was to bring him down under the stands, in full uniform, and put him into a huge 7-foot birthday cake we had stashed away under the ramp. There was a hollowed-out section in the middle of the cake, complete with a board slab for Eddie to sit on. For we had a walk-on role written in for Eddie during the celebration; we were really getting our $100 worth out of him. As a matter of fact, the cake cost us a darn sight more than Eddie did.

As I hustled down the ramp, I could hear the crowd roaring at Patkin. Eddie could hear it too. And apparently the tremendous roar, magnified underground, frightened him. "Gee," I could hear him saying, "I don't feel so good." And then, after a second or two, "I don't think I'm going to do it."

Now, Bill Durney is 6'4" and in those days he weighed 250 lbs. "Listen, Eddie," he said. "There are eighteen thousand people in this park and there's one I know I can lick. You. Dead or alive, you're going in there."

I arrived on the scene just as Bill was lifting him up to stuff him inside. Eddie was holding his bat in one hand and, at that stage of the proceedings, he was wearing little slippers turned up at the end like elf's shoes. Well, it is difficult enough, I suppose, for anybody to look calm and confident while he is being hung out like laundry. Nor do I imagine that anybody has ever managed to look like a raging tiger in elf's shoes. Taking all that into consideration, you could still see that Eddie was scared. He wanted out. "Bill," he said piteously, as he dangled there, "these shoes hurt my feet. I don't think I'll be able to go on."

We weren't about to let him duck out this late in the game. Durney dropped him in the cake, sat him down and covered the top over with tissue paper.

Up on the roof behind home plate we had a special box with a connecting bar and restaurant for the care and feeding of visiting dignitaries. By the time I got up there to join Bud Griesedieck and the rest of the Falstaff executive force, the cake had already been rolled out onto the infield grass. Along with the cake came Sir John Falstaff or, at any rate, a hefty actor dressed in Elizabethan clothes. *There* was a touch to warm the cockles and hops of the Falstaff crowd.

"Watch this," I chuckled.

Our announcer, Bernie Ebert, boomed: "Ladies and gentlemen, as a special birthday present to manager Zack Taylor, the management is presenting him with a brand-new Brownie."

Sir John tapped the cake with his gleaming cutlass and, right on cue, out through the paper popped Eddie Gaedel.

There was a smattering of applause from the stands and a light ripple of laughter.

In the Falstaff box, there was nothing but stunned silence.

"Holy smokes," Bud said, "this is what your big thing is? A little midget jumps out of a cake and he's wearing a baseball uniform and he's a bat boy or something?"

"Don't you understand?" I said. "He's a real live Brownie."

"You put funny shoes on a midget and he's a real live Brownie and that's going to get us national coverage?"

Karl Vollmer, their advertising manager, was plainly disgusted. "Aw, this is lousy, Bill," he said. "Even the cake gimmick, you've used that before in Milwaukee and Cleveland. You haven't given us anything new at all."

I begged them not to be too unhappy. "Maybe it isn't the best gag in the world," I said, "but the rest of the show was good and everybody seems happy. It will be all right."

They were determined to be unhappy, though. The gloom in that box was so thick that our Falstaff could have come up and carved it into loaves with his cutlass. (That didn't seem like a very good idea at the moment, however, because Vollmer looked as if he was just about ready to grab the cutlass and cut my throat.) "This is the explosive thing you couldn't tell us about," Vollmer muttered. "A midget jumps out of a cake and, what do you know, he's a real live Brownie."

I did my best to look ashamed of myself.

In the second game, we started Frank Saucier in place of our regular center fielder, Jim Delsing. This is the only part of the gag I've ever felt bad about. Saucier was a great kid whom I had personally talked back into the game when I bought the Browns. Everything went wrong for Frank, and all he has to show for his great promise is that he was the only guy a midget ever batted for.

For as we came up for our half of the first inning, Eddie Gaedel emerged from the dugout waving three little bats. "For the Browns," said Bernie Ebert over the loudspeaker system, "number one-eighth, Eddie Gaedel, batting for Saucier."

Suddenly, the whole park came alive. Suddenly, my honored guests sat upright in their seats. Suddenly, the sun was shining. Eddie Hurley, the umpire behind the plate, took one look at Gaedel and started toward our bench. "Hey," he shouted out to Taylor, "what's going on here?"

Zack came out with a sheaf of papers. He showed Hurley Gaedel's contract. He showed him the telegram to headquarters, duly promulgated with a time stamp. He even showed him a copy of our active list to prove that we did have room to add another player.

Hurley returned to home plate, shooed away the photographers who had rushed out to take Eddie's picture and motioned the midget into the batter's box. The place went wild. Bobby Cain, the Detroit pitcher, and Bob Swift, their catcher, had been standing by peacefully for about 15 minutes, thinking unsolemn thoughts about that jerk Veeck and his gags. I will never forget the look of utter disbelief that came over Cain's face as he finally realized that this was for real.

Bob Swift rose to the occasion like a real trouper. If I had set out to use the opposing catcher to help build up the tension, I could not have improved one whit upon his performance. Bob, bless his heart, did just what I was hoping he would do. He went out to the mound to discuss the intricacies of pitching to a midget with Cain. And when he came back, he did something I had never even dreamed of. To complete the sheer incongruity of the scene—and make the newspaper pictures of the event more memorable—he got down on both knees to offer his pitcher a target.

By now, the whole park was rocking, and nowhere were there seven more delirious people than my guests in the rooftop box. Veeck the jerk had become Willie the wizard. The only unhappy person in that box was me, good old Willie the wizard. Gaedel, little ham that he was, had not gone into the crouch I had spent so many hours teaching him. He was standing straight up, his little bat held high, his feet spraddled wide in a fair approximation of Joe DiMaggio's classic style. While the Falstaff people were whacking me on the back and letting their joy flow unrestrained, I was thinking: *I should have brought that gun up here. I'll kill him if he swings. I'll kill him, I'll kill him.*

Fortunately, Cain started out by really trying to pitch to him. The first two deliveries came whizzing past Eddie's head before he had time to swing. By the third pitch, Cain was laughing so hard that he could barely throw. Ball three and ball four came floating up about three feet over Eddie's head.

Eddie trotted down to first base to the happy tune of snapping cameras. He waited for the runner, one foot holding to the bag like a pro, and he patted Delsing on the butt in good professional exhortation before he surrendered the base. He shook hands with our first-base coach and he waved to the cheering throng.

The St. Louis dugout was behind third base, which meant that Eddie had to cut completely across the infield. If it had been difficult to get him into the cake earlier, I was worried for awhile that I would have to send Bill Durney out there again to carry him off the field. Eddie, after all, was a performer. In his small, unspectacular way he was a part of show business. He had dreamed all his life of his moment in the spotlight and now that it had come to him, he was not about to bow his head and leave quietly. He crossed that field one step at a time, stopping in between to wave his hat or bow from the waist or just to raise an acknowledging hand to the plaudits of the crowd. When he disappeared, at last, into the dugout he was the happiest little man you have ever seen.

If the thing had been done right, Delsing, running for Gaedel, would have scored and we would have won the game, 1–0. I was willing to settle for less than that. I was willing to win by one run, regardless of the final score, as long as that one run represented Eddie Gaedel. As it was, there being a limit to the amount of help you can expect from either the St. Louis Browns or fortune, Delsing got as far as third base with only one out and was then left stranded. We lost the game, 6–2.

Nothing remained but to wait for the expected blasts from league headquarters and, more particularly, from the deacons of the press, those old-timers who look upon baseball not as a game or a business but as a solemn ritual, almost a holy calling.

The press, for the most part, took the sane attitude that Gaedel had provided a bright moment in what could easily have been a deadly dull doubleheader between a 7th and an 8th place ball club. Vincent X. Flaherty of Los Angeles pretty much summed up the general reaction when he wrote, "I do not advocate baseball burlesque. Such practices do not redound to the better interests of the game— but I claim it was the funniest thing that has happened to baseball in years."

It's fine to be appreciated for a day; I recommend it highly for the soul. It's better for the box office, though, to be attacked for a full week. I was counting on the deacons to turn Gaedel into a full week's story by attacking me for spitting in their Cathedral. They didn't let me down, although I did feel the words "cheap and tawdry" and "travesty" and "mockery" were badly overworked. The spirit was willing, but I'm afraid the rhetoric was weak.

Dan Daniel, a well-known high priest from New York, wondered what "Ban Johnson and John J. McGraw are saying about it up there in Baseball's Valhalla," a good example of Dan's lean and graceful style. Non-baseball fans should understand that baseball men do not go to heaven or hell when they die; they go to Valhalla where they sit around a hot stove and talk over the good old days with Odin, Thor and the rest of that crowd. (I am assuming that the baseball people haven't driven the old Norse gods out to the suburbs. You know what guys like Johnson and McGraw do to real-estate values.)

To Joe Williams, Daniel's colleague on the New York *World-Telegram,* I was "that fellow Veeck out in St. Louis."

"It didn't matter that this made a mockery of the sport or that it exploited a freak of biology in a shameful, disgraceful way," Williams wrote. ". . . What he calls showmanship can more often be accurately identified as vulgarity."

I have never objected to being called vulgar. The word, as I never tire of pointing out to my tireless critics, comes from the Latin *vulgaris,* which means—students?—"the common people." (If you don't believe it, Joe, you could look it up.) I am so darn vulgar that I will probably never get into Valhalla, which is a shame because I would love to be able to let McGraw know how he helped that little boy who used to listen to him, enraptured, over the dinner table. From what I can remember of McGraw, he would roar with delight.

What that fellow Williams in New York didn't seem to realize—or did he?—was that it was he who was gratuitously and publicly calling Eddie Gaedel a freak. Eddie was a professional midget. He made his living by displaying himself, the only way we permit a midget to earn a living in our enlightened society. In more barbaric times, they were able to achieve a certain stature as court jesters. My use of him—*vulgaris* that I am—was the biggest thing that ever happened to him. In the week that followed, I got him bookings that earned him something between $5,000 and $10,000. I kept getting him bookings here and there for the rest of his life. Eddie hungered for another chance at the spotlight. Whenever he came to a town where I was operating he would phone and say, "OK, Boss, I'm ready."

I did use him for a couple of my gags. One of the last times was at Comiskey Park in Chicago, about a year before his death. Eddie and three other midgets, all dressed in regimental Martian clothing (gold helmets and shoes, coveralls, oxygen tanks), somehow dropped out of the heavens in a helicopter and landed directly behind second base. Quickly capturing our tiny second-base combination, Nellie Fox and Luis Aparicio, they made them honorary Martians and informed them—over the remarkably handy public-address system—that they had come down to aid them in their battle against the giant earthlings.

It was during this historic meeting that Eddie Gaedel uttered those immortal words, "I don't want to be taken to your leader. I've already met him."

The battle with league headquarters had begun before Eddie stepped into the batter's box. Will Harridge, the league president—for reasons best known to himself—had gone to his office that Sunday and had seen the report come over the Western Union teletype that I was trying to send a midget up to bat. While Hurley was still looking over the papers, our switchboard operator, Ada Ireland, sent word to me that Harridge was on the phone threatening to blow a fuse unless someone in authority came out to talk to him. I sent back word that we had all disappeared from the face of the earth.

A few minutes later, I was told that Will was trying to get me on the office teletype, which is in direct communication with headquarters. I told them to turn off the machine.

The next day, Harridge issued an executive order barring Gaedel from baseball. A new rule was promptly passed making it mandatory that all player contracts be filed with and *approved* by the president.

Naturally, I was bewildered and alarmed and shocked. I was a few other things too: "I'm puzzled, baffled and grieved by Mr. Harridge's ruling," I announced. "Why, we're paying a lot of guys on the Browns' roster good money to get on base and even though they don't do it, nobody sympathizes with us. But when this little guy goes up to the plate and draws a walk on his only time at bat, they call it 'conduct detrimental to baseball.'"

If baseball wanted to discriminate against the little people, I said, why didn't we have the courage to be honest about it, write a minimum height into the rules and submit ourselves to the terrible wrath of all right-thinking Americans. "I think," I said, "that further clarification is called for. Should the height of a player be 3 feet 6 inches, 4 feet 6 inches, 6 feet 6 inches, or 9 feet 6 inches?" Now that midgets had been so arbitrarily barred, I asked, were we to assume that giants were also barred? I made dark references to the stature of Phil Rizzuto, who is not much over five feet tall, and I implied very strongly that I was going to demand an official ruling on whether he was a short ballplayer or a tall midget.

I hammered away at the phrase "little people," which had a solid political currency in those days. I had given Eddie Gaedel a speech on that theme too. "Everybody talks about protecting the little man these days," he was supposed to say, "and now that someone has finally taken a direct step to help the plight of the little man in baseball, Harridge has stepped in and ruined my career."

Political connotations, unfortunately, were lost on Eddie. When the time came for him to deliver his statement, he blew it. "Now that someone has finally taken a direct step to help us short guys," he said, "Harridge is ruining my baseball career." Ah well, you can't win them all.

In the end I had to agree, reluctantly, to bow to superior authority. "As much as it grieves me," I said, "I will have to go along with this odd ruling." I thought that was rather big of me, especially since I had only hired Gaedel for one day.

Something else happened, though, that I was not disposed to be so amiable about. The good deacons of the press had been wailing that unless Harridge acted immediately, the name of Eddie Gaedel would desecrate the record books for all time. Harridge dutifully decreed that Gaedel's appearance be stricken from all official records. This I wouldn't stand for. I had promised Eddie that he would live forever in the record books, which are cast in bronze, carved in marble and encased in cement. Immortality I had promised him, and immortality he would have. I reminded Harridge that Gaedel had a legal contract and had been permitted to bat in an official game presided over by the league's own umpires. If Gaedel hadn't batted, I pointed out, it would also mean that Bobby Cain hadn't thrown the pitches and that Swift hadn't caught them. It would mean that Delsing had come in to run for no one, and that Saucier had been deprived of a time at bat. It would mean, in short, that the continuity of baseball was no longer intact, and the integrity of its records had been compromised. If Desecration was the game they wanted to play, then I held a pretty strong hand myself.

Eddie crept back into the record books and remains there today. When he died, he got a front-page obituary in *The New York Times,* a recognition normally accorded only to statesmen, generals and Nobel Prize winners.

I did not recognize at the time that Gaedel's moment was my moment too. I knew it was a good gag. I knew it would delight the fans and outrage the stuffed shirts. I knew, in other words, that it would be a lot of fun. It never entered my mind, however, that it would be the single act with which I would become permanently identified. Even today, I cannot talk to anybody from St. Louis without being told that they were there the day the midget came to bat. If everybody was there who says he was there, we would have had a tidy gathering of 280,000.

I have done a few other things in baseball, you know. I've won pennants and finished dead last; I've set attendance records and been close to bankruptcy. At the age of fifteen, I was taking care of Ladies' Day passes at Wrigley Field. I owned my first ball club when I was twenty-eight. I have operated five clubs—three in the major leagues and two in the minors—and in three of the towns I won pennants and broke attendance records. Two of the three teams to beat the Yankees since I came to the American League in 1946 were my teams, the 1948 Cleveland Indians and the 1959 Chicago White Sox. The only other team, the 1954 Indians, was made up for the most part of my old players.

But no one has to tell me that if I returned to baseball tomorrow, won ten straight pennants and left all the old attendance records moldering in the dust, I would still be remembered, in the end, as the man who sent a midget up to bat. It is not the identification I would have chosen for myself when I came into baseball. My ambitions were grander than that. And yet I cannot deny that it is an accurate one. I have always found humor in the incongruous, I have always tried to entertain. And I have always found a stuffed-shirt the most irresistible of all targets.

I'm Bill Veeck, the guy who sent a midget up to bat?

Fair enough.

Murray Kempton (1917–1997) grew up in Baltimore, where he worked as a copyboy for H. L. Mencken at the *Baltimore Sun* and attended Johns Hopkins University. After a stint as a labor organizer, he joined the staff of the *New York Post* in 1942. In a career that spanned six decades, Kempton wrote for several New York newspapers as well as for *The New Republic* and *The New York Review of Books*. He always rode his bicycle to work. A graceful, ardent writer, he described ballplayers with the same sympathy he brought to his labor reporting; they were all workingmen to him. This is a piece he wrote for *Sport* magazine on the return of National League baseball to New York in 1962.

Murray Kempton

◊

Back at the Polo Grounds

The return of the Polo Grounds to the National League was like the raising of a sunken cathedral. It is a place sacred in history and hallowed in the memory. Christy Mathewson used to make his home on the bluff above the Polo Grounds. When he was working, Mrs. Mathewson could look out her window at the scoreboard and, when the seventh inning came, put the roast in the oven secure in the knowledge that her husband would be finished and showered and home from the plough in an hour.

When the Mets brought the National League, or anyway its shadow, back to New York, there was no place for them except this old shrine. The Mets' permanent stadium at Flushing Meadows is a year from completion; and the City of New York had long ago leveled Ebbets Field and sowed a housing project on its site.

So George Weiss, the Mets' new president, took the Polo Grounds from necessity more than sentiment. Weiss, of course, is the deposed general manager of the Yankees; and the Yankees are the authors of that age of elegance and class distinction in baseball which really began with their Stadium Club, a response to the corporate expense account.

Weiss's prospectus for Flushing Meadows would be garish for a trotting track: "The stadium will be triple-tiered with twenty-one

escalators to speed fans to and from their seats. . . . A 1500-seat com-
fortably decorated main dining room will be available to season box
holders. . . . There are fifty-four public rest room installations conveniently located on all three levels: twenty-seven for women, twenty-
seven for men. Each women's rest room has its own lounge or powder
room."

But all is a total affront to the tradition of the National League in
New York, where Ladies Day was never for ladies and where there was
absolute democracy in the affliction of misery upon rich and poor
alike. Dodger fans had every vulgarity but the vulgarity of wealth;
Giant fans had no vulgarity at all. The mere age and squalor of the
Polo Grounds comforted its customers; you could as easily catch
some bronchial disease in its dank recesses as you used to be able to
catch malaria at night in the Roman Colosseum, and both contagions
carried the romance of history.

The New York of the Giants, Dodgers, and Yankees was an annual
re-evocation of the War between the States. The Yankees were the
North, if you could conceive a North grinding along with wealth and
weight and without the excuse of Lincoln. The Giants and Dodgers
were the Confederacy, often undermanned and underequipped and
running then because it could not hit. You went to Yankee Stadium if
you were the kind of man who enjoyed yelling for Grant at Richmond; you went to the National League parks to see Pickett's charge.
George Weiss, a displaced quartermaster-general of the Union Army,
does not understand that persons committed to endure losing causes
do not care about escalators.

The old Dodger fans were the kind of people who picket. The old
Giant fans would be embarrassed to do anything so conspicuous, but
they were the kind of people who refuse to cross picket lines. Yankee
fans are the kind of people who think they own the company the
picket line is thrown around. It is impossible for anyone who does
not live in New York to know what it truly is to hate the Yankees. As
writer Leonard Koppett has said: "The residents of other cities who
hate the Yankees really only hate New York." He has noticed they
even hate the Knicks, the most underprivileged established team in
the National Basketball Association. But, if you live in New York and
you're not a Yankee fan, you hate them the way you hate Consolidated Edison or your friendly bank.

George Weiss, being insensitive to these nuances, could not, even for one year as tenant, let the Polo Grounds rest as the raddled, gray, pigeon-speckled old rookery its mourners had left, for what everyone assumed was the last time, after sacking and looting it after the Giants lost their last game there in 1957.

Weiss has in Mrs. Joan Whitney Payson, the Mets' owner, the most generous of patronesses. He had spent $450,000 of her money decking the Polo Grounds in orange, blue, and green paint and ornamenting its walls with faintly abstract advertisements for cigars, Scotch, pomades, salamis, and breath sweeteners. As a woman, Mrs. Payson may have been enchanted at first glance; but, as a sport, she must have been saddened to see that Weiss had painted out the numbers which used to remind all present of the distance to the foul poles and which were so much the controlling mathematics of its epic history at the Polo Grounds.

It is 257 feet to the stands in right field; and, for its prior active years, the Polo Grounds had proclaimed that terrible statistic unashamedly on its fence. Bobby Thomson's home run against the Dodgers in 1951, the most famous in baseball, traveled barely 300 feet to left. Hitting in the Polo Grounds is like playing a pinball machine. Those numbers were symbols reminding us how in life we are in the midst of death and that the afternoon could end, as so many uncertain struggles had ended before it, with the ridiculous accident of a high fly 260 feet to the wrong field.

Carl Hubbell once pitched forty-six straight scoreless innings as a Giant and this string remains a National League record. Sal Maglie, a Giant almost as sacred in the memory as Hubbell himself, came closer than any other National League pitcher to breaking that record. Maglie was in the Polo Grounds one August afternoon in 1950, two-thirds of an inning away from Hubbell's scoreless total when a young Pirate outfielder named Gus Bell hit a line drive that traveled 257 feet to the foul pole for a home run. The devils who tenant the Polo Grounds had punished Maglie for affronting Hubbell; being long in memory, they have now punished Maglie for affronting Hubbell; being long in memory, they have now punished Bell by bringing him back here to finish his career as a Met. For the Polo Grounds, being storied and ancient, is also cursed.

That curse was upon the Mets on opening day in the Polo

Grounds. It had rained much of the morning; there was the chill of old night in the air. An usher pulled the collar of his new orange windbreaker up around his chin. "You better watch out," said a colleague. "Mr. Weiss wants our collars down at all times." Casey Stengel was in the dugout with photographers, reporters, and the withdrawn and brooding eminence of Rogers Hornsby, who has been hired to coach hitters who either already know how but no longer can, or, if they learn how, are unlikely to be able to.

Stengel complained that his arm was still sore from throwing plastic baseballs at the lower Broadway crowd which had welcomed the Mets to New York. Behind him, Dan Topping of the Yankees was sitting in a box; you thought of Khrushchev on a state visit to Bulgaria and there was a sudden, useless urge for Casey's Mets to get fifty runs. The Mets came out running earnestly and heavily on a wet track; they were loudly cheered by a cluster of children in right field, an odd demonstration of the persistence of buried tradition, since none of these greeters could have been older than six when the National League fled New York.

George Weiss was suffering in Mrs. Payson's box behind the Met dugout. The devils of the Polo Grounds had devised for him a special torment. The groundskeepers, in their spring-cleaning, had come upon two rusted iron chairs and, presumably to save the long walk to the scrap heap, had thrown them into Mrs. Payson's box, like dead rats in a garden. When he owned the New York Giants, Horace Stoneham would have sat unprotesting ankle deep in coffee cups and hot-dog wrappers because he took it for granted that this was the normal environment of his playground. Weiss waved a pallid hand, a fear-stricken smile upon his pallid face. "Please," he said to one of the special guards, "this is Mrs. Payson's box. Can't you do something about it?"

Down below, Stengel thrust his head through a floral horseshoe, clowning for the photographers. He rarely spoke with his players. Instead he capered and tested the rain and always posed, a reminder that he had been hired as much for his showmanship as for his managing skill; perhaps more. Showmanship and salesmanship are important to the Mets, who have more television sponsors than Jack Paar had. We describe the future they represent when we remember they started the season with one tested and still possible major-league pitcher—Roger Craig—and three tested major-league announcers.

Weiss had bet his future more on memory than on hope. Only Sherman Jones, the pitcher in his first home lineup, bore a name not indented in the memory of the customers. Six of the starters against the Pittsburgh Pirates had played in the Polo Grounds in its last prior season five years earlier. Gil Hodges, a fifteen-year man, would certainly have started if he had been able to walk; and Joe Ginsberg, Stengel's catcher, was no less pickled with brine than his colleagues and would certainly have qualified as a Polo Grounds initiate if he had not spent most of his eleven major-league years in the low-rent district of the American League.

A visitor went down to inspect the Met Lounge, which is reserved for season ticket holders only and where "gentlemen must wear coats, ladies, inclusive of girls twelve years of age and over, will not be permitted to wear slacks of any type or abbreviated clothing." There he was first inspected for dress and credentials by a pretty girl in a pin stripe jacket and with eyes like a house detective. This ordeal entitles the elite to a fifty-cent hot dog.

Stengel's old horses took the field with heart-breaking determination of stride and common impression of haunch. The noise was suddenly immense, almost a profanation at the Polo Grounds, which was always a cloister. It was also unexpected from a crowd of twelve thousand; we were back at Ebbets Field where six thousand customers used to maintain a roar in an ordinary game against the Cubs, which always left any outlander with the suspicion that the management had installed a record-player that was blasting "Crowd noise—Dempsey-Firpo 1923" somewhere in the stands. So this was a Dodger crowd; Weiss had staked his appeal there, with Hodges, Craig, Don Zimmer, and Charlie Neal. Bobby Thomson was absent; but Ralph Branca was there, with an abject grin, to be photographed pointing to the fatal spot in left field and to explain again that it would have been a home run nowhere else.

Still, an inning and two-thirds had to go by before everyone was carried back to that lost time in the mid-fifties when the Giants were sixth. Smoky Burgess got the Pirates' first hit, and then Don Hoak sliced a fly 270 feet to the wrong field, off the wall for a double to score Burgess. Jones had been introduced to that curse of the Polo Grounds, and Hoak, who knew it of old, may be excused for the indignant reflection that he had been cheated of a home run. Then Bill

Mazeroski hit a drive well over 370 feet to right center, the afternoon's first evidence of lust but normally an out in the Polo Grounds,
the tallest and thinnest park in the big leagues. Richie Ashburn and
Gus Bell ploughed and floundered and waved under it, and before
Bell could complete the salvage, Mazeroski was on third and Hoak
was home. Jones had been introduced to his outfield and was two
runs down and innocent.

In the third inning Jim Marshall entered history by walking, the
first Met to reach base safely. The first Met hit had to wait until the
next inning and belonged to the pitcher. The first Met extra-base
hit—a double—came in the fifth and could be credited more to mud
than to muscle; Marshall lifted a fly near third; Dick Groat fell chasing it. After two outs it came Jones's turn, and Stengel had to dispense
with this young man, already so much more sinned against than sin-
ning. A claque behind first base began crying for Hodges; Stengel sent
up Ed Bouchee instead and was rewarded with an honest single to
center and a run. It was the old man's first trip to his bench, a thing
of tatters; for one brief and wonderful moment, the devils had suspended their curse for Stengel's first command decision.

In the end the Mets lost 4 to 3. The first two of those four runs
were tawdry; the third was the comparatively honest consequence of
two singles and a wild pitch; and the last the direct result of two wild
pitches. That is the balance of their dreary future; and it was underlined by the reflection that, in two of the three Pirate scoring innings,
the Met pitcher had stopped the first two batters.

Groat finished the game caked with mud to his hips, from the occasions when he had fallen down, going first to his right and then to
his left. But he had made plays he had had to make. The new uniforms of the Met infielders were immaculate as they dragged home to
the clubhouse; none of them fallen down, not because they do not
have desire but they no longer have possibility. They cannot get close
enough any more to the doubtful chance to make use of the desperate dive. People are always saying that one-eighth of an inch is the
difference between winning and losing baseball. With the Mets, it is
three inches. No one could count the afternoons there would be like
this one.

But the first day had been distorted by climate and the illusion of
accident. The following Monday, the Mets greeted the new Houston

Colt .45s. Hodges was at first; the sun was out; the cries from the stands were faint and infrequent; there were only three thousand customers, the Dodger fans having already struck the colors. We were back on one of those long slow afternoons remembered from sixth place at the Polo Grounds in 1956.

The Mets went on to tie the Colts in the ninth and lose in the eleventh, a pattern picked up from the 1955–57 Giants. Those Giants were the subject of the only baseball short story written in the fifties with a legitimate claim to a place in the canon of that art form. Called "Seven Steps to Heaven," after the beer commercial, its author was E. B. White, and it was about what baseball has become in the electronic age, since its hero never went to the park but watched the disasters of the Giants as shadows on his television screen. But the Mets are not those Giants.

Those old Giants had Dusty Rhodes or Hank Sauer in left, and neither had ever pretended to be a fielder. Rhodes departed cursed and cherished. But who has a right to curse Frank Thomas?

Weiss wanted to assault the sentiment of New Yorkers with what would have been a respectable, if Mays-less, All-Star National League outfield in 1954—Thomas in left, Richie Ashburn in center, and Gus Bell in right. But it does not make you feel sentimental to see Ashburn thrown out on a deep grounder to third when he would have been safe just two years ago. It only makes you feel sad. It makes you sad, too, to see Hodges stand at the plate, trying to chip to the wrong field, a device of shortstops. These are men of great personal class; no one can enjoy seeing that what is hard for them now is what used to be precisely the easiest thing.

More than anything else, this condition must account for the brooding sorrow which chokes the Mets' dressing room after every defeat. The atmosphere has been compared to the dressing room of a team that has lost the World Series. Still a World Series is a transient thing; for those losers, there is always next year. But for the old men on the Mets, there will be no next year; this is where it ends; every afternoon is a reminder that the flesh is grass.

But then Weiss has always had a colder attitude toward old ballplayers than the rest of us do. The Met customers in left field occasionally express that difference by bringing along a banner painted "Rod Kanehl Fan Club." Rod Kanehl is a thirty-two-year-old outfielder-infielder who had never appeared in a big-league game before this year. His future is dim, but then so is his past. He carries no memory of departed glory for any spectator to regret; and this demand that he play every day is in some way a protest for the dignity of greater names. These fans would rather look at a faint hope than suffer with a damaged memory.

The Pulitzer Prize–winning journalist Jimmy Breslin was born in Jamaica, New York, and since going to work for the *New York Journal-American* in the late 1940s, he has written for just about every major New York City newspaper—living and defunct—except the *Times,* which he carefully bundles under his copy of "The Racing Form" after a trip to the newsstand. This heir to such tough-minded man-on-the-street reporters as Jimmy Cannon and Damon Runyon (of whom he wrote a 1991 biography), Breslin is one of the great populist newsmen of his time and the author of several books including *The Gang That Couldn't Shoot Straight* (1969). Breslin dedicated *Can't Anybody Here Play This Game?* (1962), his account of the hapless debut season of the New York Mets, to "the 922,530 brave souls who paid their way into the Polo Grounds in 1962. Never has so much misery loved so much company."

Jimmy Breslin

▽

from

Can't Anybody Here Play This Game?

S omeday, when George Weiss's cold, automatic methods of running an organization turn the team into just another boring winner, everything happening now probably will be forgotten. But right now, the Mets serve as more than just some comic relief while we're waiting for the ballplayers to show. The Mets are vastly important. For one who has been raised on sports in New York, the team put continuity back into life.

The only way to explain this is to tell you about the picture they had hanging on the wall of this gin mill one day last winter. It was a good picture. It was a big, clear color photo mounted on wood. The picture was of Gil Hodges. He had on a Brooklyn uniform and he was standing alongside the batting cage at Ebbets Field. His big, thick arms were bare and he was leaning on a bat. The picture was taken in 1954, and maybe nobody ever played first base much better than Hodges did that year. He hit 42 home runs, batted in 130 runs, and had an average of .304. He was a bull of a guy who came out of a little town in Indiana, but he had the kind of quickness, foot and hand, that made him different around first base. He became one of the biggest heroes Brooklyn had. Now, he is the first baseman for the New York Mets. That is, when he can play. Last year he keeled over with a kidney attack in July. Then his knee caved in and he had it operated on, and that finished him for the season. He is back for another whirl this season, but he was still limping when spring training started, so you can't count on him. The Mets probably will use him as a coach. Which is what was so hard to figure out when you looked at this picture. Here is Hodges, and all of a sudden he is old and a coach. And you have to sit down and wonder where all the years went.

You see, I always keep track of time by matching it to something that happens in sports. Take Hodges. The first time I ever read about him was in a story in the *Journal-American* early in 1947. The late Mike Gaven said something about how big this rookie Hodges' hands were, and that he was supposed to be the third-string catcher, but he could fit in at third or first too. I read the story while I was sitting in an Eighth Avenue subway train going to Madison Avenue and 53rd Street to see some man who was supposed to give me a job in his advertising agency. The girl at the reception desk in the ad agency wrote backhand on purpose and had a breathless little telephone voice, and the whole joint seemed so nice and orderly and deadly that when I finally did get in to see the guy I told him thanks, but I got this connection in the bricklayer's union and I can make more doing that. Then I walked out of the ad agency and I told myself I'd never take a job in any office that didn't let you throw cigarette butts on the floor. So far, I've made it stick. And now, if you bring up Gil Hodges, I tell you that he first came around when I made up my mind how I was going to make my living.

There is nothing strange about keeping time in this way. Some guys do it by music. You let a guy hear Tommy Dorsey's "I'll Never Smile Again" and he'll tell you what he was doing to the minute when the record was popular. Or ask a woman the first time she saw Myrna Loy in a movie. It will be the same. No difference at all. I just happen to use sports. There was a horse named Cosmic Bomb who ran out in the 1947 Kentucky Derby and cost me $10. To me, it means the first week I ever held a job for a living. The job was on a newspaper in Jamaica, Long Island, and the city room was on the first floor then, and a big man in the place was making $85 a week. But when I think of the place I always come up with Cosmic Bomb. Look him up. He ran number five in Louisville.

Two years later on Derby Day there was this old telegrapher named Frankie Dewey and he was standing at the bar of a joint called the Crossroads, up the corner from the newspaper office, and he had a straw hat tilted down over one eye and he was slapping the bar and yelling like hell. Up on the television screen, way in one corner of it, a horse called Ponder was starting to run in the stretch. Oh, did he run. Nobody ever came on like this one did. He ran past everything. "I told you," Frankie Dewey kept saying. "I told you, sonny." I had a slip from the bookmaker which said "PONDER 5–0–0" and I had put the bet down because of Frankie Dewey's tout. Ponder paid $24.80. I met a girl two nights later and had enough money to buy her a dinner because of Ponder. I wound up marrying her, and every time somebody says, "How did you two meet?" I start off by telling them about Ponder. "Steve Brooks was up," I begin.

It is like that with a lot of things in sports. But Hodges is causing me to match up with time the most. All of a sudden, from nowhere, you find he is old and shot. And you wonder where it all went. They took Hodges out of this town in 1957, and that left only the Yankees around here. Like I say, nobody ever really got close with them. So I never matched up time with baseball players for five whole years. Then the Mets come back and Hodges came with them, and I began to think again. Hodges too old to be a full-time player? Where the hell did the time go? I told that man in the advertising agency I didn't want his job, and that was only a couple of years ago. Hodges was breaking in. Yet here he is old and limping, and where did everything go? It must be a lot of years.

Those lost years changed a whole way of life for people in New York. Once you had everything. The Dodgers were in Brooklyn and the Giants were at the Polo Grounds. Madison Square Garden had fights on Friday night. Not the kind you see on television now. They had real fights. Like the night they had 18,000 in the place and in the first fight of the night, a four-rounder, a skinny kid from Brooklyn named Oliver White walked out and dropped in a right hand and put a boy named Sugar Ray Robinson on his back. Robinson got up, and you never saw anything like him. He got to White with a great left hook in the fourth. And it was only the four-round show-opener. The Ridgewood Grove operated on Saturday night, and there was a pro football team in Brooklyn, and they played sandlot baseball everywhere. People used to go out and watch events. Even sandlot games. There was one game of baseball, in a league called the Queens Alliance, that drew a crowd of 3500 to a field in Floral Park, and when the lead-off batter for a team called the Glendale Cardinals stepped in, everybody laughed. He looked like he was under five foot, and everybody thought it was a take-off on Thurber and his "You Could Look It Up."

But the little kid stayed in the batter's box, and finally the manager of the Floral Park team complained to Nick Miranda, who managed the team with the kid on it.

"A joke is a joke," he said. "But we're passing the hat for good money here. Let's not chase this crowd. Put a ballplayer in there."

"Don't you worry about this kid," Miranda said. "You just tell your third baseman look out he don't get killed."

So they pitched to this little kid. He reached up over his head for one and slammed it down the left-field line and he went into second standing up. It was the last time anybody questioned what Phil Rizzuto could do on a baseball field.

There were many things like this. Then television turned everything upside down. It produced the age of the money-hungry in sports and a whole way of life went out. People stopped going to events. Only the big games made it. Everything else died. And pretty soon normal big money was not enough for a fellow like O'Malley. He wanted more. Take a cab ride through Brooklyn and turn off Eastern Parkway at Bedford Avenue and go down the hill four blocks. Then you see what time and money-hungry people did to a way of life.

The big silver letters alongside the entrance to the apartment building said: 1700 BEDFORD AVENUE. The letters were stuck onto the red brick of the building. It is twenty-two stories high. Under the window of each apartment is a neat plaque saying that the place has been air-conditioned by General Electric.

On the sidewalk, two women stand and talk.

"I don't like that supermarket," one, in a gray coat, was saying.

"You know, you're right. I feel kind of uncomfortable in the place myself," her friend, who had blond hair and wore a kerchief, said.

"I know," the gray coat said. "I go in this place and they don't even have Purina Dog Chow. What kind of a supermarket is that?"

It was enough to make you sick. Once this was a national institution. Mention Ebbets Field and everybody in the audience would laugh. Danny Kaye did it for years. It was a standard with Fred Allen. Now it is just another address for a post office. It is twenty-two stories of apartments, and all of them are the same, and all of the people in them get to be the same after a while. Once we had Ebbets Field and a way of life. People went to games and drank beer and argued. When the Giants played the Dodgers it was nerve-racking. How a grown adult could sit in a seat and say, from the bottom of his heart, that he absolutely hated Duke Snider, whom he never met, is something for analysts. But that's what Giant fans used to do. Brooklyn fans hated right back. It was wonderful. Then we turned everything over to the moneychangers, and we wind up with twenty-two stories of red brick and plate glass and plaques by GE.

This is why the New York Mets come out as something more than a baseball team as far as an awful lot of people are concerned. The Mets are a part of life. You can start keeping track of time with them. They are not going to move for money. The owner's name is Payson, not O'Malley, and Payson stays with her own.

You ought to take a look at this picture of Hodges. It will remind you of all the years we lost because of these hustlers who came into the business. Only don't talk to Hodges about the years. He doesn't want to know anything about it.

"All I know," he was saying later this day, "is that I'm old. Nobody has to tell me that. I came into baseball yesterday. Today they throw the fast ball at me and you'd be surprised how fast it comes on top of me. A lot faster than it ever did."

Hodges was wearing an olive-drab sweater and gray slacks. He was sitting at the restaurant counter of the huge bowling establishment he owns in Brooklyn.

"Once," he was saying, "I'd be on first base and look out and we'd have Pee Wee [Reese] at short, Billy [Cox] at third, and Jackie [Robinson] at second. What an infield to look at. The games were great. No matter how far behind we fell, you knew you were never out of it.

We had seven guys who could hit home runs and put us right back in it.

"Last year with the Mets was strange. The Polo Grounds always was the enemy park. I felt strange in it. I guess it sounds funny to you. We're supposed to be playing this game for money. This 'enemy park' business sounds like something out of high school. But if you played for the Dodgers against the Giants, then the Polo Grounds will be the enemy park forever. Those games, they came down to more than a matter of money. I mean it. So it was strange to be in the Polo Grounds."

He got up from his coffee and walked across to see a repairman who was in to look at the dishwasher.

The record books say Hodges is the all-time right-handed home-run hitter in the National League. Around the dugouts he was always known as the first baseman with the fastest feet alive. A lot of times Hodges would be well off the bag when he took the throw from an in-fielder, but the umpire would always blink and call an automatic out. That would do it. Nobody ever called Hodges for not touching the bag, and in the confusion he became known as one of the great fielding first basemen of all time. Hodges had his own ideas about this, however.

"I'm going to do a story about my career when I retire," he said in the Brooklyn dressing room one day.

"What are you going to call it?" Pee Wee Reese asked him.

"'I Never Touched First Base.'"

Hodges came back and sat down at the counter. He talked about all the trouble he had over his career, trying to hit outside pitches.

"I just never could see too well when they threw an outside curve that broke away from me," he was saying. "It was a flaw I had. Everybody knew it. But it was up to the pitcher to put the ball out there, and that's not as easy as it sounds. So I had a fairly successful career."

Then he got up and walked over to the information desk. He limped a little. He'll probably be limping for a long time. But that's all right. As long as he can get back into a uniform and be around, even as a coach, he'll be familiar. I match him up with the day I made up my mind what kind of a job I wanted. He is the only one in the world I can do it with. Hell, I need the guy.

So the Mets are a bad ball club. All right, they're the worst ball club you ever saw. So what? The important thing is they are in the National League and they are familiar. The National League, to a lot of people around New York, is something hard to describe, but important. Like the chip in the table in the living room when you were growing up. It was always there. Sometimes you can buy ten new tables over a lifetime. But the one with the chip is the one that would make you feel the best. People are that way about the National League. They are more at home looking at the box score of a game between the St. Louis Cardinals and the Philadelphia Phillies than they ever could be going over one between the Cleveland Indians and the Detroit Tigers. If they came out of Cleveland it would be different. But they are from New York, and this is National League. Now we have the Mets, and that's the way it should be. We're with familiar things again.

The Mets lose an awful lot?

Listen, mister. Think a little bit.

When was the last time you won anything out of life?

Marianne Moore (1887–1972) was one of America's leading modernist poets and leading old-fashioned baseball fans. In a conversation at the Polo Grounds with Alfred Kreymborg, who had invited her to a game on the assumption that she knew nothing about baseball, Moore set Kreymborg straight and one-upped him by referring to Christy Mathewson's treatise, *Pitching in a Pinch:* "I've read his instructive book on the art of pitching and it's a pleasure to note how unerringly his execution supports his theories." Moore kept up with the literature of baseball her entire life; in a letter published in *The New York Times* before the 1968 World Series, she quoted Orlando Cepeda's *My Ups and Downs in Baseball* and Lawrence Ritter's *The Glory of Their Times* in a meandering forecast that the Cardinals would win the championship. She was wrong, but just barely: the Tigers rallied late in Game 7 to take the Series, four games to three. Moore's devotion to baseball in general and her beloved Brooklyn Dodgers in particular was sincere, and she contributed to the lore of the fabled team by writing "Hometown Piece for Messrs. Alston and Reese" during the 1956 World Series. "Baseball and Writing" comes from her 1966 collection *Tell Me, Tell Me.*

Marianne Moore

ᘐ

Baseball and Writing

Suggested by post-game broadcasts.

Fanaticism? No. Writing is exciting
and baseball is like writing.
   You can never tell with either
     how it will go
     or what you will do;
   generating excitement—
   a fever in the victim—
   pitcher, catcher, fielder, batter.
        Victim in what category?
*Owl*man watching from the press box?
      To whom does it apply?
      Who is excited? Might it be I?

It's a pitcher's battle all the way—a duel—
a catcher's, as, with cruel
    puma paw, Elston Howard lumbers lightly
      back to plate. (His spring
      de-winged a bat swing.)
    They have that killer instinct;
    yet Elston—whose catching
arm has hurt them all with the bat—
      when questioned, says, unenviously,
"I'm very satisfied. We won."
        Shorn of the batting crown, says, "We";
        robbed by a technicality.

When three players on a side play three positions
and modify conditions,
    the massive run need not be everything.
      "Going, going . . ." Is
      it? Roger Maris
    has it, running fast. You will
    never see a finer catch. Well . . .
    "Mickey, leaping like the devil"—why
      gild it, although deer sounds better—
snares what was speeding towards its treetop nest,
      one-handling the souvenir-to-be
      meant to be caught by you or me.

Assign Yogi Berra to Cape Canaveral;
he could handle any missile.
    He is no feather. "Strike! . . . Strike *two!*"
      Fouled back. A blur.
      It's gone. You would infer
    that the bat had eyes.
    He put the wood to that one.
Praised, Skowron says, "Thanks, Mel.
    I think I helped a *little* bit."
      All business, each, and modesty.
    Blanchard, Richardson, Kubek, Boyer.
      In that galaxy of nine, say which
      won the pennant? *Each.* It was he.

Those two magnificent saves from the knee—throws
by Boyer, finesses in twos—
    like Whitey's three kinds of pitch and pre-
       diagnosis
      with pick-off psychosis.
    Pitching is a large subject.
    Your arm, too true at first, can learn to
    catch the corners—even trouble
        Mickey Mantle. ("Grazed a Yankee!
My baby pitcher, Montejo!"
        With some pedagogy,
        you'll be tough, premature prodigy.)

They crowd him and curve him and aim for the knees. Trying
indeed! The secret implying:
    "I can stand here, bat held steady."
      One may suit him;
      none has hit him.
    Imponderables smite him.
    Muscle kinks, infections, spike wounds
    require food, rest, respite from ruffians. (Drat it!
        Celebrity costs privacy!)
Cow's milk, "tiger's milk," soy milk, carrot juice,
        brewer's yeast (high-potency)—
        concentrates presage victory

sped by Luis Arroyo, Hector Lopez—
deadly in a pinch. And "Yes,
    it's work; I want you to bear down,
      but enjoy it
      while you're doing it."
    Mr. Houk and Mr. Sain,
    if you have a rummage sale,
    don't sell Roland Sheldon or Tom Tresh.
        Studded with stars in belt and crown,
the Stadium is an adastrium.
        O flashing Orion,
        your stars are muscled like the lion.

The "new journalism" of the 1960s was an attempt to make nonfiction read like fiction without compromising the facts. In successful practice it featured bright, brazen writing by reporters who took on the compelling figures of their day with little compunction about what they said—or about injecting themselves into the story. Gay Talese (b. 1932) was, along with Tom Wolfe, the foremost exponent of the genre, as demonstrated in such books as *The Kingdom and the Power* (1969) and *Honor Thy Father* (1971). In this piece from *Esquire,* later collected in *Fame and Obscurity* (1970), Talese was out to show you who Joe DiMaggio really was, and nobody—not even the elusive DiMaggio himself—was going to stop him.

Gay Talese
♡
The Silent Season of a Hero

"I would like to take the great DiMaggio fishing," the old man said. "They say his father was a fisherman. Maybe he was as poor as we are and would understand."

—Ernest Hemingway, *The Old Man and the Sea*

It was not quite spring, the silent season before the search for salmon, and the old fishermen of San Francisco were either painting their boats or repairing their nets along the pier or sitting in the sun talking quietly among themselves, watching the tourists come and go, and smiling, now, as a pretty girl paused to take their picture. She was about twenty-five, healthy and blue-eyed and wearing a red turtle-neck sweater, and she had long, flowing blonde hair that she brushed back a few times before clicking her camera. The fishermen, looking at her, made admiring comments but she did not understand because they spoke a Sicilian dialect; nor did she notice the tall grey-haired man in a dark suit who stood watching her from behind a big bay window on the second floor of DiMaggio's Restaurant that over-looks the pier.

He watched until she left, lost in the crowd of newly arrived tourists that had just come down the hill by cable car. Then he sat down again at the table in the restaurant, finishing his tea and lighting another cigarette, his fifth in the last half hour. It was eleven-thirty in the morning. None of the other tables was occupied, and the only sounds came from the bar where a liquor salesman was laughing at something the headwaiter had said. But then the salesman, his briefcase under his arm, headed for the door, stopping briefly to peek into the dining room and call out, "See you later, Joe." Joe DiMaggio turned and waved at the salesman. Then the room was quiet again.

At fifty-one, DiMaggio was a most distinguished-looking man, aging as gracefully as he had played on the ball field, impeccable in his tailoring, his nails manicured, his six-foot two-inch body seeming as lean and capable as when he posed for the portrait that hangs in the restaurant and shows him in Yankee Stadium swinging from the heels at a pitch thrown twenty years ago. His grey hair was thinning at the crown, but just barely, and his face was lined in the right places, and his expression, once as sad and haunted as a matador's, was more in repose these days, though, as now, tension had returned and he chain-smoked and occasionally paced the floor and looked out the window at the people below. In the crowd was a man he did not wish to see.

The man had met DiMaggio in New York. This week he had come to San Francisco and had telephoned several times but none of the calls had been returned because DiMaggio suspected that the man, who had said he was doing research on some vague sociological project, really wanted to delve into DiMaggio's private life and that of DiMaggio's former wife, Marilyn Monroe. DiMaggio would never tolerate this. The memory of her death is still very painful to him, and yet, because he keeps it to himself, some people are not sensitive to it. One night in a supper club a woman who had been drinking approached his table, and when he did not ask her to join him, she snapped:

"All right, I guess I'm *not* Marilyn Monroe."

He ignored her remark, but when she repeated it, he replied, barely controlling his anger, "No—I wish you were, but you're not."

The tone of his voice softened her, and she asked, "Am I saying something wrong?"

"You already have," he said. "Now will you please leave me alone?"

His friends on the wharf, understanding him as they do, are very careful when discussing him with strangers, knowing that should they inadvertently betray a confidence he will not denounce them but rather will never speak to them again; this comes from a sense of propriety not inconsistent in the man who also, after Marilyn Monroe's death, directed that fresh flowers be placed on her grave "forever."

Some of the older fishermen who have known DiMaggio all his life remember him as a small boy who helped clean his father's boat, and as a young man who sneaked away and used a broken oar as a bat on the sandlots nearby. His father, a small mustachioed man known as Zio Pepe, would become infuriated and call him *lagnuso*, lazy, *meschino*, good-for-nothing, but in 1936 Zio Pepe was among those who cheered when Joe DiMaggio returned to San Francisco after his first season with the New York Yankees and was carried along the wharf on the shoulders of the fishermen.

The fishermen also remember how, after his retirement in 1951, DiMaggio brought his second wife, Marilyn, to live near the wharf, and sometimes they would be seen early in the morning fishing off DiMaggio's boat, the *Yankee Clipper*, now docked quietly in the marina, and in the evening they would be sitting and talking on the pier. They had arguments, too, the fishermen knew, and one night Marilyn was seen running hysterically, crying as she ran, along the road away from the pier, with Joe following. But the fishermen pretended they did not see this; it was none of their affair. They knew that Joe wanted her to stay in San Francisco and avoid the sharks in Hollywood, but she was confused and torn then—"She was a child," they said—and even today DiMaggio loathes Los Angeles and many of the people in it. He no longer speaks to his onetime friend, Frank Sinatra, who had befriended Marilyn in her final years, and he also is cool to Dean Martin and Peter Lawford and Lawford's former wife, Pat, who once gave a party at which she introduced Marilyn Monroe to Robert Kennedy, and the two of them danced often that night, Joe heard, and he did not take it well. He was very possessive of her that year, his close friends say, because Marilyn and he had planned to remarry; but before they could she was dead, and DiMaggio banned the Lawfords and Sinatra and many Hollywood people from her funeral. When Marilyn Monroe's attorney complained that DiMaggio was keeping her friends away, DiMaggio answered coldly, "If it weren't for those friends persuading her to stay in Hollywood she would still be alive."

Joe DiMaggio now spends most of the year in San Francisco, and each day tourists, noticing the name on the restaurant, ask the men on the wharf if they ever see him. Oh yes, the men say, they see him nearly every day; they have not seen him yet this morning, they add, but he should be arriving shortly. So the tourists continue to walk along the piers past the crab vendors, under the circling sea gulls, past the fish 'n' chip stands, sometimes stopping to watch a large vessel steaming toward the Golden Gate Bridge which, to their dismay, is painted red. Then they visit the Wax Museum, where there is a life-size figure of DiMaggio in uniform, and walk across the street and spend a quarter to peer through the silver telescopes focused on the island of Alcatraz, which is no longer a Federal prison. Then they return to ask the men if DiMaggio has been seen. Not yet, the men say, although they notice his blue Impala parked in the lot next to the restaurant. Sometimes tourists will walk into the restaurant and have lunch and will see him sitting calmly in a corner signing autographs and being extremely gracious with everyone. At other times, as on this particular morning when the man from New York chose to visit, DiMaggio was tense and suspicious.

When the man entered the restaurant from the side steps leading to the dining room he saw DiMaggio standing near the window talking with an elderly maître d' named Charles Friscia. Not wanting to walk in and risk intrusion, the man asked one of DiMaggio's nephews to inform Joe of his presence. When DiMaggio got the message he quickly turned and left Friscia and disappeared through an exit leading down to the kitchen.

Astonished and confused, the visitor stood in the hall. A moment later Friscia appeared and the man asked, "Did Joe leave?"

"Joe who?" Friscia replied.

"Joe DiMaggio!"

"Haven't seen him," Friscia said.

"You haven't *seen* him! He was standing right next to you a second ago!"

"It wasn't me," Friscia said.

"You were standing next to him. I saw you. In the dining room."

"You must be mistaken," Friscia said, softly, seriously. "It wasn't me."

"You *must* be kidding," the man said, angrily, turning and leaving the restaurant. Before he could get to his car, however, DiMaggio's nephew came running after him and said, "Joe wants to see you."

He returned expecting to see DiMaggio waiting for him. Instead he was handed a telephone. The voice was powerful and deep and so tense that the quick sentences ran together.

"You are invading my rights, I did not ask you to come, I assume you have a lawyer, you must have a lawyer, get your lawyer!"

"I came as a friend," the man interrupted.

"That's beside the point," DiMaggio said. "I have my privacy, I do not want it violated, you'd better get a lawyer. . . ." Then, pausing, DiMaggio asked, "Is my nephew there?"

He was not.

"Then wait where you are."

A moment later DiMaggio appeared, tall and red-faced, erect and beautifully dressed in his dark suit and white shirt with the grey silk tie and the gleaming silver cuff links. He moved with big steps toward the man and handed him an airmail envelope, unopened, that the man had written from New York.

"Here," DiMaggio said. "This is yours."

Then DiMaggio sat down at a small table. He said nothing, just lit a cigarette and waited, legs crossed, his head held high and back so as to reveal the intricate construction of his nose, a fine sharp tip above the big nostrils and tiny bones built out from the bridge, a great nose.

"Look," DiMaggio said, more calmly. "I do not interfere with other people's lives. And I do not expect them to interfere with mine. There are things about my life, personal things, that I refuse to talk about. And even if you asked my brothers they would be unable to tell you about them because they do not know. There are things about me, so many things, that they simply do not know. . . ."

"I don't want to cause trouble," the man said. "I think you're a great man, and . . ."

"I'm not great," DiMaggio cut in. "I'm not great," he repeated, softly. "I'm just a man trying to get along."

Then DiMaggio, as if realizing that he was intruding upon his own privacy, abruptly stood up. He looked at his watch.

"I'm late," he said, very formal again. "I'm ten minutes late. *You're* making me late."

The man left the restaurant. He crossed the street and wandered over to the pier, briefly watching the fishermen hauling their nets and talking in the sun, seeming very calm and contented. Then, after he had turned and was headed back toward the parking lot, a blue Impala stopped in front of him and Joe DiMaggio leaned out the window and asked, "Do you have a car?" His voice was very gentle.

"Yes," the man said.

"Oh," DiMaggio said. "I would have given you a ride."

Joe DiMaggio was not born in San Francisco but in Martinez, a small fishing village twenty-five miles northeast of the Golden Gate. Zio Pepe had settled there after leaving Isola delle Femmine, an islet off Palermo where the DiMaggios had been fishermen for generations. But in 1915, hearing of the luckier waters off San Francisco's wharf, Zio Pepe left Martinez, packing his boat with furniture and family, including Joe who was one year old.

San Francisco was placid and picturesque when the DiMaggios arrived, but there was a competitive undercurrent and struggle for power along the pier. At dawn the boats would sail out to where the bay meets the ocean and the sea is rough, and later the men would race back with their hauls, hoping to beat their fellow fishermen to shore and sell it while they could. Twenty or thirty boats would sometimes be trying to gain the channel shoreward at the same time, and a fisherman had to know every rock in the water, and later know every bargaining trick along the shore, because the dealers and restaurateurs would play one fisherman off against the other, keeping the prices down. Later the fishermen became wiser and organized, predetermining the maximum amount each fisherman would catch, but there were always some men who, like the fish, never learned, and so heads would sometimes be broken, nets slashed, gasoline poured onto their fish, flowers of warning placed outside their doors.

But these days were ending when Zio Pepe arrived, and he expected his five sons to succeed him as fishermen, and the first two, Tom and Michael, did; but a third, Vincent, wanted to sing. He sang with such magnificent power as a young man that he came to the attention of the great banker, A. P. Giannini, and there were plans to send him to Italy for tutoring and the opera. But there was hesitation around the DiMaggio household and Vince never went; instead he played ball with the San Francisco Seals and sportswriters misspelled his name.

It was DeMaggio until Joe, at Vince's recommendation, joined the team and became a sensation, being followed later by the youngest brother, Dominic, who was also outstanding. All three later played in the big leagues and some writers like to say that Joe was the best hitter, Dom the best fielder, Vince the best singer, and Casey Stengel once said: "Vince is the only player I ever saw who could strike out three times in one game and not be embarrassed. He'd walk into the clubhouse whistling. Everybody would be feeling sorry for him, but Vince always thought he was doing good."

After he retired from baseball Vince became a bartender, then a milkman, now a carpenter. He lives forty miles north of San Francisco in a house he partly built, he has been happily married for thirty-four years, has four grandchildren, has in the closet one of Joe's tailor-made suits that he has never had altered to fit, and when people ask if he envies Joe he always says, "No, maybe Joe would like to have what I have. He won't admit it, but he just might like to have what I have." The brother Vince most admired was Michael, "a big earthy man, a dreamer, a fisherman who wanted things but didn't want to take from Joe, or to work in the restaurant. He wanted a bigger boat, but wanted to earn it on his own. He never got it." In 1953, at the age of forty-four, Michael fell from his boat and drowned.

Since Zio Pepe's death at seventy-seven in 1949, Tom, at sixty-two the oldest brother—two of his four sisters are older—has become nominal head of the family and manages the restaurant that was opened in 1937 as Joe DiMaggio's Grotto. Later Joe sold out his share and now Tom is the co-owner of it with Dominic. Of all the brothers, Dominic, who was known as the "Little Professor" when he played with the Boston Red Sox, is the most successful in business. He lives in a fashionable Boston suburb with his wife and three children and is president of a firm that manufactures fiber-cushion materials and grossed more than $3,500,000 last year.

Joe DiMaggio lives with his widowed sister, Marie, in a tan stone house on a quiet residential street not far from Fisherman's Wharf. He bought the house almost thirty years ago for his parents, and after

their death he lived there with Marilyn Monroe; now it is cared for by
Marie, a slim and handsome dark-eyed woman who has an apartment
on the second floor, Joe on the third. There are some baseball trophies
and plaques in the small room off DiMaggio's bedroom, and on his
dresser are photographs of Marilyn Monroe, and in the living room
downstairs is a small painting of her that DiMaggio likes very much:
it reveals only her face and shoulders and she is wearing a very wide-
brimmed sun hat, and there is a soft sweet smile on her lips, an innocent curiosity about her that is the way he saw her and the way he
wanted her to be seen by others—a simple girl, "a warm bighearted
girl," he once described her, "that everybody took advantage of."

The publicity photographs emphasizing her sex appeal often offended him, and a memorable moment for Billy Wilder, who directed
her in *The Seven Year Itch,* occurred when he spotted DiMaggio in a
large crowd of people gathered on Lexington Avenue in New York to
watch a scene in which Marilyn, standing over a subway grating to
cool herself, had her skirts blown high by a sudden wind below.
"What the hell is going on here?" DiMaggio was overheard to have
said in the crowd, and Wilder recalled, "I shall never forget the look
of death on Joe's face."

He was then thirty-nine, she was twenty-seven. They had been
married in January of that year, 1954, despite disharmony in temperament and time: he was tired of publicity, she was thriving on it;
he was intolerant of tardiness, she was always late. During their honeymoon in Tokyo an American general had introduced himself and
asked if, as a patriotic gesture, she would visit the troops in Korea. She
looked at Joe. "It's your honeymoon," he said, shrugging, "go ahead if
you want to."

She appeared on ten occasions before 100,000 servicemen, and
when she returned she said, "It was so wonderful, Joe. You never
heard such cheering."

"Yes I have," he said.

Across from her portrait in the living room, on a coffee table in
front of a sofa, is a sterling-silver humidor that was presented to him
by his Yankee teammates at a time when he was the most talked-
about man in America, and when Les Brown's band had recorded a
hit that was heard day and night on the radio:

> *. . . From Coast to Coast, that's all you hear*
> *Of Joe the One-Man Show*
> *He's glorified the horsehide sphere,*
> *Jolting Joe DiMaggio . . .*
> *Joe . . . Joe . . . DiMaggio . . . we*
> *want you on our side. . . .*

The year was 1941, and it began for DiMaggio in the middle of May after the Yankees had lost four games in a row, seven of their last nine, and were in fourth place, five-and-a-half games behind the leading Cleveland Indians. On May 15th, DiMaggio hit only a first-inning single in a game that New York lost to Chicago, 13–1; he was barely hitting .300, and had greatly disappointed the crowds that had seen him finish with a .352 average the year before and .381 in 1939.

He got a hit in the next game, and the next, and the next. On May 24th, with the Yankees losing 6–5 to Boston, DiMaggio came up with runners on second and third and singled them home, winning the game, extending his streak to ten games. But it went largely unnoticed. Even DiMaggio was not conscious of it until it had reached twenty-nine games in mid-June. Then the newspapers began to dramatize it, the public became aroused, they sent him good-luck charms of every description, and DiMaggio kept hitting, and radio announcers would interrupt programs to announce the news, and then the song again: *"Joe . . . Joe . . . DiMaggio . . . we want you on our side . . ."*

Sometimes DiMaggio would be hitless his first three times up, the tension would build, it would appear that the game would end without his getting another chance—but he always would, and then he would hit the ball against the left-field wall, or through the pitcher's legs, or between two leaping infielders. In the forty-first game, the first of a double-header in Washington, DiMaggio tied an American League record that George Sisler had set in 1922. But before the second game began a spectator sneaked onto the field and into the Yankees' dugout and stole DiMaggio's favorite bat. In the second game, using another of his bats, DiMaggio lined out twice and flied out. But in the seventh inning, borrowing one of his old bats that a teammate was using, he singled and broke Sisler's record, and he was only three games away from surpassing the major-league record of forty-four set in 1897 by Willie Keeler while playing for Baltimore when it was a National League franchise.

An appeal for the missing bat was made through the newspapers. A man from Newark admitted the crime and returned it with regrets. And on July 2, at Yankee Stadium, DiMaggio hit a home run into the left-field stands. The record was broken.

He also got hits in the next eleven games, but on July 17th in Cleveland, at a night game attended by 67,468, he failed against two pitchers, Al Smith and Jim Bagby, Jr., although Cleveland's hero was really its third baseman, Ken Keltner, who in the first inning lunged to his right to make a spectacular backhanded stop of a drive and, from the foul line behind third base, he threw DiMaggio out. DiMaggio received a walk in the fourth inning. But in the seventh he again hit a hard shot at Keltner, who again stopped it and threw him out. DiMaggio hit sharply toward the shortstop in the eighth inning, the ball taking a bad hop, but Lou Boudreau speared it off his shoulder and threw to the second baseman to start a double play and DiMaggio's streak was stopped at fifty-six games. But the New York Yankees were on their way to winning the pennant by seventeen games, and the World Series too, and so in August, in a hotel suite in Washington, the players threw a surprise party for DiMaggio and toasted him with champagne and presented him with this Tiffany silver humidor that is now in San Francisco in his living room. . . .

Marie was in the kitchen making toast and tea when DiMaggio came down for breakfast; his grey hair was uncombed but, since he wears it short, it was not untidy. He said good-morning to Marie, sat down and yawned. He lit a cigarette. He wore a blue wool bathrobe over his pajamas. It was eight a.m. He had many things to do today and he seemed cheerful. He had a conference with the president of Continental Television, Inc., a large retail chain in California of which he is a partner and vice-president; later he had a golf date, and then a big banquet to attend, and, if that did not go on too long and he were not too tired afterward, he might have a date.

Picking up the morning paper, not rushing to the sports page, DiMaggio read the front-page news, the people-problems of '66: Kwame Nkrumah was overthrown in Ghana, students were burning their draft cards (DiMaggio shook his head), the flu epidemic was spreading through the whole state of California. Then he flipped inside through the gossip columns, thankful they did not have him in there today—they had printed an item about his dating "an electrifying airline hostess" not long ago, and they also spotted him at dinner with Dori Lane, "the frantic frugger" in Whiskey à Go Go's glass cage—and then he turned to the sports page and read a story about how the injured Mickey Mantle may never regain his form.

It had all happened so quickly, the passing of Mantle, or so it seemed; he had succeeded DiMaggio as DiMaggio had succeeded Ruth, but now there was no great young power hitter coming up and the Yankee management, almost desperate, had talked Mantle out of retirement; and on September 18, 1965, they gave him a "day" in New York during which he received several thousand dollars' worth of gifts—an automobile, two quarter horses, free vacation trips to Rome, Nassau, Puerto Rico—and DiMaggio had flown to New York to make the introduction before 50,000: it had been a dramatic day, an almost holy day for the believers who had jammed the grandstands early to witness the canonization of a new stadium saint. Cardinal Spellman was on the committee, President Johnson sent a telegram, the day was officially proclaimed by the Mayor of New York, an orchestra assembled in center field in front of the trinity of monuments to Ruth, Gehrig, Huggins; and high in the grandstands, billowing in the breeze of early autumn, were white banners that read: "Don't Quit Mick," "We Love the Mick."

The banners had been held by hundreds of young boys whose dreams had been fulfilled so often by Mantle, but also seated in the grandstands were older men, paunchy and balding, in whose middle-aged minds DiMaggio was still vivid and invincible, and some of them remembered how one month before, during a pre-game exhibition at Old-timers' Day in Yankee Stadium, DiMaggio had hit a pitch into the left-field seats, and suddenly thousands of people had jumped wildly to their feet, joyously screaming—the great DiMaggio had returned, they were young again, it was yesterday.

But on this sunny September day at the Stadium, the feast day of Mickey Mantle, DiMaggio was not wearing No. 5 on his back nor a black cap to cover his greying hair; he was wearing a black suit and white shirt and blue tie, and he stood in one corner of the Yankees' dugout waiting to be introduced by Red Barber, who was standing near home plate behind a silver microphone. In the outfield Guy Lombardo's Royal Canadians were playing soothing soft music; and moving slowly back and forth over the sprawling green grass between the left-field bullpen and the infield were two carts driven by groundskeepers and containing dozens and dozens of large gifts for Mantle—a six-foot, one-hundred-pound Hebrew National salami, a Winchester rifle, a mink coat for Mrs. Mantle, a set of Wilson golf clubs, a Mercury 95-horsepower outboard motor, a Necchi portable, a year's supply of Chunky Candy. DiMaggio smoked a cigarette, but cupped it in his hands as if not wanting to be caught in the act by teen-aged boys near enough to peek down into the dugout. Then, edging forward a step, DiMaggio poked his head out and looked up. He could see nothing above except the packed towering green grandstands that seemed a mile high and moving, and he could see no clouds or blue sky, only a sky of faces. Then the announcer called out his name—"*Joe DiMaggio!*"—and suddenly there was a blast of cheering that grew louder and louder, echoing and re-echoing within the big steel canyon, and DiMaggio stomped out his cigarette and climbed up the dugout steps and onto the soft green grass, the noise resounding in his ears, he could almost feel the breeze, the breath of 50,000 lungs upon him, 100,000 eyes watching his every move and for the briefest instant as he walked he closed his eyes.

Then in his path he saw Mickey Mantle's mother, a smiling elderly woman wearing an orchid, and he gently reached out for her elbow, holding it as he led her toward the microphone next to the other dignitaries lined up on the infield. Then he stood, very erect and without expression, as the cheers softened and the Stadium settled down.

Mantle was still in the dugout, in uniform, standing with one leg on the top step, and lined on both sides of him were the other Yankees who, when the ceremony was over, would play the Detroit Tigers. Then into the dugout, smiling, came Senator Robert Kennedy, accompanied by two tall curly-haired young assistants with blue eyes, Fordham freckles. Jim Farley was the first on the field to notice the Senator, and Farley muttered, loud enough for others to hear, "Who the hell invited *him*?"

Toots Shor and some of the other committeemen standing near

Farley looked into the dugout, and so did DiMaggio, his glance seeming cold, but he remaining silent. Kennedy walked up and down within the dugout shaking hands with the Yankees, but he did not walk onto the field.

"Senator," said the Yankees' manager, Johnny Keane, "why don't you sit down?" Kennedy quickly shook his head, smiled. He remained standing, and then one Yankee came over and asked about getting relatives out of Cuba, and Kennedy called over one of his aides to take down the details in a notebook.

On the infield the ceremony went on, Mantle's gifts continued to pile up—a Mobilette motor bike, a Sooner Schooner wagon barbecue, a year's supply of Chock Full O'Nuts coffee, a year's supply of Topps Chewing Gum—and the Yankee players watched, and Maris seemed glum.

"Hey, Rog," yelled a man with a tape recorder, Murray Olderman, "I want to do a thirty-second tape with you."

Maris swore angrily, shook his head.

"It'll only take a second," Olderman said.

"Why don't you ask Richardson? He's a better talker than me."

"Yes, but the fact that it comes from you. . . ."

Maris swore again. But finally he went over and said in an interview that Mantle was the finest player of his era, a great competitor, a great hitter.

Fifteen minutes later, standing behind the microphone at home plate, DiMaggio was telling the crowd, "I'm proud to introduce the man who succeeded me in center field in 1951," and from every corner of the Stadium the cheering, whistling, clapping came down. Mantle stepped forward. He stood with his wife and children, posed for the photographers kneeling in front. Then he thanked the crowd in a short speech, and, turning, shook hands with the dignitaries standing nearby. Among them now was Senator Kennedy, who had been spotted in the dugout five minutes before by Red Barber, and been called out and introduced. Kennedy posed with Mantle for a photographer, then shook hands with the Mantle children, and with Toots Shor and James Farley and others. DiMaggio saw him coming down the line and at the last second he backed away, casually, hardly anybody noticing it, and Kennedy seemed not to notice it either, just swept past shaking more hands. . . .

———

Finishing his tea, putting aside the newspaper, DiMaggio went upstairs to dress, and soon he was waving good-bye to Marie and driving toward his business appointment in downtown San Francisco with his partners in the retail television business. DiMaggio, while not a millionaire, has invested wisely and has always had, since his retirement from baseball, executive positions with big companies that have paid him well. He also was among the organizers of the Fisherman's National Bank of San Francisco last year, and, though it never came about, he demonstrated an acuteness that impressed those businessmen who had thought of him only in terms of baseball. He has had offers to manage big-league baseball teams but always has rejected them, saying, "I have enough trouble taking care of my own problems without taking on the responsibilities of twenty-five ball-players."

So his only contact with baseball these days, excluding public appearances, is his unsalaried job as a batting coach each spring in Florida with the New York Yankees, a trip he would make once again on the following Sunday, three days away, if he could accomplish what for him is always the dreaded responsibility of packing, a task made no easier by the fact that he lately has fallen into the habit of keeping his clothes in two places—some hang in his closet at home, some hang in the back room of a saloon called Reno's.

Reno's is a dimly-lit bar in the center of San Francisco. A portrait of DiMaggio swinging a bat hangs on the wall, in addition to portraits of other star athletes, and the clientele consists mainly of the sporting crowd and newspapermen, people who know DiMaggio quite well and around whom he speaks freely on a number of subjects and relaxes as he can in few other places. The owner of the bar is Reno Barsocchini, a broad-shouldered and handsome man of fifty-one with greying wavy hair who began as a fiddler in Dago Mary's tavern thirty-five years ago. He later became a bartender there and elsewhere, including DiMaggio's Restaurant, and now he is probably DiMaggio's closest friend. He was the best man at the DiMaggio-Monroe wedding in 1954, and when they separated nine months later in Los Angeles, Reno rushed down to help DiMaggio with the packing and drive him back to San Francisco. Reno will never forget the day.

Hundreds of people were gathered around the Beverly Hills home that DiMaggio and Marilyn had rented, and photographers were perched in the trees watching the windows, and others stood on the lawn and behind the rose bushes waiting to snap pictures of anybody who walked out of the house. The newspapers that day played all the puns—"Joe Fanned on Jealousy"; "Marilyn and Joe—Out at Home"—and the Hollywood columnists, to whom DiMaggio was never an idol, never a gracious host, recounted instances of incompatibility, and Oscar Levant said it all proved that no man could be a success in two national pastimes. When Reno Barsocchini arrived he had to push his way through the mob, then bang on the door for several minutes before being admitted. Marilyn Monroe was upstairs in bed, Joe DiMaggio was downstairs with his suitcases, tense and pale, his eyes bloodshot.

Reno took the suitcases and golf clubs out to DiMaggio's car, and then DiMaggio came out of the house, the reporters moving toward him, the lights flashing.

"Where are you going?" they yelled. "I'm driving to San Francisco," he said, walking quickly.

"Is that going to be your home?"

"That *is* my home and always has been."

"Are you coming back?"

DiMaggio turned for a moment, looking up at the house.

"No," he said, "I'll never be back."

Reno Barsocchini, except for a brief falling out over something he will not discuss, has been DiMaggio's trusted companion ever since, joining him whenever he can on the golf course or on the town, otherwise waiting for him in the bar with other middle-aged men. They may wait for hours sometimes, waiting and knowing that when he arrives he may wish to be alone; but it does not seem to matter, they are endlessly awed by him, moved by the mystique, he is a kind of male Garbo. They know that he can be warm and loyal if they are sensitive to his wishes, but they must never be late for an appointment to meet him. One man, unable to find a parking place, arrived a half-hour late once and DiMaggio did not talk to him again for three months. They know, too, when dining at night with DiMaggio, that he generally prefers male companions and occasionally one or two young women, but never wives; wives gossip, wives complain, wives are trouble, and men wishing to remain close to DiMaggio must keep their wives at home.

When DiMaggio strolls into Reno's bar the men wave and call out his name, and Reno Barsocchini smiles and announces, "Here's the Clipper!", the "Yankee Clipper" being a nickname from his baseball days.

"Hey, Clipper, Clipper," Reno had said two nights before, "where you been, Clipper? . . . Clipper, how 'bout a belt?"

DiMaggio refused the offer of a drink, ordering instead a pot of tea, which he prefers to all other beverages except before a date, when he will switch to vodka.

"Hey, Joe," a sportswriter asked, a man researching a magazine piece on golf, "why is it that a golfer, when he starts getting older, loses his putting touch first? Like Snead and Hogan, they can still hit a ball well off the tee, but on the greens they lose the strokes. . . ."

"It's the pressure of age," DiMaggio said, turning around on his bar stool. "With age you get jittery. It's true of golfers, it's true of any man when he gets into his fifties. He doesn't take chances like he used to. The younger golfer, on the greens, he'll stroke his putts better. The older man, he becomes hesitant. A little uncertain. Shaky. When it comes to taking chances the younger man, even when driving a car, will take chances that the older man won't."

"Speaking of chances," another man said, one of the group that had gathered around DiMaggio, "did you see that guy on crutches in here last night?"

"Yeah, had his leg in a cast," a third said. "Skiing."

"I would never ski," DiMaggio said. "Men who ski must be doing it to impress a broad. You see these men, some of them forty, fifty, getting onto skis. And later you see them all bandaged up, broken legs. . . ."

"But skiing's a very sexy sport, Joe. All the clothes, the tight pants, the fireplace in the ski lodge, the bear rug—Christ, nobody goes to ski. They just go out there to get it cold so they can warm it up. . . ."

"Maybe you're right," DiMaggio said. "I might be persuaded."

"Want a belt, Clipper?" Reno asked.

DiMaggio thought for a second, then said, "All right—first belt tonight."

Now it was noon, a warm sunny day. DiMaggio's business meeting with the television retailers had gone well; he had made a strong appeal to George Shahood, president of Continental Television, Inc., which has eight retail outlets in Northern California, to cut prices on color television sets and increase the sales volume, and Shahood had conceded it was worth a try. Then DiMaggio called Reno's bar to see if there were any messages, and now he was in Lefty O'Doul's car being driven along Fisherman's Wharf toward the Golden Gate Bridge en route to a golf course thirty miles upstate. Lefty O'Doul was one of the great hitters in the National League in the early Thirties, and later he managed the San Francisco Seals when DiMaggio was the shining star. Though O'Doul is now sixty-nine, eighteen years older than DiMaggio, he nevertheless possesses great energy and spirit, is a hard-drinking, boisterous man with a big belly and roving eye; and when DiMaggio, as they drove along the highway toward the golf club, noticed a lovely blonde at the wheel of a car nearby and exclaimed, "Look at *that* tomato!" O'Doul's head suddenly spun around, he took his eyes off the road, and yelled, "Where, *where*?" O'Doul's golf game is less than what it was—he used to have a two-handicap—but he still shoots in the 80's, as does DiMaggio.

DiMaggio's drives range between 250 and 280 yards when he doesn't sky them, and his putting is good, but he is distracted by a bad back that both pains him and hinders the fullness of his swing. On the first hole, waiting to tee off, DiMaggio sat back watching a foursome of college boys ahead swinging with such freedom. "Oh," he said with a sigh, "to have *their* backs."

DiMaggio and O'Doul were accompanied around the golf course by Ernie Nevers, the former football star, and two brothers who are in the hotel and movie-distribution business. They moved quickly up and down the green hills in electric golf carts, and DiMaggio's game was exceptionally good for the first nine holes. But then he seemed distracted, perhaps tired, perhaps even reacting to a conversation of a few minutes before. One of the movie men was praising the film *Boeing, Boeing,* starring Tony Curtis and Jerry Lewis, and the man asked DiMaggio if he had seen it.

"No," DiMaggio said. Then he added, swiftly, "I haven't seen a film in eight years."

DiMaggio hooked a few shots, was in the woods. He took a No. 9 iron and tried to chip out. But O'Doul interrupted DiMaggio's concentration to remind him to keep the face of the club closed. Di-

Maggio hit the ball. It caromed off the side of his club, went skipping like a rabbit through the high grass down toward a pond. DiMaggio rarely displays any emotion on a golf course, but now, without saying a word, he took his No. 9 iron and flung it into the air. The club landed in a tree and stayed up there.

"Well," O'Doul said, casually, "there goes *that* set of clubs."

DiMaggio walked to the tree. Fortunately the club had slipped to the lower branch and DiMaggio could stretch up on the cart and get it back.

"Every time I get advice," DiMaggio muttered to himself, shaking his head slowly and walking toward the pond, "I shank it."

Later, showered and dressed, DiMaggio and the others drove to a banquet about ten miles from the golf course. Somebody had said it was going to be an elegant dinner, but when they arrived they could see it was more like a county fair; farmers were gathered outside a big barn-like building, a candidate for sheriff was distributing leaflets at the front door, and a chorus of homely ladies were inside singing *You Are My Sunshine.*

"How did we get sucked into this?" DiMaggio asked, talking out of the side of his mouth, as they approached the building.

"O'Doul," one of the men said. "It's his fault. Damned O'Doul can't turn *anything* down."

"Go to hell," O'Doul said.

Soon DiMaggio and O'Doul and Ernie Nevers were surrounded by the crowd, and the woman who had been leading the chorus came rushing over and said, "Oh, Mr. DiMaggio, it certainly is a pleasure having you."

"It's a pleasure being here, ma'am," he said, forcing a smile.

"It's too bad you didn't arrive a moment sooner, you'd have heard our singing."

"Oh, I heard it," he said, "and I enjoyed it very much."

"Good, good," she said. "And how are your brothers Dom and Vic?"

"Fine. Dom lives near Boston. Vince is in Pittsburgh."

"Why, *hello* there, Joe," interrupted a man with wine on his breath, patting DiMaggio on the back, feeling his arm. "Who's gonna take it this year, Joe?"

"Well, I have no idea," DiMaggio said.

"What about the Giants?"

"Your guess is as good as mine."

"Well, you can't count the Dodgers out," the man said.

"You sure can't," DiMaggio said.

"Not with all that pitching."

"Pitching is certainly important," DiMaggio said.

Everywhere he goes the questions seem the same, as if he has some special vision into the future of new heroes, and everywhere he goes, too, older men grab his hand and feel his arm and predict that he could still go out there and hit one, and the smile on DiMaggio's face is genuine. He tries hard to remain as he was—he diets, he takes steam baths, he is careful; and flabby men in the locker rooms of golf clubs sometimes steal peeks at him when he steps out of the shower, observing the tight muscles across his chest, the flat stomach, the long sinewy legs. He has a young man's body, very pale and little hair; his face is dark and lined, however, parched by the sun of several seasons. Still he is always an impressive figure at banquets such as this— an *immortal*, sportswriters called him, and that is how they have written about him and others like him, rarely suggesting that such heroes might ever be prone to the ills of mortal men, carousing, drinking, scheming; to suggest this would destroy the myth, would disillusion small boys, would infuriate rich men who own ball clubs and to whom baseball is a business dedicated to profit and in pursuit of which they trade mediocre players' flesh as casually as boys trade players' pictures on bubble-gum cards. And so the baseball hero must always act the part, must preserve the myth, and none does it better than DiMaggio, none is more patient when drunken old men grab an arm and ask, "Who's gonna take it this year, Joe?"

Two hours later, dinner and the speeches over, DiMaggio is slumped in O'Doul's car headed back to San Francisco. He edged himself up, however, when O'Doul pulled into a gas station in which a pretty red-haired girl sat on a stool, legs crossed, filing her fingernails. She was about twenty-two, wore a tight black skirt and tighter white blouse.

"Look at *that*," DiMaggio said.

"Yeah," O'Doul said.

O'Doul turned away when a young man approached, opened the gas tank, began wiping the windshield. The young man wore a greasy

white uniform on the front of which was printed the name "Burt."
DiMaggio kept looking at the girl, but she was not distracted from her
fingernails. Then he looked at Burt, who did not recognize him.
When the tank was full, O'Doul paid and drove off. Burt returned to
his girl; DiMaggio slumped down in the front seat and did not open
his eyes again until they'd arrived in San Francisco.

"Let's go see Reno," DiMaggio said.

"No, I gotta go see my old lady," O'Doul said. So he dropped
DiMaggio off in front of the bar, and a moment later Reno's voice was
announcing in the smoky room, "Hey, here's the Clipper!" The men
waved and offered to buy him a drink. DiMaggio ordered a vodka and
sat for an hour at the bar talking to a half dozen men around him.
Then a blonde girl who had been with friends at the other end of the
bar came over, and somebody introduced her to DiMaggio. He
bought her a drink, offered her a cigarette. Then he struck a match
and held it. His hand was unsteady.

"Is that me that's shaking?" he asked.

"It must be," said the blonde. "I'm calm."

Two nights later, having collected his clothes out of Reno's back
room, DiMaggio boarded a jet; he slept crossways on three seats,
then came down the steps as the sun began to rise in Miami. He
claimed his luggage and golf clubs, put them into the trunk of a waiting automobile, and less than an hour later he was being driven into
Fort Lauderdale, past palm-lined streets, toward the Yankee Clipper
Hotel.

"All my life it seems I've been on the road traveling," he said,
squinting through the windshield into the sun. "I never get a sense of
being in any one place."

Arriving at the Yankee Clipper Hotel, DiMaggio checked into the
largest suite. People rushed through the lobby to shake hands with
him, to ask for his autograph, to say, "Joe, you look great." And early
the next morning, and for the next thirty mornings, DiMaggio arrived punctually at the baseball park and wore his uniform with the
famous No. 5, and the tourists seated in the sunny grandstands
clapped when he first appeared on the field each time, and then they
watched with nostalgia as he picked up a bat and played "pepper"
with the younger Yankees, some of whom were not even born when,

twenty-five years ago this summer, he hit in fifty-six straight games and became the most celebrated man in America.

But the younger spectators in the Fort Lauderdale park, and the sportswriters, too, were more interested in Mantle and Maris, and nearly every day there were news dispatches reporting how Mantle and Maris felt, what they did, what they said, even though they said and did very little except walk around the field frowning when photographers asked for another picture and when sportswriters asked how they felt.

After seven days of this, the big day arrived—Mantle and Maris would swing a bat—and a dozen sportswriters were gathered around the big batting cage that was situated beyond the left-field fence; it was completely enclosed in wire, meaning that no baseball could travel more than thirty or forty feet before being trapped in rope; still Mantle and Maris would be swinging, and this, in spring, makes news.

Mantle stepped in first. He wore black gloves to help prevent blisters. He hit right-handed against the pitching of a coach named Vern Benson, and soon Mantle was swinging hard, smashing line drives against the nets, going *ahhh ahhh* as he followed through with his mouth open.

Then Mantle, not wanting to overdo it on his first day, dropped his bat in the dirt and walked out of the batting cage. Roger Maris stepped in. He picked up Mantle's bat.

"This damn thing must be thirty-eight ounces," Maris said. He threw the bat down into the dirt, left the cage and walked toward the dugout on the other side of the field to get a lighter bat.

DiMaggio stood among the sportswriters behind the cage, then turned when Vern Benson, inside the cage, yelled, "Joe, wanna hit some?"

"No chance," DiMaggio said.

"Com'on, Joe," Benson said.

The reporters waited silently. Then DiMaggio walked slowly into the cage and picked up Mantle's bat. He took his position at the plate but obviously it was not the classic DiMaggio stance; he was holding the bat about two inches from the knob, his feet were not so far apart, and, when DiMaggio took a cut at Benson's first pitch, fouling it, there was none of that ferocious follow through, the blurred bat did not come whipping all the way around, the No. 5 was not stretched full across his broad back.

DiMaggio fouled Benson's second pitch, then he connected solidly with the third, the fourth, the fifth. He was just meeting the ball easily, however, not smashing it, and Benson called out, "I didn't know you were a choke hitter, Joe."

"I am now," DiMaggio said, getting ready for another pitch.

He hit three more squarely enough, and then he swung again and there was a hollow sound.

"Ohhh," DiMaggio yelled, dropping his bat, his fingers stung, "I was waiting for that one." He left the batting cage rubbing his hands together. The reporters watched him. Nobody said anything. Then DiMaggio said to one of them, not in anger nor in sadness, but merely as a simply stated fact, "There was a time when you couldn't get me out of there."

Willie Morris (1934–1999) grew up in Yazoo City, Mississippi, graduated from the University of Texas, and attended Oxford University as a Rhodes Scholar. In 1967, he became the youngest person ever to serve as editor-in-chief of *Harper's Magazine*. That same year he published his first book, *North Toward Home*, a memoir that won the Houghton Mifflin Literary Fellowship Award for nonfiction. In 1971 he returned to Mississippi, where he continued to write about Southern culture. Among his books are *Yazoo: Integration in a Deep-Southern Town* (1971), *Good Old Boy: A Delta Boyhood* (1971), *The Courting of Marcus Dupree* (1983), and *My Dog Skip* (1995).

Willie Morris

♢

from

North Toward Home

B ecause back home, even among the adults, baseball was all-meaning; it was the link with the outside. A place known around town simply as The Store, down near the train depot, was the principal center of this ferment. The Store had sawdust on the floor and long shreds of flypaper hanging from the ceiling. Its most familiar staples were Rexall supplies, oysters on the half shell, legal beer, and illegal whiskey, the latter served up, Mississippi bootlegger style, by the bottle from a hidden shelf and costing not merely the price of the whiskey but the investment in gas required to go to Louisiana to fetch it. There was a long counter in the back. On one side of it, the white workingmen congregated after hours every afternoon to compare the day's scores and talk batting averages, and on the other side, also talking baseball, were the Negroes, juxtaposed in a face-to-face arrangement with the whites. The scores were chalked up on a blackboard hanging on a red and purple wall, and the conversations were carried on in fast, galloping shouts from one end of the room to the other. An intelligent white boy of twelve was even permitted, in that atmosphere of heady freedom before anyone knew the name of Justice Warren or had heard much of the United States Supreme Court, a quasi-public position favoring the Dodgers, who had Jackie Robinson, Roy Campanella, and Don Newcombe—not to mention, so it was rumored, God knows how many Chinese and mulattoes being groomed in the minor leagues. I remember my father turned to some friends at The Store one day and observed, "Well, you can say what you want to about that nigger Robinson, but he's got *guts*," and to a man the others nodded, a little reluctantly, but in agreement nonetheless. And one of them said he had read somewhere that Pee Wee Reese, a white Southern boy, was the best friend Robinson had on the team, which proved they had chosen the right one to watch after him.

There were two firehouses in town, and on hot afternoons the firemen at both establishments sat outdoors in their shirt-sleeves, with the baseball broadcast turned up as loud as it would go. On his day off work my father, who had left Cities Service and was now a bookkeeper for the wholesale grocery, usually started with Firehouse No. 1 for the first few innings and then hit Number Two before ending up at The Store for the post-game conversations.

I decided not to try out for the American Legion Junior Baseball team that summer. Legion baseball was an important thing for country boys in those parts, but I was too young and skinny, and I had heard that the coach, a dirt farmer known as Gentleman Joe, made his protégés lie flat in the infield while he walked on their stomachs; he also forced them to take three-mile runs through the streets of town, talked them into going to church, and persuaded them to give up Coca-Colas. A couple of summers later, when I did go out for the team, I found out that Gentleman Joe did in fact insist on these soul-strengthening rituals; because of them, we won the Mississippi State Championship and the merchants in town took up a collection and sent us all the way to St. Louis to see the Cards play the Phillies. My main concern that earlier summer, however, lay in the more academic aspects of the game. I knew more about baseball, its technology and its ethos, than all the firemen and Store experts put together. Having read most of its literature, I could give a sizable lecture on the infield-fly rule alone, which only a thin minority of the townspeople knew existed. Gentleman Joe was held in some esteem for his strategical sense, yet he was the only man I ever knew who could call for a sacrifice bunt with two men out and not have a bad conscience about it. I remember one dismaying moment that came to me while I was watching a country semi-pro game. The home team had runners on first and third with one out, when the batter hit a ground ball to the first baseman, who stepped on first and then threw to second. The shortstop, covering second, stepped on the base but made no attempt to tag the runner. The man on third had crossed the plate, of course, but the umpire, who was not very familiar with the subtleties of the rules, signaled a double play. Sitting in the grandstand, I knew that it was not a double play at all and that the run had scored, but when I went down, out of my Christian duty, to tell the manager of the local team that he had just been done out of a run, he told me I was crazy. This was the kind of brainpower I was up against.

That summer the local radio station, the one where we broadcast our Methodist programs, started a baseball quiz program. A razor blade company offered free blades and the station chipped in a dollar, all of which went to the first listener to telephone with the right answer to the day's baseball question. If there was no winner, the next day's pot would go up a dollar. At the end of the month they had to close down the program because I was winning all the money. It got so easy, in fact, that I stopped phoning in the answers some afternoons so that the pot could build up and make my winnings more spectacular. I netted about $25 and a ten-year supply of double-edged, smooth-contact razor blades before they gave up. One day, when the jackpot was a mere two dollars, the announcer tried to confuse me. "Babe Ruth," he said, "hit sixty home runs in 1927 to set the major-league record. What man had the next-highest total?" I telephoned and said, "George Herman Ruth. He hit fifty-nine in another season." My adversary, who had developed an acute dislike of me, said that was not the correct answer. He said it should have been *Babe* Ruth. This incident angered me, and I won for the next four days, just for the hell of it.

On Sunday afternoons we sometimes drove out of town and along hot, dusty roads to baseball fields that were little more than parched red clearings, the outfield sloping out of the woods and ending in some tortuous gully full of yellowed paper, old socks, and vintage cow shit. One of the backwoods teams had a fastball pitcher named Eckert, who didn't have any teeth, and a fifty-year-old left-handed catcher named Smith. Since there were no catcher's mitts made for left-handers, Smith had to wear a mitt on his throwing hand. In his simian posture he would catch the ball and toss it lightly into the air and then whip his mitt off and catch the ball in his bare left hand before throwing it back. It was a wonderfully lazy way to spend those Sunday afternoons—my father and my friends and I sitting in the grass behind the chicken-wire backstop with eight or ten dozen farmers, watching the wrong-handed catcher go through his contorted gyrations, and listening at the same time to our portable radio, which brought us the rising inflections of a baseball announcer called the Old Scotchman. The sounds of the two games, our own and the one being broadcast from Brooklyn or Chicago, merged and rolled across the bumpy outfield and the gully into the woods; it was a combination that seemed perfectly natural to everyone there.

I can see the town now on some hot, still weekday afternoon in mid-summer: ten thousand souls and nothing doing. Even the red water truck was a diversion, coming slowly up Grand Avenue with its sprinklers on full force, the water making sizzling steam-clouds on the pavement while half-naked Negro children followed the truck up the street and played in the torrent until they got soaking wet. Over on Broadway, where the old men sat drowsily in straw chairs on the pavement near the Bon-Ton Café, whittling to make the time pass, you could laze around on the sidewalks—barefoot, if your feet were tough enough to stand the scalding concrete—watching the big cars with out-of-state plates whip by, the driver hardly knowing and certainly not caring what place this was. Way up that fantastic hill, Broadway seemed to end in a seething mist—little heat mirages that shimmered off the asphalt; on the main street itself there would be only a handful of cars parked here and there, and the merchants and the lawyers sat in the shade under their broad awnings, talking slowly, aimlessly, in the cryptic summer way. The one o'clock whistle at the sawmill would send out its loud bellow, reverberating up the streets to the bend in the Yazoo River, hardly making a ripple in the heavy somnolence.

But by two o'clock almost every radio in town was tuned in to the Old Scotchman. His rhetoric dominated the place. It hovered in the branches of the trees, bounced off the hills, and came out of the darkened stores; the merchants and the old men cocked their ears to him, and even from the big cars that sped by, their tires making lapping sounds in the softened highway, you could hear his voice, being carried past you out into the delta.

The Old Scotchman's real name was Gordon McLendon, and he described the big-league games for the Liberty Broadcasting System, which had outlets mainly in the South and the Southwest. He had a deep, rich voice, and I think he was the best rhetorician, outside of Bilbo and Nye Bevan, I have ever heard. Under his handling a baseball game took on a life of its own. As in the prose of the *Commercial Appeal's* Walter Stewart, his games were rare and remarkable entities; casual pop flies had the flow of history behind them, double plays resembled the stark clashes of old armies, and home runs deserved acknowledgment on earthen urns. Later, when I came across Thomas Wolfe, I felt I had heard him before, from Shibe Park, Crosley Field, or the Yankee Stadium.

One afternoon I was sitting around my house listening to the Old Scotchman, admiring the vivacity of a man who said he was a contemporary of Connie Mack. (I learned later that he was twenty-nine.) That day he was doing the Dodgers and the Giants from the Polo Grounds. The game, as I recall, was in the fourth inning, and the Giants were ahead by about 4 to 1. It was a boring game, however, and I began experimenting with my father's short-wave radio, an impressive mechanism a couple of feet wide, which had an aerial that almost touched the ceiling and the name of every major city in the world on its dial. It was by far the best radio I had ever seen; there was not another one like it in town. I switched the dial to short-wave and began picking up African drum music, French jazz, Australian weather reports, and a lecture from the British Broadcasting Company on the people who wrote poems for Queen Elizabeth. Then a curious thing happened. I came across a baseball game—the Giants and the Dodgers, from the Polo Grounds. After a couple of minutes I discovered that the game was in the eighth inning. I turned back to the local station, but here the Giants and Dodgers were still in the fourth. I turned again to the short-wave broadcast and listened to the last inning, a humdrum affair that ended with Carl Furillo popping out to shortstop, Gil Hodges grounding out second to first, and Roy Campanella lining out to center. Then I went back to the Old Scotchman and listened to the rest of the game. In the top of the ninth, an hour or so later, a ghostly thing occurred; to my astonishment and tit-illation, the game ended with Furillo popping out to short, Hodges grounding out second to first, and Campanella lining out to center.

I kept this unusual discovery to myself, and the next day, an hour before the Old Scotchman began his play-by-play of the second game of the series, I dialed the short-wave frequency, and, sure enough, they were doing the Giants and the Dodgers again. I learned that I was listening to the Armed Forces Radio Service, which broadcast games played in New York. As the game progressed I began jotting down notes on the action. When the first four innings were over I turned to the local station just in time to get the Old Scotchman for the first batter. The Old Scotchman's account of the game matched the short-wave's almost perfectly. The Scotchman's, in fact, struck me as being considerably more poetic than the one I had heard first. But I did not doubt him, since I could hear the roar of the crowd, the crack of the bat, and the Scotchman's precise description of foul balls that fell into the crowd, the gestures of the base coaches, and the ex-pression on the face of a small boy who was eating a lemon popsicle in a box seat behind first base. I decided that the broadcast was being delayed somewhere along the line, maybe because we were so far from New York.

That was my first thought, but after a close comparison of the two broadcasts for the rest of the game, I sensed that something more sinister was taking place. For one thing, the Old Scotchman's descrip-tion of the count on a batter, though it jibed 90 percent of the time, did not always match. For another, the Scotchman's crowd, compared with the other, kept up an ungodly noise. When Robinson stole sec-ond on short-wave, he did it without drawing a throw and without sliding, while for Mississippians the feat was performed in a cloud of angry, petulant dust. A foul ball that went over the grandstand and out of the park for short-wave listeners in Alaska, France, and the Argentine produced for the firemen, bootleggers, farmers, and myself a primitive scramble that ended with a feeble old lady catching the ball on the first bounce to the roar of an assembly that would have outnumbered Grant's at Old Cold Harbor. But the most revealing development came after the Scotchman's game was over. After the usual summaries, he mentioned that the game had been "recreated." I had never taken notice of that particular word before, because I lost interest once a game was over. I went to the dictionary, and under "recreate" I found, "To invest with fresh vigor and strength; to refresh, invigorate (nature, strength, a person or thing)." The Old Scotchman most assuredly invested a game with fresh vigor and strength, but this told me nothing. My deepest suspicions were confirmed, however, when I found the second definition of the word— "To create anew."

So there it was. I was happy to have fathomed the mystery, as perhaps no one else in the whole town had done. The Old Scotchman, for all his wondrous expressions, was not only several innings behind every game he described but was no doubt sitting in some air-conditioned studio in the hinterland, where he got the happenings of the game by news ticker; sound effects accounted for the crack of the bat and the crowd noises. Instead of being disappointed in the Scotchman, I was all the more pleased by his genius, for he made pristine facts more actual than actuality, a valuable lesson when the day finally came that I started reading literature. I must add, however, that this appreciation did not obscure the realization that I had at my disposal a weapon of unimaginable dimensions.

Next day I was at the short-wave again, but I learned with much dissappointment that the game being broadcast on short-wave was not the one the Scotchman had chosen to describe. I tried every afternoon after that and discovered that I would have to wait until the Old Scotchman decided to do a game out of New York before I could match his game with the one described live on short-wave. Sometimes, I learned later, these coincidences did not occur for days; during an important Dodger or Yankee series, however, his game and that of the Armed Forces Radio Service often coincided for two or three days running. I was happy, therefore, to find, on an afternoon a few days later, that both the short-wave and the Scotchman were carrying the Yankees and the Indians.

I settled myself at the short-wave with notebook and pencil and took down every pitch. This I did for four full innings, and then I turned back to the town station, where the Old Scotchman was just beginning the first inning. I checked the first batter to make sure the accounts jibed. Then, armed with my notebook, I ran down the street to the corner grocery, a minor outpost of baseball intellection, presided over by my young Negro friend Bozo, a knowledgeable student of the game, the same one who kept my dog in bologna. I found Bozo behind the meat counter, with the Scotchman's account going full blast. I arrived at the interim between the top and bottom of the first inning.

"Who's pitchin' for the Yankees, Bozo?" I asked.

"They're pitchin' Allie Reynolds," Bozo said. "Old Scotchman says Reynolds really got the stuff today. He just set 'em down one, two, three."

The Scotchman, meanwhile, was describing the way the pennants were flapping in the breeze. Phil Rizzuto, he reported, was stepping to the plate.

"Bo," I said, trying to sound cut-and-dried, "you know what I think? I think Rizzuto's gonna take a couple of fast called strikes, then foul one down the left-field line, and then line out straight to Boudreau at short."

"Yeah?" Bozo said. He scratched his head and leaned lazily across the counter.

I went up front to buy something and then came back. The count worked to nothing and two on Rizzuto—a couple of fast called strikes and a foul down the left side. "This one," I said to Bozo, "he lines straight to Boudreau at short."

The Old Scotchman, pausing dramatically between words as was his custom, said, "Here's the windup on nothing and two. Here's the pitch on its way— There's a hard line drive! But Lou Boudreau's there at shortstop and he's got it. Phil hit that one on the nose, but Boudreau was right there."

Bozo looked over at me, his eyes bigger than they were. "How'd you know that?" he asked.

Ignoring this query, I made my second prediction. "Bozo," I said, "Tommy Henrich's gonna hit the first pitch up against the right-field wall and slide in with a double."

"How come you think so?"

"Because I can predict anything that's gonna happen in baseball in the next ten years," I said. "I can tell you anything."

The Old Scotchman was describing Henrich at the plate. "Here comes the first pitch. Henrich swings, there's a hard smash into right field! . . . This one may be out of here! It's going, going— No! It's off the wall in right center. Henrich's rounding first, on his way to second. Here's the relay from Doby . . . Henrich slides in safely with a double!" The Yankee crowd sent up an awesome roar in the background.

"Say, how'd you know that?" Bozo asked. "How'd you know he was gonna wind up at second?"

"I just can tell. I got extra-vision," I said. On the radio, far in the background, the public-address system announced Yogi Berra. "Like Berra right now. You know what? He's gonna hit a one-one pitch down the right-field line—"

"How come you know?" Bozo said. He was getting mad.

"Just a second," I said. "I'm gettin' static." I stood dead still, put my hands up against my temples and opened my eyes wide. "Now it's comin' through clear. Yeah, Yogi's gonna hit a one-one pitch down the right-field line, and it's gonna be fair by about three or four feet— I can't say exactly—and Henrich's gonna score from second, but the throw is gonna get Yogi at second by a mile."

This time Bozo was silent, listening to the Scotchman, who described the ball and the strike, then said: "Henrich takes the lead off second. Benton looks over, stretches, delivers. Yogi swings." (There was the bat crack.) "There's a line drive down the right side! It's barely inside the foul line. It may go for extra bases! Henrich's rounding third and coming in with a run. Berra's moving toward second. Here comes the throw! . . . And they *get* him! They get Yogi easily on the slide at second!"

Before Bozo could say anything else, I reached in my pocket for my notes. "I've just written down here what I think's gonna happen in the first four innings," I said. "Like DiMag. See, he's gonna pop up to Mickey Vernon at first on a one-nothing pitch in just a minute. But don't you worry. He's gonna hit a 380-foot homer in the fourth with nobody on base on a full count. You just follow these notes and you'll see I can predict anything that's gonna happen in the next ten years." I handed him the paper, turned around, and left the store just as DiMaggio, on a one-nothing pitch, popped up to Vernon at first.

Then I went back home and took more notes from the short-wave. The Yanks clobbered the Indians in the late innings and won easily. On the local station, however, the Old Scotchman was in the top of the fifth inning. At this juncture I went to the telephone and called Firehouse No. 1.

"Hello," a voice answered. It was the fire chief.

"Hello, Chief, can you tell me the score?" I said. Calling the firehouse for baseball information was a common practice.

"The Yanks are ahead, 5–2."

"This is the Phantom you're talkin' with," I said.

"Who?"

"The Phantom. Listen carefully, Chief. Reynolds is gonna open this next inning with a popup to Doby. Then Rizutto will single to left on a one-one count. Henrich's gonna force him at second on a two-and-one pitch but make it to first. Berra's gonna double to right on a nothing-and-one pitch, and Henrich's goin' to third. DiMaggio's gonna foul a couple off and then double down the left-field line, and both Henrich and Yogi are gonna score. Brown's gonna pop out to third to end the inning."

"Aw, go to hell," the chief said, and hung up.

This was precisely what happened, of course. I phoned No. 1 again after the inning.

"Hello."

"Hi. This is the Phantom again."

"Say, how'd you know that?"

"Stick with me," I said ominously, "and I'll feed you predictions. I can predict anything that's gonna happen anywhere in the next ten years." After a pause I added, "Beware of fire real soon," for good measure, and hung up.

I left my house and hurried back to the corner grocery. When I got there, the entire meat counter was surrounded by friends of Bozo's, about a dozen of them. They were gathered around my notes, talking passionately and shouting. Bozo saw me standing by the bread counter. "There he is! That's the one!" he declared. His colleagues turned and stared at me in undisguised awe. They parted respectfully as I strolled over to the meat counter and ordered a dime's worth of bologna for my dog.

A couple of questions were directed at me from the group, but I replied, "I'm sorry for what happened in the fourth. I predicted DiMag was gonna hit a full-count pitch for that homer. It came out he hit it on two-and-two. There was too much static in the air between here and New York."

"Too much *static*?" one of them asked.

"Yeah. Sometimes the static confuses my extra-vision. But I'll be back tomorrow if everything's okay, and I'll try not to make any more big mistakes."

"Big mistakes!" one of them shouted, and the crowd laughed admiringly, parting once more as I turned and left the store. I wouldn't have been at all surprised if they had tried to touch the hem of my shirt.

That day was only the beginning of my brief season of triumph. A schoolmate of mine offered me five dollars, for instance, to tell him how I had known that Johnny Mize was going to hit a two-run homer to break up one particularly close game for the Giants. One afternoon, on the basis of a lopsided first four innings, I had an older friend sneak into The Store and place a bet, which netted me $14.50. I felt so bad about it I tithed $1.45 in church the following Sunday. At Bozo's grocery store I was a full-scale oracle. To the firemen I remained the Phantom, and firefighting reached a peak of efficiency that month, simply because the firemen knew what was going to happen in the late innings and did not need to tarry when an alarm came.

One afternoon my father was at home listening to the Old Scotchman with a couple of out-of-town salesmen from Greenwood. They were sitting in the front room, and I had already managed to get the first three or four innings of the Cardinals and the Giants on paper before they arrived. The Old Scotchman was in the top of the first when I walked in and said hello. The men were talking business and listening to the game at the same time.

"I'm gonna make a prediction," I said. They stopped talking and looked at me. "I predict Musial's gonna take a ball and a strike and then hit a double to right field, scoring Schoendienst from second, but Marty Marion's gonna get tagged out at the plate."

"You're mighty smart," one of the men said. He suddenly sat up straight when the Old Scotchman reported, "Here's the windup and the pitch coming in. . . . Musial *swings!*" (Bat crack, crowd roar.) "He drives one into right field! This one's going up against the boards!. . . . Schoendienst rounds third. He's coming on in to score! Marion dashes around third, legs churning. His cap falls off, but here he *comes*! Here's the toss to the plate. He's nabbed at home. He is *out* at the plate! Musial holds at second with a run-producing double."

Before I could parry the inevitable questions, my father caught me by the elbow and hustled me into a back room. "How'd you know that?" he asked.

"I was just guessin'," I said. "It was nothin' but luck."

He stopped for a moment, and then a new expression showed on his face. "Have *you* been callin' the firehouse?" he asked.

"Yeah, I guess a few times."

"Now, you tell me how you found out about all that. I mean it."

When I told him about the short-wave, I was afraid he might be mad, but on the contrary he laughed uproariously. "Do you remember these next few innings?" he asked.

"I got it all written down," I said, and reached in my pocket for the notes. He took the notes and told me to go away. From the yard, a few minutes later, I heard him predicting the next inning to the salesmen.

A couple of days later, I phoned No. 1 again. "This is the Phantom," I said. "With two out, Branca's gonna hit Stinky Stanky with a fast ball, and then Alvin Dark's gonna send him home with a triple."

"Yeah, we know it," the fireman said in a bored voice. "We're listenin' to a short-wave too. You think you're somethin', don't you? You're Ray Morris' boy."

I knew everything was up. The next day, as a sort of final gesture, I took some more notes to the corner grocery in the third or fourth inning. Some of the old crowd was there, but the atmosphere was grim. They looked at me coldly. "Oh, man," Bozo said, "*we* know the Old Scotchman ain't at that game. He's four or five innings behind. He's makin' all that stuff up." The others grumbled and turned away. I slipped quietly out the door.

My period as a seer was over, but I went on listening to the short-wave broadcasts out of New York a few days more. Then, a little to my surprise, I went back to the Old Scotchman, and in time I found that the firemen, the bootleggers, and the few dirt farmers who had short-wave sets all did the same. From then on, accurate, up-to-the-minute baseball news was in disrepute there. I believe we all went back to the Scotchman not merely out of loyalty but because, in our great isolation, he touched our need for a great and unmitigated eloquence.

Since 1960, when he published *Goodbye, Columbus,* the Newark, New Jersey, native Philip Roth (b. 1933) has been in the forefront of American novelists. In an essay that appeared on the op-ed page of *The New York Times* on Opening Day 1973, he explained that baseball was "this game that I loved with all my heart, not simply for the fun of playing it (fun was secondary, really), but for the mythic and aesthetic dimension that it gave to an American boy's life—particularly to one whose grandparents could hardly speak English." He continued: "Baseball was a kind of secular church that reached into every class and region of the nation and bound millions upon millions of us together in common concerns, loyalties, rituals, enthusiasms, and antagonisms . . . baseball—with its lore and legends, its cultural power, its seasonal associations, its native authenticity, its simple rules and transparent strategies, its longueurs and thrills, its spaciousness, its suspensefulness, its heroics, its nuances, its lingo, its 'characters,' its peculiarly hypnotic tedium, its mythic transformation of the immediate—was the literature of my boyhood." Baseball is threaded through several of Roth's books: *The Great American Novel* (1973), among the most eccentric baseball novels ever written; *American Pastoral* (1997), which includes a panegyric to the boys' baseball stories of John R. Tunis; and *Portnoy's Complaint* (1969), in which Alexander Portnoy daydreams, in the presence of his psychiatrist, of inhabiting the same heroic spaces as Willie, Mickey, and (most of all) the Duke.

Philip Roth

♡

from

Portnoy's Complaint

So I ran all right, out of the hospital and up to the playground and right out to center field, the position I play for a softball team that wears silky blue-and-gold jackets with the name of the club scrawled in big white felt letters from one shoulder to the other: S E A B E E S, A.C. Thank God for the Seabees A.C.! Thank God for center field! Doctor, you can't imagine how truly glorious it is out there, so alone in all that space . . . Do you know baseball at all? Because center field is like some observation post, a kind of control tower, where you are able to see everything and everyone, to understand what's happening the instant it happens, not only by the sound of the struck bat, but by the spark of movement that goes through the infielders in the first second that the ball comes flying at them; and once it gets beyond them, "It's mine," you call, "it's mine," and then after it you go. For in center field, if you can get to it, it *is* yours. Oh, how unlike my home it is to be in center field, where no one will appropriate unto himself anything that I say is *mine!*

Unfortunately, I was too anxious a hitter to make the high school team—I swung and missed at bad pitches so often during the tryouts for the freshman squad that eventually the ironical coach took me aside and said, "Sonny, are you sure you don't wear glasses?" and then sent me on my way. But did I have form! did I have style! And in my playground softball league, where the ball came in just a little slower and a little bigger, I am the star I dreamed I might become for the whole school. Of course, still in my ardent desire to excel I too frequently swing and miss, but when I connect, it goes great distances, Doctor, it flies over fences and is called a home run. Oh, and there is really nothing in life, nothing at all, that quite compares with that pleasure of rounding second base at a nice slow clip, because there's just no hurry any more, because that ball you've hit has just gone sailing out of sight . . . And I could field, too, and the farther I had to run, the better. "I got it! I got it!" and tear in toward second, to trap in the webbing of my glove—and barely an inch off the ground—a ball driven hard and low and right down the middle, a base hit, someone thought . . . Or back I go, "*I* got it, *I* got it—" back easily and gracefully toward that wire fence, moving practically in slow motion, and then that delicious DiMaggio sensation of grabbing it like something heaven-sent over one shoulder . . . Or running! turning! leaping! like little Al Gionfriddo—a baseball player, Doctor, who once did a very great thing . . . Or just standing nice and calm—nothing trembling, everything serene—standing there in the sunshine (as though in the middle of an empty field, or passing the time on the street corner), standing without a care in the world in the sunshine, like my king of kings, the Lord my God, The Duke Himself (Snider, Doctor, the name may come up again), standing there as loose and as easy, as happy as I will ever be, just waiting by myself under a high fly ball (*a towering fly ball,* I hear Red Barber say, as he watches from behind his microphone—hit out toward Portnoy; *Alex under it, under it*), just waiting there for the ball to fall into the glove I raise to it, and yup, there it is, *plock,* the third out of the inning (*and Alex gathers it in for out number three, and, folks, here's old C.D. for P. Lorillard and Company*), and then in one motion, while old Connie brings us a message from Old Golds, I start in toward the bench, holding the ball now with the five fingers of my bare left hand, and when I get to the infield—having come down hard with one foot on the bag at second base—I shoot it gently, with just a flick of the wrist, at the opposing team's shortstop as he comes trotting out onto the field, and still without breaking stride, go loping in all the way, shoulders shifting, head hanging, a touch pigeon-toed, my knees coming slowly up and down in an altogether brilliant imitation of The Duke. Oh, the unruffled nonchalance of that game! There's not a movement that I don't know still down in the tissue of my muscles and the joints between my bones. How to bend over to pick up my glove and how to toss it away, how to test the weight of the bat, how to hold it and carry it and swing it around in the on-deck circle, how to raise that bat above my head and flex and loosen my shoulders and my neck before stepping in and planting my two feet exactly where my two feet belong in the batter's box—and how, when I take a called strike (which I have a tendency to do, it balances off nicely swinging at bad pitches), to step out and express, if only through a slight poking with the bat at the ground, just the right amount of exasperation with the powers that be . . . yes, every little detail so thoroughly studied and mastered, that it is simply beyond the realm of possibility for any situation to arise in which I do not know how to move, or where to move, or what to say or leave unsaid . . . And it's true, is it not?—incredible, but apparently true—there are people who feel in life the ease, the self-assurance, the simple and essential affiliation with what is going on, that I used to feel as the center fielder for the Seabees? Because it wasn't, you see, that one was the best center fielder imaginable, only that one knew exactly, and down to the smallest particular, how a center fielder should conduct himself. And there are people like that walking the streets of the U.S. of A.? I ask you, why can't I be one! Why can't I exist now as I existed for the Seabees out there in center field! Oh, to be a center fielder, a center fielder—and nothing more!

When *Ball Four,* Jim Bouton's diary of the 1969 season he spent with the Seattle Pilots and Houston Astros, first appeared, its frank revelations about the seamy and sybaritic habits of professional ballplayers made the erstwhile heroes of American youth into extremely mortal men, and it made Bouton (b. 1939)—by then a mediocre knuckleballer—an instant and controversial best-selling author. Today most of those tales-told-out-of-clubhouse about pitchers popping pep pills and peering through keyholes at disrobing women seem like less-than-lurid peccadillos. But *Ball Four* was to baseball reporting what Watergate was to political journalism, and now we probably know more than we want to. What makes the book endure—and what has placed it on course lists at universities like Harvard—is the comic verve of Bouton's point of view. "You see, you spend a good piece of your life gripping a baseball," he writes, "and in the end it turns out that it was the other way around all the time."

Jim Bouton

♢

from

Ball Four

An outfield game is making up singer-and-actor baseball teams purely on the sound of their names. Example—Panamanian. Good speed, great arm, temperamental: shortstop Jose Greco. Or big, hard-hitting first baseman; strong, silent type: Vaughn Monroe. And centerfielder, showboat, spends all his money on cars, big ladies man, flashy dresser, drives in 75 runs a year, none of them in the clutch: Duke Ellington. Finally—great pitcher, twenty-game winner five years in a row, class guy, friendly with writers and fans alike. Stuff is good, not overpowering, but he's smart, has great control and curve ball, moves the ball around: Nat King Cole.

If you think this is a silly game, you haven't stood around in the outfield much.

———

One of the things baseball players take pride in is their crudity. The day Brandon was sent down, for example, Gary Bell, who is his friend, asked if he would mind leaving his tapes so the guys could continue to listen to his good music while he was gone. Which is like the guy in spring training who went up to a rookie and said, "Hey, if you get released, can I have your sweatshirts?" The crudity takes other forms. Like the fellow who rooms with the great chick-hustler. The hustler will spend all of his time pounding the streets, spending money in bars, working like hell at running down girls. His roommate just lounges around the room, watching television, taking it easy. And he does great just taking his roommate's leavings.

Then there's the tale Jim Gosger told about hiding in a closet to shoot a little beaver while his roommate made out on the bed with some local talent. Nothing sneaky about it, the roommate even provided the towel for Gosger to bite on in case he was moved to laughter. At the height of the activity on the bed, local talent, moaning, says, "Oh darling, I've never done it *that* way before." Whereupon Gosger sticks his head out, drawls "Yeah, surrre," and retreats into the closet.

After he told us the story, "Yeah surrre," became a watchword around the club.

"I only had three beers last night."

"Yeah, surrre."

And I've known ballplayers who thought it was great fun to turn on a tape-recorder under the bed while they were making it with their latest broad and play it back on the bus to the ballpark the next day.

———

In the bullpen tonight Jim Pagliaroni was telling us how Ted Williams, when he was still playing, would psyche himself up for a game during batting practice, usually early practice before the fans or reporters got there.

He'd go into the cage, wave his bat at the pitcher and start screaming at the top of his voice, "My name is Ted fucking Williams and I'm the greatest hitter in baseball."

He'd swing and hit a line drive.

"Jesus H. Christ Himself couldn't get me out."

And he'd hit another.

Then he'd say, "Here comes Jim Bunning, Jim fucking Bunning and that little shit slider of his."

Wham!

"He doesn't really think he's gonna get me out with that shit."

Blam!

"I'm Ted fucking Williams."

Sock!

———

I take this opportunity to present a lexicon of words and phrases encountered around baseball that are, more or less, unique to the game. There are a great many phrases having to do with a pitcher throwing at a batter. Among them are:

Chin music, as in "Let's hear a little chin music out there," this being a suggestion that the pitcher throw the baseball near the hitter's chin.

Purpose pitch, which is a pitch that knocks a batter down purposely, or perhaps may just

Spin his cap.

Keep him honest, which means, make the batter afraid if you can.

Loosen him up, meaning that if enough baseballs are thrown close to a hitter, he'll fall down easily.

Other phrases that often come up in conversation are:

Tweener, any ball hit not especially hard but directly between two outfielders, neither of whom can reach it in time.

Take him over the wall, hit a home run, as in "Horton took Bouton over the wall in the fifth."

Down the cock is the quintessence of the hitting zone. Any pitch like that is bound to be

Juiced, with some kind of power.

Parts of the body also have special appellations:

Boiler, as in "he's got the bad boiler," or upset stomach.

Hose is arm.

Moss is hair.

Shoes are *kicks* and clothes are *vines,* and when the bases are loaded they're *drunk.* A good fielder can really *pick it,* and if you want to tell a guy to go sit down, it's *go grab some bench.* Organized baseball is *O.B.,* and a stupid player has the *worst head in O.B. Wheels* are legs, and an infielder has *the good hands* or *the bad hands* as girls have *the good wheels* or *the bad wheels.* For some reason the definite article is important there. An angry man has the *red ass* or the *R.A.*

Camp-followers, whether they're eleven or sixty-five or somewhere in between, are called *Baseball Annies.* And if a player, coach or manager should bring a girl with him to another city, she's called an *import.* If an import is a *mullion,* she may have to pay her own way.

A pimple or boil is called *a bolt,* as in "get a wrench for that bolt." A hard line drive is a *blue darter, frozen rope,* or an *ungodly shot.* To think is to *have an idea,* so that when a pitcher seems to be losing his cool a coach might shout at him, "Have an idea out there."

And a fellow who talks big but appears to lack courage is said to have an *alligator mouth* and a *hummingbird ass.*

Baseball is not without its charms.

––––

I'm still trying to decide why I haven't been in more ballgames in crucial situations and all I can do is agree with Hovley that it's because they think I'm weird and throw a weird pitch. I need a new image. What I ought to do is take up chewing tobacco and let the dark brown run down the front of my uniform and walk up and down the dugout with a slight, brave limp and tape on my wrist and say things like, "goddammit" and "shit" and "let's get these guys." Then, instead of being weird, I'd be rough and tough.

I think I'd do it, except I can't stand the thought of all that brown down the front of my uniform.

––––

There's a different relationship between whites and blacks on this club than there is in Seattle. Although there was no trouble in Seattle, there was a certain distance. Generally Davis and Simpson and Harper went their separate way. Pagliaroni and Segui were quite friendly and had dinner at each other's homes and there were no strained relations. Yet there was not a lot of—what else to call it?—integration. Here it's obviously different. It's as though the blacks go out of their way to join with whites and the whites try extra hard to join in with the blacks. Blefary and Don Wilson room together on the road, and this is probably unique in baseball. In Jimmy Wynn's

room the other night the group was thoroughly mixed. Tonight
Miller and I were having milkshakes and Joe Morgan and Jimmy
Wynn came over and sat down with us. It doesn't seem forced, and
I think it's worth a lot to the ballclub.

Of course, the humor sometimes gets self-consciously heavy-
handed. Like one time Norm was supposed to play in a game against
some tough pitcher, but he had a bad ankle and at the last minute
Harry Walker decided to let him rest another night. Naturally the
word went right out that Miller had asked out of the lineup, which
everybody knew wasn't true. And soon there was a song called "Jew
the Jake," sung to the tune of Hava Nagilla.

One day Joe Pepitone inserted a piece of popcorn under his fore-
skin and went to the trainer claiming a new venereal disease. "Jesus
Christ, Joe, what the hell have you done?" the doctor said. Pepitone
didn't start laughing until the doctor had carefully used a forceps to
liberate the popcorn.

Norm Miller was doing the broadcast bit in the fourth inning
when Joe Morgan came back to the dugout after missing a big
curve ball for strike three.

"Joe, Joe Morgan, may I have a word with you?"

"Sure, Norm, how's it going?"

"Fine, Joe, fine. We wanted to ask you about that pitch you missed.
What was it?"

"Norm, that was a motherfucking curve."

"Can you tell our listeners, Joe, what's the difference between a
regular curve and a motherfucking curve?"

"Well, Norm, your regular curve has a lot of spin on it and you can
recognize it real early. It breaks down a little bit, and out. Now, your
motherfucker, that's different. It comes in harder, looks like a fastball.
Then all of a sudden it rolls off the top of the table and before you
know it, it's motherfucking strike three."

"Thank you very much, Joe Morgan."

The jazz pianist and songwriter Dave Frishberg (b. 1933) grew up in St. Paul, Minnesota, where the local St. Paul Saints of the Triple A American Association got him interested in baseball. The man who wrote "Peel Me a Grape," "You Are There," "My Attorney Bernie," and "Matty," a lyric about Christy Mathewson, has lived in New York, Los Angeles, and now lives in Portland, Oregon. Van Lingle Mungo—not to be confused with Vinegar Bend Mizell—was a slow-talking, fast-living Brooklyn Dodger speedball pitcher from the hills of South Carolina who spent some time at the end of his career pitching for the Saints' archrival, the Minneapolis Millers. The other names in the song all belong to major-leaguers of the Mungo period. Frishberg met Mungo once, before performing his song on *The Dick Cavett Show*. "First thing he asked me when does he get a check," Frishberg recalled. "I told him if he wants a check, he should write a song called 'Dave Frishberg.'"

Dave Frishberg

♢

Van Lingle Mungo

Heenie Majeski, Johnny Gee
Eddie Joost, Johnny Pesky, Thornton Lee
Danny Gardella
Van Lingle Mungo

Whitey Kurowski, Max Lanier
Eddie Waitkus and Johnny Vandermeer
Bob Estalella
Van Lingle Mungo

Augie Bergamo, Sigmund Jakucki
Big Johnny Mize and Barney McCosky
Hal Trosky

Augie Galan and Pinky May
Stan Hack and Frenchy Bordagaray
Phil Cavaretta, George McQuinn
Howie Pollett and Early Wynn
Art Passarella
Van Lingle Mungo

John Antonelli, Ferris Fain
Frankie Crosetti, Johnny Sain
Harry Brecheen and Lou Boudreau
Frankie Gustine and Claude Passeau
Eddie Basinski
Ernie Lombardi
Hughie Mulcahy
Van Lingle . . . Van Lingle Mungo

Baseball is a game that calls for bursts of inspiration within a complex rubric of formalized rules and rituals. No poet was better positioned to contemplate it as such than May Swenson (1913–1989), whose lifelong fascination with structures often expressed itself through the way her words were arranged on the page; she wrote poems in the shape of butterflies, waves, bottles. However formalistic her poems, Swenson was anything but rigid in her approach to composition. Much like a batsman who refuses to speculate on what will be thrown his way, Swenson claimed never to know what she would say—or how she would say it—until her pen began moving.

May Swenson

◊

Analysis of Baseball

It's about
the ball,
the bat,
and the mitt.
Ball hits
bat, or it
hits mitt.
Bat doesn't
hit ball, bat
meets it.
Ball bounces
off bat, flies
air, or thuds
ground (dud)
or it
fits mitt.

Bat waits
for ball
to mate.
Ball hates
to take bat's
bait. Ball
flirts, bat's
late, don't
keep the date.
Ball goes in
(thwack) to mitt,
and goes out
(thwack) back
to mitt.

Ball fits
mitt, but
not all
the time.
Sometimes
ball gets hit
(pow) when bat
meets it,
and sails
to a place
where mitt
has to quit
in disgrace.
That's about
the bases
loaded,
about 40,000
fans exploded.

It's about
the ball,
the bat,
the mitt,
the bases
and the fans.
It's done
on a diamond,
and for fun.
It's about
home, and it's
about run.

396

Roger Kahn (b. 1927) was raised in Brooklyn by a pair of Thomas Jefferson High School teachers, a father who could remember anything and talked incessantly about baseball, Brahms, botany, and Gibbon, and a mother who relished radical theater, and radical everything else. The other member of Kahn's childhood trinity was the Brooklyn Dodgers, the glorious team that he followed intently as a boy and then covered as a reporter for a glorious newspaper, the *Herald Tribune*. Both the team and the paper are gone from New York, but in memory they have surpassed even what they were back in the mid-1950s. Kahn made a major contribution to the preservation of that memory with *The Boys of Summer* (1972), his bittersweet account of his youth, his city, his paper, his team, and what became of it all. The book is nostalgic but never maudlin. Kahn captures the essential arc of a baseball career as a concentrated version of life, from the glory of youth to inevitable decline. This excerpt features Branch Rickey, the shrewd Bible-quoting impresario who ran the Dodgers, and the strident *Daily News* baseball writer Dick Young, who had a reputation for going after a story harder, and getting it more frequently, than any other New York reporter.

Roger Kahn

♡

from

The Boys of Summer

Wesley Branch Rickey arrived in Brooklyn during World War II fired by two dreams that were to falter. He would build a dynasty to surpass the Yankee empire in the Bronx. He would personally achieve enormous wealth. Rickey became Dodger president after Larry MacPhail responded to the blast of World War II and re-enlisted. MacPhail's Dodgers, assembled under a threat of bankruptcy, could not long endure. Rickey reached Brooklyn thinking in terms of generations, and, as soon as peace came, and manpower stabilized, his Dodgers emerged, formidable, aggressive and enduring. "My ferocious gentlemen," he liked to say. Although Rickey had been banished to Pittsburgh by 1952, every important Dodger pitcher, without exception, had been acquired during his remarkable suzerainty.

Raised on an Ohio farm, Branch Rickey graduated from the University of Michigan, considered becoming a Latin teacher, but chose baseball. Old records indicate that he performed marginally. He caught for the St. Louis Browns and the New York Highlanders—the paleozoic Yankees—doubling as an outfielder. In four years he batted an aggregate .239. Then he managed in St. Louis, moving from the Browns to the Cardinals. He never brought home a team higher than third. Gruff Rogers Hornsby replaced Rickey in 1925 and the Cardinals won the World Series in 1926. Rickey was forty-five that year, and without great distinction. Then he moved into the Cardinal front office and his life turned around. As an executive, Rickey let his intellect run free; broadly, as Henry Ford shaped the future of the business of automobiles, Rickey shaped the future of the game of baseball. It was Rickey who invented the so-called farm system, baseball's production line. He stocked the sources, a half dozen teams, with young, uncertain talent. As their ability allowed, ball players advanced. In one case in twenty-five, a player proved gifted enough for the majors. It was a bloodless procedure, but effective, and presently the Cardinals dominated the National League. Rickey paid execrable salaries—$7,500 a year was high pay. Considering the attrition rate, he had to curb expenses, but Rickey was also a man of principle. He had a Puritan distaste for money in someone else's hands.

In the mid-1940s he bought minor league teams for Brooklyn and the old Latinist, having organized a Dodger farm system, next created a camp where legions of players could be instructed. He chose an abandoned naval air station, four miles west of Vero Beach, Florida, as the training site. There among palms, palmettos, scrub pines and swamp, he made a world. The old Navy barracks, renamed Dodgertown, became spring housing for two hundred athletes. The mess hall now served not navigators but infielders. Outside, Rickey supervised the construction of four diamonds, five batting cages, two sliding pits and numberless pitcher's mounds, everywhere pitcher's mounds. Pitching excited Rickey. It moved him to melodramatics.

At one meeting of the Dodger command, Rickey lifted a cigar and cried, "I have come to the point of a cliff. I stand poised at the precipice. Earth crumbles. My feet slip. I am tumbling over the edge. Certain death lies below. Only one man can save me. *Who is that man?*" This meant that the Dodger bullpen needed help and would someone kindly suggest which minor league righthander should be promoted? It is a tempered irony that Rickey's sure hand failed him where he most wanted sureness. He was unable to produce a great Brooklyn pitching staff.

Pitchers, of all ball players, profit most from competitive intelligence. It is a simple, probably natural thing to throw. A child casts stones. But between the casting child and the pitching major leaguer lies the difference between a boy plunking the piano and an artist performing.

A major leaguer ordinarily has mastered four pitches. The sixty feet six inches that lie between the mound and home plate create one element in a balanced equation between pitcher and batter. No one can throw a baseball past good hitters game after game. The major league pitching primer begins: "Speed is not enough." But a fast ball moves if it is thrown hard enough. Depending on grip, one fast ball moves up and into a right-handed batter. Another moves up and away from him. A few men, like Labine, develop fast balls that sink.

The fast ball intimidates. The curve—"public enemy number one," Chuck Dressen called it—aborts careers. A curve breaks sideways, or downward or at an intervening angle, depending on how it is thrown. Branch Rickey regarded the overhand curve as the best of breaking pitches. An overhand curve, the drop of long ago, breaks straight down, and, unlike flatter curve balls, an overhand curve is equally appalling to righthanded and lefthanded batters. The pure drop, hurtling in at the eyes and snapping to the knees, carried Carl Erskine and Sandy Koufax to strikeout records (fourteen and fifteen) in World Series separated by a decade.

Finally, the technique of major league pitching requires excellent control. Home plate is seventeen inches wide; and a man does best to work the corners. A good technical pitcher throws the baseball at speeds that exceed ninety miles an hour, makes it change direction abruptly and penetrate a target area smaller than a catcher's mitt.

Art proceeds subsequently. The artful pitcher tries never to offer what is expected. Would the batter like a fast ball? Curve him, or, better, throw the fast ball at eye height. Eagerness leads to a wild swing. *Strike one.* Would the batter like another? Now throw that public enemy, down and dirty at the knees. *Strike two.* Now he's on notice for the curve. Hum that jumping fast ball letter-high. That's the pitch he wanted, but not there, not then. Sit down. *Strike three called.* Who's next?

The pitchers are different from the others. They work less often, but when they do, they can hold nothing back. Others cry at a loafing pitcher, "Bend your back. Get naked out there." Action suspends and nine others wait until the pitcher throws. All eyes are on the pitcher, who sighs and thinks. "Ya know," Casey Stengel said about a quiet Arkansan named John Sain, "he don't say much, but that don't matter much, because when you're out there on the mound, you got nobody to talk to." Pitchers are individualists, brave, stubborn, cerebral, hypochrondriacal and lonely.

There was so much that Rickey thought that he could do with pitchers. At Vero Beach three plates were crowned with an odd superstructure. This was the strike zone, outlined in string. Pitching through strings, Rickey said, let a man see where his fast ball went. He devised a curve-ball aptitude test. *Hold pitching arm with hand toward face. Grip ball along seams. Draw arm back fully so that ball touches point of shoulder. Now throw as far as you can.* One can throw neither far nor hard. The test humiliates most people, including good major league curve-ball pitchers.

Rickey erred, retrospect suggests, in overestimating the body and in underestimating the insecurity of pitchers. His favorite overhand curve tortures the arm. A line of strain runs from the elbow to the base of the shoulder. An extraordinary number of Rickey's best pitching prospects rapidly destroyed their arms. In trainer's argot, they stripped their gears.

One gentle, soft-featured Nebraskan, Rex Barney, threw overpowering fast balls, although, as Bob Cooke said so often, he pitched as though the plate were high and outside. Rickey led Barney to the strike zone strings at Vero Beach and commanded, "Please pitch with your right eye covered." Presently he said, "Pitch with your left eye covered." After months of test and experiment, Barney was still wild, and now given to periods of weeping. Rickey threw up his hands and ordered Barney to a Brooklyn psychiatrist. Before he reached thirty, Barney became a bartender. Another major talent, Jack Banta, was finished at twenty-five. Ralph Branca won twenty-one games when he was twenty-one years old. He retired to sell insurance at thirty.

Can each failure be laid at Rickey's grave? No more than one can credit Rickey with Duke Snider's 418 home runs. A model Rickey team played magnificently. A model Rickey pitching staff writhed with aching arms and nervous stomachs.

The first flaw laid bare another. Rickey treated newspapermen with condescending flattery, as one might treat stepchildren, recognizing them as an inescapable price one pays for other delights. In Pittsburgh once he invited me to his box. He was then president of the Pirate team that would lose 101 games. "Good you could come," the master began in a hoarse, intimate whisper, placing a hand on my arm. Bushy, graying eyebrows dominated the face. "I have a question on which I'd value your opinion. What do you think of Sid Gordon?"

"Well, he's slowed down, but he's a strong hitter and an intelligent hitter. His arm is fine and he can catch a fly."

Rickey nodded in excessive gratitude. "How would Sid fare at Ebbets Field?" The gnarled hand squeezed my arm. "On an *everyday* basis?"

"He'd belt a few to left."

"And right," Rickey said. "And right. Don't you think he could clear the scoreboard with regularity?"

"Why, yes. I suppose he could."

Rickey winked. "I appreciate your sharing your views. I don't mind telling you I'm concerned about the Dodgers. So many are my ball players. I'm afraid they may not win it, in which case many will blame bad luck, which would not be the entire case. Luck is the residue of design."

As I left, Rickey remarked, "You know, of course, Gordon was born in Brooklyn." His putative design was altruistic. His real intention was to have me urge the Dodgers to buy Gordon in the pages of the *Herald Tribune*. Publicity is the paradigm of salesmanship.

Balancing this deviousness, which hindered reporting, Rickey offered utter mastery of the phrase. His rolling Ohio-Oxonian dialect was a delightful instrument. Were the Pirates going to win the pennant? I asked once. "Ah, a rosebush blooms on the twelfth of May and does it pretty nearly every year. And one day it's all green and the next it's all in flower. I don't control a ball club's development the way nature controls a rosebush." Was his star home run hitter, Ralph Kiner, for sale? "I don't want to sell Ralph, but if something overwhelming comes along, I am willing to be overwhelmed." To what did he attribute the Pirates' poor record? "We are last on merit." Was he himself discouraged? "My father died at eighty-three, planting fruit trees in unpromising soil."

Once away from the days of this year, Rickey could be quite direct, but in the running of current business he was wed to intrigue. By the late 1940s his relationship with Dick Young and the *Daily News* had become catastrophic.

Where Rickey was rotund, classical and Bible Belt, Young was spiky, self-educated and New York. Rickey was shocked by alcoholism, extramarital sex and the word "shit." Young was shocked by Rickey's refusal to attend Sunday games after a week of misleading reporters. A war was inevitable. Its Sarajevo was bad pitching.

Young began baseball writing in 1943, at twenty-five, and very quickly stretched the accepted limits of the beat. He wrote not only about the games but about the athletes, giving each of the players a personality. It was traditional to present athletes as heroes. Newspaper readers learned that Babe Ruth, Lou Gehrig and Grover Cleveland Alexander were grand gentlemen and a credit to the games of baseball and life. Young had heroes—Reese and Campanella—but he fleshed out his cast with heavies. He called Gene Hermanski "a stumbling clown in the outfield." Hermanski responded by shoving Young, a compact five feet seven. But Young would not cower. He loved his job, which "a lot of very rich guys would give an arm to have," and relished the power it provided, and worked at it in original ways. He cultivated some players, argued with others, writing hard stories and soft ones, but always defending his printed words in person. If Young knocked a man on Tuesday, he sought him out on Wednesday. "I wrote what I wrote because I believe it. If you got complaints, let me hear 'em. If you want better stories, win some games."

In time Young came to know the Dodgers better than any other newspaperman and better, too, than many Dodger officials. He sensed when to flatter, when to cajole, when to threaten. As far as any lay reader of instincts can say, Young possessed a preternatural sense of the rhythms and balances of human relations.

Conversations with several Dodgers strengthened Young's harsh conclusion that a number of pitchers lacked heart and, after one losing game in 1948, he composed a polemical lead:

"The tree that grows in Brooklyn is an apple tree and the apples are in the throats of the Dodgers."

There is a nice implicit pun here on Adam's apple, but the first thrust is Young's thought. Some Dodgers cannot swallow. They are choking.

Branch Rickey had been schooled on a tame sporting press, easy to manipulate. He could not or would not recognize Young as the centurion of a new journalism. He would not even discuss choking frankly. Instead, he expressed private loathing "for *everything* about that man and what he stands for." In public he patronized Young, who above all things would not be patronized. By the time Rickey left Brooklyn in 1950, he was battling Young, Young's boss, and consequently the most widely read newspaper in the United States. In the *Daily News*, Jimmy Powers, the sports editor, identified Rickey as "El Cheapo." Young ghosted Powers' column ten times a year. The *News* would not mention Rickey's manager, Burt Shotton, by name. Instead, Young lanced the bubble of Shotton as genial paterfamilias by giving him the acronym "KOBS." The letters, forged in sarcasm, stood for Kindly Old Burt Shotton. The Dodgers lost because of, won despite, KOBS.

These assaults did not hurt Dodger attendance, but they murdered egos. When Rickey left, and Walter O'Malley became president, his first order of business was to replace KOBS with Dressen. Then O'Malley appointed Emil J. Bavasi, a warm and worldly Roman, as general manager *de facto* (at $17,500), and vice president in charge of Dick Young.

With time, one comes to regret that two such talented men as Rickey and Young fought so bitterly. Neither, I suppose, was faultless, although Rickey, being older, more secure and less tractable, probably warrants more blame. He went to his grave as a babe in public relations.

On the jacket of his ghosted memoir, *The American Diamond*, Rickey is quoted as summing up: "The game of baseball has given me a life of joy. I would not have exchanged it for any other." That's it. That's the old man exactly, still musing on the game and joy at eighty. But the introduction sounds like Rickey, too. Here, seeking a quotation from a man universally appealing, admired and beloved, Rickey began with five maundering lines from Herbert Hoover.

By the time Harold Rosenthal commended me to Dick Young's tutorship, Young and Bavasi had become friends. In addition, Young respected Dressen and enjoyed the attention and machinations of Walter Francis O'Malley. Coincidentally, he had stopped attacking management. "It is not hard to write scoops like Young does," one of the other writers remarked, "after Bavasi feeds the stuff to you." When Young found a few hours for an orientation lecture in Miami on my third day with the team, he angrily mentioned the accusation.

"You do a good job, some guy who can't do a good job says you're cheating. Have you heard that shit? You heard they feed me stuff?" Young was sipping bourbon, which Roscoe McGowen of the *Times*, who at seventy still paid dutiful visits to his mother, suggested did more for longevity than Scotch.

"I heard that, yes."

Young looked into his glass and began cursing. "I know who told you," he said, "and you're just goddamn dumb enough to believe him."

"Oh, I don't know. I'm not so dumb that I'd say who told me."

Young shook his head. "How the hell did *you* ever get this club anyway? You got pull? What the *fuck* are you doing here? Chrissake. They sent a boy."

"Look. You worry about you and the fucking *News*. I'll worry about the *Tribune*."

"I'll kill you, kid." Young's face went blank. I wanted to escape his scorn, but sat there without words. "First, though," Young said, "I gotta tell you rules. You know baseball? You ever cover a club? You know what to do or did you go to fucking Yale? Doan matter. I'm gonna take another bourbon. Hey. Another Old Crow. You're a good Jewish boy. Your mother read the *Times*. Well, you can forget that fucking paper. Rocco's a helluva man, but that don't mean a fuck. They wouldn't let him write it the right way if he fucking wanted. I'm not so sure he wants. The old *Times* way is no good any more, if it ever was any good. You following me? I'm only gonna do this once."

"The *Times* is a pretty successful paper." I winced as I heard my words. The *Times* is pretty successful. Jackie Robinson runs bases well. Dick Young is a hard man. I sit in this hotel bar, a half dozen thoughts about my brain. Who the hell are you, Young, illiterate bastard, to talk to me like this? You know what I think of the *Daily News*? My grandfather wouldn't let it in our house. It was a Fascist, Jew-baiting paper. People bought the *News* when somebody got raped. They read the details on page four. And, if by mistake they forgot to throw the paper out, they said, "Hey, look. I found it on the subway." Goddamn right Bavasi feeds you stuff. You wanna scoop me, you go ahead and try (but please, don't make me look too bad).

"It'll catch up to the *Times* the way they do things," Young said. His rage was done. "You like the way the *Times* writes baseball?" The storm had ended.

"Not much. No."

"Our paper has four times as many readers; not brokers and bank presidents, but you know what Lincoln said. '*He made so many of them.*'"

I quoted a *Times* lead I had been reading all my life: "The Yankees drew first blood yesterday and then had it spilled all over them as . . ."

"Yeah," Young said.

The son of a bitch, I thought, doesn't even give points for quoting.

"See, that was maybe okay a long time ago. Not now. I'm gonna tell you how it got to be now, once, like I say. You listening? Shit. You ain't drinking, so you must be listening. There's a lot of games in a season."

"One hundred fifty-four."

"Wrong. You're forgetting fucking spring training and playoffs and World Series. The number changes. It's always, like I said, a lot. Now you're gonna write the games most of the time. Nothing you can do about that and it ain't bad. But anytime, you hear me, *anytime* you can get your story off the game you got to do it. Because that's unusual and people read unusual things. Fights. Bean balls. Whatever. Write them, not the game."

"But most of the time you do write the games."

"That's right, and when you do, you forget the *Times*. They tell you the score, but your real fan knows the score already. When you got to write the game, the way you do it is: 'In yesterday's 3–2 Dodger victory, the most interesting thing that happened was . . .' Get that? Someone stole two bases. Someone made a horseshit pitch. Dressen made a mistake. Whatever the hell. Not just the score. Tell 'em fucking why or make them laugh. Hey. Gimme another bourbon."

Into the heavy silence, I sent forth: "Young's two rules of sportswriting." What he had articulated among curses and assaults was his credo, and a man like Dick Young, who has been hurt by life and who lives behind rings of fortification, is pained on yielding up a credo. It is like a birth. As a laboring woman, he had cried out. Now to his splendid, terse analysis of his job and mine, I had said, in condescension, "Young's two rules."

"There's a third rule, kid."

"What's that?"

"Don't be so fucking sure."

"Hey, Dick. That's goddamn good."

"It isn't mine."

"What do you mean?"

"That rule was made by a *New York Times* sportswriter whose favorite lead—you know, about the blood—you were just making fun of."

••

In his poems and his prose—particularly the long-running column he wrote for *The Village Voice*—Joel Oppenheimer (1930–1998) ranged from the personal to the social, in a voice at once garrulous and intimate, ready to leap from politics to projective verse to the art of pitching in a single sentence. A fixture of the West Village literary scene who spent hours of most summer days talking baseball with other regulars at the Lion's Head bar, Oppenheimer summed up his devotion to the Mets in *The Wrong Season* (1972). The 1972 season almost didn't happen. Anticipating the walkouts that devastated the 1981 and 1994 seasons, a 13-day players' strike at the beginning of April caused the cancellation of 86 major-league games. As this piece shows, there was plenty of arguing among writers who took sides in the dispute.

Joel Oppenheimer

♢

from

The Wrong Season

It's become increasingly chic to be involved in things like astrology, tarot, mind trips, and the like, and everybody and his brother has a good scientific reason, drawn from his favorite anthropologist or sociologist or shrinker as to why we're doing it, and why it's natural at a time like this, and how it can or can't hurt us. all i can say for myself is that the calendar has always been terribly important to me, and i tend to believe that holidays, for example, mean something, and exist for reasons, so when i looked at the calendar a few weeks ago and realized that easter, passover, and april fool's day were going to fall together this year, i decided it would have something to say about spring. indeed, along came the baseball strike, gil hodges' death, and roy campanella's rehospitalization.

a quick check with my resident astrologer, just to see if the stars as well as the calendar said anything, showed saturn and mars conjunct in gemini opposite neptune in sagittarius.

that was fine, but when i asked the resident astrologer what it told her she dove into an hour-long consultation with her familiar, and then the both of them spent forty-five minutes trying to explain their conclusions to me. i'm not blaming them, but something definitely got lost in translation. what i end up with then is what i understand of what they told me as reinforced by my poet's sense of metaphor. i see foot-dragging impetuosity in the real world, opposing pure idealism laced with rank fantasy in the world of philosophy otherwise known as games. or, in other words, total schizophrenia all around.

well, the television coverage of the beginning of the strike essentially supported this thesis. back at the ranch, in winter haven, a roving camera found some old codgers hanging around the ball park waiting for an exhibition game that wouldn't be played.

they said things like "it isn't fair," "they (the players) are spoiled," and, best of all, "why are they striking now, in the baseball season?"

i've heard this question many times during strikes, like the cabdriver asking me ten years ago why the newspapers went on strike just before christmas, when the people needed to see the ads for christmas shopping. but i guess people who spend their old age in retirement in the sunshine state on pensions won in union fights in the thirties don't ever muse on the theory of labor action, and it obviously would've fit in better with their plans and interfered less with their pleasure if the baseball players had gone out in december. i'm not mad at them, but rather at all of us.

predictably, the papers up here took off in defense of american ideals, but there was a big bonus. dick young used his news column for the strike for a while and laid off black athletes. he really couldn't blame this one on them, but he used the opportunity to transfer his venom to unions in general. somewhere along the way he dropped what has to be my favorite line when, after quoting marvin miller, the players' attorney, to the effect that a surrender at this point would see the destruction of the players' association, young said, "these are tired clichés used by every cajoling labor organizer since the abolition of the sweat shop." i'm sure everybody knows, as mr. young obviously does, that the sweat shop was the only abuse of the workers ever perpetrated by the bosses, and that the idea was dropped by the bosses themselves, of their own volition, because they discovered that it was a bad thing.

honestly, dick! i mean there are lots of arguments to make these days about a strike, and even about labor organizers—vide: every time albert shanker gets up on his hind legs and talks about the misery of being a teacher in new york city—but it is, after all, 1972, and baseball is, after all, a business.

but the news did balance his column with the loveliest of headlines and i thank them for that. across the spread it read: no game today; houk bewildered. i can see ralphie now. he's at the ball park, he has his glove, he looks bewildered indeed. and, monday, three days into the strike, phil pepe wrote a column for them, writing a little scared it seemed to me, as if maybe young were looking over his shoulder, allowing as how maybe, just maybe, the players were being bumrapped. that maybe the continual citing of the "average" thirty-grand-a-year paycheck, with no mention of the "average" four-and-a-half-year career—and no mention of the few players whose salary brings that average up—might just be telling one side of the story. sure, i find it hard to bleed for a yo-yo jock making a lot of money for playing a game, but if i had to choose i'd rather bleed for them than phil wrigley or cbs, you betcha. i been saying for a long time that nobody ever went to the stadium to watch connie mack wave his scorecard around.

those owners keep talking about how they're doing it for me, how the players are going to destroy the game. i think they don't understand something. baseball will survive or die through the kids, like with any other game. if the kids play it, get turned on by it, then we'll have baseball. if they start playing football or soccer or pool instead, and don't care about baseball, baseball will die.

the loveliest statement of this came from larry merchant, who covered opening day as usual: in the east river park, central park, washington square—anywhere kids were throwing a ball around, taking cuts, choosing up sides. he was right. the only fans who would get screwed by the disappearance of "professional baseball" are the same ones who get upset when phosphates get declared illegal and they think they're being discriminated against. they appear on television newscasts and scream about their god-given right to be clean even if it means destroying the universe. i heard one lady say that this way: "i don't care about their water, my clothes are going to be clean!" and the connection is there, too, because they are the same kind of people who think baseball consists of multicolored panels on the facade of shea stadium, or moving pictures of the stars on an exploding scoreboard. these people will indeed get screwed, because they've either forgotten or never knew how the heel of the hand ached after that first march day of throwing the ball around—and when they get hold of a signed baseball to give to their kid they yell at him if he plays with it, but he knows what a baseball is for.

there *was* one argument this week that i couldn't handle. i stopped in murray's for the organic, natural, fertile, large, fresh eggs for the week and i heard the radio tuned to wins in the background and when the sports news came on, just as murray's wife was starting to wait on me i said hold it a minute, i want to hear if anything's happening with the strike. murray went into an old leftist scream about rich athletes, and opiates of the people, and when i tried to explain why i was backing the strikers he and his wife looked at me sadly and broke, in unison, into a marvelous parody of "when i grow too old to dream" that started "when i get too old to fight i'll become a trotskyite." why supporting the players' association made me a trotskyite i don't know, but i walked around for two weeks with the song in my head.

the other thing that had been in my head before the strike was still rattling around there too and that was the season itself, because the last week of the exhibition schedule is when you start that kind of figuring, and i couldn't drop it now, just because there might not be a season.

i mean, that's the week you go to bed secure in all sorts of beliefs: like the exhibitions don't count, except the ones you've won, and that batters who aren't hitting now will start to, while the batters who are hitting are obviously raring to go already, and the pitchers are ahead of the batters anyway and *your* pitchers are going to stay that way.

will seaver ever lose? i doubt it, or at least not before the all-star break. then too, the schedule is favorable, because a preliminary check shows that the mets can't lose a game until, possibly, the sag of jetlag in l.a. at the end of april. and that'll only be the first one of the three-game set that they drop. and since it's clear that the mets will run away with the season, you settle down quiet nights with the macmillan encyclopedia and the baseball register, and you update records to see who has a shot at what.

clemente needed nine triples to make the top twenty-five triples hitters of all time. he didn't make it—he got only seven in 1972 and won't hit any more. it ain't funny—because musial is the only modern on the list, and he's got a lot more at-bats, so that's nice select company for one of our boys to be in. i mean, hardly no one hits triples these days.

despite the fact that henry aaron is becoming everybody's darling, and fickle fame has turned her glance away from willie, because of the damned homeruns, henry is still worthy of attention, because he's moving up on a lot more than that. like, this season, he should move to second in all-time hits, runs batted in, and total bases, as well as making the homerun run.

hoyt wilhelm can't really gain anything, since he leads in practically all the categories he can lead in anyhow, but ain't it a groove that he's still going at forty-eight, turning forty-nine?

tom seaver needs thirty-five wins to pass christy mathewson's total for his first six years, and he and nancy need just one more commercial to give me spasmodic nausea.

cleon jones needs to bat .375 with five hundred at-bats to have a lifetime .300 average. his middle name is joseph.

and understand that this is what baseball's about, too—this and the kids. so when you laugh at me, hunched over my transistor at the dark end of the bar, laugh quietly. remember that i don't laugh at you as you stare at the greater greensboro open, whatever that may be.

i know that ken sobol, alone in front of his stromberg-carlson on memorial day, dazed by all the radio-borne static of all those growling offenhausens, understands. i know that tommy sugar in the rain at aqueduct understands. and i know that the reasonable world does not.

the hope is eternally there—always some specific hopes; this year, before the strike, it was to see vida sign, to see that fast ball rip through. it was even to wish that bouton's knuckler kept floating through the jersey night, just like his fast ball once cut through october days, and to hope that nathaniel learned once and for all the right way to hold a bat—he's five and a half, and give me a child 'til he is six, i ain't got much time—and then, the constant hope, the thing the game is about, the moments of perfection in the long, slow drag of the game, the long, slow drag of the season. i wanted to see those.

now i have to worry, instead, if willie, poor willie, can keep his legs for one more season if i don't see him this one.

and the owners? well, they worry about things like where to put your favorite ball club when they take it away, and what color to make the uniforms this year to attract the ladies, or what kind of unopenable plastic bag to put the mustard in. ballplayers play ball, on the other hand. they understand as well as eight-year-olds playing monopoly the laying down of arbitrary rules on a nonexistent grid of the universe.

what it comes to, despite the public proclamation, is that the owners have taken their ball and gone home, and so, like always, we'll have to stuff a sock and bat it around if we want to play.

or suppose we got bill veeck to form a new league? one where, say, new york city owned the ball club and the profits did us all some good? but that, mr. young would say, smacks of socialism, and besides, since the abolition of the poorhouse, there's nothing wrong with society any more, right? all i can say is, while my soul lusts for the season like a politician lusts for november, nevertheless: off the bosses! up the players! no god, no master, one big union!

In 1966, E. B. White wrote to his stepson, and fellow *New Yorker* writer, Roger Angell (b. 1920): "Dear Rog: You are the foremost interpreter of baseball." Ten years later, White, writing again to Angell, said, "It's new and exciting to have someone exploring baseball at the depth you have ventured into." Angell's achievement was to turn quotidian baseball writing into belles lettres. In so doing he became the preeminent baseball writer of our era, a generous, appreciative, meticulous observer whose descriptions of the game are set forth with grace, brio, and wit. (Who else would refer to "the vast pastel conch of Dodger Stadium"?) Angell has Wagnerian range (Honus, that is); he is a master capable of vivid excursions into the profile (see Bob Gibson); he can make games he never saw breathtaking in their excitement (witness the 1986 National League playoffs); and he often reflects on matters philosophical ("The Interior Stadium" is the consummate baseball essay). He can write at length and, what is often more difficult, can write in brief. At heart, Angell has always been an enthusiast, a fan, and, in particular, a fan of the Red Sox, who draw out "the wild vernal hopes that leap every year, jonquil-like, in the hearts of their followers."

Roger Angell

♢

from

The Summer Game

My first visits to Shea Stadium were of the same dispiriting nature—an early, low-hit squeaker against the Reds, when the same old Mets came apart in the ninth (two hits, an error, and a wild pitch) and lost by 3–0, and a mid-May game against Atlanta, when three fast balls aimed by the Mets' skinny, hard-throwing rookie, Gary Gentry, were redirected by Hank Aaron, Orlando Cepeda, and Bob Tillman into the distant bullpens, thus providing all the runs necessary for a 4–3 Braves victory. I was not present the following night, when the Mets astonished themselves. Hitless through the sixth against Phil Niekro, they erupted for eight runs in the eighth inning, climaxed by Cleon Jones's grand-slammer, to win over Atlanta 9–3. I hurried right back the next afternoon, and my subsequent delightful hours with the Mets this year are perhaps best summarized in a game diary I began keeping at that time:

THURSDAY, MAY 15: Beautiful afternoon, beautiful game. Senior Citizens' Day at Shea, but place jam-packed with kids. Attendance: 32,130. National Pastime looks rosy, but what about schools? Hank Aaron, quickest wrists in West, wafts two (Nos. 516, 517 lifetime), and Metsies dead, down 6–2 in 7th. Metsies *not* dead. Four singles, wild pitch makes it 6–5 in 8th. Optimist fans screeching. Bud Harrelson singles, bottom 9th, Grote plunked by pitch, Agee sacrifices them along. Intentional pass loads hassocks. *Everybody* screeching. Harrelson forced at plate. Cleon Jones up, currently batting .390. (.390? Yep, .390.) Rips one—*pow!*—to right, but triumph denied as Millan, Braves' 2B, climbs invisible ladder, turns midair, & gloves pill backhand. Sudden silence. Damn!

MAY 30–JUNE 1: Mets sweep Giants 3 games while I waste Memorial Day weekend in country. Bad planning.

JUNE 3, NIGHT: Mets' 6th straight. Pass .500, take 2nd place, as Seaver 3-hits Dodgers, 5–2. First hit for good guys is Kranepool's homer in 5th; frequent recent habit with Mets. Kranepool *another* HR in 6th. Must revise Kranepool estimate; good old Eddie! Curious impression: Mets resemble vets, while young Dodgers (Sudakis, Sizemore, Grabarkewitz, etc.) are kiddie corps. What's going on here?

JUNE 4, NIGHT: Exhausted. Mets win, 1–0, in dawn's early light. 15 innings. Sweep of Giants *and* Dodgers, History made. DiLauro, elderly Met rookie hurler, lucky in early going, then implacable. Mets always look lucky these days; sign of good team. L.A. puts 12 runners on base in extra inns., scores none. Mets unflappable. Save game with incredible play in top of 15th—Al Weis, Mets' 2B, reverses gears, grabs deflected drive off pitcher's glove, throws same instant, and nails L.A. base-runner at plate. Still don't believe it. Mets win on anticlimax: Dodgers' W. Davis lopes in for Garrett's easy single, gives it the old hotdog one-hand scoop—and misses. Ball rolls to CF fence & Agee scores easily all way from first. Hoo-haw. Davis looks for place to hide. Kind of game Mets used to lose.

JUNE 15: Mets away, knocking 'em dead in West. Have just learned why Cleon Jones, Our Boy, throws left but bats right. As lad, played in Mobile sandlot with tiny right field; poke over RF wall counted as out, so Cleon switched to starboard side. Sensible. Cleon played baseball, football with T. Agee, also Our Boy, on same Mobile high-school team. Mobile High first Met farm.

JUNE 22: Sunday doubleheader, Cards. Sunshine. Mets break own record for largest '69 crowd: 55,862. (Leagues break own record for largest Sunday crowds ever: 394,008 paid.) Mets look cool, loose, rich —like old Yanks. Manager Hodges a genius. In opener, Gary Gentry shackles Cards as Mets romp, 5–1. (Gentry third straight excellent rookie hurler—Koosman last yr., Seaver yr. before. Wait till NL sees new phenom hurlers. J. Matlack, J. Bibby, now ripening on Met farms! They say Bibby looks exactly like Don Newcombe.* Mets rooters show nouveau-riche side: wildly cheer poor Swoboda, hapless Met flychaser, as he fans 5 times. Second game very tight—Koosman vs. Cards' Torrez in scoreless duel—but I am distracted by small boy, aged 10 maybe, in next box, who is intent on setting new two-game Eastern Flyweight stuffing record. Order of consumption: 1 pizza, 1 hot dog, 1 container popcorn, 1 Coke, ½ bg. peanuts, 1 Coke, 1 ice cream. No more hot dogs, so settles for 2nd pizza. Asks Pop for French fries. Mets' Boswell doubles in 5th, after 17 straight Met singles today (new record?), but still no score. Boy's dad, worn out by entreaties, leaves seat in search of French fries, thus misses Harrelson triple, Agee double that win game in 7th. Dad returns with Fr. frs., loses temper. Cries, "I knew it! The only G.-d. Fr. frs. were way the h. over behind third base!" Is placated when Rod Gaspar makes great peg in 8th to nail Brock at plate & save 1–0 nightcap. Brilliant baseball. Day to remember.

*Quite a wait. Matlack and Bibby have yet to attain the majors.

from

Five Seasons

B aseball-watchers need spring training, too. During an insignificant game between the have-not Cubs and Padres at Scottsdale, I sat in the sun-drenched open grandstand behind first base and allowed my interior clock to begin slowing itself to the pace of summer, to baseball time. As I watched the movements and patterns on the field, my interest in the game merged imperceptibly with my pleasure in the place and the weather. The sunlight was dazing, almost a

weight on my head and arms, and my shadow, thrown on the empty
bench to my right, had edge and substance. After an infield play,
I wrote "4–3" with my pencil in a box on the scorecard on my lap,
and a drop of sweat fell from my wrist and made its own blurry entry
on the same page. The Cub coaches sat together on a row of folding
chairs outside the home-plate end of their dugout, leaning back
against the foul screen with their arms folded and their caps tipped
low over their foreheads, and the Padre brain trust, over on the first-
base side, made an identical frieze. We were a scattered, inattentive
crowd, at times nearly silent, and between pitches we stared off at the
jagged, blue-tan silhouettes of low desert peaks set about the distant
rim of our gaze.

I half-closed my eyes and became aware at once that the afternoon
silence was not quite perfect but contained a running pattern of in-
nocuous baseball sounds. I could hear the murmurous play-by-play of
some radio announcer up in the press box—the words undistinguish-
able but their groups and phrases making a kind of sense just the
same—and this was accompanied by the unending sea-sound of the
crowd itself, which sometimes rose to shouts or broke apart into separate words and cries. "Hey, OK!" . . . *Clap, clap, clap, clap* . . . "Hot
dogs here" . . . "Hey, peanuts and hot dogs!" . . . *Clap, clap, clap* . . .
Whoo-wheet! (a whistle from some player in the infield). *Whoo-wheet!*
. . . *Clap-clap, clap-clap, clap-clap* . . . "The next batter, Number One,
is . . . Hosay Carr*denal, right field!" (The p.a. announcer was giving it
his best—the big, Vegas-style introduction—and the crowd tried to
respond.) "OK, *Ho*-say!" . . . "Hey-hey!" . . . "Let's *go,* Ho-say!" . . .
Clapclapclapclap . . . *Wheet!* There was a sudden short flat noise:
Whocck!—the same sound you would hear if you let go of one end of
a long one-by-eight plank, allowing it to fall back on top of a loose
stack of boards. I leaned forward and watched Cardenal sprinting
for first. He slowed as he took his turn and then speeded up again
as he saw the ball still free in the outfield, pulling into second base
with a standup double. Real cheering now, as the next batter stood in
(". . . Number Eighteen, Bill *Mad*-lock, thirrd base!"), but soon the
game wound down again and the afternoon sounds resumed. *Clap,
clap, clap* . . . "Hey, Cokes! *Get* yer ice-cold Cokes here!" . . . *Clap,
clap, clap, clap* . . . A telephone rang and rang in the press box—*pring-
pring, pring-pring, pring-pring:* a faraway, next-door-cottage sort of

noise. *Clap, clap, clap* . . . "Hey, Tim! Hey, Tim!" (a girl's voice). "Hey, Tim, over *here*!" . . . *Clap, clap* . . . "Streeough!" . . . "Aw, come *on,* Ump!" . . . *Clap, clap, clapclapclap* . . . "Get yer Cokes! Ice-cold Cokes here" . . . *Whoo-wheet!* . . . *Clapclap* . . . "*Ice*-cold." Then there was another noise, a regular, smothered slapping sound, with intervals in between: *Whug!* . . . *Whup! . . . Whug . . . Whup!*—a baseball thrown back and forth by two Padre infielders warming up in short-right-field foul territory, getting ready to come into the game. The sounds flowed over me—nothing really worth remembering, but impossible entirely to forget. They were the sounds I had missed all winter, without ever knowing it.

Agincourt and After

October 1975

Tarry, delight, so seldom met. . . . The games have ended, the heroes are dispersed, and another summer has died late in Boston, but still one yearns for them and wishes them back, so great was their pleasure. The adventures and discoveries and reversals of last month's World Series, which was ultimately won by the Cincinnati Reds in the final inning of the seventh and final game, were of such brilliance and unlikelihood that, even as they happened, those of us who were there in the stands and those who were there on the field were driven again and again not just to cries of excitement but to exclamations of wonder about what we were watching and sharing. Pete Rose, coming up to bat for the Reds in the tenth inning of the tied and retied sixth game, turned to Carlton Fisk, the Red Sox catcher, and said, "Say, this is some kind of game, isn't it?" And when that evening ended at last, after further abrupt and remarkable events, everyone—winners and losers and watchers—left the Fens in exaltation and disarray. "I went home," the Reds' manager, Sparky Anderson, said later, "and I was stunned."

The next day, during the last batting practice of the year, there was extended debate among the writers and players on the Fenway sidelines as to whether game six had been the greatest in Series history and whether we were not, in fact, in on the best Series of them all. Grizzled coaches and senior scribes recalled other famous Octobers—1929, when the Athletics, trailing the Cubs by eight runs in the fourth game, scored ten runs in the seventh inning and won; 1947, when Cookie Lavagetto's double with two out in the ninth ended Yankee pitcher Bill Bevens' bid for a no-hitter and won the fourth game for the Dodgers; 1960, when Bill Mazeroski's ninth-inning homer for the Pirates threw down the lordly Yankees. There is no answer to these barroom syllogisms, of course, but any reca-pitulation and reexamination of the 1975 Series suggests that at the very least we may conclude that there has never been a better one. Much is expected of the World Series, and in recent years much has been received. In the past decade, we have had the memorable and abrading seven-game struggles between the Red Sox and the Cardinals in 1967, the Cardinals and the Tigers in 1968, and the Orioles and the Pirates in 1971, and the astounding five-game upset of the Orioles by the Mets in 1969. Until this year, my own solid favorite—because of the Pirates' comeback and the effulgent play of Roberto Clemente—was the 1971 classic, but now I am no longer certain. Comebacks and late rallies are actually extremely scarce in baseball, and an excellent guaranteed cash-producing long-term in-vestment is to wager that the winning team in any game will score more runs in a single inning than the losing team scores in nine. In this Series, however, the line scores alone reveal the rarity of what we saw:

In six of the seven games, the winning team came from behind.

In one of the games, the winning team came from behind twice.

In five games, the winning margin was one run.

There were two extra-inning games, and two games were settled in the ninth inning.

Overall, the games were retied or saw the lead reversed thirteen times.

No other Series—not even the celebrated Giants–Red Sox thriller of 1912—can match these figures.

It is best, however, not to press this search for the greatest Series any farther. There is something sterile and diminishing about our need for these superlatives, and the game of baseball, of course, is so rich and various that it cannot begin to be encompassed in any set of seven games. This Series, for example, produced not one low-hit, low-score pitching duel—the classic and agonizing parade of double zeros that strains teams and managers and true fans to their limits as the inevitable crack in the porcelain is searched out and the game at last broken open. This year, too, the Reds batted poorly through most of the early play and offered indifferent front-line pitching, while the Red Sox made too many mistakes on the base paths, were unable to defend against Cincinnati's team speed, and committed some significant (and in the end fatal) errors in the infield. One of the games was seriously marred by a highly debatable umpire's decision, which may have altered its outcome. It was not a perfect Series. Let us conclude then—before we take a swift look at the season and the playoffs; before we return to Morgan leading away and stealing, to Yaz catching and whirling and throwing, to Eastwick blazing a fastball and Tiant turning his back and offering up a fluttering outside curve, to Evans' catch and Lynn's leap and fall, to Perez's bombs and Pete Rose's defiant, exuberant glare—and say only that this year the splendid autumn affair rose to our utmost expectations and then surpassed them, attaining at last such a level of excellence and emotional reward that it seems likely that the participants—the members of the deservedly winning, champion Reds and of the sorely disappointed, almost-champion Red Sox—will in time remember this Series not for its outcome but for the honor of having played in it, for having made it happen.

The playoffs, it will be remembered, were brief. Over in the National League, the Reds embarrassed the Pittsburgh Pirates, winners of the Eastern Division title, by stealing ten bases in their first two games, which they won by 8–3 and 6–1. Young John Candelaria pitched stoutly for the Pirates when the teams moved on to Three Rivers Stadium, fanning fourteen Cincinnati batters, but Pete Rose broke his heart with a two-run homer in the eighth, and the Reds won the game, 5–3, and the pennant, 3–0, in the tenth inning. I had deliberated for perhaps seven seconds before choosing to follow the American League championship games—partly because the Red Sox were the only new faces available (the Reds, the Pirates, and the A's have among them qualified for the playoffs fourteen times in the past six years), but mostly because I know that the best place in the world to watch baseball is at Fenway Park. The unique dimensions and properties of the Palazzo Yawkey (the left-field wall is 37 feet high and begins a bare 315 feet down the foul line from home plate—or perhaps, according to a startling new computation made by the Boston *Globe* this fall, *304* feet) vivify ball games and excite the imagination. On the afternoon of the first A's-Sox set-to, the deep green of the grass and light green of the wall, the variously angled blocks and planes and triangles and wedges of the entirely occupied stands, and the multiple seams and nooks and corners of the outfield fences, which encompass eleven different angles off which a ball or a ballplayer can ricochet, suddenly showed me that I was inside the ultimate origami.

There were two significant absentees—Jim Rice, who had suffered a fractured hand late in the campaign and would not play again this year, and Catfish Hunter, the erstwhile Oakland meal ticket, whose brisk work had been so useful to the A's in recent Octobers. Boston manager Darrell Johnson solved his problem brilliantly, moving Carl Yastrzemski from first base to Rice's spot under the left-field wall—a land grant that Yaz had occupied and prospected for many years. Oakland manager Alvin Dark found no comparable answer to his dilemma, but the startling comparative levels of baseball that were now demonstrated by the defending three-time champion A's and the untested Red Sox soon indicated that perhaps not even the Cat would have made much difference. In the bottom of the very first inning, Yastrzemski singled off Ken Holtzman, and then Carlton Fisk hit a hopper down the third-base line that was butchered by Sal Bando and further mutilated by Claudell Washington, in left. Lynn then hit an undemanding ground ball to second baseman Phil Garner, who muffed it. Two runs were in, and in the seventh the Sox added five more, with help from Oakland center fielder Bill North, who dropped a fly, and Washington, who somehow played Lynn's fly to the base of the wall into a double. Tiant, meanwhile, was enjoying himself. The Oakland scouting report on him warned he had six pitches—fastball, slider, curve, change-up curve, palm ball, and knuckler—all of which he could serve up from the sidearm, three-quarter, or overhand sectors, and points in between, but on this particular afternoon his fastball was so lively that he eschewed the upper ranges of virtuosity. He did not give up his first hit until the fifth inning or, incredibly, his first ground ball until the eighth. The Sox won, 7–1. "Tiant," Reggie Jackson declared in the clubhouse, "is the Fred Astaire of baseball."

The second game, which Alvin Dark had singled out as the crucial one in any three-of-five series, was much better. Oakland jumped away to a 3–0 lead, after a first-inning homer by Jackson, and Sal Bando whacked four successive hits—*bong! whang! bing! thwong!*—off the left-field wall during the afternoon. The second of these, a single, was converted into a killing out by Yastrzemski, who seized the carom off the wall and whirled and threw to Petrocelli to erase the eagerly advancing Campaneris at third—a play that Yaz and Rico first perfected during the Garfield Administration. The same two elders subsequently hit home runs—Yaz off Vida Blue, Rico off Rollie Fingers—and Lynn contributed a run-scoring single and a terrific diving cutoff of a Joe Rudi double to center field that saved at least one run. The Sox won by 6–3. The A's complained after the game that two of Bando's shots would have been home runs in any other park, and that both Yastrzemski's and Petrocelli's homers probably would have been outs in any other park. Absolutely true: the Wall giveth and the Wall taketh away.

Not quite believing what was happening, I followed the two teams to Oakland, where I watched the Bosox wrap up their easy pennant with a 5–3 victory. Yastrzemski, who is thirty-six years old and who had suffered through a long summer of injuries and ineffectuality, continued to play like the Yaz of 1967, when he almost single-handedly carried the Red Sox to their last pennant and down to the seventh game of that World Series. This time, he came up with two hits, and twice astonished Jackson in the field—first with a whirling throw from the deep left-field corner that cleanly excised Reggie at second base, and then, in the eighth, with a sprinting, diving, skidding, flat-on-the-belly stop of Jackson's low line shot to left that was headed for the wall and a sure triple. The play came in the midst of the old champions' courageous two-run rally in the eighth, and it destroyed them. Even though it fell short, I was glad about that rally, for I did not want to see the splendid old green-and-yallers go down meekly or sadly in the end. The Oakland fans, who have not always been known for the depths of their constancy or appreciation, also distinguished themselves, sustaining an earsplitting cacophony of hope and encouragement to the utter end. I sensed they were saying goodbye to their proud and vivid and infinitely entertaining old lineup—to Sal Bando and Campy Campaneris, to Joe Rudi and Reggie

Jackson and Gene Tenace and Rollie Fingers and the rest, who will almost surely be broken up now and traded away, as great teams must be when they come to the end of their time in the sun.

The finalists, coming together for the Series opener at Fenway Park, were heavily motivated. The Reds had not won a World Series since 1940, the Sox since 1918. Cincinnati's Big Red Machine had stalled badly in its recent October outings, having failed in the World Series of 1970 and '72 and in the playoffs of 1973. The Red Sox had a record of shocking late-season collapses, the latest coming in 1974, when they fizzled away a seven-game lead in the last six weeks of the season. Both teams, however, were much stronger than in recent years— the Reds because of their much improved pitching (most of it relief pitching) and the maturing of a second generation of outstanding players (Ken Griffey, Dave Concepcion, George Foster) to join with the celebrated Rose, Morgan, Perez, and Bench. The Red Sox infield had at last found itself, with Rick Burleson at short and Denny Doyle (a midseason acquisition from the Angels) at second, and there was a new depth in hitting and defense—Beniquez, Cooper, Carbo, and the remarkable Dwight Evans. This was a far better Boston team than the 1967 miracle workers. The advantage, however, seemed to belong to Cincinnati, because of the Reds' combination of speed and power (168 stolen bases, 124 homers) and their implacable habit of winning ball games. Their total of 108 games won had been fashioned, in part, out of an early-season streak of 41 wins in 50 games, and a nearly unbelievable record of 64–17 in their home park. The Red Sox, on the other hand, had Lynn and Tiant. . . .

Conjecture thickened through most of the opening game, which was absolutely close for most of the distance, and then suddenly not close at all. Don Gullett, a powerful left-hander, kept the Red Sox in check for six innings, but was slightly outpitched and vastly outacted over the same distance by Tiant. The venerable stopper (Tiant is listed as being thirty-four and rumored as being a little or a great deal older) did not have much of a fastball on this particular afternoon, so we were treated to the splendid full range of Tiantic mime. His repertoire begins with an exaggerated mid-windup pivot, during which he turns his back on the batter and seems to examine the infield directly behind the mound for signs of crabgrass. With men on bases, his stretch consists of a succession of minute downward waggles and pauses of the glove, and a menacing sidewise, slit-eyed, Valentino-like gaze over his shoulder at the base runner. The full flower of his art, however, comes during the actual delivery, which is executed with a perfect variety show of accompanying gestures and impersonations. I had begun to take notes during my recent observations of the Cuban Garrick, and now, as he set down the Reds with only minimal interruptions (including one balk call, in the fourth), I arrived at some tentative codifications. The basic Tiant repertoire seems to include:

(1) Call the Osteopath: In midpitch, the man suffers an agonizing seizure in the central cervical region, which he attempts to fight off with a sharp backward twist of the head.

(2) Out of the Woodshed: Just before releasing the ball, he steps over a raised sill and simultaneously ducks his head to avoid conking it on the low doorframe.

(3) The Runaway Taxi: Before the pivot, he sees a vehicle bearing down on him at top speed, and pulls back his entire upper body just in time to avoid a nasty accident.

(4) Falling Off the Fence: An attack of vertigo nearly causes him to topple over backward on the mound. Strongly suggests a careless dude on the top rung of the corral.

(5) The Slipper-Kick: In the midpitch, he surprisingly decides to get rid of his left shoe.

(6) The Low-Flying Plane (a subtle development and amalgam of 1, 3, and 4, above): While he is pivoting, an F-105 buzzes the ball park, passing over the infield from the third-base to the first-base side at a height of eighty feet. He follows it all the way with his eyes.

All this, of course, was vastly appreciated by the Back Bay multitudes, including a nonpaying claque perched like seagulls atop three adjacent rooftop billboards (WHDH Radio, Windsor Canadian Whiskey, Buck Printing), who banged on the tin hoardings in accompaniment to the park's deepening chorus of "Lu-is! Lu-is! Lu-is!" The Reds, of course, were unmoved, and only three superior defensive plays by the Sox (including another diving, rolling catch by Yastrzemski) kept them from scoring in the top of the seventh. Defensive sparks often light an offensive flareup in close games, and Tiant now started the Sox off with a single. Evans bunted, and Gullett pounced on the ball and steamed a peg to second a hair too late to nail Tiant—the day's first mistake. Doyle singled, to load the bases, and Yaz singled for the first run. Fisk walked for another run, and then Petrocelli and Burleson singled, too. (Gullett had vanished.) Suddenly six runs were in, and the game—a five-hit shutout for Tiant—was safely put away very soon after.

The next afternoon, a gray and drizzly Sunday, began happily and ended agonizingly for the Sox, who put six men aboard in the first two innings and scored only one of them, thanks to some slovenly base running. In the fourth inning, the Reds finally registered their first run of the Series, but the Sox moved out ahead again, 2–1, and there the game stuck, a little too tight for anyone's comfort. There was a long delay for rain in the seventh. Matters inched along at last, with each club clinging to its best pitching: Boston with its starter, Bill Lee, and Cincinnati with its bullpen—Borbon and McEnaney and Eastwick, each one better, it seemed, than the last. Lee, a southpaw, had thrown a ragbag of pitches—slow curves, sliders, screwballs, and semi-fastballs—all to the very outside corners, and by the top of the ninth he had surrendered but four hits. Now, facing the heaviest part of the Reds' order, he started Bench off with a pretty good but perhaps predictable outside fastball, which Bench whacked on a low line to the right-field corner for a double. Right-hander Dick Drago came on and grimly retired Perez and then Foster. One more out was required, and the crowd cried for it on every pitch. Concepcion ran the count to one and one and then hit a high-bouncing, unplayable chop over second that tied things up. Now the steal was on, of course, and Concepcion flashed away to second and barely slipped under Fisk's waist-high peg; Griffey doubled to the wall, and the Reds, for the twenty-fifth time this year, had snatched back a victory in their last licks. Bench's leadoff double had been a parable of winning baseball. He has great power in every direction, but most of all, of course, to left, where the Fenway wall murmurs so alluringly to a right-handed slugger whose team is down a run. Hitting Lee's outside pitch to right—going with it—was the act of a disciplined man.

Bill Lee is a talkative and engaging fellow who will discourse in lively fashion on almost any subject, including zero population growth, Zen Buddhism, compulsory busing, urban planning, acupuncture, and baseball. During the formal postgame press interview, a reporter put up his hand and said, "Bill, how would you, uh, characterize the World Series so far?"

Two hundred pencils poised.

"Tied," Lee said.

The action now repaired to the cheerless, circular, Monsantoed close of Riverfront Stadium. The press box there is glassed-in and air-conditioned, utterly cut off from the sounds of baseball action and baseball cheering. After an inning or two of this, I began to feel as if I were suffering from the effects of a mild stroke, and so gave up my privileged niche and moved outdoors to a less favored spot in an aux-iliary press section in the stands, where I was surrounded by the short-haired but vociferous multitudes of the Cincinnati. The game was a noisy one, for the Reds, back in their own yard, were sprinting around the Astro Turf and whanging out long hits. They stole three bases and hit three home runs (Bench, Concepcion, and Geronimo—the latter two back-to-back) in the course of moving to a 5-1 lead. Boston responded with a will. The second Red Sox homer of the evening (Fisk had hit the first) was a pinch-hit blow by Bernie Carbo, and the third, by Dwight Evans, came with one out and one on in the ninth and tied the score, astonishingly, at 5–5. The pattern of the game to this point, we can see in retrospect, bears a close resemblance to the classic sixth, and an extravagant dénouement now seemed cer-tain. Instead, we were given the deadening business of the disputed, umpired play—the collision at home plate in the bottom of the tenth between Carlton Fisk and Cincinnati pinch-hitter Ed Armbrister, who, with a man on first, bounced a sacrifice bunt high in the air just in front of the plate and then somehow entangled himself with Fisk's left side as the catcher stepped forward to make his play. Fisk caught the ball, pushed free of Armbrister (without trying to tag him), and then, hurrying things, threw to second in an attempt to force the base runner, Geronimo, and, in all likelihood, begin a crucial double play. The throw, however, was a horrible sailer that glanced off Burleson's glove and went on into center field; Geronimo steamed down to third, from where he was scored, a few minutes later, by Joe Morgan for the winning run. Red Sox manager Darrell Johnson protested, but the complaint was swiftly dismissed by home-plate umpire Larry Barnett and, on an appeal, by first-base umpire Dick Stello.

The curious thing about the whole dismal tort is that there is no dispute whatever about the events (the play was perfectly visible, and was confirmed by a thousand subsequent replayings on television), just as there is no doubt but that the umpires, in disallowing an interference call, cited apparently nonexistent or inapplicable rules. Barnett said, "It was simply a collision," and he and Stello both ruled that only an intentional attempt by Armbrister to obstruct Fisk could have been called interference. There is no rule in baseball that exempts simple collisions, and no one on either team ever claimed that Armbrister's awkward brush-block on Fisk was anything but accidental. This leaves the rules, notably Rule 2.00 (a): "Offensive interference is an act . . . which interferes with, obstructs, impedes, hinders, or confuses any fielder attempting to make a play." Rule 6.06 (c) says much the same thing (the baseball rule book is almost as thick as Blackstone), and so does 7.09: "It is interference by a batter or a runner when (1) He fails to avoid a fielder who is attempting to field a batted ball. . . ." Armbrister failed to avoid. Fisk, it is true, did not make either of the crucial plays then open to him—the tag and the peg—although he seemed to have plenty of time and room for both, but this does not in any way alter the fact of the previous interference. Armbrister should have been called out, and Geronimo returned to first base—or, if a double play had in fact been turned, *both* runners could have been called out by the umps, according to a subclause of 6.06.*

---

*I have truncated this mind-calcifying detour into legal semantics, because time proved it to be both incomplete and misleading. Shortly after the publication of this account, the news filtered out of the league offices that the Series umpires had been operating under a prior "supplemental instruction" to the interference rules, which stated: "When a catcher and a batter-runner going to first have contact when the catcher is fielding the ball, there is generally no violation and nothing should be called." This clearly exonerates Larry Barnett and explains his mystifying "It was simply a collision." What has never been explained is why the existence of this codicil was not immediately divulged to the fans and to the writers covering the Series, thus relieving the umpires of a barrage of undeserved obloquy. We should also ask whether the blanket exculpation of the supplemental instructions really does fit the crucial details of *Armbrister v. Fisk*. Subsequent pondering of the landmark case and several viewings of the Series film have led me to conclude that fairness and good sense would have been best served if Armbrister had been called out and the base runner, Geronimo, returned to first. It is still plain, however, that Carlton Fisk had the best and quickest opportunity to clarify this passionate affair, with a good, everyday sort of peg down to second; irreversibly, he blew it.

There were curses and hot looks in the Red Sox clubhouse that night, along with an undercurrent of feeling that Manager Johnson had not complained with much vigor. "If it had been me out there," Bill Lee said, "I'd have bitten Barnett's ear off. I'd have van Goghed him!"

Untidiness continued the next night, in game four, but in more likely places. The Reds did themselves out of a run with some over-ambitious base running, and handed over a run to the Sox on an error by Tony Perez; Sparky Anderson was fatally slow in calling on his great relief corps in the midst of a five-run Red Sox rally; the Boston outfield allowed a short fly ball to drop untouched, and two Cincinnati runs instantly followed. The Sox led, 5–4, after four innings, and they won it, 5–4, after some excruciating adventures and anxieties. Tiant was again at center stage, but on this night, working on short rest, he did not have full command of his breaking stuff and was forced to underplay. The Reds' pitcher over the last three innings was Rawlins J. Eastwick III, the tall, pale, and utterly expressionless rookie fireballer, who was blowing down the Red Sox hitters and seemed perfectly likely to pick up his third straight win in relief. Tiant worked slowly and painfully, running up long counts, giving up line-drive outs, surrendering bases on balls and singles, but somehow struggling free. He was still in there by the ninth, hanging on by his toenails, but he now gave up a leadoff single to Geronimo. Armbrister sacrificed (this time without litigation), and Pete Rose, who had previously hit two ropes for unlucky outs, walked. Johnson came to the mound and, to my surprise, left Tiant in. Ken Griffey ran the count to three and one, fouled off the next pitch, and bombed an enormous drive to the wall in deepest center field, four hundred feet away, where Fred Lynn pulled it down after a long run. Two outs. Joe Morgan, perhaps the most dangerous hitter in baseball in such circumstances, took a ball (I was holding my breath; everyone in the vast stadium was holding his breath) and then popped straight up to Yastrzemski, to end it. Geronimo had broken for third base on the pitch, undoubtedly distracting Morgan for a fraction of a second—an infinitesimal and perhaps telling mistake by the Reds.

Tiant, it turned out, had thrown a total of 163 pitches, and Sparky Anderson selected Pitch No. 160 as the key to the game. This was not

the delivery that Griffey whacked and Lynn caught but its immediate predecessor—the three-and-one pitch that Griffey had fouled
off. Tiant had thrown a curve there—"turned it over," in baseball
talk—which required the kind of courage that baseball men most respect. "Never mind his age," Joe Morgan said. "Being smart, having
an idea—that's what makes a pitcher."

Morgan himself has the conviction that he should affect the outcome of every game he plays in every time he comes up to bat and
every time he gets on base. (He was bitterly self-critical for that game-
ending out.) Like several of the other Cincinnati stars, he talks about
his own capabilities with a dispassionate confidence that sounds im-
modest and almost arrogant—until one studies him in action and
understands that this is only another form of the cold concentration
he applies to ball games. This year, he batted .327, led the National
League in bases on balls, and fielded his position in the manner that
has won him a Gold Glove award in each of the past two years. In
more than half of his trips to the plate, he ended up on first base,
and once there he stole sixty-seven bases in seventy-seven attempts.
A short (five foot seven), precise man, with strikingly carved features,
he talks in quick, short bursts of words. "I think I can steal off any
pitcher," he said to me. "A good base stealer should make the whole
infield jumpy. Whether you steal or not, you're changing the rhythm
of the game. If the pitcher is concerned about you, he isn't concentrating enough on the batter. You're doing something without doing
anything. You're out there to make a difference."

With the Reds leading, 2–1, in the sixth inning of the fifth game,
Morgan led off and drew a walk. (He had singled in the first inning
and instantly stolen second.) The Boston pitcher, Reggie Cleveland,
now threw over to first base seven times before delivering his first
pitch to the next Cincinnati hitter, Johnny Bench—a strike. Apparently determining to fight it out along these lines if it took all winter,
Cleveland went to first four more times, pitched a foul, threw to first
five more times and delivered a ball. Only one of the throws came
close to picking off Morgan, who got up each time and quickly resumed his lead about eleven feet down the line. Each time Cleveland
made a pitch, Morgan made a flurrying little bluff toward second.
Now Cleveland pitched again and Bench hit a grounder to right—

a single, it turned out, because second baseman Denny Doyle was in motion toward the base and the ball skipped through, untouched, behind him. Morgan flew around to third, and an instant later Tony Perez hit a three-run homer—his second homer of the day—and the game was gone, 6–2. Doyle said later that he had somehow lost sight of Bench's hit for an instant, and the box score said later that Perez had won the game with his hitting and that Don Gullett, who allowed only two Boston batters to reach first base between the first and the ninth innings, had won it with his pitching, but I think we all knew better. Morgan had made the difference.

Game Six, Game Six . . . what can we say of it without seeming to diminish it by recapitulation or dull it with detail? Those of us who were there will remember it, surely, as long as we have any baseball memory, and those who wanted to be there and were not will be sorry always. Crispin Crispian: for Red Sox fans, this was Agincourt. The game also went out to sixty-two million television viewers, a good many millions of whom missed their bedtime. Three days of heavy rains had postponed things; the outfield grass was a lush, Amazon green, but there was a clear sky at last and a welcoming moon—a giant autumn squash that rose above the right-field Fenway bleachers during batting practice.

In silhouette, the game suggests a well-packed but dangerously overloaded canoe—with the high bulge of the Red Sox' three first-inning runs in the bow, then the much bulkier hump of six Cincinnati runs amidships, then the counterbalancing three Boston runs astern, and then, *way* aft, one more shape. But this picture needs colors: Fred Lynn clapping his hands once, quickly and happily, as his three-run opening shot flies over the Boston bullpen and into the bleachers . . . Luis Tiant fanning Perez with a curve and the Low-Flying Plane, then dispatching Foster with a Fall Off the Fence. Luis does not have his fastball, however. . . .

Pete Rose singles in the third. Perez singles in the fourth—his first real contact off Tiant in three games. Rose, up again in the fifth, with a man on base, fights off Tiant for seven pitches, then singles hard to center. Ken Griffey triples off the wall, exactly at the seam of the left-field and center-field angles; Fred Lynn, leaping up for the ball and missing it, falls backward into the wall and comes down heavily. He lies there, inert, in a terrible, awkwardly twisted position, and for an instant all of us think that he has been killed. He is up at last, though, and even stays in the lineup, but the noise and joy are gone out of the crowd, and the game is turned around. Tiant, tired and old and, in the end, bereft even of mannerisms, is rocked again and again—eight hits in three innings—and Johnson removes him, far too late, after Geronimo's first-pitch home run in the eighth has run the score to 6–3 for the visitors.

By now, I had begun to think sadly of distant friends of mine— faithful lifelong Red Sox fans all over New England, all over the East, whom I could almost see sitting silently at home and slowly shaking their heads as winter began to fall on them out of their sets. I scarcely noticed when Lynn led off the eighth with a single and Petrocelli walked. Sparky Anderson, flicking levers like a master backhoe operator, now called in Eastwick, his sixth pitcher of the night, who fanned Evans and retired Burleson on a fly. Bernie Carbo, pinch-hitting, looked wholly overmatched against Eastwick, flailing at one inside fastball like someone fighting off a wasp with a croquet mallet. One more fastball arrived, high and over the middle of the plate, and Carbo smashed it in a gigantic, flattened parabola into the center-field bleachers, tying the game. Everyone out there—and everyone in the stands, too, I suppose—leaped to his feet and waved both arms exultantly, and the bleachers looked like the dark surface of a lake lashed with a sudden night squall.

The Sox, it will be recalled, nearly won it right away, when they loaded the bases in the ninth with none out, but an ill-advised dash home by Denny Doyle after a fly, and a cool, perfect peg to the plate by George Foster, snipped the chance. The balance of the game now swung back, as it so often does when opportunities are wasted. Drago pitched out of a jam in the tenth, but he flicked Pete Rose's uniform with a pitch to start the eleventh. Griffey bunted, and Fisk snatched up the ball and, risking all, fired to second for the force on Rose. Morgan was next, and I had very little hope left. He struck a drive on a quick, deadly rising line—you could still hear the loud *whock!* in the stands as the white blur went out over the infield—and for a moment I thought the ball would land ten or fifteen rows back in the right-field bleachers. But it wasn't hit quite that hard—it was traveling too fast, and there was no sail to it—and Dwight Evans, sprinting backward and watching the flight of it over his shoulder, made a last-second, half-staggering turn to his left, almost facing away from the plate at the end, and pulled the ball in over his head at the fence. The great catch made for two outs in the end, for Griffey had never stopped running and was easily doubled off first.

And so the swing of things was won back again. Carlton Fisk, leading off the bottom of the twelfth against Pat Darcy, the eighth Reds pitcher of the night—it was well into morning now, in fact—socked the second pitch up and out, farther and farther into the darkness above the lights, and when it came down at last, reillumi-nated, it struck the topmost, innermost edge of the screen inside the yellow left-field foul pole and glanced sharply down and bounced on the grass: a fair ball, fair all the way. I was watching the ball, of course, so I missed what everyone on television saw—Fisk wav-ing wildly, weaving and writhing and gyrating along the first-base line, as he wished the ball fair, *forced* it fair with his entire body. He circled the bases in triumph, in sudden company with several hundred fans, and jumped on home plate with both feet, and John Kiley, the Fenway Park organist, played Handel's "Hallelujah Chorus," *fortissimo,* and then followed with other appropriately exu-berant classical selections, and for the second time that evening I suddenly remembered all my old absent and distant Sox-afflicted friends (and all the other Red Sox fans, all over New England), and I thought of them—in Brookline, Mass., and Brooklin, Maine; in Bev-erly Farms and Mashpee and Presque Isle and North Conway and Damariscotta; in Pomfret, Connecticut, and Pomfret, Vermont; in Wayland and Providence and Revere and Nashua, and in both the Concords and all five Manchesters; and in Raymond, New Hamp-shire (where Carlton Fisk lives), and Bellows Falls, Vermont (where Carlton Fisk was *born*), and I saw all of them dancing and shouting and kissing and leaping about like the fans at Fenway—jumping up and down in their bedrooms and kitchens and living rooms, and in bars and trailers, and even in some boats here and there, I suppose, and on back-country roads (a lone driver getting the news over the radio and blowing his horn over and over, and finally pulling up and getting out and leaping up and down on the cold macadam, yelling into the night), and all of them, for once at least, utterly joy-ful and believing in that joy—alight with it.

It should be added, of course, that very much the same sort of celebration probably took place the following night in the mid-lands towns and vicinities of the Reds' supporters—in Otterbein and Scioto; in Frankfort, Sardinia, and Summer Shade; in Zanesville and Louisville and Akron and French Lick and Loveland. I am not enough of a social geographer to know if the faith of the Red Sox fan is deeper or hardier than that of a Reds rooter (although I secretly believe that it may be, because of his longer and more bitter disappointments down the years). What I do know is that this belonging and caring is what our games are all about; this is what we come for. It is foolish and childish, on the face of it, to affiliate ourselves with anything so insignificant and patently contrived and commercially exploitative as a professional sports team, and the amused superiority and icy scorn that the non-fan directs at the sports nut (I know this look—I know it by heart) is understandable and almost unanswerable. Almost. What is left out of this calculation, it seems to me, is the business of caring—caring deeply and passionately, really *caring*—which is a ca-pacity or an emotion that has almost gone out of our lives. And so it seems possible that we have come to a time when it no longer matters so much what the caring is about, how frail or foolish is the object of that concern, as long as the feeling itself can be saved. Naïveté—the infantile and ignoble joy that sends a grown man or woman to danc-ing and shouting with joy in the middle of the night over the hap-hazardous flight of a distant ball—seems a small price to pay for such a gift.

The seventh game, which settled the championship in the very last inning and was watched by a television audience of seventy-five mil-lion people, probably would have been a famous thriller in some other Series, but in 1975 it was outclassed. It was a good play that opened on the night after the opening night of *King Lear*. The Red Sox sprang away to an easy 3–0 lead in the third inning—easy because Don Gullett was overthrowing and walked in two runs in the course of striking out the side. By the fifth inning, the Sox had also left nine runners aboard, and a gnawing conviction settled on me that this was not going to be their day after all. It occurred to me simultaneously that this lack of confidence probably meant that I had finally quali-fied as a Red Sox fan, a lifelong doubter (I am *sort* of a Red Sox fan, which barely counts at all in the great company of afflicted true believers), but subsequent study of the pattern of this Series shows that my doubts were perfectly realistic. The Red Sox had led in all seven games, but in every game after the opener the Reds either tied or reversed the lead by the ninth inning or (once) put the tying and winning runs aboard in the ninth. This is called pressure baseball, and it is the absolute distinguishing mark of a championship team.

Here, working against Bill Lee, the Reds nudged and shouldered at the lead, putting their first batter aboard in the third, fourth, and fifth innings but never quite bringing him around. Rose led off with a single in the sixth. (He got on base eleven times in his last fifteen appearances in the Series.) With one out, Bench hit a sure double-play ball to Burleson, but Rose, barreling down toward second, slid high and hard into Doyle just as he was firing on to first, and the ball went wildly into the Boston dugout. Lee, now facing Perez, essayed a looping, quarter-speed, spinning curve, and Perez, timing his full swing exactly, hit the ball over the wall and over the screen and perhaps over the Massachusetts Turnpike. The Reds then tied the game in the seventh (when Lee was permitted to start his winter vacation), with Rose driving in the run.

The Cincinnati bullpen had matters in their charge by now, and almost the only sounds still to be heard were the continuous cries and clappings and shouts of hope from the Reds' dugout. Fenway Park was like a waiting accident ward early on a Saturday night. Ken Griffey led off the ninth and walked, and was sacrificed to second. Willoughby, who had pitched well in relief, had been lost for a pinch-hitter in the bottom of the eighth, and the new Boston pitcher was a thin, tall left-handed rookie named Jim Burton, who now retired a pinch-hitter, Dan Driessen, and then (showing superb intelligence, I thought) walked Pete Rose. Joe Morgan was the next batter, and Burton—staring in intently for his sign, checking the runners, burning with concentration—gave it his best. He ran the count to one and two and then threw an excellent pitch—a slider down and away, off the outer sliver of the plate. Morgan, almost beaten by it, caught it with the outer nub of his bat and lofted a little lob out to very short center field that rose slightly and then lost its hold, dropping in well in front of the onrushing, despairing Lynn, as the last runner of the year came across the plate. That was all; Boston went down in order.

I left soon, walking through the trash and old beer cans and torn-up newspapers on Jersey Street in company with hundreds of murmuring and tired Boston fans. They did not look bitter, and perhaps they felt, as I did, that no team in our time had more distinguished itself in the World Series than the Red Sox—no team, that is, but the Cincinnati Reds.

This Series, of course, was replayed everywhere in memory and conversation through the ensuing winter, and even now its colors still light up the sky. In the middle of November that fall, a Boston friend of mine dropped into a tavern in Cambridge—in the working-man's, or non-Harvard, end of Cambridge—and found a place at the bar. "It was a Monday night," he told me later, "and everybody was watching the NFL game on the TV set up at the other end of the bar. There wasn't a sound in the place, and after I'd been there about ten minutes the old guy next to me put down his beer glass and sort of shook his head and whispered to himself, 'We never should have taken out Willoughby.'"

from

Late Innings

One afternoon in Arizona, I talked about Willie Mays with Bill Rigney, who played with him on the old New York Giants and later became his manager. Rigney, who has also managed the Angels and the Twins, is now on special assignment with the Angels. He is sixty years old—a tall, trim man with straight white hair, a humorous, intelligent face, a sun-wrinkled neck, and expansively gesturing hands. He has an infielder's look and an eager, singles-hitting way of talking and thinking. We sat by the side of a deserted pool and sipped a little whiskey and talked about Willie, while a late-afternoon breeze nudged a beach ball to and fro in the water near our feet.

"What I remember most was the strength he had," Rigney said. "Besides the great plays and the hitting, I mean. He never got hurt. He played every inning, played every game, and he played hard all the time. I was still with the Giants when he came up, and you could

see that right away. There never was any Cadillacing in Willie. Another thing I marvelled at—beyond the ability, to one side of it—was
the instinct he had for the game. Mostly, you have to teach players a
lot—even the ones who are tremendous athletes. But Willie seemed
to have it all. Even in his first year, he'd get on second base, say, and
right away he'd steal the catcher's signals—within a minute he'd see
the combination. He *knew*. No matter what was going on, he knew
what it would take to win the game. I couldn't get over that. I was
thirty-two or thirty-three when he came up and joined us in '51, and
I was already thinking I'd like to manage someday, and it impressed
me that there could be a player so young who seemed to know everything. I thought that maybe that was all there was to being a manager—just sitting back and watching a man like Willie Mays play ball
for me.

"I remember the day he arrived. We were in Shibe Park, getting
ready to play the Phillies, and he turned up late but still in time for
batting practice. We'd all heard what he had done out in Minnesota
that spring, in the minors—I think he'd batted about .480 over two
months out there—but none of us was ready for the sight of him. He
got into the batting cage, and all the Phillies and all the Giants
stopped what they were doing to watch him. He hit balls up on the
roof and balls off the wall—balls ricocheting everywhere. Even in batting practice on his first day in a major-league uniform, at the age of
nineteen, he caught your eye.

"I think I saw almost all the great catches. The Vic Wertz catch in
the '54 Series. The catch off Bobby Morgan at Ebbets Field, when he
ran and dived horizontally and grabbed the ball—it was a *shot*—and
hit his head against that low concrete wall they had along the fence
in left field there, and still held on to the ball. I saw the Clemente
catch in Pittsburgh, when he caught up with the ball running with
his back to the plate and grabbed it off bare-handed. I can still see
him trotting back in with the ball in his hand and dropping it on the
mound. The one I liked best, I guess, was the play he made once in
the early season at the Polo Grounds. The grass out there had been
resodded—Horace [Horace Stoneham, the Giants' owner at the time]
had to do that every year, because the football Giants had always
chewed it up pretty good—and we'd had rain. There was a routine fly
ball hit to left, and Bobby Thomson made a move for it and slipped

and fell down flat. Willie had drifted over near him—you know, just in a routine way, to cover—and when Bobby slipped and fell, Willie made the catch with one hand, and with the other hand he reached down and pulled Bobby to his feet, all in the same motion. I can still see it.

"What a hitter he was! He *destroyed* pitchers. They all threw at him—there was a lot more of that in those days. Down he'd go, but he'd jump back up again and dig in, with that determined, surprised look of his. When I was his manager, back in the late fifties, when we'd moved out to San Francisco, there was a pitcher with the Reds named Bob Purkey, who threw at Willie every single time. Willie would step in and—bang!—here came the pitch at Willie's cap, and he'd be in the dirt. After a while, Willie wasn't hitting much more than about .150 against him. I wasn't exactly pleased by this, you understand, and at the All-Star Game that year—I think it was at Forbes Field, in Pittsburgh—I saw Warren Giles, the president of the National League, and the Commissioner, Ford Frick, sitting together, and I went over and complained about it. I'd had a couple of Bloody Marys in the pressroom, and I figured the hell with it—let it come out. So after I told them about Mr. Purkey knocking my center fielder on the seat of his pants every time, they both sort of smiled, and Mr. Giles said, 'Well, Rig, we all know that isn't in the rules, but it's part of the game, isn't it? It's part of the game of baseball.' I said, 'I'm glad to hear you say that, sir, because now I know how to solve the problem. I've promised Willie that the next time Bob Purkey comes up to bat in a game against us I'm going to switch my pitcher and my center fielder and let Willie Mays pitch against Purkey. It's all taken care of. Thank you.'

"Well, you can imagine what happened. They both said, 'Hold *on*, now, Rig! You can't do *that*! We're not going to have a race riot on our hands because of you.' And a couple of days later there came a flood of directives out from the league office and the Commissioner's office to Horace and to me, telling us to lay off. It was too bad. Willie had really been looking forward to knocking Bob Purkey's hat off, for a change. Purkey never did stop throwing at him, of course, but some of our pitchers had taken notice, and they found ways of showing Mr. Purkey that we really cared about our center fielder."

◆ ◆ ◆

July 1981

Last week, my wife and I came uptown late one night in a cab after having dinner with friends of ours in the Village. We wheeled through the warm and odorous light-strewn summer dark on the same northward route home we have followed hundreds of times over the years, I suppose: bumping and lurching up Sixth non-stop, with the successive gateways of staggered green lights magically opening before us, and the stately tall street lights (if you tipped your head back on the cab seat and watched them upside down through the back window of the cab: I had drunk a bit of wine) forming a narrowing golden archway astern; and then moving more quietly through the swerves and small hills of the Park, where the weight and silence of the black trees wrapped us in a special summer darkness. The cabdriver had his radio on, and the blurry sounds of the news— the midnight news, I suppose—passed over us there in the back seat, mixing with the sounds of the wind coming in through the open cab windows, and the motion of our ride, and the whole sense of city night. All was as always, I mean, except that now it came to me, un-surprisingly at first but then with a terrific jolt of unhappiness and mourning, that this radio news was altered, for there was no baseball in it. Without knowing it, I had been waiting for those other particu-lar sounds, for that other part of the summer night, but it was miss-ing, of course—no line scores, no winning and losing pitchers, no homers and highlights, no records approached or streaks cut short, no "Meanwhile, over in the National League," no double-zip early in-nings from Anaheim or Chavez Ravine, no Valenzuela and no Rose, no Goose and no Tom, no Yaz, no Mazz, no nothing.

The strike by this time was more than a week old, and I had so far sustained the shock of it and the change of it with more fortitude and patience than I had expected of myself. The issues seemed far re-moved from me—too expensive or too complicated, for some reason, for me to hold them clearly in my mind for long, although I am an attentive and patient fan. I would wait, then, with whatever compo-sure I could find, until it was settled, days or weeks from now, and in some fashion or other I would fill up the empty eveningtimes and morningtimes I had once spent (I did not say "wasted"; I would never say "wasted") before the tube and with the sports pages. It might even be better for me to do without baseball for a while, although I could not imagine why. All this brave nonsense was knocked out of me in an instant, there in the cab, and suddenly the loss of that murmurous little ribbon of baseball-by-radio, the ordinary news of the game, seemed to explain a lot of things about the much larger loss we fans are all experiencing because of the strike. The refrain of late-night baseball scores; the sounds of the televised game from the next room (the room empty, perhaps, for the moment, but the game running along in there just the same and quietly waiting for us to step in and rejoin it when we are of a mind to); the mid-game mid-event from some car or cab that pulls up beside us for a few seconds in traffic before the light changes; the baseball conversation in the elevator that goes away when two men get off together at the eleventh floor, taking the game with them; the flickery white fall of light on our hands and arms and the scary sounds of the crowd that suddenly wake us up, in bed or in the study armchair, where we have fallen asleep, with the set and the game still on—all these streams and continuities, it seems to me, are part of the greater, riverlike flow of baseball. No other sport, I think, conveys anything like this sense of cool depth and fluvial steadiness, and when you stop for a minute and think about the game it is easy to see why this should be so. The slow, inexorable progression of baseball events—balls and strikes, outs and innings, batters stepping up and batters being retired, pitchers and sides changing on the field, innings turning into games and games into series, and all these merging and continuing, in turn, in the box scores and the averages and the slowly fluctuous standings—are what make the game quietly and uniquely satisfying. Baseball flows past us all through the summer—it is one of the reasons that summer exists—and wherever we happen to stand on its green banks we can sense with only a glance across its shiny expanse that the long, unhurrying swirl and down-flowing have their own purpose and direction, that the river is headed, in its own sweet time, toward a downsummer broadening and debouchment and to its end in the estuary of October.

River people, it is said, count on the noises and movement of nearby water, even without knowing it, and feel uneasy and unaccountably diminished if they must move away for a while and stay among plains inhabitants. That is almost the way it is for us just now, but it is worse than that, really, because this time it is the river that has gone away—just stopped—and all of us who live along these banks feel a fretful sense of loss and a profound disquiet over the sudden cessation of our reliable old stream. The main issue of the baseball strike, I have read, concerns the matter of compensation for owners who have lost a player to free-agency, but when this difficulty is resolved and the two sides come to an agreement (as they will someday), what compensation can ever be made to us, the fans, who are the true owners and neighbors and keepers of the game, for this dry, soundless summer and for the loss of our joy?

from

Season Ticket

The split-finger fastball is baseball's Rubik's Cube of the eighties—a gimmick, a supertoy, a conversation piece, and a source of sudden fame and success for its inventor. It is thrown at various speeds and with a slightly varying grip on the ball, but in its classic mode it looks like a middling-good fastball that suddenly changes its mind and ducks under the batter's swing just as it crosses the plate. The pitch isn't exactly new—nothing in baseball is exactly new. A progenitor, the forkball, was grasped in much the same fashion, between the pitcher's forefinger and middle finger, but tucked more deeply into the hand, which took off spin and speed—a "slip-pitch," in the parlance. Elroy Face, a reliever with the Pirates, was its great practitioner in the nineteen-fifties and sixties, and he put together an amazing 18–1 won-and-lost record (all in relief) with it in 1959. Bruce Sutter—like Face, a right-handed relief specialist—came along with the first so-called split-finger fastball a decade ago while with the Cubs, and has employed it (and very little else by way of repertoire) to run up a lifetime National League record of two hundred and eighty-six saves, with a Cy Young Award in 1979; he later moved along to the Cardinals and is now with the Braves and in temporary eclipse, owing to a sore arm. The Sutter pitch seemed not only unhittable but patented, for no one else in the game has quite been able to match his way of combining the forkball grip with a mid-delivery upward thrust of the thumb from beneath, which imparted a deadly little diving motion to the ball in flight. Here matters rested until 1984, when Roger Craig, a pitching coach with the Tigers, imparted his own variant of the s.-f. fb. to several members of the Detroit mound staff, with instant effect. Craig went into retirement after that season (he has since unretired, of course, and manages the Giants), but he is an affable and enthusiastic gent, who loves to talk and teach pitching. He is tall and pink-cheeked, with a noble schnoz; as most fans know, he has endured every variety of fortune on the mound. Callers at his home near San Diego that first winter of retirement included a good many opportunistic pitchers and pitching coaches from both leagues who were anxious to get their hands on the dingus. Most prominent among them—now, not then—was Mike Scott, a large but as yet unimpressive pitcher with the Houston Astros (the Mets had traded him away after 1982, at a time when his lifetime record stood at 14–27); he spent a week with Craig and came home armed with Excalibur. With the new pitch, he went 18–8 in 1985 and 18–10 last year, when he won a Cy Young Award after leading the majors with three hundred and six strikeouts and a 2.22 earned-run average. He capped his regular-season work with a no-hitter against the Giants, clinching the Astros' divisional pennant, and then zipped off sixteen consecutive scoreless innings while winning his two starts in the championship series against the Mets, to whom he surrendered but one run over all. Indeed, the other great "what if" of this past winter (along with second-guessing the way the Red Sox played the tenth inning of Game Six in the World Series) is the speculation about the Mets' fate in the playoffs if they had been forced to face Scott for a third time, in a seventh and deciding game.

"The split-finger is mostly a changeup," Keith Hernandez told me in St. Petersburg. "It can be thrown in different ways, so you can say it's really a three-speed changeup, with the forkball action as the other half of it. Scott can make it run in or out, but when he throws it inside to me he throws it *hard*. It has so much velocity on it that it's a real fastball for him, plus it goes down. It just drops off the table. Sutter's was the best until this one, but Scott has perfected it. He has tremendous command over the pitch—he never makes a mistake." (Mike Scott, it should be added, might not agree with this generous appraisal, for Hernandez hits him better than anyone else in the league: .377 lifetime, according to the *Elias Baseball Analyst*.)

Roger Craig told me that both Scott and Morris throw the split-finger at eighty-five miles an hour or better—faster than anyone else, although Scott Garrelts, a fireballing reliever on Craig's Giants, is now approaching that level. "Jack has his fingers up higher on the ball than Mike does," Craig said. "Mike's got the ball as far out in his hand as you can get it. He throws it about sixty or seventy percent of the time now, and there was a stretch at the end of last year when he was just unhittable. The pitch was a phantom—you'd swing and it wasn't there." (A good many batters in the National League are convinced that Mike Scott also imparts another sort of witchcraft to the baseball, by scuffing it in some secret fashion, in contravention of the rules. Steve Garvey told me that retrieved balls Scott has thrown often show a patch of lightly cut concentric circles on one of the white sectors— something that might be done with an artificially roughened part of his glove or palm. Garvey made a little sidewise gesture with his hand. "That's all it moves," he said, smiling. "It's enough.")

Craig—to get back into the sunshine here—said that the best thing about the split-finger is that it can be thrown at so many different speeds. "It depends on where you've got it in your fingers, on how you cock your wrist—on a whole lot of things," he said. "But the ultimate is when it comes out off the tips of your fingers—they just slip down along the ball on the outside of the seams—and the ball *tumbles*. That's the great one, because it's the opposite spin from the fastball. People keep telling me it isn't really a fastball, but I keep saying it is, because I want that pitcher to throw it with a fastball motion. Dan Petry, back with the Tigers, used to let up on it, because it was in the back of his mind that it was an off-speed pitch, but that's wrong. Here—gimme a ball, somebody."

We were sitting out on a bullpen bench in left field on a shining morning in Scottsdale—Craig and I and one of the Giants' beat writers. Craig has large, pale, supernally clean hands—Grandpa hands, if Grandpa is a dentist—and when he got a ball he curled his long forefinger and middle finger around it at the point where the red seams come closest together. "I start with my fingers together like this, and I say 'fastball' . . . 'fastball' . . . 'fastball'"—he waggled his wrist and fingers downward again and again—"but I have them go this way each time: just a bit wider apart. By the time you're out here"—the fingers were outside the seams now, on the white, slippery parts of the ball—"you're throwing the split-finger. There's a stage where it acts sort of like a knuckleball, but it'll come. You've started."

Craig told us that he'd discovered the pitch back in 1982, while he was coaching fifteen- and sixteen-year-old boys in California. He takes great pleasure in the fact that several older or middle-level professionals have saved their careers with the pitch (Milt Wilcox, a righty with the Tigers, was one), and that subvarsity high-school and college pitchers have made the team with it. Superior pitchers sometimes resist it, by contrast. "Jack Morris thinks he's the greatest pitcher who ever lived," Craig said. "He has that great confidence. He insisted he didn't need it, even though he was getting killed with his changeup. So I said, 'Do me a favor. Pitch one game and don't throw a change—throw the split-finger instead.' He did it, and it was a two-hitter against the Orioles."

When Craig arrived at Candlestick Park in September of 1985, as the Giants' new manager, he took all the pitchers out of the bullpen on his second day and asked for a volunteer who had never essayed the split-finger. Mark Davis, a left-hander, came forward, and Craig sent the rest of the staff down to stand behind the catcher. "Well, in about twenty, twenty-five pitches he was throwing it," Roger said, "and all my other pitchers were thinkin', Well, if he can do it, *I* can do it. That way, I didn't have to go out and try to convince them one by one." Everybody on the Giants throws the pitch now, and one of Craig's starters, Mike Krukow, went 20–9 with it last year—his best year ever. Craig hasn't counted, but he believes that thirty or forty percent of the pitchers in the National League have the pitch by now, or are working on it. Five of the Dodgers' staff—Welch, Hershiser, Niedenfuer, Young, and Leary—employ the pitch, and the American League is beginning to catch up. Gene Mauch, the Angels' pilot, told Craig this spring that all his pitchers would be working on it this year.

I suggested to Roger that he should have registered the split-finger, so that he could charge a royalty every time it's thrown in a game, and his face lit up. "*That* would be nice, wouldn't it?" he said. "Just kick back and stay home, and take on a few private pupils now and then. That would be all right! But I've stopped teaching it to other teams. About ten pitching coaches called me up last winter and asked if they could come out and pick it up, but I said no. And there was this one general manager who called me up and said he'd send me and my wife to Hawaii, all expenses paid, if I'd take on his pitching coach and teach it to him. It's too late, though—I already showed it to too many guys. Dumb old me."

Not everybody, in truth, picks up the split-finger quickly or easily, and not all split-fingers are quite the same. Ron Darling, the Mets' young right-hander, mastered the delivery last summer, after a long struggle, and when he did, it became what he had needed all along—a finishing pitch, to make him a finished pitcher. (He was 15–6, with a 2.81 E.R.A., for the year, along with a hatful of strong no-decision outings.) He has never talked to Roger Craig, and, in fact, his split-finger started out as a forkball taught to him by pitching coach Al Jackson at the Mets' Tidewater farm club in 1983. But Darling, who has small hands, could never open his fingers enough to grasp the ball in the deep forkball grip, so it became a split-finger delivery instead. (Craig told me that some pitchers he knew had even gone to bed at night with a ball strapped between their fingers, in an attempt to widen their grip.) Darling had very little luck with the pitch at first, but kept at it because of Jack Morris's example—especially after Morris pitched a no-hitter against the White Sox at the beginning of the 1984 season.

"The whole idea about pitching—one of the basics of the art—is that you've got to show the batter a strike that isn't a strike," Darling said. "More than half—much more than half—of all the split-fingers that guys throw are balls. They drop right out of the strike zone. That's a problem, because you might have a great split-finger that moves a lot, and the batter is going to lay off it if he sees any kind of funny spin. So you have to throw it for a strike now and then. Hitters adjust, you know. Most of the time, you're going to throw the pitch when you're ahead in the count. But sometimes I throw it when I'm behind, too. All you have to do is make it look like a fastball for at least half the distance. A lot of times last year, I'd try to get a strike with a fastball and *then* throw a split-finger strike. If it does get over—and this began to happen for me for the first time last year—it rocks the world, because then here comes another split-finger and the bottom drops out, but the guy still has to swing. He has no other choice. Nobody can afford not to swing at that pitch—unless he's Keith Hernandez. Umpires don't call third strikes on Keith."

Fred Harris grew up in Philadelphia in the 1950s. Brendan Boyd spent his childhood in Dorchester, Massachusetts, in the same decade. In 1973, when both were living around Boston, they published *The Great American Baseball Card Flipping, Trading and Bubble Gum Book*, which is baseball writing's answer to free jazz. The book consists of a series of reproductions of 1950s baseball cards and the authors' annotations—spirited riffs on matters ranging from Smoky Burgess's heft, to Don Mossi's ears, to Vern Stephens' pop flies. Through the prism of cardboard, Boyd and Harris tell the story of what it was like to be a middle-class kid who didn't much like Ike, but worshipped Ted Williams and Richie Ashburn. The following is an excerpt from the book's introduction.

Brendan C. Boyd & Fred C. Harris

♥

from

The Great American Baseball Card Flipping, Trading and Bubble Gum Book

April 1——BASEBALL CARDS—Sure sign that the end is now in sight. The long agony of winter is almost over. The air softens and the backyard grows muddy. The last snow patches glisten and fade away.

> Dick Gernert, Paul LaPalme, Ray Scarborough,
> Jimmy Dodds, Specs O'Keefe, Madame Chiang,
> Saul Rogovin, Mike Hershberger, Dave Hillman,
> Althea Gibson, Gino Prado, C. K. Yang.

We bought our treasures in little dime stores called spas. Corner stores that were never on corners. Variety stores completely lacking in variety. They were generally owned by middle-aged men with psoriasis—paunchy citizens with sallow complexions and sour outlooks, who wore plaid woolen shirts no matter how hot it was and little felt hats that had repeatedly been stepped on. Their wives usually hung around in the background, squeezing the bread and keeping their eyes on the cash register. They wore white socks and babush-kas and fashion glasses and always asked after the health of your dead aunt. The stores were called Pete's or Mike's or Al's or Joe's or Barney's. Or sometimes Frederick's if the owner was inclined to be formal. Or Bill and Mary's if the couple was happily married. Catchy names that reflected their vibrant characters. In my neighborhood there were two dozen of these establishments, scratching lustily against each other for survival. There was Connie's Spa which was owned by a paraplegic named Connie. And Harry's Deli which carried an incom-plete selection of cold cuts. There was John's Market which had a wall of dirty magazines. And Tommy's Superette, which was quite a bit short of super. There was also B & J's, which didn't seem to stand for anything. And Lorenzo's which had sawdust on the floor. And Flan-nery's which had a stuffed codfish in the window. And Billy's Buy-Rite which sold Robitussin to winos. The one that we went to was called Eddie's. Eddie's Superteria or Eddie's Friendly Lunch—depending on Eddie's mood of the moment. It was operated by a huge Lithuanian guy named Eddie who had halitosis and was decidedly unfriendly.

Eddie sold everything from his storefront. You name it and Eddie was sure to have it—corn flakes, mustard plaster, snow tires, chili powder, teething rings, egg cups, garter belts, Nutty Putty, insecticide, light bulbs, gefilte fish, Scrabble sets. If you were interested in a deal on a forklift there was a good chance that Eddie could help you out. He even carried little packages of dehydrated night-crawlers on the chance that a stray fisherman might wander in. And all of this from just six hundred square feet of floor space—a good part of which was taken up by Mrs. Eddie (a massive woman who wore overalls and hip boots and carried what looked to be a zip gun in her budge). He had a fruit stand and a vegetable bin and a bakery counter. And the world's largest supply of canned olives. He had a pinball machine and a Coke machine and a coffee machine. And greeting cards and an ice cream freezer and a grab bag. He had hundreds of cans of mushroom lentil soup and a whole aisleful of marinated chick-peas. He had pickled pigs' feet in big jars the size of bass drums and more rhubarb pie filling than you would have thought humanly possible. If there was anything that nobody could possibly be interested in, Eddie was sure to have laid in a big supply. Fifty-pound polyethylene bags of popping corn, giant jars of green and blue Maraschino cherries, felt pennants of uninteresting historical monuments, boxes of faded monogrammed party hats and favors. He had a giant cutout of the Philip Morris midget and the largest display of sanitary napkins in the East. He kept a sale bin full of dented cans of cat food and always featured Ovaltine at 6 cents off. There was also a wall completely lined with novelty items, all mounted and neatly arranged on cardboard cards. Plastic change purses, colored rabbits' feet, copper key rings, laminated belt buckles, Confederate flags, silver nail files. Enough sewing needles to supply an army of seamstresses. More Popeye rub-ons than he could sell in fifty years. And for his customers with intellectual inclinations—the latest issues of "Argosy" and "Motor Trend." All suspended from metal clips on filigreed wires. All surrounded by paperback westerns with no covers.

But it was the candy counter that was really the center of interest, the one area that held our undivided attention. It was here that Eddie spent most of his time, although I'm sure he would have preferred it otherwise. You could spend fifteen minutes here with just a nickel, trying to decide whether to buy one old-fashioned or two. You could change your mind back and forth a dozen times or more, driving Eddie right to the brink of a nervous breakdown.

"Look, I have to wait on Mrs. Bonaturo now. Hurry up, will you, with your 8 cents' worth of crap. You kids are driving me absolutely crazy. And put that comic book down, this isn't a goddamn library."

Malted milk balls, Mary Janes, Red Hot Dollars—Fire Balls, root beer barrels, jelly beans—sugar cones, tar babies, orange slices—nonpareils, goober peanuts, wintergreens—Canada Mints, Jujubes, wax moustaches—sour balls, licorice whips, marshmallow bananas. Everything a human being could possibly wish for. Everything a Lincoln penny could possibly buy.

And baseball cards. Baseball cards. Baseball cards.

> Nippy Jones, Willard Marshall, Connie Ryan
> Burr Tillstrom, Grace Metalious, James Dean
> Charlie Keller, Billy Hitchcock, Stu Miller
> Doris Duke, Maurice Podoloff, Fulton J. Sheen

They appeared sometime during the first weeks of March when the world was beginning to thaw out around us. News of spring training was slowly drifting northward and our surviving another school year now seemed possible. Oh, they were beautiful and reassuring to behold, brand new and glistening crisply in their packages. Packed into cardboard cartons of 24 and 120, stuck behind glassed partitions and stacked on counters. An indication that the world was still in order, a promise of pleasant days and easeful nights. Bowman cards, Fleer cards, Topps cards—in green wrappers, blue wrappers, and red. And how the news spread quickly through the neighborhood—as at the coming of some inestimable personage. And we quickly down to the corner to check it out, to verify the new arrivals for ourselves. Yes, the pictures had changed a little bit. And the backs of the cards were altered oh so slightly. But they were still basically the same cards as before. There were some things even *they* couldn't change. And the joy of breaking open the year's first package. To see what Marty Marion was going to look like this year. To see if any of the old uniforms had been altered. To see if everyone was still as young as before. And the sweet pleasant smell of the bubble gum, and the sweet pleasant melting of it in your mouth. And the secure feel of the cards in your pocket, and the knowledge that they were yours and yours alone. The prospect of all the packages to be opened, the thought of all the new cards to be flipped. The possibilities of wheeling and dealing and pyramiding. The notion that maybe the Red Sox *could* win the Pennant. And above it all their splendid physical presence. Their sturdiness. Their symmetry. Their artful grace. The way they looked all stacked up on your dresser. And the mysterious things we knew they really meant.

There was Bob Allison and Moe Berg and Joe Dobson. And Gary Bell and Don Blasingame and Zeke Bella. There was Johnny Blanchard, who was extremely overrated, and Buddy Blattner, whom nobody knew. There was Steve Boros and Marshall Bridges and Lou Brissie. And Tom Brewer, who was no relation to Jim. There were team cards and manager cards and rookie cards. And cards with all sorts of interesting statistics. There was Ernie Broglio and Bill Bruton and Pete Burnside. And Wally Burnette, who had gotten a huge bonus. There was Bud Byerly and Wayne Causey and Bob Chance. And John Buzhardt—whose *h* was strangely silent. There was a card for every player, or so they said, and as many ways to collect them as collectors.

There was the dabbler and the addict and the connoisseur. There was the compilator and the fan and the gambler.

The dabbler bought seldom, if ever. He really wasn't that interested in baseball.

The addict bought often and very heavily. He didn't particularly care what he got.

The connoisseur only bought what really interested him. He bought most of his cards from private parties.

The compilator thought of himself as an artist—a totality of scope his only ambition.

The fan preferred members of the home team. A rare card meant nothing to him.

Whereas the gambler was interested primarily in quantity. Making something out of nothing, or even less.

I was a gambler I'll have to admit it—with a slight touch of the compilator and the fan. I was a gambler because that was my nature. Only later did I turn into a fan.

There was Murry Dickson, who looked about fifty. And John Goryl, who looked about twelve. There was Phil Clark, who had very high cheekbones. And Dom DiMaggio, who had no cheekbones at all. There was Lou Limmer, who had a gap between his teeth. And Harry Elliott, who wore school-teacherish glasses. And Johnny Kucks, who looked a little like Johnny Pesky, and Nelson King, who looked a lot like Andy Gump. There was Ed Charles and Nelson Chittum and Sandy Consuegra. And Ray Crone and Bert Hamric and Sam Dente. There was an endless supply of pitchers named Miller. And an infinite number of infielders named Jones.

If you wanted to collect cards you needed some business sense. A firm foundation based on sound management principle. You needed to approach it like an administrative problem. Otherwise you definitely ran the risk of going under.

First you needed a well-established line of credit—which meant getting a nickel or dime from your mother. This was not always as easy as it sounded and so alternative channels of financing were recommended.

Second you needed a provision for capital expenditure—which involved a trip to Eddie's or Lorenzo's, or whatever. This was actually the most exciting part of the deal. Fraught with every imaginable purchasing variable.

Next you needed a proper inventory management—which included dividing your new purchases into categories. There were those cards which you were definitely going to keep, and those which were more or less expendable.

Finally you needed a way of progressing with your merchandise—of utilizing all the goods you had accumulated. Sales promotion. Investment credits. Material stockpiling. Making the most of your ornate pasteboard empire.

Like the paragons of junior capitalism that we were, we used all sorts of variations on these principles. Hedging and haggling and speculating. Taking advantage of every possible angle. We used our cards to make more cards and still more cards. Turning ourselves into veritable bubble gum entrepreneurs.

There was Art Ditmar and Harry Dorish and Arnold Earley. And Doc Edwards and Dee Fondy and Don Ferrarese. There was Del Crandall, who looked upright and law-abiding, and Jim Pisoni, who looked like a second-story man. There was Art Fowler and Joe Foy and Aubrey Gatewood. And George Alusik and Mudcat Grant and Tom Morgan. And Jim Turner, who had probably been *born* a pitching coach. And Dick Donovan, who lived right in the next town. There was Howie Goss and Bob Giggie and Don Gile. And Marv Grissom and Warren Hacker and Bob Hale. And of course Don Rudolph, who was married to a stripper. And Larry Jansen, who had ten or eleven kids.

Every day at three o'clock, beginning in April, I would appear down at Eddie's with my nickel. This was my reward for maintaining my good behavior—a little bribe to keep the authorities from our door. There was usually a line of kids down there long before me, buying pimple balls and magnetic Scottie dogs and etch-a-sketch sets. I had trouble maintaining my composure at this time, such were the pressures of pure avarice building inside me. Then the nickel into Eddie's calloused palm and my hands upon the blue and orange wrapper. The wax paper very quickly under my fingernails. The smell of the gum bursting up and into the air. The feel of the virgin cards very firm against my fingertips. The hope that something marvelous was lurking there inside. Eddie Haas, rookie star of '59? But I've already got him twenty-seven times. Bill Renna—who the hell is Bill Renna? And what does he have to grin about like that? And would you believe it, another Bob Trowbridge. They must put him in every other package. Connie Grob? Well, at least that's something new. Even if he is the worst pitcher on the Senators. Oh no, not Steve Gromek again. You can't even give that guy away. And I don't think I can stand another Joe Cunningham. That's the third time I've gotten him since Wednesday. One card that I didn't have before. One card for my nickel and my effort. Well, Connie Grob into the left pocket of my jacket, and then, later, into my Red Rooster shoe box. All the rest into the back pocket of my peg pants, to be stored in my green Stoppette carton. Some cards for selling off to the rich kids, some cards for trading with adversaries and friends, some cards for keeping in my collection for the fun of it, but most cards just for matching and flipping. To see what they could turn themselves into, to see what sort of treasures they could bring. The gum neat and cracking into my mouth, and myself home in time for "Johnny Jupiter." Back up the springtime street as I had come. With the sun slowly sliding down our roof. To live another day without Sibbi Sisti. To see what all my tomorrows might possibly bring.

There was Fritz Brickell and Art Cecarelli and Johnny Groth. And Billy Harrell and Jack Harshman and Ray Herbert. Frank Baumholtz, who was always being sent down. Gair Allie, who was always being brought up. Charley Bishop. Chico Fernandez and Harry Perkowski. Billy O'Dell, Dutch Leonard and Memo Luna. Jerry Davie who was perennially promising. Johnny Briggs who would always disappoint. The Milwaukee Braves with their ball boys, Wick and Blossfield. The Detroit Tigers with their bat boys, O'Brien and Kelly. Bill Virdon, who looked like a sociology professor. Bob Skinner, who looked like a counterman at Nedicks.

What I did with my cards was I flipped them. In a desperate effort to make their numbers increase. I joined in games of chance with my fellow collectors. No quarter asked and none ever given.

How this worked was disarmingly simple (deceptively simple to the innocently uninitiated):

You drew a line in the dust or on the pavement and flipped your cards from this line toward a wall. Each player scaling his own card in turn, the winner of the previous round going last. The card closest to the wall won the pot. No leaners or doctored cards allowed. I spent 60 percent of my youth in this practice. Drilling daily and searching diligently for pigeons. Bent over cracked asphalt driveways in total silence. Scaling slivers of colored cardboard toward old garages. And I was moderately successful at it also. Amassing three shopping bags full of cards. Not a particularly creative way to spend a boyhood. But not a completely misspent youth, it seems to me. Wafting cards out across shadowy schoolyards. Seeing them float and settle softly to the ground. The hours gently rolling by until sunset. Like the fifties rolling gently through our minds. The happiness of having your card inch out another's. The agony of losing a lucky Billy Pleis. The joy of watching your stack of cards increasing. The knowledge that your youth would never end. Eighteen Lou Kretlows. Twenty-one Frank Malzones. A stack of Johnny Logans as thick as a Snickers. More Garry Roggenburks than the mind could comprehend. And over it all the sweet smile of Spring Byington. Assuring us that nothing could possibly go wrong.

Of course there were other things that you could do with your baseball cards. And other people in their various ways managed to do them. How you utilized them depended on your temperament. The possibilities for variation were practically limitless. You could play games with them on rainy afternoons, using the pictures as surrogate ballplayers. You could arrange and rearrange them in various categories and make lists of all your multiple arrangements. By position, by team, by batting average. By number, by achievement, by personal preference. You could invent various individual rating systems, make trades, construct dream teams, determine strategy. You could pile them up on your bed when you had a cold and give each and every one of them a good talking to. You could paste them on walls or on mirrors, or in scrapbooks with little plastic windows. You could mail them away to be autographed by the players, or you could sell them to an acquisitive collector. You might even have been able to eat them, although I never knew anyone who did. I didn't go in much for any of these variations. I was more interested in out and out pyramiding. I liked to gamble and take risks with my baseball cards. I liked to see what kind of booty they could bring.

There was Ted Lepcio and Don Lock and Art Mahaffey. And Lucky Lohrke and Morrie Martin and Nelson Mathews. There was Dave Hoskins not looking particularly hopeful. And Willard Nixon not looking hopeful at all. There were umpire cards and coach cards and

World Series cards. And cards of Warren Giles and Ford Frick and William Harridge. There was Ted Williams in the cockpit of a fighter. And Stan Musial giving a Little Leaguer advice. There was Lou Gehrig saying farewell in the Stadium. And Casey Stengel gagging it up with Bob Cerv. There was Buster Narum and Julio Navarro and Ray Ripplemeyer. And Don Nottebart and John Orsino and Bobo Osborne. And there was even a card of Wee Willie Keeler, although none of us knew exactly who he was.

You didn't have to play baseball to collect baseball cards. You didn't even have to be a fan, it often seemed. Although most of us rooted patiently for the Red Sox. And played pickup games the whole summer long, getting up at ungodly hours in the morning, trudging down to grassless playgrounds after dawn, playing unceasingly hour after hour; from sunup to sundown, and sometimes longer. The heat shimmering like a shock wave over the infield. The dust settling down into our lungs. Salt and sweat covering our brown necks and forearms. Our hands calloused and stinging from untaped bats. And then home again when it finally became hopeless. With the ball just a pale shadow against the night. To sit on the porch or in the backyard with the crickets. To listen to our beloved home team lose again—Norm Zauchin, Billy Goodman, Sammy White, Frank Sullivan, Mel Parnell, Ike Delock. Was there ever such a monument to futility? Was there anything that could disappoint us more? Murray Wall, Milt Bolling, Sam Mele—Karl Olson, Del Wilbur, Sid Hudson. If you haven't rooted for such a ball team you know nothing. You are innocent of the true meaning of human suffering. The only constant of my boyhood was the Red Sox—and the uninspired mediocrity of their play. That and the reassuring presence of my baseball cards: flipping back and forth through the slow summer days.

There was Stubby Overmire and Whitey Ford and Bob Porterfield. And Eddie Pellagrini who hit a home run his first time up. And Jerry Priddy and Ken Raffensberger and Bob Ramazotti. And Hal Reniff, although he might have come a bit later. And Jay Ritchie and Preacher Roe and Andre Rodgers. And Ray Scarborough and Barney Schultz and Billy Short. There was Rip Sewall who threw a pitch called the blooper ball. And Rollie Sheldon who threw pitches you couldn't name. There was Roy Smalley and Russ Snyder and Jack Spring. And

Ebba St. Claire, whose name evoked strange images. There was Bob Speake and Stuffy Stirnweiss and Pete Suder. And Don Zimmer whose name evoked nothing at all.

It is true, of course, that nothing remains totally stationary; that even the baseball cards were not an absolute constant. They changed their style very subtly through the years, although the changes were more real to us than apparent. Sometimes the players were pictured on them horizontally—sometimes they came at you straight up and down. Some years there were action pictures in the background. Some years just a head and shoulder shot. There were drawings in 1948, mostly profiles in '49 and '50. Sometimes there were reproductions of autographs on the cards; sometimes just printed or typewritten letters. And the backs of the cards varied also, in makeup and information provided. There were cartoon players' biographies some years, with capsulated major league records. Or there were one-paragraph histories of the players, with a year-by-year list of their achievements. There were quizzes and little puzzles for you to solve. "What's a pitchout?" "What does 'banjo hitter' mean?" There were blanks that you rubbed for magic answers. And always the long lists of vital statistics. The graphics and artwork got gradually better. After a while you could make out Wes Stock's face. The years went by, but I didn't see them going. The cards got better and baseball got much worse. The fifties disappeared from my memory like a daydream. I got older although I'll damned if I know how.

There was Larry Jackson and Sheldon Jones and Leo Kiely. And Jerry Kendall and Thornton Kipper and Howie Koplitz. There was Bob Elliott, who was known as Mr. Team, and Russ Nixon, who was the Chocolate Malted Kid. There was Walt Masterson and Danny McDevitt and Phil Masi. And Rudy Minarcin and Paul Minner and Billy Moran. There was Lenny Green who wasn't good, but who tried hard. And Willie Kirkland who was good, but wouldn't bother. There was Billy Rohr, who had a one-hitter as a rookie, and Dom Zanni, who really couldn't pitch at all. There was Joe Ostrowski and Max Alvis and Jim King—and Leo Posada and Marino Pieretti and Frank Funk. And Bud Podbielan, who looked a bit like death warmed over. And George Zuverink, who looked like death without the warmth.

And then one year it was all suddenly over. Mousecartoontime had finally run its course. Somehow baseball did not seem so important to us anymore. And neither, of course, did the collecting of its cards. Dick Tomanek and Bob Grim had retired. Duke Snider was very much an old man. José Melis and Frank Parker were gone forever. Snooky Lanson and his crowd had disappeared. It was 1959, almost the end of the decade. The year that Harvey Kuenn won the American League batting championship. The year that Frankie Avalon made his hit record of "Venus." The year Pat Boone composed "Twixt Twelve and Twenty." That was the year we all discovered sophistication. The year we began to put our baseball cards away.

It started out slowly enough, almost surreptitiously. Like a virus growing quietly in your blood. We had expected it, although we were not really prepared for it. It all seemed to have come on us much too soon. Our indifference was not a sudden thing after all. The habits of years are not that easily discontinued. It needed time to be absorbed by our systems. Like a best friend who suddenly moves away. But still it was there, there was no use denying it. Like the final reel of the Saturday morning serial. You could ignore it, but that wouldn't make it easier. The signs of our growing up were too readily apparent. Nobody in the neighborhood seemed interested in the new cards. Nobody played with their Erector sets anymore. Nobody played stickball against the bleachers in the town field. Nobody made walkie-talkies out of orange juice cans. We were all looking forward anxiously to high school, to record hops and class rings and making out. Nobody wanted to match pennies for Rocky Nelson. Everybody seemed to have more important things to do.

And so the cards stayed in the glass cases in Eddie's. And our nickels went for less childish things. I myself was saving up for a motor boat. The fifties sank into my consciousness like a stone. Red Buttons and Russell Arms faded from memory. Uncle Toonoose and Corporal Rusty floated away. Bobo Olson outgrew the middleweight division. George Fenneman no longer kept the secret word. And long afternoons of flipping baseball cards left us forever. Long evenings of counting our winnings disappeared. And after a while I no longer opened my shoe boxes. And soon afterward my mother put them away for good. And the surprising thing was that I never really missed them. Or even thought of them in any special way. And very gradually the memory of all of it faded. And just became another thing we used to do.

Ted Wilks, Freddy Green, Gordy Coleman
Ethyl Mertz, Silky Sullivan, Sonny Fox
Milt Graff, Walt Moryn, Brooks Lawrence
Jack Lascoolie, Bridey Murphy, Wally Cox

And that is the way you always lose your childhood.

George Plimpton (b. 1927) graduated from Harvard in 1948, and in 1953 was one of the founders of *The Paris Review.* He remains the editor. In 1961, Plimpton published *Out of My League,* an account of the day he contrived, at the behest of *Sports Illustrated,* to participate in what Marianne Moore called "the imaginary nightmare": Plimpton, the amateur, pitched against an exhibition-game lineup of professional major-league hitters including Frank Robinson and Ernie Banks. Six years later, he endured training camp with the Detroit Lions football team and then wrote the classic *Paper Lion.* In 1973 and 1974, Plimpton followed Hank Aaron as he pursued Babe Ruth's home-run record, turning in to *Sports Illustrated* this deceptively modest description of a long-anticipated event. The essay was expanded into a book, *One for the Record.*

George Plimpton

ᛩ

Final Twist of the Drama

It was a simple act by an unassuming man which touched an enormous circle of people, indeed an entire country. It provided an instant that people would remember for decades—exactly what they were doing at the time of the home run that beat Babe Ruth's great record, whether they were watching it on a television set, or heard it over the car radio while driving along the turnpike at night, or even whether a neighbor leaned over a fence and told them about it the next morning.

For those who sat in the stadium in Atlanta, their recollections would be more intimate—the sharp cork-popping sound of the bat hitting the ball, startlingly audible in the split second of suspense before the crowd began a roar that lasted for more than 10 minutes. Perhaps that is what they would remember—how people stood in front of their seats and sucked in air and bellowed it out in a sustained tribute that few athletes have ever received. Or perhaps they would remember their wonder at how easy and inevitable it seemed—that having opened the season in Cincinnati by hitting the tying home run, No. 714, with his first swing of the year, it was obviously appropriate that the man who has been called "Supe" by his teammates (for Superman) was going to duplicate the feat in Atlanta with his first swing of *that* game. That was why 53,775 had come. Or perhaps they would remember the odd way the stadium emptied after the excitement of the fourth inning, as if the crowd felt that what they had seen would be diluted by sitting through any more baseball that night.

And then finally there were those few in the core of that immense circle—the participants themselves—who would be the ones most keenly touched: the pitcher, in this case a pleasant, gap-toothed veteran named Al Downing who, of the more than 100 National League pitchers, happened to be the one who threw a fastball at a certain moment that did not tail away properly; the hitter, Henry Aaron himself, for whom the event, despite his grace in dealing with it, had become so traumatic that little in the instant was relished except the relief that it had been done; the Braves announcer, Milo Hamilton, whose imagination for months had been working up words to describe the event to the outside world; and a young bullpen pitcher named Tom House, who would reach up in the air and establish contact with a ball whose value as baseball's greatest talisman had been monetarily pegged at $25,000 and whose sentimental value was incalculable. . . .

THE PITCHER

The poor guy. All those years toiling on the mound, peering down the long alley toward the plate at those constant disturbers of his sense of well-being settling into their stances and flicking their bats—to look down one day and find Henry *Aaron* there, the large, peaceful, dark face with the big eyes and the high forehead—and knowing that one mistake, one small lapse of concentration and ability would place his name forever in the record books as having thrown the "immortal gopher."

Perhaps there are some pitchers around the league who would not mind being identified with Aaron's eclipsing of Ruth's record. Tracy Stallard, who was a young Boston Red Sox rookie when he gave up the home run to Roger Maris that broke Babe Ruth's record of 60 hit in a year, afterward rather enjoyed the back-of-the-hand notoriety that came with being a victim of Maris' clout, and he would announce, to the point of volunteering, that he was the pitcher responsible. Most pitchers, though, are sensitive enough about their craft to feel differently about such a role. Ray Sadecki once said of Stallard, "I don't want to be him. Everybody knows *who* he is. Nobody knows *where* he is."

Those scheduled in the rotation against the Atlanta Braves in the final weeks of last season and the opening days of the 1974 schedule were uncomfortably aware they were involved in a sort of cosmic game of Russian roulette, it being inevitable that one of them was going to give up the 715th home run.

The pitcher opposing Aaron in Atlanta on the last day of the 1973 season was Houston Astro lefthander Dave Roberts. Before the game he sat in front of his locker looking crestfallen. "What I should be doing is concentrating on my 17th victory of the year," he said. "But I've been thinking about *him*. I thought about him all last night. He was just deposited there in my mind. What really got me was that I knew he wasn't thinking about me at all. I wished I'd known his home telephone number, so's I could have called him every 20 minutes—'How's it going, Hank?'—just to let him know I was around."

In that game Roberts survived three Aaron turns at bat by giving up three singles that raised the batter's average to .301. Then, perhaps with his nervous system betraying him, the pitcher pulled a muscle in his back in the middle of the seventh inning and was removed. In such a situation the relieving pitcher is allowed as much time as he wants to warm up. Don Wilson, Roberts' reliever, off whom Aaron had hit his 611th home run, said later that as he stood on the mound it crossed his mind just to keep on warming up indefinitely, shaking his head and saying, "No, not yet" to the umpire until the night fell and the moon came up, and perhaps at 10:30 the next morning some sort of statute of limitations would run out the season and he would be able to pack up and go home, sore-armed but assuaged.

The pitcher who through personal experience knows more about Aaron's specialty than anyone in baseball is the tall, sidearm, whip-motion Dodger righthander, Don Drysdale, now retired from active baseball and working as a broadcaster with the California Angels. Aaron hit the astonishing total of 17 home runs off him. Next down the line is Claude Osteen, who has been touched for 13, and when his rotation comes up against the Braves, Drysdale often calls him on the phone (the two were teammates) to remind him that he'd be delighted to be taken off the hook for being Aaron's special patsy ("Now Claude, don't let down. That record is within *reach*").

Drysdale has never felt it was possible to establish much of a "book" on how to pitch to Aaron. "Besides, there never is any set way to pitch to a great hitter," Drysdale says. "If there were, he'd be hitting .220. He's one of those 'five-fingers-and-a-prayer-on-the-ball' hitters. I always used to think that he had a lot of Stan Musial in his stance. From the pitcher's mound they both seem to *coil* at you. The only sensible thing—if you couldn't get the manager to let you skip a turn against him—was to mix the pitches and keep the ball low, and if you were pitching to spots it was important to miss bad. If you missed good, and the ball got in his power zone, sometimes you were glad it went out of the park and was not banged up the middle."

Drysdale remains in awe of the concussive nature of Aaron's power. He remembers a 250-foot home run Aaron duck-hooked over the short "Chinese Wall" screen in the Los Angeles Coliseum, hit so hard that Drysdale got a crick in his neck from turning abruptly to watch it go by. "It's bad enough to have him hit any home run off you—turning and looking and saying to yourself, 'My God, how far is *that* one going to go.' But with the Coliseum home run, I ended up not only in mental anguish, but literally in physical pain."

At least Drysdale was not around to suffer the wrenching experience of facing Aaron at *this* stage in his career. As soon as Aaron was due at the plate the crowd began to stir in anticipation. In the left-field seats a forest of raised fishnets and gloved hands rose and swayed in expectation. The pitcher was practically the only person in the park who did not want to see the home run hit. Even some of his own teammates would not have been displeased, though they might have been judicious enough to keep it to themselves. In the penultimate week of the 1973 season a scuffle almost broke out in the Los Angeles dugout when a couple of the younger Dodgers, casting aside their team affiliation, carried away in their hope to see a part of history, began urging a long Aaron drive out of the park—"Get on over; get out!" They got some hard stares and shoving from one or two of the more aggressively competitive among their elders, especially Andy Messersmith, who is not only a strong team man but a pitcher hardly agreeable to seeing one of his kind humbled.

The next presentiment that the pitcher had to deal with was the flurry of activity from the umpires as Aaron left the on-deck circle and approached the plate. Since home run No. 710 a ball boy had been rushing out to provide an umpire with a clutch of specially marked balls so that, if the home run were hit, the ball could be positively identified to thwart a horde of people turning up for the $25,000 reward with fakes. Each ball was stamped, last year with an invisible diamond with a number within, this year with two sets of numbers, a marked pattern that lit up under a fluorescent lamp.

All of this could not do much to help the pitcher's confidence—the scurrying preparations of those attending to an execution. Last year Juan Marichal saw this activity, the plate umpire reaching in a special ball bag at his waist to introduce a special ball to the game, and not being aware of the procedure felt that he was the victim of some odd plot, that perhaps the ball he would get from the umpire was going to pop in two and emit smoke as he gripped it for his screwball. This year it was decided that the base umpire closest to the Braves' dugout would handle the marked balls.

The ball Aaron hit in Cincinnati with his first swing of the season (into a deep enclosure between the outfield fence and the stands known as "the pit") was marked with a pair of 14s and 1s. It was re-covered there by a policeman named Clarence Williams, holed up in his canyon with just a piece of sky overhead so that he never saw the home-run ball until it came over the fence and bounced at his feet, spattering his uniform with mud. An attendant came rushing down the enclosure toward him, holding open a small paper bag and cry-ing, "Drop it in here! Drop it in here!" And thus it was delivered to Aaron, the ball that tied Ruth's record, shielded as if contaminated from the view of the huge opening-day crowd as the attendant, flanked by two guards, hurried in from center field.

Four days later in Atlanta, Al Downing handled two of the pre-pared balls. The first was marked with 12s and 1s, the 12 arbitrarily picked by Bill Acree, the Braves' equipment manager, and the 1 to show that it was the first of a series of 24 balls specially marked. Downing used it through the first inning when he walked Aaron to massive hoots of derision. The same ball was tossed to him when Aaron came up again in the fourth. It was thrown out of the game after a pitch in the dirt. From the first-base umpire, Frank Pulli, came a ball marked with a pair of 12s and two 2s.

Downing had realized in the middle of the previous week that he was to pitch the opener in Atlanta. It did not bother him much.

Though he is not an overpowering pitcher, he has great confidence. He relies on fine control and a good change of pace. His teammates call him Ace, an encomium for winning 20 games in 1971. He is also called Gentleman Al, for his bearing not only off the field but around the mound where he behaves, according to Vince Scully, the Los Angeles broadcaster, "like a man wearing a bowler hat." Downing is very much his own boss. He shakes off his catcher's signs as many as 25 times a game, relying on his own concepts and on his sense that much of pitching is "feel" ("If you don't feel you can throw a curve at a particular time, there's not much point in trying"). He is such a student of his craft that he has always made it a point to room with a hitter, rare in a society in which there is such a confrontation between the two specialists.

Hank Greenberg, the Detroit home-run hitter, always felt that it was essential to detest the fellow opposite. He developed such an antipathy toward pitchers that he would not consider them fellow athletes. They were "throwers." He never thought much of them personally, even those on his own team. Recently he said that the only pitcher on the Tigers he had anything to do with was Fred Hutchinson. "That was because he was a kid under adversity—just coming up—and at the beginning I felt a little sorry for him."

But Downing does not hold to this principle of rancor at all. He says, "It helps a pitcher to be exposed to the enemy camp. For years I roomed with Maury Wills, and it helped my pitching considerably just listening to him talk about hitting. At the very best I knew if I ever had to pitch to him—if either of us was traded away—that I knew something of his thought process as a batter and might be able to take advantage of it.

"Aaron? Well, I'm not sure that rooming with him for 10 years would really help. You can have all the know-how, but if you make one small mistake there's no one in the league who can take advantage of it like he does. He knows what I can throw. He hit two home runs off me last year. But I'm not going to change my pattern. I mustn't go against what I've been successful with. . . . I shouldn't rearrange pitches that complement each other. If I throw 715 I'm not going to run and hide. There's no disgrace in that. On the other hand, I'm not going to run to the plate to congratulate him. It's a big home run for him, for the game, for the country, but not for me!"

THE HITTER

On occasion, as Henry Aaron sits in the Braves' dugout, he takes off his baseball cap and holds it close against his face. He moves it around until he is able to peer through one of the vent holes in the crown of the cap at the opposing pitcher on the mound. The practice, like focusing through a telescope, serves to isolate the pitcher, setting him apart in a round frame so that Aaron can scrutinize him and decide how he will deal with him once he reaches the plate.

The thought process he goes through during this is deciding what sort of a pitch he will almost surely see, engraving the possibility in his mind's eye so that when the pitch comes (almost as if dictating what he wants) he can truly rip at it. Home-run hitters must invariably be guessers of some sort since success at their craft depends on seeing a pitch come down that they expect, so they have time to generate a powerful swing. More than one pitcher has said that Aaron seems to hop on a pitch as if he had called for it. Ron Perranoski, the former Dodger relief pitcher (who in his first six seasons against Aaron held him to an .812 average, 13 for 16), once said, "He not only knows what the pitch will be, but where it will be."

Aaron describes his mental preparation as a process of elimination. "Suppose a pitcher has three good pitches: a fastball, a curve and a slider. What I do, after a lot of consideration and analyzing and studying, is to eliminate two of those pitches, since it's impossible against a good pitcher to keep all three possibilities on my mind at the plate. So in getting rid of two, for example, I convince myself that I'm going to get a fastball down low. When it comes, I'm ready. Now, I can have guessed wrong, and if I've set my mind for a fastball it's hard to do much with a curve short of nibbing it out over the infield. But the chances are that I'll eventually get what I'm looking for."

This procedure of "guessing" has many variants. Roger Maris, for example, always went up to the plate self-prepared to hit a fastball, feeling that he was quick enough to adjust to a different sort of pitch as it flew toward the plate. Most guess hitters play a cat-and-mouse game with the pitcher as the count progresses. What distinguishes Aaron's system is that once he makes up his mind what he will see during a time at bat he never deviates. Aaron has disciplined himself to sit and wait for one sort of pitch, whatever the situation.

One might suppose that a pitcher with a large repertoire of stuff would trouble Aaron—and that indeed turns out to be the case. He shakes his head when he thinks of Marichal. "When he's at the prime of his game he throws a good fastball, a good screwball, a good changeup, a good slider, a good you-have-it . . . and obviously the elimination system can't work; you can't just throw out five or six different pitches in the hope of seeing the one you want; the odds of seeing it would be too much against the batter."

What to do against a Marichal, then? "It's an extra challenge," Aaron says. "I've just got to tune up my bat a little higher. It's a question of confidence, *knowing* that the pitcher cannot get me out four times without me hitting the ball sharply somewhere."

It is this confrontation between pitcher and hitter that fascinates Aaron, and indeed it is what he likes best about baseball—what he calls "that damn good guessing game."

Obviously there have been the bad times. His manager in the mid-50s, Fred Haney, was thinking of benching him against Drysdale, who was giving him fits in their early matchups. "I had a psychological block going there," Aaron says. "Drysdale was throwing from way out by third base with that sidearm motion of his, and he was mean, and it was hard to hang in there, knowing how mean he was. I had an awful lot of respect for him.

"So much of it has to do with concentration," Aaron says. "On the day of a night game I begin concentrating at four in the afternoon. Just before I go to bat, from the on-deck circle, I can hear my little girl—she's 12 now—calling from the stands. 'Hey, Daddy! Hey, Daddy!' After the game she says to me, 'Hey, you never look around, Daddy, to wave.' Well, sometimes I look at her, I can't help it, but not too often. I'm looking at the pitcher. I'm thinking very hard about him.

"I started thinking about Al Downing of the Dodgers on the way home from Cincinnati. Basically, I knew what he would like me to hit—his fastball, which tails away and, if he's right, is his best pitch. I knew he didn't want to throw me curveballs, which from a left-hander would come inside, and which I could pull. So I set myself mentally for that one pitch I knew he'd rely on—his fastball. I can discipline myself to wait for that ball. I knew it would come sooner or later. . . ."

There is nothing in Aaron's approach to the plate to suggest such an intensity of purpose. His stride is slow and lackadaisical. (He was called Snowshoes for a time by his teammates for the way he sort of pushes himself along.) He carries his batting helmet on his way to the plate, holding two bats in the other hand. He stares out at the pitcher. He drops the extra bat. Then, just out of the batting box, resting his bat on the ground with the handle end balanced against his thighs, he uses both hands to jostle the helmet correctly into position. He steps into the box. Even here there is no indication of the kinetic possibility, none of the ferocious tamping of his spikes to get a good toehold that one remembers of Willie Mays, say, or the quick switching of his bat back and forth as he waits. Aaron steps into the batting box as if he were going to sit down in it somewhere. Downing himself has said that looking at him during his delivery, he finds it hard to believe Aaron isn't going to take every pitch.

Downing's first pitch to him in the fourth inning was a ball, a changeup that puffed up the dirt in front of the plate. Umpire Dave Davidson turned the ball over, looking at it suspiciously through the bars of his mask and tossed it out. He signaled to Umpire Pulli at first base to throw in another of the prepared balls. Downing rubbed it up a bit, then turned and, as the clock on the scoreboard behind him showed 9:07, wheeled and delivered a fastball, aiming low and expecting it to fade away off the outside corner.

The ball rose off Aaron's bat in the normal trajectory of his long hits—the arc of a four-iron shot in golf—ripping out over the infield, the shortstop instinctively bending his knees as if he could leap for it, and it headed for deep left center field. . . .

Aaron never saw it clear the fence. Hard as it is to imagine, Aaron says he has never seen one of his home runs land. "That's not what I'm supposed to do," he says. "I've seen guys miss first base looking to see where the ball went. My job is to get down to first base and touch it. Looking at the ball going over the fence isn't going to help. I don't even look at the home runs hit in batting practice. No sense to break a good habit."

So, as he has done countless times, he looked toward first as he ran, dropping his bat neatly just off the base path, and when he saw the exultation of his first-base coach, Jim Busby, he knew for sure that the long chase was over.

THE PITCHER

Al Downing did watch the ball go over the fence. He had seen the leftfielder and the centerfielder converge, and he was hoping the wind would hold the ball up. Afterward, when the ceremonies began just off home plate, he went to sit in the Dodger dugout and looked on.

The delay was of no help to his control, and he was taken out that same inning. He went to the empty Dodger locker room and dressed. A taxi was ordered for him, and he stood in the stadium tunnel waiting for it. Downing has a very cheery voice that seems to belie the gravity of any situation one might connect him with. "Well, that's that," he said. "I didn't have the rhythm, and the fastball wasn't doing what it was supposed to, which is to drop slightly. I threw a changeup, low, and then I threw a fastball right down the middle. What did I think when he hit it? Damn, there goes our lead. So I went and sat in the dugout. Nobody said anything about the home run. Why should they? We're all grown men. We don't have to console each other. One or two people came by and said, 'We'll get the runs back for you.'"

A photographer appeared with a small souvenir placard handed out by the Braves, testifying that the bearer had been on hand to see the record home run hit. It had a picture of Aaron and the number 715. The photographer wanted Downing to pose with it, hold it up and smile. Downing shook his head quickly. "I don't think that would prove anything," he said. He looked up and down the tunnel for his taxi.

"I'm more concerned about my next start," he went on. "This thing is over. It's history. It won't bother me. There's only one home run hit off me that's ever stayed in my mind. That was a grand-slam home run that Ken Boyer got in the sixth inning of the 1964 World Series—the one that beat the Yankees 4–3 and turned the whole Series around. I threw him a changeup, and there was a lot of second-guessing that I had thrown him the wrong pitch, that I should have challenged him. I thought about that for a long time. I was 23 at the time. It was a technical consideration. This one? It's more emotional. Well, pitchers don't ever like to give up home runs. But," he said in the cheery voice, "I'm not giving myself up to trauma. People will be calling to see if I've jumped out the window yet. I'm not going to wake up in the middle of the night and begin banging on the walls and looking over the sill down into the street. The next time I pitch against him I'll get him out."

A distant roar went up from the crowd. The Braves were having a good inning.

"Your team has made six errors."

"That so? They must be pressing," Downing said. "Everybody's edgy tonight." He craned his neck, looking for his taxi.

THE ANNOUNCER

At the sound of the ball hitting the bat, in the broadcast booth the chief voice of the Atlanta Braves rose against the tumult to describe the event over the air to his part of the outside world. The voice belonged to Atlanta's local broadcaster, Milo Hamilton, an announcer for the Cubs and the White Sox before coming to the Braves. It was a tremendous moment for him. True, an NBC crew (Curt Gowdy, Tony Kubek and Joe Garagiola) was on hand and so was Vince Scully, the Dodger announcer for the past 25 years, sending the game back to Los Angeles. Through their combined media, many millions would be made aware of the instant, but none had a more personal involvement than Milo Hamilton. Being with the Braves, he was the only broadcaster in the country who had known for months that at some point he would be describing Aaron's historic home run. His situation was extraordinary for a sportscaster. While he had to verbalize instantly into a microphone what he saw, in the case of Aaron's home run, since it was inevitable, Hamilton had an opportunity to prepare a sentence so perfect that if it worked, if enough people heard it and commented on it, it had an excellent chance to slip into *Bartlett's Familiar Quotations* alongside "One small step. . . ."

It was a unique situation. Almost invariably, a momentous comment in sports reporting is made spontaneously, under pressure and against the crowd noise, so that a common characteristic is often that the key sentences are repeated. There was a flurry of repetitions when Russ Hodges, ordinarily a somewhat phlegmatic sportscaster, gave his on-the-spot report of Bobby Thomson's "miracle of Coogan's Bluff" home run in the Dodger-Giant playoff game in 1951. "The Giants win the pennant! The Giants win the pennant! The Giants win the pennant! The Giants win the pennant . . . I don't believe it! I don't believe it! I DO NOT BELIEVE IT!"

Describing the extraordinary home run of Ted Williams in his last time at bat in the majors, Curt Gowdy had a brace of repeated sentences: "It's got a chance! It's got a chance! And it's gone! . . ." All of this, in fact, in somewhat restrained fashion, since in an earlier inning Williams had hit a long fly ball that Gowdy described as if it were going into the seats. He did not want to be fooled again.

Phil Rizzuto, the Yankee broadcaster, had a quasi-opportunity, much like Hamilton's, to prepare for Roger Maris' 61st home run, which was a strong possibility though hit on the last day of the 1961 season. Obviously, he did not do so, since his radio commentary, utilizing his favorite epithet, was absolutely predictable. "Holy Cow!" he cried. "That's gonna be it."

Sportscasters all take a dim view of preparing material in advance, feeling that spontaneity must be the key essential of their craft, the thing that so often produces the most noteworthy effect. Red Barber remembers that when he was broadcasting the famous Cookie Lavagetto double that destroyed Yankee Bill Bevens' no-hitter in the 1947 World Series, he described the high drive and how it hit the fence, and here came the tying run and now the winning run, and here was Lavagetto being mobbed by his own teammates, and near beaten up, and then Barber gave a sigh, worn out by all the drama, and he said memorably, "Well, I'll be a suck-egg mule."

Telecasting, obviously, gives the announcer a better chance to drop in a bon mot, since the picture on the set, if the technicians are on their toes, portrays so much. Barber was the television commentator the day Maris broke Ruth's record, and he started out, "It's a high fly ball . . ." and he paused, noting in the TV monitor that the flight of the ball was clearly shown, and then remembering that a Sacramento restaurateur had offered a large sum of money for the ball, he announced when it dropped into the stands, "It's 61 and $5,000!"

Hamilton would agree with Barber and the others about spontaneity. "It's very much my cup of tea," he says. But on his speaking tours this past winter he realized that so much curiosity was being generated by what he was going to say at the climactic moment that he felt bound to work something up. In the evenings he would sit around and let his imagination take over: as he watched the Aaron home run arch into the seats his lips murmured; the sentences formed; the facts crowded his mind, especially the similarities between Aaron and Babe Ruth—that both were born just a day apart in February, both hitting the 714th home run at the same age (40) and both as members of the Braves' organization. Hamilton decided to announce much of this material as Aaron circled the bases after hitting 715, using each base as marker along the way (". . . he steps on *second* . . . and the Babe's great record, nearly two-score years old . . . and he steps on *third* . . . a great day for Aquarians! Both Henry and the Babe . . .").

As for the phrases at the moment of impact, Hamilton decided on "Henry has tied the Babe!" for home run 714, and for 715, the tie breaker, he chose, after much thought, "Baseball has a new home-run king! It's Henry Aaron!"—not earth-shaking (nor in the case of the latter especially grammatical), but functional. Hamilton realized that anything more ornate would sound hollow and forced.

When the great moment came, however, spontaneity took over despite Hamilton's best intentions. The planned sequence of comparing Ruth and Aaron was wiped out of mind because of the speed with which Aaron circled the bases, not being one to slow down and glory in the occasion, the tremendous crowd noise and a violent eruption of fireworks exploding above the center-field rim of the stadium. Even the word "king," which he had intended to say, came out "champion." "It's gone!" he cried. "It's 715! There's a new home-run champion of all time! And it's Henry Aaron!" But mainly, Hamilton was startled during his commentary by something he had never seen before in his nine years of describing the Braves in action: as Aaron turned third base, his solemn face suddenly broke into a bright grin, as surprising to see considering his usual mien as if he had started doing an Irish jig coming down the base path toward the plate. Hamilton was struck by it, but he never had time to describe it to his audience; by the time he recovered, Aaron was running into the pack of players and dignitaries, with more streaming from both benches and the grandstand, and he had these things to describe to his listeners. But Aaron beaming was the one sight, he said later, that while it had never found its way into his commentary he would particularly remember of that day. . . .

THE HITTER

Aaron himself does not remember smiling, or very much else about that run around the bases. The tension, the long haul, the discomfiture of the constant yammering, the hate mail—perhaps all of that was symbolized by 715, and to hit it produced a welcome mental block. Aaron has always said that the most important home run in his life was 109, an undistinguished number, but it was a home run hit in the 11th inning of a 2–2 tie game that defeated the St. Louis Cardinals and gave the Braves the 1957 pennant. Aaron has a very clear memory of his reaction as he circled the base paths in that enormous tumult of rejoicing. He suddenly remembered Bobby Thomson's Miracle Home Run and how he had heard about it over somebody's radio as he was coming home from school in Mobile, Ala., and how he had begun running as if coming down from third toward his teammates waiting at an imaginary plate. "That had always been my idea of the most important homer," Aaron said after hitting his pennant-winner. "Now I've got one for myself. For the first time in my life, I'm excited." A home run of that sort, meaning one that produced a playoff or championship victory, is obviously his idea of an "important" home run.

But about 715 he remembers only his relief that it was over with and the vague happiness; that his legs seemed rubbery as he took the tour of the bases, the Dodger second baseman and shortstop sticking out their hands to congratulate him. "I don't remember the noise," he said, trying to recall, "or the two kids that I'm told ran the bases with me. My teammates at home plate, I remember seeing them. I remember my mother out there, and she hugging me. That's what I'll remember more than anything about that home run when I think back on it. I don't know where she came from, but she was there. . . ."

THE RETRIEVER

There was hardly a fan who turned up in the left-field seats for the Atlanta opener who did not firmly believe that he was going to catch the Aaron home run. Many of them brought baseball gloves. A young Atlantan from the highway department had established himself in the front row, wielding a 15-foot-long bamboo pole with a fishnet attached. He was proficient with it, sweeping it back and forth over the Braves bullpen (at home his stepsister threw up base-balls over the winter for him to practice on), though the closest he had come to catching anything with his gear had been a batting-practice home run hit into the bullpen enclosure the year before by a catcher named Freddie Velazquez. He missed sweeping it in by a couple of feet.

The left-field stands of Atlanta Stadium contain the cheapest seats in the ball park and perhaps its most knowledgeable and intractable fans. They have a close affinity with Aaron. He stands immediately in front of them when the Braves are in the field, and they look down at the big blue 44 on the back of his uniform and watch the way he rests his oversized glove ("These days I need all the glove I can get") on his hip between pitches. They rise and cheer him when he walks out to his position, and as they do he lifts his throwing hand in an awkward, shy gesture to acknowledge them.

The Braves' outfield is bordered by a six-foot-high wire-mesh fence that runs around the perimeter of the grass. In the space between it and the high wall of the stands are the two bullpens. The visitors' bullpen is in the right-field corner. The Braves' mascot, Chief Nok-A-Homa, sits in his tepee on the left-field foul line, adjacent to the Atlanta bullpen, and when a Braves batter hits a home run he steps out in his regalia and does a war dance. The Braves' bullpen being imme-diately under the left-field wall, the fans with front-row seats can look down and see the catchers resting their right knees on towels to keep their pants legs from getting dusty as they warm up the relief pitchers.

The Atlanta pitching staff was the weakest in the National League last year (one reason why the Braves, despite a Murderer's Row of Aaron, Darrell Evans, Dusty Baker, Mike Lum and Dave Johnson, who last year broke Rogers Hornsby's home-run record for second base-men, were not pennant contenders), and the left-field fans have the same sort of despairing affection for the relievers that Mets fans had for their team in its early, bleak days. "We *know* the pitchers out here," one Atlanta fan said. "In the expensive part of the stadium they never see them long enough to get acquainted. They go in and they're bombed and they're on their way to the showers, which are kept going full and heavy. They never turn off the showers once the starting pitcher is knocked out."

The main reason for sitting in the left-field corner, of course, is that the majority of Aaron's home runs are pulled toward there, either to land in the stands or in the enclosure where a denizen of the bullpen or Chief Nok-A-Homa can retrieve them. Nok-A-Homa has seen every home run Aaron has hit in Atlanta Stadium since 1969, with the exception of No. 698, which he missed because he was trying to find a chair for one of the bullpen pitchers. He has not retrieved an Aaron home run since 1972, being too busy doing his celebratory foot-stomping dance. But, brisk of foot himself and outfitted with a lacrosse stick for additional reach, he had seen himself as a possible retriever should 715 drop in the enclosure. When Aaron really tags one, the homer flies over the enclosure and drops in the general-admission areas, where a pyramid of struggling people immediately forms over the ball.

Last year a man named A. W. Kirby from Old Hickory, Tenn., sprinted down an aisle, dived over a chair and, after suffering a broken fingernail and lacerated wrists and ankles in a tremendous scuffle, came up with home run 693, coincidentally the second of those Aaron hit off Al Downing in 1973. Mr. Kirby thought the ball was worth $1,700. His son had misinformed him.

The abrasions and thumps suffered in the pileup over 715 would be worth it. A high of $25,000 (by both Sammy Davis Jr. and an anonymous Venezuelan fan) had been offered for the ball. The retriever would be photographed giving it back to Aaron, and his face would shine out of the country's sports pages, and even if on the periphery, he would know something of the excitement of being touched by the moment.

Eventually the prize would go to the Hall of Fame at Cooperstown, N.Y., to join other great talismans of baseball history under their domes of glass—among them, Roger Maris' 61st and Babe Ruth's 714th and last home run, each with the name of the retriever included.

There are several astonishing things about Ruth's last home run, the first being that it was even recovered at all. It was the *third* he hit that day (May 25, 1935), and it was the first hit out of Pittsburgh's Forbes Field since its construction in 1909, an accomplishment that lasted until 1950, when Ted Beard, a Pirate outfielder, was the first of a select group (including Willie Stargell, who has done it a number of times) to join him.

The Pirate pitcher on the mound that day against Ruth and the Boston Braves was Guy Bush, who had come in to relieve the starter, Red Lucas, off whom the Babe had hit the first of his trio. Bush, who now lives on a farm in Mississippi, remembers that the "book" on Ruth (he refers to the Bambino as the Big Bamboo) was to throw him a slow curve. "Well, sir, I threw the slow curve, and he hit this little Chinese home run down the right-field line—which was no distance at all—20 feet back into the stands for his second of the day. That made me so mad that when he came up again at the back end of the game I called Tommy Padden, my catcher, out to the mound, and I said, 'Tommy, I don't think the Big Bamboo can hit my fastball.' I *didn't* think so, sir. He had a stance at the plate where he near had his back to the pitcher; he was so far turned around that I could see the number 3 on his uniform; I didn't think the monkey could come around quick enough on my fastball to get his bat on it. So I told Tommy that I was going to challenge him with the fastball. In fact, I told Tommy to go back and *tell* the Big Bamboo what I was going to do—that I was going to *damn* him to hit my fastball. That's how confident I was. Now Tommy Padden has passed away, poor soul, and I can't tell you for sure whether he told the Bamboo what I was going to do. But I can tell you this, sir, that I threw two fastballs, and he hit the second one for the longest ball I ever saw—it cleared those whole three decks—and I was too surprised to be mad anymore."

The ball Ruth hit sailed over the heads of a group of boys who happened to be standing at the corner of Bouquet and Joncire and bounced into a construction lot, where it was retrieved by a youngster named Henry (Wiggy) Diorio. He took it around to the Schenley Hotel, where the Braves were staying, for Ruth's autograph. At that time no one, much less the Babe (who decided to retire a few games later), knew that the ball would be the last he would ever hit out of a ball park. He autographed the ball for young Wiggy and said that as far as he was concerned it was just another home run. As for Roger Maris' home run, that was caught by a young truck driver named Sal Durante. He saw the ball begin its rise, and he hopped up on his seat (No. 4 in Box 163 D in Section 33 at Yankee Stadium) and made a one-handed grab. He shouted, "I got it! I got it!" and was immediately engulfed by a tide of fans trying to wrest the ball away. The ball was worth $5,000 to him—a pleasant windfall for Durante (who was going to present the ball to Maris anyway) and made his stadium seat, according to *The New York Times* the next day, the most "profitable in baseball history."

In Atlanta most of the home runs do not reach the stands but fall in the enclosure. There, the Braves themselves had decided that if any member of the bullpen caught the ball, it should be delivered immediately to Aaron. Coach Ken Silvestri was asked to supervise the procedure. When Aaron came up he spotted his bullpen crew along the wall, about five yards apart. In the fourth inning Silvestri stationed himself close to the left-field line in the hope Aaron would pull the ball sharply. He looked around for his big flexible mitt used to catch knuckleballs and discovered that Gary Gentry, a *pitcher* what's more, had swiped it, leaving Silvestri with a regular catcher's glove, which is not the best piece of equipment to catch a long drive. He was just about to call across and cuss out Gentry when Downing began his windup and threw. . . .

The last man in the line toward center field was lefthander Tommy House, one of the staff's short relievers. He is called Puma by his teammates for the way he bounces around during the pepper games and thumps down catlike on the ball, a young Southern Cal graduate in awe of what happened.

"The whole thing blew my mind. The ball came right at me, just rising off the bat on a line. If I'd frozen still like a dummy, the ball would have hit me right in the middle of the forehead. Drop the ball? No way. It never occurred to me; it wouldn't to anyone who's been catching fly balls since he was a kid. The only vague problem was someone directly above me who had a fishnet on a pole; he couldn't get it operating in time. I've been getting a lot of kidding, particularly from the other people out in the bullpen, because I've got my masters degree in marketing and I don't suppose my professors would give me high marks for opportunism, with so much being offered for the ball. But I'm not at all sorry. What made it worthwhile was what I saw when I ran in with the ball, holding it in my gloved hand, running really fast—in fact my teammates joked afterward that it was the fastest I'd run in a couple of years—really just wanting to get rid of it, to put it in Henry's hand. In that great crowd around home plate I found him looking over his mother's shoulder, hugging her to him, and suddenly I saw what many people have never been able to see in him—deep emotion. *I'd* never seen that before. He has such cool. He never gets excited. He's so *stable*. And I looked, and he had tears hanging on his lids. I could hardly believe it. 'Hammer, here it is,' I said. I put the ball in his hand. He said 'Thanks, kid,' and touched me on the shoulder. I kept staring at him. And it was then that it was brought home to me what this home run meant, not only to him, but to all of us. . . ."

Aaron's most significant home runs have been marked where they came down—No. 500 by a white square on the Fan-A-Gram electric announcement board, No. 600 by the appropriate numerals painted in white high on the wall down the left-field foul line and No. 700 by a seat painted red amongst its baby-blue fellows in the left-field stands. The Braves management has not decided what to do about commemorating the spot where No. 715 came down. A plaque had been thought of for placement in the wall or in the stands, but no one was prepared for House's catch. Some clubhouse wags have suggested that a replica of the pitcher, life-size, should be set out there, if not the original article, stuffed, a gloved arm outstretched.

A more eloquent testimonial than anything the Braves management can probably think up is already in place just across the expressway from the stadium—a life-size concrete statue of Aaron set up in the cluttered front yard of a 70-year-old black gravestone cutter named E. M. Bailey. Bailey works only in concrete (marble is far too expensive for his customers), and each of his headstones, with the name and date chiseled on it, sells for $10. In his off time he works on pieces of sculpture—massive-winged birds with thin, curved necks, a pair of girls bent like mangrove roots in a wild dance, a memorial to John F. Kennedy with Air Force One flying above the White House— all his constructions made of Portland cement.

He began working on the Aaron sculpture last spring and had it finished and brightly painted (Aaron's uniform in appropriate blue, white and red) just in time to move it, with the assistance of three helpers, into his small front yard on the night of the opener. The statue weighs more than 2,000 pounds. It shows Aaron at the completion of the swing of a massive bat, his eyes somewhat slanted in Oriental style, watching the ball sail off on its flight. When it was in place, the children came down the street, leaning up against a chicken-wire fence to look up briefly at the statue on their way home to watch the game on TV.

Bailey, somewhat exhausted by his afternoon's labors with the statue, relaxed in his springback chair for the game. His wife sat across the room. When Aaron hit No. 715 the two could hear the shouts rising along the street from the neighbors' houses. "Just then," Bailey says, "I kind of thought back, and when I realized how far he had come and what the hardships were and what it means when one of us makes good, well, I shed a little tear over that, setting there in my chair. My wife never knew. Oh my, no! I never let on. She never saw."

In 1959, Pat Jordan was an 18-year-old bonus baby with the Milwaukee Braves, a pitching prodigy with a flaming-hot fastball who was going to make everyone forget about Warren Spahn. It never happened. Three years and many minor-league debacles later, Jordan had lost his ability to control his pitches and, as a consequence, his professional career. So he began to write about baseball, mostly pitching, and over the years produced pieces for magazines like *Sports Illustrated* and *The New York Times* and books, like his memorable *A False Spring* (1975), that display the flash of an unusually perceptive mind and the control of a careful professional. *A False Spring* is Jordan's unflinching memoir of a failed career which, as we join him here, is about to sink to the bottom of the Braves organization, Eau Claire in the Class C Northern League.

Pat Jordan

▽

from

A False Spring

I remember the first game I pitched that spring, although whether it was against Jacksonville or Cedar Rapids or Yakima, I'm not sure. I remember it was still cool in March in Waycross and I had to warm up a long time in the bullpen. I remember, too, that I did not feel right as I threw. My motion felt awkward. I had no rhythm. There was a point in my pitching motion when all the parts of my body—throwing arm, shoulders, back, hips, legs—should have been exploding in unison toward the plate. On this day those parts were out of sync. While the rest of my body was lunging forward, my throwing arm lagged behind. It was as if my arm was reaching back, too late, to grasp something it had forgotten. When both feet were planted in my follow-through and my body's rhythm was all but spent, then my arm began moving toward the plate. I released the ball without benefit from the rhythm that had been built up by the rest of my body. It was as if I were standing flat-footed and merely flipping the ball with my arm. Even as I threw I could feel what was wrong. But my arm had a will of its own that day and I could impose nothing on it. I bounced balls in the dirt and flung them over my catcher's head. And none of those wild pitches even faintly resembled the fastballs I'd once thrown in Davenport, Iowa.

I pitched to 12 batters that day and did not retire one. After every walk and wild pitch and base hit, I cursed and glared and kicked the dirt as I'd so often done at Davenport, and then, quite to my surprise, it suddenly occurred to me that what was happening at this moment was somehow different from anything I had ever experienced before. This thought startled me, like a strange and unexpected pinch hitter. I paused a moment between pitches and tried to focus on this different thing. When I finally did recognize it all rage left me and a sense of panic set in. It started as a flutter in my stomach and rose, a solid lump, to my throat. I could not swallow! For one terrifying second I thought simply of breathing, of finally catching a breath, and only when I had was my mind free to dwell on the other thing. I'd forgotten how to pitch! I had lost control over all those natural movements—arm motion, follow-through, kick—that had been merely reflex actions for so many years. I tried to remember, saw only bits and pieces, shattered fragments of a thing once whole. I sifted through the fragments, tried to fit one to another, could not remember how to make my throwing arm move in unison with my lunging body. I could not remember how I'd once delivered a baseball with a fluid and effortless motion! And even if I could remember, I somehow knew I could never transmit that knowledge to my arms and legs, my back and shoulders. The delicate wires through which that knowledge had so often been communicated were burned out, irrevocably charred, I know now, by too much energy channeled too often along a solitary and too fragile wavelength.

Terror-stricken, I looked through the home-plate screen and saw the scouts and managers sitting in their deck chairs, shaking their heads in disbelief. A cluster of ballplayers was forming around them, growing larger with each pitch as word spread from diamond to diamond. Behind them all was the rotunda—that cylindrical brick building rising high above the diamonds. On its flat roof I could see four Braves' executives—Birdie Tebbetts, John McHale, John Mullins, Roland Hemond—pointing me out to one another. I began my motion, tried in midmotion to remember, felt my arm jerk uncontrollably toward the plate. And then I saw the ball rising over the home-plate screen, over the heads of those behind the screen, higher still, over the top of the rotunda and the heads of the men standing behind it, the men glancing up, startled, and then following the ball with their eyes until it came down on Diamond Four. For a split second everyone—players, umpires, scouts, managers, executives—stared at the ball resting on the infield dirt behind second base, and then they all looked up at the point where the ball had passed over the rotunda, and then, in unison, they turned toward me, blank on the mound. Someone laughed, and then others laughed, too.

I lost it all that spring. The delicate balance I had so assiduously created at Bradenton collapsed. Just like that. One moment it was a perfectly solid-looking structure—satisfactions, potential, success, talent—and the next it was nothing but rubble. The only thing left standing was a new and impenetrable frustration.

Each game I pitched that spring was, like the first, an embarrassment. Standing on the mound, I tried to remember. The bright sun receded in the sky, grew small and distant, dissolved. Staring plateward, I saw at the end of a long, narrow tunnel, a minute fresco batter, catcher, umpire. I began my motion, heard from a great distance the shouts and nervous shifting of my fielders, pumped, raised both hands overhead, curiously felt no exertion, was moving as if in a dream, without effort, disconnected. I raised my left leg and turned it toward third base, paused—perfectly balanced on one leg, an odd looking bird, still and blank—and then my body moved toward the plate, and later, my arm. The ball traveled a great distance through the dark tunnel and I lost track of it. Moments later, sensing its return, I raised my glove and caught it, without feeling. I began my motion again, threw the ball, caught it, threw it, caught it, threw it. At times I was vaguely conscious of my fielders moving after it, and then, of myself moving, too (always the pitcher, even in a dream) drifting toward third base, straddling the bag now, aware of a runner moving toward me. He moves in agonizing slow-motion, his features twisted, his chest heaving and, curiously suspended over his right shoulder, a sunspot—the ball! The runner and the ball are approaching very fast now, growing larger and larger, are almost upon me when, with a ferocious grunt, the runner leaps into the air, momentarily obscuring the ball. He hits the dirt—whoomph—and slides. The ball, suddenly huge before my eyes, explodes in my glove, which instinctively slaps at his spikes, too late. "*Safe!*"

Amid the billowing dust, I am conscious now of the sun's glare and my labored breathing and my hot, coarse-flannel uniform dripping sweat and the heavy ball in my hand and the nauseating, oily-leather smell of my glove and the pressing shouts and whistles of my teammates and, finally, walking back to the mound, of the weariness of my limbs.

In camp that spring I became "the bonus baby who forgot how to pitch." I took to my room and locked the door. I played my records at full volume and hid behind the noise. I no longer drove into town for a beer or dinner at Ma Carter's. I took all my meals in camp. I ate either very early, before the others filled the cafeteria, or else very late, after they had eaten and gone. I seldom left my room in barracks two. I passed the time standing for hours in front of the mirror on the wall. I practiced my motion in pantomime. I threw a thousand pitches a day in front of that mirror. At first I went through my motion as quickly as if I was pitching in a game, because I hoped to slip naturally into a once familiar groove. Then, when that did not work, I went through my motion with great deliberation, step by methodical step, looking always for that point where everything started to go wrong. But all I ever saw reflected in that mirror was my own image. It hypnotized me. In midmotion my mind would drift, and by the time I forced it back I'd be in my follow-through.

No amount of throwing before that mirror, or in games, or on a warm-up mound with old "Boom-Boom" Beck beside me extolling the virtues of the fadeaway, halted my pitching decline. It generated its own momentum and I could do nothing to stop it or even slow it down. After each game in which I performed, I slid further down through the Braves' farm system—from Austin to Jacksonville to Cedar Rapids to Yakima to Boise and, finally, to Eau Claire, Wisconsin, of the Class C Northern League. I broke camp with Eau Claire, an act of kindness by the befuddled Braves' front office.

I reached Eau Claire in late April with my wife, who had joined me at the end of spring training, after a three-day drive from the southeastern corner of Georgia to the northwestern corner of Wisconsin. The land, like Nebraska, was barren of trees, but not flat. It was rich farm and dairy country of gentle undulations that had been divided into perfect square-mile plots of corn and wheat and oats and hay and grass and freshly furrowed dirt that was almost black. From the crest of one of these undulations (not even a hill, really, just a rise) one could see a gigantic patchwork quilt of green and gold and chocolate squares, the quilt rising and falling over a softly rumpled land.

Eau Claire was a neat, nondescript little city of about 30,000 people, most of them of Swedish or German ancestry. At one end of the city was a public park built on and around a hill. The base of the hill—the park's entrance—was ringed by a narrow stream crossed by only a single bridge. Across the bridge was an open area with picnic tables, swings, seesaws and jungle gyms. Higher up the hill, the park grew thick and lush with trees and shrubs and rocky gardens. At the top of the hill, at the center of another open space, was a huge, cold, stone facade—the entrance to the city's only lighted baseball stadium and the home of the Eau Claire Braves.*

Carol and I lived in a single room with a tiny kitchen on the second floor of an old two-family house. The room was so small that once we pulled the bed out of the sofa (a Castro convertible of indecipherable vintage) it was no longer possible to cross from one side of the room to the other without walking on top of the bed. In the morning, if I woke first, I had to step carefully over my sleeping wife in order to get to the kitchen. The kitchen, which was just wide enough for two people to slip by each other, contained an ancient gas stove, a sink, some wall cabinets, two fold-up chairs and a one-by-three-foot folding table that dropped out of the wall at will.

It was there that Carol prepared the first meals of our early married life. I remember, especially, the first one. She had remained at home to prepare a late supper while I went off to pitch my first game of the season. I was hurt to think she felt it of greater importance to prepare our first meal than to see me pitch, although I knew she had never been much impressed by my talent. I remembered the first time we met, in my senior year of high school. When she asked my name, I lowered my eyes and, through modestly furrowed brows, said distinctly, "Pat Jordan." Nothing! She had never heard of me! All the while we dated, I waited impatiently for the day when she would

*Hank Aaron began his baseball career as an 18-year-old second baseman with the Eau Claire Braves in the early 1950s.

acknowledge my greatness. Why else would she be interested in me? Finally, someone told her I was a baseball star. But this did not impress her much. She knew nothing about baseball, found it amazing that someone would actually pay me a large sum of money, as she put it, "Just to play a game."

"You don't understand," I said, and dismissed her ignorance. But now in Eau Claire it disturbed me that, unlike most baseball wives, mine knew nothing about the game I devoted my life to. She took her cues solely from my enthusiasms and despairs. Whenever I pitched decently enough (a rarity that year) I had to tell her so, and only then would she smile and say, "That's nice, dear." And when I was knocked out of the box in the first inning (a more common occurrence) and she saw my dejection, she commiserated, saying, "Well, it's not your fault. It's hard to do good when you only play a little bit . . . Why doesn't your manager let you play as long as the other pitchers?"

On the night of my first starting assignment I pitched less than an inning. It was like Waycross. After I was relieved, I had to sit on the bench in the dugout in 30-degree weather (it was always cold in the Northern League) until the game ended two hours later. When I returned to our apartment at midnight, I found the table set, dishes gleaming, napkins folded and a single candle, unlighted. Carol was sitting by the table, her hands folded in her lap, her eyes pink-rimmed. On the counter next to the stove was a mound of freshly peeled but uncooked potatoes and a long, thick, raw steak.

She sniffled, shivering all over as if just emerging from cold water. "I couldn't light the oven," she said, finally.

"What!"

She held up a pack of matches with only a single match left. "I tried, but it wouldn't catch!"

"Jesus, Carol, I'm starved!" She began to cry (the failed wife), and between sobs to plead forgiveness. Her martyred husband, returning from a hard night's work (less than an inning?) to find a barren table, decided, on a whim, not to grant it.

"If you can't cook, I'll eat someplace else," I said and turned toward the door. She clutched at my arm, caught it. "You can't leave me!" she screamed. "You can't! Please! Don't leave me alone!" Her eyes were glazed like a trapped animal's, and, for an instant, she frightened me. "I'll try again! *Please!*" She grabbed the book of matches and worked to light the last one. She struck the match over and over again, but it would not light. She stopped, finally, saying, "Please don't leave me alone," and then, exhausted, she sat down in a chair—a strange, frightened, hysterical girl . . . my wife! At 19! Soft and pale, with translucent skin. You could see through her, so easily . . . bluish veins and blood vessels, faint fibers in exquisite parchment.

She bruised easily, cried often that first year after she had stepped—smiling, trusting and innocent—on board a sinking ship with its mad captain. A thousand miles from home for the first time in her life, she was burdened with nothing but my black moods day after day, while I, obsessed with my disintegrating career, seldom gave her a thought. She was just there, hovering around my despairs, at times a pleasant diversion, at other times a burden. To her, I was her husband, the sole source of comfort and despair, and she wondered, secretly, if this was the way it was supposed to be? Always?

After two disastrous performances in Eau Claire I was relegated to the bullpen. Two weeks later I was the tenth pitcher on a 10-man staff. I mopped up in the last inning of lost causes, and, even then, often had to be relieved because I could not get three outs. During the next month I appeared in six games totaling 15 innings, was credited with two losses and no victories, and had an earned run average above eight.

Only three incidents stand out in that first month. I remember pitching an inning in Duluth, Minnesota, and later being asked by a Duluth player, "Aren't you the guy from Davenport? The one who could really bring it?" I nodded, embarrassed. "What happened to you? Your motion's all fucked up." Another time, I remember pitching to Lou Brock in St. Cloud, Minnesota.* At the time, Brock was leading the league in hitting with a .380 average. I struck him out on a soft, floating fastball. He swung so far ahead of the pitch that he asked the catcher if it was an off-speed pitch. At the end of the inning I sat down in the far corner of the dugout and cried. My teammates glanced over at me in disbelief. I cried uncontrollably, and my manager had to send another pitcher to the bullpen to warm up and pitch the next inning.

---

*I recall only six teams in the Class C Northern League that year: Winnipeg, Canada (Cardinals); St. Cloud, Minnesota (Cubs); Duluth, Minnesota (Tigers); Grand Forks, North Dakota (Pirates); Aberdeen, South Dakota (Orioles); and, of course, the Eau Claire, Wisconsin, Braves.

A third time, I remember a game in Winnipeg that began in weather so cold—19 degrees above zero—that we had to build small fires on the dirt floor of the dugout to keep our fingers from going numb. We huddled around the fires, simian man in gray flannel, and at the end of each inning sent one of our tribe to forage twigs and bits of paper in the open area behind the outfield fence. Because I was the player least likely to be used in that game, I was the one sent out to forage.

By June I no longer pitched, not even the last inning of hopelessly lost games (which were many, since the Braves were in last place). I spent each game in the bullpen. I warmed up constantly, inning after inning, trying to recapture what had once been as natural to me as walking. I became more obsessed and frantic as I threw, and my motion became even more distorted. I was pushing the ball now, like a shot-putter, and I remembered, without irony, Dennis Overby pushing the ball in spring training after his arm went bad. But there was nothing wrong with my arm! I could have understood a sore arm, dealt with it, accepted it eventually. What was happening to me was happening in my head, not my arm. Whenever I began to throw a ball, my head went absolutely blank, and afterwards it buzzed with a thousand discordant whispers.

After a while in that Eau Claire bullpen, no one would catch me anymore, neither our third-string catcher, nor any of my fellow pitchers, all of whom thought me mad, but comically so. I threw alone, without a ball. I stood on the warm-up mound, pumped, kicked and fired an imaginary baseball toward the plate. Behind me, my teammates sat on a bench gesturing at me with their heads and laughing.

I hadn't pitched in a game for two weeks when the Braves' minor league pitching coach, Gordon Maltzberger, passed through Eau Claire. Maltzberger spent the spring in Bradenton with Milwaukee and Louisville, while Boom-Boom Beck worked with the lower minor leaguers in Waycross. During the season, however, Boom-Boom returned to his home, while Maltzberger moved up and down the Braves' minor league system, stopping a day or two in Palatka, three days in Eau Claire, five in Cedar Rapids, a week in Jacksonville and 10 days in Louisville before beginning from the bottom all over again. He was a prim, fussy man in his late forties, who had pitched briefly in the major leagues during World War II. He wore horn-rimmed glasses and had thin lips always pressed so tightly together that a hundred tiny lines had formed like stitch marks around his mouth, which made him resemble a prissy, taciturn spinster.

At Eau Claire, Maltzberger spent his time giving encouragement to those pitchers pitching well and avoiding those, like myself, who were not. In the bullpen one night, I asked him to help me with my motion. "I'll get to you in good time," he said. I grabbed his forearm. "But you've got to—now!" I said. He looked down at my hand on his arm. I let go. "I'll get a catcher," I said. He did not hear me. He was still looking curiously at his arm. He shook it out away from his body, as if shaking off an insect. Then he walked back to the dugout, showered and left that night for Cedar Rapids.

Three more days passed. My manager, Jim Fanning, had not spoken to me in a week. He passed me with a nod and quickly averted eyes. Finally I confronted him in our deserted clubhouse one night. I demanded that he pitch me. "I haven't pitched in two weeks!" I said. I could hear my shrill voice and feel the tears sliding down my cheeks. It embarrassed me. Still, I could not stop. "Everyone pitches but me! When am I gonna pitch?"

He, too, looked at me curiously. Then warily. His features clouded —narrow eyes, long sharp nose, lipless grin, all slanting upward toward his temples like the features of a fox. He was a trim, good-looking man in his thirties who would grow trimmer and better looking with age. By forty he would resemble one of those well-tailored gentlemen sipping an expensive scotch in the pages of *The New Yorker*. A catcher in the Chicago Cubs' farm system, he had never risen higher than the American Association (AAA). There he was a bullpen catcher, who made good use of his idle time. He pasted news-paper photographs of prominent players in action on plywood and cut out their silhouettes. During each game, young boys hawked these mementos in the stands for one dollar.

Fanning called his business "Jim Fanning Enterprises," and, in truth, he was an enterprising man. Even at Eau Claire he had the distracted air of a man who had no intention of remaining a lowly minor league manager for very long. Sitting at the far end of the dugout during our games, he seemed always to be contemplating strategy—not for those games, but for his career. His players knew this. "Jim's gonna be a big man someday," they prophesied. "He don't belong in a uniform."

They were right. Today, Jim Fanning is the general manager of the Montreal Expos. I saw him a few years ago in the ballroom of the Lord Baltimore Hotel during the Orioles-Pirates World Series. The ballroom was filled with hundreds of baseball executives who had just finished dinner and now, over scotches and bourbons, were proposing trades to one another. They scribbled names on paper napkins with felt-tip pens, then hurried to another table and presented the names to a rival executive. Jim Fanning sat alone at an oval table sipping from a glass and sucking on a long cigar. In his forties now, he looked impeccably trim and distinguished in a navy blazer, gray slacks and black patent-leather loafers. While he sipped and smoked, various men came up to him, presented their napkins and waited. Jim thought for long moments, contemplated strategy while blowing smoke through puckered lips toward the ceiling, then nodded. When he was alone, finally, I went over and introduced myself.

"Remember me, Jim?" I said, standing before him. "At Eau Claire in '61?"

He grinned at me and, without rising, shook my hand. "Sure I do, Pat. How you been?" And then, really remembering, his features began to cloud exactly as they had that night years before when I'd confronted him, hysterically, in our clubhouse. On that night he had said, "Sure you're gonna pitch, Pat. Just calm down. I was gonna start you in Winnipeg on Sunday."

We left for Winnipeg, the first stop of a 13-day road trip, after a Saturday night game in Eau Claire. It was midnight when we finished storing our bags in the backs of three identical station wagons (black 1958 Chevys with a screaming Indian painted on each front door) and then got inside (three players in front, three in back) and drove off toward Winnipeg, 12 hours to the northwest. Sitting by the window in the front seat, I remember watching the highway unroll before our headlights like a beckoning white-striped carpet. We drove for hours with nothing to see but the highway and the black, limitless Minnesota woods. And then, about an hour from Fargo, North Dakota, we saw a brilliant white light in the darkness, and we stopped to eat at a truckers' cafe. The cafe glowed like a star in the center of a vast open space dotted with dimly lighted gasoline pumps. The area was crowded with small-cabbed, big-bellied diesel trucks, some of them parked off in the darkness, others being gassed up at the pumps, still others hissing steam, grinding gears and roaring off down the highway.

When we finished eating and returned to the car I sat in the middle of the front seat, my knees jammed up to my chest because of the drive shaft hump, as we crossed the flat, open plains of North Dakota. Pat Sherrill drove and I sat beside him. Around us, the others slept, their heads resting on one another's shoulders. Whenever they woke with a start they looked around, embarrassed, and tried to go back to sleep sitting straight up. After a while they began to list again, their heads drooping in stages, and before long they were sleeping just as before.

◆   ◆   ◆

We reached Fargo at dawn. Pat turned right onto Highway 29 and we drove directly north toward Canada. We drove for hours without seeing anything but the endless gray Dakota plains and an occasional farmhouse off in the distance, and when at mid-morning we crossed the Canadian border into Manitoba Province, still the land did not change. We reached Winnipeg at noon, went directly to our hotel rooms and fell asleep, fully clothed, on the bed. I woke two hours later, stiff and malodorous, and went downstairs to the coffee shop for breakfast.

We arrived at the stadium at 3:30 p.m. for a five o'clock game. We dressed into our uniforms in the clubhouse off the left-field foul line and then walked across the diamond toward our dugout along the first-base line. The Cardinals were taking batting practice, so some of us stopped at short or second base to chat with players we had known from other leagues, other years. We would take no batting practice after our exhausting drive, only infield practice. The others broke out the bats and balls from the canvas sacks and began games of catch and pepper. I stepped down into the dugout, sat on the bench and waited (the starting pitcher's privilege) for Jim Fanning to toss me a new ball and tell me to warm up. It was a simple routine, yet one that never failed to thrill me—and certainly never so much as at that moment. The manager opens a small box, withdraws a new ball from white tissue, spits on the ball (partly for luck), rubs dirt in with the spit (the ball no longer white now, but the color of rich cream), tosses it to that day's starting pitcher and says, with a wink, "Go get 'em, Pat!"

Jim Fanning tossed me a ball and told me to go to the bullpen. "But don't warm up yet," he said. I sat in the right-field bullpen and watched our team take infield practice. I grew anxious as game time drew near. Finally, one of my teammates came sprinting toward me. I stood up, flexed my shoulders, touched my toes twice. It was Hummitzsch. He tossed me a catcher's mitt. "Jim wants you to warm me up," he said. "He can't spare a catcher right now."

"But I thought . . . he told me I was starting . . ."

"I only know what he told me," Hummitzsch said, and stepped onto the mound. I caught him until he was warm, each pitch a blur through my tears. When he returned to the dugout I remained in the bullpen for a few minutes, and then I walked across the outfield to our clubhouse. I changed into my street clothes without showering, packed my blue canvas bag with "Braves" stenciled in white at both ends, and walked to the bus stop. I took a bus into town, got my other bags at the hotel and took a Greyhound bus from Winnipeg to Eau Claire.

I reached the Eau Claire bus terminal at nine o'clock in the morning and found my wife there, crying. "I didn't know what had happened to you," she said. "Everyone's looking for you. Jim Fanning called. He said you ran away . . . I didn't know . . . I thought you'd left me, too . . ." She began to laugh and cry at the same time. "I had this ridiculous vision. You were running like a madman through Canada, you were in your uniform . . ."

That night John Mullins, the farm director, telephoned. He told me that for jumping the club I was suspended without salary from the Eau Claire Braves. I told him he was too late, that I had suspended the Eau Claire Braves from my career.

"Don't be a smart-ass," he said. "We're reassigning you to Palatka in the Florida State League. You get your ass down there within two days or I'll see to it you don't get your final bonus payment."

Bernadette Mayer (b. 1945) has written in an astonishing range of genres, not a few of which she invented. An energetic participant in the literary and artistic world of New York's East Village, her many books include *The Golden Book of Words* (1978), *Utopia* (1983), *The Formal Kind of Kissing* (1990), and *The Desires of Mothers To Please Others in Letters* (1994). Among her eclectic interests, baseball has its place of honor, as this poem indicates.

Bernadette Mayer

▽

Carlton Fisk Is My Ideal

He wears a beautiful necklace
next to the beautiful skin of his neck
unlike the Worthington butcher
Bradford T. Fisk (butchers always
have a crush on me), who cannot even order veal
except in whole legs of it.
Oh the legs of a catcher!
Catchers squat in a posture
that is of course inward denying orgasm
but Carlton Fisk, I could
model a whole attitude to spring
on him. And he is a leaper!
Like Walt Frazier or, better,
like the only white leaper,
I forget his name, in the ABA's
All-Star game half-time slam-dunk contest
this year. I think about Carlton Fisk in his
modest home in New Hampshire
all the time, I love the sound of his name
denying orgasm. Carlton & I
look out the window at spring's first
northeaster. He carries a big hero
across the porch of his home to me.
(He has no year-round Xmas tree

like Clifford Ray who handles the ball
like a banana). We eat & watch the storm
batter the buds balking on the trees
& cover the green of the grass
that my sister thinks is new grass.
It's last year's grass still!
And still there is no spring training
as I write this, March 16, 1976,
the year of the blizzard that sealed our love
up in a great mound of orgasmic earth.
The pitcher's mound is the lightning mound.
Pudge will see fastballs in the wind,
his mescaline arm extends to the field.
He wears his necklace.
He catches the ball in his teeth!
Balls fall with a neat thunk
in the upholstery of the leather glove he puts on
to caress me, as told to, in the off-season.
All of a sudden he leaps from the couch,
a real ball has come thru the window
& is heading for the penguins on his sweater,
one of whom has lost his balloon
which is floating up into the sky!

Angelo Bartlett Giamatti (1938–1989) grew up an avid Boston Red Sox fan in South Hadley, Massachusetts. A respected scholar whose books include *The Earthly Paradise and the Renaissance Epic* (1966) and *Exile and Change in Renaissance Literature* (1984), Giamatti taught at Princeton and Yale, his alma mater. When he was named president of Yale in 1979, he quipped: "All I ever wanted to be was president of the American League." Declining the limousine that came with the job, he continued to navigate New Haven in his yellow Volkswagen Beetle with the Red Sox sticker on the bumper. In 1986, he became the president of the National League; the job presented him with a conflict of interest when the American League entry in that year's World Series turned out to be the Red Sox. Giamatti served as Commissioner of Baseball for five months before his death in September 1989. He wrote this lilting essay for a 1977 issue of the *Yale Alumni Magazine*.

A. Bartlett Giamatti

♥

The Green Fields of the Mind

It breaks your heart. It is designed to break your heart. The game begins in the spring, when everything else begins again, and it blossoms in the summer, filling the afternoons and evenings, and then as soon as the chill rains come, it stops and leaves you to face the fall alone. You count on it, rely on it to buffer the passage of time, to keep the memory of sunshine and high skies alive, and then just when the days are all twilight, when you need it most, it stops. Today, October 2, a Sunday of rain and broken branches and leaf-clogged drains and slick streets, it stopped, and summer was gone.

Somehow, the summer seemed to slip by faster this time. Maybe it wasn't this summer, but all the summers that, in this my fortieth summer, slipped by so fast. There comes a time when every summer will have something of autumn about it. Whatever the reason, it seemed to me that I was investing more and more in baseball, making the game do more of the work that keeps time fat and slow and lazy. I was counting on the game's deep patterns, three strikes, three outs, three times three innings, and its deepest impulse, to go out and back, to leave and to return home, to set the order of the day and to organize the daylight. I wrote a few things this last summer, this summer that did not last, nothing grand but some things, and yet that work was just camouflage. The real activity was done with the radio—not the all-seeing, all-falsifying television—and was the playing of the game in the only place it will last, the enclosed green field of the mind. There, in that warm, bright place, what the old poet called Mutability does not so quickly come.

But out here, on Sunday, October 2, where it rains all day, Dame Mutability never loses. She was in the crowd at Fenway yesterday, a gray day full of bluster and contradiction, when the Red Sox came up in the last of the ninth trailing Baltimore 8–5, while the Yankees, rain-delayed against Detroit, only needing to win one or have Boston lose one to win it all, sat in New York washing down cold cuts with beer and watching the Boston game. Boston had won two, the Yankees had lost two, and suddenly it seemed as if the whole season might go to the last day, or beyond, except here was Boston losing 8–5, while New York sat in its family room and put its feet up. Lynn, both ankles hurting now as they had in July, hits a single down the right-field line. The crowd stirs. It is on its feet. Hobson, third baseman, former Bear Bryant quarterback, strong, quiet, over 100 RBIs, goes for three breaking balls and is out. The goddess smiles and encourages her agent, a canny journeyman named Nelson Briles.

Now comes a pinch hitter, Bernie Carbo, onetime Rookie of the Year, erratic, quick, a shade too handsome, so laid-back he is always, in his soul, stretched out in the tall grass, one arm under his head, watching the clouds and laughing; now he looks over some low stuff unworthy of him and then, uncoiling, sends one out, straight on a rising line, over the center-field wall, no cheap Fenway shot, but all of it, the physics as elegant as the arc the ball describes.

New England is on its feet, roaring. The summer will not pass. Roaring, they recall the evening, late and cold, in 1975, the sixth game of the World Series, perhaps the greatest baseball game played in the last fifty years, when Carbo, loose and easy, had uncoiled to tie the game that Fisk would win. It is 8–7, one out, and school will never start, rain will never come, sun will warm the back of your neck forever. Now Bailey, picked up from the National League recently, big arms, heavy gut, experienced, new to the league and the club; he fouls off two and then, checking, tentative, a big man off balance, he pops a soft liner to the first baseman. It is suddenly darker and later, and the announcer doing the game coast to coast, a New Yorker who works for a New York television station, sounds relieved. His little world, well-lit, hot-combed, split-second-timed, had no capacity to absorb this much gritty, grainy, contrary reality.

Cox swings a bat, stretches his long arms, bends his back, the rookie from Pawtucket who broke in two weeks earlier with a record six straight hits, the kid drafted ahead of Fred Lynn, rangy, smooth, cool. The count runs two and two, Briles is cagey, nothing too good, and Cox swings, the ball beginning toward the mound and then, in a jaunty, wayward dance, skipping past Briles, fainting to the right, skimming the last of the grass, finding the dirt, moving now like some small, purposeful marine creature negotiating the green deep, easily avoiding the jagged rock of second base, traveling steady and straight now out into the dark, silent recesses of center field.

The aisles are jammed, the place is on its feet, the wrappers, the programs, the Coke cups and peanut shells, the doctrines of an afternoon; the anxieties, the things that have to be done tomorrow, the regrets about yesterday, the accumulation of a summer: all forgotten, while hope, the anchor, bites and takes hold where a moment before it seemed we would be swept out with the tide. Rice is up. Rice whom Aaron had said was the only one he'd seen with the ability to break his records. Rice the best clutch hitter on the club, with the best slugging percentage in the league. Rice, so quick and strong he once checked his swing halfway through and snapped the bat in two. Rice the Hammer of God sent to scourge the Yankees, the sound was overwhelming, fathers pounded their sons on the back, cars pulled off the road, households froze, New England exulted in its blessedness, and roared its thanks for all good things, for Rice and for a summer stretching halfway through October. Briles threw, Rice swung, and it was over. One pitch, a fly to center, and it stopped. Summer died in New England and like rain sliding off a roof, the crowd slipped out of Fenway, quickly, with only a steady murmur of concern for the drive ahead remaining of the roar. Mutability had turned the seasons and translated hope to memory once again. And, once again, she had used baseball, our best invention to stay change, to bring change on. That is why it breaks my heart, that game—not because in New York they could win because Boston lost; in that, there is a rough justice, and a reminder to the Yankees of how slight and fragile are the circumstances that exalt one group of human beings over another. It breaks my heart because it was meant to, because it was meant to foster in me again the illusion that there was something abiding, some pattern and some impulse that could come together to make a reality that would resist the corrosion; and because, after it had fostered again that most hungered-for illusion, the game was meant to stop, and betray precisely what it promised.

Of course, there are those who learn after the first few times. They grow out of sports. And there are others who were born with the wisdom to know that nothing lasts. These are the truly tough among us, the ones who can live without illusion, or without even the hope of illusion. I am not that grown-up or up-to-date. I am a simpler creature, tied to more primitive patterns and cycles. I need to think something lasts forever, and it might as well be that state of being that is a game; it might as well be that, in a green field, in the sun.

Jonathan Schwartz (b. 1938), the nation's leading connoisseur of the music of Frank Sinatra and for many years the host of a New York radio program of American musical standards, is also a superb writer. He has been a columnist for *The Village Voice* and *GQ,* and is the author of two novels and a collection of short stories. His account of his life as an over-the-top Red Sox fan appeared in 1979 in *Sports Illustrated,* whose readers received it with enthusiasm despite its somewhat satirical take on the perils of extreme fandom.

Jonathan Schwartz

♢

A Day of Light and Shadows

I didn't feel much pressure the night before the game, when the manager told me that even if Guidry went only a third of an inning I'd be the next guy out there. But I felt the pressure when I actually came into the game. More pressure than I've ever felt. Even in my personal life.

—GOOSE GOSSAGE

In the kitchen in upper Manhattan, Luis Tiant appeared to be in charge of the Red Sox' 162nd game of the year. Boston had widened a small lead over Toronto to five runs, and Tiant's impeccable control compelled even the restless woman roaming through the apartment to stop at the kitchen door and admire his performance as one would admire an exquisitely bound volume of dense theological writing in another language.

In the bedroom, the Yankees had fallen well behind Cleveland and were hitting pop-ups, always a sign late in a game that things are out of hand.

The woman was restless because her quiet Sunday afternoon was being assaulted by the babble of baseball and by what she perceived as yet another increase in my furious tension. She had retreated to the living room to sit sullenly among the Sunday editions of *Newsday, The Washington Post* and two interim New York papers born of a strike that was now in its eighth week. She had been told that this was positively *it*; that there was *no* chance that the Red Sox would advance past this Sunday afternoon; that the baseball season would be over by sundown. She had been told that there would *never* be a repetition of my impulsive flight to Los Angeles after the Yankees' four-game Fenway Park sweep three weeks before. I had simply up and left the house during the seventh inning of the last humiliating defeat. I had taken nothing with me but a Visa card and $50. I had called home from Ontario, Calif., having pulled my Avis Dodge off the road leading to the desert, though I realized it was well after midnight in New York. "I am filled with regret," I said from a phone booth without a door. "Over what?" I was asked.

Her question meant this: Was I filled with regret because the Red Sox had lost four consecutive games, or was I filled with regret because I had up and left without explanation and had not bothered to call until the middle of the night—and if you want this relationship to work you're going to have to work at it?

I replied above the roar of traffic from the San Bernardino Freeway that I was regretful about leaving, and about my insensitivity and my inability to put baseball in perspective. "A trip of this kind," I said severely, "will *never* happen again."

The truth: I was regretful because the Red Sox had lost four consecutive games, had blown an enormous lead and had handed the championship of the Eastern Division of the American League to the Yankees.

Three weeks later the phone rang for an hour after the Sunday games were over. Congratulations! From California, Palm Springs, Brentwood, San Francisco. From Stamford, Conn., and Bridgehampton, N.Y. From 73rd Street and 10th Street in Manhattan. Congratulations!

Returning from oblivion, the Red Sox had tied for first place on the last day of the season, forcing a playoff game in Boston the next afternoon. Somehow this development had moved people to seek me out with warm feelings, as if my control had been as superb as Tiant's and had contributed to the unexpected Red Sox comeback. My control, of course, had vanished after Labor Day, leaving me infuriated and melancholy. And yet I accepted congratulations that Sunday afternoon as if my behavior during September had been exemplary. In fact, I had wept and raged. I had participated in two fistfights, had terminated a close friendship and had gone out in search of a neighborhood 15-year-old who had written RED SOX STINK in orange crayon on the back window of my car. I had set out after him with vicious intent, only to return home in a minute or so, mortified. The psychiatrist, whom I immediately sought out, said to me, "This is *not* what a 40-year-old should be doing with his time. *Comprenez-vous?*"

On the triumphant Sunday evening, I drank Scotch and talked long distance. I was asked, "Are you thrilled?" I was thrilled. "Can they do it?" I doubted they could. "Are you going to the game?" Well, maybe.

I had actually thought of trying to use my connections as a radio broadcaster to round up some kind of entrée to Fenway Park for the next afternoon, but the prospect of tracking down people in their homes on a Sunday night was depressing. And there would be the scramble for the air shuttle, an endless taxi ride in a Boston traffic jam, no ticket or pass left at the press window as promised, and a frantic attempt to reach Bill Crowley, the Red Sox' cantankerous P.R. man, on the phone—"Bill, the pass was supposed to have been . . . and no one's seen it and they can't . . . and is there any possibility that I could. . . ."

No. I would watch at home, alone. I would have the apartment to myself all day. I would stand in the bedroom doorway and watch with the sound off to avoid Yankee announcer Phil Rizzuto's ghastly shrieking. At home, in the event of a Red Sox victory, I would be able to accept more congratulatory calls, this time for the real thing. "To me, it's the division championship that means the most," I had often said reasonably to whoever would listen. "After the division it's all dessert."

And yet. Had there been a more significant athletic event held in this country during my lifetime? The World Series, like the Super Bowl, is public theater, designed to entertain. Women and children gather around. Aren't the colors on the field pretty? Isn't that Howard Baker?

The NBA playoffs, even the Celtics' wild triumphs of the '60s are local affairs, presented for small numbers of people in the heat of May. And what, after all, can be seriously expected of a major professional league that has a hockey team in Vancouver?

It occurred to me that perhaps one event had been as significant as the Yankee–Red Sox playoff—the Bobby Thomson game of 1951. The circumstances had been similar: a playoff involving intense rivals home-based in relative proximity; personalities that occupied the mind at four in the morning; and startling rallies through August and September, the '51 Giants having wiped away a 13½-game Dodger lead and the '78 Yankees having fought from 14 back of the Red Sox. The difference in the two games seemed to be a small one: for the Dodgers and Giants it had been the third of a three-game playoff; for the Red Sox and Yankees it would be one game, sudden death.

In February, with a cable-television bill, a notice had arrived: COMING ATTRACTIONS. EXCITING BASEBALL ACTION. RED SOX BASEBALL ON CHANNEL F.

The notice had said nothing else, but it had stopped my heart. Having lived in New York and having been a Red Sox fan since childhood, I had spent hours sitting in parked automobiles on the East Side of the city where reception of WTIC in Hartford, which carries Red Sox games, was the clearest! Eventually I had obtained through a friend in Boston an unlisted air-check phone number that tied directly into WHDH broadcasts. From anywhere in the world one could hear whatever it was that WHDH—and, subsequently, WITS, with a different number—was airing at any moment of the day or night. WHDH was—just as WITS is—the Red Sox flagship station, and one had only to be prepared for an exorbitant phone bill to listen to any Boston game, or season. Between 1970 and 1977 I had spent nearly $15,000 listening to Red Sox broadcasts. In a hotel in Paris I had heard George Scott strike out in Seattle. From my father's home in London I had heard George Scott strike out in Detroit. From Palm Springs, Calif., I had listened to at least 100 complete games, attaching the phone to a playback device that amplified the sound. One could actually walk around the room without holding the receiver. One could even leave the room, walk down the corridor and into a bathroom to stare glumly into one's eyes in a mirror and still pick up the faint sound of George Scott slamming into a double play in Baltimore.

The most significant athletic event in my lifetime.

$15,000 in phone bills.

Endless Red Sox thoughts on beaches, and in cabs, and while watching movies with Anthony Quinn in them.

And most of the summer of 1978 spent in a darkened kitchen with Channel F.

I got on the phone to a guy who works at ABC, the network that would televise the playoff game. Their truck was up there now, I assumed, with everyone's credentials in order. The guy at ABC owed me $150 and a copy of Frank Sinatra's rare *Close to You* album that I had lent him for taping six months before.

The guy at ABC was at home asleep.

"I'll try. I'll do my best," he said, "but it's slim city."

He called me at eight in the morning. A press pass would be waiting in my name at the front desk of The Ritz Carlton Hotel in Boston. "If anyone asks, you're with Channel 7 in New York," he said. "But you've got to be dignified, or I'm in the toilet."

"Have I ever *not* been dignified?" I asked.

"Yes," he said. "Yes," he repeated softly.

LOU PINELLA: *We had dinner around eight. Me and Catfish and Thurman. After dinner, we went over to a watering hole, Daisy Buchanan's. We had a couple of drinks, and we talked about the game. I remember that we all thought it was ironic justice that these two good teams should wind up like this after 162 games. Like it was just meant to be. Some of the fans in there, they recognized us, and they ribbed us about how we were going to get beat and all. But you know, we all felt pretty confident because of the series in September when we came up to Fenway and beat 'em four straight. We all love to play at Fenway Park, and we talked about it that night.*

In the morning I got up early, around nine, and had my usual breakfast: corned beef hash, three eggs over lightly, an order of toast, orange juice. I like to play on a full stomach. It's just the way I am.

I got to the park around noon. I felt nervous, but it's good to feel nervous. It puts an edge on things. In the clubhouse about 12 guys played cards. It kind of relaxed us. I thought about Torrez. I never hit him too well.

I talked to Zimmer before the game. I wished him good luck. He's a very close friend of mine. He lives in Treasure Island, and I live in Tampa. I remember thinking during batting practice, what a beautiful autumn day in Boston. It was a beautiful day. You know?

"It's a game that blind people would pay to hear," Reggie Jackson once said of the prospect of a Frank Tanana–Ron Guidry matchup.

That comment flashed through my mind while I was riding in a taxi to Fenway Park. The season did, too. Specifics: an extra-inning loss to Cleveland in April that concluded a Sunday-afternoon double-header at 8:46 p.m.; opening day in Chicago, and the next afternoon there; two games in Texas a few weeks later. All told, five losses that came in the closing inning. Had the Red Sox held on to but one of those games, there'd be nothing cooking at Fenway today—no tie, no playoff. The Yankees would be scattered across the country like the Montreal Expos, and the Red Sox would be in a Kansas City hotel lining up tickets for friends.

I had bought the papers at The Ritz Carlton after picking up my pass, but I hadn't read them and wouldn't now as I approached Kenmore Square. After all, who wanted to stare at Ron Guidry's stats on Storrow Drive?

I arrived on the field at 1:10, exhilarated, the papers left in the taxi, my pass in hand.

I took a look in the Red Sox dugout. At the far end, Ned Martin, the team's chief radio announcer, was fumbling with a small cassette recorder while, next to him, Manager Don Zimmer waited patiently in silence. I have known Martin for 15 years and discovered early in our relationship that he has no mechanical aptitude. The tap in a kitchen sink would break away from its stem at his touch. A zippered suitcase would open only in the hands of a hotel maintenance man. The cassette machine, though it was used daily to tape the pregame show with the manager, was apt to defy Martin at any time, before any game. I saw at once that it was defying him now, on this most crucial of crucial afternoons.

Crouching on the top step of the dugout, I stared down at the two men. Perhaps three minutes elapsed, enough time for Zimmer to take notice of me. "Who's that?" he said to Martin, who was tangled in the tape of a broken cassette.

Ned looked up. "Holy Christ," he said, aware that someone who knew him well was scrutinizing his difficulties.

"I'll deal with you later," I said to him.

"Christ," Ned repeated, an utterance that to this day remains the first word on the last pregame program that Martin, a Red Sox announcer for 18 years, would conduct on the team's radio network.

Munson was hitting. Around the batting cage were the faces of the New York press, and those of some Boston writers I had gotten to know through the years. One of the Boston writers told me that moments earlier, in the clubhouse, Carl Yastrzemski had confided that he was "damned scared." A New York broadcaster, who was there only for the pleasure of it, said to me somewhat confidentially, "This is a gala occasion."

Always, when I think of baseball games that have been played, I see them as if they had taken place in the light of day. I have spent a lot of time mentally reshuffling two-hitters and leaping catches that occurred at 10 or 11 in the evening, so that they return to me grandly in afternoon sunshine. The fact that baseball is part of my daily procedure, like getting up for work or eating lunch, inspires me to conjure up sunlight for its illumination.

Forty-five minutes before the 2:30 start, I realized as I looked around the park that in all my years of journeying to Fenway, on all the summer afternoons spent peacefully in the many corners of the stadium, I had never experienced a day of such clarity, of such gentleness. Fluffy cirrus clouds appeared to have arrived by appointment. The temperature of 68° was unaccompanied by even the slightest trace of wind, which made the day seem 10° warmer than it was. For such a majestic encounter there had been provided, despite a less-than-optimistic forecast the night before, a shimmering neutral Monday, as if God, recognizing the moment, had made some hasty last-minute adjustments. It was the afternoon of my imagination, the handpicked sunlit hours during which my perpetual baseball game had always been played.

After a while I made my way up to the press room, which is on the roof of the stadium, behind the press box and the three enclosed rows of seats that stretch down both foul lines. They had been desirable seats to me as a child, because they allowed easy access to foul balls. One had only to lurk in the doorway of one of those roof boxes and await the inevitable. Other lurkers in other doorways were the competition—kids my age, ready to spring into action.

"Here it comes!"

We were off. Under or over a green railing (now red). Across the roof to the brick wall. A slide, a leap, a grapple. A major league baseball in your pocket; if not this time, the next. You always had a shot at getting one on that roof. If I competed 50 times, and surely that is a conservative guess, I emerged from my adolescence with at least 15 souvenirs—and one chipped tooth (the railing).

Before entering the press room, I looked around for a moment. I could see myself outside doorway 25-27 wearing a Red Sox cap. Oh, how quiet it had been when I raced across the top of Fenway Park—just those other feet and the whistling wind shooing me ever so gradually through the years to this very afternoon, to this very press room that I had aspired to for so long, to the tepid piece of ham and half a ring of pineapple that I would be served, to the unexpected sight of Phil Rizzuto making his way toward my table.

"You huckleberry," he said to me with a smile. "I heard what you said."

The morning before, on my radio program in New York, I had spoken harshly of Rizzuto's announcing. "He is shrill," I had said, which is true. "He roots in an unfair and unacceptable way for the Yankees," which is true.

"I heard you," Rizzuto repeated, extending his hand. "You got a nice calm show. I like it," he continued, surprising me.

Rizzuto is a charmer, an attractive, graying man with the eyes of a child. One imagines that his attention span outside a baseball park is short, but one would like to be included in whatever spare moments he has available. My distaste for his broadcasts was muted at once by the warmth of his radical innocence. Getting up from my seat, I touched his cheek in friendship. I had never met Rizzuto before and had often imagined myself dressing him down before a large and approving assembly. Instead, when he departed to make his way to the radio booth, I found myself regretting the fact that I hadn't told him that I had never come upon a better or more exciting shortstop. Never.

MIKE TORREZ: *I had my usual breakfast, just tea and a piece of toast. I don't like to pitch on a full stomach.*

As I drove to the park, I thought about a couple of games during the year. After those games I had thought that I didn't want them to be the deciding thing. Like a game in Toronto that Jim Wright pitched. It was extra innings. We got a few guys on. I think with no outs. We couldn't score and we got beat. And there was a game in Cleveland when we came back with four in the ninth. Yaz hit a homer, but we blew it. You think about those things.

When I was warming up in the bullpen I felt good. I had good motion. I didn't throw hard until the last two minutes. I looked over at Guidry and waved to him. I wished him good luck and all that. He did the same to me.

And I thought about Rivers and Munson. They're the keys. And then the
national anthem was played. And then we started to play.

A photographers' box is suspended beneath the roof seats along the
first-base line. One descends a metal ladder that is difficult to negoti-
ate. One stands throughout the game, because the early arrivals have
captured the few folding chairs scattered around.

As Mickey Rivers, the first batter, approached the plate, I said out
loud to no one, "If Torrez gets Rivers right here, the Red Sox will win."
I have a tendency to think and speak such notions. "If this light turns
green by the time I count three, I won't catch the flu all winter."

Rivers walked on four pitches and promptly stole second. "If Torrez
gets out of this with only one run, the Red Sox have a shot," I said
aloud.

Torrez got out of it unscored upon, striking out Munson with
commanding determination. I was elated. My hands were shaking. I
moved to the right corner of the box and stood by myself in a small
puddle of water left over from a rainstorm the night before.

Instilled in me from childhood is an awful fear that Whitey Ford
created: the fear not only of not winning, but of not even scoring, of
not even stroking a modest fly ball to an outfielder. Grounders and
strikeouts, and the game would be over in an hour and 40 minutes.
Done and done.

Ron Guidry is a slim man with shocking velocity and a devastating
slider. One does not imagine that one's team will defeat Guidry, or
score on Guidry, or make even the smallest contact with Guidry's
pitches. What caught my eye in the first three innings as I hung
above the field, clasping my hands together to prevent the shaking,
was that the Red Sox were not futilely opposing him. The outs were
long outs. The hitters were getting good wood on the ball.

I was astounded when Yaz connected with an inside fastball for a
leadoff second-inning homer, a blast that from my vantage point
looked foul. Fisk and Lynn followed with fly-ball outs, Lynn's drive
propelled to deep centerfield. I reasoned that Guidry, after all, was
working on only three days' rest, that he was a fragile guy, that maybe
there was a shot at him. . . . Maybe there was a shot at him.

Torrez was getting stronger as the game moved along. When the
fourth inning began, my nerves were so jumbled that I felt it im-

possible to continue standing in that puddle staring out at the field. I wanted to break away from it, soften its colors, lower its volume.

I climbed up the metal ladder and went into the men's room, a separate little building with one long urinal and two filthy sinks above which was written in large, well-formed blue Magic Marker letters and numbers, FATE IS AGAINST '78.

In the press room the ABC telecast was playing to an empty house. I sat down to watch an inning or so and was joined a moment later by Ned Martin, whose partner, an amiable, childlike man named Jim Woods, was handling the fourth. Woods' usual innings were the third, fourth and seventh. Knowing of this arrangement, I had hoped for Ned's appearance. Someone so close to it all, so immersed in it all for so many years, would have the answer. He would reassure me, calm me down.

"Well," I said.

"Torrez," he said.

"Do you think?"

"Can't tell."

Ned is usually more loquacious than he was that afternoon. He is as articulate and as creative a sportscaster as there is in the country. He is often poetic and moving. "The Yankee score is up," he had observed late in September from Toronto, where scores remain only momentarily on the electric board. "Soon it will be gone," he had continued in his usual quiet tone. "It will flash away like a lightning bug into the moist and chilly Canadian night."

From Chicago a number of seasons ago—I wrote it down at the time: "The dark clouds approaching from beyond leftfield look to be ambling across the sky in no apparent hurry. They know what trouble they are and are teasing the crowd with their distant growl."

We sat in silence through the rest of the inning.

"Well," I said finally, hoping for an encouraging word.

"You never know," Ned said.

I walked him back toward the radio booth. On the catwalk outside the visitors' radio booth, Buddy LeRoux, one of the Red Sox' new owners, was in conversation with two men wearing dark suits. I heard LeRoux use the word "cautious." He, too, was wearing a suit, pin-striped and ill-fitting. It was a baggy garment that did not complement a man of position.

I studied his eyes. This same fellow, with a younger, pudgier face, had, as the Celtics' trainer, sat next to Red Auerbach throughout my adolescence, attending thoughtfully to some of the heroes of my youth. His face is lined now, his demeanor formal, suggesting high finance. An owner: What did he know of shaky hands and midnight calls from Ontario, Calif.? There he was in conference, having missed the fourth inning—or so I imagined. I thought: If an owner can take the fourth inning off, what is so important about it all, anyway?

I returned to the puddle for the fifth and sixth innings. The Yankees stirred around against Torrez, but didn't break through. The Red Sox sixth produced a run on a line single by Jim Rice.

It also produced the play that changed the game.

Fred Lynn came to bat with two runners on, two outs and a 2–0 Red Sox lead. It was clear that Guidry was not overpowering. With Torrez so formidable, another run might put the game away. At that moment, it seemed possible to me that the Red Sox would actually win, that the nightmare would end at last.

I paced half the length of the photographers' box. With every pitch I moved a few feet to my right or left, winding up at the foot of the ladder for Guidry's 3–2 delivery.

RON GUIDRY: *I was a little tired and my pitches were up. I threw him a slider on the inside. He must have been guessing inside, because he was way out in front of it and pulled it.*

LOU PINIELLA: *Guidry wasn't as quick as usual. Munson told me that his breaking ball was hanging, so I played Lynn a few steps closer to the line than usual. I saw the ball leave the bat and then I lost it in the sun. I went to the place where I thought the ball would land. I didn't catch it cleanly, but kind of in the top of my glove. It would have short-hopped to the wall and stayed in play. Without any doubt two runs would have scored. But it was catchable.*

I watched the ball, trying to judge how deep it was hit. I realized it didn't quite have it, but I envisioned a double. Piniella seemed confused. I wanted the two runs. I felt 4–0 in my heart.

Piniella's catch was an indignity. He had appeared bollixed and off-balance, lurching about under the glaring sun in the rightfield corner.

That Lynn had unleashed so potent a smash and would go unre-warded, that *I* would go unrewarded, that the game itself would re-main within the Yankees' reach, struck me as an ominous signal that things would not, after all, work out in the end. The game and the season—the losses in Toronto, Butch Hobson's floating bone chips, Rick Burleson's injury just before the All-Star break, a thousand things that had created this day in the first place—all had spun through the early autumn sky with the ball that Lynn had struck, the ball that Piniella held in his bare right hand all the way in from rightfield, across the diamond, through the third-base coach's box and into the dark sanctuary of the visitors' dugout. He had caught it, he had held on to it, he held it even now, sitting there on the bench. The play could not be called back. The score still stood at 2–0.

In the top of the seventh inning I went into the solitary phone booth on the first-base side of the roof. I dialed my secret air-check number, realizing it was the first time I had ever sought it out as a local investment.

It was a Jim Woods inning, which frightened me all the more. Woods, like a child fumbling with a lie, cannot hide the truth of any Red Sox situation. One can tell immediately if Boston is in a favorable or thorny position, if the game is lost or won, or even tied.

Even with a 2–0 lead, Woods was somber. For Pittsburgh, New York, St. Louis, Oakland and Boston, Woods had been broadcasting baseball games ever since Dwight Eisenhower's presidency. The im-portance of Piniella's catch had not eluded him. Then he was pre-sented with singles by Chris Chambliss and Roy White that brought the lead run to the plate. I had dialed in for the security of the radio's familiar rhythm and was suddenly faced with potential disaster.

I hung up on Woods and ran back to the photographers' box, taking the steps of the ladder two at a time. Jim Spencer was pinch-hitting for the Yankees. I remembered a Spencer home run earlier in the year. Could it have been against the Angels? Jim Spencer, of all people. Spencer hit the ball fairly well to left, but Yaz was with it all the way.

Two outs.

Bucky Dent.

I had a fleeting thought that, through the years, Yankee shortstops had hurt the Red Sox at the plate. Inconsequential men—Fred Stan-ley, Gene Michael, Jim Mason—no power, .230 hitters. Shortstops.

Bucky Dent.

I leaned way over the railing, as if trying to catch a foul ball hit just below me. I was motionless, except for my shaking hands.

Dent fouled the second pitch off his shin.

Delay.

I studied Torrez. He stood behind the mound rubbing up the new ball. He did not pace, he did not turn to examine the outfield. He just rubbed up the new ball and stared in at Dent, who was bent over to the left of the plate, his shin being cared for.

MIKE TORREZ: *I lost some of my concentration during the delay. It was about four minutes, but it felt like an hour. I had thought that they'd pinch-hit for Dent with maybe Jay Johnstone or Cliff Johnson. I felt good. I just wanted to get going. That first inning really helped. My concentration was there, especially on Munson. During the delay, I thought slider on the next pitch. But Fisk and me were working so well together, I went along with his call for a fastball. When Dent hit it, I thought we were out of the inning. I started to walk off the mound. I could see Yaz patting his glove.*

I watched, hanging over the railing. I had seen too many fly balls from the roof seats on the first-base side to be fooled now. This fly ball by a Yankee shortstop with an aching shin was clearly a home run. I had no doubt from the start.

When the ball struck the net, Yastrzemski's whole body trembled for an instant. Then he froze, every muscle drawn tight in excruciating frustration.

I said out loud, "God, no! God, no!"

In minutes the Yankees had scored another run.

I climbed the ladder and walked slowly to the press room. I went into the lavatory, closed the door to the one stall and sat on the toilet with my head in my hands, wishing there was a lid on the seat. It was entirely quiet, as if I were alone in the stadium.

"You are emotionally penniless," a girl had shouted at me years before from behind a slammed and locked bathroom door.

That is what came into my mind in my own locked cubicle.

I also thought to leave the park; to take a walk, to just go away. Instead I decided to change locations, to venture to the far reaches of the leftfield roof, out near the wall.

A couple of kids were running mindlessly around, chasing each other as if they were on a beach. They pushed their way through clusters of writers and photographers who were all standing, because there were no seats to be had. I sat down on the roof and crossed my legs. I was no more than a foot from the lip, which was unprotected by a railing or other barrier.

The wind had picked up. Shadows dominated the field, except in right and right center. I noticed that the clouds were just a bit thicker. A rain delay. Would the game revert to the last complete inning? A seven-hour delay and finally a decision. Red Sox win 2–0. I saw it as the only possibility. It had to rain right at this moment. Torrentially. Monumentally. Before the new Yankee pitcher could complete this last of the seventh. The new Yankee pitcher was Gossage, and Bob Bailey was preparing to pinch-hit against him.

Bob Bailey!

I bowed my head.

GOOSE GOSSAGE: *When I saw Bailey coming up, I said to myself, with all respect to Bob, "Thank you."*

Bailey looked at strike three and went away, out of my life, off the team, out of the league, out of the country, away, away.

Reggie Jackson homered in the eighth. I affected bemusement as I watched him round the bases. I thought: Let's see, just for the fun of it, how big it's going to be. What does it matter, anyway? It's only a game.

Official bemusement on the leftfield roof.

A leadoff double by Jerry Remy in the bottom of the eighth. How nice:

A Rice fly-ball out.

Five outs left. It's only a game.

Three consecutive singles.

The score was 5–4, Yankees' favor, with Red Sox runners on first and second. Hobson and Scott, two righthanded hitters, would now face the righthanded Gossage. My bemusement vanished. I stood.

I felt that Hobson had a real crack at it, that he is a good two-strike hitter and that he would surely be hitting with two strikes before very long. I felt that if they let Scott hit I would leap from the roof in a suicidal protest. The Boomer vs. Gossage was too pathetic for me even to contemplate.

Hobson's fly-ball out to right set up the Boomer vs. Gossage. I did not leap from the roof. I sat down and rested my chin on my knees. I believe I smiled at the Boomer. I know I said aloud, "Surprise me, baby."

The Boomer did not surprise. Gossage took only a minute or so to strike him out.

I remained motionless as the teams changed sides and as they played the top of the ninth, about which I can remember little. It seems to me that Paul Blair got a hit and Dick Drago pitched. There was base running of some kind, activity around second. I know there was no scoring.

Just before the start of the last of the ninth, I imagined myself swimming in an enormous pool. I was in the desert in early summer. I thought that it was the dry heat that enabled me to move through the water so rapidly. I hardly had to move my arms or legs in order to cover the length of the pool. It was possible to swim forever.

I spotted Dwight Evans striding quickly, intensely to the plate. For whom was he hitting?

He was hitting for Frank Duffy, who had replaced Jack Brohamer, who had been hit for by Bailey. Duffy had played third in the top of the ninth, and I hadn't even noticed.

Evans was hitting for Duffy.

Why hadn't Evans come to bat instead of Bailey in the seventh?

And where was Garry Hancock? A lefthanded hitter, a slim Gary Geiger kind of guy. Where was Garry Hancock?

It looked to me as if Evans nearly got ahold of one. He missed, by God knows how small a portion of the ball, and flied routinely to left.

Gossage walked Burleson as if it had been his intention. That would give Rice a turn at bat, providing Remy stayed out of the double play.

Remy lined a shot to right. My thought was . . . double play. Piniella catches the ball and throws to Chambliss with Burleson miles off first.

LOU PINIELLA: *I didn't want the ball hit to me. It was a nightmare out there in the sun. I kept telling Blair in center to help me. When Remy hit it, I saw it for a second and then lost it. I knew it would bounce, so I moved back three steps to prevent it from bouncing over me to the wall. I moved to my left a piece. I decoyed Burleson. I didn't want him to know I couldn't see it. If Burleson had tried for third, he would have been out. There's no doubt about it. My throw was accurate and, for me, it had good stuff on it.*

JERRY REMY: *I think Burleson did 100% the right thing. It would have been very close at third. He had to play it safe. I knew I had a hit, but Rick had to hold up for just a moment between first and second. So why gamble?*

I knelt on the roof. I thought, is this actually happening? First and second, one out, last of the ninth. And Rice and Yaz. Is this actually happening?

GOOSE GOSSAGE: *I tried to calm myself down by thinking of the mountains of Colorado, the mountains that I love. I thought that the worst thing that could happen to me was, that I'd be in those mountains tomorrow. I had once hiked to a lake in the mountains. It was really quiet. I had pictured seats on the mountainsides. Thousands and thousands of seats looking down on a ball field next to the lake. I imagined myself pitching in front of all those people in the mountains.*

I didn't think Yastrzemski had a chance. I thought about it being late in the day, about his being fatigued, about how he wouldn't get around on Gossage's fastball. My hopes rode with Rice.

LOU PINIELLA: *I played Rice in right center, not deep. It cut the angle of the sun. I saw the ball clean. I caught it maybe 25 feet from the fence.*

GOOSE GOSSAGE: *When I was warming up before I came in in the seventh, I imagined myself pitching to Yaz with two outs in the ninth. The Red Sox would have a couple guys on base, and it would be Yaz and me. When it turned out that way, I thought, here it is. It was ESP. Really, I'm not kidding.*

I screamed at Yaz from the leftfield roof. "Bunt, goddam it!" I even waved my arms, thinking that I might catch his eye. He'd call time out and wander out to leftfield. "What did you say?" he'd shout up at me. "Bunt!" I'd yell back. "Interesting," he'd say.

Then Yaz would lay down a beauty.

Burleson, who had taken third after Rice's fly ball, would easily score the tying run.

Carl Yastrzemski, nearly my age.

I gazed down at him through tears.

I thought: Freeze this minute. Freeze it right here. How unspeakably beautiful it is. Everyone, reach out and touch it.

Growing up in Mount Vernon, New York, in the 1930s, Mark Harris (b. 1922) read a lot of Horatio Alger and Ring Lardner, and watched a more than equal share of his favorite ballplayer, Carl Hubbell, the New York Giants' incomparable lefthanded screwball pitcher. Then he went off to a lean-to outside Denver, Colorado, where in 1951, he created his own screwball: Henry "Author" Wiggen, the perpetually astonished, perpetually ungrammatical, perpetually self-confident star lefthanded pitcher of the New York Mammoths. The four books in which Wiggen narrates the story of his life in baseball—*The Southpaw* (1953), *Bang the Drum Slowly* (1956), *A Ticket for a Seamstitch* (1957), and *It Looked Like For Ever* (1979)—elevate the baseball novel into unmistakable art. In this scene Henry is 39, a former Mammoth (they have released him from his contract) with a weaker fastball, a weaker bladder, a new broadcasting job, and a strong desire to pitch again.

Mark Harris

◊

from

It Looked Like For Ever

The reason I drove down a day early was for a meeting in Patricia Moors's office with her and Barbara and the 2 net work negotiators and various TV people from other net works regarding throwing out the ball Opening Day. Various baseball broad casts such as Monday Night Baseball and Week End Baseball and Game of the Week protested the ceremony, saying it was 1 big advertisement for Friday Night Baseball. "Here is Wiggen," said 1 of the other net work men, "standing up there as big as life with *Friday Night Baseball* wrote across his sweater. Where will it end? The world will think Friday Night Baseball is the *official* baseball announcer for New York."

"The thing that pains me the most," said his friend, "is realizing that after he throws out the first ball he will be cheered by the crowd, for that is what they do. The world will think the crowd is *cheering* Friday Night Baseball. Is that justice or fairness? It does not sound like that to me."

Patricia's office was very cold. They always turned the heat off in the ball park by Opening Day, talking them self in to the idea the weather was perfect for baseball. The 2 negotiators from Friday Night Baseball that burned holes in my arm chairs back home were now burning holes in the chairs in Patricia's office. I had not saw Patricia since her and Ben Crowder pulled a fast 1 behind my back and I did not care who burned down her chairs and the whole place with it. We all crowded around a little electric heater. "I am amused," said Patricia, "hearing you say 'the world will think this and the world will think that' when the world will not be at tomorrow's ball game. We will be lucky if we sell 40,000 tickets."

"In fairness," said another net work man, "you should call off the game rather than permit the first ball to be threw out by Friday Night Baseball."

"Call off Opening Day?" Patricia inquired. "Opening Day is 1 century old in our family. You are a man of ambition."

Barbara spoke, saying, "The ball will not be threw out by Friday Night Baseball but by Henry Wiggen. It is an occasion showing respect for 1 man dead and another just now retiring."

"Possibly retiring," I said.

"If Friday Night Baseball throws out the first ball tomorrow why not Week End Baseball the next time?" inquired the man from Week End Baseball.

"Because," said Patricia, "you are making a mole hill out of a mountain. If you can tell me some body in your organization that pitched for me for 19 years I will gladly ask him to throw out the first ball on the next occasion."

Barbara spoke again, saying, "I am amusing my self thinking if every TV net work gets an opportunity of throwing out the first ball every radio station will have the right to throw out the first ball and every news paper and magazine that sits in the press box will have equal rights to throw out the first ball."

"I am only talking about net works," said 1 of the net work men. "No body is thinking about these god dam fly by night independents that are not even off the ground."

"Well now," said Patricia, "I must take a firm hand and tell you that Mr. Wiggen will throw out the first ball. Many of the tickets sold were sold to people expecting 1 last glimpse of him tomorrow, so there we are."

"May be not 1 last glimpse," I said. "Coming down in the car I heard a prediction where some body said I will throw out the first ball tomorrow and be back playing again soon after."

"I am groaning with in," said the first net work man, "to think about him standing up in front of all those people plus TV news with *Friday Night Baseball* wrote across his sweater."

"This is where we were," said Barbara. "He might take off his sweater."

That was a good idea. Barbara never suggests any thing I would not agree with. I did not plan to wear the sweater in the first place. I planned a dark blue blazer with gray light wool pants. I was thinking about a really flaming shirt, but in honor of the 1 minute silence for Dutch I planned a certain pearl gray and blue pin stripe instead. Neutral socks and a pair of tassel mocs. "Yes," I said, "I will be taking off my sweater all right. I did not plan on wearing it in the first place."

"Never the less," said 1 of the net work men, "you are associated with Friday Night Baseball now with all the advertising they have gave you sweater or no sweater."

"I was picturing my self slipping out of my jacket and leaving it in the box," I said.

"Well all right now," said the first net work man, "I am seeing a little justice through the clearing. He will not wear any sweater or other identifying marks."

"May be you would like him to change his name," said Barbara.

"Not necessary," the man replied, "but what is now beginning to disturb my conscience is the words I just heard. You are 'leaving it in the box.' What is the meaning of that?"

"I am leaving my jacket in the box," I replied, "while strolling out on the field to the box."

"What box?"

"The pitcher's box."

"This is gone from too much to much too much," said the net work man, shaking his head from side to side and giving out a little smile showing he would be brave no matter what. "He should throw the ball out from the owner's box. There he is concealed and can not be seen. A lot of people will hardly know who is doing it much less give Friday Night Baseball the credit for it. He should not be strolling slowly out in front of all those people, visible to many, walking ever so slowly at leisure across all the distance from the Owner's Box to the pitcher's box while 1,000's of people turn to 1 another and say, 'Oh, yes, he is now with Friday Night Baseball.' It is enough to make you cry what happened to justice."

"It is advertising pure and simple," said his friend. "Why does he not squirt his mouth and under his arm while walking to the box and collect a fee from the mouth wash and the under arm?"

"Any how," said the first man, "he will not wear the sweater."

"I am sure we are all parting good friends," said 1 of the net work men and we all stood up and shook hands all around. The joke of it was that every body was winners on the following day but me, if you recall the occasion, which I just as soon forget.

Opening Day was fair and clear and dry with some what of a nip in the air. It was Spring and Dutch Schnell was dead. New York in the Spring meant clear days after rain and a nip in the air, and Dutch above every body else. I kept thinking I heard him shouting in the park. Where was the center of the park now that Dutch was dead, for in the past you listened for him and you looked for him, and where ever he was the center was.

I and Barbara sat in the Owners Box. Often in the past Dutch walked down from the dugout to the box and shook hands and talked a little with some body there. Some times he kissed a lady for the camera, or a cripple child. When I was a young ball player I wondered why you done such things. When I was a more experienced ball player I thought you done it because the owner told you to. But when I was an older ball player I knew you done it not because any body told you to but only because that was where you were. Older people were not people you bowed and scraped to. They were your friends. You knew them. You partied with them. Your children were as old as their children. When my daughter Michele was 15 she went on a world tour with Stanton Moors La Vigne, son of Patricia, although we would not of knew they went together if the plane was not high jack. You under stood the same problems. You were all in it together.

Time and again as I grew older it was I they cared to meet, so it was I that strolled down from the dugout and shook their hand. I shook hands with many rich and famous people over the rail of the Owners Box, cripple children and ailing persons and foreign dignitaries, causing a commotion once when General Weiskopf was there 1 day during Vietnam. I said in an angry voice, "General, if you are having a war these days why are you not out dying with the young men instead of sitting in the sun at a baseball game?" His face become white and he looked at me like he was disappointed in me. Then he smiled and replied, "We are each of us caught up in our life, are we not?"

But on this particular Opening Day it was not Dutch Schnell but Ev McTaggart at the center of things. He was up against the dugout wall watching the drill, his hands jammed down in his ass pockets, focusing his eye on things when some body mentioned some thing to him and he begun walking down toward the Owners Box with out taking his eye off the ball field. When he arrived he greeted Patricia and Barbara by the hand, he give a warm kiss to Millie Schnell, and he shook my hand, giving me a wink like him and I knew some thing no body else knew and said, "How is it, Author?" and I replied, "Good luck, Ev," although it killed me.

I pitched my first complete big league baseball game Opening Day in 1952. I was not yet 21, the youngest pitcher in the league. I signed to play ball for $4,000 bonus and an automobile when numbers had a different sound from now and an automobile was a bigger thing. Now a days you can hardly get a ball player to spit on an automobile unless you throw in a small sum of cash, such as $400,000 for Beansy Binz. On Opening Day, 1952, Mayor Vincent R. Impellitteri of the City of New York threw out the first ball from the Owners Box, and Sid Goldman caught it, according to my book in title *The Southpaw,* and run over and got the Mayor's autograph. Later Sid him self run for Mayor and lost.

I remember Opening Day, 1952, clearer than any Opening Day since. I remember the players of that year clearer than the players of any year since, first names and bad habits. Nothing ever stuck so hard in my mind as the first year, and no day of that year so clear to my mind as the first day. I knew every body, or any how I thought I did. I can not now give you the names of 2 dozen present day ball players, and those I can give you are all past 30. I don't know any body low down any more, and I notice where fewer and fewer people call me "Author." People that knew me good enough to call me "Author" drift off in to the distance. When the telephone rings people ask for "Mr. Wiggen" and are flattened out with surprise when they hear that I answered my own phone.

Here was the Mammoths starting line up on Opening Day in 1952.

3b	Gonzalez
cf	Judkins
lf	V. Carucci
1b	Goldman
rf	P. Carucci
ss	Jones
2b	Park
c	Traphagen
p	Wiggen

Where have they all went I do not know. George Gonzalez, third base and leading off, left American baseball in 1956 and returned to Cuba. Some time afterwards I heard him on the radio 1 night driving between New York and Perkinsville. Some body asked him what position he played. He said, "In U. S. A. baseball I was a third baseman but in Cuba as a patriotic player I play every thing but pitch." Lucky Judkins, center field, was soon traded away, played awhile else where, left baseball in 1957 and to the best of my knowledge lives in Oklahoma to the present day.

Vincent Carucci, left field, owns a mortuary house in San Francisco. You see his advertisement on all the bill boards there. At baseball dinners he gives out little cards that look like the bill boards. When the freezer girl was all over the news he give me a phone call warning me she was a fraud, which I already knew but thanked him all the same. "Author," he said, "have your self buried in the earth, not in no fucking refridge."

Sid Goldman, first base, quit baseball in 1960, went to work for President Kennedy, run for City Council of New York and lost, run for Borough President of Manhattan and lost, run for Congress from Manhattan and lost, run for Mayor of New York and lost, and at the present writing is the director of athletics at a small college up state.

Pasquale Carucci, right field, brother of Vincent, sat on the bench at the end of his career. It was a sad sight to see. He was very unhappy and sat with his head in his hands. He felt that he should of been used. He felt that Dutch was *prejudice* against him, that it was an *injustice*. The first time Dutch asked my opinion on any subject what so ever he asked me, "What do you think of Pasquale these days?"

Maybe this was 1958, 1959. Well, I was always deeply grateful to Pasquale the way he went back for fly balls. No body caught fly balls better going away on the run or got the ball back in faster or was less afraid of the fences. He stared them down and I do not think he ever really run in to 1. But as time went by he could not turn and run back any more as good as he formerly could, and so he no longer played so shallow, and line drives he formerly caught while shallow fell in for base hits. "There been no injustice," I told Pasquale 1 time. "Dutch is prejudice against *every* body. If you are human he hates you," and Pasquale laughed a little at that, but not much. Soon he quit or was released and I and him and several other persons ate dinner together 1 night before his air plane to the Coast. I shook hands with him in front of the hotel, saying we would meet again, etc., and he replied, "If life lasts." I heard on good authority that he and Vincent fell out very badly over a business matter and stopped talking for ever. They were totally different. But when I meet Vincent 1 place or another and ask him, "How is Pasquale and why does he always stay home?" he smashes me on the back replying, "Pasquale was never greater, we are the happiest living family," but I know that is not true. Next time I will ask him for the truth if I have the courage.

Ugly Jones, shortstop, dropped from sight.

Gene Park, second base, also dropped from sight. He retired from baseball about 1960 and went home to California. A year or 2 later I met him at some sort of a get together where a fellow sold me a share in a children's game played with dice and cards and a spinning arrow called "Heads Up Baseball." The fellow said if we would put some cash in it and put our name on it we would make a lot of money. Maybe it never made a *lot* of money, but it made *some,* and I receive checks very regularly for my self and another check for Gene Park since the fellow has no address for Gene and neither do I. I put it in the bank and leave it draw interest like Suicide Alexander's account, only smaller. This been many years now. My daughter Rosemary said she believed Jones and Park were swallowed up in the Bermuda Triangle. This was at the time the Bermuda Triangle was big in the news.

Red Traphagen, catcher, taught me a great deal about baseball. In 1953 he retired, returning to San Francisco and teaching in the university there, where he been ever since. We write back and forth every year or 2 and we visit. I consider us close. Holly has wrote about Rosemary Traphagen in her book in title *Baseball Wives*. Red him self wrote several books I am sorry to say I never read except 1 in title *Backing Up First*, his own auto biography, mentioning me as follows. Notice the terrific writing. I never realized it till this minute what a clever title it was.

I have expressed my aversion to superlatives. Nevertheless, the "best" pitcher I ever caught was Henry Wiggen.

We played together during the last year of my career, at the blossoming of his. We were twelve years apart in age—one baseball generation. I think I first knew how very good he was going to be following a small incident during our year together. He pitched a pitch. The umpire called it a ball. It was a day that had not been going well for me, and I leaped upon the umpire, as one leaps upon someone—anyone—on days not going well. To my surprise, Henry came impatiently down the line, anxious to return to work, bawling at me, "Aw, fuck it, Red, it missed." It was not that he did not wish the pitch to have been a strike. It was not even that he would have morally objected to its being called wrong in his favor—wrong calls even up. It was only that he had so keen an eye for every action of his own that he hated its distortion, whether for better or for worse.

He had the instincts of a crayfish. He came with talent and desire and health. But to deliver work so good over so long a period of time requires also an independence of character sufficient to resist the mockery of people who, never having dared an art, remain ignorant of its demands. In this independence he was encouraged by his wife, Holly, a woman of wisdom and toleration and a genius in endurance; to each other they have been equally loyal and faithful; and by their four daughters Henry as father has been viewed with mingled respect and amusement.

As pitcher, he saw the game whole, the point and purpose of it. The idea of every game was not personal distinction but winning. Knowing this, he achieved both victory and distinction. Performance absorbed him. He *enjoyed* playing baseball, savoring the phenomenon of his own accruing skill. That he pitched for a full five years after his fast ball was gone testifies to his wit, wisdom, humor, enthusiasm, and to the keenness of his analysis of the tricks and realities of the art of pitching against savage hitters.

The game was a game, but life was not. He was oppressed by inequality and injustice, awed by the idea that while he was playing baseball other young men were dying in Vietnam. Many people told him it was "bad for baseball" to speak out. "Don't rock the boat," they said. But he could not resist speaking when occasions presented themselves.

"Ladies and Gentle Men. Your Attention Please. Our National Anthem." We all stood. Ev McTaggart was still walking back to the dugout with his hands in his pockets. He did not know whether he should stop or continue. There fore he stopped and removed his hat and kept walking a few steps but changed his mind and finally stopped all together, and ½ way through the song he remembered to take his other hand out of his pocket. The song ended and the cheering rose. Usually the voice of the umpire follows, calling "Play ball," but on this day the loud speaker spoke again, saying, "Ladies and Gentle Men. Your Attention Please. In honor of the late Dutch Schnell, whose name for 45 years was associated with the New York Mammoths Baseball Club, Inc., may we remain standing for 1 minute of respect full silence." We all stood standing.

I felt many eyes on our box. Only Millie Schnell stood sitting, looking down on her hands folded in her lap. I was glad I had wore the blue pin stripe instead of the flaming shirt. I remember smelling Barbara's perfume. Millie did not cry. Patricia cried like she cried at the funeral, but I was not angry at her now as I been before, nor angry at Ev McTaggart standing there with his hat still off and his 1 hand back in his pocket.

Soon the loud speaker spoke once more, saying, "Ladies and Gentle Men. Your Attention Please. May we ask Mr. Henry Wiggen to throw the baseball in to play," where before the sentence was out of the loud speaker's mouth the cheering of the crowd rose again. Dutch was forgot. I could feel it. In ½ a second all the people present turned their thought from Dutch to the next item on the program, like Hilary at the funeral thinking of nothing but the Gate Way Arch. I hated the fans. I would of loved their cheering better if I didn't know it might change to hatred and booing in another ½ a second. I sat down beside Millie, kissing her hard and sincerely and holding her close and the crowd begun to stir, becoming restless and wondering, "Well, where is he?" and I stood up and slipped off my blazer and laid it across Barbara's lap. I left my self out of the Owners Box and begun walking to the pitcher's box. I rolled up my sleeve while I walked. The cheering was very loud. If I had wore a hat I would of touched it, but wearing no hat I waved my hand instead. This felt extremely peculiar. I never before *waved* to people in a ball park. I felt insincere. Who was I waving at? I took the ball and rubbed it up and the cheering rose higher and higher. I stepped on the mound, looking in to my catcher for my sign, like this was the real thing. In my book in title *The Southpaw* I tell where Red Traphagen said to me, Opening Day, 1952, standing listening to the anthem, "Good luck, Henry, this is for the money," but today was not for the money. It was only an older ball player now retired looking in for his sign from a catcher whose name he could not even remember from September. He was the boy I pitched 2 innings to the night Dr. Schiff come to the ball game. I wound up and pitched to him and fell down.

I fell to 1 knee only, really. It must of looked worse from the seats. I popped right up again. But it could not of looked worse than it felt, falling down in the wrong clothes, all alone in front of a large crowd. The crowd first gasped. Then it laughed. Then it suddenly stopped laughing and begun cheering and applauding. Where the ball went I never knew. Every thing was standing still. No body was in motion. Suddenly from the first base side this boy Beansy Binz called out to me, "Throw it again, Author, go ahead, do it, do it," holding up a ball he was waiting to come on and pitch with, and he threw it to me and I stepped on the mound again. He was a quick thinker and I appreciated it. It was Beansy Binz actually first made me think about becoming a short relief. I should of thanked him for mentioning the idea to me, but I never did.

The reason I fell down was this. I was wearing a pair of tassel mocs by Bally. They were never meant for baseball. Maybe I should of threw from the Owners Box. But I didn't, and it never for a 1/1,000,000 of a second entered my mind to think about shoes. Who ever thought about shoes? Shoes were *on*. I pitched 4,815 innings of big league baseball and never walked out in the wrong shoes. I am not knocking Bally shoes. They are $80 shoes good for many things. I stepped off the mound where I had fell down and dug a quick hole with my toe in the grass and pitched from the hole, whipping the ball in with good speed to the catcher whose name I still can not remember. Maybe it will come to me. The crowd cheered and the umpire called out, "Play ball," and then it was for the money again, but not mine.

•••

Eric Rolfe Greenberg (b. 1945) worked in publicity for both Columbia Pictures
and the *National Lampoon* before publishing his first and only novel, *The Celebrant* (1983), the story of a relationship between the great Giants' pitcher
Christy Mathewson and a family of Jewish immigrant jewelers. Greenberg
envisioned this story of gods and heroes and children as more of a religious
novel than a baseball novel, and to this end he appropriated the tragic Mathewson, the model citizen-athlete from the early days of baseball, as a martyr
figure. The following is the beginning of a unique and widely admired novel.

Eric Rolfe Greenberg

♢

from

The Celebrant

Our family came to New York in the winter of '89, and in the
spring I saw my first game of baseball. I was eight. My mother's
brother, a jeweler, had preceded us across the Atlantic; Uncle Sid's
family was small—only four children—but the crowding was awful,
and in April my father thought to find a place of our own across the
river in Brooklyn. He inquired of a German-speaking landlord near
Prospect Park, who asked if there were children; my father answered
"nine," the German nodded, and the two men shook hands. The
following Sunday we stacked all we owned onto a rented dray and,
daunted by the spectacular height of the new bridge, crossed the river
by ferry. We returned before nightfall, much abashed. The German
had understood my father to say he had no children, and when he
arrived with nine the door was slammed in his face.

I missed this famous encounter. I'd run off to the park after my
older brother Eli and discovered there clay diamonds cut into an immense field of grass, an expanse so generous that half a dozen ballgames were underway at once, some so distant that they appeared
contests between toy miniatures. But toy players could hardly have
amazed me more than these—adults! grown men playing games!
—and many in uniforms complete with gaudy striped stockings.
Far away a bat struck a ball; seconds later I heard the sound. This

522

phenomenon was a great excitement, and I ran back and forth alter-
ing the time lapse until I was nearly trampled by an outfielder in furious pursuit of a fly ball. I dodged as he sprang, and as he stretched out
in full flight the side of his shoe caught my cheek. I reeled and fell
down. The ball bounded on, and the man who'd kicked me spat dirt
from his mouth, looked up, and said, "Well, *shit!*"—the first words
ever spoken to me on a ballfield.

The family stayed in Manhattan. We found the game everywhere,
in every imaginable variation. There were large lots along both rivers
which allowed the full exercise, and each street and alley had its own
rules and exceptions. First by imitation, then by practice, we learned
the game and the ways of the boys who played it, the angle of their
caps, the intonations of their curses and encouragements. Our ac-
cents disappeared, our strides became quick and confident. My left-
handedness, regarded by my parents as a devil's curse, turned to my
advantage in the pitcher's box. I threw a submarine ball, my knuckles
grazing the dirt as I released it. "Get those knuckles dirty, Jackie!" my
infielders would shout—Jackie, not Yakov.

The new fashion of overhand pitching soon threatened my eminence. When the National League legalized the pitch the neighborhood clubs followed suit; I tried the style but had trouble keeping
the ball low, and it's the high pitch that's hit a distance. Our team
enlisted a big fellow who could throw the overhand pitch with mustard, and to counter his advantage I attempted to learn the curve. It
was accounted a disreputable pitch, the refuge of a trickster who had
not the honest strength to power the ball over the plate. I found it
difficult, for my fingers were too short to give the ball sufficient spin.
Soon I was in the outfield, not liking the change; pitching is the core
of the game. Vowing to master the curve, I threw to Eli for an hour
every evening in the narrow alley behind our tenement. The youngsters on the block would come out and carry on as if I were pitching
for the Giants against the Orioles for the Temple Cup: "Keeler's up,
Jackie, watch it now! Ball one—come on, put it over! The curve, the
curve! Oh, he hit it! Base hit! Now Jennings—better bear down,
Jackie! McGraw's on deck!"

Finally, at fifteen, I made the curve ball work. I threw it as hard as
the fast one, and it broke just as it reached the plate, a small break but
a sharp one, straight down. It was a ground ball pitch, and it kept my

infielders busy. In tandem with the big fellow I won a good many ballgames and achieved something of a neighborhood celebrity.

At the close of the '97 season the league sponsored an awards dinner at a restaurant on Grand Street, and there I shook hands with a major league player. His name was Jack Warner. I'd watched him play shortstop for an uptown semiprofessional club, marveling at his size and power, but he lacked speed, and the professional leagues had made him first an outfielder, then a catcher. His face showed the marks of that ignoble position. At the dinner, his eyes never leaving the page, he delivered a speech analogizing baseball and life. Practice, dedication, clean living, and fair play—these guaranteed success on and off the field. We froze in a handshake while a photographer immortalized the moment, and then I took a silver cup from him. He turned to the organizer of the event and asked for his fee.

In the spring I was asked to a professional try-out at Manhattan Field, far uptown. Men with leather faces and tobacco-stained teeth examined me microscopically and stood in at bat as I pitched. A week later a letter arrived, the first I'd ever received, offering a contract with the Altoona club of the New York–Pennsylvania League.

My parents wouldn't hear of it.

Prizefighters, jockeys, ballplayers: these were professional athletes. Most celebrated were the fighters at the championship level; heavyweight Corbett could get a room at most hotels, and it was said that the better people of San Francisco welcomed him to their salons. The exemplary Gentleman Jim thus crossed once impregnable barriers, but the gulf between his status and that of the journeyman was vast. Club fighters were neighborhood heroes, yet the unspoken assumption was that they fought because they were unfit to do anything else; a man did not opt for the ring, he was condemned to it. Most jockeys were black, apprenticed to trainers or breeders; one thought of them as one thought of the horses they rode. Some professional ballplayers were locally bred, but an increasing number were itinerants from distant farmlands who lived out of cardboard suitcases in back street boarding houses. Annually they jumped from league to league and team to team for the sake of a few dollars increase in salary. To bankers and landlords and shopkeepers they were suspect, disreputable; to a man with daughters they were dangerous. An underclass supported them. Ballpark crowds were mean and roistering.

I was seventeen, and done with school; I'd stayed at it longer than most. All the pressure of a family's traditions, hopes, and plans pressed down upon me. I was the fifth son; the first had driven teams to put the second through college, and the third, Eli, sold my Uncle Sid's jewelry to see the fourth through his studies. I was obliged to provide for young Sam's higher education. I argued that I could do this on a ballplayer's salary, twenty dollars a month, but though my parents came to believe that I'd actually be paid to play ball the issue went far deeper than money. We had not crossed the ocean to find disgraceful employment.

I had not the wherewithal to resist my parents. Rather than be dead to them—for my father threatened to turn his back to me and say a kaddish for my soul—I put away the contract and assumed Eli's position at Uncle Sid's jewelry store, while Eli packed a case of samples and sought markets in faraway cities. I was no sales clerk, nor as proficient as my cousins in working the precious metals and stones, but I did show a flair for design. Should a customer find nothing on display to his liking, I'd inquire what he had in mind and quickly sketch a model; often enough, a sale would result. Once I turned this trick to delight a trio of sisters who were shopping for an anniversary present for their parents. When the piece was done I delivered it to their home, far uptown in Turtle Bay—and what a home, a mansion with fantastic wrought-iron fencing at the doors and windows and an interior elegance which to my mind quite belied the small *mezuzah* posted at the entry. That Jews could achieve such grandeur was well nigh unbelievable.

The next week the youngest of the daughters returned to the shop to thank me and to order another piece. She was merry; she kept me so long at the sketch pad with her suggestions and alterations that Uncle Sid had to bustle us out of the store at closing time. I escorted her home by trolley, and learned her name—Edith—while she learned of me everything I could babble in an hour. When our club played in Central Park the following Sunday she was there with her sisters; they carried matching parasols that spun prettily in their gloved hands. I pitched well that day, breaking off the curve ball time after time. Afterward we shared lemonade in the Ramble.

The next day I could hardly lift my arm. The curve ball was proving too great a strain. I needed a week between turns, and soon that wasn't enough. In the end I was back in the outfield, where the dream of Altoona and the big leagues faded. Playing less, I found time for afternoons with Edith; often I had to choose between her company at a concert or museum and Eli's for a ballgame. Once my brother had offered to escort all three Sonnheim girls to the Polo Grounds; the suggestion scandalized Edith's father, who coldly opined that baseball had ceased to be a gentleman's game after the Civil War, when it had been taken over by professional athletes. Might as well recommend a tour of the Tenderloin!

In deep summer, with Edith at her family's lodge on Lake George, I was ever at the ballpark—the new Polo Grounds, where the Giants were declining from their glory years of the early 'Nineties, or more frequently the Atlantic Avenue park in Brooklyn to watch the Superbas, stocked with Baltimore veterans, driving to the championships of '99 and 1900. Eli would introduce me to his sporting friends as his "expert" and make a great show of consulting me in whispers before placing a bet. It seemed he required a wager to excite his interest, whereas for me the game was all.

As the spring of 1901 turned toward summer, Eli urged me to join him on his annual "big swing" west to the Mississippi, north to Chicago, and east along the Lakes. "Sport, we'll eat a steak and see a ballgame in every city!" he swore. Uncle Sid accepted Eli's contention that my designs would be improved with a better knowledge of our markets, and Edith was away. I bought a suitcase—leather, not cardboard—and packed for my first excursion beyond the Hudson. Our first calls were in Philadelphia, where the steaks weren't much to speak of and the ballgame worse. The National League club was on the road, and we decided to test the infant American League, which had no New York franchise. The great attraction was Napoleon Lajoie, whose batting average for the Americans was a hundred points above what he'd hit for Philadelphia's Nationals the year before. His outrageous success seemed proof of the new league's inferiority. Nap was one of several former collegians courted for the club by Philadelphia's gaunt manager, Connie Mack; another was Plank, who pitched that day and easily beat the Milwaukee entry. Lajoie had three hits and scored twice.

We caught up with the Philadelphia Nationals in Pittsburgh. They missed Lajoie; the home club beat them authoritatively to move further ahead in the race. In Cincinnati dwelt a cadet branch of the family, and we stayed nearly a week. A second cousin whose face was a startling female approximation of my brother Sam's took me on an outing along the river and somehow contrived a rainstorm, a sheltering toolshed, and a blanket, but she could not contrive a different face, and the matter came to nothing. To my joy, the Cincinnati Red Stockings arrived for the latter part of our visit, and with them our own wonderful Brooklyn club, Ned Hanlon and his boys, the defending world champions. But the club was fading, the old Baltimore heroes further past their prime, and we sensed there would be no pennant flying over Atlantic Park at year's end.

On a Saturday morning in mid-July we stepped off the west-bound train into the heat of St. Louis and proceeded to the Chase Hotel. My brother always put up at the best hotels, signing as "E. Kapp." The name Kapinski would not be welcome on those registers. As I unpacked he searched out sheaths of the hotel's stationery and addressed invitations to the buyers of the town, requesting the honor of their presence at our "suite" on the Monday following. That done, he summoned an assistant manager to lay plans for breakfast, midmorning, and luncheon service: oysters and champagne, deviled eggs, a variety of sausage to suit the Swiss and Germans among our clientele. (Later Eli would cadge some kosher delicacies for our coreligionists, some of whom would first set foot in the Chase at our invitation.) He would welcome them all; he would tell the latest tales and gags; he would profess that, had he a choice, he would visit them at their offices, but to carry his samples on the dangerous streets was to court dire attack; he would show his wares and write his orders. In such ways did Eli advance the family business as it increasingly turned from retailing to manufacture. A middle-range market was emerging between the jeweler's private customer and the mail-order public, and the avenue to it was the department store. Our product line was priced below the artisan's custom work and above the C.O.D. merchandise that Eli accurately described as cheap junk. His job was to secure outlets against the efforts of dozens of direct competitors, and he shared the rails with a gaggle of salesmen hawking hardware or hose or outrageous feathered wraps; together they were inventing the business of the new century. Not all stayed at the grand hotels, but my brother would have put up at the Chase (or Boston's St. James or Baltimore's Belvedere) had his suitcase carried sandstone or cement.

Yet for all this show, his delight was to invite guests to the local ballpark. He'd staked this out as his personal form of business entertainment, leaving the burlesques and bawdy houses to his fellows of the selling trade. Here professional calculation matched his personal inclination. For himself, Eli Kapinski of New York, no fancy out-of-town attraction could rival those of home, but a major league ball-game in any city carried a sort of guarantee. For his clients—what a disarming suggestion! An afternoon at the ballpark, so refreshing, so American!

Shortly before three o'clock on a cauterizing Monday we rented a hack, collected three buyers who'd breakfasted with us that morning, and set out for League Park. St. Louis in July was the hottest place on the circuit, the hottest place God ever made a city. Our guests blamed the heat for the team's sorry record in the National League; they'd never finished above fifth place. I pointed out that the city's entry had won four championships in the old American Association in the 'Eighties. "Mildest summers on record," I was assured. This season their club had known early success but now, beset by slump and injury, they were losing ground to Pittsburgh. Still the fans prayed for a cool summer and came to League Park in record number; more than twenty thousand, an unprecedented gathering, had encircled the field for the previous game of the current series with the New York Giants.

In the matter of rooting, a boy's first team is his team forever. I'd seen my first big-league game below Coogan's Bluff ten years before, and whatever Brooklyn's current success the Giants were the club of my heart, their championships my own. But seven years' famine had followed the feast, and a dozen managers had come and gone under the club's owner, Tammany politico Andrew Freedman. A great war was waged between Freedman and my own idol, Amos Rusie, the huge righthander who'd won thirty-six games in glorious '94. Rusie refused to sign a contract in '96, came back to win forty-eight games for a lesser club in '97 and '98, and then held out for two full seasons rather than throw another pitch for Freedman. He called the owner a liar, a chiseler, a welcher, and a cheat; Freedman called Rusie a Republican. They were both right. Without Rusie or any other player of great regard the Giants finished last in 1900. They'd re-placed most of their infield and half their mound staff, but their current fifth place standing owed largely to the advent of a talented collegiate pitcher of their own, a righthander who was scheduled to throw for New York.

Play had just begun when we arrived at League Park. We watched from the outfield as the Giants mounted an early attack. Sudhoff, the elfin St. Louis pitcher, began badly: a walk, a base hit, and then a drive that skipped under the right fielder's glove and rolled to our feet. The tallest of our clients, a thin man with merry eyes, kicked the ball back toward the fielder. Far away, in the middle of the diamond, the umpire threw up his hands and shouted "Hold! Three bases!" Two Giants scored, and we moved with haste to the grandstand, a single-tiered wooden structure that rose along both foul lines. Having paid a quarter a head to enter the Park grounds, we were now charged as much again to gain the grandstand and needed fifty cents more for box seats beneath the low, shading roof. But an attendant at the box-seat turnstile swore there was no room for us in the shade, and when Eli protested he scolded us with Irish vigor: "You want to come out early these days, we're winning now, don't you know!" Finally we found room behind third base for three on one grandstand bench and for two more directly behind. The thin client and a bearded one flanked Eli while the stoutest squeezed in next to me. We doffed our jackets and loosened our collars. The Giants had scored no more, and the teams had changed sides. Little Jess Burkett stood in for St. Louis, hands high on the bat, feet spread wide. Behind him Patsy Donovan, who doubled as manager, picked at the tape around the handle of his bat. The sun burned down, the cries of the crowd floated in the humid air, and the umpire pointed a finger at the New York pitcher and bid him throw.

This pitcher was big—gigantic, compared to Wee Willie Sudhoff—yet his motion matched Sudhoff's for balance and ease until he pushed off the pitcher's slab with his right foot and drove at the plate with startling power. His follow-through ended in a light skip, and he finished on his toes, his feet well apart, his hands at the ready for a fielding play. I heard the umpire's call but didn't know if Burkett had swung and missed or taken the strike, for my eyes hadn't left the pitcher. He took the catcher's return throw and regained the hill in three strides. His broad shoulders and back tapered to a narrow waist; he wore his belt low on his hips, and his legs appeared taut and powerful beneath the billowing knickers of his uniform. A strong, muscular neck provided a solid trunk for a large head, and his cap was tipped rather far back on his forehead, revealing a handsome face and an edge of thick, light brown hair. He bent for his sign, rolled into his motion, and threw; this time I followed the ball and saw Burkett top it foul.

The fat man moved against me, reaching for his kerchief. "Who's your pitcher?" he asked.

"It's Mathewson," I said. "Christy Mathewson."

"That's Mathewson? Big kid!"

"He is that. He's bigger than Rusie, that's for sure."

"Throws hard."

"Yes, he does."

"He's winning for you, isn't he?"

"Eleven games, best on the club."

"Not bad for new corn."

"Actually, he pitched a few last year," I said.

"Win any?"

"No. As a matter of fact he lost two in relief. Then he went back to school."

Another fastball: Burkett's swing was late, and the ball bounced to first base. Ganzel gloved it and tossed underhand to Mathewson, who caught it in full stride and kicked the base for an out.

"He got over there in a hurry, too," the fat man observed.

"Hey, sport, take this and bring back some wieners and beer for us all, won't you?" said Eli, pushing a silver dollar into my hand. He winked and clapped my arm. "Hurry back now, I'm going to need your advice."

I struggled to the aisle and headed along the walkway that divided the grandstand benches from the box seats. As I reached the ramp I paused to watch Donovan at bat. His red face was lined with a manager's web of worry. Patsy fought off the pitches with short, choppy swings, hitting several foul before earning a base on balls. Ganzel met him at first, and they exchanged a greeting. Ganzel was ancient, nearly forty, and Donovan beside him looked as old. I scanned the Giants in the field: Strang and Hickman, on either side of second base, were no striplings, and Davis, New York's playing manager at third, was older yet. They were all past thirty in the outfield. The catcher was Jack Warner, he of the awards dinner years before; already he was a veteran of years. Schriver, ready at the bat for St. Louis— enough to say that they called Schriver "Old Pop." At the center stood Mathewson, young as an April morning in that sweltering July, and I, small in the crowd at the top of the ramp, turned and walked down into the shadow beneath the grandstand.

The vendors at their sizzling grills cursed loudly as fat spattered on their aprons. All about, sports in checkered vests argued, passed money, and wrote betting slips. Every inning, sometimes every pitch, was worth a wager. With my dollar I bought five pigs-in-a-blanket and as many bottles of beer, and pocketed two bits in change. I worked my way back up the ramp with some difficulty. Near our seats the fans came to my rescue, passing the food hand over hand to Eli with the efficiency of a fire brigade. I couldn't resist an urge to toss the quarter to my brother, who snared it backhanded. The section re-sounded with cheers, and the ballplayers on the field turned at the commotion.

"Still two-nothing, sport. Donovan was caught trying to steal. Hey, here we go again!" Eli cried as a base hit began the Giant second. But their game was all sock-and-run; after Strang's single, Warner flied out.

"They don't believe in the bunt, do they?" said the fat man.

"They won't win 'til they learn how," said Eli. "You've got to be able to lay it down, right, sport?"

"Here's Mathewson," I said. "He'll be bunting."

Eli looked at me. "A dollar says he brings off the sacrifice. All around?"

The clients accepted the wager. Sudhoff pitched, and Mathewson pushed the ball onto the grass and ran to first with the spritely grace of a smaller man. He was narrowly out.

"He can bunt," the thin man conceded.

"Double or nothing that they score," said Eli.

Sudhoff walked a man, and the next nailed the first pitch on a low line over second base. Two Giants crossed home.

"Double or nothing they score again!" said Eli. I pushed my knee into his back, but he looked over his shoulder and winked. The three buyers took the bet and cheered when a fly ball ended the inning and wiped out their debts. Mathewson walked slowly to the pitcher's mound, dug at the slab with his toe, smoothed the dust, and worked into his warm-ups. Again his size and youth impressed. The bearded man beside Eli studied him.

"Mathewson, his name is?"

"College kid," said Eli. "Connie Mack signed him for Philly, but he jumped to New York."

"Where's he from?"

"Pennsylvania," said Eli, at the same time that I said, "Bucknell College."

"Imagine a college man playing ball for a living!"

I mentioned Lajoie and Plank, whom we'd seen in Philadelphia, but the bearded man snorted that the new league would sign anyone, and while he knew Lajoie had played in a college uniform he doubted the boy had ever seen the inside of a classroom. Nor had Mathewson, he'd wager.

The fat man turned to me. "But you said he went back to school after last season!"

"Quit the team in September to do it," I said.

"You've seen him before?"

No, I explained; in recent seasons the more talented Brooklyn club had caught my fancy, and I hadn't been among the few at the Polo Grounds when the rookie threw his first big-league pitches that summer or won his first victories in the spring. What I knew of Mathewson came from notes in the newspapers: his age, a year greater than my own, and his home, the farming country of the Susquehanna Valley; his fame as a Bucknell foot-baller. I knew he'd pitched in professional leagues in New England and Virginia, and that while he'd put his name to a major league contract with Connie Mack he'd never worn a Philadelphia uniform. Instead he'd come to New York, and now, in his first full year, he had a third of the club's victories. If his skills were the test he belonged in the National League, but like the bearded client I wondered why a true collegian would choose the life of a professional ballplayer.

The second inning ended quickly, and while Sudhoff hit his stride in the third Eli began to orchestrate wagers with every batter. If I thought the proposition doubtful I'd signal by pressing my knee into his back, but he ignored my advice as often as he accepted it, and I came to understand that a deeper game was in progress. Eli was selling jewelry, and it wouldn't do to take too much of his clients' money. Each time he won he offered double or nothing on the next bet; at best he would finish little better than even, and at worst far worse. I engaged in chatter with the partisans around us when the Giants batted, or gazed over the midwestern crowd dotted with wide-brimmed western hats among the standard derbies and occasional boaters. Far down the right field line was the only uncrowded grand-stand section; there the coloreds sat in overalls and yellow straw hats. When St. Louis batted I studied Mathewson. He could throw hard, and with excellent control, shading the edges of the strike zone, mixing his fastball with a curve that seemed somehow erratic. Sometimes it fell an astonishing measure, while other times—what did it do? Certainly it behaved differently from the drop, but from our location I couldn't track the pitch. When St. Louis came to bat in the fifth inning I excused myself and threaded my way to a spot close behind home plate. Now I could see the inner game, the fierce battle between pitcher and batter where power and control sought mastery over instinct and guess.

Mathewson began against Padden with a pitch that came in hard at belt level and dropped abruptly and dramatically, a superb over-hand curve, and one which had wrenched my arm when I'd tried it. The second pitch was a fastball on the outside part of the plate, a second strike. Now another breaking ball, but so unlike the first, slower, and breaking in reverse, in the nature of a lefthander's curve; I'd never seen a righthander throw one. Nor had Padden, who swung late and was lucky to tip it foul. Padden stepped out of the box and shook his head like a man who'd just seen a rabbit leap out of his own hat. He took his stance a bit closer to the plate, leaning over to guard the outside corner. Then in an instant he was on his back in the dirt; comically, the bat landed on his head. Mathewson's fastball had re-claimed that disputed inside territory. Padden dusted off his knickers and took his stance farther off the plate. Mathewson stretched and threw another reverse curve, and Padden missed it badly. Strike three.

Mathewson worked through the St. Louis lineup just so. Always the first pitch was a strike, and usually the second; then a teasing pitch down low, or that strange fading curve thrown where no batter could hit it squarely, if at all. His rhythm and motion were balletic: a high kick, a swing of the hips, a stride forward, and finally the explosive release of the ball. There was intelligence as well as power behind the pitches: he had a four-run lead and found it to his purpose to walk Kruger with two out in the fifth and then retire the light-hitting Ryan, and to pass the dangerous Burkett in the sixth in favor of facing Donovan, who grounded out. When I rejoined Eli in the seventh inning Mathewson had allowed three baserunners, but no hits.

"Think they'll get to him, sport?"

I'd never witnessed a no-hit game. I'd come close to pitching one four years before, as close as the eighth inning, but a swinging bunt that squiggled up the first base line had foiled me, and in my disappointment I'd been racked for three runs. "He's doing pretty much what he wants," I said.

"A dollar says he gets by Schriver," Eli offered; the odds were heavily against a no-hitter, and betting with Mathewson seemed the safest way to protect the clients. Old Pop took a fastball for a strike, and the crowd booed. Its cries had taken on the anger of the heat and the temper of frustration. The fat man ground his cigar beneath his patent leather boot and muttered something about Schriver; the club missed its injured sluggers. Mathewson pitched, and Pop grounded weakly to Strang at second base. One out in the seventh.

"Double or nothing, all around?"

Now Padden again, and the first pitch a high strike, the second higher yet—but Padden had no wish to wait for another curve and swung, lifting a fly to center field where Van Haltren had hardly to move to glove it. Two outs now.

"Double or nothing?"

"It's a bet."

"What happens on a walk?" I asked.

"Do you think he'll pass him, sport?"

"He'll be careful with Wallace. It's his pattern."

Eli nodded. "I say he'll get him out. Double or nothing on an out." Mathewson's fastball flashed, and Wallace took it and jawed loudly at the umpire's strike call. Now that strange breaking pitch, and Wallace bounced it to third; he was out by two steps at first. The Giants came off the field as the crowd booed all the more, at Wallace, at the umpire, at the summer's merciless heat, at the cast of impending defeat.

The fat man tapped Eli on the shoulder. "It's four dollars now, right?"

"Two," said Eli.

"Four."

"No, the bet on Schriver brought us even."

"We were even before then. It's four."

"Well, if you insist," said Eli, laughing.

The Giants went down swiftly in the eighth, but New York's efforts at bat hardly mattered now; we wanted Mathewson pitching. In the St. Louis half he began with a strikeout, and the buyers' debts to Eli doubled to eight dollars apiece. The total was nearly a month's salary to me. Next was Ryan, hardly a threat; after taking two strikes he chased a high fastball and lifted it to the center fielder's range. Van Haltren loped easily across the grass and reached out to cradle it, but the web of his glove seemed to fail him, and the ball dropped at his feet.

Twenty thousand roared, but the fat man shook his head. "An error," he said.

"It's all the same," said Eli, attempting a mournful expression. "We're even."

"No, as far as I'm concerned, it's an out."

"The man's on second base," said Eli.

"But the bet is on a no-hit game, isn't it? The pitcher against the hitter. The man should have been retired. Now, double or nothing?"

It seemed it was a matter of integrity, for which the fat man had a reputation; when Eli made to forgive the debts of the men flanking him they proved no less upright than their colleague. They could play the inner game as well as my brother, for what might be lost in money was more than made in future favor. Word spread from the press benches that "error" was indeed the official call; the no-hitter was intact. Eli shifted ground: why not call the play "no bet"? The compromise was accepted, and the balance among the men reverted to eight dollars apiece.

While the party debated I studied Mathewson. He showed no annoyance in the wake of the misplay. His team still led by four runs, the inning was late, and the weak-hitting Nichols was at bat with pitcher Sudhoff to follow. Mathewson set, glanced at the baserunner, and threw. Nichols' bunt was a surprise; the score, the inning, the pitcher on deck all argued against it. Catcher Warner was slow to move after the ball, but Mathewson was upon it instantly, the ball in his glove, then in his hand, then at first base. Two outs, and sixteen dollars due to Eli from each of his clients.

"Double or nothing?"

Sudhoff, the little pitcher, hit the ball sharply, but Mathewson snatched it out of the air and the inning was over. At the Giant bench Mathewson greeted center fielder Van Haltren with a forgiving slap on the rump. He was far more cheerful than Eli, a man due ninety-six dollars of easy money. When Mathewson batted in the Giant ninth he was applauded by the home fans, and I cheered. Mathewson tugged at the bill of his cap in acknowledgment. "Imagine, a college kid!" said the bearded client. Most of the crowd had conceded the game, and many would prefer a defeat of special regard to a spoiling single in the home ninth. For myself, I wanted three clean outs and a glorious end; our clients' purses were of no matter.

"Double or nothing?"

Burkett led off. Mathewson started with a fastball; for the hundredth time he took Warner's return throw and climbed the mound. On the right knee of his knickers was a round smudge of red clay, the emblem of a hundred strides and a hundred pitches launched. He bent, stretched, and pitched again, a fastball in on Burkett's hands; it ticked the bat and sailed past Warner, who walked slowly in the heat to retrieve it.

"Oh, college boy! Oh, you college boy!"

Mathewson stood on the hill waiting for the catcher to return to position, his left leg slightly bent, his weight on the right. He gloved Warner's toss and bent for his sign, the ball resting in the pocket of his small brown glove. He seemed as fresh as when he had begun, and quite still: no heaving breath, no sleeve drawn across his face to clear the summer sweat. All question left me. This was Mathewson's place and moment; my whole being was with him. Burkett would not deny him, nor Donovan next, nor old Pop Schriver, that dark moving figure on the St. Louis bench.

"So young!" muttered the bearded man.

And I was old, I thought. I was older than Mathewson, older than Schriver, older than any of them in uniform. My youth had ended on a ragged lot by the Hudson when the curve ball had beaten my arm and my spirit—no, when I'd folded the contract into a drawer and reported for work at Uncle Sid's shop. I was on the road, yes, but as an old man, hawking samples in old men's hotels, learning how I might bet to keep old men happy. I watched Mathewson, and he became my youth; it was my fastball burning by Burkett, it was my curve that little Jess lifted to the outfield, and after the ball came back and around the infield I felt it was my glove closing around it, my arm that launched the fastball at Donovan's knees and the next that cut the black of the plate on the outside. My youth made him chase a breaking ball in the dirt, and there were two outs; here was Old Pop, and I had the game and the no-hitter in my hand.

Curve ball: Schriver lets it pass for a strike.

The other, fading curve: Schriver, off balance, swings and ticks the ball foul. Ganzel picks it up barehanded and throws it to me. Schriver is nervous; I see his hands moving on the bat, his heel twisting in the dirt.

I waste a pitch high, ball one. I take Warner's toss, wrap the ball in my glove, jam the package under my arm, reach for the resin, dust my hand. There is a lone incomprehensible cry from the grandstand, then silence. I turn, I bend, I look for Warner's sign. I toe the slab. I stretch. I throw.

Ground ball.

I reach; it is past me—but Strang is there, he takes it on a high bounce, he waits for Ganzel, old Ganzel, to set himself at first, he snaps a sidearm throw, and the ball disappears into Ganzel's mitt.

The crowd's hoarse voice rises in the heat, the Giant bench empties, the fielders race to the mound, and the team leaps to touch and embrace——

Mathewson.

Leroi Jones (b. 1934) grew up in Newark, New Jersey, went to college at Howard, lived in Greenwich Village and Harlem, and eventually returned to the city of his youth. He changed his name in 1965 as part of a radical redefinition of his goals as a writer and political activist that also found expression in poetry (*Black Magic*), plays (*Dutchman*), fiction (*The System of Dante's Hell*), essays (*Home*), and the 1984 memoir from which this excerpt is taken.

Amiri Baraka

ᐁ

from

The Autobiography of Leroi Jones

But the specialest feeling was when my father took me down to Ruppert Stadium some Sundays to see the Newark Eagles, the black pro team. Very little in my life was as heightened (in anticipation and reward) for me as that. What was that? Some black men playing baseball? No, but beyond that, so deep in fact it carried and carries memories and even a *politics* with it that still makes me shudder.

Ruppert Stadium was "Down Neck," down below the station, in the heavy industrial section, and then mostly whites, including the Portuguese, lived down there. But we were never really thinking about that when we went there. The smell or smells, and I always associate them with Newark, could be any wild thing. Sometimes straight-out rotten eggs, fart odor, or stuff for which there was no known identification. Just terrible Newark Down Neck smell.

But coming down through that would heighten my sense because I could dig I would soon be standing in that line to get in, with my old man. But lines of all black people! Dressed up like they would for going to the game, in those bright lost summers. Full of noise and identification slapped greetings over and around folks. Cause after all in that town of 300,000 that 20 to 30 percent of the population (then) had a high recognition rate for each other. They worked together, lived in the same neighborhoods, went to church (if they did) together, and all the rest of it, even played together.

The Newark Eagles would have your heart there on the field, from what they was doing. From how they looked. But these were professional ball players. Legitimate black heroes. And we were intimate with them in a way and they were extensions of all of us, there, in a way that the Yankees and Dodgers and what not could never be!

We knew that they *were* us—raised up to another, higher degree. Shit, and the Eagles, people knew, talked to before and after the game. That last fabulous year they were World Champs of the black leagues. The Negro National League. We was there opening day, jim, and Leon Day pitched a no-hitter! Opening day! And the bloods threw those seat cushions all over Ruppert Stadium and the white folks (also owners of the New York Yankees) who owned that stadium wouldn't let us have the things after that. We noted it (I know I did) but it didn't stop nothin.

That was the year they had Doby and Irvin and Pearson and Harvey and Pat Patterson, a schoolteacher, on third base, and Leon Day was the star pitcher, and he showed out opening day! But coming into that stadium those Sunday afternoons carried a sweetness with it. The hot dogs and root beers! (They have never tasted that good again.) A little big-eyed boy holding his father's hand.

There was a sense of completion in all that. The black men (and the women) sitting there all participated in those games at a much higher level than anything else I knew. In the sense that they were not excluded from either identification with or knowledge of what the Eagles did and were. It was like we all communicated with each other and possessed ourselves at a more human level than was usually possible out in cold whitey land.

Coming in that stadium with dudes and ladies calling out, "Hey, Roy, boy he look just like you." Or: "You look just like your father." Besides that note and attention, the Eagles there were something *we* possessed. It was not us as George Washington Carver or Marian Anderson, some figment of white people's lack of imagination, it was us as we wanted to be and how we wanted to be seen being looked at by ourselves in some kind of loud communion.

And we *knew*, despite the newspapers and the radio, who that was tearing around those bases. When we saw Mule Suttle or Josh Gibson or Buck Leonard or Satchel Paige and dug the Homestead Greys, Philadelphia Stars, New York Black Yankees (yes!), Baltimore Elite (pronounced E-Light) Giants, Kansas City Monarchs, Birmingham Black Barons, and even the Indianapolis Clowns! We knew who that was and what they (we) could do. Those other Yankees and Giants and Dodgers we followed just to keep up with being in America. We had our likes and our dislikes. "Our" teams. But for the black teams, and for us Newarkers, the Newark Eagles, was pure *love.*

We were wilder and calmer there. Louder and happier, without hysteria. Just digging ourselves stretch out is what and all that love and noise and color and excitement surrounded me like a garment of feeling. I know I thought that's the way life was supposed to be.

And my father was a part of that in a way that he was part of nothing else I knew. The easy comradeship among the spectators, but he even knew some of the players. And sometimes after the games he'd take me around to the Grand Hotel (used to be on West Market Street), right down the street from our church. Right next to the barbershop my father took me to. (And going to that barbershop was almost as hip as going to the Grand or the games. Them niggers was arguin in there one day about something and one guy mentions something that MacArthur had said and another dude, some old black man, said there wasn't no such thing as MacArthur! That has *always* blown my mind, what that meant!)

At the Grand Hotel, the ball players and the slick people could meet. Everybody super-clean and highlifin, glasses jingling with ice, black people's eyes sparklin and showin their teeth in the hippest way possible.

You could see Doby and Lennie Pearson and Pat Patterson or somebody there and I'd be wearin my eyes and ears out drinking a Coca-Cola, checking everything out.

The movies I dearly dug but you never got to go behind the screen and shake hands with the heroes. But at the Grand Hotel you could and my old man saw that I did.

It was black life that was celebrated by being itself at its most unencumbered. Mrs. Effa Manley, who owned the team, would even come through and Baba or somebody would buy her a drink. Or my father would push me forward for an introduction and Monte Irvin would bend down and take my little hand in his and, jim, I'd be all the way out.

In the laughter and noise and colors and easy hot dogs there was something of us celebrating ourselves. In the flying around the bases and sliding and home runs and arguments and *triumphs* there was more of ourselves in celebration than we were normally ever permitted. It was *ours*. (Not just the ownership of the teams, the Negro National League, though that had to be in it too.) But our expression unleashed for our and its own sake. It made us know that the Mantans and Stepin Fetchits and Birminghams were clowns—funny, but obviously used against us for some reason. Was it a big creep in a white hood somewhere in charge of trying to make black people feel bad? I thought so. But the clowns we knew were scarecrows, cardboard figures somebody was putting out trying to make us feel bad. Cause we knew, and we knew, that they wasn't us. Just clowns. Somebody got hooked up. We was out on the field at Ruppert Stadium, jim. And we was even up in the stands diggin it. Laid back in a yellow shirt with the collar open and white pencil-stripe pants. We was in the sun with a hot dog and a root beer having our hands shook by one of our father's friends. We was cheering for Mule Suttle or seeing Larry Doby make a double play. We was *not* clowns and the Newark Eagles laid that out clear for anyone to see!

But you know, they can slip in on you another way, Bro. Sell you some hand magic, or not sell *you*, but sell somebody somewhere some. And you be standin' there and all of a sudden you hear about—what?—Jeckie Rawbeanson. I could tell right away, really, that the dude in the hood had been at work. No, really, it was like I heard the wheels and metal wires in his voice, the imperfected humanoid, his first words "Moy nayhme is Jeckie Rawbeanson." Some Ray Bradbury shit they had mashed on us. I knew it. A skin-covered humanoid to bust up our shit.

I don't want to get political and talk bad about "integration." Like what a straight-out trick it was. To rip off what you had in the name of what you ain't never gonna get. So the destruction of the Negro National League. The destruction of the Eagles, Greys, Black Yankees, Elite Giants, Cuban Stars, Clowns, Monarchs, Black Barons, to what must we attribute that? We're going to the big leagues. Is that what the cry was on those Afric' shores when the European capitalists and

African feudal lords got together and palmed our future. "WE'RE GOING TO THE BIG LEAGUES!"

So out of the California laboratories of USC, a synthetic colored guy was imperfected and soon we would be trooping back into the holy see of racist approbation. So that we could sit next to drunken racists by and by. And watch our heroes put down by slimy cocksuckers who are so stupid they would uphold Henry and his Ford and be put in chains by both while helping to tighten ours.

Can you dig that red-faced backwardness that would question whether Satchel Paige could pitch in the same league with . . . who?

For many, the Dodgers could take out some of the sting and for those who thought it really meant we was getting in America. (But that cooled out. A definition of pathology in blackface would be exactly that, someone, some Nigra, who thunk they was *in* this! Owow!) But the scarecrow J.R. for all his ersatz "blackness" could represent the shadow world of the Negro integrating into America. A farce. But many of us fell for that and felt for him, really. Even though a lot of us knew the wholly artificial disconnected thing that Jackie Robinson was. Still when the backward Crackers would drop black cats on the field or idiots like Dixie Walker (who wouldn't even a made the team if Josh Gibson or Buck Leonard was on the scene) would mumble some of his unpatented Ku Klux dumbness, we got uptight, for us, not just for J.R.

I remained a Giant "fan," cause me fadder was, even when J.R. came on the scene. I resisted that First shit (though in secret, you know, I had to uphold my own face, alone among a sea of hostile jerks!).

(So what? So Jeckie came on down to DC town and they got his ass to put Paul Robeson down! I remember that, out of the side of my head I checked that. I wondered. What did it mean? What was he saying? And was it supposed to represent me? And who was that other guy—Paul Robeson? I heard that name . . . somewhere.)

The Negro league's like a light somewhere. Back over your shoulder. As you go away. A warmth still, connected to laughter and self-love. The collective black aura that can only be duplicated with black conversation or *music*.

Robert Creamer (b. 1922) began covering baseball for *Sports Illustrated* in 1954, the year of that magazine's inception, and continued to write and edit *S.I.* articles about the game for more than thirty years. His carefully researched, clearly written lives of Babe Ruth—*Babe: The Legend Comes to Life* (1974)—and Casey Stengel—*Stengel: His Life and Times* (1984)—defined baseball biography as a genre. Creamer's introduction to *Stengel* offers an unforgettable image of an old man working in a young man's game.

Robert Creamer

◊

from

Stengel: His Life and Times

Casey Stengel naked was a sight to remember.

At seventy, holding court after a game for a retinue of sportswriters in his office off the New York Yankees' dressing room, he would in time begin to undress. He'd take off his uniform shirt and his spikes with the rubber heels, still making telling points in his heavy, gravelly, nonstop voice. He'd take off his uniform pants, pausing perhaps to gesture in his argument. He had a lot of gestures, little flips of the hand, pulling his forearm suddenly close to his chest, a curious way of raising his chin high, his mouth closed in a grim, serious line, his eyes half closed, as he listened to someone else. He'd go on undressing, taking off his long-sleeved baseball undershirt and his baseball stockings, taking off his underwear pants, taking off the athletic supporter he wore as though he too were going into action on the ball field.

Then, naked except for slippers, he'd march out of his office and through the players' locker room, a towel hanging from one arm like a toga, looking for all the world like a Roman senator on his way to the baths. You felt that he was accompanied by a covey of courtiers as he trudged on (although it was usually only one or two last writers trying to get a clear answer), his head held high, the fierce nose canted toward a distant horizon, the diminished buttocks of age following sadly after. His long-torsoed, short-legged body had an old, dead, pale tone, gray hair on his chest and at the crotch blending with the pallor of his skin, like old snow after a few days of residual fallout. The ravages of time had pulled and tweaked the muscles of his arms and legs and trunk, leaving gullies and ravines and potholes. His right leg, broken in an accident in Boston years before, had a startling clifflike protuberance halfway down the shin, where the broken ends of the tibia had grown together unevenly in the healing.

He was a bizarre spectacle, this naked old man parading through a room full of hard-muscled young athletes, but Stengel never gave a sign that he recognized the incongruity. On the contrary, he was vain about his body, even as an old man, as he was vain about many things. He loved to pose for photographers, mugging extravagantly, twisting his leathery face into grotesque winks, wearing odd bits of clothing for props, doing almost anything the photographers wanted when he was in the mood to do it. And he was something special for them to photograph, with his craggy seamed face, jutting jaw, wide mobile mouth, huge hooked nose, amazingly blue eyes, great pendulous ears, long arms, crabbed stooped body.

On the field he was almost quaint in appearance, wearing his uniform knickers tucked in at the knee, the way knickers should be worn, the way they were worn in his youth before the fashion changed and ballplayers began to extend the legs of their baseball pants almost to their ankles. And Casey wore his dark-blue Yankee outer stockings full-length, showing the barest cuticle of white understocking just above the shoes, whereas his players pulled up the stirrups of the outer stockings to the stretching point, so that they seemed to be wearing white socks with just a narrow black clock up the sides to the bottom of the uniform pants.

Stengel wore good clothes off the field, even though his ungainly figure and leathery, worn features tended to make his expensive suits look like something bought off the rack in a cheap men's store. He always looked rumpled in a baseball uniform, and when he put on street clothes he looked a little like the hired man decked out in his store-bought Sunday-go-to-meeting suit. Nonetheless, his clothes *were* expensive. He dyed his hair (he never admitted he did) in an effort to turn the encroaching whiteness to something closer to the blond-brown (mud-gutter blond, that shade used to be called) of his youth. In his seventies he still did push-ups on the floor of whatever hotel room he was staying in, and he was proud of the strength his tough old body retained. He'd grab your arm sometimes to hold your attention, and more often than not he'd give it a squeeze to emphasize an argument—or maybe just to hurt you a little, to make you wince or pull away, to remind you (or himself) of the strength he had when he was young. He had a cruel streak ("He's a funny guy," wrote his antagonist Dave Egan of the *Boston Record* in 1942, "always funny at somebody else's expense . . . always funny in his cruel and malicious way"), and he was not at all reluctant to enjoy another's discomfort. Some of his players hated him for that, but Stengel never seemed to mind their antipathy. He'd been around too long to be upset by transient dislikes.

Yet he had keen awareness of other people's dignity—those whose dignity, or right to dignity, he respected. During ceremonies before an old-timers' game in Yankee Stadium in 1954, when Stengel, then a relatively youthful sixty-four, was managing the Yankees, Connie Mack tottered onto the field to be introduced. Mack, ninety-two, had retired as manager of the Philadelphia Athletics only a few years before, after fifty consecutive seasons managing that team. It was a hot midsummer day, and Stengel, not yet the perennial part of old-timers' doings that he would be in later years, was in the tangle of people in the Yankee dugout—old ballplayers, current ballplayers, officials, reporters, hangers-on. After Mack had been introduced and applauded, he was left alone, blinking up at the huge crowd as other old-timers were introduced, one by one. No one seemed to notice Mack except Stengel, who stirred restlessly in the dugout and then prodded an aide. "Get that old man out of the sun," he said. Gently, without fuss, Mr. Mack was led off the field and into the shade of the dugout, where Stengel sat talking quietly with him while the ceremonies droned on.

Casey respected history—baseball history—and Mack was part of it. He liked everything about the game of baseball, all its subtleties and complexities, and he particularly admired people in the game who knew what they were doing and why they were doing it. On that same old-timers' day, Stengel stood up in the dugout to watch the two-inning exhibition game played by the heroes of the past, looking out at the field over the broad backs of his young Yankee players, most of whom were sitting up on the dugout steps to watch. The players grew particularly attentive when Joe DiMaggio batted against Carl Hubbell. Hubbell, a superb left-handed pitcher for the New York Giants twenty years earlier, was in his fifties and had been out of the game a long time. DiMaggio, barely forty, had retired only two or three years before and was still strong and capable, the hero of the day for the roaring stadium crowd and for the current Yankees, too, many of whom had been his teammates. Hubbell had a 2–0 lead, but there were two men on base.

DiMaggio was greeted with tumultuous applause, and the crowd waited for him to hit one a long way for old times' sake. Hubbell, still as lean and trim as he had been in his playing days, his pitching motion as elegant as ever, kept throwing screwballs to DiMaggio, pitches that broke down and away from the batter. DiMaggio, waiting for a ball that he could pull toward the left-field seats, let them go by. The umpire called two of the pitches strikes and three of them balls. Hubbell threw again, same pitch, same spot. The umpire was in a dilemma. He didn't want to call DiMaggio out on strikes, but the big crowd didn't want Joe to walk either—they wanted to see him hit one. Before he could decide what to call the pitch, Mel Allen, the Yankee broadcaster who was handling the public address system during the old-timers' game, blithely called out, "Ball three!" again. The crowd cheered, because it meant Joe was still up. Hubbell threw another screwball to the same spot and another one, and Allen continued to call out "Ball three!" on each pitch.

The crowd was laughing, but in the Yankee dugout the players began grumbling. One of them called, "Come on, Hubbell! Put it over!" Behind him stood Stengel, his arms folded, an admiring little smile on his face as he watched Hubbell pitch. "You don't think he's gonna give him anything good to hit, do you?" he said.

The player looked around, startled. He hadn't noticed what Casey had been appreciating, that Hubbell was as serious and gifted a practitioner of his craft as DiMaggio was of his, and that he was showing what *he* could do too. Finally he eased up, laid one through the middle, and DiMaggio lifted a long fly to left that reached the seats for a home run. Three runs scored. The fans were delighted. They had seen Joe D's graceful swing and they had seen him send a ball a long way.

Stengel was pleased too. He had been uneasy in his relationship with DiMaggio during the three seasons Joe was under him as a player, but that didn't matter now. What he had enjoyed was seeing a master craftsman demonstrate a fine point in the sometimes delicate art of baseball. Not many in the stadium that day savored what Hubbell had done before DiMaggio's homer but Stengel did.

He always saw a lot of things in baseball that others didn't. He was remarkably intelligent, although with little education beyond the minimum forced on him in grammar and high school and what he picked up during two semesters or so as a dental student when he was a young man. He had a prodigious memory, a startling ability to recall relevant detail. In baseball he had the kind of understanding of a situation that is often described as intuitive—immediate comprehension of a problem and its solution without recourse to orderly, reasoned analysis—but that is probably just rapid-fire, computer-speed deduction derived from long experience. The best chess players occasionally play this way, making moves they can't immediately explain or justify; Stengel did the same in baseball, although he would often go on to explain complex or simple moves in long-winded, roundabout lectures that amused and diverted his listeners without necessarily informing them.

His explanations did not necessarily convince anyone, not even baseball adepts. Al Lopez, one of the most intelligent and successful of big-league managers, played under Casey at Brooklyn and Boston in the 1930s, managed against him in the American League in the 1950s (and was the only manager to interrupt Casey's flow of pennants) and was his good friend. Yet Lopez once said, "I swear, I don't understand some of the things he does when he manages. I've tried to figure them out, but they just don't make sense." One of the more famous of such dubious moves occurred in the 1951 World Series between the Yankees and the New York Giants. In the final game of the Series the Yankees were leading 4–1 in the ninth inning. The strength of the Giants' batting order was up, and the first three men singled, loading the bases with nobody out. The Giants thus had the tying runs on base, the winning run at bat, and their two most powerful hitters, Monte Irvin and Bobby Thomson, both right-handed batters, coming to the plate. John Sain, a right-hander, had been pitching for the Yankees, but Stengel took him out after the Giants loaded the bases. Instead of following standard baseball theory by bringing in another right-hander to pitch to the right-handed Irvin and Thomson—there were three or four available to him, including the redoubtable Allie Reynolds, who had beaten the Giants soundly a couple of days earlier—Stengel stunned baseball people by calling on an undistinguished left-hander named Bob Kuzava, who had not previously appeared in the Series. The first batter, Irvin, flied deep to left off Kuzava, scoring the man from third and advancing the other runners to second and third. The second batter, Thomson, also flied to left, driving in another run and bringing the score to 4–3, with the tying run on second base. The third successive right-handed batter, a pinch hitter named Sal Yvars, who had batted .317 that year, hit a hard, sinking line drive to right field off Kuzava which was caught for the final out.

Stengel's tactic had worked—somehow. Three hard-hit balls, but the Giants had not been able to tie the score and the Yankees had won the game and the World Series. No one has ever been able to fully decipher Stengel's tortuous reasoning for bringing in Kuzava. Perhaps he had anticipated that the Giants' right-handed batters would be likely to hit fly balls that would be caught without too much trouble in the spacious Yankee Stadium outfield. But how could he be so sure that not one of those fly balls would go through for a double or a triple or reach the seats for a home run?

Besides, ground balls are what you want in a situation like that, grounders that will let your infielders come up with a double play while a run is scoring, grounders that, even if one did get through into the outfield for a base hit, would most likely score only one run, not the devastating three or four that a long hit might bring across. Stengel could point out that Kuzava had the best earned-run average on his staff that year and had excellent control, a desirable talent when the bases are full. But even so, a lefty? And, after all, he *did* give up three hard-hit balls.

Nonetheless—and this is where Al Lopez would shake his head in wonder—it worked. Kuzava *had* saved the game, the Giants had not caught up, and the Yankees had won the World Series.

The only fair conclusion is that Stengel *sensed* something deep in the information bank of the runaway computer that was his brain, some retrieval of data on what the Giants' right-handed batters had done or could do combined with what his left-hander had done or could do, tied in with the lovely spaciousness of the outfield in

Yankee Stadium and the cushion of a three-run lead. *Whirr, bzzzz, click-click-click,* and Kuzava was the answer.

Baseball absorbed Stengel. It was his life, and if that sounds like a cliché it is still true. He was born in Kansas City, Missouri, in 1890 and died in Glendale, California, in 1975, and for most of the eighty-five years in between baseball mattered more to him than almost anything else. During his life he grew famous and came to know and talk with kings, presidents, generals, actors, writers. That was important to him—he *liked* being famous—but it was secondary to baseball. Baseball was the thread his life hung on. "He doesn't talk about anything else," his wife said. "He doesn't think about anything else. He has only one life, and that's baseball. That way he's happy, and I'm happy for him."

John McGraw liked horseracing and gambling. Babe Ruth golfed, bowled, hunted, ate, drank and chased women. Ted Williams was almost as fascinated by the intricacies of fishing as he was by hitting. Reggie Jackson likes the glitter of the social ramble. George Brett talks earnestly of settling down on a ranch someday. Stengel said, "I don't play cards, I don't play golf, and I don't go to the picture show. All that's left is baseball."

He did like to drink and had the reputation of absorbing large amounts of liquor (bourbon, usually) without adverse effect. One night during a World Series in Los Angeles a sportswriter taking a shortcut down a flight of service stairs in a hotel was stunned to find Stengel on the bare cement floor of a landing, his shoulders and head leaning against the wall, his eyes closed. "I thought he was dead," the writer said. He shook Casey, and Stengel aroused himself, mumbled something, shook off the offer of assistance and made his way stiffly and awkwardly on up the staircase to his room. "I thought he was sick," the writer said. "I felt bad. I couldn't help but think he was getting close to the end." The next morning the writer, not feeling too perky himself, made his way downstairs for coffee and there was Stengel at a table, eating breakfast, waving his hands and talking, apparently as sound as ever.

Some of his friends insist that his drinking was exaggerated. "He drank to be sociable," Lopez claimed. "It was his way of staying up all night," Lee MacPhail said. "While other people were drinking, he was talking."

He was always talking and performing. During a game, when he came out of the dugout to talk to his pitcher or argue with an umpire, the crowd sat up and paid attention. When he spoke—at banquets or luncheons or just sitting around a table—he performed with his body as well as with his mouth, making his odd little gestures, lifting his head this way and that. His speeches rambled incredibly, sliding from one subject to another in midsentence as one thought led him to another. "Casey babbles in front of an audience," a writer once claimed, "because he gets flustered. He's afraid to stop, so he says anything that comes into his head." Another newspaperman said, "If somebody talks as though he's crazy, there are only two possible explanations. Either he *is* crazy, or he's putting on an act. No one ever accused Stengel of being crazy."

Much of the attention he received focused on him as Stengel the Clown. He was a very funny man, a quick-witted wisecracker, a physical comic, a natural mime who could wonderfully mimic other people. And his restless energy and exuberant spirits led him into one amusing scrape after another. "There was never a day around Casey that I didn't laugh," said his old Brooklyn teammate Zack Wheat.

Yet he was always serious about the game of baseball, about how it should be played, and particularly about his role as manager. Red Smith wrote, "It is erroneous and unjust to conceive of Casey Stengel merely as a clown. He is something else entirely—a competitor who always had fun competing, a fighter with a gift of laughter."

He could be clear and even concise when he had to be. Red Barber said that when he switched from the Dodgers to become a Yankee broadcaster after the 1953 season, he had to learn a lot in a hurry about his new ball club. Early in spring training he approached Casey and asked him if he could spare some time someday to go over his players. Stengel understood at once that Barber wanted to be briefed on the particular talents and on-field idiosyncrasies of the various Yankee players, things that would help the broadcaster as he did the play-by-play of a game. "Sure," he said. "Let's do it right now." The two sat together on a bench, and Casey took a small printed roster of the team from a back pocket. "He went down the list man by man in detail," Barber said. "There was no double-talk, none at all. In thirty minutes he gave me a detailed, analytical report on every last man on his roster. It was remarkable. And all season long, everything he told me about every man held up."

On the other hand, sometimes when he tried to explain something precisely, his efforts to enhance his listeners' knowledge would get hopelessly tangled. There was a pronounced stream-of-consciousness effect in his monologues, one thing reminding him of another *ad infinitum*, although he usually tried, sometimes with hilarious success, to get back to the starting subject at the very end of his answer. If you had a general idea of what he was talking about—John McGraw's theories of baserunning, say, or Mickey Mantle's speed—it wasn't always that hard to follow him, but at times he could be very confusing. He would switch from point A to related point B and on to remotely connected point C without bothering to explain the reasons for the sudden switches, and it was easy to get lost. At a baseball dinner early in 1954, talking about the rings members of the winning team in the World Series receive, he said, "That ring don't cost so much. I got four or five rings and don't know whether I'm going to wear five of them when I go out. Unless you're broke, the ring is the best thing you can get which money comes in handy all the time. If a player don't shoot he can go and play against us which is all right in the first place too. The situation is for five years and they still haven't found the end of it, the other guys. They say the owners are rich, so what? We must have the umpires, not the same ones. It's the money the Yankees got. On the ball club you can't write it all down. You do it. So they say it's the lively ball and the damn bunting. . . . What about the shortstop Rizzuto who got nothing but daughters but throws out the left-handed hitters in the double play?"

Casey could be wildly amusing, but there was burning ambition in him too. He enjoyed being funny, but he wanted to be recognized for his accomplishments, which were many. He faced a lot of problems in his life, and he coped with them. "I'm a man that's been up and down," he told Harry Paxton, when Paxton was working with him on the autobiography Casey published in 1961. He never gave in. He kept coming back. And always in baseball.

Roy Blount (b. 1941) grew up in Decatur, Georgia, attended Vanderbilt and Harvard, and worked as a reporter and editorial writer for the *Atlanta Journal*. In 1968 he went to work for *Sports Illustrated,* and seven years later he resigned to begin a successful freelance career. He is the author of the memoir *Be Sweet* (1998), the editor of *Roy Blount's Anthology of Southern Humor* (1994), and has written about everything from mixed-breed dogs to gender issues to collard greens to Mark Twain. A frequent subject is baseball, which he has described as "a game of waiting, spitting, and nuance." His enthusiastic appreciation of *The Sporting News* first appeared in *Sports Illustrated* in 1986.

Roy Blount, Jr.

ᗐ

The Sporting News

I had been into 1886 for no more than an hour, and lo!

"I've just found the first time the hidden-ball trick was played! In history!" I cried.

Mac Mac Farlane's eyes—as they were not reluctant to do, for all their venerability—twinkled. "Good going, Kid," he said.

Here it was on page 1 of the Sept. 13 issue of *The Sporting News*:

FOUTZ'S SHARP TRICK.
He Catches Pete Browning Napping at Second Base,
And Puts Him Out Without the Assistance of Captain Comiskey

"It happened in a game between St. Louis and Louisville," I went on. "On September 8, 1886. 'In the presence of 6,000 persons, Foutz played the sharpest trick ever seen on the ball field.' Pete Browning was on first for Louisville, and took a big lead because Charley Comiskey was playing way off the base in rightfield. 'Pete had his back turned toward second base, and was keeping an eye on the movements of Comiskey, while he eagerly pranced back and forth to show the crowd that he was not afraid to steal off a bag. Foutz pretended not to watch Browning, but suddenly. . . .'

"Wait a minute," I said, my heart sinking. "What position did this guy Foutz play?"

Mac Farlane did not know, but moved to look it up in one of many volumes. This time, I was quicker. I advanced the microfilm to the box scores. They were old. They were faint. But there was the game in question, and there was Foutz.

"His name was Dave," said Mac Farlane. "He was . . ."

"He was pitching," I said. I had not found the first hidden-ball trick after all.

But I had found something pretty amazing. Something from the days when organized ball was as young as I was when I became a fan of it. The days when baseball was so young that almost anything could happen. I had found not only the first time but surely the last time that a pitcher picked a man with a .343 lifetime batting average off first base *without making a throw*.

. . . suddenly Bushong [the catcher] signaled; and Foutz dashed over toward first base with the ball in hand, touching Browning before the latter knew what had happened. Such a play was never before seen, and the spectators howled with delight. Pete was mighty mad and, as he has a faculty for being caught napping, the play was
DOUBLY EMBARRASSING

"Pete Browning," mused Mac Farlane with relish. "An odd fellow. He didn't slide. Wouldn't slide. Another thing, he thought every bat had a certain number of hits in it, so when old Betsy got 19 hits he'd hang her up in his cellar. Had old Betsys hanging all over the place. He also thought it was smart when riding a train to open a window, stick his head out and catch soot from the smokestack. In his eyes. He thought that made his eyes water and cleaned out his sight."

"Wow," I observed. I had not observed "wow" in a number of years.

Pete Browning stories! Oh, I knew Browning was the guy who got Hillerich and Bradsby into the bat business when he brought them a wagon tongue or something and asked them to see what kind of old Betsy they could turn out on their lathe. It was the birth of the Louisville Slugger. But I had never heard any *other* Pete Browning stories.

"Neat," I observed, nearly aloud. The last time I had observed "neat" nearly aloud was when I took my son John to the Hall of Fame and he stood in Babe Ruth's actual locker and he observed "neat" aloud. It isn't easy to get young people to observe "neat" aloud about something that you think is just as neat as they do.

Now I am not in Babe Ruth's locker, but I am in a place just as wondrous. I am in the cubbyhole of Paul (Mac) Mac Farlane, 66, official historian of *The Sporting News*. I am unscrolling the Bible of Baseball. And as I do so, it is annotated by a high priest.

Mac Farlane used to pitch batting practice to Joe Cronin!

Mac Farlane had hung around with Hugh Duffy! One of the first things I remember learning in life, on my own, was that Hugh Duffy hit .438, the alltime major league standard, back before the modern era. Never in my wildest dreams—even when those dreams included being a baseball immortal myself—did I expect to hang around with anybody who had hung around with Hugh Duffy!

Mac Farlane has a stack of three-by-five cards, on which is recorded every time anybody hit for the cycle in the big leagues before 1977! Mac Farlane thinks all this is as neat as I think it is.

"Look at this," he says. He shows me a photograph taken around 1879 of the Providence Grays and the Boston Nationals lounging in shallow rightfield at the Messer Street baseball field in Providence. He points to one of the Grays.

"Paul Hines," he says. "Got hit by a pitch in the ear and turned deaf as a haddock. Invented the electrical acoustical cane. Sometimes, in the dark, deaf people have trouble getting their balance. Hines invented the electrical acoustical cane [Mac Farlane repeats this term with pleasure] so he could get a feeling of where he was. I don't know whether I ought to tell you how he died."

"Oh, come on."

"Got caught shoplifting. He was teched at the time and had the walkarounds. He was as old as the hammers of Hades. He didn't know what he was doing. Shock of it killed him."

I'd never heard anybody say "old as the hammers of Hades" before. I am in a place where baseball is as old as the hammers of Hades, and as fresh.

I am in heaven.

March 17 is the 100th anniversary of *The Sporting News*, the weekly tabloid published in St. Louis that stood for decades as the Bible of Baseball, but in recent years has restructured itself into a condensation of the week's news in all major sports. For 91 years *The Sporting*

News was owned by the Spink family, who devoted it to the idiosyn-
cratic gratification of themselves and everyone else who was obsessed
with baseball. In 1977 it was sold to the Times Mirror Company,
which has more than doubled the paper's circulation, to 711,000,
by appealing (in the words of *Sporting News* chief executive officer
Richard Waters) to "the yuppie group and on up." *The Sporting News* is
still baseball's publication of record: Every major league box score
since 1886 has been printed—with strict triple-checked accuracy—in
its pages. There is talk now of dropping the box scores so that the
eight pages they take up will be available for (in editor Tom Barnidge's
words) "really dynamite feature stories."

But who wants to dwell for long upon contemporary publishing
practices when we can contemplate mythological figures? Recently
I spent a week in the offices of *The Sporting News* on Lindbergh
Boulevard in St. Louis and I kept gravitating toward its historical
storehouse, where Mac Farlane keeps the sacred relics, the temple
jewels, the idols' eyes.

It doesn't look like a shrine. Things are lying around or stuffed
away and Mac Farlane has to dig them out for you. But that is exactly
what Mac Farlane loves to do, when the moment arises.

The Ty Cobb letters for instance. I was deep into 1908. "Here's a
great Cobb story," I said.

"Cobb, you know, was the Joe Namath of the American League,"
said Mac Farlane. "There was no denying it was a major league, with
Cobb in it."

"I never thought of that," I said. I read aloud from the Cobb story,
which appeared on Jan. 16, 1908.

WILL WATCH COBB.
OFTEN SNEAKED IN EXTRA BASE LAST SEASON.
*Tricks Can Not Be Turned if Members of
Fielding Side Are Always on the Alert.*

*A safe bet is that when the several American League teams get down to
training, each manager will take his first baseman aside and tell him in no
uncertain tones that he must watch Ty Cobb more closely this year. The
champion batsman of the league had a habit last season, when on first
base, of going from that sack way around to third on a bunt or slow infield
grounder. . . . . Let an infielder or a pitcher fumble a bunt ever so little, and*

Ty was sure to attempt to take two bases. Let the first baseman be pulled off the bag a trifle in making the catch, and Ty was certain to go the limit. This year, however, all the first basemen will be watching out for just this play and Cobb will be lucky if he pulls it off as regularly as he did in 1907.

"Did I show you these?" Mac Farlane asked. He handed me a thick handful of handwritten letters. They were written to the late J. G. Taylor Spink, from 1914 to 1962 the publisher of *The Sporting News.* They were written by Cobb.

"Wow," I said. "Have Cobb's biographers read these?"

"Nah," said Mac Farlane.

I started reading them: "Anything I write you can be *assured* no one will know where it comes from . . . I will throw up a phoney story to hide real source."

This was dated 1955. Cobb was filling Spink in on Wahoo Sam Crawford, who had not yet been enshrined in the Hall of Fame. I knew Crawford hated Cobb during the years they played together. But I had never realized their non-speaking terms went as far as this. Crawford, Cobb wrote to Spink, "never helped in the outfield by calling, plenty of room, you take it, Etc." Not only that, but when Cobb tried to steal second to get into scoring position with Crawford at bat, Crawford would foul the ball off so Cobb would have to go back and the first baseman would have to hold him on, giving Crawford a bigger hole to hit through. According to Cobb, "I ran hundreds of miles in all and had to return to first."

However, Cobb urged Spink to support Crawford's Hall of Fame candidacy. Cobb said he had written on Crawford's behalf to Grantland Rice and other influential sportswriters. "Sam has had copies of my letters. I like the decent way, I like to return good for what I considered say evil. So I have been his booster and he knows it from me."

How Crawford must have hated that.

"Cobb was a bastard," said Mac Farlane. "But he was a factual bastard."

"And a fast bastard," I said.

"Mm," said Mac Farlane. "Did you see this?" He pointed to a handwritten quotation tacked to his wall:

> *"If You Don't Live to get Old, You Die Young!"*
> —*Cool Papa Bell*

"Ah, yes," I said. "Talking about fast." I had heard about Cool Papa
Bell, the great star of the Negro leagues long before blacks were admitted to the teams that *The Sporting News* covered. Bell was said to be
so fast he once hit a line drive up the middle and the ball hit his foot
as he was sliding into second. "How fast was he really?" I asked Mac
Farlane.

"Clocked in 12 seconds around the bases."

"*Really?*"

Mac Farlane's expression seemed to say, "What do you think I deal
in here, but 'really'?"

"I mean . . ." I said, "I'd always heard Mantle had the fastest time,
at 13.1 or something. Although I guess Vince Coleman and some of
these later guys. . . . Twelve seconds?"

"Jamie will tell you himself," Mac said.

I tried to think who Jamie was. Must be somebody I ought to recognize. "I wish I could talk to Cool Papa himself," I said.

"Jamie," said Mac Farlane. "That's what I call him, but that's family. You should just call him Cool Papa at first." He picked up the
phone, and the next thing I knew I had an appointment to visit
Cool Papa Bell in his house on James "Cool Papa" Bell Avenue in
St. Louis.

Cool Papa, who will be 83 on May 17, sat nonchalantly on his
living room couch and told me how fast he was. In 1948, Satchel
Paige talked him into playing against some barnstorming major
league all-stars in Los Angeles. Bell didn't want to play because he
was out of shape and hadn't felt quite himself since somebody practiced witchcraft on him and poisoned his food when he was in the
Mexican League. But he agreed. Then he had to drag Paige out to
the park and by the time they got there they had no time to loosen
up. Bell hit a single off the all-stars' pitcher, Bob Lemon, and Paige
laid down a sacrifice bunt. Bell had studied Lemon on television, so
as soon as the pitcher looked over at him hard once and then
turned back to the plate, Bell took off. Everybody converged on
Paige's bunt except the shortstop, who covered second. By the time
catcher Roy Partee started to throw to second, Bell was rounding
it. And nobody was covering third. So Partee ran toward third. By
the time Partee got to third, Bell was rounding it. And nobody was
covering home. As Bell scored, Partee was running down the line

hollering "Time! Time!" But you can't call time when the ball is in play, even against Cool Papa Bell.

"I got that on paper," Cool Papa said. "All on paper's not true, but that's true. I was sick, I was 45 years old when I did that. I did that a gang of times. They clocked me going around the bases in 12 seconds, but then another time I went from home plate to third in eight seconds. They wanted me to break my 12-second record but then it rained. And the league broke up."

What if *The Sporting News* had covered Cool Papa the way it covered the Georgia Peach? Bell doesn't let it bother him. "We never had no reading lessons in school, in Mississippi," he said. "Sitting on a hill, that's the only way it was a high school. I had to learn myself. I'd read *The Sporting News,* about Babe Ruth, Bill Terry, Chuck Klein. Seemed like everything it was, Chuck Klein was leading in it. I just liked a ballplayer."

I returned to Mac Farlane. "Cool Papa says he ran from first to third in eight seconds," I said. "That's . . ."

"Jamie," said Mac, "is factual."

Mac Farlane can be a factual bastard himself, at least from official baseball's viewpoint. Five years ago he uncovered evidence that in 1910 somebody altered the batting records of Cobb and Napoleon Lajoie. His research established that Lajoie, not Cobb, had won the batting championship that year and that Cobb's lifetime batting average was .366 instead of .367, and his career hit total was 4,190 instead of 4,191. But .367 and 4,191 are sacred numbers. Bowie Kuhn, then baseball's commissioner, refused to allow the new figures to be etched in stone. Mac Farlane can't get over this: "Baseball could never live with facts!" he says.

Mac Farlane can. There are no books of baseball statistics, except the ones painstakingly produced by *The Sporting News,* that Mac Farlane can't find mistakes in. He pulls out a copy of the *Official American League Batting Averages for 1973,* corrected by him in ink. Sal Bando hit .287, not .286; Brooks Robinson hit .257, not .256; it was George Brett, not Ken, who hit .125; Larry, not Fred, Haney hit .500 (1 for 2), not .000 (0 for 1), and so on. I must say I found this unsettling. What if I had been Haney? I would have turned to Mac Farlane.

In the May 24, 1886, issue, I read the following story filed by a Cincinnati correspondent but headlined in St. Louis:

AKIN TO REAL DEMONS.
That is What They say of the Saint Louis Browns.
All Cincinnati Jealous of the Club that
Beat the Coming Champions

If it is any satisfaction for a player to maim or cripple a brother player, then let him continue in his good (?) work. If not then cry a halt before disastrous results ensue. The game that was lost to us [the Reds] Friday was due to Comiskey's throwing himself

FULL TILT

against McPhee, causing Bid to throw wild to first. . . .
The Browns personally are a clever set of men, but on the field they are akin to demons.
Oh, my! Oh, my oh!

"I thought these old guys were tough," I said. "Here's Charley Comiskey being called a 'demon' for going into the second baseman hard enough to break up a double play."

"Who's the second baseman?" asked Mac Farlane with asperity.

"Bid McPhee," I said. "I think I've heard of him."

Mac Farlane looked at me with an expression he was not reluctant to use when I fell short of his expectations. "Bid McPhee should be in the Hall of Fame," he said. "Wouldn't *you* let into the Hall of Fame a man who was voted by his peers the greatest second baseman up to 1900?"

"Oh, *I* would," I said hastily. "I guess I . . . don't go any further back, in second basemen, than Lajoie."

There was a pause. I had pronounced it—just as I have been pronouncing it in my mind since I was nine years old—La-*jo*-ey.

"He pronounced it *La*-jho-ay," said Mac Farlane, who then began speaking in French! Something about . . . *lanceurs*. . . . I couldn't follow it—oh, my, oh. Maybe I had no business in this sanctum after all. *French.* Was I being tested? I turned, meekly, from the microfilm machine. Mac Farlane was reading a letter aloud. A request for information.

"When letters come from France," explained Mac Farlane, "I translate."

"How did you learn such good French?" I asked.

He smiled like an owl in pleasant recollection. "Mm," he said. He looked over his glasses. "I'd rather not repeat it."

Mac Farlane will repeat many other things, however, such as what Hugh Duffy once said about what it takes to hit .400. Only I can't repeat that. I know an unprintable story about Hugh Duffy!

I also know, on Mac Farlane's authority, that Babe Ruth once described Lou Gehrig as "built like a four-car garage with five buses in it." I hadn't realized that Ruth ever said anything about anybody except himself. "You know, Ruth's favorite dessert was eels and ice cream," said Mac Farlane.

"It was?" I answered.

"Yes," said Mac Farlane.

But there is plenty of Ruth lore in circulation. Mac Farlane has Hugh Duffy lore. Duffy, a Hall of Famer whose career ended in 1906, was a scout for the Red Sox in the 1940s. Mac Farlane's father was a minority stockholder in the Sox, and Mac grew up around the team—talking to Harry Hooper while Hooper shagged flies, and getting to know Duffy "very well. You know he worked Jackie Robinson out before the Dodgers did. Thought Robinson was a little old to be a rookie and the Red Sox . . ."

"The *Red Sox?*"

". . . and Duffy thought he was excessively ding-toed at the time."

"You mean pigeon-toed?"

There was a pause such as might follow were an eminent jazz historian to describe Count Basie as cool and you were to say, "You mean groovy?"

"Ding-toed," said Mac Farlane.

The true story of baseball's color line has never been told, according to Mac Farlane, and it involves actual exclusionary legislation that has never come to light. He has been trying to get people to listen to the whole story, but they won't. Now he hopes to develop a TV documentary on the subject. "Branch Rickey was interested in Robinson as a gate attraction," he says. "My description of Rickey is a Bible-quoting thief."

Once, when Mac Farlane was a semi-pro player at Arlington, Mass., in 1937, he batted against Satchel Paige. "The ball looked like a ribbon," he says. "I struck out on three pitches."

Mac Farlane never batted against Walter Johnson, but he knew plenty of people who did. "From the tip of his finger to his wrist was 14 inches. People say he came over the top, but he threw sidearm.

And he'd whip those long fingers around. . . . Three guys gave up and left the plate against him with only two strikes."

I don't remember how Johnson came up, but we got into Rube Waddell when I was reading "Gossip of the Players" from 1908. During the off-season in those days *The Sporting News* had four great tidbits columns: "Gossip of the Players," "Scribbled by Scribes," "Tips by the Managers" and "Said by the Magnates." I find it interesting that the money men have always had an important place in *Sporting News* coverage. This headline appeared on Nov. 24, 1910:

> *O, YOU MAGNATES!*
> *CONTINUE TO OCCUPY LIMELIGHT*
> *WITH THEIR TROUBLES.*

But "Gossip of the Players" was by far my favorite. I was reading some 1908 quotes from Waddell, whom I always loved as a kid because his legend had to do with his chasing a fire engine or playing catch with kids or wrestling alligators when he was supposed to be pitching. As recorded by some period scribe, this is what Waddell was saying in 1908:

> *I have had good luck fishing, so far, and ought to be satisfied, but since I have been associated with that advanced financier, Jack O'Connor, I have developed a hankering for lucre. Jack has drilled it into me that I owe it to myself to go get the money. He may be right, but it is not clear to me how a fellow can owe himself anything in any way.*

Ah, Rube. Here he was a few weeks earlier.

> *I want to call attention to the fact that few freak or fool stories were printed about me [during the preceding season] in the papers. Why up to this year I never knew when I got out of bed what I would read about myself. . . . I am not conservative or discreet, but I am not 'bughouse,' but if I have done all that has been said or written about me, I ought not to be at large.*

Did Rube really talk like that? Well, did Samson or Delilah really talk the way *they* do in the Bible? All we can say is this: that legendary sports flakes have been saying that last thing (if they had really done all that has been said or written . . .) at least since Rube Waddell. After that winter Waddell pitched only two more years in the big leagues, and six years later, at 37, he was dead of tuberculosis. Cocaine was not a problem among players in those days, but liquor was. I read Waddell's quotes to Mac Farlane.

"One time," said Mac Farlane, "a detective brought Waddell into the hotel lobby and told Connie Mack he was arresting him. Said Rube had been making fresh remarks to ladies and disturbing the peace. Mack asked if there was any way to keep Waddell out of jail. The detective said, well, he supposed if Mack paid the $10 fine. . . . So Mack did. A little later Mack walked past a saloon down the street and through the window he saw Rube and the 'detective'—he was no detective, he was a friend of Rube's—drinking up Mack's $10."

The Sporting News was founded by Al Spink as a local magazine of all sports. In 1886, there was an item about W. C. Manning, THE CHAMPION ONE-LEGGED WRESTLER OF THE WORLD, which declared, "Manning has never been thrown, though he has met several two-legged men."

But when Al's brother Charles took over *The Sporting News* in 1887, he concentrated solely on baseball, and made it national. When Charles's son, Taylor, became publisher in 1914, baseball became the publication's holy cause. Taylor Spink was as obsessed with being the driving force behind the Bible of Baseball as Cobb was with being a better player than anybody else. "To Spink," says Mac Farlane, "the word 'vacation' was absolute blasphemy." The staff labored six or seven days a week, and Spink would call them up in the middle of the night to make sure they were thinking about *The Sporting News* in their sleep. "Pappy Spink drilled into us, Get everything right even if you have to call God Almighty. And if anything was wrong he raised *hell*."

Most of the writing was contributed by "beat guys," the newspaper reporters who followed the baseball teams everywhere and kept the nation's devotees up to date with weekly reports from the field. These days *The Sporting News* takes as its purview the whole sporting scene and, in order to make room for what is most topical across that broad scene each week, a beefed-up editorial staff boils down the beat guys' copy. "People today want a five-to-10-minute quick read—so they can go to a cocktail party and sound knowledgeable," says C.E.O. Waters. Editor Barnidge points out that "readers today are not as willing to work at reading." But in the old days, when scribes were paid by the inch and the Bible of Baseball was scripture. . . .

Do you have a few extra minutes?

Oct. 7, 1893. Harry Leach reporting from Chicago (again with one of those St. Louis headlines):

RESULTS OF OVER-EXERTION
How It Effects Some of Chicago's Nervous Scribes

There are times when sobriety of temper is an essential precaution. Too much excitement is detrimental to the gearing of the nervous system. However thrilling an event may be, it is best to be calm. It is a medical fact that over exertion of the aexota, where the nerve center is situated, will, without fail, lead to cataclasm of the semi-colon and watery consummation of the lower lobe of the apocalypse. These facts were secured at the Pan-American congress of physicians after a large outlay of time and money. They are particularly pertinent at this time, because about 1000 cranks who witnessed that game of ball between Baltimore and Chicago last Friday are wandering around in the great throbbing world this morning with their semi-colons terribly cataclasted.

For eight innings neither side made a run.

There follows—well, here is some of what follows:

Never More Decker, eager to shatter anything he could, came up. There was a reverberating roar and the ball whistled away through the air in an opposite direction. McGraw and the ball met and stuck together like two lone girls when a tramp is trying to break in through the back door. That retired the side. . . .

And here is some more:

The air thumped like a volcano with the crater plugged up. Many a horny tongued son of toil on the bleacheries buried his teeth in the soft pine boards and pulled out knots in sheer anguish. . . .

And more:

Reitz seized himself passionately and bore down on the plate. Irwin shot the ball in with a scream of triumph and Reitz died. . . .

And then, finally, at the end of the 12th long paragraph, comes the end of the story, which is also the first mention of the final score:

That was the run of the game. It was to exciting too tell about.

And I believe it.

Have you ever wondered how ball players joshed in the early days of the 20th century? Here is how the Baltimore Orioles joshed in 1908, according to J. M. Cummings in the May 28 *The Sporting News*, under this headline:

ORIOLES' OFF DAYS.
PASSED PLEASANTLY IN LOBBY OF HOTEL.
"Waiter, remove these peas," he [manager Jack Dunn] demanded. "They won't stay on me knife. Bring me some split in half, that will. . . . Boys," he began. "I am seriously thinking about organizing the Baltimore Club into a minstrel troupe at the end of the season. Prithee, what thinkest thou? . . . Dessau and Pearson could figure as the P.-C.-M. kids in a knockabout comedy I have in mind to be called 'The higher up we go the better we like it, because it's so different, yet it ain't.'"

Hearne rose at this thrilling juncture, threw up his hands and in a stage whisper remarked, "I'm getting foolish."

"Not 'getting,'" replied the manager, and "Hughie" fell under the table.

"How do you feel, Pfyl?" inquired the manager. "Do you feel as though you could feel your way through some minor f-e-e-l-ing-in part? Just some little piece eloquent in -er-er-er its silence, for instance. Methinks thou wouldst fairly shine in some thinking part."

"Aw, quit your joshing, you distract my attention from my victuals," was all that could be got from the ambassador from the New York Giants.

In those days, Baltimore was in the minors. *The Sporting News* covered the minor leagues almost as thoroughly as it did the majors, hence headlines such as this one, from Wilkes-Barre:

BARONS STRONGER.
LEZOTTE HAS WEEDED OUT DUMB ELEMENT.

And nine long paragraphs from Keokuk headlined UNJUST TO OSKALOOSA, all about the inequities of the Central Association schedule. Such coverage made *The Sporting News* not only the Bible but the *Variety* of baseball, and what is left of that coverage is still a big reason why players can be seen reading *The Sporting News* in clubhouses—checking up on their friends in the bushes.

An operation called *Baseball America* provides the most comprehensive coverage of the minor leagues, and *USA Today* prints a wealth of big-league statistics five days a week. By the time box scores come out in *The Sporting News* they are as much as 10 or 11 days old. It's a great thing for baseball writers to know they can always lay their hands on the season's box scores if they save *The Sporting News*. "But I don't know how many of our 700,000 readers are baseball writers," says Barnidge.

The Sporting News's advertising revenues have doubled since 1981. It's a considerably more accessible and professional-looking product now than it was as holy writ under Taylor Spink. Old hands on the staff, who remember Pappy Spink the way old soldiers remember General Patton, say that the paper got better when Taylor died in 1962 and his mild-mannered son, C. C. Johnson Spink, started making some of the changes that the present owners have accelerated.

But there are several up-to-date sports publications. Only *The Sporting News* has 100 years of baseball fever behind it. Only *The Sporting News* can show you in its pages an endorsement of Coca-Cola by Hughie (Ee-yah) Jennings, in which he maintained that "the hardest thing a ball player has to contend with is thirst, because if you try to satisfy it with water, you either get loggy or lose your 'Ginger' or it makes you sick, while alcoholic beverages are fatal to good ball."

The newsstands are loaded with analyses of how baseball has been affected by artificial turf and free agency. Only *The Sporting News* can take you back to the days when scribes speculated that base stealing was on the decline because catchers were wearing "the fat glove of the modern type. . . . When the catchers took the force of the fiercely projected ball on the thin glove of years ago their fingers gave way, forming a sort of spring box to receive the shock. So heavy was the impact that the hand naturally unconsciously recoiled, and the ball was delayed a fraction of a second before the catcher would gather it up and shoot it down to second. . . . It's different with the big glove, the ball whangs into the great fat cushion and its shock is killed instanter." (To counteract this development, a beat guy proposed in 1899 that second base to moved eight feet closer to first when a runner was on first; then if he reached second, second would be moved eight feet closer to third.)

The Sporting News has another unique resource. "The FBI uses this," says Mac Farlane. It's a huge card catalog containing the transactional careers of everybody who *ever* signed a professional baseball contract, major or minor. "Everybody? Are you *sure*?" I asked Mac Farlane. His expression, while kindly, suggested that if there was anything he was unsure of, it was whether I knew what "sure" meant.

So I looked up the best player *I* ever threw batting practice to, the only kid from my high school team who signed a contract, Bobby DeFoor. And there he was: William Robert DeFoor, who kicked around a couple of years and then was put on injured reserve. (After that, I knew, came the Baptist ministry, but that was for a higher card catalog.)

You might think it struck me with a certain finality that I myself was not in that card catalog, what with my being 44 now and not gaining any steps. But it didn't. I was too busy turning over in my mind the possibility that Johnny Evers and I might have a lot in common.

I had been reading "Gossip of the Players" for Nov. 12, 1908. Johnny Evers had been giving a lot of thought to this whole problem of what to do when the other team has men on first and third. This is a problem that may seem primitive to fans of big-time baseball today. But it is a problem never resolved, very firmly, at any level of ball that I myself attained. As Evers put it: *If the catcher threw to second, the man on third would race home and the throw was too long from second to get him. Then the trick of the second baseman running in behind the pitcher on such occasions and stopping the throw and shooting it back to the plate was started. This worked for a while, but then the runner on third got to sticking to the bag and as a result the man going from first to second would be safe at second.*

Exactly. What was Evers's solution?

With much practice, I was able to run in on such plays, thus holding the runner at third, and with a good throw from the catcher I could take the ball and with the same movement pass it between my knees back to second base in time to nab the other runner. The catcher, of course, must make a good throw for the play to be a success.

Here we have Johnny Evers. The Evers of Tinker-to-Evers-to-Chance. The Evers who stole a pennant from the Giants in 1908 by calling for the ball when Merkle failed to touch second base. Here we have Johnny Evers with his thinking cap on, figuring out a way to avoid either going all to pieces or sitting there sullenly when the other team has men on first and third.

Exactly the kind of thing I worried about when I played ball. And if I had ever been able to do more than one thing—or even one whole thing—in the same movement, *I think that I might have come up with this same between-the-knees trick!*

I have problems identifying with contemporary baseball stars. They are so much richer than I am, and their gloves are so much better. They play in and on sleek synthetic fibers. They have got the other-team-with-the-guys-on-first-and-third problem licked. And if they're so great, where were they when I was a kid?

I know where Johnny Evers was. He was in my head, in undying verse ("pricking our [the Giants'] gonfalon bubble"), in a glove as scruffy and a uniform as baggy as mine.

A baseball fan, no matter how old, is always a kid, right? If only we could get back to baseball that kids and old guys—as opposed to yuppies and on up—can identify with.

Then again, in the bright lexicon of baseball, why should there be any "if only"? What happened when I told Mac Farlane I wished I could meet Cool Papa Bell? And what did Cool Papa himself reply, when I asked him the obligatory question: Did he regret having been excluded from the white majors? With a calm assurance not unlike Mac Farlane's, Bell replied: "People say, 'Isn't it a shame you couldn't play in the major leagues?' Unh-uh: I *could* play. Like they used to say, 'You can't eat in this place.' And I would say, 'I *can*. Maybe you're not going to let me in there. But I can *eat* anywhere.' And I could play."

I thought of that as I peered at faint but enduring microfilm. Mac Farlane was saying, "Johnny Evers. A very *brainy* player. There haven't been many brainy players. Lots of *smart* players, but . . ."

You know what I was reminded of? One of those movies where there's a kid and there's this old guy who knows karate mysteries or can train your foal to be Seabiscuit or has a time machine.

David Remnick (b. 1958) grew up in New Jersey, attended Princeton, and was hired as a sportswriter by *The Washington Post* in 1982. Eventually he became the newspaper's Moscow correspondent, and his book *Lenin's Tomb: The Last Days of the Soviet Empire* won the Pulitzer Prize for 1993. He was named editor of *The New Yorker* five years later. This piece, which first appeared in *Esquire* in 1987 and was included in Remnick's essay collection *The Devil Problem and Other True Stories* (1996), is as much a commentary on the nature of fame at a certain point in American history as it is a profile of a fading slugger.

David Remnick

ᑌ

The September Song of Mr. October

(June 1987)

In the last weeks before spring training, Reggie Jackson drove down the freeway from his home in the Oakland hills to the ball park where he began his career in 1968. He ran sprints across the outfield, fielded fungoes, and took batting practice with players half his age, boys who looked at him with the same slack-jawed regard he once had for Mantle, Maris, and Mays. They studied his easy looping warm-up swings, his murderous slashes at the ball, even the vicious way he spit through his teeth after every pitch, and as they watched him, they may have remembered seeing the same motions a decade ago on television or, if they were lucky, from a seat in the upper deck. Jackson was a part of their boyhood. Now they were professional ballplayers and an audience for the September song of Mr. October.

The youngest of them could hardly imagine Reggie Jackson in gold, green, and white; for them, he was born in pinstripes. But all knew him as a man of swaggering qualities, a name as resonant in their imagination as Ali, Elvis, or even the Babe. At least a dozen players in Reggie's era, from Clemente to Schmidt to Mattingly, were better players, more complete and consistent, but he was the Promethean among them. He defined an Age of Jackson.

Statistically, he is king only of strikeouts, the all-time leader in that category, but his legacy is the big stroke, the electric moment. He won three championships with the Athletics, two with the Yankees. He played in the postseason in eleven of his nineteen years. No player ever had a single day greater than his October 18, 1977. On the cool night when the Yankees won their first World Series in fifteen years, Jackson hit three home runs on three swings. No one else had ever done that. Likely, no one would again. "I have been to the mountain-top, and I have seen the promised land," he said. "I've seen it more than any man alive."

The brilliant light was out. It was like watching the movements of a shadow on the grass. His swing—which often left him screwed into the clay, his helmet falling over his eyes, his number, 44, stretched grotesquely across his back—his swing still had the old ferocious look. But something was wrong. The eyes, the concentration, the re-flexes, something. Jackson was not past heroics—he could still send the ball screaming into the outer dark—but he was past the *expectation* of heroics. His home runs now had the quality only of nostalgia and accident. He was forty years old.

In the fall of 1986, he seemed sure to play in another World Series. "I might have gone out on that," he said. His California Angels were one strike away from beating the Boston Red Sox. Horribly, the Angels let go their grip, and the Red Sox advanced instead. It mat-tered little to Jackson that in the Series against the Mets, Boston would imitate California's collapse, and, somehow, surpass it. Only one thing resonated in his mind. His last at-bat had been a strikeout, and his team had lost. "Of course, you can't blame the Angels," he said. "They'd never won anything. They didn't know how. I was a different story. I'd been there." When it was over, California no longer wanted him. They had already forced one of the game's most superb batsmen, Rod Carew, into a ragged, undignified end. Now to the sixth-leading home-run hitter of all time, the Angels said, in no uncertain terms, find another team, quit. Suddenly, Reggie Jackson was just an overpaid .240 hitter without a glove. Jackson waited for offers. Thirty-six hours after the owners of the A's called him, he signed a one-year contract with them for $525,000, little more than half his old salary. He was already worth millions in stocks, real es-tate, and other investments. He had homes in Carmel, Oakland, and

Los Angeles; his own Cessna jet; and a car collection worth two and a half million dollars. He had a china collection featuring a six-hundred-dollar teacup. The money was meaningless. He would not go out on strike three. "It wouldn't be right," he said. "Someone like me is supposed to leave the game in a different way. That's not how it ends for Reggie Jackson."

A couple of days before his next workout at the Coliseum, Jackson flew in his private plane to Las Vegas. A Canadian auto-painting-supply company called Spraybake had invited him to the auto show there, where they were displaying Jackson's favorite, a 1955 Chevrolet Bel Air. The license plate read R JAX 55. Normally Jackson gets ten to fifteen thousand dollars to lend what he himself calls the Reggie aura, but Spraybake was one of his "best relationships," he said, and he would do it for expenses. "They like me. They're Reggie guys."

Jackson walked in a half-hour late, wearing a blue sweatshirt and faded, pressed jeans. His hair, which he used to wear in a woolly Afro style, now had the patchy look of a putting green on an abandoned course. There were flecks of gray in his beard. More than one visitor noted that he seemed shorter than his "official height" of six feet. "I thought he'd be a giant," said one young girl. "He's just plain."

Jackson found a central spot on the carpet, spread his legs, folded his arms over his chest, and waited. Warily, all the Spraybake men formed a circle around the star. They made small talk about Jackson's hundred or so cars, about his feelings on having just joined the Oakland A's. And as their nerve increased and their imagined sense of fraternity took hold, they asked his opinion of a passing girl in silver tights. They had seen the photographs through the years of Reggie with dozens of beautiful women, mostly blondes. "Not bad," Jackson allowed. "Not bad."

Clubhouse talk with Reggie: even fifteen thousand dollars would have been a small price to pay. Still, the men were uncomfortable. They appeared to concentrate very hard on what they said before they said it. If Jackson does not care for a question, he will often ignore it. If he thinks a query too obvious, he will say, "You mean you don't know?" Disgust is one of his moods. They shift easily, inexplicably. But he was in a good mood now, and he received even banalities with cheer.

After a while, the crowd thinned out and Reggie was almost alone. There were no balls to sign, no absurdities to answer. And so he picked up a soft towel and began polishing the fingerprints off his Chevrolet. "I hate fingerprints," he said. "Why do people put their fingers all over something like this?" As he buffed the chrome, he said, "It's like I've lived a dream. If you're talking about a standard for success, they're Steve Jobs in computers, Lee Iacocca in cars, and Reggie Jackson in baseball. I was the standard in clutch situations for ten years. I wasn't the best hitter, but I was the most feared. I was the baddest motherfucker on the block. I was Jesse James, Wyatt Earp. But even they slow down. Even they deteriorate.

"From 1972 to 1979, when you needed a home run in the ninth, and the pennant was riding on it, I was going to the plate to hit that cocksucker over the fence. And not just hit it over. I mean, like forty rows deep. You know what I'm saying? But it didn't last forever. It wasn't just last year or the year before that. It goes as far back as the 1981 Series against the Dodgers. I was out hurt at the beginning. I got back in it, but I couldn't turn it around. I couldn't do it anymore."

Jackson sat down on a couch and drank a cup of orange juice. The crowds returned as quickly as they had gone.

"Hi! I'm a Ziebart girl!" said an almost-blonde in a pair of white hot pants. "I thought you were giving balls out."

"Reggie. Hey, Reggie! I just want to shake your hand. No questions asked. Is that okay?"

"Hey, Reggie Jackson. You're always selling something, aren't you?"

One after another. The strangeness of being Reggie. In public, he is like a ferocious animal in a zoo cage: people admire him, poke him, measure themselves against him. Then they go away, perhaps frightened, disappointed, or thrilled. Usually Jackson endures it. Sometimes he snaps back. It depends on his mood.

Once, when all of New York wanted to know when Reggie would recover from an injury and return to right field, a young boy said to him in an elevator, "Hey, when are you gonna play, Reg?"

Jackson grabbed himself by the crotch and said, "Play with this."

Sometimes it is not his fault. In bars, people try to pick a fight. In New York, someone took a shot at him with a pistol. It is part of the idiocy of being that famous.

Finally, Jackson rose from the sofa and told the Spraybake men, "The crowds are a little thick. I'll be back in fifteen minutes." He said he'd take a walk and let them thin out. He was gone for hours. When he finally returned, it was time to go.

Jackson left the convention center that evening with Everett Moss and Ted Kay, two of his buddies from California. Moss is Jackson's closest friend and one of six people on the Reggie payroll. Ted Kay is a scarred former football player from Kent State who met Jackson in a pickup basketball game. Ted told Reggie he was out of work, and the next day he had a job caring for the "L.A. division" of Reggie's car collection. "Reggie saved me," Ted said. "Now I live over the garage."

As they left the hall, 1984 Playmate of the Year Barbara Edwards, who was at the convention selling Snap-on tools, caught up to Jackson. A calendar photo of Edwards wearing a farmer's-daughter outfit and clutching a Snap-on tool hangs near the desk in his L.A. garage. In Las Vegas she wore fur.

"You ever see anything that gorgeous?" Ted said to Everett as they kept a respectable distance behind their man.

"Yes, I have," Everett said. He has been with Jackson for twenty years. "Sometimes even a bit better," Everett added.

The streets were clogged with conventioneers, and Jackson and Barbara Edwards could not get a cab. One cabdriver slowed, as if in response to Jackson's signal, but then he drove away. All he wanted was a closer look.

"My Gawd," said Barbara Edwards. "What kinda town is this?" Jackson ran across the street in an attempt to flag a cab, but it was filled, and defiantly sped away. Finally, he gave up and took a place in line at a nearby hotel. He was reduced to the sort of patience required of bunters and long relievers. It hurt. When Barbara Edwards climbed into her cab, Reggie leaned into the backseat and kept his face very close to hers for almost a minute. Then he said goodbye.

Someone mentioned that perhaps her beauty exceeded her intellectual strengths. "It's true. She doesn't seem too sharp," Reggie said, "but it's probably the whole thing of meeting Reggie Jackson for the first time. If I spent time with her, she'd get over it."

The next cab was supposed to be Jackson's, but a woman in the line insisted otherwise. Exasperated, he offered to split the ride with the woman, who called herself Roxanne. In the front seat, Roxanne turned to Jackson and said, "I drive eighteen-wheelers. Whadda you do?"

Ted and Everett laughed nervously. Then Reggie laughed, too. He knew it was just a joke, but when he dropped her off he made no motion to let her skip the fare. As the cab rode toward the airport he said, "Fuck her. She wasn't too impressed with me."

Then, to the driver, he said, "You like this job? It's not bad, is it? Six months from now I'll be out here in Vegas with a checker cab, cigarette breath, and a T-shirt. I'll be great. Won't I?"

As the car pulled up to the airport gate, Reggie had one more question for the driver. "Hey, you ever get a blowjob in the cab?"

The walls of Reggie's plane are covered with Ultrasuede. The seats are deep and embracing. Before he fell asleep, Reggie put his feet up on a seat and said, "This plane doesn't make economic sense. It's seven thousand eight hundred dollars an hour. But I'm buying time. I'm buying solitude."

That winter he needed quiet more than ever. His father was very sick. Several times in the weeks before spring training, Reggie flew to Philadelphia to visit him in the hospital. "For a while we weren't sure if he was gonna make it," Reggie said.

Martinez Jackson ran a cleaning store when Reggie was growing up, and brewed corn liquor in the basement to make a little extra money. To keep the cold out of the house, they draped blankets across the doors.

One day when Reggie was around six, he was riding with his father in the delivery truck when he noticed his father was crying.

"What's wrong?" Reggie asked.

"Your mom and I are splitting up," he said. "She's leaving today." In his autobiography, written with Mike Lupica, Jackson put it this way: "The next thing I knew, my mother was just kind of gone. Her other three natural children went with her. I stayed with my dad. . . . There are things that happen to you in your life that you don't question, maybe because you're afraid of what the answer will be. My mom leaving me behind is one of those things. I never asked her why."

Martinez and Reggie grew closer. Then, when he was a senior at Cheltenham High School and the best athlete in the Philadelphia area, Reggie saw police cars parked in front of his house. A court sentenced Martinez Jackson to six months in jail for making liquor illegally. For a while, Reggie was as alone as a boy can be. With his father gone, Reggie helped run the business, finished school, handled the recruiters, and, finally, left for Arizona State. He visited his father only once in prison. He could not stand the sight of the old man in prison grays.

And now Martinez Jackson was worn out. Reggie did not know what more he could do for his father. He had been a good and grateful son. Long ago, when times were tough, his father dreamed of owning a red Cadillac. Reggie bought him one. He helped him build his cleaning business. So his dad could make some extra money, Reggie even got him a "job" as a scout for the Angels. ("The only scouting he's got to do is scout the mailbox for his check every month.") He had always done for his father what every son hopes he will be in the position to do. But he could not make it all right, not with fame or money or words.

In feeling his own decline, Jackson was himself learning a little of what it is to grow old. "You don't retire at your convenience. You don't die when you're ready," he said. Below, the lights of Los Angeles blurred through the fog. "It's an inconvenience to die. You don't retire at the top. There are no announcements. There are no invitations. You're just gone."

He had a date in town that night, but by morning he was alone. He woke at 6:00 A.M., made a few business calls, and rode a stationary bike for twenty minutes. At seven-thirty he drove his garnet Porsche to Super Bodies, a storefront gym near Newport Beach. Another "Reggie guy," a hulking blond named Walt Harris, met Jackson on the sidewalk, and the two men went inside to stretch. "I used to tear my muscles up all the time," Reggie said. "Now I don't run fast enough to tear nothing."

Jackson worked harder than anyone else in the gym. "When I quit I'll become a body builder," he said with a load of weights on his back. "Just for the hell of it. For vanity." He worked his quadriceps, his calves, his triceps and biceps. Between sets, he ran in place with the quick, short steps of a shadowboxer. He wore a baseball cap, sweatpants, and a blue rubber shirt. Sweat washed over his face and dripped off the point of his chin. He had always looked more like a heavyweight fighter than a ballplayer.

To strengthen the muscles that power his baseball swing, Jackson took a twenty-five-pound barbell and mimicked the motions of batting. Many players disdain heavy weight training, saying it makes them bulky, but Reggie was not lifting for singles or doubles to the opposite field. He was training his muscles for a last season of all-or-nothing.

Jackson climbed on a computerized exercise bike to get his heart beating faster. "When I was twenty-eight years old I didn't have any of this," he said over the whir. "I did nothing. I did, like, a million five hundred thousand dollars in the off-season just hustling business."

He finished his workout with a series of abdominal exercises. Some days he did thirteen hundred sit-ups.

At last he rested and drank a glass of blended fruits. A few friends dropped by the gym to say hello, including a young woman named Anne Appleby, who brought her one-month-old daughter, Kimberley Nicole. Reggie cradled the baby in his arms and stood in front of a mirror. "How do I look?" he said. "Like a daddy?" The mother laughed. Kimberley cried. Reggie gave the baby back to Anne. "Hey, so it's only Reggie Jackson," he said. "Who cares, right?"

Before every game at Yankee Stadium, old clips of Ruth and Gehrig, DiMaggio and Mantle flicker on the big screen above the bleachers.

When he visits the stadium, Jackson sometimes tries to take his batting practice while his own image—younger, faster, reliably heroic—is on the screen. Once, while warming up on an August afternoon with the Angels, he belted one ball straight at his own looming icon. Afterward he told *The Washington Post,* "I'm still Reggie, but not as often."

Inevitably, the stadium's film shows Jackson's performance against the Dodgers in the sixth and final game of the 1977 World Series. As he hits his three home runs, the PA system plays the old rock standard "Lightnin' Strikes (again and again and again)."

"It was the worst year of my life," Jackson said behind the wheel of a van. "I was a walking-around mental case." It began with a disastrous interview in which he said that he, and not the team's gritty catcher, Thurman Munson, was the "straw that stirs the drink." Every morning in the *Times,* the *Post,* and the *News,* the protagonists continued their *opéra bouffe.* Billy and George and Reggie. Thurman and Graig and Sparky. That one season generated more books than the Korean War. Though he never avoided the clubhouse and dugout madness, Jackson would spend hour after hour that year sitting on the terrace of his Fifth Avenue apartment, depressed and weary. "I used to read the Bible and take little sayings out of it because I needed support, I needed help," he said. "Sounds like I was nuts, huh?"

Then the autumn came. In the postseason most hitters do not perform nearly as well as they do in the spring or summer. It is not only the pressure that oppresses them, it is the cold air, the truncated and superior pitching staffs, the constant night games.

Reggie Jackson lived for October. That he could focus so clearly on a speeding ball amid all the turbulence—that was always his gift. After five games, the Yankees had a 3–2 lead over the Dodgers. Reggie left Los Angeles on his second homer of the Series, a long shot off Don Sutton. He wanted the season to end, and, somehow, he had an idea of just how it would.

Driving toward a body shop where he often hangs out, Jackson turned down the oldies station he listens to and let it all roll back over him like a wave.

"The day of game six, well, everybody has asked me, what did you do? And I just kinda said I relaxed and listened to the radio. The truth is I spent the afternoon relaxing with a lady. Relaxing, baby, I was relaxed.

"I knew I was swinging the bat good in batting practice. I probably hit two dozen balls out. The crowd in right field was going crazy.

"I was on the money. I was like a guy rolling a three hundred game. I was like a basketball shooter, and when he lets go you know it's gonna be all net. So I was ready. Sometimes you just know.

"The first time up against Burt Hooton, I didn't get to swing. Got walked on four pitches. The next time up, Thurman was on base and they had to give me a ball to hit. It was the first pitch he threw. It felt like I'd hit it hard enough to go five hundred feet, but I hit over the ball because I thought it was going to sink. But Yankee Stadium has a short right field, and the ball stayed up just long enough.

"The next time up, in the fifth, Hooton was out of the game and Elias Sosa was in. Sosa was a hard thrower, and I knew he was going to try to bust me with a pitch inside. That's always been the thing to do. Even when I was on deck I was saying to myself, Please, dear God, let him hurry up and get ready so I can get it.

"I knew as soon as Sosa let go of the ball I was going to hit it out of the ballpark. It was the best ball I hit all night, like a one-iron shot. Now I could hear the crowd starting to chant my name. '*Reg*-gie. *Reg*-gie.' Jesus.

"I knew I was going to get up again, and I figured I might as well go for another one. It wouldn't matter even if I struck out. No matter what I did I'd still get another ovation.

"And so they brought in Charlie Hough. We were up seven–three in the bottom of the eighth. A knuckler! I probably have more career home runs off knucklers than any pitchers I'd ever faced. I couldn't lose. All I wanted him to do was throw a strike. And, man, he threw a cookie."

The second-base umpire, Ed Sudol, could not believe it. "Hough threw him a tremendous knuckleball," he said. "I don't know how Reggie even got his bat on it, let alone hit it about four hundred and twenty feet." The Dodger first baseman, Steve Garvey, began to applaud in his glove. In the dugout, all the year's tensions melted. Munson hugged Reggie, and so did Martin. Graig Nettles, who would later get in a fistfight with Jackson at a party, said, "It was magic. And it didn't matter in the slightest whether you liked him or detested him. After the third home run, I walked out to the on-deck circle as the crowd was cheering and cheering, and I took my helmet off and waved at everybody as though they were cheering me, and I enjoyed my little fantasy as the noise swirled over the whole stadium."

When Jackson trotted out to right field, they chanted his name, louder and louder, *Reg*-gie . . . *Reg*-gie . . . *Reg*-gie. Confetti, most of it torn flecks of programs, napkins, and toilet paper, showered over him. For once, the sound was clear and unanimous. No one who appreciated the difficulty of what he had done could withhold his admiration or affection.

He never grew bored remembering his perfect night. He pulled the van off the highway, turned off the engine, and gripped the wheel with both hands. A hard sun shone through the window, and Reggie put his face in the light. He was quiet awhile. Then he said,

"When all is said and done, people like me. They like me. That's something."

Reggie drove back home. His condominium was packed with Reggie memorabilia: a wood clock with Reggie's image carved into the face; a gilt baseball, a tribute to the home run that propelled Reggie past Mickey Mantle; two copies of his autobiography, *Reggie*; a videotape labeled REGGIE JACKSON, POSITIVE AT-BATS, 1985; a batch of Reggie clips stacked on a director's chair emblazoned with its owner's name.

Earlier he had read with evident sadness a story about George Foster, a once-extraordinary hitter for the Reds and Mets who had squandered his fortune. "You see it all the time," Reggie said. "Sometimes it's the player, sometimes it's these agents who are telling them what to do. They're just a bunch of white guys with Samsonite brief cases and bad suits." He was in his bedroom, dressing while he watched the Financial News Network on cable. His eyes fixed on the stock ticker that ran across the bottom of the screen. Every few minutes or so he stopped to place a call to his lawyer in Oakland, his agent in New York, his real estate partner in Phoenix, a car dealer in Los Angeles. He seemed to love this part of being him.

"Are you in?" he asked his broker. They were talking about a "very hot" jeans company. "It was up to three and heading toward four. You in? Hang in there, at least today. If it gets hairy, I'll call you."

He got up from the bed and began to sway to the electronic bounce of FNN's theme songs. "I'm a capitalist," he said. "And I'm a Reagan supporter. But mostly in politics I'm a fence-sitter. I don't want to put myself in a position to say too many controversial things, because a lot of the people I'm in contact with are CEOs. They can affect my future." He shimmied during the bond report, hopped during the NASDAQ index. When the report on the top ten stocks of the day came on, Reggie sat perched on the edge of his bed and watched every second.

"I think you're getting to see that there are all sides to Reggie," he said after it was over. "I may not necessarily be better than anyone, but I'm unique. There's Reggie the ballplayer and Reggie the media guy and Reggie who's into cars. But Reggie's also meeting with the main players of the eighties. I call Boone Pickens for advice on high-end economics. I look hard at what Steve Jobs is doing. Tonight I'm supposed to have dinner with John Sculley, the head of Apple. You think I won't come away with any wisdom?"

A report came on the television about the scandals on Wall Street. "Boesky just got caught," Reggie said. "I'm not condoning what he did. It's just not wrong. They say that pigs get fat, hogs go to market."

Jackson made a few more calls. Then he pulled out his suitcases. The next morning he had practice at the Coliseum in Oakland. He stepped into a walk-in closet filled with dozens of shirts, and fingered sleeve after sleeve. When he emerged with the chosen shirts draped across his arm, Jackson's whole expression had changed. "Let me ask you something," he said. "What kind of story are you doing?" There was a painful, nervous pause. "Is it a Reggie profile? A 'Reggie retires' kind of thing? See, I think the media get some kind of weird enjoyment out of asking, 'What are you going to do when you're not the center of attention anymore? What are you going to do when all the adulation is dried up and all the cheers die down? Huh?' It's like they want you to say, 'I'll collapse. I won't be able to make it in society. I'll end up in a halfway house.' Well, you can see that baseball is just a part of me. Reggie Jackson is not your average baseball player."

Reggie cannot get over the completeness of himself, his multifaceted self. "I guess I underestimated the magnitude of me," he has said. No one, he is convinced, has told his story adequately. He has already written two autobiographies and is considering a third. When he contracted Lupica to write *Reggie* with him, there were hermeneutic debates of every sort. *Reggie,* Jackson believed, did not contain all that is Reggie. "It was on the best-seller list, but it could have been a huge book, you know what I'm saying? It could have been something. It could have been another fucking Hemingway, but for that I would've needed a . . . James Michener."

He checked his watch, a chunky gold Rolex. "It's getting late," he said. "We've got a couple of things to do before we fly to Oakland, and I've got that dinner with John Sculley tonight. Did I mention that? He's the head of Apple."

At lunch, Reggie, Ted, and Walt stood in front of a big-screen TV that was playing old baseball highlights. As the tape rolled they quizzed each other on averages, plays, nicknames—all the ephemera of the game. Jackson never missed a question.

"You're the king," Walt said.

"Yes," Reggie said.

They drove back to the garage—Ted and Walt on motorcycles, Jackson in one of his vintage "muscle" cars. There to greet them was one of Reggie's girlfriends—a young, blond student from Golden West College. ("About the ladies. Keep the names out of it," Reggie said. "I don't want one of them getting mad about another. I mean, they know, but, well, you understand.")

"I thought we were going to lunch," she complained. "I've been here for like an hour."

"I said one o'clock, didn't I?" Reggie said.

"I was here early," she said. "You guys were gone."

"*Ahh*, well," Reggie said, and he enveloped her in his arms.

For the next hour or so Reggie watched Ted hose down a buddy's Oldsmobile. They talked carburetors and camshafts. Jackson walked from one car to the next, admiring the Corniche, perusing the Corvette, checking out the "fat fender" on the custom Mercedes-Benz. The blonde looked for something to do. She helped Ted polish the hood of the Oldsmobile. Reggie watched her while he spoke once more on the phone to his broker.

"Honey!" he said when he hung up. "It's long strokes. Not across. Not short. *Looong* strokes."

"I didn't—"

"I know, honey, you're learning."

Reggie and the blonde drove back to his condominium, leaving Walt and Ted to work in the garage. "I've got the plane set to go in a couple of hours," he told them. "I've got some packing to do."

Jackson was once married to a woman named Jennie Campos. They were divorced, after four years, in 1972. Since then he has come close to marrying once, lived with at least one other woman, and has dated "a lot." "Reggie's girls all look pretty much the same," Walt said. "Blond, pretty, twenty-one or twenty-two, perfect bods, kind of beachy." He said he wants a family "after baseball sometime," but for the moment one of the biggest portraits in his house is of Reggie and his Chevrolet. "So I'm not married," he said. "Whoopee shit. The only thing about not being married is I don't have children, or I don't have someone to share my life with all the time. So I'm missing a couple of things, but I'm not exactly . . . I don't need a goddam psychoanalyst."

Walt checked his watch, smiled, and said, "That should be enough time." He drove Jackson's van back to the condominium. When Walt arrived, Reggie was standing outside surrounded by his bags. He was fidgety, scowling. He was in a panic. Once more the mood had shifted.

"You see a little white sack?" he asked Walt.

"No, what's in it? What are you talking about?"

"I can't find the thing," Reggie said, louder now. "I hid it and now I don't know where I put it."

"What's in it? How big is it?"

"It's a little bank sack with ten thousand dollars in it, that's what it is, and now I can't find it. Jesus."

"Maybe you hid it in the garage."

For the next couple of hours, Reggie, Ted, and Walt looked everywhere in the garage, in the condominium. They shuttled back and forth following one false lead after another. Finally Jackson went back home and emptied his bags all over his driveway. A neighbor named Heather walked over from the condominium next door.

"Hi! What's goin' on?" she chirped through her gum.

"Oh, I just misplaced something," he said. The sun was getting dim, and the appointment four hundred miles away with John Sculley, one of the main players of the 1980s, was drawing close. "It's driving me crazy," he said.

Then Heather began laughing. "Hah, hah, hah." It was inexplicable.

"Yeah, well . . ." Reggie said, containing himself.

"How's that ball team up in California?"

Reggie blinked. Wasn't he in California?

"Oh, they're all right," he said.

Heather just stood there.

"Well . . ." Reggie said hopefully.

"Well," Heather replied. Then, after a cruel silence, she added, ". . . see ya 'round."

"See ya 'round, Heather."

Reggie drove once more to the garage, where he leaned on his Chevrolet. "Ten thousand bucks," he said. "Ten thousand bucks." He called San Francisco and canceled his dinner with John Sculley.

"All right, now, we're not going home until we find it," he announced. Ted and Walter never stopped looking, no doubt out of good fellowship, but also, one could not help thinking, in an effort to obliterate suspicion. They were Reggie guys.

"Wait," Jackson said. "I think I know where it is." Jackson's relief was considerable, though nothing compared with Ted's and Walt's. Walt drove Jackson back to the condominium. Reggie opened the trunk of his garnet Porsche and found a black box used for holding compact disks. Inside was the sack, and inside that was the ten thousand dollars.

On February 26, 1935, the Yankees released Babe Ruth. He played two months for the Boston Braves, hitting just .181. Fat, tired, and looking for an exit line, he hit three home runs one afternoon at Forbes Field. But those home runs had the quality of nostalgia and accident. Ruth retired that June at the age of forty. For the rest of his life he tried to win a job as a manager. No one would hire him.

Twelve years later, Ruth was dying of throat cancer. Commissioner Happy Chandler declared a "Babe Ruth Day" at Yankee Stadium. Wearing a camel's-hair coat, Ruth stepped slowly up to the microphone and spoke in a rasp. "You know, this baseball game of ours comes up from the youth," he said to the crowd. "That means the boys. The only real game in the world, I think, is baseball."

Yogi Berra was there, and he later said, "When he finished talking, the Babe waved a salute and turned around and walked back to the dugout. Nobody made a move to help him. I remember one of the ballplayers saying, 'Do you think we ought to go out and give him a hand?' And somebody said, 'Leave him alone. He knows where the dugout is.'"

In his last days, Ruth still had a strong appetite, but he could no longer chew. Some days Babe would eat a mound of chopped meat. As he grew worse he ate soft-boiled eggs. At least the cancer had not robbed him of his memory. He could summon pleasure in an instant. One day shortly before he died Ruth looked down at his egg and said, "To think of the steaks . . ."

"You compare me to Babe Ruth and I'll look silly," Reggie said, driving the Oakland freeway. In athletic terms, he is right. It is as a folk hero, not as a player, that Reggie reaches across time to Babe.

Now Reggie was trying to end a little better than the Babe. He would be a designated hitter, he would play first base. He would change if he had to. But he could not humiliate himself. He would not go out on .181. That would be torture to him. "I'm not going to embarrass myself," he said. "You talk about the way Ted Williams went out on a home run. Who wouldn't want that?"

As he sat now in the Coliseum's dim and tiny clubhouse, Jackson looked around at all the kids. Who had worked as hard as he had? Who among them understood the importance of the game, and the short time they had to play it? Jackson saw players with better reflexes but with rolls of fat around their middles; he saw young men charged by the pleasures of their game but ignorant of its subtleties. Even their lack of financial savvy annoyed him. He saw young Tony Phillips dressing and joking about the "great salary deal" he was going to make. That did it.

"'Great'? How great?" Reggie said. "What did you make last year?"

"Three-fifty, four hundred thou with incentives," Phillips said.

"And now you're in arbitration?"

"Yeah."

"What are your numbers? How many hits did you have last year?"

"I don't know exactly."

"How many runs?"

"I'm not sure."

"You don't know?"

"Not sure."

"You've *gotta* know," Reggie said. "If you're in arbitration how can you *not* know? You have an agent?"

"Yeah, sure I do." Phillips was getting more and more defensive. He wanted out, he wanted to hit and run and get out of the jaws of Reggie Jackson.

"Who is he? Your brother? Your best friend? Why don't you do your own deal?"

To Phillips's astonishment, Reggie began to explain the way "agents can cut you," the sort of studying he'd better do, the interest-free loans he could ask for. "You have to make the deal that's good for you," Jackson said. "Are you gonna have any left when you're done? Can you buy your own home? Can you structure a bank loan? I'm giving you the third degree, man, because you gotta know what you're doing."

Phillips was silent. Vaguely, he understood that Jackson, of all people, knew what he was talking about. Still, he wanted out.

Reggie smiled. "Hey, man, don't listen to me. I'm just an old shit. I don't know nothing."

"No, brother, what have you been around? Twenty years?"

"Don't mean nothing. I'm just an old man."

The other players left for the field, Phillips included. Reggie waited until the others were gone before he put on his jade-colored Athletics jacket, his shades, and his shoes.

"You think Phillips will listen?" someone asked him.

Jackson spit through his teeth as he walked through the shadowy hall toward the field. His spikes clicked on the concrete. "I don't give a shit if he listens or not, to be honest," he said. "I just don't care."

The morning was clear and cool, and the grass brilliant in the hard winter light. So direct was the sun that it burned off the previous day's rain in a couple of hours. Only twenty players came to the optional workout. The manager, Tony LaRussa, was out of town, and most of the veterans had better things to do. Spring training was still weeks away. The emptiness of the seats made an echo chamber of the Coliseum, so that a sharp line drive sounded like the report from a .22.

In the dugout, a young outfielder named Michael Williams slammed a ball into his glove. He played awhile for the Cleveland Indians in 1986, but they released him. Now he was hoping to land a job in the A's system. "Class A would be fine with me," he said. "I've gotta start somewhere." Williams grew up in Hayward, California, just a short drive from the Coliseum, and when he was six or seven years old he and a friend came to the ballpark to see their first game.

"Just about the second I walked into the park, Reggie put one over the fence. Right over there," Williams said, pointing to left center field. "It was incredible, the way he hit it, and he'd just drop his bat at home plate and watch the ball and admire it going over the wall. Man! I followed every move he made. I didn't watch anyone else."

After the players did a few stretching exercises and ran laps around the grass, Jackson seized the privilege of seniority and took the first turn at bat. His own bats had not yet arrived in Oakland, so he selected a thirty-four-ounce Adirondack of white ash from a heap on the grass. "I used to use a thirty-six or a thirty-seven. Biggest bat in the league for five years," he said, taking a few warm-up swings. "Now I use a thirty-three or a thirty-four."

With his old Yankee teammate Bob Watson watching him, with nearly everyone in the park watching him, Jackson stepped into the cage. He tapped his bat on home plate, then bunted three pitches to the left, three more to the right.

"Okay now, Reg, let it rip," Watson said. It was unlikely that the A's would ask him to do any bunting.

Jackson took the first pitch, then hit three pop flies to short right field. They were too shallow for the outfielders to bother with them.

Jackson tapped once more on the plate, then cracked a line drive to center field.

"Better," Watson said. "But you're lifting that back foot."

"It's February," Jackson said, and he stepped in once more. He hit another drive, which echoed through the empty park, then a dozen pops to center and right. He smacked a foul back into the cage. At the finish of his swing his body had dropped close to the dirt and his arms and bat described a pretzel. "Damn," he said.

Jackson unwound himself and took on a more determined air. Sweating freely now, he kicked the dirt and nodded to the pitcher. He hit a couple of drives that would have been singles, then another series of shallow fly balls that were sure outs. "That's slow hands right there," he grumbled. The big hits were just not coming: foul, foul, fly, single, fly, single, single. No numbers on the board. "It takes a while for my hands to get ready," he said.

"Keep that back foot down," Watson said.

Then the pitcher grooved one in, chest-high, medium-fast. Reggie cocked his elbows and lunged at the pitch. The ball exploded off the bat, arcing into the cloudless sky and sailing over a group of fielders who were chatting in center field. Reggie dropped his bat and, along with everyone else, followed the flight of the ball. It was beautiful what the man could do. Finally, the ball cleared the fence and smacked sharply off the empty seats. A lovely, lonely sound. A home run in wintertime.

The novelist, poet, and nature writer Annie Dillard (b. 1945) grew up in Pittsburgh during the 1950s. She is the author of many books including *Teaching a Stone to Talk* (1982), *Living by Fiction* (1982), and *Pilgrim at Tinker Creek* (1974), for which she was awarded the Pulitzer Prize. The home-brewed etymology that follows, taken from her memoir *An American Childhood* (1987), would have pleased H. L. Mencken, who mused, in *The American Language,* that "the history of baseball terms also deserves to be investigated."

Annie Dillard

ᗐ

from

An American Childhood

One Sunday afternoon Mother wandered through our kitchen, where Father was making a sandwich and listening to the ball game. The Pirates were playing the New York Giants at Forbes Field. In those days, the Giants had a utility infielder named Wayne Terwilliger. Just as Mother passed through, the radio announcer cried—with undue drama—"Terwilliger bunts one!"

"Terwilliger bunts one?" Mother cried back, stopped short. She turned. "Is that English?"

"The player's name is Terwilliger," Father said. "He bunted."

"That's marvelous," Mother said. "'Terwilliger bunts one.' No wonder you listen to baseball. 'Terwilliger bunts one.'"

For the next seven or eight years, Mother made this surprising string of syllables her own. Testing a microphone, she repeated, "Terwilliger bunts one"; testing a pen or a typewriter, she wrote it. If, as happened surprisingly often in the course of various improvised gags, she pretended to whisper something else in my ear, she actually whispered, "Terwilliger bunts one." Whenever someone used a French phrase, or a Latin one, she answered solemnly, "Terwilliger bunts one." If Mother had had, like Andrew Carnegie, the opportunity to cook up a motto for a coat of arms, hers would have read simply and tellingly, "Terwilliger bunts one." (Carnegie's was "Death to Privilege.")

Growing up in Brooklyn, Stephen Jay Gould (b. 1941) was the borough's rare Yankee fan. Today this paleontologist, essayist, and winner of a MacArthur Foundation prize, whose books include *Wonderful Life: The Burgess Shale and the Nature of History* and *The Mismeasure of Man,* is the rare Harvard professor who sometimes wears a Yankee cap to lecture. In those lectures, he has been known to weave his theories about the extinction of the .400 hitter into discussions concerning the decline of extreme variation in a truly evolved system. The star outfielder for that lesson was Ted Williams. Here, in an essay first published in *The New York Review of Books* in 1988, Gould puts his mind to another aspect of evolution and probability—the streak.

Stephen Jay Gould

ʊ

The Streak of Streaks

My father was a court stenographer. At his less than princely salary, we watched Yankee games from the bleachers or high in the third deck. But one of the judges had season tickets, so we occasionally sat in the lower boxes when hizzoner couldn't attend. One afternoon, while DiMaggio was going 0 for 4 against, of all people, the lowly St. Louis Browns (now the even lowlier Baltimore Orioles), the great man fouled one in our direction. "Catch it, Dad," I screamed. "You never get them," he replied, but stuck up his hand like the Statue of Liberty—and the ball fell right in. I mailed it to DiMaggio, and, bless him, he actually sent the ball back, signed and in a box marked "insured." Insured, that is, to make me the envy of the neighborhood, and DiMaggio the model and hero of my life.

I met DiMaggio a few years ago on a small playing field at the Presidio of San Francisco. My son, wearing DiMaggio's old number 5 on his Little League jersey, accompanied me, exactly one generation after my father caught that ball. DiMaggio gave him a pointer or two on batting and then signed a ball for him. One generation passeth away, and another generation cometh: but the earth abideth forever.

My son, uncoached by Dad, and given the chance that comes but once in a lifetime, asked DiMaggio as his only query about life and career: "Suppose you had walked every time up during one game of your fifty-six-game hitting streak? Would the streak have been over?" DiMaggio replied that, under 1941 rules, the streak would have ended, but that this unfair statute has since been revised, and such a game would not count today.

My son's choice for a single question tells us something vital about the nature of legend. A man may labor for a professional lifetime, especially in sport or in battle, but posterity needs a single transcendant event to fix him in permanent memory. Every hero must be a Wellington on the right side of his personal Waterloo; generality of excellence is too diffuse. The unambiguous factuality of a single achievement is adamantine. Detractors can argue forever about the general tenor of your life and works, but they can never erase a great event.

In 1941, as I gestated in my mother's womb, Joe DiMaggio got at least one hit in each of fifty-six successive games. Most records are only incrementally superior to runners-up; Roger Maris hit sixty-one homers in 1961, but Babe Ruth hit sixty in 1927 and fifty-nine in 1921, while Hank Greenberg (1938) and Jimmy Foxx (1932) both hit fifty-eight. But DiMaggio's fifty-six–game hitting streak is ridiculously and almost unreachably far from all challengers (Wee Willie Keeler and Pete Rose, both with forty-four, come second). Among sabremetricians*—a contentious lot not known for agreement about anything—we find virtual consensus that DiMaggio's fifty-six–game hitting streak is the greatest accomplishment in the history of baseball, if not all modern sport.

The reasons for this respect are not far to seek. Single moments of unexpected supremacy—Johnny Vander Meer's back-to-back nohitters of 1938, Don Larsen's perfect game in the 1956 World Series—can occur at any time to almost anybody, and have an irreducibly capricious character. Achievements of a full season—Maris's sixty-one homers, Ted Williams's batting average of .406, also posted in 1941 and not equaled since—have a certain overall majesty, but they don't demand unfailing consistency every single day; you can slump for a while, so long as your average holds. But a streak must be absolutely exceptionless; you are not allowed a single day of subpar play, or even bad luck. You bat only four or five times in an average

---

*A happy neologism based on an acronym for members of the Society for American Baseball Research, and referring to the statistical mavens of the sport.

game. Sometimes two or three of these efforts yield walks, and you get only one or two shots at a hit. Moreover, as tension mounts and notice increases, your life becomes unbearable. Reporters dog your every step; fans are even more intrusive than usual (one stole DiMaggio's favorite bat right in the middle of his streak). You cannot make a single mistake.

Thus Joe DiMaggio's fifty-six–game hitting streak is both the greatest factual achievement in the history of baseball and a principal icon of American mythology. What shall we do with such a central item of our cultural history?

◆   ◆   ◆

Statistics and mythology may seem the most unlikely bedfellows. How can we quantify Caruso or measure *Middlemarch*? But if God could mete out heaven with the span (Isaiah 40:12), perhaps we can say something useful about hitting streaks. The statistics of "runs," defined as continuous series of good or bad results (including baseball's streaks and slumps), is a well-developed branch of the profession, and can yield clear—but wildly counterintuitive—results. (The fact that we find these conclusions so surprising is the key to appreciating DiMaggio's achievement, the point of this article, and the gateway to an important insight about the human mind.)

Start with a phenomenon that nearly everyone both accepts and considers well understood—"hot hands" in basketball. Now and then, someone just gets hot, and can't be stopped. Basket after basket falls in—or out as with "cold hands," when a man can't buy a bucket for love or money (choose your cliché). The reason for this phenomenon is clear enough; it lies embodied in the maxim: "When you're hot, you're hot; and when you're not, you're not." You get that touch, build confidence; all nervousness fades, you find your rhythm; swish, swish, swish. Or you miss a few, get rattled, endure the booing, experience despair; hands start shaking and you realize that you shoulda stood in bed.

Everybody knows about hot hands. The only problem is that no such phenomenon exists. The Stanford psychologist Amos Tversky studied every basket made by the Philadelphia 76ers for more than a season. He found, first of all, that probabilities of making a second basket did not rise following a successful shot. Moreover, the number of "runs," or baskets in succession, was no greater than what a standard random, or coin-tossing, model would predict. (If the chance of making each basket is 0.5, for example, a reasonable value for good shooters, five hits in a row will occur, on average, once in thirty-two sequences—just as you can expect to toss five successive heads about once in thirty-two times, or 0.5^5.)

Of course Larry Bird, the great forward of the Boston Celtics, will have more sequences of five than Joe Airball—but not because he has greater will or gets in that magic rhythm more often. Larry has longer runs because his average success rate is so much higher, and random models predict more frequent and longer sequences. If Larry shoots field goals at 0.6 probability of success, he will get five in a row about once every thirteen sequences (0.6^5). If Joe, by contrast, shoots only 0.3, he will get his five straight only about once in 412 times. In other words, we need no special explanation for the apparent pattern of long runs. There is no ineffable "causality of circumstance" (if I may call it that), no definite reason born of the particulars that make for heroic myths—courage in the clinch, strength in adversity, etc. You only have to know a person's ordinary play in order to predict his sequences. (I rather suspect that we are convinced of the contrary not only because we need myths so badly, but also because we remember the successes and simply allow the failures to fade from memory. More on this later.) But how does this revisionist pessimism work for baseball?

My colleague Ed Purcell, Nobel laureate in physics but, for purposes of this subject, just another baseball fan,* has done a comprehensive study of all baseball streak and slump records. His firm conclusion is easily and swiftly summarized. Nothing ever happened in baseball above and beyond the frequency predicted by coin-tossing models. The longest runs of wins or losses are as long as they should be, and occur about as often as they ought to. Even the hapless Orioles, at 0 and 21 to start this season, only fell victim to the laws of probability (and not to the vengeful God of racism, out to punish major league baseball's only black manager).

---

*Richard Sisk of the New York *Daily News* Sunday magazine (March 27, 1988) wrote a funny article about the sabremetric studies of three Harvard professors—Purcell, Dudley Herschbach, and myself. It ran with the precious title: "Buncha Pointyheads Sittin' Around Talkin' Baseball."

But "treasure your exceptions," as the old motto goes. There is one major exception, and absolutely only one—one sequence so many standard deviations above the expected distribution that it should not have occurred at all: Joe DiMaggio's fifty-six–game hitting streak in 1941. The intuition of baseball aficionados has been vindicated. Purcell calculated that to make it likely (probability greater than 50 percent) that a run of even fifty games will occur once in the history of baseball up to now (and fifty-six is a lot more than fifty in this kind of league), baseball's rosters would have to include either four lifetime .400 batters or fifty-two lifetime .350 batters over careers of one thousand games. In actuality, only three men have lifetime batting averages in excess of .350, and no one is anywhere near .400 (Ty Cobb at .367, Rogers Hornsby at .358, and Shoeless Joe Jackson at .356). DiMaggio's streak is the most extraordinary thing that ever happened in American sports. He sits on the shoulders of two bearers—mythology and science. For Joe DiMaggio accomplished what no other ballplayer has done. He beat the hardest taskmaster of all, a woman who makes Nolan Ryan's fastball look like a cantaloupe in slow motion—Lady Luck.

◆ ◆ ◆

Amos Tversky, who studied "hot hands," has performed a series of elegant psychological experiments with Daniel Kahneman.* These long-term studies have provided our finest insight into "natural reasoning" and its curious departure from logical truth. To cite an example, they construct a fictional description of a young woman: "Linda is thirty-one years old, single, outspoken, and very bright. She majored in philosophy. As a student, she was deeply concerned with issues of discrimination and social justice, and also participated in anti-nuclear demonstrations." Subjects are then given a list of hypothetical statements about Linda: they must rank these in order of presumed likelihood, most to least probable. Tversky and Kahneman list eight statements, but five are a blind, and only three make up the true experiment:

---

*See several of their essays in Amos Tversky, Daniel Kahneman, and Paul Slovic, eds., *Judgment Under Uncertainty: Heuristics and Biases* (Cambridge University Press, 1982).

Linda is active in the feminist movement;
Linda is a bank teller;
Linda is a bank teller and is active in the feminist movement.

Now it simply must be true that the third statement is least likely, since any conjunction has to be less probable than either of its parts considered separately. Everybody can understand this when the principle is explained explicitly and patiently. But all groups of subjects, sophisticated students who ought to understand logic and probability as well as folks off the street corner, rank the last statement as more probable than the second. (I am particularly fond of this example because I know that the third statement is least probable, yet a little homunculus in my head continues to jump up and down, shouting at me—"but she can't just be a bank teller; read the description.")

Why do we so consistently make this simple logical error? Tversky and Kahneman argue, correctly I think, that our minds are not built (for whatever reason) to work by the rules of probability, though these rules clearly govern our universe. We do something else that usually serves us well, but fails in crucial instances: we "match to type." We abstract what we consider the "essence" of an entity, and then arrange our judgments by their degree of similarity to this assumed type. Since we are given a "type" for Linda that implies feminism, but definitely not a bank job, we rank any statement matching the type as more probable than another that only contains material contrary to the type. This propensity may help us to understand an entire range of human preferences, from Plato's theory of form to modern stereotyping of race or gender.

We might also understand the world better, and free ourselves of unseemly prejudice, if we properly grasped the workings of probability and its inexorable hold, through laws of logic, upon much of nature's pattern. "Matching to type" is one common error; failure to understand random patterning in streaks and slumps is another—hence Tversky's study of both the fictional Linda and the 76ers' baskets. Our failure to appreciate the uniqueness of DiMaggio's streak derives from the same unnatural and uncomfortable relationship that we maintain with probability. (If we understood Lady Luck better, Las Vegas might still be a roadstop in the desert, and Nancy Reagan might not have a friend in San Francisco.)

My favorite illustration of this basic misunderstanding, as applied to DiMaggio's hitting streak, appeared in a recent article by baseball writer John Holway, "A Little Help from his Friends," and subtitled "Hits or Hype in '41" (*Sports Heritage*, November/December, 1987). Holway points out that five of DiMaggio's successes were narrow escapes and lucky breaks. He received two benefits-of-the-doubt from official scorers on plays that might have been judged as errors. In each of two games, his only hit was a cheapie. (In game sixteen, a ball dropped untouched in the outfield and had to be ruled a hit, even though the ball could have been caught, had it not been misjudged; in game fifty-four, DiMaggio dribbled one down the third base line, easily beating the throw because the third baseman, expecting the usual, was playing far back.) The fifth incident is an oft-told tale, perhaps the most interesting story of the streak. In game thirty-eight, DiMaggio was 0 for 3 going into the last inning. Scheduled to bat fourth, he might have been denied a chance to hit at all. Johnny Sturm popped up to begin the inning, but Red Rolfe then walked. Slugger Tommy Henrich, up next, was suddenly swept with a premonitory fear: suppose I ground into a double play and end the inning. An elegant solution immediately occurred to him: why not bunt (an odd strategy for a power hitter)? Henrich laid down a beauty; DiMaggio, up next, promptly drilled a double to left.

Holway's account is interesting, but his premise is entirely, almost preciously, wrong. First of all, none of the five incidents represents an egregious miscall. The two hits were less than elegant, but they were undoubtedly legitimate; the two boosts from official scorers were close calls on judgment plays, not gifts. As for Henrich, I can only repeat manager Joe McCarthy's comment when Tommy asked him for permission to bunt: "Yeah, that's a good idea." Not a terrible strategy either—to put a man into scoring position for an insurance run when you're up 3–1.

But these details do not touch the main point—Holway's premise is false because he accepts the conventional mythology about long sequences. He believes that streaks are unbroken runs of causal courage—so that any prolongation by hook-or-crook is an outrage against the deep meaning of the phenomenon. But extended sequences are no such thing. Long streaks always are, and must be, a matter of extraordinary luck imposed upon great skill. Please don't make the vulgar mistake of thinking that Purcell or Tversky or I or anyone else would attribute a long streak to "just luck"—as though everyone's chances are exactly the same, and streaks represent nothing more than the lucky atom that kept moving in one direction. Long hitting streaks happen to the greatest players— Sisler, Keeler, DiMaggio, Rose—because their general chance of getting a hit is so much higher than average. Just as Joe Airball cannot match Larry Bird for runs of baskets, Joe's cousin Bill Ofer, with a lifetime batting average of .184, will never have a streak to match DiMaggio's with a lifetime average of .325. The statistics show something else, and something fascinating: there is no "causality of circumstance," no "extra" that the great can draw from the soul of their valor to extend a streak beyond the ordinary expectation of coin-tossing models for a series of unconnected events, each occurring with the characteristic probability for that particular player. Good players have higher characteristic probabilities, hence longer streaks.

Of course DiMaggio had a little luck during his streak. That's what streaks are all about. No long sequence has ever been entirely sustained in any other way (the Orioles almost won several of those twenty-one games). DiMaggio's remarkable achievement—its uniqueness, in the unvarnished literal sense of that word—lies in whatever he did to extend his success well beyond the reasonable expectations of random models that have governed every other streak or slump in the history of baseball.

Probability does pervade the universe—and in this sense, the old chestnut about baseball imitating life really has validity. The statistics of streaks and slumps, properly understood, do teach an important lesson about epistemology, and life in general. The history of a species, or any natural phenomenon that requires unbroken continuity in a world of trouble, works like a batting streak. All are games of a gambler playing with a limited stake against a house with infinite resources. The gambler must eventually go bust. His aim can only be to stick around as long as possible, to have some fun while he's at it, and, if he happens to be a moral agent as well, to worry about staying the course with honor. The best of us will try to live by a few simple rules: do justly, love mercy, walk humbly with thy God, and never draw to an inside straight.

DiMaggio's hitting streak is the finest of legitimate legends because it embodies the essence of the battle that truly defines our lives. DiMaggio activated the greatest and most unattainable dream of all humanity, the hope and chimera of all sages and shamans: he cheated death, at least for a while.

Stephen King (b. 1947) had lived near Bangor, Maine, for nearly twenty years when he wrote this piece about the fortunes of his son's Little League team. The same nuanced development of a suspenseful plot that is a hallmark of King's fiction is fully evident in this account of a series of important games played by children. In other respects, however, it is far removed from the gothic and apocalyptic tone of *The Stand, The Shining,* and his other novels of horror and the uncanny. Of this piece, King has written: "My proximity to the Bangor West All-Star team when it mounted its unlikely charge on the State Championship was either pure luck or pure fate, depending on where you stand in regard to the possible existence of a higher power. I tend toward the higher power thesis, but in either case, I was only there because my son was on the team. . . . For a month or so it was like living inside one of those corny sports novels with which many of us guys have whiled away our duller afternoon study-halls: *Go Up for Glory, Power Forward,* and occasional bright standouts like John R. Tunis's *The Kid from Tomkinsville.*" This essay originally appeared in *The New Yorker* in 1990.

Stephen King

◻

Head Down

Head down! Keep your head *down!*"

It is far from the most difficult feat in sports, but anyone who has ever tried to do it will tell you that it's tough enough: using a round bat to hit a round ball squarely on the button. Tough enough so that the handful of men who do it well become rich, famous, and idolized: the Jose Cansecos, the Mike Greenwells, the Kevin Mitchells. For thousands of boys (and not a few girls), their faces, not the face of Axl Rose or Bobby Brown, are the ones that matter; their posters hold the positions of honor on bedroom walls and locker doors. Today Ron St. Pierre is teaching some of these boys—boys who will represent Bangor West Side in District 3 Little League tournament play—how to put the round bat on the round ball. Right now he's working with a kid named Fred Moore while my son, Owen, stands nearby, watching closely. He's due in St. Pierre's hot seat next. Owen is broad-shouldered and heavily built, like his old man; Fred looks almost painfully slim in his bright green jersey. And he is not making good contact.

"Head down, Fred!" St. Pierre shouts. He is halfway between the mound and home plate at one of the two Little League fields behind the Coke plant in Bangor; Fred is almost all the way to the backstop. The day is a hot one, but if the heat bothers either Fred or St. Pierre it does not show. They are intent on what they are doing.

"Keep it *down!"* St. Pierre shouts again, and unloads a fat pitch.

Fred chips under it. There is that chinky aluminum-on-cowhide sound—the sound of someone hitting a tin cup with a spoon. The ball hits the backstop, rebounds, almost bonks him on the helmet. Both of them laugh, and then St. Pierre gets another ball from the red plastic bucket beside him.

"Get ready, Freddy!" he yells. "Head down!"

Maine's District 3 is so large that it is split in two. The Penobscot County teams make up half the division; the teams from Aroostook and Washington counties make up the other half. All-Star kids are selected by merit and drawn from all existing district Little League teams. The dozen teams in District 3 play in simultaneous tournaments. Near the end of July, the two teams left will play off, best two out of three, to decide the district champ. That team represents District 3 in State Championship play, and it has been a long time—eighteen years—since a Bangor team made it into the state tourney.

This year, the State Championship games will be played in Old Town, where they make the canoes. Four of the five teams that play there will go back home. The fifth will go on to represent Maine in the Eastern Regional Tournament, this year to be held in Bristol, Connecticut. Beyond *that,* of course, is Williamsport, Pennsylvania, where the Little League World Series happens. The Bangor West players rarely seem to think of such dizzy heights; they will be happy just to beat Millinocket, their first-round opponent in the Penobscot County race. Coaches, however, are allowed to dream—are, in fact, almost *obligated* to dream.

This time Fred, who is the team joker, *does* get his head down. He hits a weak grounder on the wrong side of the first-base line, foul by about six feet.

"Look," St. Pierre says, taking another ball. He holds it up. It is scuffed, dirty, and grass-stained. It is nevertheless a baseball, and Fred eyes it respectfully. "I'm going to show you a trick. Where's the ball?"

"In your hand," Fred says.

Saint, as Dave Mansfield, the team's head coach, calls him, drops it into his glove. "Now?"

"In your glove."

Saint turns sideways; his pitching hand creeps into his glove. "Now?"

"In your hand. I think."

"You're right. So watch my hand. Watch my hand, Fred Moore, and wait for the ball to come out in it. You're looking for the ball. Nothing else. Just the ball. I should just be a blur to you. Why would you want to see me, anyway? Do you care if I'm smiling? No. You're waiting to see how I'll come—sidearm or three-quarters or over the top. Are you waiting?"

Fred nods.

"Are you watching?"

Fred nods again.

"O.K.," St. Pierre says, and goes into his short-arm batting-practice motion again.

This time Fred drives the ball with real authority: a hard sinking liner to right field.

"All *right!*" Saint cries. "That's *all right,* Fred Moore!" He wipes sweat off his forehead. "Next batter!"

Dave Mansfield, a heavy, bearded man who comes to the park wearing aviator sunglasses and an open-neck College World Series shirt (it's a good-luck charm), brings a paper sack to the Bangor West–Millinocket game. It contains sixteen pennants, in various colors. BANGOR, each one says, the word flanked by a lobster on one side and a pine tree on the other. As each Bangor West player is announced on loudspeakers that have been wired to the chain-link backstop, he takes a pennant from the bag Dave holds out, runs across the infield, and hands it to his opposite number.

Dave is a loud, restless man who happens to love baseball and the kids who play it at this level. He believes there are two purposes to All-Star Little League: to have fun and to win. Both are important, he says, but the most important thing is to keep them in the right order.

The pennants are not a sly gambit to unnerve the opposition but just for fun. Dave knows that the boys on both teams will remember this game, and he wants each of the Millinocket kids to have a souvenir. It's as simple as that.

The Millinocket players seem surprised by the gesture, and they don't know exactly what to do with the pennants as someone's tape player begins to warble out the Anita Bryant version of "The Star-Spangled Banner." The Millinocket catcher, almost buried beneath his gear, solves the problem in unique fashion: he holds his Bangor pennant over his heart.

With the amenities taken care of, Bangor West administers a brisk and thorough trouncing; the final score is Bangor West 18, Millinocket 7. The loss does not devalue the souvenirs, however; when Millinocket departs on the team bus, the visitors' dugout is empty save for a few Dixie cups and Popsicle sticks. The pennants—every single one of them—are gone.

"Cut *two!*" Neil Waterman, Bangor West's field coach, shouts. "Cut *two*, cut *two!*"

It's the day after the Millinocket game. Everyone on the team is still showing up for practice, but it's early yet. Attrition will set in. That is a given: parents are not always willing to give up summer plans so their kids can play Little League after the regular, May–June season is over, and sometimes the kids themselves tire of the constant grind of practice. Some would rather be riding their bikes, trying to hang ten on their skateboards, or just hanging around the community pool and checking out the girls.

"Cut *two!*" Waterman yells. He is a small, compact man in khaki shorts and a Joe Coach crewcut. In real life he is a teacher and a college basketball coach, but this summer he is trying to teach these boys that baseball has more in common with chess than many would ever have believed. Know your play, he tells them over and over again. Know who it is you're backing up. Most important of all, know who your cut man is in every situation, and be able to hit him. He works patiently at showing them the truth that hides at the center of the game: that it is played more in the mind than with the body.

Ryan Iarrobino, Bangor West's center fielder, fires a bullet to Casey Kinney at second base. Casey tags an invisible runner, pivots, and throws another bullet to home, where J. J. Fiddler takes the throw and tosses the ball back to Waterman.

"Double-play ball!" Waterman shouts, and hits one to Matt Kinney (not related to Casey). Matt is playing shortstop at practice today. The ball takes a funny hop and appears to be on its way to left center. Matt knocks it down, picks it up, and feeds to Casey at second; Casey pivots and throws to Mike Arnold, who is on first. Mike feeds it home to J.J.

"All right!" Waterman shouts. "Good job, Matt Kinney! *Good job! One-two-one!* You're covering, Mike Pelkey!" The two names. Always the two names, to avoid confusion. The team is lousy with Matts, Mikes, and guys named Kinney.

The throws are executed flawlessly. Mike Pelkey, Bangor West's number two pitcher, is right where he's supposed to be, covering first. It's a move he doesn't always remember to make, but this time he does. He grins and trots back to the mound as Neil Waterman gets ready to hit the next combination.

"This is the best Little League All-Star team I've seen in years," Dave Mansfield says some days after Bangor West's trouncing of Millinocket. He dumps a load of sunflower seeds into his mouth and begins to chew them. He spits hulls casually as he talks. "I don't think they can be beaten—at least not in this division."

He pauses and watches as Mike Arnold breaks toward the plate from first, grabs a practice bunt, and whirls toward the bag. He cocks his arm back—then holds the ball. Mike Pelkey is still on the mound; this time he has forgotten that it is his job to cover, and the bag is undefended. He flashes Dave a quick guilty glance. Then he breaks into a sunny grin and gets ready to do it again. Next time he'll do it right, but will he remember to do it right during a game?

"Of course, we can beat ourselves," Dave says. "That's how it usually happens." And, raising his voice, he bellows, "*Where were you, Mike Pelkey? You're s'posed to be covering first!*"

Mike nods and trots over—better late than never.

"Brewer," Dave says, and shakes his head. "Brewer at their field. That'll be tough. Brewer's *always* tough."

Bangor West does not trounce Brewer, but they win their first "road game" without any real strain. Matt Kinney, the team's number one pitcher, is in good form. He is far from overpowering, but his fastball has a sneaky, snaky little hop, and he also has a modest but effective breaking pitch. Ron St. Pierre is fond of saying that every Little League pitcher in America thinks he's got a killer curveball. "What they think is a curve is usually this big lollipop change," he says. "A batter with a little self-discipline can kill the poor thing."

Matt Kinney's curveball actually curves, however, and tonight he goes the distance and strikes out eight. Probably more important, he walks only four. Walks are the bane of a Little League coach's existence. "They kill you," Neil Waterman says. "The walks kill you every time. Absolutely no exceptions. Sixty per cent of batters walked score in Little League games." Not in this game: two of the batters Kinney walks are forced at second; the other two are stranded. Only one Brewer batter gets a hit: Denise Hewes, the center fielder, singles with one out in the fifth, but she is forced at second.

After the game is safely in the bag, Matt Kinney, a solemn and almost eerily self-possessed boy, flashes Dave a rare smile, revealing a set of neat braces. "She could *hit!*" he says, almost reverently.

"Wait until you see Hampden," Dave says dryly. "They *all* hit."

When the Hampden squad shows up at Bangor West's field, behind the Coke plant, on July 17th, they quickly prove Dave right. Mike Pelkey has pretty good stuff and better control than he had against Millinocket, but he isn't much of a mystery to the Hampden boys. Mike Tardif, a compact kid with an amazingly fast bat, rips Pelkey's third pitch over the left-field fence, two hundred feet away, for a home run in the first inning. Hampden adds two more runs in the second, and leads Bangor West 3–0.

In the third, however, Bangor West breaks loose. Hampden's pitching is good, Hampden's hitting is awesome, but Hampden's fielding, particularly infielding, leaves something to be desired. Bangor West puts three hits together with five errors and two walks to score seven runs. This is how Little League is most often played, and seven runs should be enough, but they aren't; the opposition chips stubbornly away, getting two in its half of the third and two more in the fifth. When Hampden comes up in the bottom of the sixth, it is trailing by only three, 10–7.

Kyle King, a twelve-year-old who started for Hampden this evening and then went to catcher in the fifth, leads off the bottom of the sixth with a double. Then Mike Pelkey strikes out Mike Tardif. Mike Wentworth, the new Hampden pitcher, singles to deep short. King and Wentworth advance on a passed ball, but are forced to hold when Jeff Carson grounds back to the pitcher. This brings up Josh Jamieson, one of five Hampden home-run threats, with two on and two out. He represents the trying run. Mike, although clearly tired, finds a little extra and strikes him out on a one-two pitch. The game is over.

The kids line up and give each other the custom-ordained high fives, but it's clear that Mike isn't the only kid who is simply exhausted after the match; with their slumped shoulders and lowered heads, they all look like losers. Bangor West is now 3–0 in divisional play, but the win is a fluke, the kind of game that makes Little League such a nerve-racking experience for spectators, coaches, and the players themselves. Usually sure-handed in the field, Bangor West has tonight committed something like nine errors.

"I didn't sleep all night," Dave mutters at practice the next day. "Damn, we were outplayed. We should have lost that game."

Two nights later, he has something else to feel gloomy about. He and Ron St. Pierre make the six-mile trip to Hampden to watch Kyle King and his mates play Brewer. This is no scouting expedition; Bangor has played both clubs, and both men have copious notes. What they are really hoping to see, Dave admits, is Brewer getting lucky and putting Hampden out of the way. It doesn't happen; what they see isn't a baseball game but gunnery practice.

Josh Jamieson, who struck out in the clutch against Mike Pelkey, clouts a home run over everything and into the Hampden practice field. Nor is Jamieson alone. Carson hits one, Wentworth hits one, and Tardif hits a pair. The final score is Hampden 21, Brewer 9.

On the ride back to Bangor, Dave Mansfield chews a lot of sunflower seeds and says little. He rouses himself only once, as he wheels his old green Chevy into the rutted dirt parking lot beside the Coke plant. "We got lucky Tuesday night, and they know it," he says. "When we go down there Thursday, they'll be waiting for us."

The diamonds on which the teams of District 3 play out their six-inning dramas all have the same dimensions, give or take a foot here or an outfield gate there. The coaches all carry the rule book in their back pockets, and they put it to frequent use. Dave likes to say that it never hurts to make sure. The infield is sixty feet on each side, a square standing on the point that is home plate. The backstop, according to the rule book, must be at least twenty feet from home plate, giving both the catcher and a runner at third a fair chance on a passed ball. The fences are supposed to be 200 feet from the plate. At Bangor West's field, it's actually about 210 to dead center. And at Hampden, home of power hitters like Tardif and Jamieson, it's more like 180.

The most inflexible measurement is also the most important: the distance between the pitcher's rubber and the center of the plate. Forty-six feet—no more, no less. When it comes to this one, nobody ever says, "Aw, close enough for government work—let it go." Most Little League teams live and die by what happens in the forty-six feet between those two points.

The fields of District 3 vary considerably in other ways, and a quick look is usually enough to tell you something about the feel any given community has for the game. The Bangor West field is in bad shape— a poor relation that the town regularly ignores in its recreation budget. The undersurface is a sterile clay that turns to soup when the weather is wet and to concrete when the weather is dry, as it has been this summer. Watering has kept most of the outfield reasonably green, but the infield is hopeless. Scruffy grass grows up the lines, but the area between the pitcher's rubber and home plate is almost completely bald. The backstop is rusty; passed balls and wild pitches frequently squirt through a wide gap between the ground and the chain link. Two large, hilly dunes run through short-right and center fields. These dunes have actually become a home-team advantage. Bangor West players learn to play the caroms off them, just as Red Sox left fielders learn to play caroms off the Green Monster. Visiting fielders, on the other hand, often find themselves chasing their mistakes all the way to the fence.

Brewer's field, tucked behind the local IGA grocery and a Marden's Discount Store, has to compete for space with what may be the oldest, rustiest playground equipment in New England; little brothers and sisters watch the game upside down from the swings, their heads down and their feet in the sky.

Bob Beal Field in Machias, with its pebble-pocked-skin infield, is probably the worst of the fields Bangor West will visit this year;

Hampden, with its manicured outfield and neat composition infield, is probably the best. With its picnic area beyond the center-field fence and a rest-room-equipped snack bar, Hampden's diamond, behind the local VFW hall, looks like a rich kids' field. But looks can be deceiving. This team is a combination of kids from Newburgh and Hampden, and Newburgh is still small-farm and dairy country. Many of these kids ride to the games in old cars with primer paint around the headlights and mufflers held in place by chicken wire; they wear sunburns they got doing chores, not while they were hanging out at the country-club swimming pool. Town kids and country kids. Once they're in uniform, it doesn't much matter which is which.

Dave is right: the Hampden-Newburgh fans are waiting. Bangor West last won the District 3 Little League title in 1971; Hampden has never won a title, and many local fans continue to hope that this will be the year, despite the earlier loss to Bangor West. For the first time, the Bangor team really feels it is on the road; it is faced with a large hometown rooting section.

Matt Kinney gets the start. Hampden counters with Kyle King, and the game quickly shapes up as that rarest and richest of Little League commodities, a genuine pitchers' duel. At the end of the third inning, the score is Hampden 0, Bangor West 0.

In the bottom of the fourth, Bangor scores two unearned runs when Hampden's infield comes unglued once more. Owen King, Bangor West's first baseman, comes to bat with two on and one out. The two Kings, Kyle on the Hampden team and Owen on the Bangor West team, are not related. You don't need to be told; a single glance is enough. Kyle King is about five foot three. At six foot two, Owen King towers over him. Size differences are so extreme in Little League that it's easy to feel disoriented, the victim of hallucination.

Bangor's King raps a ground ball to short. It's a tailor-made double play, but the Hampden shortstop does not field it cleanly, and King, shucking his two hundred or so pounds down to first at top speed, beats the throw. Mike Pelkey and Mike Arnold scamper home.

Then, in the top of the fifth, Matt Kinney, who has been cruising, hits Chris Witcomb, number eight in Hampden's order. Brett Johnson, the number nine hitter, scorches one at Casey Kinney, Bangor West's second baseman. Again, it's a tailor-made double-play ball, but

Casey gives up on it. His hands, which have been automatically dipping down, freeze about four inches off the ground, and Casey turns his face away to protect it from a possible bad hop. This is the most common of all Little League fielding errors, and the most easily understood; it is an act of naked self-preservation. The stricken look that Casey throws toward Dave and Neil as the ball squirts through into center field completes this part of the ballet.

"It's O.K., Casey! Next time!" Dave bawls in his gravelly, self-assured Yankee voice.

"New batter!" Neil shouts, ignoring Casey's look completely. "New batter! Know your play! We're still ahead! Get an out! Just concentrate on getting an out!"

Casey begins to relax, begins to get back into the game, and then, beyond the outfield fences, the Hampden Horns begin to blow. Some of them belong to late-model cars—Toyotas and Hondas and snappy little Dodge Colts with U.S. OUT OF CENTRAL AMERICA and SPLIT WOOD NOT ATOMS stickers on the bumpers. But most of the Hampden Horns reside within older cars and pick-up trucks. Many of the pick-ups have rusty doors, FM converters wired up beneath the dashboards, and Leer camper caps built over the truck beds. Who is inside these vehicles, blowing the horns? No one seems to know—not for sure. They are not parents or relatives of the Hampden players; the parents and relatives (plus a generous complement of ice-cream-smeared little brothers and sisters) are filling the bleachers and lining the fence on the third-base side of the diamond, where the Hampden dugout is. They may be local guys just off work—guys who have stopped to watch some of the game before having a few brewskis at the VFW hall next door—or they may be the ghosts of Hampden Little Leaguers Past, hungry for that long-denied State Championship flag. It seems at least possible; there is something both eerie and inevitable about the Hampden Horns. They toot in harmony—high horns, low horns, a few foghorns powered by dying batteries. Several Bangor West players look uneasily back toward the sound.

Behind the backstop, a local TV crew is preparing to videotape a story for the sports final on the eleven o'clock news. This causes a stir among some of the spectators, but only a few of the players on the Hampden bench seem to notice it. Matt Kinney certainly doesn't. He is totally intent on the next Hampden batter, Matt Knaide, who taps one turf shoe with his aluminum Worth bat and then steps into the batter's box.

The Hampden Horns fall silent. Matt Kinney goes into his windup. Casey Kinney drops back into position just east of second, glove down. His face says it has no plans to turn away if the ball is hit to him again. The Hampden runners stand expectantly on first and second. (There is no leading away from the bag in Little League.) The spectators along the opposing arms of the diamond watch anxiously. Their conversations die out. Baseball at its best (and this is a very good game indeed, one you would pay money to see) is a game of restful pauses punctuated by short, sharp inhalations. The fans can now sense one of those inhalations coming. Matt Kinney winds and fires.

Knaide lines the first pitch over second for a base hit, and now the score is 2–1. Kyle King, Hampden's pitcher, steps to the plate and sends a low, screeching line drive straight back to the mound. It hits Matt Kinney on the right shin. He makes an instinctive effort to field the ball, which has already squiggled off toward the hole between third and short, before he realizes he is really hurt and folds up. Now the bases are loaded, but for the moment no one cares; the instant the umpire raises his hands, signalling time out, all the Bangor West players converge on Matt Kinney. Beyond center field, the Hampden Horns are blowing triumphantly.

Kinney is white-faced, clearly in pain. An ice pack is brought from the first-aid kit kept in the snack bar, and after a few minutes he is able to rise and limp off the field with his arms around Dave and Neil. The spectators applaud loudly and sympathetically.

Owen King, the erstwhile first baseman, becomes Bangor West's new pitcher, and the first batter he must face is Mike Tardif. The Hampden Horns send up a brief, anticipatory blat as Tardif steps in. King's third pitch goes wild to the backstop. Brett Johnson heads home; King breaks toward the plate from the mound, as he has been taught to do. In the Bangor West dugout, Neil Waterman, his arm still around Matt Kinney's shoulders, chants, *"Cover-cover-COVER!"*

Joe Wilcox, Bangor West's starting catcher, is a foot shorter than King, but very quick. At the beginning of this All-Star season, he did not want to catch, and he still doesn't like it, but he has learned to live with it and to get tough in a position where very few small players survive for long; even in Little League, most catchers resemble human Toby jugs. Earlier in this game he made an amazing one-handed stab of a foul ball. Now he lunges toward the backstop, flinging his mask aside with his bare hand at the same instant he catches the rebounding wild pitch. He turns toward the plate and tosses to King as the Hampden Horns chorus a wild—and premature, as it turns out—bray of triumph.

Johnson has slowed down. On his face is an expression strikingly similar to that worn by Casey Kinney when Casey allowed Johnson's hard-hit grounder to shoot through the hole. It is a look of extreme anxiety and trepidation, the face of a boy who suddenly wishes he were someplace else. *Anyplace* else. The new pitcher is blocking the plate.

Johnson starts a halfhearted slide. King takes the toss from Wilcox, pivots with surprising, winsome grace, and tags the hapless Johnson out easily. He walks back toward the mound, wiping sweat from his forehead, and prepares to face Tardif once more. Behind him, the Hampden Horns have fallen silent again.

Tardif loops one toward third. Kevin Rochefort, Bangor's third baseman, takes a single step backward in response. It's an easy play, but there is an awful look of dismay on his face, and it is only then, as Rochefort starts to freeze up on what is an easy pop fly, that one can see how badly the whole team has been shaken by Matt's injury. The ball goes into Rochefort's glove, and then pops out when Rochefort—dubbed Roach Clip first by Freddy Moore and then by the whole squad—fails to squeeze it. Knaide, who advanced to third while King and Wilcox were dealing with Johnson, has already broken for the plate. Rochefort could have doubled Knaide up easily if he had caught the ball, but here, as in the majors, baseball is a game of ifs and inches. Rochefort doesn't catch the ball. He throws wild to first instead. Mike Arnold has taken over there, and he is one of the best fielders on the team, but no one issued him stilts. Tardif, meanwhile, steams into second. The pitchers' duel has become a typical Little League game, and now the Hampden Horns are a cacophony of joy. The home team has their thumping shoes on, and the final score is Hampden 9, Bangor West 2. Still, there are two good things to go home on: Matt Kinney is not seriously hurt, and when Casey Kinney got another tough chance in the late innings he refused to choke, and made the play.

After the final out is recorded, the Bangor West players trudge into their dugout and sit on the bench. This is their first loss, and most of them are not coping with it very gracefully. Some toss their gloves disgustedly between their dirty sneakers. Some are crying, others look close to tears, and no one is talking. Even Freddy, Bangor's quip-master general, has nothing to say on this muggy Thursday evening in Hampden. Beyond the center-field fence, a few of the Hampden Horns are still tooting happily away.

Neil Waterman is the first person to speak. He tells the boys to get their heads up and look at him. Three of them already are: Owen King, Ryan Iarrobino, and Matt Kinney. Now about half the squad manages to do as he's asked. Several others, however—including Josh Stevens, who made the final out—continue to seem vastly interested in their footgear.

"Get your *heads* up," Waterman says again. He speaks louder this time, but not unkindly, and now they all manage to look at him. "You played a pretty good game," he says softly. "You got a little rattled, and they ended up on top. It happens. It doesn't mean they're better, though—that's something we're going to find out on Saturday. Tonight all you lost was a baseball game. The sun will still come up tomorrow." They begin to stir around on the bench a little; this old homily has apparently not lost its power to comfort. "You gave what you had tonight, and that's all we want. I'm proud of you, and you can be proud of yourselves. Nothing happened that you have to hang your heads about."

He stands aside for Dave Mansfield, who surveys his team. When Dave speaks, his usually loud voice is even quieter than Waterman's. "We knew when we came down here that they had to beat us, didn't we?" he asks. He speaks reflectively, almost as if he were talking to himself. "If they didn't, they'd be out. They'll be coming to our field on Saturday. That's when *we* have to beat *them*. Do you want to?"

They are all looking up now.

"I want you to remember what Neil told you," Dave says in that reflective voice, so unlike his practice-field bellow. "You are a team. That means you love each other. You love each other—win or lose—because you are a team."

The first time anyone suggested to these boys that they must come to love each other while they were on the field, they laughed uneasily at the idea. Now they don't laugh. After enduring the Hampden Horns together, they seem to understand, at least a little.

Dave surveys them again, then nods. "O.K. Pick up the gear."

They pick up bats, helmets, catching equipment, and stuff everything into canvas duffel bags. By the time they've got it over to Dave's old green pick-up truck, some of them are laughing again.

Dave laughs with them, but he doesn't do any laughing on the ride home. Tonight the ride seems long. "I don't know if we can beat them on Saturday," he says on the way back. He is speaking in that same reflective tone of voice. "I want to, and *they* want to, but I just don't know. Hampden's got mo on their side, now."

Mo, of course, is momentum—that mythic force which shapes not only single games but whole seasons. Baseball players are quirky and superstitious at every level of play, and for some reason the Bangor West players have adopted a small plastic sandal—a castoff of some young fan's baby doll—as their mascot. They have named this absurd talisman Mo. They stick it in the chain-link fence of the dugout at every game, and batters often touch it furtively before stepping into the on-deck circle. Nick Trzaskos, who ordinarily plays left field for Bangor West, has been entrusted with Mo between games. Tonight, for the first time, he forgot to bring the talisman.

"Nick better remember Mo on Saturday," Dave says grimly. "But even if he remembers . . ." He shakes his head. "I just don't know."

There is no admission charge to Little League games; the charter expressly forbids it. Instead, a player takes around a hat during the fourth inning, soliciting donations for equipment and field maintenance. On Saturday, when Bangor West and Hampden square off in the year's final Penobscot County Little League game, at Bangor, one can judge the growth of local interest in the team's fortunes by a simple act of comparison. The collection taken up at the Bangor-Millinocket contest was $15.45; when the hat finally comes back in the fifth inning of the Saturday-afternoon game against Hampden, it's overflowing with change and crumpled dollar bills. The total take is $94.25. The bleachers are full; the fences are lined; the parking lot is full. Little League has one thing in common with almost all American sports and business endeavors: nothing succeeds like success.

Things start off well for Bangor—they lead 7–3 at the end of three—and then everything falls apart. In the fourth inning, Hampden scores six runs, most of them honest. Bangor West doesn't fold, as it did after Matt Kinney was hit in the game at Hampden—the players do not drop their heads, to use Neil Waterman's phrase. But when they come to bat in the bottom of the sixth inning they are down by a score of 14–12. Elimination looks very close and very real. Mo is in its accustomed place, but Bangor West is still three outs away from the end of its season.

One kid who did not need to be told to get his head up following Bangor West's 9–2 loss was Ryan Iarrobino. He went two for three in that game, played well, and trotted off the field *knowing* he had played well. He is a tall kid, quiet, with broad shoulders and a shock of dark-brown hair. He is one of two natural athletes on the Bangor West team. Matt Kinney is the other. Although the two boys are physical opposites—Kinney slim and still fairly short, Iarrobino tall and well muscled—they share a quality that is uncommon in boys their age: they trust their bodies. Most of the others on the Bangor West squad, no matter how talented, seem to regard feet, arms, and hands as spies and potential traitors.

Iarrobino is one of those boys who seem somehow more *there* when they are dressed for some sort of competition. He is one of the few kids on either team who can don batting helmets and not look like nerds wearing their mothers' stewpots. When Matt Kinney stands on the mound and throws a baseball, he seems perfect in his place and time. And when Ryan Iarrobino steps into the right-hand batter's box and points the head of his bat out toward the pitcher for an instant before raising it to the cocked position, at his right shoulder, he also seems to be exactly where he belongs. He looks dug in even before he settles himself for the first pitch: you could draw a perfectly straight line from the ball of his shoulder to the ball of his hip and on down to the ball of his ankle. Matt Kinney was built to throw baseballs; Ryan Iarrobino was built to hit them.

Last call for Bangor West. Jeff Carson, whose fourth-inning home run is really the difference in this game, and who earlier replaced Mike Wentworth on the mound for Hampden, is now replaced by Mike

Tardif. He faces Owen King first. King goes three and two (swinging wildly for the fences at one pitch in the dirt), then lays off a pitch just inside to work a walk. Roger Fisher follows him to the plate, pinch-hitting for the ever-gregarious Fred Moore. Roger is a small boy with Indian-dark eyes and hair. He looks like an easy out, but looks can be deceptive; Roger has good power. Today, however, he is overmatched. He strikes out.

In the field, the Hampden players shift around and look at each other. They are close, and they know it. The parking lot is too far away here for the Hampden Horns to be a factor; their fans settle for simply screaming encouragement. Two women wearing purple Hampden caps are standing behind the dugout, hugging each other joyfully. Several other fans look like track runners waiting for the starter's gun; it is clear they mean to rush onto the field the moment their boys succeed in putting Bangor West away for good.

Joe Wilcox, who didn't want to be a catcher and ended up doing the job anyway, rams a one-out single up the middle and into left-center field. King stops at second. Up steps Arthur Dorr, the Bangor right fielder, who wears the world's oldest pair of high-top sneakers and has not had a hit all day. This time he rifles one, but right at the Hampden shortstop, who barely has to move. The shortstop whips the ball to second, hoping to catch King off the bag, but he's out of luck. Nevertheless, there are two out.

The Hampden fans scream further encouragement. The women behind the dug out are jumping up and down. Now there are a few Hampden Horns tootling away someplace, but they are a little early, and all one has to do to know it is to look at Mike Tardif's face as he wipes off his forehead and pounds the baseball into his glove.

Ryan Iarrobino steps into the right-hand batter's box. He has a fast, almost naturally perfect swing; even Ron St. Pierre will not fault him on it much.

Ryan swings through Tardif's first pitch, his hardest of the day—it makes a rifle-shot sound as it hits Kyle King's glove. Tardif then wastes one outside. King returns the ball; Tardif meditates briefly and then throws a low fastball. Ryan looks at it, and the umpire calls strike two. It has caught the outside corner—maybe. The ump says it did, anyway, and that's the end of it.

Now the fans on both sides have fallen quiet, and so have the coaches. They're all out of it. It's only Tardif and Iarrobino now, balanced on the last strike of the last out of the last game one of these teams will play. Forty-six feet between these two faces. Only, Iarrobino is not watching Tardif's *face*. He is watching Tardif's *glove*, and somewhere I can hear Ron St. Pierre telling Fred, *You're waiting to see how I'll come—sidearm, three-quarters, or over the top.*

Iarrobino is waiting to see how Tardif will come. As Tardif moves to the set position, you can faintly hear the *pock-pock, pock-pock* of tennis balls on a nearby court, but here there is only silence and the crisp black shadows of the players, lying on the dirt like silhouettes cut from black construction paper, and Iarrobino is waiting to see how Tardif will come.

He comes over the top. And suddenly Iarrobino is in motion, both knees and the left shoulder dipping slightly, the aluminum bat a blur in the sunlight. That aluminum-on-cowhide sound—*chink,* like someone hitting a tin cup with a spoon—is different this time. A *lot* different. Not *chink* but *crunch* as Ryan connects, and then the ball is in the sky, tracking out to left field—a long shot that is clearly gone, high, wide, and handsome into the summer afternoon. The ball will later be recovered from beneath a car about 275 feet away from home plate.

The expression on twelve-year-old Mike Tardif's face is stunned, thunderstruck disbelief. He takes one quick look into his glove, as if hoping to find the ball still there and discover that Iarrobino's dramatic two-strike, two-out shot was only a hideous momentary dream. The two women behind the backstop look at each other in total amazement. At first, no one makes a sound. In that moment before everyone begins to scream and the Bangor West players rush out of their dugout to await Ryan at home plate and mob him when he arrives, only two people are entirely sure that it did really happen. One is Ryan himself. As he rounds first, he raises both hands to his shoulders in a brief but emphatic gesture of triumph. And, as Owen King crosses the plate with the first of the three runs that will end Hampden's All-Star season, Mike Tardif realizes. Standing on the pitcher's rubber for the last time as a Little Leaguer, he bursts into tears.

"You gotta remember, they're only twelve," each of the three coaches says at one time or another, and each time one of them says it, the listener feels that he—Mansfield, Waterman, or St. Pierre—is really re-minding himself.

"When you are on the field, we'll love you and you will love each other," Waterman tells the boys again and again, and in the wake of Bangor's eleventh-hour, 15–14 win over Hampden, when they all did love each other, the boys no longer laugh at this. He continues, "From now on, I'm going to be hard on you—very hard. When you're playing, you'll get nothing but unconditional love from me. But when we're practicing on our home field some of you are going to find out how loud I can yell. If you're goofing off, you're going to sit down. If I tell you to do something and you don't do it, you're going to sit down. Recess is over, guys—everybody out of the pool. This is where the hard work starts."

A few nights later, Waterman hits a shot to right during fielding practice. It almost amputates Arthur Dorr's nose on the way by. Arthur has been busy making sure his fly is zipped. Or inspecting the laces of his Keds. Or some damn thing.

"*Arthur!*" Neil Waterman bellows, and Arthur flinches more at the sound of that voice than he did at the close passage of the baseball. "*Get in here!* On the bench! *Now.*"

"But—" Arthur begins.

"In here!" Neil yells back. "You're on the pine!"

Arthur trots sullenly in, head down, and J. J. Fiddler takes his place. A few nights later, Nick Trzaskos loses his chance to hit away when he fails to bunt two pitches in five tries or so. He sits on the bench by himself, cheeks flaming.

Machias, the Aroostook County/Washington County winner, is next on the docket—a two-out-of-three series, and the winner will be District 3 champion. The first game is to be played at the Bangor field, behind the Coke plant, the second at Bob Beal Field in Machias. The last game, if needed, will be played on neutral ground between the two towns.

As Neil Waterman has promised, the coaching staff is all encourage-ment once the national anthem has been played and the first game starts.

"That's all right, no damage!" Dave Mansfield cries as Arthur Dorr misjudges a long shot to right and the ball lands behind him. "Get an out, now! Belly play! Let's just get an out!" No one seems to know exactly what "belly play" is, but since it seems to involve winning ball games, the boys are all for it.

No third game against Machias is necessary. Bangor West gets a strong pitching performance from Matt Kinney in the first one and wins 17–5. Winning the second game is a little tougher only because the weather does not cooperate: a drenching summer downpour washes out the first try, and it is necessary for Bangor West to make the 168-mile round trip to Machias twice in order to clinch the division. They finally get the game in, on the twenty-ninth of July. Mike Pelkey's family has spirited Bangor West's number two pitcher off to Disney World in Orlando, making Mike the third player to fade from the team, but Owen King steps quietly in and pitches a five-hitter, striking out eight before tiring and giving way to Mike Arnold in the sixth inning. Bangor West wins, 12–2, and becomes District 3 Little League champ.

At moments like these, the pros retire to their air-conditioned locker rooms and pour champagne over each other's heads. The Bangor West team goes out to Helen's, the best (maybe the only) restaurant in Machias, to celebrate with hot dogs, hamburgers, gallons of Pepsi-Cola, and mountains of French fries. Looking at them as they laugh at each other, razz each other, and blow napkin pellets through their straws at each other, it is impossible not to be aware of how soon they will discover gaudier modes of celebration.

For now, however, this is perfectly O.K.—great, in fact. They are not overwhelmed by what they have done, but they seem tremendously pleased, tremendously content, and entirely *here*. If they have been touched with magic this summer, they do not know it, and no one has as yet been unkind enough to tell them that it may be so. For now they are allowed the deep-fried simplicities of Helen's, and those simplicities are quite enough. They have won their division; the State Championship Tournament, where bigger and better teams from the more heavily populated regions downstate will probably blow them out, is still a week away.

Ryan Iarrobino has changed back into his tank top. Arthur Dorr has a rakish smear of ketchup on one cheek. And Owen King, who struck terror into the hearts of the Machias batters by coming at them with a powerful sidearm fastball on 0-2 counts, is burbling happily into his glass of Pepsi. Nick Trzaskos, who can look unhappier than any boy on earth when things don't break his way, looks supremely happy tonight. And why not? Tonight they're twelve and they're winners.

Not that they don't remind you themselves from time to time. Halfway back from Machias after the first trip, the rainout, J. J. Fiddler begins to wriggle around uneasily in the back seat of the car he is riding in. "I gotta go," he says. He clutches at himself and adds ominously, "Man, I gotta go bad. I mean big time."

"J.J.'s gonna do it!" Joe Wilcox cries gleefully. "Watch this! J.J.'s gonna flood the car!"

"Shut up, Joey," J.J. says, and then begins to wriggle around again.

He has waited until the worst possible moment to make his announcement. The eighty-four-mile trip between Machias and Bangor is, for the most part, an exercise in emptiness. There isn't even a decent stand of trees into which J.J. can disappear for a few moments along this stretch of road—only mile after mile of open hayfields, with Route 1A cutting a winding course through them.

Just as J.J.'s bladder is going to DEFCON-1, a providential gas station appears. The assistant coach swings in and tops up his tank while J.J. splits for the men's room. "Boy!" he says, brushing his hair out of his eyes as he jogs back to the car. "That was close!"

"Got some on your pants, J.J.," Joe Wilcox says casually, and everyone goes into spasms of wild laughter as J.J. checks.

On the trip back to Machias the next day, Matt Kinney reveals one of the chief attractions *People* magazine holds for boys of Little League age. "I'm sure there's one in here someplace," he says, leafing slowly through an issue he has found on the back seat. "There almost always is."

"What? What are you looking for?" third baseman Kevin Rochefort asks, peering over Matt's shoulder as Matt leafs past the week's celebs, barely giving them a look.

"The breast-examination ad," Matt explains. "You can't see everything, but you can see quite a lot. Here it is!" He holds the magazine up triumphantly.

Four other heads, each wearing a red Bangor West baseball cap, immediately cluster around the magazine. For a few minutes, at least, baseball is the furthest thing from these boys' minds.

———

The 1989 Maine State Little League Championship Tournament begins on August 3, just over four weeks after All-Star play began for the teams involved. The state is divided into five districts, and all five send teams to Old Town, where this year's tourney is to be held. The participants are Yarmouth, Belfast, Lewiston, York, and Bangor West. All the teams but Belfast are bigger than the Bangor West All-Stars, and Belfast is supposed to have a secret weapon. Their number one pitcher is this year's tourney wunderkind.

The naming of the tourney wunderkind is a yearly ceremony, a small tumor that seems to defy all attempts to remove it. This boy, who is anointed Kid Baseball whether he wants the honor or not, finds himself in a heretofore unsuspected spotlight, the object of discussion, speculation, and, inevitably, wagering. He also finds himself in the unenviable position of having to live up to all sorts of pretournament hype. A Little League tournament is a pressure situation for any kid; when you get to Tourney Town and discover you have somehow become an instant legend as well, it's usually too much.

This year's object of myth and discussion is Belfast's southpaw Stanley Sturgis. In his two outings for Belfast he has chalked up thirty strikeouts—fourteen in his first game, sixteen in his second. Thirty K's in two games is an impressive statistic in any league, but to fully understand Sturgis's accomplishment one has to remember that Little League games consist of only six innings. That means that 83 per cent of the outs Belfast recorded with Sturgis on the hill came on strikeouts.

Then there is York. All the teams that come to the Knights of Columbus field in Old Town to compete in the tourney have excellent records, but York, which is undefeated, is the clear favorite to win a ticket to the Eastern Regionals. None of them are over five-ten, and their best pitcher, Phil Tarbox, has a fastball that may top seventy miles an hour on some pitches—extravagant by Little League standards. Like Yarmouth and Belfast, the York players come dressed in special All-Star uniforms and matching turf shoes, which make them look like pros.

Only Bangor West and Lewiston come wearing mufti—which is to say, shirts of many colors bearing the names of their regular-season team sponsors. Owen King wears Elks orange, Ryan Iarrobino and Nick Trzaskos wear Bangor Hydro red, Roger Fisher and Fred Moore wear Lions green, and so on. The Lewiston team is dressed in similar fashion, but they have at least been provided with matching shoes and stirrups. Compared with Lewiston, the Bangor team, dressed in a variety of baggy gray sweatpants and nondescript street sneakers, looks eccentric. Next to the other teams, however, they look like out-and-out ragamuffins. No one, with the possible exception of the Bangor West coaches and the players themselves, takes them very seriously. In its first article on the tourney the local newspaper gives more coverage to Sturgis, of Belfast, than it does to the entire Bangor West team.

Dave, Neil, and Saint, the odd but surprisingly effective brain trust that has brought the team this far, watch Belfast take infield and batting practice without saying much. The Belfast kids are resplendent in their new purple-and-white uniforms—uniforms that have not worn so much as a speck of infield dirt until today. At last, Dave says, "Well, we finally got here again. We did that much. Nobody can take that away from us."

Bangor West comes from the district in which the tournament is being held this year, and the team will not have to play until two of the five teams have been eliminated. This is called a first-round bye, and right now it's the biggest, perhaps the only, advantage this team has. In their own district, they looked like champions (except for that one awful game against Hampden), but Dave, Neil, and Saint have been around long enough to know that they are now looking at an entirely different level of baseball. Their silence as they stand by the fence watching Belfast work out acknowledges this eloquently.

In contrast, York has already ordered District 4 pins. Trading pins is a tradition at the regional tournaments, and the fact that York has already laid in a supply tells an interesting tale. The pins say York means to play with the best of the East Coast, in Bristol. The pins say they don't think Yarmouth can stop them; or Belfast, with its wunderkind southpaw; or Lewiston, which clawed its way to the Division 2 championship through the losers' bracket, after dropping their first game 15–12; or, least of all, fourteen badly dressed pipsqueaks from the west side of Bangor.

"At least we'll get a chance to play," Dave says, "and we'll try to make them remember we were here."

But first Belfast and Lewiston have *their* chance to play, and after the Boston Pops has steamed through a recorded version of the national anthem, and a local writer of some repute has tossed out the obligatory first pitch (it sails all the way to the backstop), they have at it.

Area sports reporters have spilled a lot of ink on the subject of Stanley Sturgis, but reporters are not allowed on the field once the game starts (a situation caused by a mistake in the rules as they were originally laid out, some of them seem to feel). Once the umpire has commanded the teams to play ball, Sturgis finds himself on his own. The writers, the pundits, and the entire Belfast hot-stove league are now all on the other side of the fence.

Baseball is a team sport, but there is only one player with a ball at the center of each diamond and only one player with a bat at the diamond's lowest point. The man with the bat keeps changing, but the pitcher remains—unless he can no longer cut it, that is. Today is Stan Sturgis's day to discover the hard truth of tourney play: sooner or later, every wunderkind meets his match.

Sturgis struck out thirty men in his last pair of games, but that was District 2. The team Belfast is playing today, a tough bunch of scrappers out of Lewiston's Elliot Avenue League is a different plate of beans altogether. They are not as big as the boys from York and don't field as smoothly as the boys from Yarmouth, but they are pesky and persistent. The first batter, Carlton Gagnon, personifies the gnawing, clawing spirit of the team. He singles up the middle, steals second, is sacrificed to third, then bolts home on a steal play sent in from the bench. In the third inning, with the score 1–0, Gagnon reaches base again, this time on a fielder's choice. Randy Gervais, who follows this pest in the lineup, strikes out, but before he does, Gagnon has gone to second on a passed ball and stolen third. He scores on a two-out base hit by Bill Paradis, the third baseman.

Belfast comes up with a run in the fourth, briefly making a game of it, but then Lewiston puts them, and Stanley Sturgis, away for good, scoring two in the fifth and four more in the sixth. The final tally is 9–1. Sturgis strikes out eleven, but he also gives up seven hits, while Carlton Gagnon, Lewiston's pitcher, strikes out eight and allows only three hits. When Sturgis leaves the field at the end of the game, he looks both depressed and relieved. For him the hype and hoopla are over. He can quit being a newspaper sidebar and go back to being a kid again. His face suggests that he sees certain advantages in that.

Later, in a battle of the giants, tourney favorite York knocks off Yarmouth. Then everybody goes home (or, in the case of the visiting players, back to their motels or to the homes of their host families). Tomorrow, Friday, it will be Bangor West's turn to play while York waits to meet the winner in the closer.

Friday comes in hot, foggy, and cloudy. Rain threatens from first light, and an hour or so before Bangor West and Lewiston are scheduled to square off the rain comes—a deluge of rain. When this sort of weather struck in Machias, the game was quickly cancelled. Not here. This is a different field—one with a grass infield instead of dirt—but that isn't the only factor. The major one is TV. This year, for the first time, two stations have pooled their resources and will telecast the tournament final statewide on Saturday afternoon. If the semifinal between Bangor and Lewiston is postponed, it means trouble with the schedule, and even in Maine, even in this most amateur of amateur sports, the one thing you don't jiggle is the media's schedule.

So the Bangor West and Lewiston teams are not dismissed when they come to the field. Instead, they sit in cars or cluster in little groups beneath the candy-striped canvas of the central concession booth. Then they wait for a break in the weather. And wait. And wait. Restlessness sets in, of course. Many of these kids will play in bigger games before their athletic careers end, but this is the biggest to date for all of them; they are pumped to the max.

Someone eventually has a brainstorm. After a few quick phone calls, two Old Town schoolbuses, gleaming bright yellow in the drenching rain, pull up to the nearby Elks Club, and the players are whisked off on a tour of the Old Town Canoe Company factory and the local James River paper mill. (The James River Corporation is the prime buyer of ad time on the upcoming championship telecast.) None of the players look particularly happy as they climb aboard the buses; they don't look much happier when they arrive back. Each player is carrying a small canoe paddle, about the right size for a well-built elf. Freebies from the canoe factory. None of the boys seem to know just what they should do with the paddles, but when I check later they're all gone, just like the Bangor pennants after that first game against Millinocket. Free souvenirs—good deal.

And there will be a game after all, it seems. At some point—perhaps while the Little Leaguers were watching the fellows at the James River mill turn trees into toilet paper—the rain stopped. The field has drained well, the pitcher's mound and the batters' boxes have been dusted with Quick-Dry, and now, at just past three in the afternoon, a watery sun takes its first peek through the clouds.

The Bangor West team has come back from the field trip flat and listless. No one has thrown a ball or swung a bat or run a single base so far today, but everybody already seems tired. The players walk toward the practice field without looking at each other; gloves dangle at the ends of arms. They walk like losers, and they talk like losers.

Instead of lecturing them, Dave lines them up and begins playing his version of pepper with them. Soon the Bangor players are razzing each other, catcalling, trying for circus catches, groaning and bitching when Dave calls an error and sends someone to the end of the line. Then, just before Dave is ready to call the workout off and take them over to Neil and Saint for batting practice, Roger Fisher steps out of the line and bends over with his glove against his belly. Dave goes to him at once, his smile becoming an expression of concern. He wants to know if Roger is all right.

"Yes," Roger says. "I just wanted to get this." He bends down a little farther, dark eyes intent, plucks something out of the grass, and hands it to Dave. It is a four-leaf clover.

In Little League tournament games, the home team is always decided by a coin toss. Dave has been extremely lucky at winning these, but today he loses, and Bangor West is designated the visiting team. Sometimes even bad luck turns out to be good, though, and this is one of those days. Nick Trzaskos is the reason.

The skills of all the players have improved during their six-week season, but in some cases attitudes have improved as well. Nick started deep on the bench, despite his proven skills as a defensive player and his potential as a hitter; his fear of failure made him unready to play. Little by little, he has begun to trust himself, and now Dave is ready to try starting him. "Nick finally figured out that the other guys weren't going to give him a hard time if he dropped a ball or struck out," St. Pierre says. "For a kid like Nick, that's a big change."

Today, Nick cranks the third pitch of the game to deep center field. It is a hard, rising line drive, over the fence and gone before the center fielder has a chance to turn and look, let alone cruise back and grab it. As Nick Trzaskos rounds second and slows down, breaking into the home-run trot all these boys knows so well from TV, the fans behind the backstop are treated to a rare sight: Nick is grinning. As he crosses home plate and his surprised, happy teammates mob him, he actually begins to laugh. As he enters the dugout, Neil claps him on the back, and Dave Mansfield gives him a brief, hard hug.

Nick has also finished what Dave started with his game of pepper: the team is fully awake now, and ready to do some business. Matt Kinney gives up a lead-off single to Carl Gagnon, the pest who began the process of dismantling Stanley Sturgis. Gagnon goes to second on Ryan Stretton's sacrifice, advances to third on a wild pitch, and scores on another wild pitch. It is an almost uncanny repetition of his first at bat against Belfast. Kinney's control is not great this afternoon, but Gagnon's is the only run the team from Lewiston can manage in the early going. This is unfortunate for them, because Bangor comes up hitting in the top of the second.

Owen King leads off with a deep single; Arthur Dorr follows with another; Mike Arnold reaches when Lewiston's catcher, Jason Auger, picks up Arnold's bunt and throws wild to first base. King scores on the error, putting Bangor West back on top, 2–1. Joe Wilcox, Bangor's catcher, scratches out an infield hit to load the bases. Nick Trzaskos strikes out his second time up, and that brings Ryan Iarrobino to the plate. He struck out his first time up, but not now. He turns Matt Noyes's first pitch into a grand-slam home run, and after an inning and a half the score is Bangor West 6, Lewiston 1.

Up to the sixth, it is an authentic four-leaf-clover day for Bangor West. When Lewiston comes to bat for what the Bangor fans hope will be the last time, they are down by a score of 9–1. The pest, Carlton Gagnon, leads off and reaches on an error. The next batter, Ryan Stretton, also reaches on an error. The Bangor fans, who have been cheering wildly, begin to look a little uneasy. It's hard to choke when you're eight runs ahead, but not impossible. These northern New Englanders are Red Sox fans. They have seen it happen many times.

Bill Paradis makes the jitters worse by singling sharply up the middle. Both Gagnon and Stretton come home. The score is now 9–3, runner on first, nobody out. The Bangor fans shuffle and look at each other uneasily. *It can't really get away from us this late in the game, can it?* their looks ask. The answer is, Of course, you bet it can. In Little League, anything can and often does happen.

But not this time. Lewiston scores one more time, and that's it. Noyes, who fanned three times against Sturgis, fans for the third time today, and there is finally one out. Auger, Lewiston's catcher, hits the first pitch hard to the shortstop, Roger Fisher. Roger booted Carl Gagnon's ball earlier in the inning to open the door, but he picks this one up easily and shovels it to Mike Arnold, who feeds it on to Owen King at first. Auger is slow, and King's reach is long. The result is a game-ending 6–4–3 double play. You don't often see around-the-horn d.p.s. in the scaled-down world of Little League, where the base paths are only sixty feet long, but Roger found a four-leaf clover today. If you have to chalk it up to anything, it might as well be that. Whatever you chalk it up to, the boys from Bangor have won another one, 9–4.

Tomorrow, there are the giants from York.

It is August 5, 1989, and in the state of Maine only twenty-nine boys are still playing Little League ball—fourteen on the Bangor West squad and fifteen on York's team. The day is an almost exact replica of the day before: hot, foggy, and threatening. The game is scheduled to begin promptly at 12:30, but the skies open once again, and by 11 it looks as though the game will be—must be—cancelled. The rain comes pouring down in buckets.

Dave, Neil, and Saint are taking no chances, however. None of them liked the flat mood the kids were in when they returned from their impromptu tour of the day before, and they have no intention of allowing a repeat. No one wants to end up counting on a game of pepper or a four-leaf clover today. If there *is* a game—and TV is a powerful motivator, no matter how murky the weather—it will be for all the marbles. The winners go on to Bristol; the losers go home.

So a makeshift cavalcade of vans and station wagons driven by coaches and parents is assembled at the field behind the Coke plant, and the team is ferried the ten miles up to the University of Maine field house, a barnlike indoor facility where Neil and Saint rally them through their paces until the boys are soaked with sweat. Dave has arranged for the York team to use the field house, too, and as the Bangor team exits into the overcast the York team, dressed in their natty blue uniforms, troops in.

The rain is down to isolated dribbles by three o'clock, and the ground crew works frantically to return the field to playable shape. Five makeshift TV platforms have been constructed on steel frames around the field. In a nearby parking lot is a huge truck with MAINE BROADCASTING SYSTEM LIVE REMOTE painted on the side. Thick bundles of cable, held together with cinches of electrician's tape, lead from the cameras and the temporary announcer's booth back to this truck. One door stands open, and many TV monitors glimmer within.

York hasn't arrived from the field house yet. The Bangor West squad begins throwing outside the left-field fence, mostly to have something to do and keep the jitters at bay; they certainly don't need to warm up after the humid hour they just spent at the University. The camerapersons stand on their towers and watch the ground crew try to get rid of the water.

The outfield is in fair shape, and the skin parts of the infield have been raked and coated with Quick-Dry. The real problem is the area between home plate and the pitcher's mound. This section of the diamond was freshly resodded before the tournament began, and there has been no time for the roots to take hold and provide some natural drainage. The result is a swampy mess in front of home plate— a mess that slops off toward the third-base line.

Someone has an idea—an inspiration, as it turns out—that involves actually removing a large section of the wounded in-field. While this is being done, a truck arrives from Old Town High School and two industrial-size Rinsenvacs are off-loaded. Five minutes later, the ground crew is literally vacuuming the subsurface of the infield. It works. By 3:25, the groundkeepers are replacing chunks of sod like pieces in a large green jigsaw puzzle. By 3:35, a local music teacher, accompanying herself on an acoustic guitar, is winging her way through a gorgeous rendition of "The Star-Spangled Banner." And at 3:37 Bangor West's Roger Fisher, Dave's dark-horse pick to start in place of the absent Mike Pelkey, is warming up. Did Roger's find of the day before have anything to do with Dave's decision to start him instead of King or Arnold? Dave only puts his finger on the side of his nose and smiles wisely.

At 3:40, the umpire steps in. "Send it down, catcher," he says briskly. Joey does. Mike Arnold makes the sweep tag on the invisible runner, then sends the baseball on its quick journey around the infield. A TV audience that stretches from New Hampshire to the Maritime Provinces of Canada watches as Roger fusses nervously with the sleeves of his green jersey and the gray warm-up shirt he wears beneath it. Owen King tosses him the ball from first base. Fisher takes it and holds it against his hip.

"Let's play ball," the umpire invites—an invitation that umpires have been extending to Little League players for fifty years now—and Dan Bouchard, York's catcher and leadoff hitter, steps into the box. Roger goes to the set position and prepares to throw the first pitch of the 1989 State Championship game.

Five days earlier:

Dave and I take the Bangor West pitching staff up to Old Town. Dave wants them all to know how the mound feels when they come up here to play for real. With Mike Pelkey gone, the staff consists of Matt Kinney (his triumph over Lewiston still four days in the future), Owen King, Roger Fisher, and Mike Arnold. We get off to a late start, and as the four boys take turns throwing, Dave and I sit in the visitors' dugout, watching the boys as the light slowly leaves the summer sky.

On the mound, Matt Kinney is throwing one hard curve after another to J. J. Fiddler. In the home dugout, across the diamond, the three other pitchers, their workouts finished, are sitting on the bench with a few teammates who have come along for the ride. Although the talk comes to me only in snatches, I can tell it's mostly about school—a subject that comes up with greater and greater frequency during the last month of summer vacation. They talk about teachers past and teachers future, passing on the anecdotes that form an important part of their preadolescent mythology: the teacher who blew her cool during the last month of the school year because her oldest son was in a car accident; the crazy grammar-school coach (they make him sound like a lethal combination of Jason, Freddy, and Leatherface); the science teacher who supposedly once threw a kid against his locker so hard the kid was knocked out; the home-room teacher who will give you lunch money if you forget, or if you just say you forgot. It is junior high apocrypha, powerful stuff, and they tell it with great relish as twilight closes in.

Between the two dugouts, the baseball is a white streak as Matt throws it again and again. His rhythm is a kind of hypnosis: Set, wind, and fire. Set, wind, and fire. Set, wind, and fire. J.J.'s mitt cracks with each reception.

"What are they going to take with them?" I ask Dave. "When this is all over, what are they going to take with them? What difference does it make for them, do you think?"

The look on Dave's face is surprised and considering. Then he turns back to look at Matt and smiles. "They're going to take each other," he says.

It is not the answer I have been expecting—far from it. There was an article about Little League in the paper today—one of those think pieces that usually run in the ad-littered wasteland between the obituaries and the horoscopes. This one summarized the findings of a sociologist who spent a season monitoring Little Leaguers, and then followed their progress for a short time thereafter. He wanted to find out if the game did what Little League boosters claim it does—that is, pass on such old-fashioned American values as fair play, hard work, and the virtue of team effort. The fellow who did the study reported that it did, sort of. But he also reported that Little League did little to change the *individual* lives of the players. School troublemakers were still school troublemakers when classes started again in September; good scholars were still good scholars; the class clown (read Fred Moore) who took June and July off to play some serious Little League ball was still the class clown after Labor Day. The sociologist found exceptions; exceptional play sometimes bred exceptional changes. But in the main this fellow found that the boys were about the same coming out as they were going in.

I suppose my confusion at Dave's answer grows out of my knowledge of him—he is an almost fanatic booster of Little League. I'm sure he must have read the article, and I have been expecting him to refute the sociologist's conclusions, using the question as a springboard. Instead, he has delivered one of the hoariest chestnuts of the sports world.

On the mound, Matt continues to throw to J.J., harder than ever now. He has found that mystic place pitchers call "the groove," and even though this is only an informal practice session to familiarize the boys with the field, he is reluctant to quit.

I ask Dave if he can explain a little more fully, but I do so in a gingerly way, half expecting that I am on the verge of hitting a hitherto unsuspected jackpot of clichés: night owls never fly in the daytime; winners never quit and quitters never win; use it, don't lose it. Maybe even, God save us, a little Hummm, baby.

"Look at them," Dave says, still smiling. Something in that smile suggests he may be reading my mind. "Take a good look."

I do. There are perhaps half a dozen of them on the bench, still laughing and telling junior high school war stories. One of them breaks out of the discussion long enough to ask Matt Kinney to throw the curve, and Matt does—one with a particularly nasty break. The boys on the bench all laugh and cheer.

"Look at those two guys," Dave says, pointing. "One of them comes from a good home. The other one, not so good." He tosses some sunflower seeds into his mouth and then indicates another boy. "Or that one. He was born in one of the worst sections of Boston. Do you think he'd know a kid like Matt Kinney or Kevin Rochefort, if it wasn't for Little League? They won't be in the same classes at junior high, wouldn't talk to each other in the halls, wouldn't have the slightest idea the other one was alive."

Matt throws another curve, this one so nasty J.J. can't handle it. It rolls all the way to the backstop, and as J.J. gets up and trots after it the boys on the bench cheer again.

"But this changes all that," Dave says. "These boys have played together and won their district together. Some come from families that are well-to-do, and there's a couple from families as poor as used dishwater, but when they put on the uniform and cross the chalk they leave all that on the other side. Your school grades can't help you between the chalk, or what your parents do, or what they don't do. Between the chalk, what happens is the kids' business. They tend it, too, as well as they can. All the rest—" Dave makes a shooing gesture with one hand. "All left behind. And they know it, too. Just look at them if you don't believe me, because the proof is right there."

I look across the field and see my own kid and one of the boys Dave has mentioned sitting side by side, heads together, talking something over seriously. They look at each other in amazement, then break out laughing.

"They played together," Dave repeats. "They practiced together, day after day, and that's probably even more important than the games. Now they're going into the State Tournament. They've even got a chance to win it. I don't think they will, but that doesn't matter. They're going to be there, and that's enough. Even if Lewiston knocks them out in the first round, that's enough. Because it's something they did together between those chalk lines. They're going to remember that. They're going to remember how that felt."

"Between the chalk," I say, and all at once I get it—the penny drops. Dave Mansfield *believes* this old chestnut. Not only that, he can *afford* to believe it. Such clichés may be hollow in the big leagues, where some player or other tests positive for drugs every week or two and the free agent is God, but this is not the big leagues. This is where Anita Bryant sings the national anthem over battered PA speakers that have been wired to the chain-link behind the dugouts. This is where, instead of paying admission to watch the game, you put something in the hat when it comes around. If you want to, of course. None of these kids are going to spend the off-season playing fantasy baseball in Florida with overweight businessmen, or signing expensive baseball cards at memorabilia shows, or touring the chicken circuit at two thousand bucks a night. When it's all free, Dave's smile suggests, they have to give the clichés back and let you own them again, fair and square. You are once more allowed to believe in Red Barber, John Tunis, and the Kid from Tomkinsville. Dave Mansfield believes what he is saying about how the boys are equal between the chalk, and he has a right to believe, because he and Neil and Saint have patiently led these kids to a point where *they* believe it. They do believe it; I can see it on their faces as they sit in the dugout on the far side of the diamond. It could be why Dave Mansfield and all the other Dave Mansfields across the country keep on doing this, year after year. It's a free pass. Not back into childhood—it doesn't work that way—but back into the dream.

Dave falls silent for a moment, thinking, bouncing a few sunflower seeds up and down in the palm of his hand.

"It's not about winning or losing," he says finally. "That comes later. It's about how they'll pass each other in the corridor this year, or even down the road in high school, and look at each other, and remember. In a way, they're going to be on the team that won the district in 1989 for a long time." Dave glances across into the shadowy first-base dugout, where Fred Moore is now laughing about something with Mike Arnold. Owen King glances from one to the other, grinning. "It's about knowing who your teammates are. The people you had to depend on, whether you wanted to or not."

He watches the boys as they laugh and joke four days before their tournament is scheduled to begin, then raises his voice and tells Matt to throw four or five more and knock off.

Not all coaches who win the coin toss—as Dave Mansfield does on August 5, for the sixth time in nine postseason games—elect to be the home team. Some of them (the coach from Brewer, for instance) believe the so-called home-team advantage is a complete fiction, especially in a tournament game, where neither team is actually playing on its home field. The argument for being the visitors in a jackpot game runs like this: At the start of such a game, the kids on both teams are nervous. The way to take advantage of those nerves, the reasoning goes, is to bat first and let the defending team commit enough walks, balks, and errors to put you in the driver's seat. If you bat first and score four runs, these theorists conclude, you own the game before it's barely begun. QED. It's a theory Dave Mansfield has never subscribed to. "I want my lasties," he says, and for him that's the end of it.

Except today is a little different. It is not only a tournament game, it is a *championship* tournament game—a *televised* championship game, in fact. And as Roger Fisher winds and fires his first pitch past everything for ball one, Dave Mansfield's face is that of a man who is fervently hoping he hasn't made a mistake. Roger knows that he is a spot starter—that Mike Pelkey would be out here in his place if Pelkey weren't currently shaking hands with Goofy down in Disney World—but he manages his first-inning jitters as well as one could expect, maybe a little better. He backs off the mound following each return from the catcher, Joe Wilcox, studies the batter, fiddles with his shirt-sleeves, and takes all the time he needs. Most important of all, he understands how necessary it is to keep the ball in the lowest quarter of the strike zone. The York lineup is packed with power from top to bottom. If Roger makes a mistake and gets one up in the batter's eyes—especially a batter like Tarbox, who hits as powerfully as he throws—it's going to get lost in a hurry.

He loses the first York batter nevertheless. Bouchard trots down to first, accompanied by the hysterical cheers of the York rooting section. The next batter is Philbrick, the shortstop. He bangs the first pitch back to Fisher. In one of those plays that sometimes decide ball games, Roger elects to go to second and try to force the lead runner. In most Little League games, this turns out to be a bad idea. Either the pitcher throws wild into center field, allowing the lead runner to get to third, or he discovers that his shortstop has not moved over to cover second and the bag is undefended. Today, however, it works. St. Pierre has drilled these boys well on their defensive positions. Matt Kinney, today's shortstop, is right where he's supposed to be. So is Roger's throw. Philbrick reaches first on a fielder's choice, but Bouchard is out. This time, it is the Bangor West fans who roar out their approval.

The play settles most of Bangor West's jitters and gives Roger Fisher some badly needed confidence. Phil Tarbox, York's most consistent hitter as well as their ace pitcher, strikes out on a pitch low and out of the strike zone. "Get him next time, Phil!" a York player calls from the bench. "You're just not used to pitching this slow!"

But speed is not the problem the York batters are having with Roger; it's location. Ron St. Pierre has preached the gospel of the low pitch all season long, and Roger Fisher—Fish, the boys call him—has been a quiet but extremely attentive student during Saint's ball-yard seminars. Dave's decisions to pitch Roger and bat last look pretty good as Bangor comes in to bat in the bottom of the first. I see several of the boys touch Mo, the little plastic sandal, as they enter the dugout.

Confidence—of the team, of the fans, of the coaches—is a quality that can be measured in different ways, but whatever yardstick you choose, York comes out on the long side. The hometown cheering section has hung a sign on the lower posts of the scoreboard. YORK IS BRISTOL BOUND, this exuberant Fan-O-Gram reads. And there is the matter of those District 4 pins, all made up and ready for trading. But the clearest indicator of the deep confidence York's coach has in his players is revealed in his starting pitcher. All the other clubs, including Bangor West, pitched their number one starter in their first game, bearing an old playoff axiom in mind: if you don't get a date, you can't dance at the prom. If you can't win your prelim, you don't have to worry about the final. Only the coach from York ran counter to this wisdom, and pitched his number two starter, Ryan Fernald, in the first game, against Yarmouth. He got away with it—by a whisker— as his team outlasted Yarmouth, 9–8. That was a close shave, but today should be the payoff. He has saved Phil Tarbox for the final, and while Tarbox may not be technically as good as Stanley Sturgis, he's got something going for him that Sturgis did not. Phil Tarbox is *scary.*

Nolan Ryan, probably the greatest fastball pitcher ever to play the game of baseball, likes to tell a story about a Babe Ruth League tournament game he pitched in. He hit the opposing team's leadoff batter in the arm, breaking it. He hit the second batter in the head, splitting the boy's helmet in two and knocking him out for a few moments. While this second boy was being attended to, the number three batter, ashen-faced and trembling, went up to his coach and begged the man not to make him hit. "And I didn't blame him," Ryan adds.

Tarbox is no Nolan Ryan, but he throws hard and he is aware that intimidation is the pitcher's secret weapon. Sturgis also threw hard, but he kept the ball low and outside. Sturgis was polite. Tarbox likes to work high and tight. Bangor West has got to where they are today by swinging the bat. If Tarbox can intimidate them, he will take the bats out of their hands, and if he does that Bangor is finished.

Nick Trzaskos doesn't come anywhere near a leadoff home run today. Tarbox strikes him out with an intimate fastball that has Nick ducking out of the box. Nick looks around unbelievingly at the home-plate umpire and opens his mouth to protest. "Don't say a word, Nick!" Dave blares from the dugout. "Just hustle back in there!" Nick does, but his face has resumed its former narrow look. Once inside the dugout, he slings his batting helmet disgustedly under the bench.

Tarbox will try to work everyone but Ryan Iarrobino high and tight today. Word on Iarrobino has got around, and not even Phil Tarbox, confident as he appears to be, will challenge him. He works Ryan low and outside, finally walking him. He also walks Matt Kinney, who follows Ryan, but now he is high and tight again. Matt has superb reflexes, and he needs them to avoid being hit, and hit hard. By the time he is awarded first base, Iarrobino is already at second, courtesy of a wild pitch that came within inches of Matt's face. Then Tarbox settles down a little, striking out Kevin Rochefort and Roger Fisher to end the first inning.

Roger Fisher continues to work slowly and methodically, fiddling with his sleeves between pitches, glancing around at his infield, occasionally even checking the sky, possibly for UFOs. With two on and one out, Estes, who reached on a walk, breaks for third on a pitch that bounces out of Joe Wilcox's glove and lands at his feet. Joe recovers quickly and guns the ball down to Kevin Rochefort at third. The ball is waiting for Estes when he arrives, and he trots back to the dugout. Two out; Fernald has gone to second on the play.

Wyatt, York's number eight hitter, dribbles one up the right side of the infield. The ball's progress is slowed further by the soggy condition of the ground. Fisher goes for the ball. So does King, the first baseman. Roger grabs it, then slips on the wet grass and *crawls* for the bag, ball in hand. Wyatt beats him easily. Fernald comes all the way home on the play to score the first run of the game.

If Roger is going to crack, one would expect it to happen right here. He checks his infield, and examines the ball. He appears ready to pitch, and then steps off the rubber. His sleeves, it seems, are not quite to his liking after all. He takes his time fixing them while Matt Francke, the York batter, grows old and mouldy in the batter's box. By the time Fisher finally gets around to throwing, he all but owns Francke, who hits an easy hopper to Kevin Rochefort at third. Rochefort throws on to Matt Kinney, forcing Wyatt. Still, York has drawn first blood and leads, 1–0, at the end of an inning and a half.

Bangor West doesn't put any runs on the board in the second inning, either, but they score against Phil Tarbox just the same. The rangy York pitcher trotted off the mound with his head up at the end of the first inning. Going in after pitching the second, he trudges with his head down, and some of his teammates glance at him uneasily.

Owen King, who bats first in Bangor's half of the second, isn't intimidated by Tarbox, but he is a big boy, much slower than Matt

Kinney. After running the count full, Tarbox tries to jam him inside. The fastball runs up and in—too much of both. King is hit hard in the armpit. He falls to the ground, clutching the hurt place, too stunned to cry at first, but obviously in pain. Eventually, the tears do come— not a lot of them, but real tears, for all that. At six foot two and over two hundred pounds, he's as big as a man, but he's still only twelve and not used to being hit by seventy-mile-an-hour inside fastballs. Tarbox immediately rushes off the mound toward him, his face a mask of concern and contrition. The umpire, already bending over the downed player, waves him off impatiently. The on-duty paramedic who hurries out doesn't even give Tarbox a second look. The fans do, however. The fans are giving him all kinds of second looks.

"Take him out before he hits someone else!" one yells.

"Pull him before someone *really* gets hurt!" another adds, as if being hit in the ribcage by a fastball weren't really getting hurt.

"Warn im, ump!" a third voice chimes in. "That was a deliberate brushback! Warn im what happens if he does it again!"

Tarbox glances toward the fans, and for a moment this boy, who has formerly radiated a kind of serene confidence, looks very young and very uncertain. He looks, in fact, the way Stanley Sturgis did as the Belfast-Lewiston game neared its conclusion. As he goes back to the mound, he slams the ball into his glove in frustration.

King, meanwhile, has been helped to his feet. After making it clear to Neil Waterman, the paramedic, and the umpire that he wants to stay in the game and is capable of doing so, he trots down to first base. Both sets of fans give him a solid round of applause.

Phil Tarbox, who of course had no intention of hitting the leadoff batter in a one-run game, immediately shows how shaken he is by grooving one right down the middle to Arthur Dorr. Arthur, the second-smallest boy in Bangor West's starting lineup, accepts this unexpected but welcome gift by driving it deep to right center.

King is off at the crack of the bat. He rounds third, knowing he can't score but hoping to draw the throw that will assure Arthur of second base, and, as he does, the wet conditions become a factor. The third-base side of the diamond is still damp. When King tries to put on the brakes, his feet go out from under him and he lands on his ass. The relay has come in to Tarbox, and Tarbox will not risk a throw; he charges King, who is making feeble efforts to regain his feet. At the end, Bangor's biggest player just raises his arms in an eloquent, touching gesture: *I surrender.* Thanks to the slippery conditions, Tarbox now has a runner on second with one out instead of runners on second and third with none out. It is a big difference, and Tarbox displays his renewed confidence by striking out Mike Arnold.

Then, on his third pitch to Joe Wilcox, the next batter, he hits him smack in the elbow. This time, the cries of outrage from the Bangor West fans are louder, and tinged with threat. Several of them direct their ire at the home-plate umpire, demanding that Tarbox be taken out. The ump, who understands this situation completely, does not bother even to warn Tarbox. The stricken look on the boy's face as Wilcox jogs shakily down to first undoubtedly tells him it isn't necessary. But York's manager has to come out and settle the pitcher down, to point out the obvious: *You have two outs and first base was open anyway. There's no problem.*

But for Tarbox there *is* a problem. He has hit two boys this inning, hit both of them hard enough to make them cry. If that weren't a problem, he would need a mental examination.

York puts together three singles to score two runs in the top of the third, opening up a 3–0 lead. If these runs, both solidly earned, had come in the top of the first, Bangor would have been in serious trouble, but when the players come in for their raps they look eager and excited. There is no feeling among them that the game is lost, no whiff of failure.

Ryan Iarrobino is Bangor's first batter in the bottom of the third, and Tarbox works him carefully—too carefully. He has begun to aim the ball, and the result is fairly predictable. With the count at 1-2, he plinks Iarrobino on the shoulder. Iarrobino turns and pounds his bat once on the ground—whether in pain, frustration, or anger is impossible to tell. Most probably it is all three. Reading the mood of the crowd is much easier. The Bangor fans are on their feet, yelling angrily at Tarbox and at the ump. On the York side, the fans are silent and bewildered; it is not the game they were expecting. As Ryan trots down to first, he glances over at Tarbox. It is brief, that glance, but it seems clear enough: *That's the third time, you. Make it the last time.*

Tarbox confers briefly with his coach, then faces Matt Kinney. His confidence is in shambles, and his first pitch to Matt, a wild one, suggests that he wants to continue pitching this game about as much as a cat wants a bubble bath. Iarrobino beats York catcher Dan Bouchard's throw to second easily. Tarbox walks Kinney. The next batter is Kevin Rochefort. After two failed bunt attempts, Roach settles back and allows Phil Tarbox the chance to dig his hole a little deeper. He does, walking Kevin after having him 1-1. Tarbox has now thrown more than sixty pitches in less than three innings.

Roger Fisher also goes 3-2 with Tarbox, who is now relying almost exclusively on soft breaking stuff; he seems to have decided that if he does hit another batter he will not hit him hard. There is no place to put Fish; the bases are jammed. Tarbox knows it and takes a calculated risk, grooving another one, believing Fish will lay off in the hope of a walk. Roger snaps hungrily at it instead, bouncing one between first and second for a base hit. Iarrobino trots home with Bangor's first run.

Owen King, the player who was at bat when Phil Tarbox started to self-destruct, is the next batter. The York coach, suspecting his ace will work even less successfully to King this time, has seen enough. Matt Francke comes in to relieve, and Tarbox becomes York's catcher. As he squats behind the plate to warm Francke up, he looks both resigned and relieved. Francke doesn't hit anyone, but he is unable to stop the bleeding. At the end of three innings, Bangor West has only two hits, but they lead York, 5–3.

It is now the fifth inning. The air is full of gray moisture, and the YORK IS BRISTOL BOUND banner tacked to the scoreboard uprights has begun to sag. The fans look a little saggy themselves, and increasingly uneasy. *Is* York Bristol bound? *Well, we're supposed to be,* their faces say, *but it's the fifth inning now, and we're still two runs behind. My God, how did it get so late so early?*

Roger Fisher continues to cruise, and in the bottom of the fifth Bangor West puts what appear to be the final nails in York's coffin. Mike Arnold leads off with a single. Joe Wilcox sacrifices pinch-runner Fred Moore to second, and Iarrobino doubles off Francke, scoring Moore. This brings Matt Kinney to the plate. After a passed ball advances Ryan to third, Kinney hits an easy grounder to short, but it squirts off the infielder's glove and Iarrobino trots home.

Bangor West takes the field jubilantly, owning a 7–3 lead and only needing three more outs.

When Roger Fisher takes the mound to face York in the top of the sixth, he has thrown ninety-seven pitches, and he's a tired boy. He shows it at once by walking pinch-hitter Tim Pollack on a full count. Dave and Neil have seen enough. Fisher goes to second base, and Mike Arnold, who has been warming up between innings, takes over on the mound. He is ordinarily a good reliever, but it's not his day. Tension, maybe, or maybe it's just that the damp dirt of the mound has caused a change in his normal motion. He gets Francke to fly out, but then Bouchard walks, Philbrick doubles, and Pollack, the runner charged to Fish, scores, and Bouchard is held up at third; by itself, Pollack's run means nothing. The important thing is that York now has runners on second and third, and the potential tying run is coming to the plate. The potential tying run is someone with a very personal interest in getting a hit, because he is the main reason York is only two outs away from extinction. The potential tying run is Phil Tarbox.

Mike works the count to 1-1, and then throws a fastball right down the middle of the plate. In the Bangor West dugout, Dave Mansfield winces and raises one hand toward his forehead in a warding-off gesture even as Tarbox begins his swing. There is the hard sound of Tarbox accomplishing that most difficult of baseball feats: using the round bat to hit the round ball squarely on the button.

Ryan Iarrobino takes off the instant Tarbox connects, but he runs out of room much too early. The ball clears the fence by twenty feet, bangs off a TV camera, and bounces back onto the field. Ryan looks at it disconsolately as the York fans go mad, and the entire York team boils out of the dugout to greet Tarbox, who has hit a three-run homer and redeemed himself in spectacular fashion. He does not step on home plate but *jumps* on it. His face wears an expression of near-beatific satisfaction. He is mobbed by his ecstatic teammates; on his way back to the dugout, his feet are barely allowed to touch the ground.

The Bangor fans sit in silence, utterly stunned by this awful reversal. Yesterday, against Lewiston, Bangor flirted with disaster; today they have swooned in its arms. Mo has changed sides again, and the fans are clearly afraid that this time it has changed for good. Mike Arnold confers with Dave and Neil. They are telling him to go on back and pitch hard, that the game is only tied, not lost, but Mike is clearly a dejected, unhappy boy.

The next batter, Hutchins, hits an easy two-hopper to Matt Kinney, but Arnold is not the only one who is shaken; the usually dependable Kinney boots the ball, and Hutchins is on. Andy Estes pops out to Rochefort at third, but Hutchins advances to second on a passed ball. King grabs Matt Hoyt's pop-up for the third out, and Bangor West is out of trouble.

The team has a chance to put it away in the bottom of the sixth, except that doesn't quite happen, either. They go one-two-three against Matt Francke, and all at once Bangor West is in its first extra-innings game of postseason play, tied 7–7 with York.

During the game against Lewiston, the muddy weather eventually unravelled. Not today. As Bangor West takes the field in the top of the seventh, the skies grow steadily darker. It's now approaching six o'clock, and even under these conditions the field should still be clear and fairly bright, but fog has begun to creep in. Watching a videotape of the game would make someone who wasn't there believe something was wrong with the TV cameras; everything looks listless, dull, underexposed. Shirtsleeve fans in the center-field bleachers are becoming disembodied heads and hands; in the outfield, Trzaskos, Iarrobino, and Arthur Dorr are discernible chiefly by their shirts.

Just before Mike throws the first pitch of the seventh, Neil elbows Dave and points out to right field. Dave immediately calls time and trots out to see what's the matter with Arthur Dorr, who is standing bent over, with his head almost between his knees.

Arthur looks up at Dave with some surprise as he approaches. "I'm O.K.," he says in answer to the unspoken question.

"Then what in hell are you doing?" Dave asks.

"Looking for four-leaf clovers," Arthur responds.

Dave is too flabbergasted, or too amused, to lecture the boy. He simply tells Arthur it might be more appropriate to look for them after the game is over.

Arthur glances around at the creeping fog before looking back at Dave. "I think by then it's gonna be too dark," he says.

With Arthur set to rights, the game can continue, and Mike Arnold does a creditable job—possibly because he's facing the substitute-riddled bottom of York's order. York does not score, and Bangor comes up in the bottom of the seventh with another chance to win it.

They come close to doing just that. With the bases loaded and two out, Roger Fisher hits one hard up the first-base line. Matt Hoyt is right there to pounce on it, however, and the teams change sides again.

Philbrick flies out to Nick Trzaskos to open the eighth, and then Phil Tarbox steps in. Tarbox is not finished working Bangor West over yet. He has regained his confidence; his face is utterly serene as he takes Mike's first pitch for a called strike. He swings at the next one, a pretty decent changeup that bounces off Joe Wilcox's shin guard. He steps out of the box, squats with the bat between his knees, and concentrates. This is a Zen technique the York coach has taught these boys—Francke has done it several times on the mound while in tight spots—and it works for Tarbox this time, along with a little help from Mike Arnold.

Arnold's final pitch to Tarbox is a hanging curve up in the batter's eyes, exactly where Dave and Neil hoped no pitch would be today, and Tarbox creams it. It goes deep to left center, high over the fence. There is no camera stanchion to stop this one; it ends up in the woods, and the York fans are on their feet again, chanting "Phil-Phil-Phil" as Tarbox circles third, comes down the line, and jumps high in the air. He doesn't just jump on home plate; he *spikes* it.

Nor, it seems at first, will that be all. Hutchins bangs a single up the middle and gets second on an error. Estes follows this by hitting one to third, and Rochefort throws badly to second. Luckily, Roger Fisher is backed up by Arthur Dorr, saving a second run, but now York has guys at first and second with only one out.

Dave calls Owen King in to pitch, and Mike Arnold moves over to first. Following a wild pitch that moves the runners up to second and third, Matt Hoyt bangs one on the ground to Kevin Rochefort. In the game that Bangor West lost to Hampden, Casey Kinney was able to come back and make the play after committing an error. Rochefort does it today, and in spades. He comes up with the ball, then holds it for a moment, making sure Hutchins isn't going to break for the plate. *Then* he throws across the diamond to Mike, getting the slow-running Matt Hoyt by two steps. Considering the wringer these boys have been through, it is an incredibly canny piece of baseball. Bangor West has recovered itself, and King works Ryan Fernald—who hit a three-run homer against Yarmouth—perfectly, nipping at the corners, using his weirdly effective sidearm delivery to supplement the over-the-top fastball. Fernald pops weakly to first and the inning is over. At the end of seven and a half, York leads Bangor, 8–7. Six of York's RBIs belong to Philip Tarbox.

Matt Francke, York's pitcher, is as tired as Fisher was when Dave finally elected to replace him with Mike Arnold. The difference is that Dave *had* a Mike Arnold and, behind Mike, an Owen King. The York coach has no one; he used Ryan Fernald against Yarmouth, making him ineligible to pitch today, and now it's Francke forever.

He starts off the eighth well enough, striking out King. Arthur Dorr comes up next, one for four on the day (a double off Tarbox). Francke, obviously struggling now but just as obviously determined to finish this game, goes full with Arthur, then serves one up that's way outside. Arthur trots down to first.

Mike Arnold comes up next. It wasn't his day on the mound, but he does well this time at the plate, laying down a perfect bunt. The intent is not to sacrifice; Mike is bunting for the base hit, and almost gets it. But the ball will not quite die in that soggy patch between home and the pitcher's mound. Francke snatches it, glances toward second, and then elects to go to first. Now there are two men out with a runner at second. Bangor West is an out away from the end.

Joe Wilcox, the catcher, is up next. With the count 2-1, he hits a chalk hugger up the first-base line. Matt Hoyt grabs it, but just an instant too late; he takes the ball less than half a foot into foul territory, and the first-base umpire is right there to call it. Hoyt, who has been ready to charge the mound and embrace Matt Francke, instead returns the ball.

Now the count on Joey is 2-2. Francke steps off the rubber, stares straight up into the sky, and concentrates. Then he steps back on and delivers one high and out of the strike zone. Joey goes for it anyway, not even looking, swinging in self-defense. The bat makes contact with the ball—pure luck—and it bounces foul. Francke does the concentration bit again, then throws—just outside. Ball three.

Now comes what may be the pitch of the game. It *appears* to be a high strike, a game-ending strike, but the umpire calls ball four. Joe Wilcox trots down to first base with a faint expression of disbelief on his face. It is only later, watching the slow-motion replay on the TV tape of the game, that one can see how right, and how good, the umpire's call was. Joe Wilcox, so anxious that he is pinwheeling the bat in his hands like a golf club right up to the moment of the pitch, rises on his tiptoes as the ball approaches, and this is the reason it appears to be letter-high to him as it crosses the plate. The umpire, who never moves, discounts all of Joe's nervous tics and makes a major league call. The rules say you cannot shrink the strike zone by crouching; by the same token, you cannot expand it by stretching. If Joe hadn't gone up on his toes, Francke's pitch would have been throat-high instead of letter-high. So, instead of becoming the third out and ending the game, Joe becomes another base runner.

One of the TV cameras was trained on York's Matt Francke as he made the pitch, and it caught a remarkable image. A video replay shows Francke light up as the ball breaks downward just a moment too late to earn the strike. His pitching hand comes up in a victorious fisted salute. At this moment, he begins to move to his right, toward the York dugout, and the umpire blocks him out. When he returns to view a second later, his expression has become one of unhappiness and incredulity. He does not argue with the call—these kids are taught not to do that in their regular seasons, and to never, never, *never* do it in a championship situation—but as he prepares to work the next batter Francke appears to be crying.

Bangor West is still alive, and as Nick Trzaskos approaches the plate they come to their feet and begin to yell. Nick is obviously hoping for a free ride, and he gets one. Francke walks him on five pitches. It is the eleventh walk given up by York pitching today. Nick trots down to first, loading the bases, and Ryan Iarrobino steps in. Again and again, it has been Ryan Iarrobino in these situations, and now it is Ryan once more. The Bangor West fans are on their feet, screaming. The Bangor players crowd the dugout, fingers hooked through the mesh, watching anxiously.

"I can't believe it," one of the TV commentators says. "I can't believe the script of this game."

His partner chips in, "Well, I'll tell you what. Either way, this is how both teams would want the game to end."

As he speaks, the camera offers its own ghastly counterpoint to the comment by focusing on the stricken face of Matt Francke. The image strongly suggests that this is the *last* thing the York lefty wanted. Why would he? Iarrobino has doubled twice, walked twice, and been hit by a pitch. York hasn't retired him a single time. Francke throws high and outside, then low. These are his 135th and 136th pitches. The boy is exhausted. Chuck Bittner, the York manager, calls him over for a brief conference. Iarrobino waits for the conference to end, then steps in again.

Matt Francke concentrates, head back and eyes closed; he looks like a baby bird waiting to be fed. Then he winds up and throws the last pitch of the Maine Little League season.

Iarrobino has not been watching the concentration bit. His head is down; he is only watching to see how Francke will come, and his eyes never leave the ball. It is a fastball, low and tailing toward the outside corner of the plate. Ryan Iarrobino dips a little. The head of the bat whips around. He catches all of this one, really cranks it, and as the ball flies out of the park to deep right-center field, his arms shoot up over his head and he begins to tap-dance deliriously down the first-base line.

On the mound, Matt Francke, who was twice within inches of winning this game, lowers his head, not wanting to look. And as Ryan rounds second and starts back toward home, he seems to finally understand what he has done, and at that point he begins to weep.

The fans are in hysterics; the sports commentators are in hysterics; even Dave and Neil seem close to hysterics as they block the plate, making room for Ryan to touch it. Rounding third, he passes the umpire there, who is still twirling one magisterial finger in the gray air, signalling home run.

Behind the plate, Phil Tarbox takes off his mask and walks away from the celebration. He stamps his foot once, his face clenched with deep frustration. He walks off-camera and out of Little League for good. He will play Babe Ruth ball next year, and probably he will play it well, but there will be no more games like this for Tarbox, or for any of these boys. This one is, as they say, in the books.

Ryan Iarrobino, laughing, crying, holding his helmet on his head with one hand and pointing straight up to the gray sky with the other, leaps high, comes down on home plate, and then leaps again, straight into the arms of his teammates, who bear him away in triumph. The game is over; Bangor West has won, 11–8. They are Maine's 1989 Little League Champions.

I look toward the fence on the first-base side and see a remarkable sight: a forest of waving hands. The parents of the players have crowded against the chain-link and are reaching across the top to touch their sons. Many of the parents are also in tears. The boys all wear identical expressions of happy disbelief, and all these hands— hundreds of them, it seems—wave toward them, wanting to touch, wanting to congratulate, wanting to hug, wanting to *feel*.

The boys ignore them. Later, there will be touches and hugs. First, however, there is business to take care of. They line up and slap hands with the boys from York, crossing at home plate in the ritual manner. Most of the boys on both teams are crying now, some so hard they can barely walk.

Then, in the instant before the Bangor boys go to the fence, where all those hands are still waving, they surround their coaches and pummel them and each other in joyful triumph. They have held on to win their tournament—Ryan and Matt, Owen and Arthur, Mike and Roger Fisher, finder of four-leaf clovers. At this moment they are cheering each other, and everything else will just have to wait. Then they break for the fence, going toward their crying, cheering, laughing parents, and the world begins to turn in its ordinary course once again.

"How long are we gonna keep on playing, Coach?" J. J. Fiddler asked Neil Waterman after Bangor clinched the division against Machias.

"J.J.," Neil replied, "we're gonna play until someone makes us stop."

The team that finally made Bangor West stop was Westfield, Massachusetts. Bangor West played them in the second round of the Eastern Regional Little League Championship, at Bristol, Connecticut, on August 15th, 1989. Matt Kinney pitched for Bangor West and threw the game of his life, striking out nine, walking five (one intentional), and giving up only three hits. Bangor West, however, got only one hit off Westfield pitcher Tim Laurita, and that one belonged, predictably enough, to Ryan Iarrobino. The final score was 2–1, Westfield. Credit Bangor's one RBI in the game to King, on a bases-loaded walk. Credit the game-winning RBI to Laurita, also on a bases-loaded walk. It was a hell of a game, a purist's game, but it couldn't match the one against York.

In the pro world, it was a bad year for baseball. A future Hall of Famer was banned from the sport for life; a retired pitcher shot his wife and then took his own life; the commissioner suffered a fatal heart attack; the first World Series game to be played at Candlestick Park in over twenty years was postponed when an earthquake shook northern California. But the majors are only a small part of what baseball is about. In order places and in other leagues—Little League, for instance, where there are no free agents, no salaries, and no gate admissions—it was a pretty fine year. The Eastern Regional Tournament winner was Trumbull, Connecticut. On August 26, 1989, Trumbull beat Taiwan to win the Little League World Series. It was the first time an American team had won the Williamsport World Series since 1983, and the first time in fourteen years that the winner had come from the region in which Bangor West plays.

In September, the Maine division of the United States Baseball Federation voted Dave Mansfield amateur coach of the year.

Molly O'Neill (b. 1954) worked for ten years as a professional chef, specializing in Italian and American cooking, before switching to feature writing for the *Boston Globe, Boston, New York Newsday,* and *The New York Times,* where she served as the Sunday magazine's food columnist. She is the author of three books including *The New York Cookbook.* Her youngest brother, Paul, played nine of his sixteen years in the major leagues as rightfielder for the New York Yankees. This article appeared in *The New York Times* during the 1990 World Series.

Molly O'Neill

ꗠ

Coming to the Plate, One Family's Ethos

W hen Paul O'Neill steps to the plate for the Cincinnati Reds tonight, he will embody the hopes of most of the 52,000 fans at Riverfront Stadium and, for at least one pitch, he will be the focal point of over 50 million televisions across America. He will also be at the center of our family's field of dreams. Since 1928, when our father, a former minor league pitcher, began throwing screwballs on his family's farm, the Series has been manifest destiny. Baseball kept our father alive.

Tonight will be Paul's first official World Series appearance. But it isn't his first World Series experience. He has been playing baseball as if his life depended on it since he was 2 years old. He had to. His four older brothers would have used him as a base if he hadn't learned how to swing a bat. In addition, our father had quite a lot on his mind—a baseball career that ended in a World War II paratrooping accident, a dicey ditch-digging business, six children and an achieving wife—and he never seemed to remember any of his sons' names until he heard them announced over the public address system at the Little League park.

For 10 years, my mother said, her sons seemed like an endless progression of different-colored flannel uniforms that needed to be washed. My brothers were all baseball stars. It was the roll of some very large cosmic dice that kept Paul playing the game. Two others were scouted and chose early retirement over the major leagues. One became a poet; another grew his hair long and became an entrepreneur. We all knew the consequence of these acts. "I could end up T. S. Eliot and Michael could be Donald Trump," my brother Robert said last week. "For Dad, it wouldn't come close to what Paul's doing."

We grew up in Columbus, Ohio. In a neighborhood where most children grew up Lutheran or Methodist, we grew up Baseball. It is a way of life that is as whimsical and superstitious as any other religion. Our neighbors, who were primarily academics from Ohio State University, weren't always tolerant of our rituals. The ecstasy of winning a round of home run derby by slamming a tennis ball over the fence that divided our dusty back yard from the manicured lawn next door completely escaped Mr. Walter, the owner of the manicured lawn.

His complaints ignited a slow-seething battle between my parents. To my mother, who was loath to offend, the solution was obvious: stop hitting balls. "Children can read," she would proclaim. "Children can take music lessons or ballet lessons." This irreverence astounded my father, who also didn't understand why parking his backhoe in the driveway embarrassed my mother. While they battled, a steady stream of balls continued to sail over the fence.

Mr. Walter, a soft-spoken widower, decided that we were incorrigible and spent the afternoons huddled on his back porch holding a rosary. When the ball hit the plywood backstop, he would pass a bead, when it smacked off the bat, he prayed harder. When a ball passed over the fence, he dropped his rosary, retrieved the offending sphere and retired it to his house. He thought that we possessed an exhaustible supply of balls. He was wrong. On a given afternoon, we might run out of tennis balls but there were soft balls, hard balls, Wiffle balls, soccer balls, Nerf balls, kick balls. . . .

We moved from that neighborhood when Paul was 6 years old. On moving day, Mr. Walter delivered hundreds of different balls, all neatly packaged in oversized cardboard storage boxes. It was his offering; his prayers had been answered. I was 15, had retired from softball three years before, and it seemed like providence that I would have my own bedroom where I could scribble deep and meaningful poetry in my diary and listen to top 40 music. My brothers were jubilant because the new house was set in the middle of four acres of potential baseball diamond.

By that time, they were a team. They had begun a 10-year reign over Central-Ohio Little League. Cincinnati had the Big Red Machine; Columbus had the O'Neill Boys. My oldest brother, Michael, was 13 and had an 80-mile-an-hour fastball. My brother Pat, who was 11, had a mean curveball. Kevin was a catcher. Robert was a pitcher. My father was the Little League coach. Paul wanted to play, but he was too young for anything more than the backyard games.

The backyard games had become very serious. My brothers weren't just a team, they were a franchise. They built a baseball diamond and worked as the grounds crew to keep the infield grass groomed. They acted as park security and cleaned the clubhouse, which in off-game times doubled as a shed for our pony, Tonka. As players, they only appeared in full equipment. They looked like miniature major leaguers, so many sawed-off chess pieces in a game that began before any of us were born.

We all knew that some day we would play the game for real. It just took a couple of decades to figure out the positions we would play.

A lot of the figuring occurred intra-brother. There was brutal competition for the mound. Winning mattered most, so the position usually belonged to Michael. Kevin, who was 4 years younger, was the catcher, and because Michael pitched as wild as he did fast, Kevin had a strong attachment to his face guard, chest guard, shin guards and helmet. It didn't surprise any of us when, at 13 years old, Kevin retired from baseball and started playing football. He liked the equipment.

Games of "hot box"—one player on first, another on second and a runner in between—proved that Pat, who loved the game more than any other brother, possessed the least physical gift. He is built a little too low to the ground. Robert, although five years younger, was Mike's singular competition for the mound. He pitched smart and steady. Paul was stuck with leftovers. He was just a little boy when the rest of my brothers entered adolescence, en masse. He started facing Michael when he was 8 years old. The others were sick of being hit by pitches. Paul took any pitches he could get.

His earliest training as a competitor was as a sort of pillow for his older brothers' Gestalt therapy. In the years when Robert fought to unseat Michael on the pitcher's mound, he relaxed by challenging Paul to 25-point games of one-on-one basketball. Coolly, Robert would allow a 23-point lead. And then, with the same dramatic effortlessness every afternoon, Robert would take the next 25 points from Paul.

The game never changed, and neither did Paul's reaction. "You cheater," he would shriek, hurling the basketball and storming into the house to call our mother at the hospital where she worked. "Mom," he would sob into the phone, after our mother had been paged from a death bed or an emergency room. "Robert cheated."

Paul had a sense of injustice early on. He criminalized his individual tormentors. If an older brother was in the process of winning, he was "lucky." If he won, he had "cheated," and Paul would follow the winner around with challenges for rematches phrased in a sportsmanlike manner: "What's the matter, cheater? Afraid you won't get lucky again?" My father interceded occasionally. "Quit torturing the darned baby, will ya?" he'd say.

Although usually, a game was a game in our house, a winner was a winner and only losers needed umpires. During his early childhood, the injustice for Paul was birth order. In the end, it may have been a lucky break. He was 2 years old when the older boys began to dominate Plain City.

Cincinnati had Crosley Field; Ohio Little League had Plain City. It was a Little League–scale replica of a major league park in an Amish community 25 miles northwest of Columbus. Plain City had a grass infield, dugouts, and uniformed umpires. It had a scoreboard, a concession stand and stadium-style stands. The Plain City games were our World Series. My father, the coach, would sit on the bench chewing like Don Zimmer. My brothers would play out their Catfish Hunter fantasies.

My mother and I would sit in the stands with Paul. He wore little sunsuits and I remember the way his blond curls smelled, the way the mosquitoes buzzed around us on those muggy Midwestern summer evenings. My attendance was mandatory. I was furious and bored and carried books like Sylvia Plath's "Bell Jar" to read during the game. But

Paul, from whom I was inseparable for the first eight years of his life, kept me connected to the game.

There was a dirt race track surrounding the Plain City ball park and one night, an Amish man steered his horse and buggy around the track during the bottom of the sixth and final inning. In his Abraham Lincoln hat and top coat, the buggy driver looked like something out of a 19th century museum. Michael was playing right field in that game. His team was one run up, with a runner on base and two out, when a routine fly ball landed at his feet. He was watching the horse and buggy. "He missed the ball, Ollee," Paul said, his earliest and enduring pronunciation of my name recalling the boxer Muhammad Ali. "Tell him to get it," he screamed.

He was too old to sit on my lap when Robert began pitching. If he had persevered, I suppose Robert would have been a reliever. He'd do anything to prevent a batter getting ahead of him. If they did, he collapsed. In one tied game at Plain City, with the bases loaded on walks and a full count, he began sobbing into the mitt on his left hand and consoling himself with his right hand, which was slipped down the front of his flannel, green and white pinstriped pants. "My god," whispered our horrified mother.

Maybe Paul learned from his older brothers' mistakes; he certainly learned the symmetry between baseball and life. Like the rest of us, he wasn't surprised when Robert, who was already being looked at by major league scouts, retired from baseball at age 15 and took up poetry and tennis. Even more than batters getting ahead of him, Robert loathed fielders who blew the play on a perfect groundball pitch.

He is the only brother who believes that he might have made a mistake about baseball. When Paul negotiates his contract, Robert, who is now 30 years old and weighs 220 pounds, is quick to point out that he, not Paul, was the m.v.p. of Plain City. "It's on the records," he says. "M.v.p. 1972. Paul only got most valuable pitcher and that was in 1974."

In a reversal of their one-on-one games, Robert calls Paul "lucky." "He's the only one who could go to the Ohio State Fair and blow the balloon off the clown's mouth, or get the ring around the bottle and come home with all the prizes," he says.

Paul's luck went as unnoticed as his performance on the Little League field did. A few years later, when he broke his ankle sliding into second base in Plain City, nobody thought it was any big deal that he played right field in a cast and led the team in batting. That's what O'Neill Boys do.

Besides, the world had started to change. As an all-city high school player, Michael was engaged in a hair-cut battle. Today, he says that it was symptomatic of his "uncoachableness." Then, he said, "What difference does it make how long my hair is if I am blowing away the batters?" Scouts still watched him, but he realized that his career potential was limited during his first year of college. "During a game after a particularly rough fraternity party," he told me yesterday, "I saw three balls coming at me instead of one."

Something similar happened to Pat in his senior year of high school. He quit baseball so that he could work in a grocery store and buy a car.

Paul was too young to drive a car or suffer the long-reaching ripples of Woodstock nation that washed over the rest of our adolescence. He kept playing baseball. My father, his top four prospects benched for life, focused exclusively on Paul. He called his youngest son "Mike, Pat, Kev or Rob, no, Paul." By the time he was in high school, Paul was the only one living at home. The rest of us were being socially relevant in places like Haight Ashbury and Provincetown.

Paul was at home when our parents began to look older. He called our father Little Buddy, and Old Timer. In 1980, when the telephone rang in our parents' kitchen with the news that Paul was Cincinnati's fourth-round draft pick, the Old Timer cried.

Nobody else was surprised. Nevertheless, the process of Paul's career pulled us back together, back into the story of our childhood, complete with the unresolved challenges and the echoes of "Cheater!" and "Luck!"

As Paul moved between single, double and triple A baseball, our other brothers drifted between careers. I suppose they tended some demons and doubt. Nobody talked about it. Everybody rooted for Paul. But since we grew up in the church of Baseball, we know why our father has outlived four of his brothers, we know what kept him alive during emergency bypass surgery the year that Paul moved up to the majors, we know about teams, we know for what we cheer.

None of it surprises us. Last week, sitting in a Broadway theater, in the middle of the second act of "Lettice and Lovage," I had an irrepressible urge to put on my Walkman, which was tuned to WFAN. Paul had called me from the locker room before the game; I just had this feeling. I tuned into an announcer yelling. "It's over the right field fence! A home run for O'Neill." My companion was amazed. I wasn't surprised.

Several nights later, I was watching the game on television when the Reds clinched the pennant. A few minutes passed before my brother Robert called. He was watching the post-game shows at his home in Cincinnati. "I haven't seen Paul on the screen," he said. "I have this feeling, he's standing by his locker, waiting for somebody to come and tell him he's the m.v.p." We listened to each other breathe and listened as our separate televisions announced that two relief pitchers had been named joint m.v.p.'s.

"Oh man," said Robert, "O.K., look. I have this big pumpkin, O.K.? I am going to carve it to look like something Charlie Brown might do, O.K.? It's going to say "REDS" in big victorious letters and I am going to put a candle in it and I'm going to take it over and put it on Paul's front porch before he gets home. He'll spend the whole night trying to figure out who did it. It might give him a laugh. He might think it's lucky."

After a pause, my brother Robert continued his declaration of full adulthood. "Look I gotta go, O.K.?" he said. "See you at the game on Tuesday. Wear red."

The dominant emotion any batter must overcome is his fear of a hard object thrown at high speed in the general direction of his solar plexus. Few writers have expressed that fear better than Richard Ford (b. 1944) did at the climax of his Pulitzer Prize–winning novel *Independence Day* (1995). Ford and his wife were once devotees of sports radio and habitués of minor-league ballparks, but he says that's all over now; players' enormous salaries have made a business out of the sport and made him sure that he "won't write, think or watch baseball ever again." When this piece appeared in *Harper's* in 1992, Ford's perspective on the game had yet to acquire that alienated edge.

Richard Ford

A Minors Affair

One of the keenest of my peculiarly transcontinental American memories is of driving across the wide state of Nebraska one summer in the Seventies—late at night, with the cold farm air whipping in the window—listening to the Denver Bears play the Iowa Oaks in Denver, 400 or so miles away. Denver then was the minor-league affiliate of the big-league Montreal Expos, which meant that the Expos could reach into the Bears' lineup on any day of the week and bring a player up to the parent club for duty.

That summer Denver sported a wonderful minor-league spectacular named Bombo Rivera, who was hitting balls hard and far and in all directions, catching everything in the yard, and throwing lightning bolts to every base. And it was Bombo who came in late for Denver that summer night and rocketed a home run high up into the lights (or so I envisioned it) and out into that rarefied mountain air to win the game. "Bombo, Bombo, Bombo," my wife and I heard the crowd chanting from within our dimly lighted radio out upon that vast and empty American plain. Bombo was the hero in Denver that night, and also in Nebraska. Though in Iowa he was a villain.

Later that summer and back in the East I happened to click into Bombo on TV—a chunky, bunch-shouldered, high-waisted black kid, or so I remember him now. The Expos, in the philosophical humor of a losing campaign, had brought him up to infuse whatever excitations he'd caused in Denver into the waning weeks of a long season in Quebec. Once that afternoon he struck out. Once he hit a ball high up into the pale afternoon sky, though that was caught. Later, and rather unexpectedly, he was replaced for defensive purposes. And in a couple of weeks, I read in the papers, he was gone. Back to Denver, I guessed. Back to the minor leagues. Or worse.

The essentials of the game are what, in some respects, the minor leagues are about. The minors are all those 170 or so teams scattered in professional leagues and associations from Edmonton to El Paso to East Jesus making up the infrastructure of the big leagues, those 26 (soon to be 28) teams serving major markets instead of just playing for cities, places where rich players sport big contracts, employ abusive agents, tape Nike endorsements, make insincere public apologies for their drug and sexual peccadilloes; where the World Series is often played, and so is the best baseball in the world.

The minors, all those *other* teams dotting America's heartland in hierarchical order of relative excellence (Triple-A better than Double-A, much better than just Single-A, a lot better than the Rookie League), are nominally where promising young prospects sharpen their baseball skills by playing beside and against other promising young prospects, summer upon blissful summer, in a cloistered Freudeo-Darwinian struggle up the ladder toward major-league proficiency and prominence. In point of fact, the minor leagues are somewhat different from that pastoral ideal. Precious few prospects can ever, it turns out, make the "bigs," baseball being the sweetly but disarmingly difficult game it is. So that, somewhat coldly speaking, the minors are there principally to provide organized competition for the pricey few players who'll make it to the major leagues, with the rest, like Bombo maybe, and a couple of guys I went to high school with, once their dreams turned to black and white, playing because they love the game and are good at it and because they hate to say "quit."

Importantly, though, the minors are where the basic matters of baseball can most conveniently and lovingly be observed. Television is almost never an option (one must attend), and ballparks are small, seats close in, crowds often modest, and the players' and grounds' proportions to one's own tender, human dimensions appreciable, as is the quality of play. Stars are few—only an occasional phenom passing through, or a wounded big leaguer bullying himself into shape—so that there's rarely the distraction of hoopla or household names, franchise or impact players, or controversies of any kind, except small ones. There's rarely even the controversy of great play —which, to some minor-league connoisseurs, is just one more distracting form of solipsistic virtuosity, one found chiefly in the big leagues and giving rise to the old aspersion that they play a somewhat different game up there.

They don't. Everywhere, from Portland to Pawtucket, baseball's the same slow, sometimes stately, sometimes tedious game governed by extensive, complexly arbitrary rules, and practiced according to arcane, informal mores and runic vocabularies which compel that almost every act of play be routine. Even the great smashes, the balletic defensive turns, and the unparalleled pitching performances—by being so formally anticipated, so contemplated and longed-for by the fans—become ritual, even foregone. It's a Platonic game in this way, with all visible excellence (and even unexcellence) ratified by a prior scheme of invisible excellence which is the game itself.

A well-versed *aficionada* of baseball, my wife, pointed out to me once, as we sat contentedly through a rain delay one September evening in Dodger Stadium, Great Falls, Montana, that there are no surprises in baseball. "It's always the same," she said. "A routine grounder—out at first. A routine pop fly to center. Two away. That's what I like about it." "Me, too," I might've said, sighing at the pink sky going blue behind the storm-swept mountains, feeling upon me that deep languor native to baseball's lack of urgency. "Me, too."

Why else would you go to see a game you loved played not even so well? Cutoff men missed? Throws to the wrong side of second? Failing to line up on the rundown? Not laying down the bunt with the go-ahead run on first? Only for love of the game, I suppose; for the essentials, which the minor leagues, synonymous with the second-rate in almost everything, stand for as a sort of fondly sentimental emblem.

What's *really* important about all of it? Probably nothing, and that in itself is a blessing. "In the great department store of life, baseball is the toy department," a sportscaster in L.A. used to say, and the bush leagues are proof of it. Rivalries among minor-league cities are never anything momentous. Players arrive in Billings and Memphis from hometowns far away, spend a few weeks, get chummy with a few locals, pick up a girlfriend, lose one, perform brief heroics or yeoman service on the field, then travel on, bags and bats in hand, to some new small town up or down the ladder. It's life for a while.

The tendency among spoilsport sportswriters to make it all so elegiac and bittersweet—to like us to see our own lives (easier for men, of course) in these boys' prospects; to make it all a gooey-nostalgic allegory for trying and failing while still young, an emblem for rum life lived well instead of just being an emblem for itself—is baloney, and I'm not wrong about it. Believe me, I don't see myself in those boys' lives. They're not my vicars, and I don't fantasize—at least not about them. I go to the game to *quit* thinking about my life, to sit and stare at a pleasant field I know on which is played a game I also know by players whose lives, wives, drug and betting habits, child-hood tragedies, and religious infatuations I *don't* know and don't want to. I'm just there to watch, to be pleased, maybe even thrilled, but not, God help me, to take moral instruction.

Maybe, just maybe, there's a soupçon of minor civic misfeasance in a town that *won't* support a minor-league team, *won't* provide its citizens entertainment on a small scale proportioned to certify their very existence by attesting that they lead the lives they think they lead—the life all Americans half-crave and half-hate—the small one, in a town that hasn't gotten too big for its britches, like Miami or Denver used to be, snugged into the culture's fabric as into a featherbed.

In the spirit that says it's good to understand one's institutions for fear we'll lose the knack of merely liking them and become their un-witting servants, it's cagey of us to keep baseball in its place, low upon the horizon, uninvested with too many of our national hopes and epiphanic longings. Baseball holds up nicely enough just as itself, in its small essentials.

Yusef Komunyakaa (b. 1947) grew up in the segregated paper-mill town of Bo-
galusa, Louisiana (the public library did not admit blacks), received a bronze
star for his service in Vietnam, and now teaches at Princeton University. Race,
the war, and black popular culture—everything from jazz to Negro League
baseball—are central concerns of this poet whose collection *Neon Vernacular:
New and Selected Poems 1977–1989* was awarded the Pulitzer Prize. This tribute
to black baseball appears in *Magic City* (1992).

Yusef Komunyakaa

Glory

Most were married teenagers
Working knockout shifts daybreak
To sunset six days a week—
Already old men playing ball
In a field between a row of shotgun houses
& the Magazine Lumber Company.
They were all Jackie Robinson
& Willie Mays, a touch of
Josh Gibson & Satchell Paige
In each stance & swing, a promise
Like a hesitation pitch always
At the edge of their lives,
Arms sharp as rifles.
The Sunday afternoon heat
Flared like thin flowered skirts
As children & wives cheered.
The men were like cats
Running backwards to snag
Pop-ups & high-flies off
Fences, stealing each other's glory.
The old deacons & raconteurs
Who umpired made an *Out* or *Safe*
Into a song & dance routine.

Runners hit the dirt
& slid into homeplate,
Cleats catching light,
As they conjured escapes, outfoxing
Double plays. In the few seconds
It took a man to eye a woman
Upon the makeshift bleachers,
A stolen base or homerun
Would help another man
Survive the new week.

Don DeLillo (b. 1936) has defined his subject matter as "the inner life of the culture," and in his eleven novels, beginning with *Americana* in 1971 and including *The Names* (1982), *White Noise* (1985), and *Libra* (1988), he has established himself as a great chronicler of modern America's rituals, obsessions, subcultures, and secret dream quests. In "The Triumph of Death," the prologue to his long and ambitious *Underworld* (1997), DeLillo takes as his point of departure the legendary third and final game of the 1951 New York Giants–Brooklyn Dodgers playoff series. With extraordinary intricacy he weaves in details both historical and imagined to create a fresco at once exuberant and charged with darker implications. It was first published in *Harper's* under the title "Pafko at the Wall."

Don DeLillo

▽

from

Underworld

He speaks in your voice, American, and there's a shine in his eye that's halfway hopeful.

It's a school day, sure, but he's nowhere near the classroom. He wants to be here instead, standing in the shadow of this old rust-hulk of a structure, and it's hard to blame him—this metropolis of steel and concrete and flaky paint and cropped grass and enormous Chesterfield packs aslant on the scoreboards, a couple of cigarettes jutting from each.

Longing on a large scale is what makes history. This is just a kid with a local yearning but he is part of an assembling crowd, anonymous thousands off the buses and trains, people in narrow columns tramping over the swing bridge above the river, and even if they are not a migration or a revolution, some vast shaking of the soul, they bring with them the body heat of a great city and their own small reveries and desperations, the unseen something that haunts the day—men in fedoras and sailors on shore leave, the stray tumble of their thoughts, going to a game.

The sky is low and gray, the roily gray of sliding surf.

He stands at the curbstone with the others. He is the youngest, at fourteen, and you know he's flat broke by the edgy leaning look he hangs on his body. He has never done this before and he doesn't know any of the others and only two or three of them seem to know each other but they can't do this thing singly or in pairs so they have found one another by means of slidy looks that detect the fellow foolhard and here they stand, black kids and white kids up from the subways or off the local Harlem streets, lean shadows, bandidos, fifteen in all, and according to topical legend maybe four will get through for every one that's caught.

They are waiting nervously for the ticket holders to clear the turnstiles, the last loose cluster of fans, the stragglers and loiterers. They watch the late-arriving taxis from downtown and the brilliantined men stepping dapper to the windows, policy bankers and supper club swells and Broadway hotshots, high aura'd, picking lint off their mohair sleeves. They stand at the curb and watch without seeming to look, wearing the sourish air of corner hangabouts. All the hubbub has died down, the pregame babble and swirl, vendors working the jammed sidewalks waving scorecards and pennants and calling out in ancient singsong, scraggy men hustling buttons and caps, all dispersed now, gone to their roomlets in the beaten streets.

They are at the curbstone, waiting. Their eyes are going grim, sending out less light. Somebody takes his hands out of his pockets. They are waiting and then they go, one of them goes, a mick who shouts *Geronimo*.

There are four turnstiles just beyond the pair of ticket booths. The youngest boy is also the scrawniest, Cotter Martin by name, scrawny tall in a polo shirt and dungarees and trying not to feel doomstruck—he's located near the tail of the rush, running and shouting with the others. You shout because it makes you brave or you want to announce your recklessness. They have made their faces into scream masks, tight-eyed, with stretchable mouths, and they are running hard, trying to funnel themselves through the lanes between the booths, and they bump hips and elbows and keep the shout going. The faces of the ticket sellers hang behind the windows like onions on strings.

Cotter sees the first jumpers go over the bars. Two of them jostle in the air and come down twisted and asprawl. A ticket taker puts a headlock on one of them and his cap comes loose and skims down his back and he reaches for it with a blind swipe and at the same time—everything's at the same time—he eyes the other hurdlers to keep from getting stepped on. They are running and hurdling. It's a witless form of flight with bodies packed in close and the gate-crashing becoming real. They are jumping too soon or too late and hitting the posts and radial bars, doing cartoon climbs up each other's back, and what kind of stupes must they look like to people at the hot dog stand on the other side of the turnstiles, what kind of awful screwups—a line of mostly men beginning to glance this way, jaws working at the sweaty meat and grease bubbles flurrying on their tongues, the gent at the far end going dead-still except for a hand that produces automatic movement, swabbing on mustard with a brush.

The shout of the motley boys comes banging off the deep concrete.

Cotter thinks he sees a path to the turnstile on the right. He drains himself of everything he does not need to make the jump. Some are still jumping, some are thinking about it, some need a haircut, some have girlfriends in woolly sweaters and the rest have landed in the ruck and are trying to get up and scatter. A couple of stadium cops are rumbling down the ramp. Cotter sheds these elements as they appear, sheds a thousand waves of information hitting on his skin. His gaze is trained on the iron bars projected from the post. He picks up speed and seems to lose his gangliness, the slouchy funk of hormones and unbelonging and all the stammering things that seal his adolescence. He is just a running boy, a half-seen figure from the streets, but the way running reveals some clue to being, the way a runner bares himself to consciousness, this is how the dark-skinned kid seems to open to the world, how the bloodrush of a dozen strides brings him into eloquence.

Then he leaves his feet and is in the air, feeling sleek and unmussed and sort of businesslike, flying in from Kansas City with a briefcase full of bank drafts. His head is tucked, his left leg is clearing the bars. And in one prolonged and aloof and discontinuous instant he sees precisely where he'll land and which way he'll run and even though he knows they will be after him the second he touches ground, even though he'll be in danger for the next several hours—watching left and right—there is less fear in him now.

He comes down lightly and goes easy-gaiting past the ticket taker groping for his fallen cap and he knows absolutely—knows it all the way, deep as knowing goes, he feels the knowledge start to hammer in his runner's heart—that he is uncatchable.

Here comes a cop in municipal bulk with a gun and cuffs and a flashlight and a billy club all jigging on his belt and a summons pad wadded in his pocket. Cotter gives him a juke step that sends him nearly to his knees and the hot dog eaters bend from the waist to watch the kid veer away in soft acceleration, showing the cop a little finger-wag bye-bye.

He surprises himself this way every so often, doing some gaudy thing that whistles up out of unsuspected whim.

He runs up a shadowed ramp and into a crossweave of girders and pillars and spilling light. He hears the crescendoing last chords of the national anthem and sees the great open horseshoe of the grandstand and that unfolding vision of the grass that always seems to mean he has stepped outside his life—the rubbed shine that sweeps and bends from the raked dirt of the infield out to the high green fences. It is the excitement of a revealed thing. He runs at quarter speed craning to see the rows of seats, looking for an inconspicuous wedge behind a pillar. He cuts into an aisle in section 35 and walks down into the heat and smell of the massed fans, he walks into the smoke that hangs from the underside of the second deck, he hears the talk, he enters the deep buzz, he hears the warm-up pitches crack into the catcher's mitt, a series of reports that carry a comet's tail of secondary sound.

Then you lose him in the crowd.

In the radio booth they're talking about the crowd. Looks like thirty-five thousand and how do you figure it. When you think about the textured histories of the teams and the faith and passion of the fans and the way these forces are entwined citywide, and when you think about the game itself, live-or-die, the third game in a three-game play-off, and you say the names Giants and Dodgers, and you calculate the way the players hate each other openly, and you recall the kind of year this has turned out to be, the pennant race that has brought the city to a strangulated rapture, an end-shudder requiring a German loanword to put across the mingling of pleasure and dread and suspense, and when you think about the blood loyalty, this is what they're saying in the booth—the love-of-team that runs across the boroughs and through the snuggled suburbs and out into the apple counties and the raw north, then how do you explain twenty thousand empty seats?

The engineer says, "All day it looks like rain. It affects the mood. People say the hell with it."

The producer is hanging a blanket across the booth to separate the crew from the guys who've just arrived from KMOX in St. Louis. Have to double up since there's nowhere else to put them.

He says to the engineer, "Don't forget. There wasn't any advance sale."

And the engineer says, "Plus the Giants lost big yesterday and this is a serious thing because a crushing defeat puts a gloom on the neighborhoods. Believe me, I know this where I live. It's demoralizing for people. It's like they're dying in the tens of thousands."

Russ Hodges, who broadcasts the games for WMCA, he is the voice of the Giants—Russ has an overworked larynx and the makings of a major cold and he shouldn't be lighting up a cigarette but here he goes, saying, "That's all well and good but I'm not sure there really is a logical explanation. When you deal with crowds, nothing's predictable."

Russ is going jowly now but there are elements of the uncomplicated boy in his eyes and smile and in the hair that looks bowl-cut and the shapeless suit that might belong to almost anyone. Can you do games, can you do play-by-play almost every day through a deep summer and not be located in some version of the past?

He looks out at the field with its cramped corners and the overcompensating spaces of the deep alleys and dead center. The big square Longines clock that juts up from the clubhouse. Strokes of color all around, a frescoing of hats and faces and the green grandstand and tawny base paths. Russ feels lucky to be here. Day of days and he's doing the game and it's happening at the Polo Grounds—a name he loves, a precious echo of things and times before the century went to war. He thinks everybody who's here ought to feel lucky because something big's in the works, something's building. Okay, maybe just his temperature. But he finds himself thinking of the time his father took him to see Dempsey fight Willard in Toledo and what a thing that was, what a measure of the awesome, the Fourth of July and a hundred and ten degrees and a crowd of shirtsleeved men in straw hats, many wearing handkerchiefs spread beneath their hats and down to their shoulders, making them look like play-Arabs, and the greatness of the beating big Jess took in that white hot ring, the way the sweat and blood came misting off his face every time Dempsey hit him.

When you see a thing like that, a thing that becomes a newsreel, you begin to feel you are a carrier of some solemn scrap of history.

In the second inning Thomson hits a slider on a line over third.

Lockman swings into an arc as he races toward second, looking out at left field.

Pafko moves to the wall to play the carom.

People stand in both decks in left, leaning out from the rows up front, and some of them are tossing paper over the edge, torn-up scorecards and bits of matchbook covers, there are crushed paper cups, little waxy napkins they got with their hot dogs, there are germ-bearing tissues many days old that were matted at the bottoms of deep pockets, all coming down around Pafko.

Thomson is loping along, he is striding nicely around first, leaning into his run.

Pafko throws smartly to Cox.

Thomson moves head-down toward second, coasting in, and then sees Lockman standing on the bag looking at him semi-spellbound, the trace of a query hanging on his lips.

Days of iron skies and all the mike time of the past week, the sore throat, the coughing, Russ is feverish and bedraggled—train trips and nerves and no sleep and he describes the play in his familiar homey ramble, the grits-and-tater voice that's a little scratchy today.

Cox peers out from under his cap and snaps the ball sidearm to Robinson.

Look at Mays meanwhile strolling to the plate dragging the barrel of his bat on the ground.

Robinson takes the throw and makes a spin move toward Thomson, who is standing shyly maybe five feet from second.

People like to see the paper fall at Pafko's feet, maybe drift across his shoulder or cling to his cap. The wall is nearly seventeen feet high so he is well out of range of the longest leaning touch and they have to be content to bathe him in their paper.

Look at Durocher on the dugout steps, manager of the Giants, hard-rock Leo, the gashouse scrapper, a face straight from the Gallic Wars, and he says into his fist, "Holy fuggin shit almighty."

Near the Giants' dugout four men are watching from Leo's own choice box when Robinson slaps the tag on Thomson. They are three-quarters show biz, Frank Sinatra, Jackie Gleason and Toots Shor, drinking buddies from way back, and they're accompanied by a well-dressed man with a bulldog mug, one J. Edgar Hoover. What's the nation's number one G-man doing with these crumbums? Well, Edgar is sitting in the aisle seat and he seems to be doing just fine, smiling at the rude banter that rolls nonstop from crooner to joke-smith to saloonkeeper and back. He would rather be at the racetrack but is cheerful enough in this kind of company whatever the venue. He likes to be around movie idols and celebrity athletes, around gossip-meisters such as Walter Winchell, who is also at the game today, sitting with the Dodger brass. Fame and secrecy are the high and low ends of the same fascination, the static crackle of some li-bidinous thing in the world, and Edgar responds to people who have access to this energy. He wants to be their dearly devoted friend pro-vided their hidden lives are in his private files, all the rumors col-lected and indexed, the shadow facts made real.

Gleason says, "I told you chumps, it's all Dodgers today. I feel it in my Brooklyn bones."

"What bones?" says Frank. "They're rotted out by booze."

Thomson's whole body sags, it loses vigor and resistance, and Robinson calls time and walks the ball to the mound in the pigeon-toed gait that makes his path seem crooked.

"The Giants'll have to hire that midget if they want to win, what's-his-name, because their only hope is some freak of nature," Gleason says. "An earthquake or a midget. And since this ain't California, you better pray for an elf in flannels."

Frank says, "Fun-nee."

The subject makes Edgar nervous. He is sensitive about his height even though he is safely in the middle range. He has added weight in recent years and when he sees himself in the mirror getting dressed, thick-bodied and Buddha-headed, it is a short round man that looks back at him. And this is something the yammerheads in the press have reported to be true, as if a man can wish his phantom torment into public print. And today it's a fact that taller-than-average agents are not likely to be assigned to headquarters. And it's a further fact that the midget his pal Gleason is talking about, the three-foot seven-inch *sportif* who came to bat one time for the St. Louis Browns some six weeks ago in a stunt that was also an act, Edgar believes, of political subversion—this fellow is called Eddie Gaedel and if Gleason recalls the name he will flash-pair Eddie with Edgar and then the short-man jokes will begin to fly like the storied shit that hits the fan. Gleason got his start doing insult comedy and never really stopped—does it for free, does it for fun and leaves shattered lives behind.

Toots Shor says, "Don't be a shlump all your life, Gleason. It's only one-zip. The Giants didn't come from thirteen and a half games back just to blow it on the last day. This is the miracle year. Nobody has a vocabulary for what happened this year."

The slab face and meatcutter's hands. You look at Toots and see a speakeasy vet, dense of body, with slicked-back hair and a set of chinky eyes that summon up a warning in a hurry. This is an ex-bouncer who throws innocent people out of his club when he is drinking.

He says, "Mays is the man."

And Frank says, "This is Willie's day. He's due to bust loose. Leo told me on the phone."

Gleason does a passable clipped Britisher saying, "You're not actually telling me that this fellow stepping up to the wicket is going to do something extraordinary."

Edgar, who hates the English, falls forward laughing even as Jackie takes a breathless bite of his hot dog and begins to cough and choke, sending quidbits of meat and bread in many directions, pellets and smithereens, spitball flybys.

But it is the unseeable life-forms that dismay Edgar most and he faces away from Gleason and holds his breath. He wants to hurry to a lavatory, a zinc-lined room with a bar of untouched oval soap, a torrent of hot water and a swansdown towel that has never been used by anyone else. But of course there is nothing of the kind nearby. Just more germs, an all-pervading medium of pathogens, microbes, floating colonies of spirochetes that fuse and separate and elongate and spiral and engulf, whole trainloads of matter that people cough forth, rudimentary and deadly.

The crowd, the constant noise, the breath and hum, a basso rumble building now and then, the genderness of what they share in their experience of the game, how a man will scratch his wrist or shape a line of swearwords. And the lapping of applause that dies down quickly and is never enough. They are waiting to be carried on the sound of rally chant and rhythmic handclap, the set forms and repetitions. This is the power they keep in reserve for the right time. It is the thing that will make something happen, change the structure of the game and get them leaping to their feet, flying up together in a free thunder that shakes the place crazy.

Sinatra saying, "Jack, I thought I told you to stay in the car until you're all done eating."

Mays takes a mellow cut but gets under the ball, sending a routine fly into the low October day. The sound of the ash bat making contact with the ball reaches Cotter Martin in the left-field stands, where he sits in a bony-shouldered hunch. He is watching Willie instead of the ball, seeing him sort of shrug-run around first and then scoop his glove off the turf and jog out to his position.

The arc lights come on, catching Cotter by surprise, causing a shift in the way he feels, in the freshness of his escapade, the airy flash of doing it and not getting caught. The day is different now, grave and threatened, rain-hurried, and he watches Mays standing in center field looking banty in all that space, completely kid-size, and he wonders how the guy can make those throws he makes, whirl and sling, with power. He likes looking at the field under lights even if he has to worry about rain and even if it's only afternoon and the full effect is not the same as in a night game when the field and the players seem completely separate from the night around them. He has been to one night game in his life, coming down from the bluff with his oldest brother and walking into a bowl of painted light. He thought there was an unknown energy flaring down out of the light towers, some intenser working of the earth, and it isolated the players and the grass and the chalk-rolled lines from anything he'd ever seen or imagined. They had the glow of first-time things.

The way the runner skid-brakes when he makes the turn at first.

The empty seats were Cotter's first surprise, well before the lights.

On his prowl through the stands he kept seeing blank seats, too many to be explained by people buying a beer or taking a leak, and he found a spot between a couple of guys in suits and it's all he can do to accept his good luck, the ease of an actual seat, without worrying why there's so many.

The man to his left says, "How about some peanuts hey?"

Peanut vendor's coming through again, a coin-catching wiz about eighteen, black and rangy. People know him from games past and innings gone and they quicken up and dig for change. They're calling out for peanuts, *hey, here, bag,* and tossing coins with thumb flicks and discus arcs and the vendor's hands seem to inhale the flying metal. He is magnet-skinned, circus-catching dimes on the wing and then sailing peanut bags into people's chests. It's a thrill-a-minute show but Cotter feels an obscure danger here. The guy is making him visible, shaming him in his prowler's den. Isn't it strange how their common color jumps the space between them? Nobody saw Cotter until the vendor appeared, black rays phasing from his hands. One popular Negro and crowd pleaser. One shifty kid trying not to be noticed.

The man says, "What do you say?"

Cotter raises a hand no.

"Care for a bag? Come on."

Cotter leans away, the hand going to his midsection to mean he's already eaten or peanuts give him cramps or his mother told him not to fill up on trashy food that will ruin his dinner.

The man says, "Who's your team then?"

"Giants."

"What a year hey?"

"This weather, I don't know, it's bad to be trailing."

The man looks at the sky. He's about forty, close-shaved and Brylcreemed but with a casual quality, a free-and-easy manner that Cotter links to small-town life in the movies.

"Only down a run. They'll come back. The kind of year it's been, it can't end with a little weather. How about a soda?"

Men passing in and out of the toilets, men zipping their flies as they turn from the trough and other men approaching the long receptacle, thinking where they want to stand and next to whom and not next to whom, and the old ballpark's reek and mold are consolidated here, generational tides of beer and shit and cigarettes and peanut shells and disinfectants and pisses in the untold millions, and they are thinking in the ordinary way that helps a person glide through a life, thinking thoughts unconnected to events, the dusty hum of who you are, men shouldering through the traffic in the men's room as the game goes on, the coming and going, the lifting out of dicks and the meditative pissing.

Man to his left shifts in the seat and speaks to Cotter from off his shoulder, using a crafty whisper. "What about school? Having a private holiday?" Letting a grin slide across his face.

Cotter says, "Same as you," and gets a gunshot laugh.

"I'd a broken out of prison to see this game. Matter of fact they're broadcasting to prisoners. They put radios in cell blocks in the city jails."

"I was here early," Cotter says. "I could have gone to school in the morning and then cut out. But I wanted to see everything."

"A real fan. Music to my ears."

"See the people showing up. The players going in the players' entrance."

"My name's Bill Waterson by the way. And I'd a gladly gone AWOL from the office but I didn't actually have to. Got my own little business. Construction firm."

Cotter tries to think of something to say.

"We're the people that build the houses that are fun to live in."

Peanut vendor's on his way up the aisle and headed over to the next section when he spots Cotter and drops a knowing smile. The kid thinks here comes trouble. This gatemouth is out to expose him in some withering way. Their glances briefly meet as the vendor moves up the stairs. In full stride and double-quick he dips his hand for a bag of peanuts and zings it nonchalant to Cotter, who makes the grab in a one-hand blur that matches the hazy outline of the toss. And it is one sweetheart of a moment, making Cotter crack the smile of the week and sending a wave of goodwill through the area.

"Guess you got one after all," says Bill Waterson.

Cotter unrolls the pleated top of the brown bag and extends it to Bill. They sit there shelling the peanuts and rubbing off the tissuey brown skin with a rolling motion of thumb and index finger and eating the oily salty flesh and dropping the husks on the ground without ever taking their eyes off the game.

Bill says, "Next time you hear someone say they're in seventh heaven, think of this."

"All we need is some runs."

He pushes the bag at Bill once more.

"They'll score. It's coming. Don't worry. We'll make you happy you skipped school."

Look at Robinson at the edge of the outfield grass watching the hitter step in and thinking idly, Another one of Leo's country-boy krauts.

"Now there's a law of manly conduct," Bill says. "And it states that since you're sharing your peanuts with me, I'm duty-bound to buy us both some soda pop."

"That sounds fair enough."

"Good. It's settled then." Turning in his seat and flinging up an arm. "A couple of sportsmen taking their ease."

Stanky the pug sitting in the dugout.

Mays trying to get a jingle out of his head, his bluesy face slightly puffed, some catchy tune he's been hearing on the radio lately.

The batboy comes down the steps a little daydreamy, sliding Dark's black bat into the rack.

The game turns inward in the middle innings. They fall into waiting, into some unshaped anxiety that stiffens the shoulder muscles and sends them to the watercooler to drink and spit.

Across the field Branca is up in the Dodger bullpen, a large man with pointy elfin ears, tight-armed and throwing easily, just getting loose.

Mays thinking helplessly, Push-pull click-click, change blades that quick.

In the stands Special Agent Rafferty is walking down the stairs to the box-seat area behind the home team dugout. He is a thickset man with a mass of reddish hair—a shock of red hair, people like to say—and he is moving with the straight-ahead look of someone who doesn't want to be distracted. He is moving briskly but not urgently, headed toward the box occupied by the Director.

Gleason has two sudsy cups planted at his feet and there's a hot dog he has forgotten about that's bulging out at each end of his squeezed fist. He is talking to six people at once and they are laughing and asking questions, season box holders, old-line fans with their spindly wives. They see he is half swacked and they admire the clarity of his wit, the fine edge of insult and derision. They want to be offended and Jackie's happy to do it, bypassing his own boozy state to do a detailed imitation of a drunk. He goes heavy-lidded and growly, making sport of one man's ragmop toupee, ridiculing a second for the elbow patches on his tweed jacket. The women enjoy it enormously and they want more. They watch Gleason, they look at Sinatra for his reaction to Gleason, they watch the game, they listen to Jackie do running lines from his TV show, they watch the mustard slide down his thumb and feel too shy to tell him.

When Rafferty reaches Mr. Hoover's aisle seat he does not stand over the Director and lean down to address him. He makes it a point to crouch in the aisle. His hand is set casually near his mouth so that no one else can make out what he is saying. Hoover listens for a moment. He says something to his companions. Then he and Rafferty walk up the stairs and find an isolated spot midway down a long ramp, where the special agent recites the details of his message.

It seems the Soviet Union has conducted an atomic test at a secret location somewhere inside its own borders. They have exploded a bomb in plain unpretending language. And our detection devices indicate this is clearly what it is—it is a bomb, a weapon, it is an instrument of conflict, it produces heat and blast and shock. It is not some peaceful use of atomic energy with home-heating applications. It is a red bomb that spouts a great white cloud like some thunder god of ancient Eurasia.

Edgar fixes today's date in his mind. October 3, 1951. He registers the date. He stamps the date.

He knows this is not completely unexpected. It is their second atomic explosion. But the news is hard, it works into him, makes him think of the spies who passed the secrets, the prospect of warheads being sent to communist forces in Korea. He feels them moving ever closer, catching up, overtaking. It works into him, changes him physically as he stands there, drawing the skin tighter across his face, sealing his gaze.

Rafferty is standing on the part of the ramp that is downhill from Mr. Hoover.

Yes, Edgar fixes the date. He thinks of Pearl Harbor, just under ten years ago, he was in New York that day as well, and the news seemed to shimmer in the air, everything in photoflash, plain objects hot and charged.

The crowd noise breaks above them, a chambered voice rolling through the hollows in the underbody of the stadium.

Now this, he thinks. The sun's own heat that swallows cities.

Gleason isn't even supposed to be here. There's a rehearsal going on right now at a midtown studio and that's where he's supposed to be, preparing a skit called "The Honeymooners," to be shown for the first time in exactly two days. This is material that's close to Jackie's heart, involving a bus driver named Ralph Kramden who lives with his wife Alice in a shabby Brooklyn flat. Gleason sees nothing strange about missing a rehearsal to entertain fans in the stands. But it's making Sinatra uneasy, all these people lapping at their seat backs. He is used to ritual distances. He wants to encounter people in circumstances laid out beforehand. Frank doesn't have his dago secret service with him today. And even with Jackie on one flank and Toots on the other—a couple of porkos who function as natural barriers—people keep pressing in, showing a sense of mission. He sees them decide one by one that they must speak to him. The rigid grins floating near. And the way they use him as a reference for everything that happens. Somebody makes a nice play, they look at Frank to see how he reacts. The beer vendor trips on a step, they look at Frank to see if he has noticed.

He leans over and says, "Jack, it's a great boot being here but you think you can put a towel over your face so these people can go back to watching the game?"

People want Gleason to do familiar lines of dialogue from the show. They're calling out the lines they want him to do.

Then Frank says, "Where the hell is Hoover by the way? We need him to keep these women off our beautiful bodies."

The catcher works up out of his squat, dirt impacted in the creases that run across the back of his ruddled neck. He lifts his mask so he can spit. He is padded and bumpered, lips rough and scored and sun-flaked. This is the freest thing he does, spitting in public. His saliva bunches and wobbles when it hits the dirt, going sandy brown.

Russ Hodges is over on the TV side for the middle innings, talking less, guided by the action on the monitor. Between innings the statistician offers him part of a chicken sandwich he has brought along for lunch.

He says to Russ, "What's the wistful look today?"

"I didn't know I had a look. Any look. I don't feel capable of a look. Maybe hollow-eyed."

"Pensive," says the statman.

And it's true and he knows it, Russ is wistful and drifting and this is so damn odd, the mood he's been in all day, a tilting back, an old creaky easing back, as of a gray-haired man in a rocker.

"This is chicken with what?"

"I'm guessing mayonnaise."

"It's funny, you know," Russ says, "but I think it was Charlotte put the look in my face."

"The lady or the city?"

"Definitely the city. I spent years in a studio doing re-creations of big league games. The telegraph bug clacking in the background and blabbermouth Hodges inventing ninety-nine percent of the action. And I'll tell you something scout's honor. I know this sounds far-fetched but I used to sit there and dream of doing real baseball from a booth in the Polo Grounds in New York."

"Real baseball."

"The thing that happens in the sun."

Somebody hands you a piece of paper filled with letters and numbers and you have to make a ball game out of it. You create the weather, flesh out the players, you make them sweat and grouse and hitch up their pants, and it is remarkable, thinks Russ, how much earthly disturbance, how much summer and dust the mind can manage to order up from a single Latin letter lying flat.

"That's not a bush curve Maglie's throwing," he says into the mike.

When he was doing ghost games he liked to take the action into the stands, inventing a kid chasing a foul ball, a carrot-topped boy with a cowlick (shameless, ain't I) who retrieves the ball and holds it aloft, this five-ounce sphere of cork, rubber, yarn, horsehide and spiral stitching, a souvenir baseball, a priceless thing somehow, a thing that seems to recapitulate the whole history of the game every time it is thrown or hit or touched.

He puts the last bite of sandwich in his mouth and licks his thumb and remembers where he is, far from the windowless room with the telegraph operator and the Morse-coded messages.

Over on the radio side the producer's saying, "See that thing in the paper last week about Einstein?"

Engineer says, "What Einstein?"

"Albert, with the hair. Some reporter asked him to figure out the mathematics of the pennant race. You know, one team wins so many of their remaining games, the other teams wins this number or that number. What are the myriad possibilities? Who's got the edge?"

"The hell does he know?"

"Apparently not much. He picked the Dodgers to eliminate the Giants last Friday."

The engineer talks through the blanket to his counterpart from KMOX. The novelty of the blanket has these men talking to each other in prison slang. When they switch to black dialect the producer gets them to stop but after a while they're at it again, doing a couple of reefer Negroes in the fumy murmurs of some cellar room. Not loud enough to be picked up on mike of course. An ambient noise like random dugout buzz—a patter, a texture, an extension of the game.

Down in the field boxes they want Gleason to say, "You're a dan-dan-dandy crowd."

Russ makes his way back to the radio side after the Giants go down in their half of the sixth still trailing by a run. He's glad he doesn't have a thermometer because he might be tempted to use it and that would be demoralizing. It's a mild day, glory be, and the rain's holding off.

Producer says, "Going to the wire, Russ."

"I hope I don't close down. My larynx feels like it's in a vise."

"This is radio, buddy. Can't close down. Think of what's out there. They are hugging their little portables."

"You're not making me feel any better."

"They are goddamn crouched over the wireless. You're like Murrow from London."

"Thank you, Al."

"Save the voice."

"I am trying mightily."

"This game is everywhere. Dow Jones tickers are rapping out the score with the stock averages. Every bar in town, I guarantee. They're smuggling radios into boardrooms. At Schrafft's I hear they're breaking into the Muzak to give the score."

"All those nice ladies with their matched sweater sets and genteel sandwiches."

"Save the voice," Al says.

"Do they have tea with honey on the menu?"

"They're eating and drinking baseball. The track announcer at Belmont's doing updates between races. They got it in taxicabs and barbershops and doctors' offices."

They're all waiting on the pitcher, he's a faceful of boding, upper body drawn forward, glove hand dangled at the knee. He's reading and reading the sign. He's reading the sign. Hitter fidgeting in the box. This son of a buck can bring it.

The shortstop moves his feet to break the trance of waiting.

It's the rule of confrontation, faithfully maintained, written across the face of every slackwit pitcher since there were teams named the Superbas and the Bridegrooms. The difference comes when the ball is hit. Then nothing is the same. The men are moving, coming out of their crouches, and everything submits to the pebble-skip of the ball, to rotations and backspins and airstreams. There are drag coefficients. There are trailing vortices. There are things that apply unrepeatably, muscle memory and pumping blood and jots of dust, the narrative that lives in the spaces of the official play-by-play.

And the crowd is also in this lost space, the crowd made over in that one-thousandth of a second when the bat and the baseball are in contact. A rustle of murmurs and curses, people breathing soft moans, their faces changing as the play unrolls across the grassy scan. John Edgar Hoover stands among them. He is watching from the wide aisle at the head of the ramp. He has told Rafferty he will remain at the game. No purpose served by his leaving. The White House will make the announcement in less than an hour. Edgar hates Harry Truman, he would like to see him writhing on a parquet floor, felled by chest pains, but he can hardly fault the President's timing. By announcing first, we prevent the Soviets from putting their own sweet spin on the event. And we ease public anxiety to some degree. People will understand that we've maintained control of the news if not of the bomb. This is no small subject of concern. Edgar looks at the faces around him, open and hopeful. He wants to feel a compatriot's nearness and affinity. All these people formed by language and climate and popular songs and breakfast foods and the jokes they tell and the cars they drive have never had anything in common so much as this, that they are sitting in the furrow of destruction. He tries to feel a belonging, an opening of his old stop-cocked soul. But there is some bitter condition he has never been able to name and when he encounters a threat from outside, from the moral wane that is everywhere in effect, he finds it is a balance to this state, a restoring force. His ulcer kicks up of course. But there is that side of him, that part of him that depends on the strength of the enemy.

Look at the man in the bleachers who's pacing the aisles, a neighborhood crazy, he waves his arms and mumbles, short, chunky, bushy-haired—could be one of the Ritz Brothers or a lost member of the Three Stooges, the Fourth Stooge, called Flippo or Dummy or Shaky or Jakey, and he's distracting the people nearby, they're yelling at him to siddown, goway, meshuggener, and he paces and worries, he shakes his head and moans as if he knows something's coming, or came, or went—he's receptive to things that escape the shrewdest fan.

It is a stone-faced Director who returns to his seat for the seventh-inning stretch. He says nothing of course. Gleason is shouting down a vendor, trying to order beers. People on their feet, shaking off the tension and fret. A man slowly wiping his glasses. A staring man. A man flexing the stiffness out of his limbs.

"Get me a brandy and soda," Toots says.

Jackie tells him, "Don't be a clamhead all your life."

"Treat the man nice," Frank says. "He's come a long way for a Jew who drinks. He's best buddies with world leaders you never even heard of. They all roll into his joint sooner or later and knock back a brandy with Toots. Except maybe Mahatma Gandhi. And *him* they shot."

Gleason flares his brows and goggles his eyes and shoots out his arms in a nitwit gesture of revelation.

"That's the name I couldn't think of. The midget that pinch-hits."

People around them, hearing part of this and reacting mainly to inflection and gesture—they've seen Jackie physically building the remark and they knock together laughing even before he has finished the line.

Edgar is also laughing despite the return of the midget business. He admires the rough assurance of these men. It seems to flush from their pores. They have a size to them, a natural stamina that mocks his own bible-school indoctrination even as it draws him to the noise. He's a self-perfected American who must respect the saga of the knockabout boy emerging from a tenement culture, from back-streets slant with danger. It makes for gusty egos, it makes for ap-petites. The pussy bandits Jackie and Frank have a showy sort of ease around women. And it's true about Toots, he knows everybody worth knowing and can drink even Gleason into the carpeting. And when he clamps a sympathetic paw on your shoulder you feel he is some provident force come to guide you out of old despond.

Frank says, "This is our inning."

And Toots says, "Better be. Because these shit-heel Dodgers are making me nervous."

Jackie is passing beers along the row.

Frank says, "Seems to me we've all made our true loyalties known. Shown our hearts' desire. We got a couple of old-timey Giant fans. And this porpoise with a haircut from Brooklyn. But what about our friend the G-man. Is it G for Giants? Fess up, Jedgar. Who's your team?"

J. Edgar. Frank calls him Jedgar sometimes and the Director likes the name although he never lets on—it is medieval and princely and wily-dark.

A faint smile creeps across Hoover's face.

"I don't have a rooting interest. Whoever wins," he says softly. "That's my team."

He is thinking of something else entirely. The way our allies one by one will receive the news of the Soviet bomb. The thought is grimly cheering. Over the years he has found it necessary to form joint ven-tures with the intelligence heads of a number of countries and he wants them all to die a little.

Look at the four of them. Each with a hanky neatly tucked in his breast pocket. Each holding his beer away from his body, leaning forward to tease the high scud from the rim of the cup. Gleason with a flower in his lapel, a damp aster snatched from a vase at Toots' place. People are still after him to do lines from the show.

They want him to say, "Harty har-har."

The plate umpire stands mask in hand, nearly blimpish in his out-fitting. He is keeping the numbers, counting the pitcher's warm-up tosses. This is the small dogged conscience of the game. Even in re-pose he shows a history thick with embranglement, dust-stomping men turning figures in the steep sun. You can see it in his face, chin thrust out, a glower working under his brow. When the number reaches eight he aims a spurt from his chaw and prepares to take his whisk-broom to the rubber slab.

In the stands Bill Waterson takes off his jacket and dangles it lengthwise by the collar. It is rippled and mauled and seems to strike him as a living body he might want to lecture sternly. After a pause he folds it over twice and drops it on his seat. Cotter is sitting again, surrounded by mostly vertical people. Bill looms above him, a sizable guy, a one-time athlete by the look of him, getting thick in the middle, his shirt wet under the arms. Lucky seventh. Cotter needs a measly run to keep him from despairing—the cheapest eked-out un-earned run ever pushed across. Or he's ready to give up. You know that thing that happens when you give up before the end and then your team comes back to perform acts of valor and you feel a queasy shame stealing over you like pond slick.

Bill says down to him, "I take my seventh-inning stretch seriously. I not only stand. I damn well make it a point to stretch."

"I've been noticing," says Cotter.

"Because it's a custom that's been handed down. It's part of some-thing. It's our own little traditional thing. You stand, you stretch—it's a privilege in a way."

Bill has some fun doing various stylized stretches, the bodybuilder, the pet cat, and he tries to get Cotter to do a drowsy kid in a class-room.

"Did you ever tell me your name?"

"Cotter."

"That's the thing about baseball, Cotter. You do what they did be-fore you. That's the connection you make. There's a whole long line. A man takes his kid to a game and thirty years later this is what they talk about when the poor old mutt's wasting away in the hospital."

Bill scoops his jacket off the seat and puts it on his lap when he sits down. Seconds later he is standing again, he and Cotter watching Pafko chase down a double. A soft roar goes up, bushy and dense, and the fans send more paper sailing to the base of the wall. Old shopping lists and ticket stubs and wads of fisted newsprint come falling around Pafko in the faded afternoon. Farther out in left field they are dropping paper on the Dodger bullpen, on the working figure of Labine and the working figure of Branca and the two men who are catching them and the men sitting under the canted roof that juts from the wall, the gum-chewing men with nothing to say.

Branca wears the number thirteen blazoned on his back.

"Told you," Bill says. "What did I tell you? I told you. We're coming back."

"We still have to score the run," Cotter says.

They take their seats and watch the hitter steer a look right up the line at Durocher dummying through the signs from the coach's box at third. Then Bill is on his feet again, rolling up his sleeves and shouting encouragement to the players, common words of spark and heart.

Cotter likes this man's singleness of purpose, his insistence on faith and trust. It's the only force available against the power of doubt. He figures he's in the middle of getting himself befriended. It's a feeling that comes from Bill's easy voice and his sociable sweaty gymnasium bulk and the way he listens when Cotter speaks and the way he can make Cotter believe this is a long and close association they share—boon companions goes the saying. He feels a little strange, it's an unfamiliar thing, talking to Bill, but there's a sense of something protective and enclosing that will help him absorb the loss if it should come to that.

Lockman squares around to bunt.

There's a man in the upper deck leafing through a copy of the current issue of Life. There's a man on 12th Street in Brooklyn who has attached a tape machine to his radio so he can record the voice of Russ Hodges broadcasting the game. The man doesn't know why he's doing this. It is just an impulse, a fancy, it is like hearing the game twice, it is like being young and being old, and this will turn out to be the only known recording of Russ' famous account of the final moments of the game. The game and its extensions. The woman cooking cabbage. The man who wishes he could be done with drink. They are the game's remoter soul. Connected by the pulsing voice on the radio, joined to the word-of-mouth that passes the score along the street and to the fans who call the special phone number and the crowd at the ballpark that becomes the picture on television, people the size of minute rice, and the game as rumor and conjecture and inner history. There's a sixteen-year-old in the Bronx who takes his radio up to the roof of his building so he can listen alone, a Dodger fan slouched in the gloaming, and he hears the account of the misplayed bunt and the fly ball that scores the tying run and he looks out over the rooftops, the tar beaches with their clotheslines and pigeon coops and splatted condoms, and he gets the cold creeps. The game doesn't change the way you sleep or wash your face or chew your food. It changes nothing but your life.

The producer says, "At last, at least, a run."

Russ is frazzled, brother, he is raw and rumpled and uncombed. When the teams go to the top of the eighth he reports that they have played one hundred and fifty-four regular season games and two play-off games and seven full innings of the third play-off game and here they are tied in a knot, absolutely deadlocked, they are stalemated, folks, so light up a Chesterfield and stay right here.

The next half inning seems to take a week. Cotter sees the Dodgers put men on first and third. He watches Maglie bounce a curve in the dirt. He sees Cox bang a shot past third. A hollow clamor begins to rise from the crowd, men calling from the deep reaches, an animal awe and desolation.

In the booth Russ sees the crowd begin to lose its coherence, people sitting scattered on the hard steps, a priest with a passel of boys filing up the aisle, paper rolling and skittering in the wind. He hears the announcer from St. Louis on the other side of the blanket, it is Harry Caray and he sounds like his usual chipper self and Russ thinks of the Japanese term for ritual disembowelment and figures he and Harry ought to switch names about now.

Light washing from the sky, Dodgers scoring runs, a man dancing down the aisle, a goateed black in a Bing Crosby shirt. Everything is changing shape, becoming something else.

Cotter can barely get out the words.

"What good does it do to tie the score if you're going to turn around and let them walk all over you?"

Bill says, "They're going into that dugout and I guarantee you they're not giving up. There's no quit in this team. Don't pull a long face on me, Cotter. We're buddies in bad times—gotta stick together."

Cotter feels a mood coming on, a complicated self-pity, the strength going out of his arms and a voice commencing in his head that reproaches him for caring. And the awful part is that he wallows in it. He knows how to find the twisty compensation in this business of losing, being a loser, drawing it out, expanding it, making it sickly sweet, being someone carefully chosen for the role.

The score is 4–1.

It should have rained in the third or fourth inning. Great rain drenching down. It should have thundered and lightning'd.

Bill says, "I'm still a believer. What about you?"

The pitcher takes off his cap and rubs his forearm across his hairline. Big Newk. Then he blows in the cap. Then he shakes the cap and puts it back on.

Shor looks at Gleason.

"Still making with the mouth. Leave the people alone already. They came here to see a game."

"What game? It's a lambasting. We ought to go home."

"We're not going home," Toots says.

Jackie says, "We can beat the crowd, clamhead."

Frank says, "Let's take a vote."

Toots says, "You're tubercular in the face. Sit back and watch the game. Because nobody goes until I go and I ain't going."

Jackie waves down a vendor and orders beer all around. Nothing happens in the home half of the eighth. People are moving toward the exit ramps. It is Erskine and Branca in the bullpen now with the odd paper shaving dropped from the upper deck. Dodgers go down in the top of the ninth and this is when you sense a helpless scattering, it is tastable in the air, audible in the lone-wolf calls from high in the stands. Nothing you've put into this is recoverable and you don't know whether you want to leave at once or stay forever, living under a blanket in the wind.

Engineer says, "Nice season, boys. Let's do it again sometime."

The closeness in the booth, all this crammed maleness is making Russ a little edgy. He lights another cigarette and for the first time all day he does not reproach himself for it. He hears the solitary wailing, he hears his statistician reciting numbers in fake French. It is all part of the same thing, the feeling of some collapsible fact that's folded up and put away, and the school gloom that traces back for decades—the last laden day of summer vacation when the range of play tapers to a screwturn. This is the day he has never shaken off, the final Sunday before the first Monday of school. It carried some queer deep shadow out to the western edge of the afternoon.

He wants to go home and watch his daughter ride her bike down a leafy street.

Dark reaches for a pitch and hits a seeing-eye bouncer that ticks off the end of the first baseman's glove.

A head pops up over the blanket, it's the engineer from KMOX and he starts telling a joke about the fastest lover in Mexico—*een May-heeko*. An amazing chap named Speedy Gonzalez.

Russ is thinking base hit all the way but glances routinely at the clubhouse sign in straightaway center to see if the first E in CHESTER-FIELD lights up, indicating error.

Robinson retrieves the ball in short right.

"So this guy's on his honeymoon in Acapulco and he's heard all the stories about the incredible cunning of Speedy Gonzalez and he's frankly worried, he's a highly nervous type and so on the first night, the night of nights, he's in bed with his wife and he's got his middle finger plugged up her snatch to keep Speedy Gonzalez from sneaking in there when he's not looking."

Mueller stands in, taking the first pitch low.

In the Dodger dugout a coach picks up the phone and calls the bullpen for the eighteenth time to find out who's throwing good and who ain't.

Mueller sees a fastball belt-high and pokes a single to right.

"So then he's dying for a smoke and he reaches over for a second to get his cigarettes and matches."

Russ describes Dark going into third standing up. He sees Thomson standing in the dugout with his arms raised and his hands held backwards gripping the edge of the roof. He describes people standing in the aisles and others moving down toward the field.

Irvin dropping the weighted bat.

"So then he lights up quick and reaches back to the bed finger-first."

Maglie's already in the clubhouse sitting in his skivvies in that postgame state of disrepair and pit stink that might pass for some shambles of the inner man, slugging beer from the bottle.

Irvin stands in.

Russ describes Newcombe taking a deep breath and stretching his arms over his head. He describes Newcombe looking in for the sign.

"And Speedy Gonzalez says, Sen-yor-or, you got your finger up my a-ass."

Russ hears most of this and wishes he hadn't. He does a small joke of his own, half standing to drape the mike with his suit coat as if to keep the smallest syllable of raunchy talk from reaching his audience. Decent people out there.

Fastball high and away.

The crowd noise is uncertain. They don't know if this is a rally in the works or just another drag-tail finish that draws out the pain. It's a high rackety noise that makes Russ think of restive waiting in a train station.

Irvin tries to pull it, overeager, and Russ hears the soul of the crowd repeat the sorry arc of the baseball, a moaned vowel falling softly to earth. First baseman puts it away.

Decent people out there. Russ wants to believe they are still assembled in some recognizable manner, the kindred unit at the radio, old lines and ties and propinquities.

Lockman stands in, the towhead from Caroline.

How his family used to gather around the gramophone and listen to grand opera, the trilled r's of old Europe. These thoughts fade and return. They are not distractions. He is alert to every movement on the field.

A couple of swabbies move down to the rail near third base.

How the records were blank on one side and so brittle they would crack if you looked at them cross-eyed. That was the going joke.

He is hunched over the mike. The field seems to open outward into nouns and verbs. All he has to do is talk.

Saying, "Carl Erskine and fireballer Ralph Branca still throwing in the bullpen."

Pitch.

Lockman fouls it back into the netting.

Now the rhythmic applause starts, tentative at first, then spreading densely through the stands. This is how the crowd enters the game. The repeated three-beat has the force of some abject faith, a desperate kind of will toward magic and accident.

Lockman stands in once more, wagging the yellow bat.

How his mother used to make him gargle with warm water and salt when he complained of a sore throat.

Lockman hits the second pitch on a low line over third. Russ hears Harry Caray shouting into the mike on the other side of the blanket. Then they are both shouting and the ball is slicing toward the line and landing fair and sending up a spew of dirt and forcing Pafko into the corner once again.

Men running, the sprint from first to third, the man who scores coming in backwards so he can check the action on the base paths. All the Giants up at the front of the dugout. The crowd is up, heads weaving for better views. Men running through a slide of noise that comes heaving down on them.

The pitch was off the plate and he wrong-wayed it and Harry started shouting.

The hit obliterates the beat of the crowd's rhythmic clapping. They're coming into open roar, making a noise that keeps enlarging itself in breadth and range. This is the crowd made over, the crowd renewed.

Harry started shouting and then Pafko went into the corner and Russ started shouting and the paper began to fall.

One out, one in, two runs down, men on second and third. Russ thinks every word may be his last. He feels the redness in his throat, the pinpoint constriction. Mueller still on the ground at third, in-jured sliding or not sliding, stopping short and catching his spikes on the bag, a man in pain, the flare of pulled tendons.

Paper is falling again, crushed traffic tickets and field-stripped ciga-rettes and work from the office and scorecards in the shape of air-planes, windblown and mostly white, and Pafko walks back to his position and alters stride to kick a soda cup lightly and the gesture functions as a form of recognition, a hint of some concordant force between players and fans, the way he nudges the white cup, it's a little onside boot, completely unbegrudging—a sign of respect for the sly contrivances of the game, the patterns that are undivinable.

The trainer comes out and they put Mueller on a stretcher and take him toward the clubhouse. Mueller's pain, the pain the game exacts—a man on a stretcher makes sense here.

The halt in play has allowed the crowd to rebuild its noise. Russ keeps pausing at the mike to let the sound collect. This is a rumble of a magnitude he has never heard before. You can't call it cheering or rooting. It's territorial roar, the claim of the ego that separates the crowd from other entities, from political rallies or prison riots—everything outside the walls.

Russ nuzzles up to the mike and tries to be calm although he is very close to speaking in a shout because this is the only way to be heard.

Men clustered on the mound and the manager waving to the bullpen and the pitcher walking in and the pitcher leaving and the runner for Mueller doing kneebends at third.

They are banging on the roof of the booth.

Russ says, "So don't go way. Light up that Chesterfield. We're gonna stay right here and see how big Ralph Branca will fare."

Yes. It is Branca coming through the dampish glow. Branca who is tall and stalwart but seems to carry his own hill and dale, he has the aura of a man encumbered. The drooping lids, leaden feet, the thick ridge across the brow. His face is set behind a somber nose, broad-bridged and looming.

The stadium police are taking up posts.

Look at the man in the upper deck. He is tearing pages out of his copy of Life and dropping them uncrumpled over the rail, letting them fall in a seesaw drift on the bawling fans below. He is moved to do this by the paper falling elsewhere, the contagion of paper—it is giddy and unformulated fun. He begins to ignore the game so he can waft pages over the rail. It brings him into contact with the other paper throwers and with the fans in the lower deck who reach for his pages and catch them—they are all a second force that runs parallel to the game.

Not far away another man feels something pulling at his chest, arms going numb. He wants to sit down but doesn't know if he can reach an arm back to lower himself to the seat. Heart, my heart, my god.

Branca who is twenty-five but makes you think he exemplifies ancient toil. By the time he reaches the mound the stretcher bearers have managed to get Mueller up the steps and into the clubhouse. The crowd forgets him. They would forget him if he were dead. The noise expands once more. Branca takes the ball and the men around the mound recede to the fringes.

Shor looks at Gleason.

He says, "Tell me you want to go home. What happened to let's go home? If we leave now, we can beat the crowd."

He says, "I can't visualize it enough, both you crumbums, you deserve every misery in the book."

Jackie looks miserable all right. He loosens his necktie and undoes the top button of his shirt. He's the only member of the quartet not on his feet but it isn't the shift in the game that has caused his discomfort. It's the daylong booze and the greasy food.

Shor says, "Tell me you want to go home so I can run ahead and hold the car door open and like *usher* you inside."

Paper is coming down around the group, big slick pages from a magazine, completely unremarkable in the uproar of the moment. Frank snatches a full-page ad for something called pasteurized process cheese food, a Borden's product, that's the company with the cow, and there's a color picture of yellowish pressed pulp melting horribly on a hot dog.

Frank deadpans the page to Gleason.

"Here. This will help you digest."

Jackie sits there like an air traveler in a downdraft. The pages keep falling. Baby food, instant coffee, encyclopedias and cars, waffle irons and shampoos and blended whiskeys. Piping times, an optimistic bounty that carries into the news pages where the nation's farmers record a bumper crop. And the resplendent products, how the dazzle of a Packard car is repeated in the feature story about the art treasures of the Prado. It is all part of the same thing. Rubens and Titian and Playtex and Motorola. And here's a picture of Sinatra himself sitting in a nightclub in Nevada with Ava Gardner and would you check that cleavage. Frank didn't know he was in this week's Life until the page fell out of the sky. He has people who are supposed to tell him these things. He keeps the page and reaches for another to stuff in Gleason's face. Here's a Budweiser ad, pal. In a country that's in a hurry to make the future, the names attached to the products are an enduring reassurance. Johnson & Johnson and Quaker State and RCA Victor and Burlington Mills and Bristol-Myers and General Motors. These are the venerated emblems of the burgeoning economy, easier to identify than the names of battlefields or dead presidents. Not that Jackie's in the mood to scan a magazine. He is sunk in deep inertia, a rancid sweat developing, his mouth filled with the foretaste of massive inner shiftings.

Branca takes the last of his warm-up tosses, flicking the glove to indicate a curve. Never mind the details of manner or appearance, the weight-bearing body at rest. Out on the mound he is strong and loose, cutting smoothly out of his windup, a man who wants the ball.

Furillo watching from right field. The stone-cut profile.

The bushy-haired man still pacing in the bleachers, moaning and shaking his head—call the men in the white suits and get him outta here. Talking to himself, head-wagging like a street-corner zealot with news of some distant affliction dragging ever closer. Siddown, shaddap, they tell him.

Frank keeps putting pages in Gleason's face.

He tells him. "Eat up, pal. Paper clears the palate."

When in steps Thomson.

The tall fleet Scot. Reminding himself as he gets set in the box. See the ball. Wait for the ball.

Russ is clutching the mike. Warm water and salt. Gargle, said his mother.

Thomson's not sure he sees things clearly. His eyeballs are humming. There's a feeling in his body, he's digging in, settling into his stance, crowd noise packing the sky, and there's a feeling that he has lost the link to his surroundings. Alone in all this rowdy-dow. See the ball. Watch and wait. He is frankly a little fuddled is Bobby. It's like the first waking moment of the day and you don't know whose house you're in.

Russ says, "Bobby Thomson up there swinging."

Mays down on one knee in the on-deck circle half leaning on his cradled bat and watching Branca go into a full windup, push-pull click-click, thinking it's all on him if Thomson fails, the season riding on him, and the jingle plays in his head, it's the radio embrace of the air itself, the mosaic of the air, and it will turn itself off when it's ready.

There's an emergency station under the stands and what the stadium cop has to do is figure out a way to get the stricken man down there without being overrun by a rampant stomping crowd. The victim looks okay considering. He is sitting down, waiting for the attendant to arrive with the wheelchair. All right, maybe he doesn't look so good. He looks pale, sick, worried and infarcted. But he can make a fist and stick out his tongue and there's not much the cop can do until the wheelchair arrives, so he might as well stand in the aisle and watch the end of the game.

Thomson in his bent stance, chin tucked, waiting.

Russ says, "One out, last of the ninth."

He says, "Branca pitches, Thomson takes a strike called on the inside corner."

He lays a heavy decibel on the word strike. He pauses to let the crowd reaction build. Do not talk against the crowd. Let the drama come from them.

Those big rich pages airing down from the upper deck.

Lockman stands near second and tries to wish a hit onto Thomson's bat. That may have been the pitch he wanted. Belt-high, a shade inside—won't see one that good again.

Russ says, "Bobby hitting at two ninety-two. He's had a single and a double and he drove in the Giants' first run with a long fly to center."

Lockman looks across the diamond at home. The double he hit is still a presence in his chest, it's chugging away in there, a body-memory that plays the moment over. He is peering into the deltoid opening between the catcher's knees. He sees the fingers dip, the blunt hand make a flapping action up and left. They'll give him the fastball high and tight and come back with the curve away. A pretty two-part scheme. Seems easy and sweet from here.

Russ says, "Brooklyn leads it four to two."

He says, "Runner down the line at third. Not taking any chances."

Thomson thinking it's all happening too fast. Thinking quick hands, see the ball, give yourself a chance.

Russ says, "Lockman without too big of a lead at second but he'll be running like the wind if Thomson hits one."

In the box seats J. Edgar Hoover plucks a magazine page off his shoulder, where the thing has lighted and stuck. At first he's annoyed that the object has come in contact with his body. Then his eyes fall upon the page. It is a color reproduction of a painting crowded with medieval figures who are dying or dead—a landscape of visionary havoc and ruin. Edgar has never seen a painting quite like this. It covers the page completely and must surely dominate the magazine. Across the red-brown earth, skeleton armies on the march. Men impaled on lances, hung from gibbets, drawn on spoked wheels fixed to the tops of bare trees, bodies open to the crows. Legions of the dead forming up behind shields made of coffin lids. Death himself astride a slat-ribbed hack, he is peaked for blood, his scythe held ready as he presses people in haunted swarms toward the entrance of some hell-trap, an oddly modern construction that could be a subway tunnel or office corridor. A background of ash skies and burning ships. It is clear to Edgar that the page is from Life and he tries to work up an anger, he asks himself why a magazine called Life would want to reproduce a painting of such lurid and dreadful dimensions. But he can't take his eyes off the page.

Russ Hodges says, "Branca throws."

Gleason makes a noise that is halfway between a sigh and a moan. It is probably a sough, as of rustling surf in some palmy place. Edgar recalls the earlier blowout, Jackie's minor choking fit. He sees a deeper engagement here. He goes out into the aisle and up two steps, separating himself from the imminent discharge of animal, vegetable and mineral matter.

Not a good pitch to hit, up and in, but Thomson swings and tomahawks the ball and everybody, everybody watches. Except for Gleason who is bent over in his seat, hands locked behind his neck, a creamy strand of slime swinging from his lips.

Russ says, "There's a long drive."

His voice has a burst in it, a charge of expectation.

He says, "It's gonna be."

There's a pause all around him. Pafko racing toward the left-field corner.

He says, "I believe."

Pafko at the wall. Then he's looking up. People thinking where's the ball. The scant delay, the stay in time that lasts a hairsbreadth. And Cotter standing in section 35 watching the ball come in his direction. He feels his body turn to smoke. He loses sight of the ball when it climbs above the overhang and he thinks it will land in the upper deck. But before he can smile or shout or bash his neighbor on the arm. Before the moment can overwhelm him, the ball appears again, stitches visibly spinning, that's how near it hits, banging at an angle off a pillar—hands flashing everywhere.

Russ feels the crowd around him, a shudder passing through the stands, and then he is shouting into the mike and there is a surge of color and motion, a crash that occurs upward, stadium-wide, hands and faces and shirts, bands of rippling men, and he is outright shouting, his voice has a power he'd thought long gone—it may lift the top of his head like a cartoon rocket.

He says, *"The Giants win the pennant."*

A topspin line drive. He tomahawked the pitch and the ball had topspin and dipped into the lower deck and there is Pafko at the 315 sign looking straight up with his right arm braced at the wall and a spate of paper coming down.

He says, *"The Giants win the pennant."*

Yes, the voice is excessive with a little tickle of hysteria in the upper register. But it is mainly wham and whomp. He sees Thomson capering around first. The hat of the first-base coach—the first-base coach has flung his hat straight up. He went for a chin-high pitch and coldcocked it good. The ball started up high and then sank, missing the facade of the upper deck and dipping into the seats below—pulled in, swallowed up—and the Dodger players stand looking, already separated from the event, staring flat into the shadows between the decks.

He says, *"The Giants win the pennant."*

The crew is whooping. They are answering the roof bangers by beating on the walls and ceiling of the booth. People climbing the dugout roofs and the crowd shaking in its own noise. Branca on the mound in his tormented slouch. He came with a fastball up, a pitch that's tailing in, and the guy's supposed to take it for a ball. Russ is shouting himself right out of his sore throat, out of every malady and pathology and complaint and all the pangs of growing up and every memory that is not tender.

He says, *"The Giants win the pennant."*

Four times. Branca turns and picks up the rosin bag and throws it down, heading toward the clubhouse now, his shoulders aligned at a slant—he begins the long dead trudge. Paper falling everywhere. Russ knows he ought to settle down and let the mike pick up the sound of the swelling bedlam around him. But he can't stop shouting, there's nothing left of him but shout.

He says, "Bobby Thomson hits into the lower deck of the left-field stands."

He says, "The Giants win the pennant and they're going crazy."

He says, "They're going crazy."

Then he raises a pure shout, wordless, a holler from the old days—it is fiddlin' time, it is mountain music on WCKY at five-thirty in the morning. The thing comes jumping right out of him, a jubilation, it might be *heyyy-ho* or it might be *oh-boyyy* shouted backwards or it might be something else entirely—hard to tell when they don't use words. And Thomson's teammates gathering at home plate and Thomson circling the bases in gamesome leaps, buckjumping—he is forever Bobby now, a romping boy lost to time, and his breath comes so fast he doesn't know if he can handle all the air that's pouring in. He sees men in a helter-skelter line waiting at the plate to pummel him—his teammates, no better fellows in the world, and there's a look in their faces, they are stunned by a happiness that has collapsed on them, bright-eyed under their caps.

He tomahawked the pitch, he hit on top of it and now his ears are ringing and there's a numbing buzz in his hands and feet. And Robinson stands behind second, hands on hips, making sure Thomson touches every base. You can almost see brave Jack grow old.

Look at Durocher spinning. Russ pauses for the first time to catch the full impact of the noise around him. Leo spinning in the coach's box. The manager stands and spins, he is spinning with his arms spread wide—maybe it's an ascetic rapture, a thing they do in mosques in Anatolia.

People make it a point to register the time.

Edgar stands with arms crossed and a level eye on Gleason folded over. Pages dropping all around them, it is a fairly thick issue—laxatives and antacids, sanitary napkins and corn plasters and dandruff removers. Jackie utters an aquatic bark, it is loud and crude, the hoarse call of some mammal in distress. Then the surge of flannel matter. He seems to be vomiting someone's taupe pajamas. The waste is liquidy smooth in the lingo of adland and it is splashing freely on

Frank's stout oxford shoes and fine lisle hose and on the soft woven wool of his town-and-country trousers.

The clock atop the clubhouse reads 3:58.

Russ has got his face back into the mike. He shouts, "I don't believe it." He shouts, "I don't believe it." He shouts, "I do *not* believe it."

They are coming down to crowd the railings. They are coming from the far ends of the great rayed configuration and they are moving down the aisles and toward the rails.

Pafko is out of paper range by now, jogging toward the clubhouse. But the paper keeps falling. If the early paper waves were slightly hostile and mocking, and the middle waves a form of fan commonality, then this last demonstration has a softness, a selfness. It is coming down from all points, laundry tickets, envelopes swiped from the office, there are crushed cigarette packs and sticky wrap from ice-cream sandwiches, pages from memo pads and pocket calendars, they are throwing faded dollar bills, snapshots torn to pieces, ruffled paper swaddles for cupcakes, they are tearing up letters they've been carrying around for years pressed into their wallets, the residue of love affairs and college friendships, it is happy garbage now, the fans' intimate wish to be connected to the event, unendably, in the form of pocket litter, personal waste, a thing that carries a shadow identity—rolls of toilet tissue unbolting lyrically in streamers.

They are gathered at the netting behind home plate, gripping the tight mesh.

Russ is still shouting, he is not yet shouted out, he believes he has a thing that's worth repeating.

Saying, "Bobby Thomson hit a line drive into the lower deck of the left-field stands and the place is going crazy."

Next thing Cotter knows he is sidling into the aisle. The area is congested and intense and he has to pry his way row by row using elbows and shoulders. Nobody much seems to notice. The ball is back there in a mighty pileup of shirts and jackets. The game is way behind him. The crowd can have the game. He's after the baseball now and there's no time to ask himself why. They hit it in the stands, you go and get it. It's the ball they play with, the thing they rub up and scuff and sweat on. He's going up the aisle through a thousand pounding hearts. He's prodding and sideswiping. He sees people dipping frantically, it could be apple-bobbing in Indiana, only slightly violent.

Then the ball comes free and someone goes after it, the first one out of the pack, a young guy in a scuttling crawl with people reaching for him, trying to grab his jacket, a fistful of trouser-ass. He has wiry red-dish hair and a college jacket—you know those athletic jackets where the sleeves are one color and leathery looking and the body is a darker color and probably wool and these are the college colors of the team.

Cotter takes a guess and edges his way along a row that's two rows down from the action. He takes a guess, he anticipates, it's the way you feel something will happen and then you watch it uncannily come to pass, occurring almost in measured stages so you can see the wheel-work of your idea fitting into place.

He coldcocked the pitch and the ball shot out there and dipped and disappeared. And Thomson bounding down on home plate mobbed by his teammates, who move in shuffled steps with hands extended to keep from spiking each other. And photographers edging near and taking their spread stances and the first of the fans appearing on the field, the first strays standing wary or whirling about to see things from this perspective, astonished to find themselves at field level, or running right at Thomson all floppy and demented, milling into the wedge of players at home plate.

Frank is looking down at what has transpired. He stands there hands out, palms up, an awe of muted disgust. That this should happen here, in public, in the high revel of event—he feels a puzzled wonder that exceeds his aversion. He looks down at the back of Jackie's glossy head and he looks at his own trouser cuffs flaked an intimate beige and the spatter across his shoe tops in a strafing pattern and the gumbo puddle nearby that contains a few laggard gobs of pinkoid stuff from deep in Gleason's gastric sac.

And he nods his head and says, "My shoes."

And Shor feels offended, he feels a look come into his face that carries the sting of a bad shave, those long-ago mornings of razor pull and cold water.

And he looks at Frank and says, "Did you see the homer at least?"

"I saw part and missed part."

And Shor says, "Do I want to take the time to ask which part you missed so we can talk about it on the phone some day?"

There are people with their hands in their hair, holding in their brains.

Frank persists in looking down. He allows one foot to list to port so he can examine the side of his shoe for vomit marks. These are handcrafted shoes from a narrow street with a quaint name in oldest London.

And Shor says, "We just won unbelievable, they're ripping up the joint, I don't know whether to laugh, shit or go blind."

And Frank says, "I'm rooting for number one or number three."

Russ is still manning the microphone and has one last thing to say and barely manages to get it out.

"The Giants won it. By a score of five to four. And they're picking Bobby Thomson up. And carrying him off the field."

If his voice has an edge of disquiet it's because he has to get to the clubhouse to do interviews with players and coaches and team officials and the only way to get out there is to cross the length of the field on foot and he's already out of breath, out of words, and the crowd is growing over the walls. He sees Thomson carried by a phalanx of men, players and others, mostly others—the players have run for it, the players are dashing for the clubhouse—and he sees Thomson riding off-balance on the shoulders of men who might take him right out of the ballpark and into the streets for a block party.

Gleason is suspended in wreckage, drained and humped, and he has barely the wit to consider what the shouting's about.

The field streaked with people, the hat snatchers, the swift kids who imitate banking aircraft, their spread arms steeply raked.

Look at Cotter under a seat.

All over the city people are coming out of their houses. This is the nature of Thomson's homer. It makes people want to be in the streets, joined with others, telling others what has happened, those few who haven't heard—comparing faces and states of mind.

And Russ has a hot mike in front of him and has to find someone to take it and talk so he can get down to the field and find a way to pass intact through all that mangle.

And Cotter is under a seat handfighting someone for the baseball. He is trying to get a firmer grip. He is trying to isolate his rival's hand so he can prise the ball away finger by finger.

It is a tight little theater of hands and arms, some martial test with formal rules of grappling.

The iron seat leg cuts into his back. He hears the earnest breathing of the rival. They are working for advantage, trying to gain position.

The rival is blocked off by the seat back, he is facedown in the row above with just an arm stuck under the seat.

People make it a point to read the time on the clock atop the notched facade of the clubhouse, the high battlement—they register the time when the ball went in.

It is a small tight conflict of fingers and inches, a lifetime of effort compressed into seconds.

He gets his hands around the rival's arm just above the wrist. He is working fast, thinking fast—too much time and people take sides.

The rival, the foe, the ofay, veins stretched and bulged between white knuckles. If people take sides, does Cotter have a chance?

Two heart attacks, not one. A second man collapses on the field, a well-dressed fellow not exactly falling but letting himself down one knee at a time, slow and controlled, easing down on his right hand and tumbling dully over. No one takes this for a rollick. The man is not the type to do dog tricks in the dirt.

And Cotter's hands around the rival's arm, twisting in opposite directions, burning the skin—it's called an Indian burn, remember? One hand grinding one way, the other going the other, twisting hard, working fast.

There's a pause in the rival's breathing. He is pausing to note the pain. He fairly croons his misgivings now and Cotter feels the arm jerk and the fingers lift from the ball.

Thomson thrusting down off the shoulders of the men who carry him, beating down, pulling away from grabby hands—he sees players watching intently from the clubhouse windows.

And Cotter holds the rival's arm with one hand and goes for the ball with the other. He sees it begin to roll past the seat leg, wobbling on the textured surface. He sort of traps it with his eye and sends out a ladling hand.

The ball rolls in a minutely crooked path into the open.

The action of his hand is as old as he is. It seems he has been sending out this hand for one thing or another since the minute he shot out of infancy. Everything he knows is contained in the splayed fingers of this one bent hand.

Heart, my heart.

The whole business under the seat has taken only seconds. Now he's backing out, moving posthaste—he's got the ball, he feels it hot and buzzy in his hand.

A sense of people grudgingly getting out of his way, making way but not too quickly, dead-eye sidewalk faces.

The ball is damp with the heat and sweat of the rival's hand. Cotter's arm hangs lank at his side and he empties out his face, scareder now than he was when he went over the turnstile but determined to look cool and blank and going down the rows by stepping over seat backs and fitting himself between bodies and walking on seats when it is convenient.

Look at the ushers locking arms at the wrists and making a sedan seat for the cardiac victim and hauling him off to the station under the grandstand.

One glance back at the area above, he allows himself a glance and sees the rival getting to his feet. The man stands out, white-shirted and hulking, and it's not the college boy he thought it might be, the guy in the varsity jacket who'd been scrambling for the ball.

And the man catches his eye. This is not what Cotter wants, this is damage to the cause. He made a mistake looking back. He allowed himself a glance, a sidewise flash, and now he's caught in the man's hard glare.

The raised seams of the ball are pulsing in his hand.

Their eyes meet in the spaces between rocking bodies, between faces that jut and the broad backs of shouting fans. Celebration all around him. But he is caught in the man's gaze and they look at each other over the crowd and through the crowd and it is Bill Waterson with his shirt stained and his hair all punished and sprung—good neighbor Bill flashing a cutthroat smile.

The dead have come to take the living. The dead in winding-sheets, the regimented dead on horseback, the skeleton that plays a hurdy-gurdy.

Edgar stands in the aisle fitting together the two facing pages of the reproduction. People are climbing over seats, calling hoarsely toward the field. He stands with the pages in his face. He hadn't realized he was seeing only half the painting until the left-hand page drifted down and he got a glimpse of rust brown terrain and a pair of skeletal men pulling on bell ropes. The page brushed against a woman's arm and spun into Edgar's godfearing breast.

Thomson is out in center field now dodging fans who come in rushes and jumps. They jump against his body, they want to take him to the ground, show him snapshots of their families.

Edgar reads the copy block on the matching page. This is a sixteenth-century work done by a Flemish master, Pieter Bruegel, and it is called *The Triumph of Death*.

A nervy title methinks. But he is intrigued, he admits it—the lefthand page may be even better than the right.

He studies the tumbrel filled with skulls. He stands in the aisle and looks at the naked man pursued by dogs. He looks at the gaunt dog nibbling the baby in the dead woman's arms. These are long gaunt starveling hounds, they are war dogs, hell dogs, boneyard hounds beset by parasitic mites, by dog tumors and dog cancers.

Dear germ-free Edgar, the man who has an air-filtration system in his house to vaporize specks of dust—he finds a fascination in cankers, lesions and rotting bodies so long as his connection to the source is strictly pictorial.

He finds a second dead woman in the middle ground, straddled by a skeleton. The positioning is sexual, unquestionably. But is Edgar sure it's a woman bestraddled or could it be a man? He stands in the aisle and they're all around him cheering and he has the pages in his face. The painting has an instancy that he finds striking. Yes, the dead fall upon the living. But he begins to see that the living are sinners. The cardplayers, the lovers who dally, he sees the king in an ermine cloak with his fortune stashed in hogshead drums. The dead have come to empty out the wine gourds, to serve a skull on a platter to gentlefolk at their meal. He sees gluttony, lust and greed.

Edgar loves this stuff. Edgar, Jedgar. Admit it—you love it. It causes a bristling of his body hair. Skeletons with wispy dicks. The dead beating kettledrums. The sackcloth dead slitting a pilgrim's throat.

The meatblood colors and massed bodies, this is a census-taking of awful ways to die. He looks at the flaring sky in the deep distance out beyond the headlands on the left-hand page—Death elsewhere, Conflagration in many places, Terror universal, the crows, the ravens in silent glide, the raven perched on the white nag's rump, black and white forever, and he thinks of a lonely tower standing on the Kazakh

Test Site, the tower armed with the bomb, and he can almost hear the wind blowing across the Central Asian steppes, out where the enemy lives in long coats and fur caps, speaking that old weighted language of theirs, liturgical and grave. What secret history are they writing? There is the secret of the bomb and there are the secrets that the bomb inspires, things even the Director cannot guess—a man whose own sequestered heart holds every festering secret in the Western world—because these plots are only now evolving. This is what he knows, that the genius of the bomb is printed not only in its physics of particles and rays but in the occasion it creates for new secrets. For every atmospheric blast, every glimpse we get of the bared force of nature, that weird peeled eyeball exploding over the desert—for every one of these he reckons a hundred plots go underground, to spawn and skein.

And what is the connection between Us and Them, how many bundled links do we find in the neural labyrinth? It's not enough to hate your enemy. You have to understand how the two of you bring each other to deep completion.

The old dead fucking the new. The dead raising coffins from the earth. The hillside dead tolling the old rugged bells that clang for the sins of the world.

He looks up for a moment. He takes the pages from his face—it is a wrenching effort—and looks at the people on the field. Those who are happy and dazed. Those who run around the bases calling out the score. The ones who are so excited they won't sleep tonight. Those whose team has lost. The ones who taunt the losers. The fathers who will hurry home and tell their sons what they have seen. The husbands who will surprise their wives with flowers and chocolate-covered cherries. The fans pressed together at the clubhouse steps chanting the players' names. The fans having fistfights on the subway going home. The screamers and berserkers. The old friends who meet by accident out near second base. Those who will light the city with their bliss.

Cotter walks at a normal pace in the afterschool light. He goes past rows of tenements down Eighth Avenue with a small solemn hop in his stride, a kind of endless levered up-and-down, and Bill is positioned off his shoulder maybe thirty yards back.

He sees the Power of Prayer sign and carries the ball in his right hand and rubs it up several times and looks back and sees the college boy in the two-tone jacket fall in behind Bill, the guy who was involved in the early scuffle for the ball.

Bill has lost his buckaroo grin. He barely shows an awareness that Cotter exists, a boy who walks the earth in high-top Keds. Cotter's body wants to go. But if he starts running at this point, what we have is a black kid running in a mainly white crowd and he's being followed by a pair of irate whites yelling thief or grief or something.

They walk down the street, three secret members of some organized event.

Bill calls out, "Hey Cotter buddy come on, we won this game together."

Many people have disappeared into cars or down the subways, they are swarming across the walkway on the bridge to the Bronx, but there are still enough bodies to disrupt traffic in the streets. The mounted police are out, high-riding and erect, appearing among the cars as levitated beings.

"Hey Cotter I had my hand on that ball before you did."

Bill says this good-natured. He laughs when he says it and Cotter begins to like the man all over again. Car horns are blowing all along the street, noises of joy and mutual salute.

The college boy says, "I think it's time I got in this. I'm in this too. I was the first one to grab ahold of the ball. Actually long before either one of you. Somebody hit it out of my hand. I mean if we're talking about who was first."

Cotter is watching the college boy speak, looking back diagonally. He sees Bill stop, so he stops. Bill is stopping for effect. He wants to stop so he can measure the college boy, look him up and down in an itemizing way. He is taking in the two-tone jacket, the tight red hair, he is taking in the whole boy, the entire form and structure of the college boy's status as a land animal with a major brain.

And he says, "What?" That's all. A hard sharp *what*.

And he stands there agape, his body gone slack in a comic dumbness that's pervaded with danger.

He says, "Who the hell are you anyway? What are you doing here? Do I *know* you?"

Cotter watches this, entertained by the look on the college boy's face. The college boy thought he was part of a team, it's us against him. Now his eyes don't know where to go.

Bill says, "This is between my buddy Cotter and me. Personal business, understand? We don't want you here. You're ruining our fun. And if I have to make it any plainer, there's going to be a family sitting down to dinner tonight minus a loved one."

Bill resumes walking and so does Cotter. He looks back to see the college boy following Bill for a number of paces, unsurely, and then falling out of step and beginning to fade down the street and into the crowd.

Bill looks at Cotter and grins narrowly. It is a wolfish sort of look with no mercy in it. He carries his suit jacket clutched and bunched in his hand, wadded up like something he might want to throw.

With advancing dark the field is taking on a deeper light. The grass is incandescent, it has a heat and sheen. People go running past, looking half ablaze, and Russ Hodges moves with the tentative steps of some tourist at a grand bazaar, trying to hand-shuffle through the crowd.

Some ushers are lifting a drunk off the first-base line and the man warps himself into a baggy mass and shakes free and begins to run around the bases in his oversized raincoat with long belt trailing.

Russ makes his way through the infield and dance-steps into an awkward jog that makes him feel ancient and extraneous and he thinks of the ballplayers of his youth, the men with redneck monickers whose endeavors he followed in the papers every day, Eppa Rixey and Hod Eller and old Ivy Wingo, and there is a silly grin pasted across his face because he is a forty-one-year-old man with a high fever and he is running across a ball field to conduct a dialogue with a pack of athletes in their underwear.

He says to someone running near him, "I don't believe it, I still don't believe it."

Out in dead center he sees the clubhouse windows catch the trigger-glint of flashbulbs going off inside. He hears a shrill cheer and turns and sees the raincoat drunk sliding into third base. Then he realizes the man running alongside is Al Edelstein, his producer.

Al shouts, "Do you believe it?"

"I do not believe it," says Russ.

They shake hands on the run.

Al says, "Look at these people." He is shouting and gesturing, waving a Cuban cigar. "It's like I-don't-know-what."

"If you don't know what, then I don't know what."

"Save the voice," says Al.

"The voice is dead and buried. It went to heaven on a sunbeam."

"I'll tell you one thing's for certain, old pal. We'll never forget today."

"Glad you're with me, buddy."

The running men shake hands again. They are deep in the outfield now and Russ feels an ache in every joint. The clubhouse windows catch the flash of the popping bulbs inside.

In the box seats across the field Edgar sets his hat at an angle on his head. It is a dark gray homburg that brings out the nicely sprinkled silver at his temples.

He has the Bruegel folded neatly in his pocket and will take these pages home to study further.

Thousands remain in the stands, not nearly ready to leave, and they watch the people on the field, aimless eddies and stirrings, single figures sprinting out of crowds. Edgar sees someone dangling from the wall in right-center field. These men who drop from the high walls like to hang for a while before letting go. They hit the ground and crumple and get up slowly. But it's the static drama of the dangled body that Edgar finds compelling, the terror of second thoughts.

Gleason is on his feet now, crapulous Jack all rosy and afloat, ready to lead his buddies up the aisle.

He rails at Frank. "Nothing personal, pal, but I wonder if you realize you're smelling up the ballpark. Talk about stinko. I can smell you even with Shor on the premises. Usually with Shor around, blind people are tapping for garbage cans in their path."

Shor thinks this is funny. Light comes into his eyes and his face goes crinkly. He loves the insults, the slurs and taunts, and he stands there beaming with balloonhead love. It is the highest thing that can pass between men of a certain mind—the stand-up scorn that carries their affections.

But what about Frank? He says, "It's not my stink. It's your stink, pal. Just happens I am the one that's wearing it."

Says Gleason, "Hey. Don't think you're the first friend I ever puked on. I puked on better men than you. Consider yourself honored. This is a form of flattery I extend to nearest and dearest." Here he waves his cigarette. "But don't think I am riding in any limousine that has you in it."

They march toward the exit ramp with Edgar going last. He turns toward the field on an impulse and sees another body dropping from the outfield wall, a streaky length of limbs and hair and flapping sleeves. There is something apparitional in the moment and it chills and excites him and sends his hand into his pocket to touch the bleak pages hidden there.

The crowd is thinning quickly now and Cotter goes past the last of the mounted police down around 148th Street.

"Hey Cotter now let's be honest. You snatched it out of my hand. A clear case of snatch and run. But I'm willing to be reasonable. Let's talk turkey. What do you say to ten dollars in crisp bills? That's a damn fair offer. Twelve dollars. You can buy a ball and a glove for that."

"That's what you think."

"All right, whatever it takes. Let's find a store and go in. A fielder's glove and a baseball. You got sporting goods stores around here? Hell, we won the game of our lives. There's cause for celebration."

"The ball's not for sale. Not this ball."

Bill says, "Let me tell you something, Cotter." Then he pauses and grins. "You got quite a grip, you know. My arm needs attention in a big way. You really put the squeeze on me."

"Lucky I didn't bite. I was thinking about it."

Bill seems delighted at the way Cotter has entered the spirit of the moment. The side streets are weary with uncollected garbage and broken glass, with the odd plundered car squatting flat on its axle and men who stand in doorways completely adream.

Bill runs toward Cotter, he takes four sudden running steps, heavy and overstated, arms spread wide and a movie growl rolling from his throat. Cotter sees it is a joke but not until he has run into the street and done a loop around a passing car.

They smile at each other across the traffic.

"I looked at you scrunched up in your seat and I thought I'd found a pal. This is a baseball fan, I thought, not some delinquent in the streets. You seem to be dead set on disappointing me. Cotter? Buddies sit down together and work things out."

The streetlights are on. They are walking briskly now and Cotter isn't sure who was first to step up the pace. He feels a pain in his back where the seat leg was digging in.

"Now tell me what it's going to take to separate you from that baseball, son."

Cotter doesn't like the tone of this.

"I want that cotton-pickin' ball."

Cotter keeps walking.

"Hey goofus I'm talking to you. You maybe think this is some cheapo entertainment. String the guy along."

"You can talk all you want," Cotter says. "The ball's not yours, it's mine. I'm not selling it or trading it."

A car comes veering off the avenue and Cotter stops to let it go by. Then he feels something shift around him. There's a ripple in the pavement or the air and a scant second in a woman's face nearby—her eyes shift to catch what's happening behind him. He turns to see Bill coming wide and fast and arm-pumping. It seems awful heavy traffic for a baseball. The color coming into Bill's face, the shiny fabric at his knees. He has a look that belongs to someone else entirely, a man out of another experience, desperate and propelled.

Cotter stands there for one long beat. He wastes a head-fake, then starts to run down the empty side street with Bill right on his neck and reaching. He cuts sharp and ducks away, skidding to his knees and wheeling on his right hand, the ball hand, pressing the ball hard in the tar and using it to pivot. Bill goes past him in a drone of dense breath, a formal hum that is close to speech. Cotter sees him stop and turn. He is skewed with rage, face bloated and quirked. A sleeve hangs down from the jacket in his hand and brushes softly on the ground.

Cotter runs back up to the avenue with the sound of rustling breath behind him. They are past the ballpark crowd, this is unmixed Harlem here—all he has to do is get to the corner, to people and lights. He sees barroom neon and bedsheets strung across a lot. He sees Fresh Killed Chickens From The Farm. He reads the sign, or maybe gathers it whole, and there's an odd calm completion in it, a gesturing of safety. Two women step aside when he gets near—they glance past him to his pursuit and he notes the alertness in their faces, the tapering of attention. Bill is close, banging the asphalt in his businessman's shoes.

Cotter goes south on the avenue and runs half a block and then he turns and does a caper, he does a physical jape—running backwards for a stretch, high-stepping, mocking, showing Bill the baseball. He's a cutup in a sour state. He holds the ball chest-high and turns it in his fingers, which isn't easy when you're running—he rotates the ball on its axis, spins it slowly over and around, showing the two hundred and sixteen raised red cotton stitches.

Don't tell me you don't love this move.

The maneuver makes Bill slow down. He looks at Cotter back-pedaling, doing a danceman's strut, but he doesn't detect an opening here. Because the maneuver makes him realize where he is. The fact that Cotter's not scared. The fact that he's parading the baseball. Bill stops completely but is too smart to look around. Best to limit your purview to straight ahead. Because you don't know who might be looking back at you. And the more enlightened he becomes, the more open grows the space for Cotter's anger. He doesn't really know how to show it. This is the second time today he has taunted someone but he doesn't feel the spunky rush of dodging the cop. The high heart of the gate-crash is a dimness here—he is muddled and wrung out and can't get his bad-ass glare to function. So he stands there flatfoot and looks at Bill with people walking by and noticing and not noticing and he spins the ball up and over the back of his hand and catches it skipping off his wrist with a dip and twist of the same hand, like fuck you mister who you messing with.

He looks at Bill, a flushed and panting man who has vainly chased along a railroad track for the five-oh-nine.

Then he turns his back and walks slowly down the street. He begins to think about the game's amazing end. What could not happen actually happened. He wants to get home, sit quiet, let it live again, let the home run roll over him, soaking his body with a kind of composure, the settled pleasure that comes after the thing itself.

A man calls from a window to a man on a stoop.

"Hey baby I hear she put your nightstick in a sling."

Cotter turns here, looks there, feeling a sense of placeness that grows more familiar.

He sees a kid he knows but doesn't stop to show him the ball or brag on the game.

He feels the pain from the seat leg.

He sees a street-corner shouter making a speech, a tall man in a rag suit with bicycle clips nipping his pants at the ankles.

He feels a little bringdown working in his mind.

He sees four guys from a local gang, the Alhambras, and he crosses the street to avoid them and then crosses back.

He gets to his street and goes up the front steps and into the sour air of his building and he feels the little bringdown of fading light that he has felt a thousand times before.

Shit man. I don't want to go to school tomorrow.

Russ Hodges stands on an equipment trunk trying to describe the scene in the clubhouse and he knows he is making no sense and the players who climb up on the trunk to talk to him are making no sense and they are all talking in unnatural voices, failed voices, creaturely night screaks. Others are pinned to their lockers by reporters and family members and club officials and they can't get to the liquor and beer located on a table in the middle of the room. Russ holds the mike over his head and lets the noise sweep in and then lowers the mike and says another senseless thing.

Thomson goes out on the clubhouse veranda to respond to the sound of his chanted name and they are everywhere, they are on the steps with stadium cops keeping them in check and there are thousands more spread dense across the space between jutting bleacher walls, many arms extended toward Thomson—they are pointing or imploring or making victory fists or stating a desire to touch, men in suits and hats down there and others hanging over the bleacher wall above Bobby, reaching down, half falling over the edge, some very near to touching him.

Al says, the producer, "Great job today, Russ buddy."

"We did something great just by being here."

"What a feeling."

"I'd smoke a cigar but I might die."

"But what a feeling," Al says.

"We sure pulled something out of a hat. All of us together. Damn I just realized."

"What's a ball game to make us feel like this?"

"I have to go back. Left my topcoat in the booth."

"We need a walk to settle us down."

"We need a long walk."

"That's the only coat you've ever loved," says Al.

They leave by way of the Dodger clubhouse and there's Branca all right, the first thing you see, stretched facedown on a flight of six steps, feet touching the floor. He's still in uniform except for shirt and cap. He wears a wet undershirt and his head is buried in his crossed arms on the top step. Al and Russ speak to a few of the men who remain. They talk quietly and try not to look at Branca. They look but tell themselves they aren't. Next to Branca a coach sits in full uniform but hatless, smoking a cigarette. His name is Cookie. No one wants to catch Cookie's eye. Al and Russ talk quietly to a few more men and all of them together try not to look at Branca.

The steps from the Dodger clubhouse are nearly clear of people. Thomson has gone back inside but there are fans still gathered in the area, waving and chanting. The two men begin to walk across the outfield and Al points to the place in the left-field stands where the ball went in.

"Mark the spot. Like where Lee surrendered to Grant or some such thing."

Russ thinks this is another kind of history. He thinks they will carry something out of here that joins them all in a rare way, that binds them to a memory with protective power. People are climbing lampposts on Amsterdam Avenue, tooting car horns in Little Italy. Isn't it possible that this midcentury moment enters the skin more lastingly than the vast shaping strategies of eminent leaders, generals steely in their sunglasses—the mapped visions that pierce our dreams? Russ wants to believe a thing like this keeps us safe in some undetermined way. This is the thing that will pulse in his brain come old age and double vision and dizzy spells—the surge sensation, the leap of people already standing, that bolt of noise and joy when the ball went in. This is the people's history and it has flesh and breath that quicken to the force of this old safe game of ours. And fans at the Polo Grounds today will be able to tell their grandchildren—they'll be the gassy old men leaning into the next century and trying to convince anyone willing to listen, pressing in with medicine breath, that they were here when it happened.

The raincoat drunk is running the bases. They see him round first, his hands paddling the air to keep him from drifting into right field. He approaches second in a burst of coattails and limbs and untied shoelaces and swinging belt. They see he is going to slide and they stop and watch him leave his feet.

All the fragments of the afternoon collect around his airborne form. Shouts, bat-cracks, full bladders and stray yawns, the sand-grain manyness of things that can't be counted.

It is all falling indelibly into the past.

Martin Espada (b. 1957) was born in New York, worked as a lawyer in Massachusetts, a radio journalist in Nicaragua, and as a groundskeeper at Ned Skeldon Stadium, home of the Detroit Tigers Triple A minor-league franchise, the Toledo Mud Hens. He has published five volumes of poetry including *City of Coughing and Dead Radiators* (1993) and *Imagine the Angels of Bread* (1996) in which appears "Rain Delay: Toledo Mud Hens, July 8, 1994."

Martin Espada

Rain Delay: Toledo Mud Hens, July 8, 1994

Despite the rumors of rain,
the crowd spreads across the grandstand,
a hand-sewn quilt, red and yellow shirts,
blue caps. The ballgame is the county fair
in a season of drought, the carnival
in a town of boarded factories,
so they sing the anthem as if ready
for the next foreign war.
Billboards in the outfield
sell lumber, crayons, newspapers,
oldies radio, three kinds of beer.

The ballplayers waiting for the pitch:
the catcher coiled beneath the umpire's alert leaning;
the infielders stalking with poised hands;
then the pitcher, a weathervane spinning in wind;
clear echo of the wood, a ground ball,
throw, applause. The first baseman
shouts advice in Spanish to the pitcher,
and the pitcher nods.

The grandstand celebrates
with the team mascot
prancing pantomime in a duck suit,
a lightning bug called Louie
cheerleading for the electric company.
Men in Caterpillar tractor hats
rise from seats to yell at Louie
about their electric bills.

Ballpark lit in the iron-clouded storm,
a ghost dirigible floating overhead
and a hundred moons misting in the grey air.
A train howls in the cornfields.
When the water strikes down,
white uniforms retreat from the diamond,
but in the stands
farm boys with dripping hair
holler their hosannas to the rain.

During his 17 major-league seasons with the Cardinals, Mets, and Indians, Keith Hernandez (b. 1953) could be relied upon for skillful, intelligent play during the game and for keen analytical commentary after it. Hernandez would settle into the seat in front of his locker, crack open a beer—he kept a bucket with two or three of them on ice by his feet—and discuss the events just past with a level of insight rarely found among reporters and athletes. Hernandez retired from active play in 1990, and in 1994, with the help of a collaborator, Mike Bryan, he wrote *Pure Baseball,* a pitch-by-pitch dissection of two games he watched on television. The results redefine the term "inside baseball." Hernandez's thoughts on peeking come after a pitch from the Yankees' Scott Kamienecki to Detroit Tigers' slugger Cecil Fielder.

Keith Hernandez

◊

from

Pure Baseball

Kamieniecki's first pitch to Cecil is a big-breaking curve for a ball, and his second offering is a big-breaking curve for a strike, and already we have reaped a reward from watching this game on television. In the stands, you have to have the right seats and be watching carefully to see that Yankees catcher Jim Leyritz gives the sign and slides inside, then back outside just as Kamieniecki goes into his delivery. Leyritz is not the steady catcher—Mike Stanley is getting the night off before tomorrow's day game, and Matt Nokes is on the disabled list—and this may just be the way he works behind the plate, but it could also mean that Cecil Fielder has the reputation of sneaking a peek at the catcher's location now and then, and this is a way to cross him up. He peeks, you're set up inside, he focuses on the pitcher, you shift outside. Clever. Some hitters have this reputation of peeking, sometimes it's merited, sometimes it's probably not. I have no idea regarding Cecil, nor do I care. Maybe I say this because I peeked myself, now and then, not too often.

In my case, the rumor started that I was peeking when I looked at my hands gripping the bat to make certain the knuckles were lined up properly. That was a blasphemous lie because I checked those knuckles before the catcher settled in. I believe Orel Hershiser started this rumor. No, no, no, Orel. I like to believe I was a little more clever than you suggest. And, anyway, with you on the mound, I didn't need to! I picked my spots for peeking, usually facing left-handers in late-game, tight-game RBI situations, and here's how I did it. The pitcher takes his stretch. *Precisely* when he glances toward the runner at first base, I shift my eyes backward *without* moving my head. This is the critical point, obviously. The head cannot move because the catcher would pick this up. With my quick motionless glance backward, if I could glimpse the catcher, he was set up outside. If I could not see him, he was inside. Dennis Martinez caught me doing this one time and got mad. He stepped off the mound, glared in, and shouted, "Don't you &%#$@ peek!" He caught Ray Knight, too, and maybe a lot of other guys, I don't know.

When I played with the Cardinals, Steve Carlton threw me (and most batters) 95 percent sliders. It was a great pitch, as good as J. R. Richard's, but he had even better control of it than Richard. Carlton threw the slider like an automaton: outside corner black, at the knees, every time. And Carlton beat the Cards like a drum—payback, I guess, for when Augie Busch wouldn't pay him $100,000 (!) and traded him instead to the Phillies for Rick Wise. That was 1972. In any event, I peeked on Steve a few times. I glanced back one game, didn't see Tim McCarver, and concluded this was one of Carlton's rare pitches inside to me. I hit that pitch against the scoreboard. The next day Tony Taylor, the Phillies' first-base coach, accused me of peeking. He wrapped an arm around my shoulders and said, "After all those sliders, he throws one fastball inside and you hit it for a homer? No, no. I don't believe that. You were peeking."

What could I say? Deny. Deny. Deny. Another time I pulled off the same trick against Carlton—another homer—and this time he confronted McCarver in the dugout after the inning: "You see? Forget the fastball!"

McCarver defended himself, and they had quite a tiff.

After one of these Hernandez homers—I forget which one—McCarver suggested from behind his mask that I was peeking. Furthermore, he suggested I cut it out. "You know," he said, "you can get hurt doing that."

Deny. Deny. Deny. But Tim was right. If you get caught peeking you deserve to get drilled. It's as simple as that. It's also simple for the pitcher to pull off. The catcher sets up outside, you peek and look outside, the pitcher ignores the target and fires it right at your heart or head. Nevertheless, a lot of guys peek in one way or another, but they must be very selective. Do it often and you'll get caught. Also, the pitcher often misses his target, so your advance knowledge can screw you up!

Is peeking cheating? Absolutely not. Poor sportsmanship? No more so than stealing signs or doctoring the ball. I consider all these tricks as part of the art and craft of playing baseball, not as cheating. Now, hitting with a corked bat, that is cheating because there's no way to catch this trick on the field. But if you can stand on the mound and somehow scuff the baseball in full view of the umpires and everyone else and not get caught, more power to you. I admire the guys like Mike Scott, Don Sutton, Rick Rhoden, who scuffed the ball with regularity and no one ever figured out how. (Or maybe their catchers did the deed for them. Rumor has it that Yogi Berra hid a razor blade in his shin guard to mark the ball for Whitey Ford. Yogi allegedly scraped the ball across the blade as he was retrieving it from his mitt for the return throw to the mound.)

Vern Hoscheit, the Mets' bullpen coach who had been around forever and seen it all in baseball, would spend the first several innings watching Mike Scott from the dugout whenever he started against us, and Vern never detected anything suspicious. But after nine innings of hard work against Scott, we had a bucket full of baseballs at Shea Stadium with the same scuff mark on the same part of the ball: three lines, like a chicken scratch. Coincidence?

Or Bob Forsch. He gave himself extensive manicures on his off days, working hard on his index and middle fingers. Sharpen, lacquer, sharpen, lacquer. Five days later, those nails were like razors. If the umps go out to check, where's the foreign object? Or Don Sutton. Lou Brock collected balls thrown by him, and many had what looked like *and were* razor-blade marks. But where was the blade, or whatever? Or the legendary Nolan Ryan. National Leaguers thought he scuffed the change-up, and I gather that some guys in the American League—Yankees manager Buck Showalter among them—also believe he doctored some pitches in this league. They said as much after he got in the big fight with Robin Ventura. I think Nolan doctored his change-up to make it drop like a split-fingered fastball. What was his technique? Well, a collection of balls thrown by Ryan had the same telltale chicken scratch as the bucket of balls collected after Mike Scott pitched. Nolan and Mike were teammates in Houston. Therefore . . . "Elementary, my dear Watson." Ask Mike Scott how Nolan Ryan doctored the baseball—or vice versa. The difference was that Mike used the trick to make his fastball move in or out, while Nolan used it to make his change-up sink inordinately sharp and late.

The way I look at it, any benefit I or any other batter might have gotten from peeking—and it wasn't that much, to be honest—is more than offset by doctored baseballs. But I say it's all an art! Hats off to all the old-time craftsmen who doctor the ball, peek, steal the catcher's and the third-base coach's signs—and deke the runners. "Deke." You know the term? Yes, surely, but just in case, it comes from football. The runner "dekes" the defender with a fake to the left, then cuts right. In baseball, fielders try to deke runners, and maybe I'm an admirer of this particular skill because I was the victim of the cleverest deke I have ever seen, much less been a part of, on any baseball field.

The Cardinals were playing the Reds in Cincinnati, and I was charging home from first base on a double. Ken Oberkfell scored in front of me, and I don't know whether Ken was signaling me to stand or to slide as I approached the plate. He may have been urgently signaling a slide, but I was too mesmerized by Johnny Bench's performance in front of the plate. Bench was standing there holding his mask in his throwing hand against his hip, watching lackadaisically but also with disgust as the ball was being kicked around by the other fielders. He had nothing to do on this play; that much was obvious to me. Then, at the last conceivable moment. Johnny threw down his mask, took one giant step back directly onto home plate and directly beneath my foot as I tried to plant it on the plate, took the throw, and swiped me with the tag. I was stunned at how instantly the play had gone from a ho-hum score to "You're out!" Johnny's teammates hadn't been kicking the ball around after all. He had known all along he had a shot at me *if* I didn't slide, so for my benefit he put on a show Olivier would have been proud of. He saw where my foot was going to land and got his directly underneath it. I never touched the plate and I knew it, but I yelled and screamed at umpire Ed Vargo anyway. George Hendrick, who saw it all from the on-deck circle, told me bluntly, "Keith, you were out." Of course I was out. I was just embarrassed. What a fabulous play by Bench. Nevertheless, I had to tell him the next time I came to bat that if he tried that again, I'd level him. He never did, but I don't believe the opportunity came up, either. You now see this kind of charade often when the third baseman, waiting for the throw from the right fielder, stands as if nothing is happening, then tries for the last-moment catch and tag. But it's overused and rarely works anymore. The rule: When in doubt, slide.

Robert Stanbury "Buster" Olney (b. 1964) grew up in Randolph Center, Vermont, and has covered pro baseball for the *Nashville Banner,* the *San Diego Union-Tribune,* the *Baltimore Sun,* and, for the past six years, *The New York Times.* This tale of Albert Belle's purloined bat is the consummate baseball yarn, a shaggy-dog story *par excellence* that just happens to be true.

Buster Olney

❥

Yankee Ends Real Corker of a Mystery

Jason Grimsley, a relief pitcher in his first season with the New York Yankees, was among those who flocked to see the movie *Mission: Impossible* in 1996, and as he watched Tom Cruise and an accomplice crawl through an air duct to steal secret information, memories of Grimsley's own impossible mission came back to him.

Grimsley didn't steal government secrets, but he was at the center of a heist that is part of baseball lore for its audacity and ingenuity. For the first time, Grimsley acknowledged last week that it was he who crawled through the innards of the Chicago's Comiskey Park into the umpires' dressing room on July 15, 1994, to exchange an illegally corked bat of his Cleveland Indians teammate Albert Belle for one that was cork-free.

"That was one of the biggest adrenaline rushes I've ever experienced," Grimsley said.

The Indians were in a playoff race with the White Sox as they played in Chicago, and Belle, the Indians' left fielder, was obliterating American League pitching—when the season was ended by a strike on Aug. 12, he had a .357 average and 36 home runs.

Chicago's manager, Gene Lamont, had been tipped off that Belle might have hollowed out the barrel of his bat and filled it with cork, which makes the head of the bat lighter, increasing the speed of the swing. As is the prerogative of any manager, Lamont challenged the legality of Belle's bat in the first inning, a process that automatically prompted an umpire, Dave Phillips, to take the bat and lock it in his dressing room for later examination.

As the bat was removed from the field, the Cleveland dugout was seized with concern. Belle's teammates knew it contained the illegal substance, and once that was discovered, their best hitter would certainly be suspended.

Grimsley, who was one of the Indians' starting pitchers but was not working that night, said, "As I was sitting there, the thought came to my mind: I can get that bat."

Grimsley said he knew that the clubhouse contained a false ceiling, with removable square tiles, and he surmised that the umpires' dressing room, situated on the same level, had the same kind of ceiling. Grimsley walked back toward the clubhouse and down a hallway to do some reconnaissance—he noted the whereabouts of the umpires' room, and the cinder-block walls that framed the rooms.

If he climbed above the ceiling, Grimsley figured, he could crawl atop the cinder-block walls and work his way from the Indians' clubhouse to the umpires' room. He estimated the distance between the clubhouse and the umpires' room to be at least 100 feet.

Grimsley, who was born and reared in Cleveland, Tex., is 6 feet 3 inches and 180 pounds—as tall and lanky as a saguaro cactus. He had never done this sort of thing before, but he had never been afraid of adventure. He climbed trees aggressively as a child, loved to ride his bike and his motorcycle over jumps. When he was 12, he ran a motorcycle over a stump and lost his big left toe.

"This was like a puzzle to be solved," he said. "It's like the game we play—this was a challenge."

Grimsley, who was the primary operative but said he was aided by another member of the organization who was not a player, procured a yellow flashlight and a cork-free bat, then climbed onto the desk in the office of Manager Mike Hargrove, removed a ceiling tile and climbed on top of the cinder-block wall.

The wall Grimsley had to balance on was about 18 inches wide. A slip and he would fall through the ceiling.

Grimsley aimed his flashlight and located a wall at which he knew he would have to turn. Some light seeped through the tile cracks, but it was very dark, and very hot.

"It was pretty hairy up there," said Grimsley, whose journey was complicated by piping that hung from wires and crossed the cinder-block walls. Grimsley and his accomplice had to move slowly and carefully over the pipes, lest they rupture them and destroy the operation. Grimsley figures it took them 35 to 40 minutes to traverse the distance to where they guessed the umpires' locker room would be.

Grimsley made two turns, and as he moved closer to the umpires' room, the slant of the stands slowly reduced his headroom. As he neared his destination, Grimsley had to pull himself along on his stomach, the flashlight in his mouth.

At last, he reached what he thought was the umpires' room and removed a tile. But he had miscalculated.

"There was a groundskeeper in there, sitting in there on a couch," he said. "I put the tile back down, but he had to know. Thank goodness he didn't say anything."

Now knowing precisely where he was, Grimsley moved a few feet to his right and lifted a tile to the umpires' dressing room.

"My heart was going 1,000 miles an hour," Grimsley said. "And in I went. I just rolled the dice. A crapshoot."

What if an umpire had walked in at that moment?

"I'm nailed," he said. "I'm busted."

Grimsley said he quickly dropped from the top of a refrigerator to a counter and down, and immediately spotted Belle's bat in an umpire's locker. He made the exchange, as imperfect as it was: according to another member of the Indians' organization, Grimsley had to switch Belle's bat with one belonging to Paul Sorrento because every one of Belle's bats was corked.

Grimsley said he climbed back out, paused to make sure his footprints were not apparent in the dust on top of the refrigerator, and replaced the tile.

"As soon as I got back up, somebody came back in the room," he said. "I had to sit there for about two minutes; I was about 20 or 30 feet from somebody."

Grimsley doesn't know for sure if the person was an umpire, but whoever it was left, and Grimsley and his accomplice returned to the Cleveland clubhouse, four innings after the operation began, and he said he informed the rest of the Indians of his success.

They could not believe he had reclaimed the bat. "They were pretty excited," he said.

After the game, which the Indians won by 3–2, the umpires had no doubt that the bats had been switched—the one now in their possession bore Sorrento's name. White Sox officials were apoplectic, and there was talk of bringing in the F.B.I. Ultimately, the Indians were told that if they returned Belle's original bat, there would be no punishment for whoever made the switch. They complied, and Belle was given a 10-game suspension, a penalty that was appealed and reduced to 7 games.

Grimsley's role was not disclosed at the time, but since the bat was returned, Belle was punished and nearly five years have passed, it is highly unlikely that baseball officials will pursue the matter further with the now 31-year-old pitcher.

Grimsley said his teammates were supportive of his action, for there was no doubt about his motivation. "I had the interests of the Cleveland Indians at heart," said Grimsley, who was later treated to a round of golf by Belle.

The next day, Grimsley—whose identity as the culprit was unknown to the White Sox—was standing in the outfield with a couple of teammates when Mike LaValliere, a Chicago catcher, walked over to them.

"Hey, I heard you guys had a mission impossible last night," LaValliere said, smiling. "That's beautiful."

And he walked away, leaving Grimsley grinning behind him.

Sources and Acknowledgments

Great care has been taken to trace all owners of copyright material included in this book. If any have been inadvertently omitted or overlooked, acknowledgment will gladly be made in future printings.

E. L. Thayer, Casey at the Bat: *San Francisco Examiner*, June 3, 1888.

Will Hough & Frank Adams, The Umpire Is a Most Unhappy Man: Liner notes, *Hurrah for Our National Game: Jewels from the Baseball Diamond 1858–1913*, Newport Classics recording 85576.

Jack Norworth, Take Me Out to the Ball Game: *Take Me Out to the Ball Game* (New York: The York Music Co., 1908).

Newspaper Verse: Franklin P. Adams, Baseball's Sad Lexicon: *In Other Words* (Garden City, N.Y.: Doubleday, Page, 1912). George E. Phair, The Old-Fashioned Pitcher: Lawrence Ritter, *The Glory of Their Times* (New York: Macmillan, 1966). Reprinted by permission of Lawrence S. Ritter.

Charles E. Van Loan, Baseball as the Bleachers Like It: *The Outing*, September 1909.

Owen Johnson, *from* The Varmint: *The Varmint* (New York: The Baker and Taylor Company, 1910).

George Jean Nathan, Baiting the Umpire: *Harper's Weekly*, September 10, 1910.

Albert G. Spalding, *from* America's National Game: *America's National Game* (New York: American Sports Publishing Company, 1911).

Damon Runyon, Hail! Roger Merkle, Favorite of Toledo: *New York American*, July 10, 1911. Rajah's Pride Falls Before 'G. Hooks-em': *New York American*, July 11, 1911.

Lawrence S. Ritter, *from* The Glory of Their Times: Sam Crawford: *The Glory of Their Times* (New York: Macmillan, 1966). Copyright © 1966. Reprinted by permission of Lawrence S. Ritter.

Ring Lardner, *from* You Know Me Al: *You Know Me Al: A Busher's Letters* (New York: George H. Doran, 1916). Where Do You Get That Noise?: *Saturday Evening Post*, October 23, 1915.

Carl Sandburg, Hits and Runs: *Cornhuskers* (New York: Henry Holt and Company, 1918). *from* Always the Young Strangers: *Always the Young Strangers* (New York: Harcourt, Brace and Company, 1953). Copyright © 1953, 1952 by Carl Sandburg and renewed © 1981, 1980 by Margaret Sandburg, Helga Sandburg Crile, and Janet Sandburg. Reprinted by permission of Harcourt, Inc.

Heywood Broun, Ruth Comes Into His Own with 2 Homers, Clinching Second for Yanks, 4 to 2: *New York World*, October 12, 1923.

Jerome Holtzman, *from* No Cheering in the Press Box: *No Cheering in the Press Box* (New York, Holt, Rinehart and Winston, 1974). Copyright © 1974 Jerome Holtzman. Reprinted by permission of the author.

William Carlos Williams, The crowd at the ball game: A. Walton Litz and Christopher Macgowan, eds., *The Collected Poems of William Carlos Williams. Vol. 1: 1909–1939* (New York: New Directions, 1986). Copyright © 1938 New Directions Publishing Corp. Reprinted by permission. *from* White Mule: Fourth of July Doubleheader: *White Mule* (New York: New Directions, 1937). Copyright © 1937 New Directions Publishing Corp. Reprinted by permission.

Donald Honig, *from* Baseball When the Grass Was Real: James "Cool Papa" Bell: *Baseball When the Grass Was Real: Baseball from the Twenties to the Forties Told by the Men Who Played It* (New York: Coward, McCann & Geoghegan, 1975). Copyright © 1975 by Donald Honig. Reprinted by permission of the University of Nebraska Press.

James Weldon Johnson, *from* Along This Way: *Along This Way: The Autobiography of James Weldon Johnson* (New York: Viking Press, 1933). Copyright © 1933 by James Weldon Johnson, renewed © 1961 by Grace Nail Johnson. Used by permission of Viking Penguin, a division of Penguin Putnam Inc.

Thomas Wolfe, *from* Of Time and the River: *Of Time and the River* (New York: Charles Scribner's Sons, 1935). Copyright © 1935 by Charles Scribner's Sons; copyright renewed © 1963 by Paul Gitlin, Administrator C.T.A. Reprinted with the permission of Scribner, a Divison of Simon & Schuster, Inc.

Paul Gallico, Inside the Inside: *Farewell to Sport* (New York: Knopf, 1938). Copyright © 1937, 1938, 1964, 1966 by Paul Gallico. Reprinted by permission of Harold Ober Associates, Incorporated.

Moe Berg, Pitchers and Catchers: *Atlantic Monthly*, September 1941. Copyright © 1941. Reprinted with permission of Irwin M. Berg.

James Thurber, You Could Look It Up: *My World—And Welcome To It* (New York: Harcourt, Brace and Company, 1942). Copyright © 1942 by James Thurber. Copyright © renewed 1970 by Helen Thurber and Rosemary A. Thurber. Originally published in *The Saturday Evening Post*, April 15, 1941. Reprinted by arrangement with Rosemary A. Thurber and The Barbara Hogenson Agency. All rights reserved.

Rolfe Humphries, Polo Grounds: *Collected Poems* (Bloomington: Indiana University Press, 1965). Copyright © 1965 Indiana University Press. Reprinted by permission.

Wendell Smith, It Was a Great Day in Jersey: *Pittsburgh Courier*, April 19, 1946. Copyright © 1946, reprinted by permission of Wyonella Smith / National Baseball Hall of Fame Library, Cooperstown, N.Y.: Wendell Smith Papers.

J. F. Powers, Jamesie: *Prince of Darkness, and Other Stories* (Garden City, N.Y.: Doubleday & Company, 1947). Copyright © 1947. Reprinted by permission of the Powers Family Literary Trust, Katherine A. Powers, Trustee.

James A. Maxwell, Shine Ball: *The New Yorker*, October 7, 1950. Copyright © 1950 by James A. Maxwell.

Nelson Algren, *from* Chicago: City on the Make: *Chicago: City on the Make* (Garden City, N.Y.: Doubleday & Co., 1951). Copyright © 1951. Reprinted by permission of McGraw-Hill Education, A Division of The McGraw-Hill Companies.

Jimmy Cannon, Nice Work: *Who Struck John?* (New York: Dial, 1956). Copyright © 1953. Reprinted by permission of *The New York Post*.

Tallulah Bankhead, *from* Tallulah: *Tallulah: My Autobiography* (New York: Harper and Bros, 1952). Copyright © 1952 by Tallulah Bankhead.

Bernard Malamud, *from* The Natural: *The Natural* (New York: Harcourt, Brace and Company, 1952). Copyright © 1952, renewed © 1980 by Bernard Malamud. Reprinted by the permission of Russell & Volkening as agents for the author.

Red Smith, Dodgers Defeat Yanks, 3–2, as Erskine Fans 14: *Red Smith on Baseball* (Chicago: I. R. Dee, 2000). Copyright © 2000 by Phyllis W. Smith, reprinted by permission of Ivan R. Dee, Publisher. Originally published in the *New York*

Herald Tribune, October 3, 1953. The Terrible-Tempered Mr. Grove: *To Absent Friends* (New York: Atheneum, 1983). Copyright ©1982 Atheneum Publishers, Inc. Originally published in *The New York Times*, March 3, 1974. Reprinted with permission of Scribner, a Division of Simon & Schuster.

Jacques Barzun, *from* God's Country and Mine: *God's Country and Mine: A Declaration of Love Spiced with a Few Harsh Words* (Boston: Little, Brown, 1954). Copyright © 1954 by Jacques Barzun, © renewed 1982 by Jacques Barzun. Reprinted with permission of Little, Brown and Company, Inc.

Robert Frost, Perfect Day—A Day of Prowess: *Sports Illustrated,* July 23, 1956. Copyright © 1956. Reprinted by permission of the Estate of Robert Lee Frost.

James T. Farrell, My Grandmother Goes to Comiskey Park: *My Baseball Diary* (New York: A.S. Barnes, 1957). Copyright © 1957. Reprinted by permission of the James T. Farrell Estate.

from Damn Yankees: *Damn Yankees*. Text Copyright © 1956 by George Abbott, Richard Bissell and Douglass Wallop, Renewed © 1982. Lyrics Copyright © 1955 by Frank Music Corp. Renewed © 1983 by Richard Adler Music and J. & J. Ross Co. This excerpt from the play *Damn Yankees* is owned by and used here with permission of the copyright owners. All Rights Reserved. The right to perform *Damn Yankees* must be secured from Music Theatre International, exclusive licensing agent for live stage performance rights.

W. C. Heinz, The Rocky Road of Pistol Pete: *What A Time It Was: The Best of W.C. Heinz on Sports* (San Francisco: Da Capo Press, 2001). Copyright © W.C. Heinz. First published in *True Magazine*.

Jim Brosnan, *from* The Long Season: *The Long Season* (New York: Harper and Brothers, 1960). Copyright © 1960, 1975 by Jim Brosnan. Reprinted by permission of HarperCollins Publishers, Inc.

Robert Francis, Pitcher; The Base-Stealer: *Collected Poems 1936–1976* (Amherst: University of Massachusetts Press, 1976). Copyright © 1976 by Robert Francis. Reprinted by permission of Wesleyan University Press. Both poems were originally published in Francis' collection *The Orb Weaver* (1960).

John Updike, Hub Fans Bid Kid Adieu: *Assorted Prose* (New York: Knopf, 1965). Copyright © 1965 by John Updike. Used by permission of Alfred A. Knopf, a division of Random House, Inc.

Satchel Paige, Rules for Staying Young: Satchel Paige (as told to David Lipman), *Maybe I'll Pitch Forever* (Garden City, N.Y.: Doubleday, 1962). Copyright © 1962. Reprinted by permission of the University of Nebraska Press.

Bill Veeck (with Ed Linn), A Can of Beer, a Slice of Cake—and Thou, Eddie Gaedel: *Veeck As In Wreck* (New York: G. P. Putnam's Sons, 1962). Copyright © 1962. Reprinted by permission of Sterling Lord Literistic, Inc.

Murray Kempton, Back at the Polo Grounds: Al Silverman, ed., *The Best of Sport 1946–1971* (New York: Viking, 1971). Copyright © 1971 Sport Magazine.

Jimmy Breslin, *from* Can't Anybody Here Play This Game?: *Can't Anybody Here Play This Game?* (New York: Viking, 1963). Copyright © 1963 by Jimmy Breslin. Reprinted by permission of Jimmy Breslin.

Marianne Moore, Baseball and Writing: *The Complete Poems of Marianne Moore* (New York: Viking, 1967). Originally published in *Tell Me, Tell Me* (1966). Copyright ©1961 by Marianne Moore, © renewed 1989 by Lawrence E. Brinn and Louise Crane, Executors of the Estate of Marianne Moore. Used by permission of Viking Penguin, a division of Penguin Putnam, Inc.

Gay Talese, The Silent Season of a Hero: *Fame and Obscurity* (New York: World Publishing Co., 1970). Copyright © 1970 by Gay Talese. Reprinted by permission of the author.

Willie Morris, *from* North Toward Home: *North Toward Home* (Boston: Houghton Mifflin, 1967). Copyright © 1967 by Willie Morris. Reprinted by permission of Raines & Raines.

Philip Roth, *from* Portnoy's Complaint: *Portnoy's Complaint* (New York: Random House, 1969). Copyright © 1969 by Philip Roth. Used by permission of Random House, Inc.

Jim Bouton, *from* Ball Four: *Ball Four: My Life and Hard Times Throwing the Knuckleball in the Big Leagues*. Edited by Leonard Shecter. (New York: World Publishing Co., 1970). Copyright © 1970 by Jim Bouton. Reprinted with permission of Jim Bouton.

Dave Frishberg, Van Lingle Mungo: Lyrics provided courtesy of the author. Copyright © 1969, 1997 Kohaw Music, Inc. All Rights Reserved. Used by Permission.

May Swenson, Analysis of Baseball: *More Poems to Solve* (New York: Scribner, 1971). Copyright © 1971 by May Swenson. Reprinted with permission of the Literary Estate of May Swenson.

Roger Kahn, *from* The Boys of Summer: *The Boys of Summer* (New York: Harper and Row, 1972). Copyright © 1971, 1972 by Roger Kahn. Reprinted by permission of Hookslide, Inc.

Joel Oppenheimer, *from* The Wrong Season: *The Wrong Season* (Indianapolis: Bobbs-Merrill, 1973). Copyright © 1973 by Joel Oppenheimer. Reprinted by permission of the Oppenheimer Literary Estate, which wishes to note that Oppenheimer was a "poet, columnist, Brooklyn Dodgers fan by birth, Mets fan by choice or lack thereof."

Roger Angell, *from* The Summer Game: Excerpt is from "The Leaping Corpse and Other Mysteries" in *The Summer Game* (New York: Viking, 1972). Copyright © 1972 by Roger Angell, used by permission of Viking Penguin, a division of Penguin Putnam Inc. *from* Five Seasons: *Five Seasons* (New York: Simon & Schuster, 1977). Copyright © 1977 by Roger Angell, reprinted by permission of International Creative Management, Inc. *from* Late Innings: *Late Innings* (New York: Simon & Schuster, 1982). Copyright © 1982 by Roger Angell, reprinted by permission of Simon and Schuster. *from* Season Ticket: *Season Ticket* (Boston: Houghton Mifflin, 1988). Copyright © 1988 by Roger Angell, reprinted by permission of Houghton Mifflin Company. All rights reserved.

Brendan C. Boyd and Fred C. Harris, *from* The Great American Baseball Card Flipping Trading and Bubble Gum Book: *The Great American Baseball Card Flipping Trading and Bubble Gum Book* (Boston: Little, Brown and Co., 1973). Copyright © 1973 by Brendan C. Boyd and Frederick C. Harris. Reprinted with permission of Fred Harris.

George Plimpton, Final Twist of the Drama: *Sports Illustrated*, April 22, 1974. Copyright © 1974 by George Plimpton. Reprinted with permission of George Plimpton.

Pat Jordan, *from* A False Spring: *A False Spring* (New York: Dodd, Mead, 1975). Copyright © 1973, 1974, 1975 by Pat Jordan. Reprinted with permission of the author.

Bernadette Mayer, Carlton Fisk Is My Ideal: *A Bernadette Mayer Reader* (New York: New Directions, 1992). Copyright © 1968 Bernadette Mayer. Reprinted by permission of New Directions Publishing Corp.

A. Bartlett Giamatti, The Green Fields of the Mind: Kenneth S. Robson, ed., *A Great and Glorious Game: Baseball Writings of A. Bartlett Giamatti* (Chapel Hill, N.C.: Algonquin Books, 1998). Copyright © 1998. Reprinted by permission of Algonquin Books of Chapel Hill, a division of Workman Publishing.

Jonathan Schwartz, A Day of Light and Shadows: *Sports Illustrated*, February 26, 1979. Copyright © 1979 by Jonathan Schwartz. Reprinted by permission of the author.

Mark Harris, *from* It Looked Like For Ever: *It Looked Like For Ever* (New York: McGraw-Hill, 1979). Copyright © 1979 by Mark Harris. Reprinted by permission of the author.

Eric Rolfe Greenberg, *from* The Celebrant: *The Celebrant* (New York: Everest House, 1983). Copyright © 1983 by Eric Rolfe Greenberg. Reprinted by permission of University of Nebraska Press.

Amiri Baraka, *from* The Autobiography of Leroi Jones: *The Autobiography of Leroi Jones* (New York: Freundlich Books, 1984). Copyright © 1984. Reprinted by permission of Lawrence Hill Books, an imprint of Chicago Review Press, Inc.

Robert Creamer, *from* Stengel: His Life and Times: *Stengel: His Life and Times* (New York: Simon and Schuster, 1984). Copyright © 1984 by Robert Creamer. Reprinted by permission of Sterling Lord Literistic.

Roy Blount, Jr., The Sporting News: *Sports Illustrated*, March 17, 1986. Copyright © 1986 by Roy Blount, Jr. Reprinted by permission of International Creative Management, Inc.

David Remnick, The September Song of Mr. October: *The Devil Problem and Other True Stories* (New York: Random House, 1996). Copyright © 1996 by David Remnick. Used by permission of Random House, Inc.

Annie Dillard, *from* An American Childhood: *An American Childhood*. Copyright © 1987 by Annie Dillard. Reprinted by permission of HarperCollins Publishers, Inc.

Stephen Jay Gould, The Streak of Streaks: *The New York Review of Books*, August 18, 1988. Copyright © 1988 by Stephen Jay Gould. Reprinted by permission of the author. The section of the essay which reviews *Streak: Joe DiMaggio and the Summer of 1941* by Michael Seidel has been omitted here.

Stephen King, Head Down: *Nightmares and Dreamscapes* (New York: Viking, 1993). Copyright ©1993 by Stephen King. Used by permission of Viking Penguin, a division of Penguin Putnam, Inc.

Molly O'Neill, Coming to the Plate, One Family's Ethos: *The New York Times*, October 16, 1990. Copyright © 1990, The New York Times Co. Reprinted by permission.

Richard Ford, A Minors Affair. *Harper's*, September 1992. Copyright © 1991 by *Harper's Magazine*. Reprinted by permission.

Yusef Komunyakaa, Glory. *Magic City* (Hanover, N.H.: Wesleyan University Press,

1992). Copyright © 1992 by Yusef Komunyakaa. Reprinted by permission of Wesleyan University Press.

Don DeLillo, *from* Underworld: *Underworld* (New York: Scribner, 1997). Subsequent edition, *Pafko at the Wall* (New York: Scribner, 2001). Copyright © 1997 by Don DeLillo. Reprinted with permission of Scribner, a Divison of Simon & Schuster, Inc.

Martin Espada, Rain Delay: Toledo Mud Hens, July 8, 1994. *Imagine the Angels of Bread* (New York: W.W. Norton and Co., 1996). Copyright © 1996 by Martin Espada. Used by permission of W. W. Norton & Company, Inc.

Keith Hernandez and Mike Bryan, *from* Pure Baseball: *Pure Baseball* (New York: HarperCollins, 1994). Copyright © 1994 by Keith Hernandez and Mike Bryan. Reprinted by permission of HarperCollins Publishers, Inc.

Buster Olney, Yankee Ends Real Corker of a Mystery: *The New York Times*, April 11, 1999. Copyright © 1999 by The New York Times Co. Reprinted by permission.